Chamorro-English Dictionary

PALI LANGUAGE TEXTS: MICRONESIA

Social Science Research Institute
University of Hawaii

Donald M. Topping
Editor

CHAMORRO-ENGLISH DICTIONARY

DONALD M. TOPPING
PEDRO M. OGO
BERNADITA C. DUNGCA

University of Hawaii Press
Honolulu

The original publication of this book was subsidized
by the government of the
Trust Territory of the Pacific Islands.

Library of Congress Catalog Card Number 74-16907
ISBN 978-0-8248-0353-7

Printed in the United States of America

19   23 22

University of Hawai‘i Press books are printed on acid-
free paper and meet the guidelines for permanence
and durability of the Council on Library Resources.

www.uhpress.hawaii.edu

CONTENTS

PREFACE

Although this work bears the word *dictionary* in its title, it is not, in the compilers' opinions, truly a dictionary of Chamorro. To qualify as a genuine dictionary, all the definitions would be in Chamorro, etymologies would be given, and more Chamorro entries included. Such a dictionary will have to be produced by the Chamorro people themselves if a genuine Chamorro dictionary worthy of that title is ever compiled.

The present work might be considered an intermediate step along the way towards a full dictionary of Chamorro. It goes beyond the previous dictionaries of Callistus, Von Preissig, Vera, Arnold, Donlon, and "Val" in the following ways: (1) a larger number of entries; (2) fuller English glosses; and (3) the inclusion of sample sentences to illustrate usage.

It is hoped that this work will be of interest to Chamorro speakers who want to learn more about their language, to Chamorro speakers who want to expand their English vocabulary, and to non-Chamorro speakers who want to learn something of the Chamorro language.

This dictionary was begun in 1967 when Pedro M. Ogo of Rota and I were working on the material that went into *Spoken Chamorro* (Topping 1969 *b*). Our original intention was to develop a lexicon that would be included in that textbook. After we had accumulated more than three thousand lexical entries we decided to start working in earnest towards a more complete Chamorro-English dictionary. A grant from the University of Hawaii Office of Research Administration made it possible for Mr. Ogo to remain in Honolulu through the spring of 1968 to continue work on the dictionary.

I spent the summer of 1968 in the Mariana Islands collecting new data and checking with other native speakers of Chamorro the entries that Mr. Ogo and I had made. During this period I was able to check our data with speakers from Guam, Rota, and Saipan. This phase of the work was made possible through a grant (No. GS–2118) from the National Science Foundation.

Work on the dictionary was then suspended until Mrs. Bernadita C. Dungca of Guam came to the University of Hawaii in the fall of 1971 with the Pacific Language Development Project. From that time until June 1973 Mrs. Dungca and I worked as time permitted at expanding and correcting items in the dictionary and adding new items as we found them in the course of our work on the language.

Publication of the final results has been made possible through a grant from the Government of the Trust Territory of the Pacific Islands.

Although the three of us did most of the work in compiling the dictionary, numerous other people from the Marianas assisted over the years. While there are too many individuals who contributed to list them all by name, I would like to give special acknowledgement to Judge Ignacio V. Benavente and Mr. José S. Pangelinan of Saipan, and to Mr. Thomas T. Cruz ("Andai") of Yoña, Guam, for their contributions. I would also like to acknowledge the combined efforts of Professors Robert Hsu and Ann Peters, and of Mrs. Melody Moir Actouka, for their help in getting this work through the computer and into its final printed form.

The sources for all the Chamorro data are entirely native; any faults in the English glosses and translations should be attributed to me.

Speaking for the other two compilers and myself, this dictionary is far from exhaustive. There are probably several thousand Chamorro words that we simply did not think of. We hope that the Chamorro people will take upon themselves the task of expanding this work into a full-fledged dictionary that will serve either to help keep the language alive or as a fitting tribute to its demise.

DONALD M. TOPPING

INTRODUCTION

1.0 The Chamorro Language. Chamorro is the native language of the people indigenous to the Mariana Islands. At the time of writing there are approximately 52,000 native speakers of the language in the Marianas, 40,000 of whom live on Guam, the southernmost island of the chain.

Chamorro belongs to the Austronesian family of languages (sometimes called Malayo-Polynesian). Prominent grammatical features of the language suggest that it is most closely related to the languages of the Philippines. We cannot at this point determine to which of the Philippine languages Chamorro is most closely related, for it shares common grammatical features and vocabulary with several of them. The most outstanding features of Chamorro grammar that suggest its Philippine roots are the verb affixes *-um-*, *-in-*, *ma-*, and reduplication; the articles *i*, *si*, and *ni*; and the "focus" system. The grammar of Chamorro has been described in several published works (see Bibliography), most recently by Topping 1973*a*.

The shared vocabulary may not be a good basis for determining the closeness of the relationship between Chamorro and other languages because Chamorro and the Philippine languages borrowed extensively from Spanish vocabulary during the more than three hundred years that Spain ruled in this area. (See Fischer 1961.)

Chamorro has traditionally been the language of home and church. Most formal education in the Mariana Islands has been conducted in an alien language, that is, Spanish, Japanese, and English. Literacy in Chamorro has been taught in the schools of the islands sporadically. Hence, there exists very little in the way of written Chamorro literature, aside from that produced by the church.

At present English is the official medium of instruction in all the schools of the Mariana Islands, except for the bilingual education classes in selected schools of Guam, Rota, and Saipan. There are strong indications of a growing desire among Chamorro parents for the schools to take on the responsibility of teaching their children to read and write in Chamorro as well as in English. This desire appears to be motivated by the fear that Chamorro may become extinct because the young people are more and more using English to the exclusion of Chamorro.

According to surveys taken by Carol Odo and George Riley between 1971 and 1973, most Chamorro parents on Guam speak English at home to their young children. Many Guamanian children enter kindergarten able to communicate only in English. If this trend continues, there is a very great possibility that Chamorro will cease to be spoken by Guamanians within another generation. Whether this will actually happen remains to be seen. It is foolhardy to make predictions concerning the future of any language.

1.1   Dialects of Chamorro. In the way people speak Chamorro there are some minor differences that may be considered dialectal. These differences are not great enough to cause any difficulty in communication, yet they can be recognized instantly by the native speakers of Chamorro.

The major dialect differences are between Rota and all the other islands. The dialects of Saipan and of central and northern Guam are quite similar, while the dialects of southern Guam and Rota have certain common features. The major differences between the dialects of Saipan and Guam are found in vocabulary; Saipanese tend to use more loanwords from Japanese, while Guamanians use more loanwords from English. The Rota dialect has pre-served a few Chamorro words that are no longer used in Saipan and Guam. These vocabulary differences are marked in the dictionary by the initials (R), (S), and (G) for Rota, Saipan, and Guam respectively. This means that the vocabulary item so marked is used primarily in that dialect. (Of course, some speakers from Rota may use a word that has been marked (G) or (S), and vice versa. The initials indicate only that the word is used more widely in that particular dialect area).

The major nonlexical features that distinguish the Rota dialect (from those spoken in Saipan and Guam) can be summarized as follows. (The cross-references are to the sections in the *Chamorro Reference Grammar* [Topping 1973*a*], hereafter referred to as CRG.)

a.   "Sing-song" intonation. (See 1.5)
b.   Absence of geminate consonants. (See 2.4.3)
c.   Absence of syllable-final *h*. (See 2.4.3)
d.   Insertion of *h* in Spanish loan words, especially preceding glides.

Some examples illustrating the last three dialect differences are given here:

Guam/Saipan		*Rota*
b.	tommo 'knee'	tomo
	meggai 'many'	megai
c.	mamahlao 'bashful'	mamalao
	tohge 'stand up'	toge
d.	espia 'look for'	espiha
	tieras 'scissors'	tiheras

1.2   Dialect Forms in the Dictionary. The Guam/Saipan pronunciation was chosen as the basis for making dictionary entries. Rotanese (and other alter-nate) pronunciations are frequently, though not always, given. For example, the word meaning 'to stir' is entered under *lehgua'* with the syllable-final *h*.

The alternate form *legua'* is also listed under this entry, but it is not listed separately. On the other hand, the word meaning 'look for' is listed as both *espia* and *espiha* with a cross listing under both entries. A double listing was made when the compilers found it difficult to determine whether one pronunciation was used more widely than the other.

When the alternate Rotanese pronunciation of a word is not listed, the reader can determine what it is by observing the three rules (b, c, and d) given in the preceding section.

It should be pointed out that the compilers of this dictionary did not aim to list only the "proper" pronunciations in the entries. Rather, we have tried to list the words as they are currently pronounced by various mature speakers of the language. The Guam/Saipan dialect form was most often selected as the main lexical entry, not because it is more correct or proper, but because more people use it.

There are probably more formal and subtle differences in the dialects of Chamorro that are not covered here or in the CRG. We have limited ourselves to only the most noticeable differences.

2.0 Aim of This Work. One aim in compiling this dictionary has been to provide an alphabetized listing of as many Chamorro words as could be collected, spelled according to the principles adopted by the Marianas Orthography Committee in February 1971, with each word given a fairly comprehensive English definition. Sample sentences have been provided for many of the entries to illustrate how the word in question can be used. Cross-references have been made to other Chamorro words that are semantically related.

An English-Chamorro Finder List generated from selected words in the English definitions of the Chamorro words is also provided. Not every English word found in the definitions of the Chamorro words appears in the English-Chamorro Finder List. Those English words that do appear in the list were selected on the basis of their frequency in American English, as determined by the opinions of the compilers with the aid of the *Computational Analysis of Present-Day American English* and the *Thorndike-Century Junior Dictionary*. The English glosses are not intended to be definitive or authoritative. Rather, they are intended to show as accurately as possible the current meanings and connotations of the Chamorro words. They are the result of many, many hours of discussion and explanation between a native speaker of Chamorro and a native speaker of English. There undoubtedly have been many omissions of meaning, and probably some distortions. This is to be expected in a bilingual dictionary, the two languages of which are the products of vastly different cultures, and compilers of which are not completely fluent in each other's language.

This work is also viewed as a companion piece to the CRG, in which the author attempts to give a fairly detailed description of the phonology, the

,pelling system, and the grammar of Chamorro. Since grammatical information is presented in that work, such information is not included in this dictionary.

In sum, this dictionary aims to provide the most recent and complete record of the lexicon of the Chamorro language as it is used by the Chamorro people in 1974. In this respect, it is a *descriptive* dictionary, not a *prescriptive* one. We hope, however, that the spelling used in this dictionary will help toward standardizing the spelling system of Chamorro.

2.1 Methodology. When the compilation of this dictionary first began, all the entries, definitions, and cross-references were handwritten on cards that were alphabetized and filed daily. When we had five thousand or so entries it was suggested that we store them in a computer at the University of Hawaii Computing Center. The major advantages of the computerized filing system were: (1) it could be updated at any time without going through the arduous task of manual realphabetization, and (2) it was possible to program an automated reverse English-Chamorro Finder List.

The disadvantages of using the computer in the early stages of the dictionary work were: (1) the computer could accept and print only standard upper-case letters, and (2) it required that the English gloss in the English-Chamorro Finder List be no more than 72 letters and spaces long. These limitations had a lasting effect on the English glosses found in the present work. Later on, when newer computer hardware provided both upper- and lower-case letters, a considerable amount of work went into recasting thousands of words.

The major advantage in using the computer is one that was not anticipated when work first began, namely automated typesetting. Had it not been for this technological development, our limited resources would have required that this dictionary be published in mimeographed or typewritten form.

2.2 Some Limitations. The most obvious limitations of this work are (1) that it contains only a part of the total Chamorro lexicon, and (2) that the English glosses are sometimes less than satisfactory. That is to say, the English glosses don't explain the full meaning of the Chamorro words. Furthermore, some of them may be completely misleading when the words appear out of context.

Another limitation is that not all of the common Chamorro words we could think of were included. To have done so would have produced a dictionary of such volume as to be too expensive and cumbersome to use. We deliberately excluded thousands of *derived words,* that is, words that are derived from roots by adding affixes. For example, it is possible to derive twenty-three different words from the root word *sangan* 'to say' simply by adding affixes. The same could be done with any Class I word. Since most of the meanings of the derived forms are fully predictable, neither the derived words nor their definitions are included in the dictionary.

Some derived forms are included when the meanings are not predictable, and some others are included to illustrate how a particular affix, for example, *achá-*, combines with root words to form other words.

3.0 Sources of This Work. The primary source for the majority of the items in this dictionary is the spoken language. Tape recordings of conversations and monologues were used extensively. The compilers also made conscious efforts to detect any previously unlisted words as they listened to live conversations.

All the Chamorro dictionaries cited in the Bibliography were carefully examined for new lexical items. We included all words that were recognized by native speakers, but did not include words that are no longer in use. We considered including archaic forms for purposes of historical interest, but decided not to (except for archaic forms that could be verified) because the spelling system used in the older dictionaries has proved too unreliable.

All the entries in this work were either spoken or verified by a native speaker of Chamorro.

3.1 Names of Flora and Fauna. Most of the names of the flora of the Marianas were taken from a prepublication copy of "The Flora of Guam" by Benjamin C. Stone. Stone's spellings of the Chamorro names were changed to conform to the new orthography. The pronunciations we have listed were verified by several Guamanian men and women who were consulted during the summer of 1968. Some of the entries for plants are followed by a question mark in parentheses (?). This means that nobody was found who could verify the accepted pronunciation of the name of that plant, in which case the hypothetical pronunciation is given.

The names of the birds were taken from a prepublication copy of the "Check List of Guam Birds" compiled by Mr. Francisco P. DeLeon of the Division of Fish and Wildlife, Territory of Guam.

The names of the fishes came from two sources. The more reliable identifications were taken from a prepublication copy of the "Check List of Guam Fishes" compiled by Harry T. Kami, Isaac I. Ikehara, and Francisco P. DeLeon of the Division of Fish and Wildlife, Territory of Guam. This document gives the Chamorro names and the scientific names of the fishes of Guam.

The other source for fish names was Leonard P. Schultz's *Fishes of the Marshall and Marianas Islands*. In using this work the compilers provided the Chamorro names based upon pictures of various fishes. Since the compilers are not ichthyologists, our identifications are somewhat questionable.

3.2 Nicknames. More than one hundred nicknames, most of which were supplied by Mr. Rufino Tudela of Saipan, were included in this work, mainly for the purpose of showing the Chamorro method of deriving nicknames from given names, and to call attention to the tradition of playing with names, a tradition that seems to be dying out as more and more children are given American-type names, such as Robert, William, and Jon-Jon.

The most striking difference between the American and Chamorro methods of nickname derivation is that Americans tend to alter the first part of a given name (for example, "Bob" from Robert, "Chris" from Christina), while Chamorros tend to utilize the latter part of a given name (for example, "Ina" from Alfonsina, "Elo" from Cornelio). In many instances the nickname bears no phonological resemblance to the given name (for example, "Umbai" from Jesus).

3.3 Place-names. Some place-names have been included, mainly for the purpose of providing the current Chamorro pronunciation based upon adult speech. As more foreigners, with their faulty pronunciations of the place-names, come to the islands, the Chamorros—and particularly the Chamor-ros of Guam—are changing their own pronunciation to conform to that of the foreigners. The traditional spellings have been used in accordance with the principles of the Marianas Orthography Committee, even though the spell-ings do not always reflect the Chamorro pronunciation. Hopefully, a sepa-rate listing of place-names of the Marianas will be published before the indigenous names and their pronunciations, which contain much of the his-tory of the islands, are lost forever.

4.0 Orthography. The orthography—or spelling system—used in this work is based upon the recommendations of the Marianas Orthography Committee's report of February 1971. We have occasionally departed from the rules when the pronunciation of the word seemed to warrant it. The rules adopted by the Orthography Committee represent some drastic changes from the traditional spelling system.

The rationale for changing the spelling system is to make it systematic and to bring it more in line with the recently adopted spelling systems for other Oceanic languages, such as Indonesian, Malay, Cebuano, and Ilokano. The compilers of this work realize that it will take a long while before a standard-ized spelling system is used by everyone who writes in Chamorro.

4.1 The New Spelling. A new spelling system for Chamorro was officially adopted in February 1971, in the hope of standardizing the orthography. It is hoped that this dictionary will also serve that end. (The companion CRG also uses the orthography of this dictionary).

At present most people who write Chamorro follow their own intuition about how all but the most common words should be spelled. The result has been many personalized spelling systems rather than a standard one.

The complete set of recommendations for the new spelling system is given in the CRG, pp. 58–67. Some of the more important changes will be dis-cussed briefly here.

4.1.1 GLOTTAL STOP. The glottal stop (represented by ' in the new spelling system and called *glota* by some Chamorros) is shown wherever it occurs, except at the beginning of words. Von Preissig sometimes shows the glottal stop by use of the circumflex mark (^) over the preceding vowel, as in *hagâ* 'blood'. None of the other lexicographers or grammarians made any attempt to show the occurrence of this consonant in the spelling system, probably because it is not a significant consonant in any western European language. The apostrophe symbol was adopted by the Marianas Orthography Committee primarily because it is available on any standard typewriter.

It was determined by the Orthography Committee that the glottal consonant should be written in Chamorro whenever it occurs, except in initial position. The following words will illustrate the glottal stop as it appears in the writing system:

Chamorro	English Gloss
ha'i	forehead
li'e'	to see
gua'ot	stairs
agua'	step over

4.1.2 ELIMINATION OF *c, j,* and *q*. The letters *c, j,* and *q* are no longer used in the system except in spelling proper names. The letter *j* has been replaced by *h;* the letter *c* (when it occurs before *a, o,* or *u),* and the letter *q* have been replaced by the letter *k*. The words below will illustrate the old spelling (from the Von Preissig dictionary) contrasted with the new:

Old Spelling	New Spelling	English Gloss
canô	kanno'	to eat
cálulot	kálulot	finger, toe
jaáne	ha'ani	day
jao	hao	you
quílolog	kílulok	to turn
quinilag	kinilak	diarrhea

4.1.3 FINAL *g*. Many common words in Chamorro have traditionally been spelled with a final *g*, such as *mauleg* 'good', *somnag* 'sun', and *dogdog* 'breadfruit'. In the new spelling system, *g* never occurs at the end of a word; it has been replaced by *k* which was considered a more accurate representation of the actual sound that occurs. Hence, the above words spelled in the new system are as follows: *maolek, somnak,* and *dokdok*. This is probably the most controversial change in the spelling system.

4.1.4 THE SEQUENCE *gu*. The sequence of letters *gu* was used by Von Preissig to represent the simple consonant *g* when followed by the vowels *e* or *i*. This sound is now written with a single *g*, as in *gimen* 'to drink', *gigon* 'as soon as', and *geftao* 'big hearted'.

The sequence *gu* is used in the new spelling system to represent the phonetic sequence [gw] as in the following words: *guiya* 'him, her', *guenao* 'there', and *gua'ot* 'stairs'.

4.1.5 *ng* BEFORE *k*. The sound written as *ng* is a velar nasal. When the sound occurs before a *k*, *n* is used to represent the sound that is represented by *ng* elsewhere. The following words (the second pair respelled phonemically) will serve to illustrate:

> ababang   'butterfly'
> nginge'   'sniff'
>
> banko /bangko/ 'bench'
> tankat /tangkat/ 'cage'

4.1.6 DIPHTHONGS. There are several diphthongs in Chamorro, most of them found in loan words. In the earlier writings one often finds the diphthong *au*, as in *lau* 'but', and *tautau* 'people', and *mauleg* 'good'. This same sound was sometimes written *ao*. In the new spelling system this diphthong is always spelled *ao*. The above words are now spelled *lao, taotao*, and *maolek*. The other diphthongs of Chamorro are listed below with sample words and English glosses:

> | ai | taitai | 'to read' |
> |----|--------|-----------|
> | oi | boi | 'boy' |
> | ia | espia | 'look for' |
> | oe | hagoe | 'pond' |
> | iu | tiu | 'uncle' |
> | ie | fiét | 'proud' |

All of the diphthongs except *ai* and *ao* occur only in loan words from other languages.

4.1.7 VOWELS. Although Chamorro has six distinct phonemic vowels, the spelling system uses only the vowels *a, e, i, o, u*. Thus, one of the distinctive vowels in the language is not specified in the new writing system. There is no way to distinguish between the /æ/ of *baba* 'open' and the /a/ of *baba* 'bad'. The Committee felt that it would not be necessary to show this distinction since the meaning of a word spelled with *a* could always be determined on the basis of the context.

In this dictionary, the words which have the low front vowel [æ] in a stressed syllable are marked as follows:

> baba [æ] 'open'

Only the main entries which have [æ] as a stressed vowel are so marked.

4.1.8 PROBLEMS WITH VOWELS. The problem of how certain vowels of Chamorro should be spelled is one of long standing, and it has not been completely resolved by the new spelling system. The rules formulated by the Orthography Committee are explicit. (See CRG, pp. 61–62.) However, the compilers of this dictionary at times felt that to follow the rules would distort the actual pronunciation of certain words. Hence, the rules were not always observed.

The major problem centers on the pronunciation of unstressed vowels when it is difficult, if not impossible, to determine whether the vowel should be *i* or *e*, or, in the case of a back vowel, whether it should be *u* or *o*.

To resolve this problem for the dictionary we have followed the spelling rules except where we felt the actual pronunciation required that an exception to the rule be made. Following are some examples of words that are exceptions to the spelling rules governing the vowels. Two spellings are given. Those in the first column show the word spelled according to the general spelling rules; those in the second column are the dictionary entries.

Spelled by Rule	*Dictionary Entry*	*English Gloss*
che'lo	che'lu	'sibling'
dankulu	dankolo	'big'
dilengdeng	dilingdeng	'ring bell'
desatende	disatende	'disregard'
deskatga	diskatga	'unload'
ensigidas	insigidas	'promptly'
ensutta	insutta	'insult'

A thorough study of the exceptions to the spelling rules would show that most of the exceptions are made for Spanish and English loanwords. The spelling rules work for at least 98 percent of native Chamorro words. Some additional exceptions must be made to accommodate the words borrowed from foreign sources that were not made to conform completely to the sound system of Chamorro.

4.1.9 INCONSISTENCIES IN SPELLING. Since the initial compilation of this dictionary began in 1967, the spelling system has been revised at least three times. Each revision has required a complete respelling of all the affected items in the dictionary.

Although the compilers of this work have made every effort to achieve consistency in spelling in the dictionary, a careful reader may find that we have not always been successful.

By way of apology, we might add that the spelling of such a widely used language as English, which has had innumerable dictionaries since Robert Cawdrey's *A Table Alphabeticall* (1604), the first English dictionary, still suffers from inconsistencies in spelling. Users of English have managed to live with these minor problems. Hopefully those who use written Chamorro can also develop a tolerant attitude toward the vagaries of the written language.

4.2 Primary Stress. Primary stress (the loudest syllable) is predictable for most Chamorro words. It falls on the next to last syllable. Where primary stress is predictable it is not shown in the dictionary entries. Primary stress is shown by an acute accent mark (´) over the stressed vowel in words with an unpredictable primary stress. Some examples are: *asút* 'blue', *dánkolo* 'big', *garañón* 'lustful', *gá'umessitan* 'joker'.

5.0 Guide to Pronunciation. This brief guide to pronunciation is included for the benefit of the non-Chamorro user who is not familiar with the sounds of the language. Phonetic respelling of each individual word was considered unnecessary since the spelling system itself provides a very good representation of the way the Chamorro words are pronounced, with the exception of the low front vowel [æ].

The symbols below are presented in alphabetical order. The letters of the Chamorro alphabet are presented first, followed by a phonetic representation. Two Chamorro words containing the sound are then given with the appropriate letter in italics. The Chamorro words are followed by a broad phonetic respelling and an English gloss.

Alphabetical Symbol	Phonetic Symbol	Chamorro Words	Phonetic Respelling	English Gloss
a	[æ]	baba	[bæba]	'open'
		katu	[kætu]	'cat'
a	[a]	baba	[baba]	'bad'
		katta	[katta]	'letter'
b	[b]	batu	[batu]	'a game'
		pabu	[pabu]	'turkey'
ch	[ts]*	chagi	[tsægi]	'try'
		uchan	[utsan]	'rain'
d	[d]	dagi	[dægi]	'lie'
		gada'	[gada']	'young fruit'
e	[e]	echong	[etsoŋ]	'crooked'
		sage'	[sage']	'pain'
f	[f]	fugo'	[fugo']	'squeeze'
		hafa	[hafa]	'what'
g	[g]	go'te	[go'te]	'support'
		nigap	[nigap]	'yesterday'

Alphabetical Symbol	Phonetic Symbol	Chamorro Words	Phonetic Respelling	English Gloss
h	[h]	hatsa	[hattsa]	'lift'
		mamahlao	[mamahlao]	'shy'
i	[i]	ipe'	[ipe']	'split'
		hayi	[hadzi]	'who'
'	[']	li'e'	[li'e']	'see'
		haga'	[haga']	'blood'
k	[k]	kadidak	[kadidak]	'tickle'
		niyok	[nidzok]	'coconut'
l	[l]	lahi	[lahi]	'male'
		alu	[alu]	'barracuda'
m	[m]	macheng	[matseŋ]	'monkey'
		homhom	[homhom]	'dark'
n	[n]	napu	[napu]	'wave'
		alunan	[alunan]	'pillow'
ñ	[ñ]	ñalang	[ñalaŋ]	'hungry'
		años	[años]	'years'
ng	[ŋ]	nginge'	[ŋiŋe']	'sniff'
		echong	[etsoŋ]	'crooked'
o	[o]	oppop	[oppop]	'lie face down'
		hihot	[hihot]	'hear'
p	[p]	pacha	[patsa]	'touch'
		nigap	[nigap]	'yesterday'
r	[r]	ratu	[ratu]	'moment'
		para	[pæra]	'towards'
s	[s]	susu	[susu]	'breast'
		lassas	[læssas]	'skin'
t	[t]	tommo	[tommo]	'elbow, knee'
		hihot	[hihot]	'near'
u	[u]	utot	[utot]	'cut'
		hagu	[hagu]	'you'
y	[dz]	yan	[dzæn]	'and'
		huyong	[hudzoŋ]	'outside'

*One will hear this sound ranging from [ts] to [č].

6.0   Dictionary Entries. There are several different types of information in each entry. These will each be explained separately as they are likely to occur in the various types of entries.

6.1   Headwords. The headword is in **boldface type.** It may be a full word, or it may be an affix. If it is a prefix it will be followed by a hyphen, for example, **chát-.** If the headword is a suffix, it will be preceded by a hyphen, for example, **-guan.** If the headword is an infix, it will be preceded and followed by a hyphen, for example, **-um-.** The hyphens indicate that the headword is not a full word.

Letters of the alphabet have also been listed as headwords. They are listed according to their Chamorro pronunciation.

6.2   Word Classification. For the purposes of this dictionary four different classes of words are identified. Three of the classes are identified by a number (1, 2, or 3) following the headword. The fourth class has no designating number to mark it.

A Class I word is any word that can take the *passive voice* prefix and the *goal focus* infix. All Class I words may function as transitive verbs.

A Class 2 word takes either *-um-* or *ma-* when it occurs as a predicate in an intransitive statement.

A Class 3 word is any one of several *defective verbs.*

The unclassified words include expletives, proper names, words such as *hunggan* 'yes' and *ahe'* 'no', and other words that proved impossible to classify with any precision.

A more complete discussion of word classes in Chamorro can be found in CRG, pp. 76–82.

6.3   Definitions of Chamorro Entries. All definitions are given in English; hence, they are more properly called glosses. The compilers have tried to give a variety of English words that will help illustrate the range of meaning of the Chamorro entry.

6.4   Alternate Pronunciations. In many cases we have included alternate pronunciations. In some instances we have advised the reader to *see* another entry which might show the more common pronunciation. In some other cases, we have indicated that there is an alternate pronunciation by using the word *also.*

6.5   Cross-references. Many of the dictionary entries contain a cross-reference to another word, or words. This type of cross-reference is marked by the letters *Cf.* The words following *Cf.* are either similar or related in meaning, and are included to help the user find a word that might be more suitable for his purposes.

6.6 Masculine-Feminine Distinctions. Chamorro has retained many Spanish gender distinctions in the Class 2 words. When the masculine form differs from the feminine form, this is indicated by the initials m and f in parentheses.

6.7 Sample Sentences. Sample sentences have been provided for a large number of the entries. Limitations of space prevented us from providing a sentence for every entry. Since the purpose of the sample sentences was to illustrate usage, we tried to choose dictionary entries that we felt might be troublesome for a beginner in the language.

We tried to keep the sentences as short and simple as possible for reasons of economy. The English glosses of the sentences are sometimes quite literal translations, and consequently often sound awkward. The glosses were kept literal in the hope of helping the beginning language learner locate all the meaningful words in the Chamorro and English sentences.

6.8 Taboo and Slang Words. Since it was the intention of the compilers that this dictionary reflect current usage of Chamorro, we have followed the basic principles of current lexicography by including words that some language purists might consider improper. Those words have been marked by the labels *slang* or *taboo* to indicate different degrees of social unacceptability. Words included in the category of *slang* would be used very commonly among peer groups but not in formal situations. Those words marked *taboo* should never be used by anyone who does not have a full understanding of the linguistic and social implications of such words.

6.9 Summary of Symbols and Abbreviations Used.

> 1, 2, or 3: word class code
> (m) masculine; (f) feminine: gender distinction
> Also, see: alternate pronunciation
> Cf.: cross-reference
> esp.: especially
> fr.: from
> G (Guam), R (Rota), S (Saipan): dialect variants
> Pron.: pronunciation
> Sp.: Spanish

7.0 Old Chamorro Numbers. Chamorro speakers frequently talk about the pre-Spanish numbers. We have never met anyone who remembers them or who remembers having heard them used. In the interest of preserving what little is known about these numbers they are presented here as taken from the *Chamorro-Wörterbuch* by Fr. P. Callistus.

Simple numbers, also for days, months, etc.	For living things	For inanimate things	For long objects
1. hacha	maisa	hachiyai	taghachun
2. hugua	hugua	hugiyai	taghuguan
3. tulo	tato	tolgiyai	tagtulun
4. fatfat	fatfat	fatfatai	tagfatun
5. lima	lalima	limiyai	tagliman
6. gunum	guagunum	gonmiyai	taggunum
7. fiti	fafiti	fitgiyai	tagfitun
8. gualu	guagualu	guatgiyai	taggualun
9. sigua	sasigua	sigiyai	tagsiguan
10. manot	maonot	manutai	tagmaonton
100. gatus	gatus	gatus	manapo (gatus)

According to the phonological rules of Chamorro, which were operative even during the time of Fr. Callistus, some of the above words could not have been pronounced as they are spelled here, for examples, *tagfia, tolgiyai*. By the rules of modern Chamorro pronunciation, a more accurate spelling for these numbers would be *takfia* and *totgiyai*. The initial *tag-* of all the words in the last column would have been pronounced *tak-*, with the possible exception of *taggunum* which has a geminate consonant.

It will be noticed that the only one of the above words still in use in modern Chamorro is *maisa,* meaning 'alone' or 'oneself'.

8.0 How to Locate Derived Words. The user of this dictionary may not be able to locate Chamorro words that he has heard or seen. It is quite possible that the compilers have omitted the word he is looking for. It is more likely, however, that the missing word is actually a *derived word* which has deliberately not been included. For example, the word *manachálokka'* 'to be of the same height' is not in the dictionary. However, the root word *lokka'*, and the prefixes *man-* and *achá-* are all listed. The problem is that the user may not know how to discover the root of the word he is looking for. He must be able to look for the *root word* and construct the meaning of the derived word for himself.

As was pointed out in 2.2 above, it is possible to derive an extremely large number of Chamorro words from root words. For obvious reasons we have not attempted to include all of the derived words in the language in this work.

In order to determine the meaning of derived words, the user must be aware of the processes of affixation in Chamorro so that he can determine what the root word is. For a full description of these processes and affixes see CRG, pp. 169–201. The affixes are all listed separately in this dictionary. The following is a brief outline that will list some of the more common affixes and processes that tend to disguise the root words.

8.1 Infixes *-um-* **and** *-in-*. The infixes *-um-* and *-in-* are both used very frequently in Chamorro, and may cause some difficulty in locating root words. These infixes are always placed just before the first vowel of the word to which they are attached. Following are some examples of root words and their derived forms using *-um-*:

Root Word	Derived Word
saga	sumaga
gupu	gumupu
taitai	tumaitai
agang	umagang
ba'	buma'

The infix *-in-* sometimes causes additional changes to take place in the root word through the process of vowel fronting (see CRG, pp. 52–53). Following are some examples of root words and their derived forms using *-in-:*

Root Word	Derived Word
atan	inatan
malago'	minalago'
taitai	tinaitai
huchom	hinichom
godde	ginedde

Notice in the last two examples above that the stressed vowel of the root word is different in the derived word. This change is known as vowel fronting, and it will always happen when a back vowel is preceded by the infix *-in-*.

8.2 Reduplication. The process of reduplication is used widely in Chamorro, and at times it can obscure the structure of the root word. The different types of reduplication in Chamorro are discussed in different sections of CRG. The most common types with examples are as follows:

(a) Reduplication of stressed vowel and preceding consonant, if any.

Root Word	Derived Word
táotao	tátaotao
ádda'	á'adda'
malágu	malálagu
gúpu	gúgupu
ñálang	ñáñalang

(b) Reduplication of final consonant and vowel.

Root Word	Derived Word
guatu	guátutu
fine'na (from *fo'na*)	finé'nana
magi	mágigi
dánkolo	dánkololo
ñalang	ñálalang

Notice that the last items in groups (a) and (b) above contain the same root word *ñalang* 'hungry'. The reduplicated form in the (a) group— *ñáñalang*—might be glossed as 'being hungry', while the reduplicated form of the (b) group—*ñálalang*—means 'very hungry'.

8.3 Prefixes. There are numerous prefixes in Chamorro that are written as part of the word. These are all given in the dictionary with definitions and sample sentences. They are listed here without glosses as a quick reference point which the user can consult if he is having difficulty locating a word in the dictionary.

Prefixes

á-	ga'-	mí-
achá-	ge'-	mina'-
an-	gi-	na'-
cha'-	ha- (hah-)	pinat-
chát-	ka-	san-
fa'-	ke-	tai-
fama'-	la'-	tak-
fan . . . (y) an	ma-	ya-
	man-	

8.4 Suffixes. Suffixes are also written as part of the word in Chamorro, and thus may obscure the structure of the root word. All of the suffixes are listed and glossed in the dictionary. They are listed here as a quick reference for the user.

Suffixes

-an	-hun	-ñaihon
-guan	-i	-on
-gui	-iyi	-yi
-guiyi	-ña	-yiyi
		-yon

8.5 Prefix *man-* Several of the prefixes and suffixes cause changes to take place in the structure of the root word. The very common prefix *man-* (and its alternate form *fan-*) causes certain changes that tend to obscure the structure of the root word. These changes are described fully in CRG, pp.

48–50, and are summarized briefly here with examples. Notice that when the prefix *man-* is added to a root word, the initial consonant of the root word may change.

Root Word man- +	*Root Word*	*Consonant Change*
po'lo	mamo'lo	n→m; p→ø*
taña'	manaña'	t→ø
kati	mangati	n→ng; k→ø
fa'om	mama'om	n→m; f→ø
ngangas	mangngangas	n→ng
saga	mañaga	n→ñ; s→ø
chagi	mañagi	n→ñ; ch→ø

If the user is not able to find the word he is looking for in this dictionary, and if the word begins with the letters *ma* plus a nasal consonant (*m, n, ñ, ng*), then the word probably contains the prefix *man-*. The root can then be located by reconstructing what the initial consonant of the root was before the prefix was added. The above list of consonant changes should help in determining what the initial consonant might be.

8.6 Affixes and Reduplication. When prefixes, infixes, suffixes, and reduplication all occur together with one root—and they often do—the actual root word can become almost totally obscured. Such words are not at all uncommon in Chamorro. Given below are some examples that will illustrate how combinations of affixes can come together to form Chamorro words.

Chamorro Word	*Component Parts*
mangekematai	Prefix *man-*
	Prefix *ke-*
	Reduplication
	Root word *matai*
manmasanganenñaihon	Prefix *man-*
	Prefix *ma-*
	Root word *sangan*
	Suffix -*i* (spelled *e*)
	Excrescent consonant *n*
	Suffix -*ñaihon*
manacháchama' a' ñao	Prefix *man-*
	Prefix *achá-*
	Reduplication
	Prefix *ma-*
	Root word *a'ñao*

*ø is a linguistic symbol meaning "zero." → is a symbol meaning "becomes."

Introduction

Chamorro is a language that forms new words by combining affixes and root words extensively. It has not been possible to list all of the potential Chamorro words in this dictionary. In order to determine what some words mean, one simply has to know the affixes of the language, and the rules for combining them with the root words.

BIBLIOGRAPHY

Direct Sources for Dictionary Material

Callistus, P. (O. Capuchin). 1910. *Chamorro-Wörterbuch: nebsteiner Chamorro-Grammatik.* Hong Kong: Typis Societatis Missionum ad Exteros.

DeLeon, Francisco P. n.d. "Check List of Guam Birds." Mimeographed. Territory of Guam: Division of Fish and Wildlife.

Donlon, Adelbert (O.F.M. Cap.). 1946. *English-Chamorro Dictionary.* Mimeographed at Garrison, New York. Copy available at the Micronesian Area Research Center, University of Guam.

F. "Val" C. 1967. *Chamorro-English Dictionary.* Hong Kong: The Green Pagoda Press.

Fritz, G. 1908. *Chamorro Wörterbuch.* Berlin: G. Reimer.

Kami, Harry T., Isaac I. Ikehara, and Francisco P. deLeon. n.d. "Check List of Guam Fishes." Mimeographed. Territory of Guam: Division of Fish and Wildlife.

Kučera, Henry, and W. Nelson Francis. 1967. *Computational Analysis of Present-Day American English.* Providence: Brown University Press.

Preissig, Edward R. von. 1918. *Dictionary and Grammar of the Chamorro Language of the Island of Guam.* Washington, D.C.: Government Printing Office.

Schultz, Leonard P. 1953–1966. *Fishes of the Marshall and Marianas Islands.* Washington, D.C.: Government Printing Office.

Stone, Benjamin C. 1970. "The Flora of Guam." *Micronesica: Journal of the University of Guam,* 6 (1970–1971).

Thorndike, E.L. 1935. *The Thorndike-Century Junior Dictionary.* Chicago: Scott-Foresman.

Vera, Roman Maria de. 1932. *Diccionario Chamorro–Castellano.* Manila: Cacho Hermanos.

Related Studies

Augon, Katherine B. 1971. *Let's Chat in Chamorro.* Agaña, Guam: Guam Economic Development Authority.

Burrus, E. J. 1954. "Sanvitores' Grammar and Catechism in the Mariana Language." *Anthropos* 49:934–960.

Callistus, P. (O. Capuchin). n.d. *Chamorro-Grammar.* Translated from the German original by James R. Grey, edited and arranged by Junior

Pangelinan. Saipan, M. I. Mimeographed. Copy available in the Micronesian Area Research Center, University of Guam.

Carano, Paul, and Pedro C. Sanchez. 1964. *A Complete History of Guam.* Tokyo and Rutland, Vt.: Charles E. Tuttle Co.

"Chamorro in Micronesia." 1965. *Anthropological Linguistics* 7(2): 265–297.

Conant, Carlos E. 1911. "Consonant Changes and Vowel Harmony in Chamorro." *Anthropos* 6:136–146.

Costenoble, H. 1940. *Die Chamoro Sprache.* 'S-Gravenhage: M. Nijhoff.

Dyen, Isidore. 1962. "The Lexicostatistical Classification of the Malayo-Polynesian Languages." *Language* 38:38–46.

F. "Val" C. 1967. *Chamorro-English Guidebook; Words and Phrases of the Marianas Islands.* Hong Kong: The Green Pagoda Press.

Fischer, J. L. 1961. "The Retention Rate of Chamorro Basic Vocabulary." *Lingua* 10 (1961): 255–266.

Fritz, G. 1908. *Chamorro Grammatik.* Herausgegeben von dem Seminar für Orientalische Sprachen. Berlin: G. Reimer.

Kats, J. 1919. *Het Tjamoro van Guam en Saipan Vergeleken meteenige verwante talen.* 'S-Gravenhage: M. Nijhoff.

Mata y Araujo, Luis de. 1865. *Grammatica Chamorro.* Manila: Giraudier.

Mathiot, Madeleine. 1955. *Chamorro Phonemics.* Master's thesis, Georgetown University.

Safford, William E. 1909. *The Chamorro Language of Guam.* Washington, D. C.: W. H. Lowdermilk and Co.

Sanvitores, Diego Luis de. 1954. "Lingua Mariana." *Micro-Bibliotheca Anthropos*, vol. 14. Freiburg, Switzerland: Anthropos-Institut.

Seidin, William. 1960. "Chamorro Phonemes." *Anthropological Linguistics* 2:6–35.

Solenberger, Robert R. 1953. "Recent Changes in Chamorro Direction Terminology." *Oceania* 24:132–141.

Spoehr, Alexander. 1954. *Saipan: The Ethnology of a War-Devastated Island.* Chicago: Natural History Museum.

———. 1957. *Marianas Prehistory: Archaeological Survey and Excavations on Saipan, Tinian, and Rota.* Chicago: Natural History Museum.

Thompson, Laura M. 1932. *Archaeology of the Marianas Islands.* Bernice P. Bishop Museum Bulletin 100. Honolulu: B. P. Bishop Museum.

———. 1945. *The Native Culture of the Marianas Islands.* Bernice P. Bishop Museum Bulletin 185. Honolulu: B. P. Bishop Museum.

———. 1947. *Guam and Its People.* Princeton, N. J.: Princeton University Press.

Topping, Donald M. 1963a. *Chamorro Structure and the Teaching of English.* Ph.D. dissertation, Michigan State University.

———. 1963b. "Loanblends: a Tool for Linguists." *Language Learning* 13:281–287.

———. 1968. "Chamorro Vowel Harmony." *Oceanic Linguistics* 8:67–79.

———. 1969*a*. "A Restatement of Chamorro Phonology." *Anthropological Linguistics* 11:62–77.

———. 1969*b*. *Spoken Chamorro*. Honolulu: University of Hawaii Press.

———. 1973*a*. *Chamorro Reference Grammar*. Honolulu: The University Press of Hawaii.

———. 1973*b*. "Spoken Chamorro Tomorrow?" *Guam Recorder*, 2nd ser. 3(1):45–48.

CHAMORRO-ENGLISH DICTIONARY

a A—letter.

a- Reciprocal marker, do (something) to each other - prefix. May be affixed to verbs. *Atungo' na dos.* Know each other or be acquainted with each other. *Aguaiya na dos.* Love each other. *Afa'na'gue na dos.* Teach each other.

a'a' 2. Open mouth (wide). *A'a' fan.* Open your mouth please.

á'abang [æ] 2. Type of plant-eugenia reinwardtiana. Hardwood tree, formerly used for bullcart.

á'ada' [æ] 2. Mimicker, imitator, mocker.

á'adahi [æ] 2. Protector, guard, caretaker, body guard. Cf. **Adahi.**

á'addak [æ] 2. Knocker—one who or that which knocks. Pounder. Cf. **Addak.**

á'aga [æ] 2. Type of fish-family labridae. Wrasses.

á'akonseha [æ] 2. Adviser, counselor. Cf. **Konseheru.**

á'amte [æ] 2. Physician, doctor, nurse, healer. Cf. **Na'homlo, amte.**

á'aposta [æ] 2. Gambler, one who bets, wagers. Cf. **Aposta.**

á'arekla [æ] 2. Fixer, repairman, arranger. Cf. **Arekla.**

á'atte [æ] 2. Magician, wizard, sorcerer, trickster, clairvoyant, sleight-of-hand artist. Cf. **Atte.**

á'ayuda [æ] 2. Helper, collaborator, aid, assistant. Cf. **Ayudante, ayuda.**

á'baba' [æ] 2. Feeble-minded, stupid, crazy. Cf. **Ba'ba'.**

ababang [æ] 2. Butterfly, butterfly fish ornamented with black and yellow stripes. Also **guihan ababang** 'butterfly fish'. Refers to many small fish of the families zanclidae and chaetodontidae.

ababang amariyu 2. Type of fish-chaetodon auriga. Yellow butterfly.

ababang gupalao 2. Type of fish-family zanclidae. Moorish idols.

ababang kahet 2. Type of insect—papilo xuthus l. Citrus swallowtail.

abahakat 2. Type of plant—used by Carolinian women as perfume.

abahu 1. Clear land—by felling all trees and bushes, tear a house down, take down everything.

abak [æ] 2. Lost, gone astray, take something by mistake. *Abak i taotao.* The man is lost. *Abak chalan-ña.* He took the wrong road.

ábaka 2. Type of plant-musa textilis. Manila hemp, rope.

ábalansa 1. Balance—by making two sides of scale equal.

ábale' [æ] 2. Intercourse.

abandona Abandon, relinquish, evacuate, leave behind, forsake, desert. Cf. **Dingu.**

abandonáo 2. Abandoned, left, forsaken, left alone.

abaniku 2. Fan (Japanese style), folding fan. Cf. **Goia.**

ábansa 2. Bear out, stick with something out of obligation even though it is very disagreeable.

abansa 2. Advance, go forward. Cf. **Atbansa.**

abanse 2. Advance pay, payment in advance.

abas 2. Type of plant-psidium guavaja.

abeha 2. Honeybee, bumblebee, bee, drone. Also **abea.**

abettura 2. Aperture, opening, slit, hole. Also **atbettura.**

abiba 1. Encourage, give encouragement, inspire, incite. Cf. **Biba.**

abietto 2. Open, unfastened. Also **atbietto.**

abilidát 2. Ability, capacity. Cf. **Kapasidat.**

abirigua 1. Interrogate, question, ask. Cf. **Faisen, kuestiona, imbestiga.** *Ha abirigua i patgon.* He interrogated the child.

abiriguadót 2. Interrogator, examiner, prober, investigator. Cf. **Imbestigadot.**

abisa 1. Advise, notify, alarm—give, warning--give, inform.

abisu 2. Alarm, warning sound for notifying of danger, notice of danger, danger signal.

ábiu 2. Support, help, supply. Stronger in meaning than *ayuda.* *Manmanggagagao abiu i taotao Luta.* The people of Rota are asking for help.

abok [æ] 2. Friend, buddy, pal, mate. Cf. **Amigu.**

abona 1. Side with, take sides, as to conceal the fault of the one being favored, back someone, support someone. Cf. **Alaba**. *Si nana-hu ha abona yo'.* My mother sided with me.

abona 1. Pay, purchase, buy. Cf. **Fahan**.

abonu 2. Fertilizer, manure.

abrasa 1. Encompass, cover a certain area. Unit of measurement from fingertip of outstretched arm to opposite shoulder.

abrasu 1,2. Hug (by having arms meet together), enfold in the arms, encircled in someone's arms. (R) Cf. **Toktok**. *Ha abrasu i patgon-ña.* She embraced her child. *I abrasu-hu ni palao'an apmam-ña kinu i abrasu-mu ni patgon.* My embrace of the woman was longer than your embrace of the child.

abrebiasión 2. Abbreviation.

abríbiet 1. Abbreviate.

abrilata 2. Can opener. Cf. **Baban lata**.

Abrít 2. April. Cf. **Lumuhu**.

abubon pápago' 2. Physalia, Portuguese Man of War. Lit. irritating balloon.

abubu 2. Balloon.

abubu 2. Type of plant-stictocardia tiliaefolia. Morning glory.

abuchuelas 2. Type of plant-phaseolus vulgaris.

abugadu 2. Lawyer, attorney, counselor, prosecutor, defender. Also **abugao, difensot**.

abugáo 2. Lawyer, attorney, counselor, defender. Also **abugadu**.

abundansia 2. Abundance, profusion, plenty, opulence, overflow.

abundante 2. Abundant, plentiful, opulent.

ábuni [æ] 2. Food sac—esp. in crustacean family, fleshy part of crustaceans, testicle (slang), brain (slang).

aburidu 2. Ruckus, disturbance, racket, fuss, riot, confused—in mind. *Umaburidu i taotao gi halom guma'.* The man made a noise in the house.

abusu 2. Abuse, maltreatment, ill-treatment, outrage, ill-use.

abuttáo 2. Piled up, amassed.

achá- [æ] As—as, indicating equality (prefix), similative affix. Also **cha-**. *Achabrabu ham na dos.* We are both healthy. *Achayayas si Juan yan si Jose gi bola.* John is as tired as Joseph in the ball game.

acha [æ] 1. Pound, beat, as pounding roots, etc. Cf. **Attan**.

achágigu [æ] At same time, simultaneously, occurred simultaneously. *Achagigu hit humanao asta Guam.* We left for Guam simultaneously. *Achagigu hit maigo'.* We went to sleep at the same time.

áchago' [æ] 2. Distance.

achago'ña Farther, more distant.

acháguasguas [æ] 2. Peer, equal.

achahet 2. Peer. From *acha-* plus *hit*. Cf. **Achataotao**. *Mandaña' ham yan i manachahet-hu.* We got together, my peers and I.

achai 2. Chin.

achá'igi [æ] 2. Compete, contend. Cf. **Kompetensia**. *Umacha'igi i dos umamigu.* The two friends competed.

achaigua 2. Similar, alike, akin, analogous, parallel, homogeneous, uniform, resemble, equal, likeness. Cf. **Parehu**. *Ti achaigua-mu yo'.* You are not my equal. *Achaigua-ña i amiga-ña.* She is similar to her friend. *Este na lepblo achaiguan ayu.* This book is like that one.

achá'ikak [æ] 2. Race, run, to compete at high speed. Cf. **Karera**. *Ta acha'ikak asta i tenda.* We will race to the store. *Acha'ikak yan si Juan.* Race with John.

achá'ikak [æ] 2. Plunge down, tumble.

achaka 1. Blame, reproach, hold responsible. Also **akacha**. *I lahi ha achaka i ga'lagu.* The man blamed the dog.

achaki 2. Trouble, pester, problem, incident. *Si Juan gai achaki gi ega'an.* Juan had some trouble this morning.

achakma' [æ] 2. Having an affair, shacking up, common-law marriage, having a mistress. *Mapribi umachakma' gi relihon Katoliku.* It is prohibited by the Catholic religion to keep a mistress.

achamcham [æ] 2. Jawbone (lower), jaw, the lower or nether jaw.

achang 2. Lower class in older Chamorro society. See **manachang**.

achátaotao [æ] 2. Peer, equal in age and status; people.

achá'ungak [æ] 1. Balance, make equal weights.

achetge 1. Wink, blink. Cf. **Chalamlam, señas.** *I lahi ha achetge i palao'an.* The man winked at the girl.

achiak 2. Gecko, small lizard (lives in houses). Cf. **Guali'ek.**

áchibao 2. Troublemaker, having a bad record. Cf. **Achaka, mahaderu, palacha'.**

achigo' 2. Close eyes, shut eyelids deliberately. *Achigo'.* Close your eyes.

achita 2. Hatchet, pickax, mattock. Also **hachita.**

acho' 2. Rock, stone, pebble. Cf. **Baras.**

Acho' Nickname for Ignacio.

acho' atupat 2. Sling stone.

acho' dagon haya 2. Type of coral, fire coral, millepora. Causes burning sensation if it touches bare skin.

acho' mulinu 2. Millstone, grinding stone.

acho' ñañak 2. Coral. Cf. **Cho'cho'.**

acho' tasi 2. Coral, generic term for any kind of hard coral.

achok [æ] At least. *Ti mangganna yo' lao achok i amigu-hu.* I didn't win but, at least, my friend did.

áchokka' [æ] Although, even though, not even. From *achok* plus *ha'. Achokka' malago' yo' humanao lao taya' salape'-hu.* Although I wanted to go I have no money. *Hanao para i lancho achokka' malangu hao.* Go to the farm even though you are sick. *Achokka' si Maria ti kumonfotme fatto ha' magi.* Although Maria doesn't agree , just come here.

achom [æ] 2. Sneeze. Cf. **Hatcheng.** *Umachom si Pedro.* Pete sneezed.

achón 2. Torch. Also **hachon.**

achoti 2. Type of plant-bixa orellana. Anatto. A small tree bearing red prickly capsules containing seeds which are used for coloring rice, known as *hineksa' agaga'.*

achoti 2. Working middle class of pre-Spanish Chamorro society. Cf. **Atcha'ot.**

adá [æ] Oh (interjection). Implies interrogative. *Ada, un espiha yo' nigap?* Oh, you searched for me yesterday?

ada lao But, have decided not to, change of mind, change of decision, maybe not, but that's all right. (R) *Konne' yo' guatu asta i espitat, ada*

lao munga sa' mitinane' hao. Take me there to the hospital but that's all right , you have lots of things to do.

adaba 2. Padlock. Also **andaba.**

adahi [æ] What do you know (exclamation). *Adahi sa' anakko' este na fina'okso'.* What do you know, this hilly place is long.

adahi [æ] 1. Guard, protect, take care of, collect and lay up. Also **hadahi.**

adahi [æ] 2. Careful, watch out, look out, beware.

adai 2. Friend. Probably from *adahi*, or two who care for each other.

ádai [æ] For pete's sake, for crying out loud, goodness sake. Also an expression showing politeness in addressing a friend of the opposite sex of the same age group.

ádalak [æ] 2. Reciprocal system of work exchange.

adamelong 2. Round, circular, spherical, globular, oval. Cf. **Aredondo.**

adanggua' 1. Step over, jump over. (R) Cf. **Goppe, agua'.** *Hu adanggua' i fache'.* I stepped over the mud puddle.

ádaose [æ] 2. Piled up, stacked on top of one another, intertwined. *Ha na'fanadaose gi hilo' i recorder.* He piled them up on the recorder.

adapta 1. Adopt, select, adapt, adjust, accommodate. Also **adopta.** Cf. **Adotta.** *Ha adapta i patgon.* She adopted the child. *In adapta ham gi kleman Hawaii.* We adapted to the climate in Hawaii.

adda' [æ] 1,2. Mimick, ridicule (by imitating), ape, copy, imitate closely. Mimickry. *Ha adda' i haohao ga'lagu.* He mimicked the barking of the dog. *Ha adda' i sinangan-ña.* He ridiculed his speech.

addak 1. Knock, rap, strike with a quick sharp blow. Cf. **Dakdak, dakot.** *Ha addak i ilu-hu ni baston-ña.* He rapped my head with his cane.

addeng [æ] 2. Foot—human, feet, leg (human). Cf. **Patas.**

addet [æ] 2. Severe, strict, austere, rigid. *Addet i minahalang-ña.* His loneliness was severe.

ádespatta [æ] 2. Disconnect, separate, break away. Cf. **Dipatta, sipara, adingu.** Also **despatta.** *Hu* *na'adespatta i alamle*. I separated the wires.

Adet   Nickname for Margarita.

adetfa 2.   Type of flower-oleander.

adibina   Prophesy, predict, foretell. *Hu adibina i tiempo para agupa'*. I foretold the weather for tomorrow.

adibina 2.   Riddle.

adiktáo 2.   Addict.

adilanta 1.   Improve, progress, advance, ameliorate. *Adilanta i tiningo'-mu.* Improve your knowledge.

adilantáo 2.   Advanced, progressing, improving, improved, precocious, brash.

adilanto 2.   Improvement, progress, advancement, advantage.

adimás   Rather than, apart from that, moreover, besides. Cf. **Fuera di.** *Adimas ki un hugando maolek-ña na un fanestudia.* Rather than playing, it is better that you study.

ádingan [æ] **2.**   Converse, talk, speak, utter. *Umadingan yo' yan i ma'gas.* I conversed with the boss. *Malago' yo' na un adingan.* I want you to talk.

adingani [æ] **1.**   Speak to, talk to. *Hu adingani i ma'estro.* I talked to the teacher.

adinganiyi 1.   Intercede, speak in favor of someone.

ádingu [æ] **2.**   Departure, separation, leave behind. Cf. **Dipatta, sipara, adespatta, desparati.** *Umadingu si Juan yan si Jose.* Juan and Jose went separate ways.

adiós 2.   Good-by, farewell, adieu.

ado' [æ] **2.**   Type of seaweed—very popular as an edible plant.

adobu 2.   Type of food, meat seasoned with vinegar, garlic, or onion.

adonse 1.   Stack up, pile on top of each other. Also **adaose.**

adopta 1.   Adopt, select. Also **adapta.**

adora 1.   Adore, worship, idolize, adorate.

adorasión 2.   Adoration, worship.

adotgan 2.   Hole, tunnel, a hole through something. *Umadotgan i hilu esta i otro banda.* The thread went through to the other side.

adotna 1.   Beautify, adorn, decorate—with ornaments. Cf. **Beste.**

adotno 2.   Beautification, adornment, ornament, decoration.

adotse 2.   Type of berry, grows on a bush.

adotta 1.   Adopt, take as one's own child. Cf. **Adapta, adopta.**

adottera 2.   Adulterous (woman), adulteress, a woman who commits adultery. Also **adotteria.** Cf. **Adotteru.**

adotteru 2.   Adulterous (man), adulterer, one who commits adultery. Also **adotteriu.** Cf. **Adottera.**

adu [æ] **1.**   Peep, peek at, keep a watch on. Cf. **Ngelo'.** Also **ado'.** *Hu adu i patgon gi bentana.* I peeped at the child through the window.

aduana 2.   Taxes, revenue.

aduanayon 2.   Taxable, subject to revenue.

adubáo 2.   Pot roast, roast. Cf. **Adobu.**

á'duko' [æ] **2.**   Imbecile, idiot, idiotic, moron. Cf. **Attamos, duko'.**

adulisensia 2.   Adolescence.

adumídide'   A little bit (at a time), gradual, by degrees. *Sigi ha' manhanao adumidide' i taotao siha gi miteng.* The people continued to leave the meeting a few at a time.

adutteria 2.   Adultery.

a'ef 2.   Torch—made from the dried shoot of the coconut tree. Also **ha'ef.**

afabilidát 2.   Courtesy, friendliness, pleasantness.

afabót 2.   In favor of.

afa'fa' [æ] **2.**   Armpit, crotch.

afa'fa'i [æ] **1.**   Carry—under the armpit. *Ha afa'fa'i i lepblo.* He carried the book under his armpit.

afagao [æ] **2.**   Hoarse, husky voice, harsh voice.

afamáo 2.   Famous, distinguished. Cf. **Distenggidu.**

áfa'maolek [æ] **2.**   Collaborate, form a group, help out, cooperate with, be friends. Cf. **A'ayuda.** *Umafa'maolek hit.* We became friends—we cooperated. *Manafa'maolek i mañe'lu-hu siha.* My brothers and sisters helped each other.

afan-   Reciprocal marker, plural. Combined form of *a-* plus *fan-*. Used in direct address to a group. *Hafa afanatungo'.* Hello, friends. *Afangga'chong, nihi ta fanhanao.* Let's go, friends.

áfana' [æ] 2. Face (each other), confront (one another). *Maila' ta afana'.* Let's face each other.

afañe'los 2. Comrades, brotherhood, fellowmen, friends—form of direct address. *Afañe'los, ayuda yo'.* Comrades, help me.

afao 2. Fog, mist, haze. (R) Cf. **Asgon.**

afatigáo 2. Fatigue, weariness, comatose; condition just preceding death.

a'fe 1,2. Sling, bandage for supporting an injured arm. To put in a sling. Cf. **Ha'fe.** *Hu a'fe i kannai-hu.* I use a sling for my arm. *Malingu i a'fe-ku.* I lost my sling.

afekta 1. Affect, involve, implicate in guilt. *Ti ha afekta yo' i fino'-mu.* Your talk didn't affect me.

áffulo' [æ] 2. Wrestling, wrestle. *Ya-hu umegga' affulo'.* I like to watch wrestling.

afgue 1. Add lime to betel nut mixture. From *afuki.* Cf. **Afok.**

afitma 1. Affirm, allege, assert.

aflagu 2. Groin, lower part of the abdomen.

aflitu 1. Fry. Cf. **Kema.**

afloha 1. Loosen, slacken. Cf. **Gomgom, kamkam.** *Ha afloha i tali.* He slackened the rope.

afok 2. Lime, birdlime, limestone (soft), quicklime. *Hu na'ye afok i mai'es.* I put lime on the corn.

afottunáo 2. Fortunate, lucky.

afte 1. To roof, cover with roof, install a roof. *Hu afte i gima'-hu.* I roofed my house.

afuera 2. Keep out. Cf. **Suhayi.**

afuetsáo 2. Obligation, required. Cf. **Fuetsao.**

afuetsas 1. Force, demand, compel, require. Cf. **Opbliga.** *Hu afuetsas i taotao na u funhayan i che'cho'-ña.* I forced the man to finish his work.

afuki 1. Put lime—on betel nut. Cf. **Afok.** *Hu afuki i pigua'.* I put lime on the betel nut.

afula' 2. Type of fish-family dasyatidae. Manta ray, sting ray, leopard ray, skate. Also **hafula'.** Cf. **Fanihen tasi.**

afulu 2. Hem lining of skirt, cuff—of shirt sleeve.

afuluyi 1. Wrap in, to line a garment, to put in a hem.

afuyot 1. Sandwich in, wrap up, infold, cover by winding around or folding, roll up. make ball—of something by pressing palms of hands together, as in making a riceball, snowball, etc. Cf. **Balutan, falulon, royu, puhot.** *Hu afuyot i patgon ni sabanas.* I wrapped the baby in the blanket. *Ma'afuyot i guihan ni titiyas.* The fish was wrapped in the tortilla. *Hu afuyot i hineksa' ni kannai-hu.* I made a rice-ball with my hands. *Hu afuyot i kesu ni pan.* I sandwiched the cheese with the bread.

aga 2. Type of bird-corus kubaryi, Marianas crow, all black.

aga' [æ] 2. Banana (ripe).

aga' guahú 2. Kind of banana-similar to Taiwan banana, but smaller tree.

aga'ga' 2. Neck.

agaga' [æ] 2. Red (color).

agaga' chada' 2. Egg yolk. Cf. **Yemma.**

agaliya 2. Stretcher, carrying stretcher for sick person. Also **anggariya.**

agaliya 2. Type of plant-ricinus communis. Castor bean.

Agaña Principal town of Guam. Pron. hagatña.

Agaña Heights Village in central Guam. Pron. agaña haits. Formerly known as Tutujan.

agang 1. Call (someone), beckon, summon. *Ha agang yo' si nana.* Mother called me.

a'gang [æ] 2. Loud, noise, booming, resounding. *A'gang dimasiao i batkon aire.* The plane is too loud.

agangi 1. Call, send for, invite. *Hu agangi i asagua-hu.* I invited my wife.

agangñaihon 1. Announce, declare, beckon, gossip. *Si Josepha ha agangñaihon yo'.* Josepha spread gossip about me.

ágaode [æ] 1. Cross legs, cross arms, cross one thing over another. Also **agaole.**

ágaole [æ] See agaode.

agapa' [æ] 2. Right (direction), opposite from left. *Agapa' na kannai.* Right hand. *Chule' i agapa' na direksion gi adinga' chalan.* Take the right direction of the road at the intersection.

agapa' fafayiña 2. Right-handed.

agara 1.   Covet, grab up, claim another's property. *Ha agagara gue' ni iyon taotao.* He claimed another person's property.

agasi 2.   Type of plant-cassytha filiformis. Parasite plant.

Agat   Village in central Guam. Pron. hagat.

agate'lang 2.   Type of plant-eugenia palumbis, hardwood tree.

Aget   Nickname for Margaret.

agi [æ] **2.**   Liquor, a local distilled liquor made from fermented fruit. Cf. **Aguayente, inestila.**

ágila 2.   Eagle, hawk.

a'go [æ] **1.**   Change, shift, substitute, exchange. *Hu a'go i sabanas gi katre.* I changed the blanket on the bed.

ágofli'e' [æ] **2.**   Friend, pal, partner. Cf. **atungo', amigu, ga'chong.**

agon 2.   Staple food, such as rice, taro, yam, etc. Starchy food. *Na'i ham kada ha'ani ni agon-mami.* Give us this day our daily bread.

agon [æ]   Really, are you sure? Used when addressing speaker to verify information on a statement just made. *Manggos suette hamyo agon.* You all are really fortunate.

agon- [æ]   Re- (a prefix denoting again), again. Cf. **Ta'lo.** *Agonchule'.* Recover, regain, etc. *Agonestablesi.* Re-establish. *Agonfatto.* Come back again.

agonias 2.   Agony, pangs of death. Cf. **Pinadesi.**

agonta'lo   Repeat, do (something) again, again. Cf. **Ta'lo.** *Agonta'lo kumanta i kanta-mu.* Repeat singing your song.

Agosto 2.   August. Cf. **Tenhos.**

ágo'te [æ] **2.**   Embrace each other, shake hands, hold hands. Cf. **Amantieni, asostieni.** *Umago'te i dos.* They held hands.

agradapble 2.   Agreeable, pleasing, obliging.

agradesi 1.   Appreciate, value, cherish, prize, treasure.

agradesidu 2.   Receivable. Also **atgradesidu.**

agradesimiento 2.   Gratitude, thanks, reward. Cf. **Gratifikasion.**

agramensora 2.   Surveyor (f), land surveyor.

agramensót 2.   Surveyor.

Agrihan 2.   Agrihan—name of an island located in the northern part of the Marianas District, the sixth island north of Saipan. Pronounced agrigan.

agrikuttura 2.   Agriculture.

agua 2.   Type of fish-chanos chanos. (Family chanidae). Milkfishes.

agua 2.   Water—used only in liturgical language. *Agua bendita.* Holy water. *Nuestra Señora de las Agua.* Our Lady of the Water.

agua' [æ] **1.**   Step over. Cf. **Goppe, adanggua'.**

agua bendita 2.   Holy water.

aguada 2.   Water supply.

águaguat 2.   Stubborn, perverse, naughty, mischievous, obstinate, pertinacious, dogged. Cf. **Ataktak.**

aguaguati 1.   Quarrel, disagree. Cf. **Resiste.**

aguahnon 2.   Become watery—from a cream base. Cf. **Aguanon.**

águaiya [æ] **2.**   Amour, love affair. Cf. **Guaiya.**

aguanon 2.   Become watery—from a cream base. Also **aguahnon.** *I atuli aguanon.* The pudding became watery.

aguanta 1.   Endure, restrain oneself, resist, aggravate—esp. wound, bear. Cf. **Sungon.**

aguas 2.   Type of fish-neomyxus chaptalii. Family mugilidae. Baby mullet.

aguas 2.   Gill—of fish. Also **guasang, atgayas.**

aguayente 2.   Liquor, brandy, hard liquor, a local distilled liquor made from fermented fruits. Cf. **Agi, inestila.**

aguet 1.   Throw, cast, fling.

aguguiyi 1.   Take sides—esp. applies to an attack of many upon one, side with. Cf. **Agululumi.** *Hu aguguiyi si Pete as Maria.* I took sides with Pete against Maria. *Hu aguguiyi i patgon ni palao'an.* I sided with the child against the woman.

aguhi 2.   Ghost crab. Also **haguihi.**

Aguigan   Second island south of Saipan. Also **Aguihan.**

Aguihan 2.   The second island south of Saipan. Also spelled Aguijan, Aguigan.

agululumi 1.   Band together against, run together, gang up. Cf. **Asaguani,**

aguguiyi. *Nihi ta agululumi si Jose.* Let's band together against Jose. *I taotao siha ma agululumi i guaka.* The men grouped together to catch the cow.

agumento 2. Argument. Also **atgumento.**

agupa' 2. Tomorrow.

agupa'ña 2. Day after tomorrow. Cf. **Nakpa'ña.**

a'guyon 2. Changeable, variable, fickle, inconstant. Cf. **A'go.** *A'guyon este i biyas sinturon-hu.* My belt buckle is changeable.

ahe' 2. No—negative reply to yes-no question; contrast with *munga.* Also **ahi'.**

ahensia 2. Agency.

ahente 2. Agent. Cf. **Eyente.**

ahgaga 2. Type of plant-melothria guamensis. Also **agaga.** Medicinal vine.

ahgao 2. Type of plant-premna obtusifolia. A small tree. Hardwood —used for building materials.

ahonholi 2. Type of plant-sesamum orientale. Sesame seed. Sesame.

ahos 2. Type of plant-allium sativum. Garlic.

ahu 2. Kind of food, coconut dumpling. A mixture of young coconut meat, water, starch, sugar cooked by boiling.

ahusta 1. Adjust. Cf. **Na'ahustao, templa.**

ai Interjection, oh, ouch, wow.

aidentifika 1. Identify.

aidentifikasión 2. Identification.

aire 1. Ventilate, air out.

aire 2. Air, wind. Cf. **Manglo'.**

ais 2. Ice.

ais baks 2. Ice box, refrigerator. Also **kahon ais.**

ais krim 2. Ice cream.

aka' See **akka'.**

akabosse 2. Twenty-one points in tres siete (card game), the winning score. Also **kabosse.**

akacha [æ] 2. Troublesome, troublemaker, teaser. Cf. **Palacha', achaka.**

akachayi [æ] 1. Tease, harass, vex, irritate by petty requests, deceive, defraud, cheat, dupe.

akademia 2. Academy, preparatory school, seminary, school for instruction in a particular science or art.

akadémiku 2. Academic, scholastic.

akadidok 2. Sharp point, fine point, keen edge.

akado' 2. Nipple, teat, mammilla. (R) Cf. **Chaflake', chipon.**

akague [æ] 2. Left (direction), opposite from right. *Akague na banda gi tataotao-mu.* Left side of your body. *Akague gi filan tinanom.* The row of plants on the extreme left.

akague fafayiña 2. Left-handed.

ákakam 2. Molar tooth. Cf. **Nifen.**

á'kalaye' [æ] 2. Hang, suspend. *Hu na'a'kalaye' i babui.* I hung the pig up.

akaleha' 1. Snail, large land snail in Guam. African snail. Cf. **Dengdeng.**

ákaleng 2. Dislocated, twisted, deformed. *I kannai-hu umakaleng nigap.* My hand twisted yesterday.

akankang [æ] 2. Type of vine— creeper. A twining vine used for herb medicine. Usually grows near beach area.

akankang [æ] 2. Molar, tooth. Also **akakam.**

akankang dankolo 2. Type of plant-stizolobium.

akankang kalaton [æ] 2. Type of plant-phaseolus sp. Sea bean.

akankang malulasa [æ] Alternate form of *akankang manulasa.*

akankang manulasa 2. Type of plant-vigna marina. Beach pea.

akankang tasi 2. Type of plant-canavalia rosea.

aka'on 2. Type of tree—pandanus, different from *pahong* and *kafo'.*

aka'on 2. Type of plant—pandanus. A rare type of pandanus on Guam. Screw pine.

akaontan 2. Accountant. Cf. **Kontadot.**

akaparas 2. Type of plant. A weed that grows on rocky ground near the ocean. Also **atkaparas.**

akapuku 2. Type of plant-cassia alata. Candle bush. A Mexican shrub. Cf. **Take' biha.** Also called acapulco.

akasu If, in case. Short form for *siakasu.* Also **enkasu.** *Akasu ma na'i yo' ni kareta bai hu espiha hao.* If they give me the car, I will look for you.

9

akda' [æ] 2. Mimicker, imitator. Cf. A'ada'.

akeyo' 1,2. Plait. Hair that is coiled on top of the head, braid, tress, hair bun.

akgak 2. Type of tree—pandanus. Screw pine--its leaves are famous for weaving. Cf. Kafo', pahong.

akidi It takes so much time, so much time passes. *Siempre madingu hao gi che'cho'-mu akidi un amomotsa fine'na.* You will be late for your work if you are going to eat your breakfast first. *Akidi un na'funhayan tumaitai i lepblo-mu manana ha'.* It takes you so long to finish reading your book, it will be morning. *Akidi un arekla i kareta-mu makpo' ha' i karera.* It takes so long to fix your car that the race will be over.

akihom 1. Clench, grip, grip tightly with hand, hold or grasp firmly.

akka' 1. Bite, nip, bite into, grip with teeth, clench—with teeth.

ákkaga [æ] 2. Miss, daughter, girl, expression used by older people when addressing a young female. *Akkaga, hanao asta i eskuela.* Miss, go to school.

ákkamo' [æ] 2. Marriage, married. Cf. Umakkamo', kasamiento.

aklara 1. Declare, clarify. Cf. Na'klaru. *Hu aklara na magahet.* I declared that it's true.

akli'e' 2. Sharp sighted, perceptive—of physical objects, a good watchman or lookout. *I akli'e' na taotao ha li'e' i submarine gi halom tasi.* The sharp sighted man saw the submarine in the sea.

akmangao [æ] 2. Type of crab-scylla serrata. (Fortunidae). Mangrove crab.

akompaña 1. Accompany, escort. Cf. Esgaihon, ga'chungi.

akompañamento 2. Convoy, escort, accompaniment.

akompara 1. Compare, make a comparison, contrast. *Hu akompara i dos kareta.* I compared the two cars.

akomparasión 2. Comparison. Also komparasion.

akomprende 2. Agree, understand one another, reach an understanding, reach an agreement.

akonseha 1. Advise, counsel, warn, apprise, inform.

akonseheru 2. Counselor, adviser, councilman. Also akonsehera (f).

akong [æ] 2. Scorched, dirt, dirty, filthy, soiled with dirt. Cf. Dokngos , tostos, kossos, lakulakong, kulakong. *Akong i hineksa'.* The (cooked) rice is scorched.

akostombra 2. Become accustomed, habituate, make familiar by use.

akotdión 2. Accordion. Also atmoniku.

akredót 2. Creditor (m).

aksepta 1. Accept, receive, take.

akseptasión 2. Acceptance, acceptancy.

aksidente 2. Accident, mishap, by chance. Cf. Desgrasia. *Umaksidente si Juan gi chalan.* John had an accident on the road.

aksión 2. Action, deed, behavior.

akson 2. Type of plant-pandanus fragrans. Or pandanus guamensis. Pandanus.

akta [æ] 2. Actor.

aktibu 2. Active, alert, vivacious, having power of quick motion. Cf. Makalamya.

akto 2. Fact, actual, reality, exact, act—pertaining to legislation, actuality. Cf. Fakto.

akudi 1. Assist, help, aid. Cf. Ayuda, aosiliu. *Akudi hulo' i patgon gi tapbla.* Assist the child up from the floor.

akusa 1. Accuse, incriminate, charge with, indict, lodge a complaint. *Ha akusa na guahu chumule' i pan.* He accused me of taking the bread.

akusadót 2. Accuser, plaintiff, demandant. Cf. Demandadot.

akusáo 2. Accused, blamed, called to account.

ala 2. Nest—for brooding hen.

ala 2. Basket—usually made from coconut leaves, sack, bag.

ala [æ] O'clock, of the clock, particle used in telling time for one o'clock. For two o'clock and up, *alas* is used. *Ala una.* One o'clock. *Alas dos.* Two o'clock.

alaba 1. Side with, take sides, as to protect, defend, conceal, etc. Cf. Abona. *Hu alaba i patgon gi linachi-ña.* I sided with the child in his error.

alabadu 2. Embrace.

alabastro 2. Alabaster.

aladu 1,2. Plow.

alafrís 2. Carpenter's plane for cutting grooves for interlocking pieces of wood.

alagatapeha' 2. Avocado. Also **alageta.**

alageta 2. Type of plant-persea americana. Avocado. Also **alagatapeha'.**

alaguan 2. Kind of food, rice soup. A mixture of ripe coconut milk, rice, water, cooked by boiling.

alahas 2. Jewelry, ornament, jewel.

alaihai tasi 2. Type of plant-ipomoea tuba. Morning glory.

álaisen 2. Miss (each other), fail to meet with someone, fail to fall in with someone. Cf. **Laisen.** *Umalaisen ham yan i amigu-hu nigap.* My friend and I failed to meet each other yesterday. *Manalaisen siha.* They missed each other.

alakrán 2. Type of insect, a scorpion like insect with three pairs of legs and pincers.

alalak [æ] 2. Type of plant-ipomoea tiliaefolia. Beach morning glory.

alalak tasi 2. Type of plant-ipomoea pes-caprae. Morning glory—with pink flowers.

Alamagan 2. Alamagan, the fourth island north of Saipan.

alambriyu 2. Type of plant-lygodium scandens.

alamle 2. Wire, cable, metallic thread. Cf. **Uaia'.**

alamlen manunu 2. Gridiron, grill—for cooking over open fire.

alamlen tituka' 2. Barbed wire.

á'langa' [æ] 2. Loco, crazy (slang).

alangilang 2. Type of tree-canagium odoratum. Also **ilangilang.**

alapát 2. Parallel, side by side. Cf. **Atparehu.** *Umalapat i dos fila.* The two lines were parallel.

alapika 1,2. Rattle, clack. Noise resulting from clacking two objects together, as a Hallowe'en noise maker.

alatga 1. Give away excess, fill up beyond its capacity, overflow. *Alatga muna'i i guihan siha sa' bula.* You give away lots of fish because there are plenty of them.

alatgayi 1. Give out, play out. *Ha alatgayi i guaka ni tali-ña.* He made the cow's rope longer.

alayi 1. Carry (in woven basket), put (something) into a woven basket. To carry something in a skirt held up by the front. Cf. **Ala.**

albom [æ] 2. Album.

ale' [æ] 1. Insult, bring disgrace upon, do someone wrong.

alegria 2. Merriment, glee, rejoicing.

Alemán 2. German—a native or one of the people of Germany.

Alemania 2. Germany.

alenken 2. Capsize, stumble, turn over, trip in walking, running, etc. *Adahi na un alenken gi hemhom.* Be careful so you don't stumble in the dark.

alentos 2. Energy, power, strength, force, might. Cf. **Fuetsa, alimento.**

alesna 2. Ice pick, awl.

aletses 2. Type of fish-spratelloides delicatulus (family dussumieridae). Round herrings.

ali [æ] 2. Giddyap—to cow or horse to speed it up. Also **hali.** Cf. **Lachaddek.**

aliansa 2. Alliance, league, coalition, confederacy, federation. Cf. **Inetnon.**

aliba See **alibia.**

alibia 1. Ease, relieve, alleviate, facilitate. Also **aliba.** *Ha alibia yo' ni kinatga-ku.* He relieved me of my load.

alibiu 2. Relief, freed from pain, suffering or grief. *Atrasao matto i alibiu.* The relief came late.

alientos 2. Breath. Cf. **Hinagong.**

aligao 1. Search for, seek, be in quest of, try to find. Cf. **Espiha, buska, bando.** *I nana ha aligao i patgon-ña.* The mother searched for her child.

alikates 2. Pliers.

alileng 2. Cateye shell.

alimasat 2. Type of fish. Also **alimasak.**

alimenta 2. Nutrition, energy. *Tai alimenta sa' ti chumocho kasi ki sinko dias.* She is suffering from malnutrition because she has not eaten for almost five days.

alimento 2. Energy, power, strength, force, might. Cf. **Fuetsa, alentos.**

alimentosu 2. Nutritious. Cf. **Sustansia.**

aliña 1. Take care of, take pride in. *Ha aliñañayi gue'.* She takes pride in herself.

aliñao 2. Tidy, neat.

alipika 2. Last bell for mass. *Ma'alipika
i misa.* The last bell for mass has
rung.

alitos 2. Earring.

alitos 2. Lobe, ear lobe.

alitos ababang 2. Cocoon.

alof [æ] 1. Beckon, signal, summon by
signs, call by signs, wave. *Ha alof
yo'.* He beckoned to me.

alok 3. Say—imperative, also used with
hu-pronouns. Cf. **Ilek.** *Alok, hafa dai
gi Amerikanu.* Say hello to the
American. *Hafa na un alok tailayi
gue'?* Why did you say he is bad?

alom 2. Type of plant-melanolepis
multiglandulosa. A small native
somewhat weedy euphorbiaceous
tree.

alon laiguan 2. Type of fish-family
sphyraenidae. Barracuda resembling
a large mullet.

alon le'u 2. Type of fish-saurida gracilis.
(Synodontidae). Similar to barracuda,
but different family.

alosuttimo At the very end, eventually,
ultimately. Cf. **Gi uttimo, pot uttimo.**
*Alosuttimo siempre mumalate' hao
yanggen sigi ha' hao umeskuela.*
Eventually, you will be smart if you
keep on attending school.

alu 2. Type of fish-(family
sphyraenidae). Barracuda.

aluda 2. Type of fish-cirrihtus
pinnulatus.

alugat di Instead of. (R) Cf. **Enlugat di.**
*Alugat di un maigo' maolek-ña na
un fanestudia.* Instead of you
sleeping, it is better for you to study.

alula 2. Hurry, swift. Cf. **Inalula,
sahyao.** *Alula para i eskuela.* Hurry
to the school. *Inalula yo' asta i
gima'-mami.* I hurried to our house.

alulayi 1. Expedite, hurry, hasten. Cf.
Apura. *Alulayi ya un funhayan.*
Hurry and be finished.

aluminom 2. Aluminum.

alunan 2. Pillow. Cf. **Atmohada.**

alunan hayu 2. Wooden pillow, made of
short piece of wood.

alutong 2. Granite, type of volcanic
rock, basalt rock.

ama 2. Mistress, owner, boss.

amaka 2. Hammock, swing, hanging
bed or couch.

ámama [æ] 1. Play up to, brown-nose,
apple polishing. *Ha amamama si

nana-ña para u nina'i ni malago'-ña.*
He is playing up to his mother so
that she will give him what he
wants.

ámamang [æ] 2. Lower lip. Also
amang.

amante 2. Lovely, lovable.

amantes 2. Lovers.

ámantieni [æ] 2. Embrace each other,
shake hands, hold hands. Cf. **Ago'te,
asostieni.** *Fanamantieni kannai.*
Hold hands.

amanu Where, which. Also manu.
Amanu nai gaige si Juan? Where is
Juan?

amang 2. Lower lip. Also amamang.

amapble 2. Friendly, kind, amiable.

amara 1. Stack deck, shuffle (cards)—by
putting good ones together in the
deck, shuffler fixes deck of cards so
that he deals himself good ones.

amara 1. Tie a knife to the cock's foot.
Ha amara i gayu. He tied the knife
to the cock's foot.

amarasión 2. Stacking deck, the act of
shuffling cards by putting good ones
together.

amariyu 2. Yellow.

amaru 2. Type of plant-nephrolepis.
Fern. Also amari.

amasa 1. Knead dough. Cf. **Yaka'.**

amaska 1,2. Add tobacco to betel nut
mixture. Chewing tobacco.

amasohan 2. Scar, wound mark. Cf.
Maso', paladan.

ambasadót 2. Ambassador.

ambiento 2. Greedy, avaricious, glutton.
Also **hambiento, hambrento.**

ambo 2. Term used in game of bingo
when two numbers next to each
other horizontally are called.
Partners.

ambos Both. *Maolek para ambos.* It's
good for both of us.

ambos 2. Share (something)—esp. the
cost of something, pitch in, share
benefits, split (a bet). *Maila' ya ta
ambos gi che'cho'.* Come and we will
share the work.

ambre 2. Hungry, starved, starving,
famished. Cf. **Ñalang.**

ambros 2. Share (something)—esp. the
cost of something, pitch in, share
benefits, split (a bet). Also **ambos.**

ámbulan 2. Ambulance, mobile hospital.

ame' 1,2. To screen, as a door or window. (R) Wire screen.

ame' 2. Rain. (S) Cf. **Uchan.**

Ame' Nickname for Carmen.

amen Okay, fine. *Amen yo' na enao un cho'gue.* It is okay with me for you to do that.

amen 2. Amen.

amen 2. A term used with small children when directing them to kiss the hand of an elder. Cf. **nginge'.**

amenda 2. Amend. Cf. **Enmienda.**

Amerikanon pao asu 2. A derogatory term for Chamorro who puts on airs. Literally American of smoky odor.

Amerikanon pao take' 2. Derogatory term for Chamorro who puts on airs. Cf. **pao, take'.**

Amerikanon papa' patas 2. Derogatory term for Chamorro who puts on airs. Literally American under foot.

Amerikanu 2. American (m). Also **Amerikana** (f).

amiga 2. Friend (f), Buddy, pal, comrade. Cf. **Ga'chong, kume'.**

amigu 2. Friend, buddy, pal, partner, companion, comrade (m). Also *amiga* (f). Cf. **Ga'chong, kume'.**

amín I mean, that is to say. From English 'I mean'.

aminasa 1. Threaten, menace, frighten, scare. Cf. **Espanta, hongang, fa'ñagui.** *Ha aminasa yo' ni papet kotte.* He threatened me with court papers.

aminasáo 2. Threatening, menacing, sinister, defiant.

aminasayon 2. Easy to frighten.

aminasu 2. Threat, menace. Cf. **Espanto.**

aminudu See atminudu.

amista 2. Fidelity, integrity, loyalty, friendliness.

amistosamente 2. In a friendly way.

amko' 2. Old, worn out, ancient, not new, old person, aged, adult. Cf. **Bihu.**

amme [æ] **1,2.** Cud, chewing tobacco, remnant of betel nut or chewing tobacco. Chew betel nut—for someone, usually a toothless person. Cf. **Mohmo, bagasu.**

amonestasión 2. Warning, admonition. Cf. **Abisa.**

amontona 1. Heap, pile. *Ha amontona i kamuti.* He piled up the sweet potatoes.

amot 1. Dispossess, deprive by force, bereave, debar, hinder from possessing, take (something) away, grab from, snatch from. *Hu amot i patgon ni bola.* I snatched the ball from the child.

amot 2. Medicine, herb, drug, narcotic drug.

amot agaga' 2. Iodine, merthiolate, reddish medicine.

amot chetnot 2. Medicine applied to a wound or injured part. Cf. **Amot hirida.**

amot chetnot maipe 2. Medicine—for drinking when a patient is restless in his sleep or has sore in his mouth caused from unknown sources. Cf. **Amot fresko.**

amot dagga' Medicine—applied for swelling or inflammation. Cf. **Amot pokpok.**

amot fresko 2. Medicine—for drinking when patient is restless in his sleep or has sore in the mouth.

amot gapotulu 2. Hair spray—medicine for hair.

amot guesgues nifen 2. Toothpaste, tooth powder.

amot hirida 2. Medicine applied to a wound or injured part. Cf. **Amot chetnot.**

amot lila 2. Gentian violet, a purple medicine.

amot makpong 2. Medicine—for urinary troubles, bed-wetting.

amot mapga' 2. Medicine—to stop bleeding after child delivery and for dislocation of the pelvic bone, taken internally.

amot muna'maigo' 2. Sleeping pill, soporific, anything to induce sleep.

amot nifen 2. Poultice—for aching tooth.

amot palai 2. Liniment, a medicated liquid for rubbing into the skin.

amot sinagu 2. Medicine—for common cold.

amot tininu 2. Medicine—for piles or back pain.

amot tumaga' 2. Type of plant-cassia occidentalis. Senna.

amot tumaga' karabao 2. Type of plant-cassia sophera.

amot ulo' 2. De-worming pill.

amotsa 2. Breakfast, lunch, morning meal; for some speakers any meal.

amotsát 2. Breakfast time, time for lunch, eating time.

ampaia' 2. Umpire, referee.

Ampan Nickname for Amparo.

ampara 1. Protect. Cf. **Difende, hulof, protehi.**

amsong [æ] **2.** Baby clam that is edible.

amtao 2. Experienced. Cf. **Susedi.** *Amtao na makinista gue'.* He is an experienced machinist.

amte 1. Apply first aid, treat wound, cure sickness. *Ha amte yo' si Daniel.* Daniel treated my wound.

amtiyon 2. Curable, can respond to treatment.

amu 2. Boss, master, employer, head. Cf. **Ma'gas.**

amuráo 2. Enamored, in love, infatuated. *Hu na'amurao si Maria.* I caused Maria to fall in love with me.

án- [æ] Leftover of (something). *Ansopbla.* Leftover of what's left. *Anbali.* The dust or the leftover from the sweeping. *Ansupiyu.* Wood shavings. *Ankanno'.* Slop, leftover food.

an [æ] Abbreviated form for *yanggen, anggen. An humanao hao agupa', adahi na ti un agang si Maria.* If you leave tomorrow, be sure to call Maria.

anadót 2. Baby walker, a ring on wheels inside which a baby stands when learning to walk.

anai [æ] When (subordinator). Also **annai.** Cf. **Nai, gigon.** *Anai matto yo' Hawaii ha na'manman yo'.* When I came to Hawaii it surprised me. *Humanao yo' anai matto gue'.* I left when he came.

anai maolilek Just right, perfect fit.

anakko' 2. Long, extended in time or length, not short. *Anakko' tataotao-ña lao dikike' patas-ña.* He has a long body, but he has small feet.

analisa 1. Analyze, examine critically, study. Cf. **Estudiayi.**

Anatahan 2. Anatahan, the first island north of Saipan.

ánbasihu [æ] **2.** Empty container. Cf. **Basiu.**

Ancha' Nickname for Esperansa.

ancho 2. Wide, spacious, roomy, deep. Cf. **Fedda'.** *Ancho hinasso-ña si Juan.* John's thoughts are deep.

Anchon Nickname for Esperansa.

Anda Nickname for Candelaria.

andaba 2. Padlock, lock. Cf. **Aseradura.** Also **adaba.**

andadót 2. Baby walker. Cf. **Anadot.**

andami 2. Scaffold, platform used by builders working on the wall of a building.

andas 2. Barrow, stretcher, litter.

ande' [æ] **2.** Show off, showy, gaudy. Cf. **Banidosu, dudos.**

andi'i 1. Flirt with, show off to. Cf. **Ande'.** *Ha andi'i yo' si Thomas.* Thomas flirted with me.

anduyo' 2. Bunch of tobacco leaves.

anes Honest, truly. From English honest.

anibat 2. Syrup, honey. Cf. **Miet.**

anibetsariu 2. Anniversary.

aniles 2. Type of plant-indigofera suffruticosa. Small bush.

ánima 1. Elate, inspire, encourage, strengthen, raise the spirit of.

ánimas 2. Soul, spirit, ghost. Cf. **Ante.**

animát 2. Animal—used figuratively most of the time. Cf. **Ga'ga'.**

animosu 2. Courageous, valiant, stouthearted, valorous, spirited, dauntless, intrepid. Also **animosa.** Cf. **Butmuchachu.**

animu 2. Mettle, courage, spirit, effort.

ánineng [æ] **2.** Shadow, seclusion.

anít 2. Bluing agent—for laundering.

aniti 2. Devil, satan. Cf. **Diablo, satanas, hudas, maknganiti, demoniu.**

aniyon kannai 2. Ring for the finger.

aniyu 2. Ring, rim, any circular band.

ánkanno' [æ] **2.** Garbage, left over food.

ankas 1. Share. *Ta ankas gi atkilon.* Let's share together on the rent.

ankas 2. Ride together—either in front of or behind, as on a passenger seat of a motorcycle, on horseback, etc.

ankas 2. Free-loader, moocher. *Ta ankas gi atkilon Maria.* We will free-load at Maria's rented place.

ankla 1,2. Anchor. *Ma ankla i batko.* They anchored the ship. *Tinake' i ankla.* The anchor is rusty.

ánlasgue [æ] 2. Wood shaving, a thin slice pared off with a knife, plane, blade, etc. Cf. **Ansupiyu.**

ánmaso'on [æ] 2. Scar, weal. Cf. **Paladan.**

annai When. Also **anai.**

annok [æ] 2. Exposed, can be seen with the naked eyes, apparent, come into sight. *Annok iya Guam ginen Rota yanggen malinao i tasi.* Guam can be seen from Rota when the sea is calm.

anobiu 2. Lover (m). Also **anobia.**

anokupáo 2. Unoccupied, idle.

anonas 2. Type of plant-annona reticulata. Custard apple, bullock's heart.

ansianu 2. Experienced, initiated, skillful, ancient. Cf. **Eksperiensia.** *Esta ansianu gue' guenao na cho'cho'.* He is already experienced in that work.

ansias 2. Anxious, longing, eagerness.

ánsupiyu [æ] 2. Wood shaving, a thin slice pared off with a knife, plane, blade, etc. Cf. **Anlasgue.**

antagonista 2. Antagonist, opposer, foe.

antes di Before, prior to, beforehand, before time, previous to.

anti 2. Soul, spirit, ghost. Cf. **Animas.**

antigon 2. Ancient. Also **antigu.**

antigu 2. Ancient, dark ages, primitive.

antiguamente 2. Olden times, long time ago.

antiguayon 2. Very old.

antihos 2. Eyeglasses, pince-nez, face mask—for skin diving, sunglasses. Also **antiohos, antios.**

antikamara 2. Vestibule, front chamber.

antikristo 2. Anti-Christ.

antiohos 2. Eyeglasses, goggles, face mask, monocle, pince-nez—a lens of glass or rock crystal used to correct defects of vision. Also **antios, antihos.**

antios 2. Eyeglasses, pince-nez, sunglasses, face mask—for skin diving. Cf. **Antiohos.**

antisipa 1. Anticipate.

antisipante 2. Anticipant.

antisipasión 2. Foretaste, anticipation.

anto'asi At least. Also **atto'asi, ato'asi.** *Chule' anto'asi hu nana'i hao.* Take it, at least I am giving it to you.

antohu 2. Occasionally—if I feel like it, whim. *Chumocho yo' pot antohu.* I eat if I feel like it.

Antong Nickname for Antonio.

antula 1. Mock, ridicule. Cf. **Adda'.** *I famagu'on ma antulayi i bihu.* The children mocked the old man.

ántupa [æ] 2. Debris, rubbish, scrap.

anula 1. Annul. Cf. **Kansela.**

anunsia 1. Announce, publicize, broadcast, inform.

anunsiáo 2. Can be announced, capable of being announced, can be broadcast.

anunsiu 2. Announcement, message. Cf. **Infotmasion, notisia.**

aña [æ] 1. Beat up, overpower, punish, harm, hurt, injure. Cf. **Fueges, kastiga, galuti, lamen.**

añadi 1. Increase, add to. Cf. **A'umenta, atisa.** *Ha añadi dos na niyok gi monton.* He added two coconuts to the pile.

a'ñao 1. Overpower, defeat, vanquish, overwhelm.

añehu 2. Old things.

años 2. Age, years. Cf. **Idat, sakkan.**

añu 2. Year. Cf. **Sakkan.**

añu feskat 2. Fiscal year.

Añu Nuebu 2. The new year.

anggariya 1,2. Stretcher, litter. *I anggariya ma'usa gi malangu.* The stretcher is used for the patient. *Ma'anggariya i malangu asta i espitat.* The patient was carried on the stretcher to the hospital.

anggen [æ] If, when (usually used to connect clauses or phrases). Cf. **Yanggen.** *Anggen humanao yo' bai hu espiha hao.* When I leave I will look for you.

angglo' 2. Dry, arid, not wet or moist, dried, dried up.

anggosto 2. Narrow. Cf. **Estrecho, ma'i'ot.**

anggosto na chalan 2. Narrow road.

ángheles 2. Angels. Cf. **Anghet.**

anghet 2. Angel. Cf. **Angheles.**

angilao 2. Type of plant-grewia crenata. A type of tree.

angla'a' 2. Gape, open mouth wide. Also **langa'.**

angokko 1. Trust, rely on, put confidence in, have faith in, place reliance in, confide in. Cf. **Dipende, apela.** *Ti hu angokko hao.* I don't trust you.

15

angokkuyon 2. Trustful, truthful, trustworthy, dependable. Cf. **Angokko.**

aodensia 2. Audience.

aoditoriu 2. Auditorium.

aoditót 2. Auditor, accountant. Cf. **Kontadot.**

a'ok [æ] 2. Wedding gift, of the bridegroom to the bride.

aomenta 1. Expand, enlarge, extend, increase, broaden, widen, thicken, amplify, magnify, augment, dilate. Also umenta. Cf. **Atisa, ekstende.**

aosiliu 1,2.. Aid, help, assist, give support. Cf. **Ayuda.** *Manggagao i atministradot aosiliu para Luta.* The administrator requested aid for Rota. *Hu aosiliu i peskadot gumoddiyi ni boti-ña gi pantalan.* I helped the fisherman tie his boat to the dock.

aotoridát 2. Authority, right to command, sovereignty, jurisdiction. Also aturidat.

aotorisa 1. Authorize, permit, empower, give authority to, license, commission. Also aturisa.

aotorisasión 2. Authorization. Also aturisasion.

apa [æ] 1. Place hand on the shoulder of someone, put arm around the shoulder of another person while strolling or standing. *Hu apa i amigu-hu.* I put my arm around the shoulder of my friend.

apacha' 2. Grasshopper, mantis.

apacha' a'me' 2. Type of insect-orthoptera tettigoniidae. Katydid.

apacha' matai 2. Type of insect-acridiidae family, brown-spotted grasshopper.

apacha' suette 2. Type of insect-licustidae, green grasshopper.

apaga 1,2. Carry (something)—on the shoulder. Shoulder. *Hu po'lo i kinatga gi apaga-hu.* I placed the things that were to be carried on my shoulders.

apagayi 1. Carry on shoulder. *Hu apagayi i kahon.* I carried the box on my shoulder.

a'pagon 2. Go out, damp, expire. *Este na chupa a'pagon.* This cigarette goes out often.

apahigai 2. Type of insect-orthoptera phasmidae. Walking stick, mantis.

á'paka 2. White, light-colored skin.

apaka' 2. Type of bird-gallicolumba xanthonura, white-throated ground dove.

á'paka' chada' 2. Egg white.

ápaniti [æ] 1. Box, fight with each other. Cf. **paniti.**

ápannak [æ] 2. Clash, strike violently together, spank. *Umapannak i dos.* The two spanked each other.

aparadót 2. Closet, cabinet, clothes wardrobe, clothes closet, hot-locker. Cf. **Tanso', komuda.**

aparatos 2. Equipment, apparatus.

aparehu 1. Prepare. Cf. **Pripara.**

aparehu 2. Mule pack.

apas 2. Wage, salary, stipend, fee, recompense for service rendered. Cf. **Suetdo.**

apas kontribusión 2. Revenue, taxes. Cf. **Reditu.**

apasi 1. Pay, make payment, compensate, remunerate, reimburse. *Ha apasi yo' ni che'cho'-hu.* He paid me for my work.

apasigua 1. Help, aid, assist, pacify, calm, appease.

apasoti 2. Type of plant-chenopodium ambrosioides. Wormseed. Also **alapasotes.**

apatta 1. Remove, take away, send away, separate, disconnect, isolate, set apart.

apattáo 2. Separated, isolated, divided.

ápatte [æ] 2. Divide, share, split evenly. Cf. **Dibidi, patte.** *Ha na'apatte ham ni guinaha-ña.* He shared some of his possessions with us.

apayu'ak 2. Large spider. See **apayuhak.**

apayuhak 2. Large spider (generic). Also apayu'ak. Cf. **Sanye'ye'.**

ápayuni [æ] 1. Get used to, be acquainted with, know well, accustom, be accustomed, become accustomed. Also payuni. Cf. **Payon.** *Hu apayuni drumaiba i kareta-hu.* I am used to driving my car.

apbladora 2. Gossiper (f). Also atbladora.

apbladoria 2. Gossip. Also atbladoria.

apbladót 2. Slanderer, gossiper. (m). Also **Apbladora** (f).

a'pe' [æ] 2. Harelip, congenitally divided lips, like that of a hare, or this deformity. Cf. **Pire'**.

apecheng 1. Cling, carry (something) under the arm, hold.

apédelok 1. Crumple. Cf. **Hemmot**. *Ha apedelok i magagu.* He crumpled the clothes.

apehu 2. Type of plant-acrostium aureum. Mangrove fern.

apela 1. Trust, depend on, rely on. Cf. **Angokko, dipende**. *Apela hao giya guahu.* Trust me.

apela 1. Appeal—a case at court.

apenas 2. Rarely, seldom, hardly, infrequent, not often. Cf. **Hassan, eskasu**. *Apenas yo' matto gi gima'-mu.* I seldom go to your house.

apigasa 2. Goose pimples, goose flesh, goose bumps.

apiu 2. Celery.

apiyidu 2. Surname, family name, last name. Also **apuyidu**.

aplaka 1. Make peace, placate, soothe feelings of.

aplakáo 1. Attack. Cf. **Ataki, hatme**. *Ma aplakao ni sendalu.* They were attacked by the soldiers.

aplasu 1,2. Applaud, applause, praise, approval, cheer. *Ma aplasu hao gi huegu.* They applauded you at the game . *Mana'i gue' aplasu pot i maolek na che'cho'-ña.* He was applauded for his good work.

aplika 1. Apply for, put to use, apply. Cf. **Na'sietbe**. *Hu aplika i tiningo'-hu.* I applied my knowledge. *Ha aplika i che'cho'.* He applied for the work.

aplikáo 2. Applicable, fit, suitable, relevant.

aplikapble 2. Applicable. Cf. **Aplikao**.

aplikasión 2. Application, utilization, diligence.

aplohkateng 2. Type of plant-psychotria mariana. A type of tree.

aplok 2. Coconut (without any meat), young coconut.

apmam 2. Ago, past, gone, awhile, for sometime, since olden times. Also **atmam, atman**. Cf. **Hagas**. *Apmam na tiempo.* Since olden times.

apo' [æ] 2. Lean against, rest in a recumbent position, lean the head back. Cf. **Aso'**.

aposta 1,2. Bet, wager. *Hu aposta i salape'-hu.* I bet my money. *Mapedde gue' ni aposta.* He lost the bet.

apóstoles 2. The apostles, the disciples, follower, scholar. Cf. **Disipulu**.

apostóliku 2. Apostolic—pertaining to the apostles, or to the Pope and his authority.

apótalang 2. Crab—box. Cf. **Atopalang**.

apoyu 2. Prop, support. Cf. **Gu'ot, sague**. *Apoyu i tapbla ni acho'.* Support the wood with the rock.

appan 2. Recede (water), dry up, become dry, evaporate. *Ha na'appan i hineksa'.* She caused the water in the rice to dry up.

ápplacha' [æ] 2. Dirty, unclean, dirt, impure, impurity. Cf. **Kuchinu**.

appleng [æ] 2. Sprained, dislocate, twisted muscle or bone.

appleng [æ] 2. Slang, markedly colloquial language, nonsense, incoherent speech. *Appleng kuentos-mu.* Your speech is incoherent.

aprebáo 2. Approved. Cf. **Apreba**. Also **apruebao**. *Aprebao i che'cho'-mu.* Your work is approved.

aprehende 1. Apprehend, sieze, arrest.

aprendes 1. Fasten—with small tacks. *Ha aprendes i litratu gi liga.* He fastened the picture to the wall.

apreta 1. Speed up, make fast, force to hurry, cause to hurry, hurry, hasten. Cf. **Chaddek**. *Apreta manungo' ya un funhayan umeskuela.* Hurry your learning and you will be finished with school.

apretadót 2. One who presses or hurries others. *Mampos si Antonio apretadot na taotao.* Tony is a very hard driver.

apretáo 2. Hasty, speedy, expeditious, done or made quickly. Cf. **Apurao, pakiao**. *Apretao na cho'cho' enao.* That work was hastily done.

apretát 2. Hasty, speedy, expeditious, hurried, done without deliberation or due caution. Cf. **Apretao**. *Mampos apretat este na cho'cho'.* This was a rush job (hasty work).

aprobecha 1. Use, make use of. *Hu aprobecha i kareta-ña i che'lu-hu.* I used my brother's car.

apropósitu 2. Fit, suitable, appropriate. Cf. **Umaya**.

aprueba 1. Approve, test, verify, agree. Also **apreba**. *Hu aprueba i fino'-mu.* I agreed with your statement. *Si tata-hu ha aprueba i che'cho'-hu.* My father approved my work.

apruebasión 2. Approval, approbation. Also **aprebasion**.

apsolusión 2. Absolution, acquittal.

apsolutamente 2. Absolutely, without limits.

apsolutu 2. Absolute.

apsom [æ] 2. Type of plant-desmodium triflorum or oxalis corniculata.

apson [æ] 2. Sour. Cf. **Ma'aksom**. *Ma'apson i kahet.* The orange is sour.

apstinensia 2. Abstinence. *Ha'anen apstinensia.* A fast day.

apstrakto 2. Obstruction, obstacle, block.

apu 2. Ash—the remaining substance of what was burned.

apudera 1. Covet, claim—someone else's property. Cf. **Agara**. *Hu apudera yo' ni siya.* I'm claiming the chair.

ápula' [æ] 1. To take off for each other. *Apula' na dos sapatos.* You take off each other's shoes.

apula'i 1. Take off for each other, remove for each other, untie for each other, translate for each other.

apunta 1. Aim, note down, write down, point at, direct at. Cf. **Tancho'**.

apunta 1. Appoint. *I ma'estro ha apunta yo' para hu kanta gi dimimoria.* The teacher appointed me to sing at the program.

apura 1. Expedite, facilitate, hurry, hasten. Cf. **Alulayi**.

apuráo 2. Restless, hasty, eager, fervent, excited, intense, enthusiastic. Cf. **Apretao**.

apusento 2. Bedroom, lodging, room.

apuya' 2. Navel.

apuya' tasi 2. Deep, deepest part of the ocean, central part of the ocean, equator. Lit. navel of the ocean.

apuyidu 2. Surname. Also **apiyidu**.

Arabia 2. Arab, Arabian.

arak [æ] 2. Liquor, distilled liquor made from fermented coconut sap. Also **agi, inestila**.

arandela 2. Washer (metal), axle guard.

aranka 1. Budge, move. Cf. **Rempua**. *Ta aranka i banko siha gi eskuela anai ta balle i satge.* We moved the benches at school when we swept the floor.

arañas 2. Candelabra.

aras 2. Wedding ring, ring, jewelery given by groom to bride. Pledge, earnest money.

aras 2. Favoritism, to favor one person over another. *Hu na'i aras si Maria.* I show favoritism to Maria.

arasa 1. Raze, destroy completely. *I pakyo ha arasa todu i tinanom.* The typhoon razed all of the plants.

arastra 1. Drag, pull along, draw along wearily. Cf. **Batangga, batsala**. *Hu arastra i katga-ku asta i gima'.* I dragged my load to the house.

area 1. Hurry up, hustle up, used to describe action of male mammal chasing after an animal in heat. Cf. **Apreta, alulayi**.

arebatáo 2. Reckless, careless, heedless of consequences. Cf. **Bronko**.

arekla 1. Fix, arrange, repair.

areklamento 2. Rule, regulation, condition, measure. Cf. **Areklo**.

arekláo 2. Fixable, can be fixed, arranged; orderly. Cf. **Atmao**.

arekláo 2. Disciplined, conditioned, regulated.

areklayon 2. Fixable.

areklo 2. Rule, regulation, measure, condition. Cf. **Areklamento**.

arendatariu 2. Lessor.

aresmetika 2. Arithmetic. Also **arofmetika**.

aresta 1. Arrest, seize, apprehend.

arestáo 2. Arrested, capable of being arrested, under arrest.

arias 2. Unit of measurement—approximately 100 square meters.

aridedót 2. Surround, all around, all over. Also **ridedot**. *Aridedot taotao gi plasan batkon aire.* The airport was surrounded by people.

aridondeha 1. Enclose.

aridondo 2. Round, circular, spherical, globular. Also **ridondo**. Cf. **Adamelong**.

arienda 1,2. Pay rent, lease (land). Cf. **Atkila**. *I arienda guaguan.* The rental is expensive.

ariendo 2. Rental, lease, rent, a piece of leased land or property. Also **arendo**.

ariendót 2. Renter, rental, amount of rent. Also **arendot**. Cf. **Atkilon**.

ariesga 1. Dare, risk. Cf. **Atotga**. *Si Jose ti ha ariesga gue' humuyong gi tasi.* Jose did not dare to go into the ocean.

arima 2. Get close, draw near, bring one's self nearer. *Umarima yo' gi hoyu.* I bring myself near the hole. *Arima gi fi'on i matai.* Bring yourself close to the corpse.

arina 2. Flour.

arofmetika 2. Arithmetic. Cf. **Kuentas, aresmetika**.

aroma 2. Type of plant-acacia farnesiana. A spiny shrub.

arurú 2. Type of plant-maranta arundinacea. Arrowroot. Also **sagu**.

as 2. Ace—as in cards.

as [æ] Article, non-focus marking personal article. Cf. **Si**. *Gaige as Maria i lepblo-ku.* My book is at Maria's. *Guinaiya si Juan as Maria.* It is Juan that Maria loves.

asa 1. Cause to blow away. Also **hasa**. *I boti inasa ni manglo'.* The boat was blown away by the wind.

asada 1,2. To plow. Pickax, hoe, mattock, plow. *Hu asada i tano' ni asada.* I plowed the land with a plow.

asadót 2. Roasting spit.

ásagua [æ] 2. Wed, marry, get married. *Umasagua si Emi yan si Pete.* Pete and Emi got married.

asagua [æ] 2. Spouse, husband, wife, mate. *Hu li'e' i dos asagua.* I saw the two married ones.

asaguan maga'lahi 2. First lady. Also **maga'haga**.

asaguani 1. Band together against, run together. (R) Cf. **Agululumi, aguguiyi**.

asaina Show disgust—expletive. *Asaina na aguaguat patgon hao.* Gosh, you are a naughty child.

Asaina 2. Lord, God.

asaite 2. Oil, cod oil, salad oil, coconut oil, mainly used for medicine or food. Cf. **Laña**.

asaitera 2. Grease gun, oil can, oil cruet (bottle for the table).

Asan [æ] Village in central Guam. Pron. **assan**.

asayon 2. Nauseated. Cf. **Atsayon**.

asensión 2. Ascension of Christ.

asensión 2. Type of plant—curacao milkweed.

asentadu 2. Decorous, pleasing. Also **asientadu**.

aseradura 2. Padlock, lock. Also **seradura, seladura**. Cf. **Andaba**.

aserín 2. Sawdust.

aseru 2. Magnet, steel.

asetga 2. Type of plant-beta vulgaris. Garden beet.

asga' [æ] 2. Spark-producer, that which produces spark, such as flint, wheel on cigarette lighter, match head and carborundum, flint, match head.

asgon 2. Fog, mist, haze, blurry. Cf. **Afao**.

asgue 1. Smoke out. Cf. **Fohne, pohne**.

asi komu Like this. *Asi komu un cho'gue este maolek.* If you do it like this, it's good.

ásidu 2. Acid.

asienta 1. Press (clothes with an iron), act upon by steady pushing or thrusting while in contact, wet clothes—for ironing. Cf. **Prensa**.

asientadu 2. Decent, appropriate, proper, suitable, pleasing, moderate. Cf. **Disente**. Also **asentadu**.

asiento 2. Starch, carbohydrate.

asiga 2. Salt.

asigura 1. Assure, secure against change or risk, insure, confirm, give confidence to, ensure.

asiguráo 2. Assured, insured, sure, indubitable, make sure.

asi'i 1. Forgive, pardon, excuse, condone, grant forgiveness, exculpate. Cf. **Despensa**. *Hu asi'i i palao'an ni bida-ña.* I forgave the woman for what she did.

asi'iyon 2. Excusable, pardonable, forgivable.

asikna 1. Assign, appoint.

asipudera Even if. Also **sipudera**. *Asipudera ta manana lao ta saga ha' ya ta na'funhayan i che'cho'-ta.* Even if it takes till morning (but) we'll stay and finish our work.

asiste 1. Assist, help, succor, be of service, give aid. Cf. **Ayuda, faboresi, faiche'chu'i**.

asistensia 2. Assistance.

asistente 2. Assistant, helper.

askerosu 2. Fetish for cleanliness, afraid of being dirty or contaminated. Also **skerosu.**

asne 1. Pickle, apply salt.

asnentukon 2. Pickled fish, small fish soaked in brine.

asnentukon 2. Briney, anything soaked in brine, such as salted fish. Also **anestukon.**

aso' [æ] **2.** Tilted, leaning, bent, bend over, lean against. Cf. **Ma'ngak, apo'.**

ásodda' [æ] **2.** Meet with, fall in with. Cf. **Sodda'.** *Hu na'asodda' i dos taotao gi chalan.* I let the two people meet on the road.

asolas 2. Occasionally (for business). *Asolas humahanao yo' para Guam.* Occasionally I go to Guam for business.

asosiasión 2. Association.

ásostieni [æ] **2.** Embrace each other, support each other. Cf. **Amantieni, ago'te.** *Asostieni na dos sa' en peddong.* Hold each other before you fall.

aspirina 2. Aspirin.

assemble 2. Assemble, assembly. *Guaha assemble gi plasa.* There was an assembly at the plaza.

assohne 1. Lie down with. From **asson.** *Assohne i patgon.* Lie down with the child.

asson 2. Recline, lie down. *Asson sa' yayas hao'.* Lie down because you are tired.

asta [æ] Until, to, toward, up to, preposition word (usually used for past time). *Mata'chong yo' guihi asta i oran alas tres.* I sat there until three o'clock.

asta ki [æ] Until, if—usually used to connect phrases or clauses, when. *Ti siña i patgon umegga' telebision solu asta ki ha na'funhayan i leksion-ña.* The child can not watch television only until he finishes his lesson. *Nangga asta ki humanao yo' para i eskuela.* Wait until I go to school.

asta ngai'an Until when, when. *Asta ngai'an hao magi ta'lo?* (Until) when are you coming back again?

astaimanu Contracted form for *hafa taimanu.*

astetema Type of plant-ammannia coccinea.

astronomia 2. Astronomy.

asu 2. Smoke, smudge, steam, vapor, fog, the gaseous products of burning organic materials which finally settle as soot.

asuela 2. Gouge, chisel, adze. *Ma guaguaddok ni asuela.* They are digging with a gouge.

ásufa' [æ] **2.** Collide, clash, bump into.

asugi 2. Quicksilver, mercury.

asugiyi 1. Cover with quicksilver. Cf. **Asugi.**

asuguat 2. Support—for rafters in a house.

asukat 2. Sugar.

asulen palos 2. Type of eel-conger noordziek (family congridae). White eels.

asuli 2. Type of eel-anguilla marmorata (family anguillidae). Fresh-water eels. Also **hasuli.**

asuma 1. Assume.

asunsion 2. Type of plant-asclepias curassavica.

Asunsión 2. Asuncion, the seventh island north of Saipan.

asunto 2. Notice, topic, news, reason, affair, concern, report, subject. *Maolek i asunto pot i tiempo.* The report about the weather is good. *Hafa na asunto na para un hanao?* What is the reason for your leaving?

ásupak [æ] Cf. **Hasupak.**

asusena 2. Type of flower—tuberose. Cf. **flores asusena.**

asusta 1. Frighten. Cf. **Aminasa, fa'ñague.**

asustáo 2. Frightened. Cf. **Luhan.**

asút 2. Blue, azure.

atachuelas 2. Tack, thumb tack. Also **tachuelas.**

átadok 2. Eye, eyeball. Cf. **Mata.**

atadok haguha 2. Needle's eye.

átaga' [æ] **1.** Cut each other. Cf. **Taga'.** *Umataga' i dos taotao.* The two men cut each other.

atagga' [æ] Reddish (color), as when one blushes, flushing, complexion of a person when sun-burned.

ataha 1. Counteract, halt, prevent, contravene, stop, forestall, impede. Also **taha.** Cf. **Pribeni, chomma'.**

átahgue [æ] **2.** Alternate.

atahu 2. Bunch of tamales.

ataka 1. Do repeatedly, to do something in large doses or amounts, to do a lot. Usually followed by an action word. Also **atraka**. *Hu ataka muna'chocho hao ayuyu.* I let you eat a lot of coconut crab. *Ha ataka mama'baba gi bola.* He fooled around quite a bit during the ball game.

ataka Assault.

ataken guha 2. Asthma attack.

ataken korasón 2. Heart attack.

atakeru 2. Attacker, the one on the offensive.

ataki 1. Attack—as in an ailment.

átaktak [æ] 2. Stubborn, slow-witted, feather-brained, forgetful, unmindful, naughty, unheedful, disobedient.

atalak [æ] 2. Stare, open eye wide, act of staring, a fixed look. Also **talak**.

atalaki [æ] 1. Scowl, look at menacingly, to give a dirty look. *Ha atalaki i patgon.* He scowled at the child.

á'tamos 2. Imbecile, idiotic. Cf. **Kaduku**. Also **attamos**.

atan [æ] 1. Look at, glance, perceive. *Hu atan hulo' ya momotmot uchan gi sabana.* I looked up and there was much rain on the mountain.

atan seguet 1. Look secretly.

atani 1. Nail, attach, join, fix, fasten, pin. *Ma'atani i litratu gi liga.* The picture was nailed to the wall.

atanon [æ] 2. Handsome, good looking, pretty, appearance.

atarantáo 2. Undecided, unsettled, debatable, tentative.

atarantáo 2. Dizziness—resulting from brain injury, a little touched in the head. *Despues di aksidente, atarantao ilu-ña.* After the accident, he was a little off in the head.

ataska 2. Muddy, bog.

ata'út 2. Coffin, casket. Also **ata'ot**.

átayo' [æ] 2. Small of the back, portion of the back just above the hips.

atba 2. Dawn, first church bell—in the morning.

atbahakat 2. Type of plant-ocimum basilicum. Sweet basil.

átbanet 2. Mason, brick layer.

atbansa 1. Advance, move forward, promote, progress, improve.

atbeti 1. Advised. *Ha atbeti hao na munga humanao.* He advised you not to go.

atbettura 2. Aperture, opening, hole, slit. Also **abettura**.

átbidon 1,2. Add starch. Starch (for ironing).

atbiento 2. Advent.

atbietto 2. Opened, left open, aperture, advertise by keeping door open. Cf. **Binaba**. *Umatbietto i petta anai guinaife ni manglo'.* The door was opened when the wind blew it.

atbinu 2. Albino (person).

atbladora 2. Gossiper. Also **apbladora**.

atbladoria 2. Gossip. Also **apbladoria**.

atbladót 2. Slanderer (m), gossiper. Also **hatbladot**. (R) Also **apbladot**.

atbola 1. Hoist, uplift, raise up, lift.

atboladura 2. Roof frame, the frame to which the tin or thatch is attached.

atborota 1. Disturb, upset, bother, annoy, vex, irk, instigate, incite, stir up.

atborotu 2. Fuss, trouble, annoyed with trifles, inconvenience, worry, troublesomeness, uproar, disturbance, riot, disadvantage. Cf. **Plaitu, yinaoyao, enkebukao**. *Meggai na atborotu guini na guma'.* There is too much trouble in this house.

atborutáo 2. Troublesome, out of control, fuss, irritating activity.

atbot 2. Type of plant-delonix regia, flame tree. Any large tree.

atbot det fuegu 2. Type of plant-delonix regia. Formal name of flame tree used on Guam. Flame tree, poinciana.

atbuetto Ajar, open. Also **atbietto**.

atcha'ot 2. Archaic form which refers to middle class of earlier Chamorro society. Now replaced by *achoti*.

atdao 2. Sun.

atderecho 2. Right side up, correct position, the state of being in the right manner. Also **direcho**.

atdet [æ] 2. Severe, strict, serious, austere, rigorous, strenuous, rigid, strong (spirit), robust. Cf. **Fotte**.

atektok 2. Leprosy, leper. Cf. **Nasarinu, lasarinu**.

atende 1. Attend, heed, pay attention, take care of, take into account or consideration, be attentive. Cf. **Atituyi**. *Hu atende i fino' saina-hu.* I pay attention to my parents' words.

atendidu 2. Courteous, attentive, sociable, agreeable, complimentary, showing good manners (m). Atendida (f). Cf. **Atende**.

atensión 2. Attention.

atento 2. Attentive, courteous, polite. Cf. **Atendidu**.

ateng 2. Black ant—very large. Also **hateng**.

ates 2. Type of plant-annona squamosa. Sweetsop, sugar apple.

ates aniti 2. Type of plant-desmodium gangeticum.

atfabetikamente 2. Alphabetically.

atfabetu 2. Alphabet.

átfilet 2. Pin, safety pin.

atfilet kabesa 2. Pin, straight pin.

atfilet makandalu 2. Pin, safety pin.

atfombra 2. Rug, carpet, floor covering.

atgayas 2. Gill, hook by gill. Cf. **Guasang**.

átgidon 2. Cotton, cotton wadding. Also **atgodon**.

atgimat 1. Enamor, cause to fall in love, bewitch. *Inatgimat ni bunita-ña.* He was enamored of her beauty.

atgodon di Manila 2. Type of plant-ceiba pentandra. Kapok. Also **atgidon Manila**.

atgon [æ] 2. One of group. *Atgon un taotao chumo'gue.* One of those people did it.

atgon [æ] 2. Particular, some. *Atgon lugat.* Some (particular) place. *Atgon na bes.* Some times.

atgoya 1,2. Tie rope on the ring or through the nose of a cow, nose ring (of animal), hole for nose ring, tie down—figurative sense. *Atgoya i asagua-mu sa' mampos machalek.* Tie your wife down because she is too free.

atgradesidu 2. Receivable, capable of being received. Also **atgradesiyon, agradesidu**.

atgradesiyon 2. Receivable, capable of being recived, thankful, grateful. Cf. **Atgradesidu**.

átguaset 2. Foreman.

atgumento 2. Argument, debate, deliberation. Cf. **Debati**. Also **agumento**.

atguyosu 2. Self-opinionated. Also **otguyosu**.

Atika Nickanme for Escolastica.

atilek 2. Tweak (by the ear), ear-twist, pinch. Cf. **De'on**. *Ha atilek yo' si nana.* My mother pinched my ears.

atinget 2. Type of fish-kuhlia taeniura (family kuhlidae).

atisa 1. Increase—the speed, the glow of light, etc., accelerate. *I draiba ha atisa i finalagon i kareta.* The driver increased the speed of the car.

átiteng 1. Carry each other. Also **atiten**. Cf. **Titeng**.

atiteng 1. Carry for.

atitu 2. Observant. If Jose lends Pedro something and Pedro forgets about it but Maria remembers it, then Maria is *atitu*.

atituyi 1. Heed, pay attention, be attentive. Cf. **Atende**. *Atituyi hafa ilek saina-mu!* Heed what your parents say!

atituyiyon 2. Remarkable, extraordinary.

atka 2. Ark, Noah's ark.

atkadi 2. Commissioner, mayor, chief, head of the community, justice of the peace.

atkagueti 2. Hindrance, troublesome, impediment, obstruction—to accomplishment of something.

atkahót 2. Alcohol. Also **atkot**.

atkángheles 2. Archangels, angels.

atkaparas 2. Type of plant-capparis cordifolia. Wild caper.

atkayadas 2. Gills—of a fish.

atkila 1. Rent, lease (house). Cf. **Arienda**. *Ha atkila i gima'.* He rented the house.

atkilón 2. Rental, rent, renter. Cf. **Arendot**.

atkitrán 2. Tar.

atkiya 1,2. Pin up hair, large hairpin—usually used to hold up braid.

atkos 2. Arch—of a building, house, archway.

atkos 2. Bow, arch.

átlibes 2. Opposite, upside-down, inside out. *Atlibes i chinina-mu.* Your shirt is inside-out.

atma 1,2. Invent, assemble, machinery, set trap, set up.

atma 2. Arms—of war, armaments.

atmadót 2. Scarf, wrap.

atmadót 2. One who sets traps. Also **atmadora** (f).

atmagosu 2. Type of plant-momordica charantia. Bermuda grass.

atmahayan 2. Type of plant-melochia villosissima, or boehmeria tenacissima. Fibre plant.

atmangao [æ] 2. Spotted sea crab.

atmao 2. Assembled, put back together, finished (by being assembled).

atmariáo 2. Lunatic, one who is insane, demented, fool, idiot, crazy, maniac. Cf. **Kaduku, brutu, loku.**

atmas 2. Weapon, fire-arms, gun, rifle, pistol.

atmayas 2. Kind of food. Gruel. A mixture of ripe coconut milk, ground eskomme, water, and salt cooked by boiling.

atmayi 1. Restore order, reassemble, put back correctly, assemble. Cf. **atma. Atmayi yo' ni bisikleta.** Reassemble the bicycle.

atmayon 2. Fixable, repairable. From *atmao.* Cf. **Areklao.**

atministradót 2. Administrator.

atministrasión 2. Administration.

atmiñudu 1. Chip in, help out—in little bits. (R) Also **aminudu.** *Maila' ya ta atmiñudu ya ta chule' i kareta.* Come and we will chip in and take the car. *Atmiñudu fan na dos ya u libianu.* Help one another and it will be easy for you.

atmirante 2. Admiral.

atmirapble 2. Admirable, wonderful.

atmiti 1. Admit, allow, grant, concede. *Ha atmiti na guiya chumule'.* He admitted that he took it.

atmohada 2. Pillow. Cf. **Alunan.**

atmoneda 2. Auction, vendue, public sale, bid, mortgage. *Para u matutuhon i atmoneda agupa'.* The auction will begin tomorrow.

atmonesta 1. Admonish, advise, warn. (R) *Hu atmonesta i taotao na u bira gue'.* I admonished the man to turn back.

atmoniku 2. Accordion.

atmoniu 2. Organ.

atnibat 2. Syrup. Also **anibat.**

ato' 1. Take, snatch, grab, seize, nab, get hold of. (R)

ato' 2. Back up, reverse, move back. (R) *Umato' i kabayu.* The horse backed up.

atof 1,2. Roof, to put roof on a house. Cf. **techo.**

atof higai 2. Roof made of palm leaves.

atof sin 2. Tin roof, roof—made of tin.

atok [æ] 2. Conceal, hide—imperative form. Cf. **Na'na'.** *Hu na'atok i salape'.* I hid the money.

atópalang 2. Crab—box (calappa calappa, linnaeus). Also **apotalang.**

atot [æ] 2. Filipino (slang Guam). Name of a fish that stays in fresh water mud or swampy area.

atot [æ] 2. Type of fish-petroscirtes mitratus (family blenniidae). Also **hatot.**

atotga 1. Risk, venture, hazard, dare. Cf. **Atrebi.** *Hu atotga humanao asta i taddong tasi.* I dared to go to the deep ocean.

atotgante 2. Daring, venturous, fearlessly bold.

atotgayi 1. Speculate.

átotpe [æ] 2. Collide, clash, bump into, meet head on. Cf. **Asufa'.** *Umatotpe i dos kareta.* The two cars collided.

atotta 1. Make a cement floor. *Ha atototta i gima'.* He put a cement floor in the house.

atpa 2. Harp. Also **hatpa.**

atpahon 2. Proverb, maxim.

atparehu 2. Parallel, side by side. (R) Cf. **Alapat.** *Umatparehu i dos kareta gi chalan.* The two cars were parallel on the road.

atrabisañu See **trabisañu.**

atrabisáo 2. Traverse, lying across, cross in opposition, go counter to, crosswise. Also **attrabisao.** Cf. **Trabisañu.**

atraka 1. Extravagant in buying, purchasing more than one needs. *Baratu i guihan ya hu atraka.* The fish were on sale, and I bought (many of them).

atrasáo 2. Late, tardy, not being on time.

atrebi 1. Risk, venture, hazard, dare. Cf. **Atotga.**

atrebidu 2. Bold, daring, insolent.

atrebidu 2. Borrows without permission.

atrebimiento 2. Nosey, touching something. Cf. **Embilikeru, kamten.**

atrisión 2. Attrition.

atropeya 1. Interfere, meddle.

atsadu 2. Stray (animal), gone astray, as a domestic animal that leaves its home. Also **hatsadu.**

atsayon 2. Nauseated, affect or become affected with nausea. (R) Also **asayon.** *Atsayon yo' gi painge.* I was nauseated last night.

atta 2. Dischargee (from hospital), a patient who has been discharged from the hospital. *Atta i che'lu-hu gi espitat.* My brother was discharged from the hospital.

áttamos 2. Foolish, frivolous, irresponsible. *Mampos hao attamos gi che'cho'.* You are very foolish at work.

attan 1. Pound, to hammer. *Hu attan i lilok.* I pounded the nail.

attat 2. Altar.

áttayo' 2. Loins, portion of back immediately above the buttocks.

atte 1. Pour in, pour slowly. *Ha atte i basu ni lemonada.* He poured the lemonade into the cup. *Ha atte i batde.* He poured (something) into the bucket.

atte 1,2. Trick, play a trick. Stratagem, artifice, wile, maneuver, magic, feint. *Maila' ya hu atte hamyo.* Come and I'll play a trick on you.

áttikulu [æ] **2.** Article, item.

áttilong 2. Black.

attisa 2. Artist.

atto' [æ] **1.** Hide oneself. Cf. **Atok.** *Atto' sa' inaliligao hao as Juan.* Hide because Juan is looking for you.

attura 2. Position, posture, pose.

attura 2. Height, altitude. Cf. **Linekka'.**

átugan [æ] **1.** Band together, form a group in order to catch something such as an animal or a person. *Nihi ta atugani i mannok.* Let's band together to catch the chicken.

atuhong 2. Type of fish-family scaridae. Large parrot fish with big bump on forehead.

atulai 2. Type of fish-trachurops crumenophthalmus. Big eye scad, small. Also **hatulai.**

átulaika [æ] **2.** Interchange, exchange, in lieu of. Cf. **Tulaika.**

atuli 2. Broth, mush, ground corn boiled and seasoned with coconut milk, porridge, puree.

átungo' [æ] **1.** Acquaint, apprise, know about. *Para ta atungo' pot i gipot.* We should acquaint ourselves about the party.

átungo' [æ] **2.** Friend, pal, partner, acquaintance.

atupat 2. Sling—type David used when he fought Goliath.

atupat 2. Container—for boiling rice, woven from a strand of the coconut leaf. Also **katupat.**

aturidát 2. Authority, jurisdiction. Also **aoturidat.**

aturisa 1. Authorize, empower, commission, permit. Also **aoturisa.**

aya [æ] **2.** Match, fit, suit, appropriate, resembling, equal. *Hu na'aya i chinina-hu yan i katsunes-hu.* I match my shirt with my trousers.

ayao [æ] **1.** Borrow, opposite of lend. Cf. **Presta.** *Hu ayao i salape' as Pedro.* I borrowed the money from Pedro. *Hu ayao gue' ni kareta.* I borrowed the car from him. *Hu na'ayao gue' ni kareta.* I lent the car to him.

ayek [æ] **1.** Choose, select, pick out.

ayenda 2. Agenda.

ayu [æ] That, those, which (demonstrative). *Ayu na lahi.* That man.

ayu guatu Over there—away from speaker and addressee.

ayu ha' That's all, that's it, all there is— the thing far from the addressee and speaker. *Ayu ha' lini'e'-mami na guihan.* That was all the fish we saw.

ayu na That is why (something is done), that is the reason—talking about a third person or persons. Also **taiguihi na.** *Bula piligru gi tasi ayu na debidi un gof adahi hao.* There are lots of dangers in the ocean, that is why you must be very careful.

ayu na tiempo 2. Era, at that time.

ayu nai That is where, that is when, that is the time or place (away from speaker and addressee). *Ayu nai pumasehu yo' para Saipan nai umasodda' hit.* That was the time we met when I toured Saipan.

ayuda 1. Help, aid, assist, succor, be of service, give aid. Cf. **Asiste, faboresi, faiche'chu'i, aosiliu, akudi.**

ayudante 2. Helper, collaborator, aid, assistant.

ayugue' There is, stating existence (object far from both speaker and addressee). *Ayugue' i kafi-ña.* There is his coffee.

ayunat 2. Fast, Lenten fast, Lent, time of fasting. Cf. **Kuaresma.**

ayunu 2. Fast, do without food for moral or religious reasons. *Umayunu* *gue' gi tiempon kuaresma.* He fasted during Lent.

ayu'os 1,2. Wave goodby, signal by waving. Probably fr. Adios. Cf. **Alof.**

ayuyu 2. Coconut crab, robber crab—generally found in Micronesia, birgus latro, linneus.

ba' 2. Crawl—on hands and feet. *Esta buma' i patgon.* The child crawls already.

ba'a Short form for *ñaba'.*

ba'an [æ] **2.** Wake up (late)—esp. in the morning, oversleep. *Ba'an yo' pa'go gi ega'an.* I got up out of bed late this morning.

ba'ba' 2. Seed—undeveloped when ripe, defective, hollow seed, shrunken seed, deformed. Sterile, unable to reproduce.

ba'ba' 2. Retarded, stunted, fail to reach full growth.

baba 2. Bad, spoiled, evil, worthless. *Baba i katne.* The meat went bad.

baba' 2. Kind of taro—grows in pond or swampy area.

ba'ba' [æ] **1.** To spank, to whip. Cf. **Saolak, kastiga, sakudi.**

baba [æ] **1.** Open, unroll, disclose, reveal, divulge, expand.

bábaba 2. Silly, thickheaded, stupid. *Ha fa' i bababa gue'.* He is pretending to be a silly person.

bábale' [æ] **2.** Moth. Also **babali.**

bábale' [æ] **2.** Eyelash. Also **babali.**

bábali [æ] **2.** Eyelash, eyelid. Also **babale'.**

bábali [æ] **2.** Moth—esp. the type that flies around lights at night. Also **babale'.**

báballe [æ] **2.** Sweeper, one who sweeps, esp. using the broom.

baban boteya 2. Bottle opener.

baban lata 2. Can opener. Cf. **Abrilata.**

babarias 2. Foolishness, stupidity, folly. Cf. **Binaba.**

babas 2. Chin. Cf. **Achai.**

babas 2. Drool, saliva running from chin of infant.

bábasbas 2. Type of fish-family mullidae. General term for goatfish. From batbas.

baberu 2. Bib.

babuen baksia' 2. Type of pig—with *short snout.*

babuen halom tano' 2. Wild pig, wild boar.

babuen kuaresma 2. Type of pig—legendary. Used as a threat to small children, much like 'the bogey man will get you.'

babuen lansa 2. Pig—with long snout.

babuen machalek 2. Wild pig.

babui [æ] **2.** Pig, swine; a term used in keeping track of score by counting the number of games won in tres siete (card game).

bach [æ] **2.** Badge.

bachet 2. Blind.

bá'chigo' [æ] **2.** Mongol-eyed. Also **batchigo'.**

badu 2. Humpback, hunchback, crooked back.

bafa 2. Buffer, any tool used for buffing a surface. Cf. **skwiyi.**

bagai 1,2. Clothing, sarong, wrap loin cloth around oneself. *Hu bagai yo' nu i tu'aya.* I wrapped myself with a towel.

bagamondo 2. Loafer, moocher, vagabond. Cf. **Flohu, gago'.**

bagasu 2. Dregs, waste pulp, sediment, grated coconut after the milk is extracted, coffee grounds, tea leaves, matter which settles to the bottom of liquid.

bagen 2. Type of plant-derris. (?).

baggai 1,2. Have intercourse (slang), coitus, (taboo). Cf. **Dalle, sirek, kichi.**

baggai 2. Fight. *Umabaggai i dos.* The two people fought each other.

bagón 2. Gondola car—a railroad car with sides and end but without a top. Flat car (for freight). Cf. **Karu.**

bagón 2. Salted seafood.

bagu 2. Lazy, indolent, shiftless, unindustrious, vagabond.

baha' [æ] **1.** Take down, bend down. Cf. **Dilok, dengha.**

baha' [æ] **2.** Bend down, droop, low. Cf. **takpapa'.**

bahada 2. Descent, slope, dip (in a road).

báhadot 2. Tool of bamboo used for collecting tuba from tree. Also **Bahdot.**

bahakke 2. Work clothes, worn clothing that may be used for work, non-dressy clothes.

bahdot 2. Bamboo container—used for collecting sap in larger quantities from the bongbong which are

attached to the individual trees. Also
bahadot.

báhia 2. Bay, harbor.

bahu Under. *Bahu kondision na...*
'Under condition that...'

bahu 2. Bass voice.

bahu 2. Slowpoke, lazy person. Cf.
Flohu.

bai Will (future marker)—used with
first person, sing. and pl., going to.
Bai hu hatsa gue'. I will lift him. *Bai
in e'mak gi tasi.* We will swim in the
ocean.

Bai' Nickname for Jesus.

baias 2. Bias, as used in sewing.

baila 1. Dance—either alone or with
others, sway, vibrate, waver, swing.
Cf. **Dansa.**

bailadora 2. Dancer (f), one who likes to
dance.

bailadót 2. Dancer , one who dances
(m).

bailan fayao 2. Stick dance—performed
by women.

bailarina 2. Ballerina, ballet dancer.

baina 2. Sheath, scabbard, pod, cover
for blade of knife.

bainan niyok 2. Covering for shoot of
coconut tree.

baitamina 2. Vitamins, vitality. Also
baitamin.

baka 2. Cow.

bakaláo 2. Cod liver oil, cod.

bakana 2. Bay.

bakante 2. Vacant, unoccupied, leisure,
free time.

bakasión 2. Vacation, holiday.

bakauaine 2. Type of plant-lumnitzera
littorea. (?).

bakeru 2. Herdsman, employed on a
ranch to care for cows, horses,
carabaos. *I bakeru
muna'fanggigimen i guaka an
pupuenge.* The herdsman gives
water to the cows in the evening.

baketa 1. To beat up, wallop, knock
down, hit, smack, slug, to have
intercourse (slang). Cf. **Sapblasos,
yagai, dalle.**

baketa 2. Ramrod—for rifle, cleaning
rod.

baketasu 2. Punished, hurt, injured,
harm. (R) *Kao un tungo' i
mabaketasu na palao'an?* Do you
know the woman that was punished?

bakiya 2. Calf (f), cow—young.

bákudang 2. Bomb, high explosive
charge dropped from an aircraft. (R)

bakuko' 2. Negro, black complexion. Cf.
Negro, attilong.

bákulu 2. Crutch, cane, aid, support,
staff.

bákulu 2. Shooter (marbles), the marble
used to shoot with in game of
marbles.

bakuna 1,2. Vaccinate, vaccination.

bala 2. Bullet.

bala' 1. Open—by separating two things
in contact, such as a book, envelope,
sac, etc. (R) Cf. **Baleng.** *Bala' i
mata-ña ya u fakmata.* Open his
eyes so he could wake up. *Hu bala' i
paketi para bai hu li'e' hafa
sanhalom-ña.* I unwrapped the
package in order to find out what
was in it.

balaha 1,2. Cards (playing), shuffle—
playing cards. *Hu balaha meggai
siha na kattan balaha.* I shuffle
many playing cards.

balahan sakke 2. Type of card game.

balakbak [æ] 2. Handbag, small
baggage, suitcase. Cf. **Katpeta.**

balakiyu 2. Young boar, shoat, shote.

balaku 2. Boar, principle actor or star
of a play (slang).

balan granada 2. Hand grenade. Cf.
Terudang.

balan petdigón 2. Shotgun shell,
shotgun pellet.

balansa 2. Balance, scales.

balansa 2. Seesaw, teeter-totter,
balance, play at seesaw. *Hu
na'balansa i lapes gi gui'eng-hu.* I
balanced the pencil on my nose.

balanse 2. Balance, balance of credit,
the remainder of cash or credit in a
business transaction. Cf. **Fondo.**

balansea 2. Rocking motion.

balas 1,2. Whip, spank, bean pole,
trellis, riding whip, tomato stake,
stick, twig. *Ha balas i aguaguat na
patgon.* He whipped the naughty
child. *Malingu i balas.* The whip is
lost.

balaskes 2. Type of chicken; small. Also
bulaskes. *Familian balaskes si Juan.*
Juan is from the family that is small.

balaso' [æ] 2. Marrow—of the
breadfruit, soursop, sugar apple,
pineapple .

balate' 2. Sea cucumber, sea slug—a holothurian (esp. of the genus cucumaria). Beche-de-mer, trepang.

balensiana 1,2. Cook Spanish rice, Spanish rice. *Hu tungo' fuma'tinas i balensiana.* I know how to cook the Spanish rice. *Agaga' kulot-ña i balensiana.* The color of the Spanish rice is red. *Ha balensiana i hineksa'.* She cooked the rice Spanish style.

balenten pachot 2. Braggart, courageous of the mouth.

balentia 2. Fight (to the finish), try to outlast an opponent in a fight, a type of fighting in which only one contestant survives, preliminary fighting, esp. in cockfighting. Cf. **Palitada, gayera.**

baleng [æ] 1. Open, open up, skin back foreskin, to turn inside out—as a sack, to turn a pocket inside-out. Cf. **La'mok, bala'.** *Hu baleng i mata-ña i amigu-hu anai mamaigo' gue'.* I opened my friend's eyes when he was sleeping.

bali 1, 2. Worth, value.

balibagu 2. Lazy person, worthless person.

baliente 2. Courageous, brave, daring. Also **balente.** Cf. **Subetbiu.**

baliles 2. Barrel—wood. Also **bariles.**

balisa 2. Suitcase, valise.

balisa 2. Buoy, channel marker, device for marking channels. Cf. **Boya.**

balle 1. Sweep, rake, brush. *Hu balle i satge nigap.* I swept the floor yesterday.

balotu 2. Ballot, voting ticket, political ticket. Cf. **Botu.**

balua 1. Evaluate, estimate, calculate approximately. *Hu balua i presion i kareta-hu.* I evaluated the price of my car.

balutan 1,2. Infold, wrap up, swathe, swaddle, bundle, pregnant, cover by winding around or folding, roll up. Cf. **Afuyot, falulon, royu.**

bam 1,2. Bombard, bomb. Cf. **Kampo'.**

bampa 2. Bumper—of vehicle.

banaderu 2. Waterhole—esp. for pigs or carabao, mud wallow. Also **bañaderu.**

banalu 2. Type of plant-thespesia populnea. Tree. Also **kilu.**

Bancho' Nickname for Bonifacio.

banda 2. Side, corner, edge.

bándaras 1. Cover—by wrapping, wrap around. *Ha bandaras gue' ni tu'aya.* He wrapped himself with a towel.

bandeha 2. Tray, platter, serving tray.

bándera 1. Strap on.

bandera 2. Flag.

bando 1. Look for—by shouting, call out for someone not in sight, a public notice. Cf. **Buska, espiha, aligao.**

bandoleru 2. Bandit.

bandoñaihon 1. Announce, proclaim.

bandulina 2. Mandolin, banjo.

banek 2. A hollow form where two or more roots join the trunk of a tree, hollow of dead tree.

banes 2. Varnish. Also **batnís.**

banidát 2. Vanity, boastfulness, bragging. Also **banida.**

banidosa 2. Showy, show off, gaudy, pretentious, ostentatious, pompous, flaunt, strut (f). Cf. **Ande', dudos.**

banidosu 2. Show off, showy, gaudy, flaunt, strut, proud, conceited (m). Cf. **Ande'.**

bankas 2. Type of chicken—resembling black-breasted red game, old English.

bankera 2. Banker, money changer (f); dealer—in card game.

bankeru 2. Banker, money changer, exchanger (m).

banko 2. Bank—an establishment for exchange of money.

banko 2. Bench, seat, desk.

bankon addeng 2. Foot-stool.

banna 2. Swollen, swell. *E'kat muna'kalamten i mañetnot adeng-mu sa' u banna.* Don't move your injured leg so much because it might swell.

banyo 2. Banjo.

bañaderu 2. Mud-hole, mud, wet ground, wet floor, muddy pond. Also **banaderu.**

baño 2. Shower, bathroom.

Bang Nickname for Juan.

bangheliu 2. Gospel. (R) Also **ebangheliu.**

baobao 2. Hollow sounding—as an overripe watermelon. Cf. **Gueko.** *Hu ekungok i baobao-ña i chandia.* I listened for the ripe sound of the watermelon.

baobao 2. Plump, a fat person full of liquid.

baotismo 2. Baptism, christening.

baotista 2. Baptist, baptizer. *Si Juan Baotista.* John the Baptist.

bapót 2. Ship—large with engine. Cf. **Batko.**

bapót lumi'of 2. Submarine. Cf. **Batkon lumi'of.**

bapót situ 2. Launch, pleasure boat.

bara 2. Arm's length, yard (measurement).

barakilan 2. Rafter, beam giving form to a roof, sloping member sustaining a roof covering.

Baran Nickname for Barbara.

baranda 2. Veranda, porch. Cf. **Kahida.**

baranka 2. Rocky, rugged road, bumpy.

baras 2. Gravel, pebbles, small stones.

baratu 2. Cheap, inexpensive.

baratura 2. Sale, discount sale, on sale, cheapen, lower the price of.

barena 1. Bore into. *Ha barena i hayu.* He bored into the wood.

bareta 1,2. Dig (with a digging iron). Digging iron, crowbar, large iron bar, a long, heavy rod used for digging holes in hard soil.

bariapble 2. Variable, inconstant, changeable.

barigada 2. Flank, soft area on sides underneath rib cage.

barigeta 2. Fly, opening in men's trousers.

barigón 2. Big-bellied, potbelly (m).

barigona 2. Big-bellied, potbelly (f).

bariles 2. Barrel. Cf. **Tina.**

barilitu 2. Keg, small barrel.

bariu 2. Country, district.

bariya 2. Ribs—of umbrella, rod used for support, spoke (bicycle), steel rod, reinforcing steel.

baró 1,2. Drill, driller, auger bit. Also **barohu.** *I katpenteru ha baro i hayu.* The carpenter drills the wood. *I baro malingu.* The drill is lost.

baro' 2. Crowbar, lever.

barohu 2. Drill. Also **baró.**

barometro 2. Barometer.

baroti 2. Headrest, wood pillow.

Barrigada Village in central Guam. Cf. **Barigada.**

bas 2. Bus.

basia 1. Pour out, empty. Cf. **Chuda'.**

basihu 2. Empty container. Also **basiu.**

basiu 2. Empty container. Also **anbasiu, basihu.**

basnak [æ] 2. Fall, drop, stumble, fall down. Cf. **Poddong.** *I patgon basnak gi tronkon hayu.* The child fell down from the tree.

basta 2. Stop, quit, suffice, enough (command). Cf. **Para.** *Basta.* Stop (whatever you are doing).

basta hiya' No kidding.

bastante 2. Enough, sufficient, ample, adequate. *Bastante nu hagu para un ayuda yo'.* You are sufficient to help me.

bastatdo 2. Bastard, illegitimate child.

baston 2. Cane, staff, stick—walking.

baston San Jose 2. Type of plant-cordyline fruticosa. Tea leaf.

bastos 2. Rough, harsh, rugged, scabrous, uneven, not neat, coarse, not smooth. *Bastos na taotao macho'cho'.* The man is not a neat worker. *Bastos lassas-ña si David.* David has rough skin.

bastos 2. Clubs—card in the suit of.

basu 2. Tumbler, glass cup, drinking glass.

basula 2. Trash, rubbish, garbage, scraps, refuse, useless or worthless matter.

basuleru 2. Trash man, rubbish man, street cleaner.

bata' 2. Baptismal gown, esp. for infants.

bátadot 2. Urinal—used for bed patients.

batakasu 1. Punish, hurt. Cf. **Baketasu.**

bátalan 2. Plank, diving board.

batangga 1. Drag, pull. Cf. **Batsala.**

batangga 2. A type of sled for carrying things, pulled by a cow or carabao.

batatas 2. Potato.

bataya 2. War, battle. Cf. **Gera.** Also **batiya.**

batayón 2. Battalion, infantry, regiment.

batbaridat 2. Foolishness, nonsense, stupidity, imbecility. Cf. **Bobada.**

bátbaru 2. Daring, bold, venturesome, rash, wild, brave. Also **batbara** (f).

batbas 1,2. Trim, shave, cut hair. Beard, mustache, whiskers. *Hu batbas i flores.* I trimmed the flowers. *Hu pacha i batbas-ña si tata-hu.* I touched my father's beard.

batbas guihan 2. Whisker—of fish, especially of goatfish or catfish.

batbas mai'es 2. Corn silk.

batbas uhang 2. Feelers—of crayfish or shrimp.

batbena 2. Type of plant-heliotropium indicum. Wild heliotrope.

batberia 2. Barber shop.

batberu 2. Barber (m). Also **batbera** (f).

batbon 2. Bearded person, person with a long beard.

batbuda 2. Hairy, shaggy, hirsute (f). Cf. **Mepplo.**

batbudu 2. Hairy, hirsute (m). Also **batbuda** (f). Cf. **Mepplo.**

bátchigo' [æ] **2.** Mongol-eyed, slant-eyed, eyelids very close together (characteristic of oriental people). Also **ba'chigo'.**

batde 2. Pail, bucket.

batdeha 1. Pour—water on deck, floor, etc., wash surface--by pouring on deck. Also **batdea.**

ıatdo 2. No pairs or members of the same suit in card game.

ateha 2. Laundry (hand), a place where one washes clothes by hand, washtub. Also **batea.**

batehan mama'gasi 2. Washboard—esp. for clothes.

bateria 2. Battery, dry cell.

batidót 2. Mixer, beater, one who mixes.

batingting 2. Triangle—musical instrument.

batiya 2. War, battle. Also **bataya.**

batkadót 2. Branding iron.

batko 2. Ship, any large seagoing vessel.

batkón 2. Balcony.

batkon aire 2. Airplane. Cf. **Eroplanu.**

batkon gera 2. Warship, battleship.

batkon layak [æ] **2.** Sailing boat.

batkon lumi'of 2. Submarine. Cf. **Bapot lumi'of.**

batnís 1,2. Varnish. Also **banes.**

batṣa 2. Raft, barge. Also **batsai.**

bátsala 1. Drag (something)—on any surface, pull. Cf. **Batangga, arastra.**

batso 2. Waltz.

batte 1. Stir, mix, agitate. Cf. **Lehgua', yaka', daña'.**

batte 1. Brew, make liquor.

batu 2. Type of game. The equipment consists of a round stick four to six inches long, one to one and a half inches in diameter, and flat on both ends, discs made of stone or metal, approximately three inches in

diameter. Players stand ten or more feet away from the stick, which has been placed on end, and take turns trying to knock down the stick with their discs. Whoever knocks down the stick is declared the winner.

batunes 1,2. Button. *Ma batunes i chininan-ñiha.* They buttoned their shirts.

batunes 2. Type of plant-hyptis capitata. A type of grass.

ba'út 2. Trunk, chest. (R)

baya' [æ] **1.** Fed up, satiated, flood with (something). *Hu na'baya' i amigu-hu mangga.* I flooded my friend with mangoes. *Binaya' yo' mangga.* I'm satiated with mangoes.

ba'yak [æ] **2.** Midrib—of coconut frond.

ba'yak [æ] **2.** Type of fish-aulostomus chinensis (family aulostomidae). Trumpet fish. Cf. **Hankot.**

ba'yak [æ] **2.** Type of fish-fistularia petimba (fistularidae).

bayena 2. Whale.

bayi 2. Vale, valley. Cf. **Kañada.**

bayila' 2. Trachoma, a chronic, contagious form of conjunctivitis, characterized by inflammatory granulation of the mucous membrane of the surface of the eyelid. In Guam is known as *puten matan Saipan.*

bayineru 2. Whaler, person who hunts whales, sailor.

bayineta 2. Bayonet. Also **bayuneta.**

bayogon dankolo 2. Type of plant-entada pursaetha. Snuff box.

bayogon dikike' 2. Type of plant-mucuna gigantea. Wild bean. Cf. **Gaye', gaogao, dalalai.**

bayogon halom tano' 2. Type of plant-flagellaria indica.

bayogu 2. Ankle bone, knuckle, knee cap.

bayogu 2. Seed of a *gaye'* plant.

be B—letter.

be' 2. Calf, young cow, call of cattle. Cf. **Bakiya.**

bebe' 2. Vagina, female sex organ. Cf. **Chada', iyon palao'an.**

bebe' Underwood 2. Type of plant, a popular name for *chaioti* in Guam.

be'i 1,2. Bandage.

Bek Nickname for Isabel.

bela 1,2. Wake, vigil, a wake for a dead or dying person. *Ma bela i matai gi painge.* They held a wake for the dead person last night. *Bula na taotao gi bela.* There are lots of people at the wake.

belemba 2. Blowing, twirling, whirling. *Bumelemba i manglo' taftaf gi ega'an.* The wind was blowing early in the morning. *Bumelemba i kuttina gi bentana.* The drapery was blowing at the window.

belembao 2. Shaking, swaying—as leaves of palm tree swaying in the breeze. (R)

belembao 2. Jews harp. Cf. **Belembao tuyan.**

belembao pachot 2. Mouth harmonica.

belembao tuyan 2. Musical string instrument which is held against the belly while the musician plays. The belly is used as a sounding device.

belu 2. Tottering, as a child just learning to stand, balanced (upright). (R) *Hu na'belu i lapes.* I balanced the pencil upright (caused to stand on its end).

belu 2. Veil—esp. that used in wedding ceremony.

Benbenidu Nickname for Benaventura.

béndabat 2. Direction midway between two cardinal points of compass, such as northeast.

béndabat 2. Western wind; a wind that comes from a direction that is not normal, usually bringing rough seas and rain.

bendas 1,2. Blindfold, bandage, put on a bandage.

bende 1. Sell, exchange commodities for money, vend. Cf. **Despacha, tulaika.** *Ha bende i tano'-ña pot sien pesos.* He sold his land for one hundred dollars.

bende gi chalan 1. Peddle, sell from door to door.

bendisi 1. Bless. *I pale' ha bendisi i taotao siha.* The priest blessed the people.

bendisión 2. Blessed, capable of being blessed, blessing.

benditu 2. Praying pose, with hands together close to chin, and with head slightly bowed.

bendiyon 2. Salable, vendable, can be sold, for sale.

bene' 1,2. Apply lipstick. (S) Lipstick. *I palao'an ha bene' i labios-ña.* The woman put lipstick on her lips.

benediksión 2. Benediction.

benefisiu 1,2. Benefit, profit, deed of charity, benefaction. *Guaha benefisiu pot i che'cho'-hu para i eskuela.* There are some benefits from my work for the school. *Bula na benefisiu siha manmasangan lao ti manmakumple.* There are lots of benefits mentioned but they are not accomplished.

Benet Nickname for Bernadita.

benifaktót 2. Benefactor.

benikno 2. Benign, gentle, mild, kind.

Bénkile' Nickname for Vicente.

benne 2. Plywood.

bense 1. Persuade, induce (one) to believe or do something, plead with, urge, impress. *Ha bense si nana-ña humanao asta Guam.* He persuaded his mother to go to Guam. *Ti ha bense yo' eyu na taotao.* That man does not impress me.

bense 1. Defeat. *Mabense i kontrariu.* My opponent was defeated.

benta 2. Merchandise, commodities, stock. Cf. **Fektos.**

bentaha 2. Advantage, benefit, profit, gain, odds, bonus. *Bula bentaha para i taotao ni mitano'.* There are lots of advantages for a person with a lot of land.

bentana 2. Window.

bente 2. Twenty.

bente i unu 2. Twenty-one.

benteron magagu 2. Clothing salesman.

benteru 2. Salesman, agent (m). Also **bentera** (f).

bentura 2. Venture. Cf. **Atotga, arebi.**

bengbeng 2. Drone, buzz, buzzing sound, as of an insect in flight. Also **bilengbeng.**

bengbeng 2. Type of bird-coturnix chinesis liteata, painted quail.

bengbingi 1. Drone at, buzz at, making a buzzing sound at, like flying an airplane over someone. Also **bilengbingi.** *I sasata ha bengbingi yo'.* The bee buzzed around me.

bengga 1. Revenge, avenge. Cf. **Emmok.**

benggadót 2. Avenger, revenger, retaliator.

benggansa 2. Vengeful, revengeful, serving to gain vengeance.

benggatibu 2. Vengeful, vengeance-seeker, grudge-bearing.

berebere' 2. Beriberi.

bes 2. Time, round. Also **beses.** Cf. **Bi'ahi.** *Atrasao yo' gi che'cho' tres beses.* I was late to work three times.

bes 2. Base. Cf. **Di'u.**

besbes 2. Zoom, flash, hissing sound—as of leaking gas, or water poured on a fire, squirt. Cf. **Petsan.** *Besbes i kareta gi chalan.* The car zoomed down the road. *Besbes i hanom gi grifu.* The water squirted out of the faucet.

besbes 2. Sizzle—as frying fat, fizz.

béspira 2. Vigil, vesper.

bespiran Añu Nuebu 2. New year's eve.

bespiran gupot 2. Evening before a festivity.

bespiran nochebuena 2. Christmas eve.

beste 1,2. Decorate, adorn, garnish, decoration, ornament. *Bunitu na beste.* It is a beautiful decoration. *Ha beste i eskuela.* She decorated the school.

bestida 2. Gown, dress, clothes for women. Cf. **Magagu, bestidura.**

bestidu 2. Suit, clothes.

bestidura 2. Frock, dress, gown, garb, garment. Cf. **Bestidu.**

betbena 2. Type of plant-heliotropium indicum. A type of grass.

betbo 2. The word—from God, told by the angel to Joseph that the Son of God was to become a man born of the Virgin Mary.

betde 2. Green (color).

betdugu 2. Executioner, hangman. Also **betduhu.**

betduhu 2. Executioner, killer. Also **betdugu.**

beteranu 2. Veteran.

betguelas 2. Small pox, pox.

betmehu 2. Blonde, pale, fair complexion (m). Also **betmeha** (f). Cf. **Blandina.**

betmehu 2. Mold, cavity, decay.

betnechu See **buen echu.**

Betnes 2. Friday.

Betnes Santo 2. Good Friday.

betso 2. Verse.

biaheru 2. Traveler, voyager, adventurer, wanderer. Also **biahera** (f).

biahi 2. Journey, trip, voyage, excursion. Cf. **Hinanao.** *I bunitu na biahi.* The beautiful trip. *Bumiahi yo' para Hawaii.* I took a trip to Hawaii.

biahi 2. Time, round. Also **bi'ahi.** *Este i mina'tres biahi na hu agang hao.* This is the third time I called you. *Dos biahi.* Two times.

biátiku Beatitude.

biatiku 2. Ringing of bell when the priest is on his way to administer the sacrament of Extreme Unction. Administer Extreme Unction. Last rites. Cf. **Santos Olios.**

biatu 2. Blessed, beatified.

biba 1. Hurrah (shout), scatter, viva. Cf. **Rega, chalapon.** *I patgon ha biba i biyat.* The child scattered the marbles.

Biban Nickname for Oliva.

bibek 2. Harmonica, horn, whistle. Cf. **Hamonika.**

bibenda 2. Story (of building), floors (of building). *Sumaga yo' gi bente bibenda na guma'.* I stayed in a twenty-story building. *Ya-hu sumaga gi yahululo' na bibenda.* I like to stay on the highest floor of a building.

bíbende 2. Shopkeeper, seller, salesman.

bibenka 2. Type of food, rice pudding, rice pancake.

bíberes 2. Beverage (alcoholic). Cf. **Maneska.**

bíbinenu 2. Poisoner—one who or that which poisons. Cf. **Hihina, Tatatse.**

bíblia 2. Bible. Cf. **Historia sagrada.**

bibliku 2. Biblical.

bíbotda 2. One who embroiders.

bibu 2. Fast, rapid, quick, hurried, good. Cf. **Guse', sahyao, apreta, alula, chaddek.** *Bibu i kareta-ña.* His car is fast. *Ina binibu i fandanggo.* The party was good.

bíburas 2. Angry person, one who destroys things when angry.

bida 1. Do, work, act. Cf. **Cho'gue.** *Hafa bida-mu nigap?* What did you do yesterday?

bida 2. Existence, life.

bien binidu 2. Welcome, greeting, hearty reception.

bienabenturansa 2. Blessedness, beatitude, bliss.

bienecho See **buenecho.**

bigoti 2. Moustache, whisker.

biha 2. Grandmother, old woman.

bíhiga 2. Bladder, specif. the urinary bladder.

bihu 2. Grandfather, old man, ancient, old person, not young, aged. Cf. **Amko'.**

Bik Nickname for David.

biknai 2. Type of plant-antidesma bunius. (?).

biktima 2. Victim.

biktoria 2. Victory, conquest, triumph. Cf. **Ginanna.**

biktoriosu 2. Winner, victorious, prize-winning, triumphant, conquering.

bíkulo' 2. Ghost, evil spirit (baby talk). Cf. **Fafa'ñague, birak.**

bilembines 2. Type of plant-averrhoa carambola. Star apple.

bilén 2. Type of plant-coix lachryma-jobi. Job's tears.

bilén 2. Manger, a trough or box where baby Jesus was placed, crib—of Jesus.

Bilen 2. Bethlehem.

bileng 2. High—caused by drinking liquor or any intoxicating agent, intoxicated (slightly), excited with drink, in one's cups.

bilengbeng 2. Buzz, buzzing sound, as of an insect, droning sound, as of a distant airplane, spinning top. Also **bengbeng.**

bilengbingi 1. Drone at, buzz at, make a buzzing sound at, like flying an airplane over someone. Also **bengbingi.**

bilikeru 2. Meddler, snooper, intruder, poke into one's business (m) , **bilikera** (f). Also **embilikeru.**

binaba [æ] 2. Opened, left open, aperture. Cf. **Atbietto.**

binaba [æ] 2. Foolishness, stupidity, folly, evil. *Basta i binaba siha.* Stop the foolishness.

binadu 2. Deer.

binadu 2. Warped lumber, lumber that is not straight. *Ina binadu este na pidason hayu.* This piece of wood is not straight.

binakle [æ] 2. Vinegar.

binanidosu 2. Assumption, pride.

binatte [æ] 2. Cake batter.

binatten tiratira 2. Ice cream, syrup mixture for coconut candy.

binaya' [æ] 2. Satiated. *Binaya' yo' ni hanom.* I've had my fill of water.

binebolensia 2. Benevolence.

bineleta 2. Violetish, containing violet color.

binenu 2. Poison, poisonous, venomous.

binenuyi 1. Poison. Cf. **Hina, tatse.**

binetde 2. Greenish, containing green color.

binibu 2. Very good, surprisingly good. *Ina binibu i fandanggo gi as Camacho.* The fandango at Camacho's was surprisingly good.

binibu 2. Fast. *Ai, na binibu na kareta.* Oh, what a fast car.

binibu 2. Anger. Cf. **Bubu, linalalo'.** *Gai binibu si Rufino as Juan.* Rufino was angered by Juan.

binila 2. Bloated, distended belly, made full.

binilachu 2. Drunkenness, intoxication, state of being intoxicated, or drunk.

binu 2. Wine.

binga 1, @2. To bud, new bud or shoot of a plant. *Bibinga i flores gi tronkon rosat.* The rose bush is blooming.

biola 2. Viola.

biombo 2. Room divider, screen for dividing a room.

bira 1. Turn, revolve, rotate, invert, change direction, divert, turnabout.

birada 2. Corner, curve, bend (of road).

birada 2. Round trip, make trip to a place and back, corner. Cf. **Dibuetta.**

biradót 2. One who turns, one who returns. (R)

biradót 2. Tool for twisting, esp. for making rope or cord from fibers.

birak 2. Ghost, demon, disembodied soul, specter, spook. Cf. **Taotao mo'na.**

birayon 2. Capable of being turned.

birenghenas 2. Type of plant-solanum melongena. Eggplant. Also **berengenas.**

birenghenas halom tano' 2. Type of plant-solanum guamense. Also solanum melongena.

bisabuella 2. Great-grandmother.

bisabuello 2. Great-grandfather.

bisagra 2. Hinge.

bisi 1. Extinguish (fire with liquid). (R)

bisikleta 2. Bicycle, tricycle.

bisinu 2. Neighborhood, vicinity, neighbor.

bisio 2. Habit, custom. Cf. **Kustumbre.**

bisio 2. Vice.

bisiosu 2. Vicious.

bisita 1,2. Visit, visitor.

bisko 2. Floating eye.

biskuchu 2. Biscuit, cracker. Cf. **Krakas.**

bisnes 2. Business.

bisnieta 2. Great-granddaughter.

bisnietu 2. Great-grandson.

bithen 2. Virgin, maiden.

bittot 2. Virtue.

bitu'osu 2. Virtuous, having virtue.

bi'uda 2. Widow.

bi'udu 2. Widower.

biyas 2. Buckle, a fastening for two loose ends. Also **hebiyas.**

biyát 2. Billards, marbles (play).

biyeti 2. Ticket, fare.

blandina 2. Blonde, a blonde person (f). Cf. **Betmeha.**

blandinu 2. Blonde, a blonde person (m). Cf. **Betmehu.**

blanka 2. White (color). Cf. **A'paka'.**

blankeha 1. Paint white, make something white.

blankeha 1. Throw, hurl, cast, fling. Also **blankea.** Cf. **Blanko.** *Ha blankeha i katga-ña asta i halom kareta.* He hurled his load into the car.

blanko 1. Throw, cast, fling, hurl, pitch, sling. Cf. **Yotte, daggao, yute', foyang, blankeha.**

blanko 2. Out in the open, in full view, wide open. *Blanko nai gaige i gima'-hu.* My house is out in the open.

blet 2. Blade, the cutting part of an instrument.

blusa 2. Blouse.

Bo Nickname for Ramon.

bo'an 2. Foam, froth, scum, foamy.

bo'bo' 2. Spring—fresh water. Place where fresh water and salt water come together, usually by the seashore. Brackish spring by the seashore.

bóbolong 2. Meatless coconut, a fully grown coconut with no meat.

bóbolong 2. Tuba container—made of bamboo or coconut and used for collecting tuba. Also **bongbong.**

bocha 2. Blackeye, swelling (from bee sting). Cf. **Pokpok.** *Bocha yo' anai ha akka' yo' i sasata.* I swelled up when the bee stung me. Also **botcha.**

boddek 2. Slob, lazy person who is large.

bohao 1,2. To fan, ventilate manually, aerate, fan, blower, instrument to cause air to blow. Cf. **Gueha, abaniku.**

bohbo 1. Spray out—mouthful of water or something like chewed coconut meat. Also **bobu.** Cf. **Luga'.**

bohbo 2. Crowded, many, filled. Cf. **Bula.** *Bohbo taotao gi gima' Yu'us.* There was a crowd of people at the church.

bohbo 2. Swollen, puffed up.

boi Older form for *bai.* Future marker used with first person only.

boka 2. Eaten, devoured, consumed, food, eat. Cf. **Chocho.**

bokáo 2. Mouthful, morsel, bite.

bokbok 1. Uproot, break loose, pull out, tear out by the roots. Cf. **Bo'ok.**

bokbok lulok 2. Nail puller.

bokka' 2. Bump, hilly, steep, full, swelling, heap, mound, knoll, pile of soil.

boksion 2. Pale, ghastly, wan, deathlike, ashen, pallid. Cf. **Chupon, betmehu.**

bókugo' 2. Cave—man-made, used for shelter during storms or war, tunnel. Also **bokungo'.** Cf. **Liyang.**

bókungo' 2. Man-made cave. Also **bokugo'.**

bola 2. Ball, ball game, baseball, softball, play (ball). *Nihi ta bola.* Let's play ball. *Kao un li'e' i bola gi Damenggo?* Did you see the ball game on Sunday?

bolabola 2. Testicle, global shape, a round object. Cf. **Dammot, dollan.**

bollan 2. Foam—refers to spoiled coconut or soupy cooking.

bolu 2. Long machete.

bomba 1,2. Pump, bombard. *Bomban hanom.* Water pump. *Si Manuel ha bomba i hanom gi halom tanke.* Manuel pumps the water out from the tank. *I bomba mayulang.* The pump is broken. *Ma bomba Saipan gi tiempon gera.* Saipan was bombarded during the war.

bomban guafi 2. Fire extinguisher, extinguisher. Cf. **Bomban kimason.**

bomban kimasón 2. Fire extinguisher, extinguisher. Cf. **Bomban guafi.**

bombatdea 1. Bombardment.

bona 1. Favor, show favoritism, side with. *I tata ha bona i patgon-ña.* The father sided with his child.

bona 1. Buy, purchase. Cf. **Abona.** *Un bona i kareta-mu pot kuanto?* How much did you buy the car for?

Boninas 2. Bonin islands.

bonita 2. Type of fish-caesio caerulaureus. Family lutjanidae. Snapper.

boñelos 2. Doughnut, fritters, pastry— in the shape of small balls.

boñelos aga' 2. Banana doughnut.

boñelos dagu 2. Yam doughnut.

boñelos kamuti 2. Sweet potato doughnut.

boñelos lemmai 2. Breadfruit doughnut.

boñelos manglo' 2. Doughnut—made from flour, shortening and yeast. Lit. doughnuts of wind.

boñelos uhang 2. Shrimp doughnut.

bongbong 2. Bamboo container—used to hold any liquid.

bongbong fagot [æ] 2. Bamboo rod used to carry tuba. Also **bahadot.**

bo'ok 1. Uproot, break loose, pull out, tear out. Cf. **Bokbok.** *Si Taga' ha bo'ok i tronkon niyok.* Taga pulled up the coconut tree by the roots.

bos 2. Voice.

bosbos 2. Swarm—as bees when leaving a hive, spurt of liquid, flow of liquid from an opening such as a water faucet, skin rash--sudden appearance. *Mambosbos i sasata gi me'na-hu.* The bees swarmed in front of me. *Bosbos i hanom gi grifu.* The water spurted from the faucet.

bosbusi Swarm at, spurt (something) on or at. *Hu bosbusi mata-ña ni hanom.* I spurted water in his eyes. *I sasata siha ma bosbusi yo'.* The bees swarmed at me.

bosong 2. Boss, foreman. Also **boson.**

bossat 2. Bridle—made of rope, halter--for leading an animal. Gag--for tying a person's mouth.

bossat 2. Pouch in fishing net where fish are trapped.

bossat 2. Condom (slang).

bota 2. Vote for, vote—cast a. *Hu bota si Señot Guerrero.* I voted for Mr. Guerrero.

botana 2. Botany.

botas 2. Boots.

botasión 2. Election, plebescite, popular vote on a question of public policy.

botcha 2. Blackeye. Also **bocha.**

botda 1. Embroider, stitch.

botdadura 2. Design, embroidery, fancy work used to decorate something. Not limited to embroidery.

botdáo 2. Embroidery, lace.

botdo 2. Zigzag, tacking. Term used when boat is circling while waiting to enter a harbor. Also **batdo.** *I boti bumotdo.* The boat zigzagged.

botdo 2. Aimless, wandering around aimlessly.

botdo lagas 2. Type of plant-portulaca oleracea. Type of vine—used for medicinal purposes.

boten layak 2. Sail boat.

boti 2. Boat, small craft, small vessel.

botkán 2. Volcano, volcanic. Also **botkanu.**

botkanu 2. Volcano, volcanic. Also **botkan.**

botlas 2. Sarcasm—plural form. Cf. **Botleha.**

botlas 2. Ornament, decorations worn on clothes.

botleha 1. Sarcasm, mock, ridicule, bitter remark. Cf. **Despresio, despresia, botlehu.** *Ma botleha i kandidatu gi miteng.* They ridiculed the candidate at the meeting.

botlehu 2. Sarcasm, ridicule, mockery, insult, harsh remark.

botlón 2. One who ridicules, mocker (m); one who mocks.

botlona 2. One who ridicules, mocker (f); one who mocks.

botlonu 2. Mocker, insulter, taunter, jeerer, hooter, ridiculer. Also **botlona** (f). Cf. **Botlon.**

Botneo 2. Borneo.

botosaiko' 2. Motorcycle, motorscooter. Also **motosaiko', botosaikot.** Cf. **Otobai'.**

botosaikot 2. Motorcycle. Also **botosaiko'.**

botsa 1,2. Pocket, insert (something) in the pocket. *Hu botsa i salape'.* I pocketed the money. *Guaha maddok gi betsa-ku.* There is a hole in my pocket.

botsan alunan 2. Pillow case.

botsiyu 1,2. Sack (small), put in purse.

botto 2. Figure, mass, bulk, magnitude, size, figuration, configuration, statue, silhouette. Cf. **Figura.**

botu 2. Vote, suffrage, franchise, plebescite, referendum, poll, ballot, selection of choice. Cf. **Balotu.**

boya 2. Buoy, float. Cf. **Balisa.**

boyo' 1. Spit out (mouthful). See **boyok.**

boyo' 2. Give drink, especially alcoholic drink. *Na'fan boyo' yo'.* Give me a drink.

boyo' Shave the head, bald—from haircut. Type of haircut when the head is shaved bald.

boyok 1. Spit out (mouthful), to spew or spray out of mouth by blowing, such as mouthful of chewed coconut meat after juice is gone. Also **boyo'.** Cf. **Bobu.**

brabu 2. Healthy, industrious, hard working person. Cf. **Butmuchachu.**

brasa 2. Fathom, measurement from finger tip to finger tip, with both arms outstretched, at arm's length.

braseha 1,2. Embrace, encircle with arms, measure—with arms outstretched or encircling something. Cf. **Brasa.** *Hu braseha i petta.* I measured the door with arms outstretched. *Hu braseha i sentura-mu.* I encircled your waist with my arms.

brasu 2. Arm, thoracic limb, forearm.

breablanka 2. Type of plant-canarium. Type of flower.

brilu 2. Brillo, steel wool.

brin 2. Canvas. Cf. **Trapat.**

brinabu [æ] 2. Health, soundness of body, freedom from disease or ailment, well-being, healthfulness, clean bill of health. Cf. **Brabu.**

brinda 2. Toast (in drinking), bottoms up, skoal. An exclamation pledging health in drinking. Cf. **Kampai'.** *Nihi ta brinda si Mr. Pangelinan.* Let's have a toast to Mr. Pangelinan.

broas 2. Sponge cake. Also **brohas.** Cf. **kek.**

brochas 1,2. Brush (something). Duster, brush. Cf. **Guesgues, gue'gue'.**

brochas magagu 2. Clothes brush, used for washing clothes.

brohas 2. Sponge cake. Also **broas.**

broka 2. Drill (hand), brace and bit.

bronka 2. Reckless, careless, heedless of consequences. (f). Cf. **Arebatao.**

bronko 2. Reckless, careless, heedless of consequences (m). Cf. **Arebatao.**

bronse 2. Brass, bronze.

bruha 2. Witch, sorceress, wizard.

bruñi 1. Rub, wash by scrubbing, scrub. Cf. **Hotyat.**

brusia 2. Brassiere. Also **brasia.**

bruta 2. Foolish, idiotic, imbecilic, moronic, stupid, loony, brainless, dumb (f). Cf. **Loka, kaduka.**

brutu 2. Brute, scoundrel, man without honor or virtue, unwise, foolish. Also **bruta.**

bu 2. Pig's call. Cf. **Nena'.**

bu'a 2. Type of fish-lutjanus vaigiensis (family lutjanidae). Snapper.

bubu 2. Mad, enraged, angry. Cf. **Lalalo'.**

bubulao 2. Scary, a frightening person or thing.

buchi 2. Mumps, goiter, tumor on the neck.

buchibuchi 2. Turnover (pastry).

budega 2. Cellar, basement, vault, storeroom.

budu 2. Type of plant-inocarpus fagiferus. (?).

buelu 1,2. To put ruffle on dress.

buen 2. Approval, approbation, sanction, agreeing to, good (as in approval).

buen binidu 2. Welcome, toast, salute. Also **bien binidu.**

buen echu Good for you, see what happened (slang). *Buen echu na un ganna siha.* Good for you for beating them. *Buen echu na matomba hao sa' hu abisa hao na munga malagu.* See, you have fallen down because I warned you not to run.

buen probecho You are welcome.

buena 1,2. Lethal area of the heart, kill —by damaging heart. *Hu buena i binadu.* I killed the deer in the heart. *Hu danche i binadu gi buena-ña.* I hit the deer in the lethal area (of the heart).

buena 2. Weakest spot, vulnerable spot.

buenaplanta 2. Nice shape, beautiful, well built, well constructed.

buenas 2. Twelve or more points in tres siete (card game).

buenas Greetings. A shortened form for *buenas dias,* etc.

buenas dias Good morning, good day, hello.

buenas noches Good evening, good night.

buenas tatdes Good afternoon.

buenecho Better, preferable. Used in a disdainful manner. Also **bienecho.** *Buenecho ya u hanao.* It's better that he is gone.

buente 2. Maybe, perhaps. Cf. **Fa'na'an.**

buenu 2. Good, all right, okay. Cf. **Esta, maolek.**

buetta 2. Travel, journey, round trip, make a tour, cruise, tour. *Hu buetta yo' tatte gi hinanao-hu.* I traveled back from my trip.

buf 2. Booth.

bufón 2. Mask—covering the entire face and head. Cf. **Maskara.**

bukadutse 2. Type of fish-polydactylus sexfilis (family polynemidae). Threadfins.

bukayu 2. Coconut candy—made of sugar and grated coconut after oil has been extracted.

bukiki 2. Type of plant-olitorea ternatea. A type of flower.

bukiya 2. Valve—of innertube, where air is put in.

bula 2. Much, plenty, lots of, full. *Bula i tasi.* High tide. Cf. **Lahyan, meggai.**

bulacheru 2. Drunkard, tippler. Also **buklacheru, butlacheru.**

bulachon tasi 2. Seasick.

bulachon ulu 2. Nausea, dizziness.

bulachu 2. Drunk, intoxicated, dizzy, seasick, airsick.

bulaskes 2. Type of chicken—resembling hamburg, small. Also **balaskes.**

bulenchok 2. Pointed nose. Also **bulenchot.**

bulenchot 2. Long nose. Also **bulenchok.**

bulengngo' 2. Flat nose, dented, dull point, crumpled. Cf. **Daloggai, maheffong.**

buleru 2. Baseball player.

buliku 2. Jackass, donkey.

bulokbok 2. Bubbling sound, gurgling, boiling sound, gurgling as in a flowing stream, or pouring from a full bottle. *Bulokbok i matokcha' na guihan gi halom hanom.* The speared fish gurgles in the water. *I buseru bulokbok gi halom hanom.*

The diver was making bubbles in the water.

bulokbok 2. Stab. *I palao'an ha na'bulokbok i taotao.* The woman stabbed the man.

bulontariamente 2. Voluntarily, willingly, deliberately, intentionally.

bulontariu 2. Voluntary, volunteer. *Bumulontariu yo' manlaknos dies pesos.* I volunteered to donate ten dollars.

bulontát 2. Voluntary.

bumá' 2. Crawl, act like a cow. (From *ba'* the call of a cow.)

bumábaba 2. Talk silly, talk nonsense.

bumaranka 1. Flaunt, behave impudently.

bumasta 2. Interrupt, delay, stop.

bumuchachu 2. Industrious. Cf. **butmuchachu.**

bundak 2. Forest, jungle, woods.

buninas 2. Type of fish-lutjanus kasmira (lutjanidae). Snapper.

bunita 2. Pretty, pleasing, nice, gracious, neat (f).

bunitu 2. Handsome, pretty, nice, gracious (m).

bunitu 2. Type of fish-family thunnus saliens.

bunituyan 2. Slightly handsome. Cf. **Bunitu.**

bunmuchachu 2. Industrious, hard-working. Also **butmuchachu.**

bu'o' 2. Bubble, foam, lather. Cf. **Bo'an.**

burego' 2. Incognito, person in disguise, clown. *Hu li'e' burego' gi duranten selebrasion.* I saw a clown during the celebration.

buremos 2. Type of chicken—resembling plymouth rock (barred). Also **bremos.**

burón 2. Blotch, messy writing, scratched out writing, blotchy printing.

buru 2. Burro.

buruka 2. Noise, racket, loud noise. *Buruka i kareta-ña.* His car is noisy. *Bumuruka gue'.* He is noisy - he made noise.

burukenta 2. Noisy (f).

burukento 2. Noisy (m).

buseru 2. Diver. Cf. **Lili'of.**

busina 2. Siren, whistle.

busisi 2. Drill—kind of hand-made drill turned by hand.

buska 1. Search for, seek, look for. Cf. **Bando, espiha, aligao.**

buskabida Used when asking someone what he is doing when he is obviously idle or wasting time. *Hafa buskabidada-mu?* What are you doing?

buskaplaiteru 2. Troublemaker.

buskaplaito 2. Troublemaker, argumentative. Cf. **Kahaderu, palacha'.** *Si Antonio buskaplaito na taotao.* Tony is a troublemaking person. *Basta bumuskaplaito.* Stop looking for trouble.

buso' 2. Lump—a protuberance, as a swelling, hump.

busu 1. Dive. Cf. **Li'of.**

butdosa 2. Bulldozer, earth mover.

buteten malulasa 2. Type of fish-arothron nigropunctatus. A member of the large group of puffer fishes.

buteten pento 2. Type of fish-family canthigasteridae. Spotted blow fish.

buteten tituka' 2. Type of fish-diodon hystrix (family diodontidae). Porcupine fish.

buteti 2. Type of fish-family canthigasteridae. Blow fish, puffer fish.

buteya 2. Bottle, flask, beaker.

buteyón 2. Bottle (half gallon).

butlacheru 2. Drunkard, boozer, alcoholic, dipsomaniac—one with whom drunkenness has become a habit. Also **bulacheru.**

butmuchachu 2. Industrious, hard-working, laborious, diligent. (R) Also **bunmuchachu.**

butón agaga' 2. Type of plant-gomphrena globosa. A type of flower.

butonsiyu 2. Type of plant-cyperus kyllingia. (?) Cf. **Cha'guan humatak.**

butto 2. Statue, silhouette, indistinct form or image.

buya 2. Quarrel, unruly argument. Cf. **Plaito.**

buyada 2. Lot of, crowd, many. Cf. **Meggai , bula.** *Un buyada na guihan kinnene'-hu gi painge.* I caught a lot of fish last night.

cha 2. Type of plant-camellia sinensis, tea.

cha'- [æ] Better not, don't, should not —with possessive pronouns. Also

chacha'. *Cha'-mu ume'essitan.* You'd better not joke. *Cha'-miyu manhahanao sin guahu.* You'd better not leave without me.

cha ttano' [æ] **2.** Barren, infertile, unproductive, esp. worn out land or insufficient soil. Cf. **Kansadu.**

cháthinallom [æ] **2.** Vexation, anger.

chaba 1. Interrupt, chop, cut with a quick blow as in karate. Also **chabba.** *Hu chaba i dos taotao nu i mumumu.* I stopped the two men from fighting.

chaba 2. Cut notches in trunk of tree to facilitate climbing. Cf. **Matuba.**

chabba 1. Interrupt. Cf. **Chaba.**

chacha 2. Type of plant-cyclosorus spp. (?).

chacha [æ] **2.** Type of plant-cyathea lunulata. A type of bush, fern.

chacha' [æ] **2.** Fussy, choosey, squeamish, particular, hard to please.

chacha'- [æ] Better not, don't. Used with possessive pronouns. Also **cha'.** *Chacha'-mu umessitan.* You'd better not joke.

cháchaga' [æ] **2.** Thigh, upper part of leg of any two legged animal, refers only to the back legs of a four legged animal. Cf. **Pietna.**

chachak 1,2. Saw, cut, slice. Cutter, slicer, saw.

chachak mañisi 2. Rip saw.

chachak trumosu 2. Saw—large, cross-cut saw.

chachalani 1. Demonstrate, show the way, give good advice, show how to do something. *Chachalani si Maria taimanu nai siña mama'salape'.* Advise Maria as to how to make money.

cháchalon [æ] **2.** Fat (fried), the fat of a pig cut in squares and fried until all the oil is removed, like crisp bacon. Also **chacharon.**

Chacho' Nickname for Ignacio.

chada' 2. Egg, ovum, vagina (slang).

chaddek [æ] **2.** Hurried, fast , quick. Cf. **Guse', sahyao, alula, apreta, bibu.**

cháflaki 2. Nipple. Cf. **Akado', chipon.**

chaflalak [æ] **1.** Twist, wring, as in twisting rope. Cf. **Chaflilek.** *I palao'an ha chaflalak i aggak para godde.* The woman twisted (wove) the aggak leaves for tying.

chaflek [æ] 2. Quiver, jerk—give a quick and suddenly arrested push, pull, or twist, esp. when someone is dying, twitch, as in dying. Critically ill, at point of death. Cf. **Mañague'**. *Chaflek i mannok.* The chicken quivered in dying.

chaflilek 1. Twist (something), wrap around, twist around.

chagga' [æ] 1. Pinch (on the thigh). Cf. **De'on.**

chagi [æ] 1. Try, taste, attempt, test.

chago' 2. Far, afar, distant. *Chago' iya Hawaii ginen Guam.* Hawaii is far from Guam.

chago'ña 2. Further, more distant.

chagua 1. Extinguish partially (fire), partly extinguish a fire by using sand or soil, to lessen the heat of a fire, cause to calm, die down. *Hu chagua i guafi.* I reduced the fire. *Machagua i manglo'.* The wind died down.

cha'guan 2. Grass, weed, vine, lawn.

cha'guan agaga' [æ] 2. Type of plant-echinochloa colonum. Jungle rice.

cha'guan kakaguetes 2. Type of plant-teramnus labialis. Grass.

cha'guan lemmai 2. Type of plant-cyperus kyllingia. Grass.

cha'guan mannok 2. Type of plant-adenostemma. A type of grass, used for making brooms.

cha'guan Saigón 2. Type of plant-synedrella nodiflora. A type of grass.

cha'guan Santa Maria 2. Type of plant-vernonia cinerea. Grass.

cha'guan tasi 2. Type of plant-diplanthera uninervis. Sea grass.

cha'guan Umatac 2. Type of plant-cyperus rotundus. Nutgrass.

chaguangguan 2. Type of bird-myiagra oceanica freycineta, Micronesian broadbill—blue, white, and buff.

chahan 1,2. Cook—in an underground pit, oven (underground), underground pit.

chahlao 1. Catch—in the air. Also **chalao.**

Chai' Nickname for Rosa.

Chaife Name of a devil.

chaiguan 2. Type of plant, type of seaweed.

chaioti 2. Type of plant-sechium edule. Type of vine.

chak 2. Chalk. Cf. **yesu.**

cha'ka 2. Rat, mouse, shrew (family soricidae).

cha'ka 2. Bicep, type of muscle.

cha'kan akaleha' 2. Rat—long nose and feeds on snails. Lit. Snail rat.

cha'kan dikike' 2. Mouse.

cha'kan yomson 2. Rat—large, any especially large rat.

chakchak [æ] 2. Crack (the bones of a joint), dawn—break of, pop the knuckles. Cf. **Chakka', chekchek.**

chakchak manana [æ] 2. Dawn, daybreak, aurora, dawning.

chakka' [æ] 2. Titter, chuckle, crack (the bones of a joint), to pop the bones of a joint. Cf. **Chakchak, chekchek.**

cha'lak 1. Cut—small opening, as though to make slices in a fish to season it. Make small cut in flesh.

cha'lak Type of fish-family holocentridae. Squirrel fish.

chalakiles 2. Cf. **Charakiles.**

chalamlam [æ] 2. Blink, wink, twinkle. Cf. **Achetgue.**

chalan 2. Road, highway, street, path. Cf. **Katsada.**

Chalan Kanoa 2. The capital of Saipan, name of village on Saipan.

chalan kaskáo 2. Gravel road.

Chalan Pago Village in central Guam linked with village of Ordot.

chalan simento 2. Paved road.

chalani 1. Lead, guide, instruct, give advice, give counsel, advise. Cf. **Chachalani.**

chalao 1. Catch—the ball, etc. Also **chahlao.**

chalaochao 1. Shake—esp. liquid, rattle, move or sway with short quick irregular motions, bouncy.

chalapon [æ] 1. Scatter, disperse, dispel, dissipate, distribute. Cf. **Biba.**

chalehgua' 1. To stir, agitate. Cf. **Batte, lehgua'.** *Hu chalehgua' i fina'tinas-hu.* I stirred my cooking.

chalek 2. Laughter, laugh, smile.

chaleku 2. Vest, waistcoat, undershirt—for babies, shirt--sleeveless.

chambara' 2. Sword fight. (S)

Chamorri 2. Highest class in pre-Spanish Chamorro society.

Chamorrita 2. Young Chamorro (female).

Chamorritu 2. Young Chamorro (male).

Chamorro 2. Native people in the Marianas or the language spoken there .

chamosga 1. Burning off hair—as in dressing animals or preparing them for cooking, sear.

chamoskadu 2. Pot pourri, a mixture or blend of edibles in a stew-like dish.

champa 1. Compete, challenge, show off, to keep up with the Joneses. *Ha champa hao gi feria.* He competed with you at the fair. *Hu champa hao nigap.* I challenged you yesterday.

champan 2. Scow, large flat-bottomed boat with a square end, sampan.

champuladu 2. Type of food. Rice gruel cooked with chocolate.

cha'-mu [æ] Do not, don't. Cf. **Cha'-**. *Cha'-mu pumapacha i paki.* Don't touch the gun. *Cha'-mu humahanao gi gima'.* Don't leave the house.

Chana' Nickname for Susana.

chanda 1. Challenge, contradict, interrupt, object to, shove, push. Cf. **Chaba'**.

chandia 2. Type of plant-citrullus vulgaris. Watermelon. Also **chandiha**.

chanka' [æ] **1.** Hang, suspend (with a strap), carry—over shoulder from a strap.

chankletas 2. Sandal, slipper.

chanko 2. Limping, club foot, bow-legged. Cf. **Makabebe'**.

chankocha Boil, cook (in water)— usually refers to protein food or when sterilizing things.

channo 2. Taking big steps while walking, walk—with arms swinging briskly. *Bunitu chumanno si Antonio.* Tony looked nice while walking rapidly.

chansa 1,2. Chanceful, chance.

chansa 2. Joke, jest. *Mampos chansa na taotao.* He jests a lot.

chanseru 2. One who chances, a person or animal that takes risks or chances, joker.

changa 2. Lusterless, shade of color— lighter when compared with another shade of the same color. Often used when referring to a type of betel nut. Cf. **Kachang**.

chaochao 1,2. Shake, rattle. Rough water—when waves are breaking, trembling. Cf. **Chalaochao**. *Hu chaochao i hanom gi halom i tanke.* I shook the water inside the tank. *Chaochao i tasi.* The sea is rough.

chaole 2. Wag (tail), swing (hips), switch tail. *Ha na'chaole i ga'lagu dadalak-ña anai hu agang i na'an-ña.* The dog wagged its tail when I called its name.

cha'ot [æ] **2.** Allergic, allergy. *Cha'ot-hu i mangga.* I'm allergic to mangoes.

Chapanes 2. Japanese. Cf. **Hapones**.

chapeta 2. Washer, a ring of metal, as around a bolt or screw to form a seat for the head or nut, a perforated plate to form a seat for the head of a nail when roofing a house, heel taps. Cf. **Tachuelas**.

chapon 2. Become pale, turn white. *Anai hu sangani na ma'a'agang gue' gi polisia, chapon ha'.* When I told him the police were calling him, he suddenly turned pale. Also **chupon**, **chipon**.

chapós 2. Clumsy.

chappak 1. Detach, rip off—something that is stuck, as an adhesive bandage. *Hu chappak i kandalu gi petta.* I detached the lock from the door.

chapuseru 2. Cheater, deceiver.

chara 2. Type of plant-sesuvium portulacastrum. Grass—that grows near the sea.

charakiles 2. Type of food—a stew-like dish of chicken, coconut crab, or clams to which toasted ground rice or corn is added. Seasoned with achoti. Also **chalakiles**.

Charanka' 2. Chalan Kanoa (slang). Cf. **Chalan Kanoa**.

charera 2. Teakettle, pot, a metallic vessel for boiling liquids.

Charo' Nickname for Amparo.

chasko 2. Trace, speck. Also **chatko**. *Ni chasko ti sopbla despues di gipot.* There wasn't a trace of anything left after the party.

chat [æ] Slightly, hardly. Same as prefix *chat-*, but may modify whole phrases. *Chat ha hasso si Juan enao.* Juan hardly ever thinks of that.

chat- [æ] Slightly (prefix), hardly, barely. Also **chatta'**. *Chatbunita.* Slightly pretty. *Chatmalagu si Juan.*

John is not a good runner. *Chatespiha hao nu guahu.* You hardly searched for me.

chat- [æ] Prefix giving a negative or derogatory meaning to words. For example, *hallom* 'surmise', *chathinallom* 'anger'. See others listed below.

cháta'an [æ] **2.** Rainy, rainy season, not a good day, bleak, dreary weather. From *chatha'ani.*

cha'tan 2. Particular, individual, distinct from others, choosy, selective.

chatanmak [æ] **2.** Morning—before dawn, morning--before daybreak.

chátanti [æ] **2.** Bad spirit.

chatda' [æ] **2.** Shortage, insufficient amount—such as food or money. *Chatda' i nenkanno' gi gipot.* There was not enough food at the party.

chatda' [æ] Short form of *chatta' ha'.*

chátfañagu [æ] **2.** Miscarriage, birth given prematurely.

chátfino' [æ] **2.** Profanity, blasphemy, cursing, swearing, foul language, foul talk.

chatfinu'i 1. Swear at, curse at, blaspheme at. *Un chatfinu'i i digeru.* You cursed at the cheater.

chatge [æ] **1.** Laugh at—for being funny, laugh at someone by mocking, laugh at someone showing friendship, kindness, gratitude. *Hu chatge i na'chalek na taotao.* I laughed at the clown.

chatgon [æ] **2.** Smiley, smile easily or often.

chatguahu [æ] I am not feeling well. Lit. not very myself. *Chat* plus *guahu.* Nausea. Cf. **Chatguiya.**

chatguaiya [æ] **1.** Despise, dislike.

chatguiya Not feeling well, nausea. Cf. **Chatguahu.** *Chatguiya i patgon.* The child is not feeling well. *Chatguiya ham na dos.* The two of us are not feeling well. *Manchatguiya siha.* They are not feeling well.

cháthinasso [æ] **2.** Worry, be concerned. Cf. **Hasso.** *Mampos yo' chathinasso pot hagu.* I worried a lot about you.

chathinengge 2. Superstition, disbelief. Cf. **Hongge.**

chátilu [æ] **2.** Stubborn, hard-headed.

chatko 2. Stain, spot, discolored with foreign matter. Cf. **Mancha, pekas.**

chatko Cf. **Chasko.**

chátkuentos [æ] **1.** Gibber, speak incoherently.

chatli'e' 1. Hate, detest, abhor, abominate, loathe.

chátli'e' [æ] **1.** Fail to see (something) clearly.

chátmafañagu [æ] **2.** Ill-born.

chátmanhula [æ] **1.** Perjure, swear falsely.

chátmasa [æ] **2.** Unripe, immature, not cooked.

chátmata [æ] **2.** Eyesight (poor), nearsighted, myopic.

chátpachot [æ] **2.** Foul-mouthed.

chátpa'go [æ] **2.** Ugly, unpleasant, disagreeable, contrary to beauty, offensive to the sight. Cf. **Chura.**

chátsaga [æ] **2.** Difficult, hard. Incapacitated, incapable, disabled, preoccupied. Cf. **Mapot, makkat.** *Chatsaga mabira i boti.* It is difficult to maneuver the boat. *Chatsaga yo' na hu ayuda hao pa'go.* I am too preoccupied to help you now.

chatta' [æ] Hardly, barely, slightly (prefix). Also **chat.**

chattao [æ] **2.** Selfish, greedy, niggardly, avaricious, caring unduly or supremely for oneself. Cf. **Intereseo, otguyosu, meskinu.**

che C—letter.

chebbang 1. Nick, chip, put a nick in piece of wood or metal. Chop off, break off. Cf. **Mafte'.**

chebot 2. Fat, corpulent, fleshy, chubby, plump, stocky, obese, stout, portly. Cf. **Yommok.**

Checha' Nickname for Teresa.

che'che' 2. Midget, esp. as a relatively small member of a litter, very diminutive, small in size.

chechet 1,2. Hiss, call by hissing sound, call attention to. *I taotao ha chechet i amigu-ña.* The man hissed at his friend.

chechet 2. Attached to, fond of, love. *I patgon chechet as tata-ña.* The child is fond of his father.

checho 2. Adjacent, next to, bordering, boundary line. Also **chehcho.** *Chumecho i tano'-mu yan i tano'-hu.* Your land is next to my land.

che'cho' baba 2. Bungle.

cheddok 1. Insert partially between two objects for support or carrying. *Hu*

cheddok i lepblo gi papa' afa'fa'-hu.
I held the book under my armpit. *I
katpenteru ha cheddok i lapes gi
talanga-ña.* The carpenter put the
pencil behind his ear. *I gaseta
macheddok gi entalo' i dos lepblo.*
The newspaper was put between the
two books.

cheddok 1. To tuck something under
fold of garment at the waist.

chefchef 1. Dislocate, break partially (as
a green branch). *Hu chefchef i
ramas.* I partially broke the tree
branch. *Machefchef i kannai-hu.* My
arm was dislocated.

cheffla 2. Whistle (with lips).

chefflague 1. Whistle at, whistle to. *Hu
cheflague i ga'lagu.* I whistled to the
dog.

cheggai 2. Type of shell-cypraeidae.
Small cowrie, money cowrie.

cheggai pápaguan 2. Vagina (slang).

chehcho 2. Adjacent. Also **checho.**

chek 2. Check.

chekchek 2. Titter, chuckle, crack
(bones of a joint), to pop the bones
of the joint. Cf. **Chakka', chakchak.**

chekchek 2. Squeaky, noise from
squeaking or grinding together (as
the teeth in anger). *Chekchek i petta
anai hu baba.* The door squeaked
when I opened it. *Hu hungok i
chekchek i nifen-ña.* I heard the
grinding of her teeth.

chekeru 2. Pigpen, pigsty. Also **chikeru.**

chekka' 2. Weak, delicate, susceptible to
sickness or illness, an animal that
dies easily, such as a duck. Cf.
Hamlangu. *Chekka' na ga'ga' i
nganga'.* The duck is a delicate
animal.

chekle' 2. Robber, thief, stealer. Cf.
Sakke, ladron.

chekpa 2. Heavy smoker, smoking too
much, one who smokes someone
else's cigarettes.

che'lu 2. Sibling, brother, sister. *Che'lon
lahi.* Brother. *Che'lon palao'an.*
Sister.

chenche 2. Bedbug.

chenchule' 2. Present (money),
donation, thing that is given away,
gift. Cf. **Regalu, nina'i.**

chenchulu 2. Net, seine, long fish net, a
large net, one edge having sinkers
and the other floats.

chengle 1. Keep—something that was
borrowed temporarily, fail to return
something borrowed, stuck, remain
attached. Cf. **Gaddon, chenglong.** *Ha
chengle si Jose i lepblo.* Jose kept the
book.

chenglong 2. Stuck, caught in
something, become immovable.
Chenglong i rueda gi fache'. The
wheel was stuck in the mud.

che'op 2. Basket—woven from coconut
leaves and made for carrying on the
back.

chepchop tasi 2. Water—by the shore,
seashore, coast, water at the edge of
the seashore. Cf. **Kanton tasi,
chepchop unai.**

chepchop unai 2. Seashore, sand at the
edge of the sea. Cf. **Chepchop tasi,
kanton tasi.**

cheribiyan apaka' 2. Type of
plant-dolichos lablab. Vine—similar
to lima beans.

che'tan 2. Injury—esp. to a joint, pain
in the back or joint resulting from
an injury.

chetnot 2. Wound, sore. Cf. **Hirida.**

chetnot manman 2. Type of condition
when a person stares blankly into
space and can't remember anything.

chetnudan 2. Injured, hurt, wounded,
injury. Cf. **Hiridao.** *Chetnudan yo'
nigap gi tasi.* I was injured yesterday
at the sea. *Ha na'chetnudan yo' i
kareta.* The car injured me. *Ha
ripara i chetnudan-hu.* He became
aware of my injury.

chetta' kalalamten 2. Not budge, hardly
move. *Chetta' kalalamten i kareta.*
The car would not budge.

chetton 2. Stick to, adhere, cohere,
cling to, connect. *Chetton i lilok gi
tapbla.* The nail clings to the
lumber. *Chetton i danges i mangga
gi kannai-hu.* The sap of the mango
sticks to my hand.

chi- How far, to what extent, limit,
boundary. *Hafa chi-mu gi eskuela?*
How far did you go in school? *Hafa
chi-mu gi tinaitai-mu?* How far did
you read? *Manu chi-ña i tano'-mu?*
Where is the boundary of your
property?

Chian Nickname for Lucia.

chiba 2. Goat.

chibaleng [æ] 2. Blink.

chibe' 2. Tiny, minute, small, relatively little. Smaller than *dikike'*. Cf. **Dikike', dichicheng, po'yet.**

Chicha' Nickname for Luisa.

chícharos 2. Peas.

chiche' 2. Grin (showing teeth), smile (toothy), gritting teeth.

chíchiget 2. Pincher, as a crab's pincher, clip, hair pin, clothespin.

chíchiget 2. Type of insect. A black insect with pincer at one end.

chichigua 2. Baby-sitter.

chichi'i 1. Show contempt—by baring teeth. *I patgon ha chichi'i i ma'estra-ña.* The child bared his teeth at his teacher.

chichiton 2. Type of plant-achyranthes aspera. (?).

chigalu 2. Cigar.

chigando' 2. Suck thumb, thumb-sucker. *Chumigagando' i patgon.* The child is sucking his thumb.

chigando' 2. Pipe (for tobacco).

chigando' pi'ao 2. Bamboo pipe.

chiget 1,2. Over-run, run over, crowd together, press, compress, stifle, clip, crush, sandwich in, tuck in. Hairpin, tweezer, clothes pin. Cf. **Kañase'.** *Hu chiget i cha'ka ni kareta gi chalan.* I ran over a rat with a car on the road. *Chiget magagu.* Clothespin. *Chiget gapotulu.* Hair pin. *Hu chiget i pahina ni klip papet.* I clipped the pages together with a paper clip.

chigu'an 2. Brine, salt-brine, any strong saline solution.

chihet 2. Friendly—baby or girl, affable, docile. Usually describes a baby that is very outgoing and friendly.

chikas 2. Ten points in tres siete (card game).

chikeru 2. Fence, pen, corral, pigsty, pigpen, stockade.

chikitu 2. Tiny, very small (m). Also chikita (f).

chiku 1. Kiss, touch or press with the lips.

chiku 2. Type of plant-manilkara zapodilla. A type of tree.

chikulati 2. Chocolate. (R) Also chokolati.

Chilang Nickname for Cecilia.

chili 2. Penis, male sex organ. Cf. **Iyon lahi, paluma.**

chilong 2. Proportionate, equal, uniform, of like measure. *Chilong i*

tiningo'-mu yan i che'cho'-mu. Your knowledge is proportionate to your work.

chimboko' 2. Penis, male sex organ. (R) Cf. **Chili, iyon lahi, paluma, chingcheng.**

chiminea 2. Chimney.

chin How far, how much, to what degree. Cf. **Chi.** *Ti hu tungo' chin minaolek-ña.* I don't know how good he is.

China 2. China, Chinese (f).

chinachak [æ] 2. Slash, long cut, slice, dismember.

chinachalani 2. Instruction.

chinada' [æ] 2. Inguinal rupture, the groin is enlarged to an abnormal size. Used to describe person who walks with bent back or straddle legged.

chinaddek [æ] 2. Speed, haste, swiftness, briskness. Cf. **Chaddek.**

chinagi [æ] 2. Examination, test, trial.

chinago' [æ] 2. Remote, isolated.

chinakguat [æ] See chinatguat.

chinatguat [æ] 2. Lymph glands (swollen), usually caused by infection, bee stings, etc. Also chinakguak.

chinathasso [æ] 1. Project evil thoughts, imagine bad conduct in others. *Chinathasso si Juan ni asagua-ña.* Juan's wife imagined bad things about his behavior.

chinatkinemprende 2. Misunderstanding. *Ma na'suha i chinatkinemprende.* They eliminated the misunderstanding.

chinatpachot [æ] 2. Blasphemy.

chinatsaga [æ] 2. Suffering, poor.

chinatsaga [æ] 2. Discomfort.

chinepchop 1. Swallow up, absorb.

chinikulati na kulot 2. Brownish, containing brown color.

chinile' 2. Taken, seized, grasped, clutched, snatched, grabbed. Cf. **Chule'.**

chinilong 2. Proportion.

chinina 2. Dress, shirt, clothes, apparel, attire, raiment.

Chinu 2. Chinese (m), stingy, selfish (slang), miser.

chingcheng 2. Penis, male sex organ. Cf. **Chili, iyon lahi, paluma.**

chi'ok 2. Dew, drops of rain on leaves of plant. Also chi'op.

chi'op 2. Dew. Cf. **Chi'ok.**

chipón 2. Nipple—esp. of baby bottle. Cf. **Akado', chaflake'.**

chipon 2. Become pale. Cf. **Chapon, chupon.**

chirigame' 2. Toilet paper, or tissue. (S) Cf. **Papet etgue.**

chispas 2. Splatter, zoom by, squirt, spurt, spark, rush out, take off—with high speed. Cf. **Besbes, petsan.** *Chispas i hanom gi grifu.* The water squirted from the faucet. *Chispas i guafi gi feggon.* The fire sparked from the stove. *Chispas yo' gi fi'on-mu.* I moved quickly by your side.

chita 2. Flower prints (of cloth).

chitan Hawaiian 2. Hawaiian print.

cho Whoa, halt, stay, hold. Used mainly when driving a bull cart.

cho'cho' 1. Reach into—an opening, extend into by reaching, grab (something)--from inside something. *Hu cho'cho' halom i maddok ni kannai-hu.* I reached into a hole with my hand.

cho'cho' 2. Work, job, employment, task, position. *Bula na cho'cho' guaha giya Hawaii.* There is lots of work in Hawaii.

cho'cho' 2. Coral rock.

chocho 2. Eat, devour, consume. Does not take specific object. Cf. **Boka.** *Malago' yo' chumocho.* I want to eat.

choffe 1. Push gently; to push a lightweight object aside, such as paper or a leaf. *Hu choffe i hagon.* I pushed the leaf aside.

choffe 1. Shield from, to screen—esp. from wind, to block the wind. Cf. **Lenge.** *Hu choffe i manglo' anai hu tototnge i guafi.* I blocked off the wind when I was building the fire.

cho'gue 1. Do, render, perform, work. Cf. **Bida.** *Hu cho'gue i leksion-hu.* I did my lesson.

cho'guiyi 1. Serve, work for others, to wait on.

chokolati 2. Chocolate. Also **chikulati.**

Cholai' Nickname for Concepcion.

cho'le 2. Cyst, lump—bladder-like sac containing fluid morbid matter, protuberance. Enlarged lymph gland.

chomchom 2. Type of sickness, usually afflicting babies, symptoms include low grade fever.

chomchom Bushy, cluster of bees on hive. *I tronkon hayu chomchom.* The tree is bushy. *Chomchom na yanu.* A field overgrown with bushes.

chomchom abea 2. Bee's nest.

cho'me 1. Pour briskly, dash (liquid on something), spill (liquid).

chomma' 1. Forbid, prevent, impede, obstruct. Cf. **Pruibi.** *Ma chomma' i patgon gumimen setbesa.* They forbid the child to drink beer.

Chonai' Nickname for Concepcion.

chonchon 2. Nest, haunt, den, sex organ (f). Slang.

chonchon sasata 2. Wasp hive.

chonka 2. Type of game played by two persons only. The players have a wood tray with several cups carved into the top of the tray. Each player has a handful of marbles or small shells which he places in the cups successively. *Chonka* also names the equipment used in the game. Also **chonga.**

Chonke' Nickname for Concepcion.

chonnek 1. Push, shove, thrust, propel. Cf. **Su'on.**

Chong Nickname for Consolacion, Concepcion, Asuncion.

chopak 2. Type of plant-mammea odorata. Type of tree.

chopchop 1. Suck, absorb, draw in (as smoke from a cigarette), take up moisture.

Chopia Nickname for Estefania.

Choseng 2. Korean.

chosgo 2. Type of plant-glochidion. A type of tree.

chotda 2. Green banana, banana tree.

chotdan bunita 2. Type of banana— very rare in Guam. Pinkish color meat when ripe.

chotdan dama 2. Banana—similar to *chotdan Manila.*

chotdan gálayan 2. Type of banana— long, light green in color when almost ripe. Soft in texture.

chotdan guahú 2. Type of banana— grows on a short tree.

chotdan halom tano' 2. Type of banana —wild banana that is found in the jungle.

chotdan lakatán 2. Type of banana— similar to *chotdan Makao.* Skin is only slightly yellow when ripe.

chotdan long 2. Type of banana—usually cooked before eating.

chotdan Makáo 2. Type of banana—longer than *chotdan Manila.* Chinese banana.

chotdan Manila 2. Short banana.

chotdan pahong 2. Type of banana—grows on very large tree. Bunches grow very close together.

chotdan paladang 2. Type of banana—similar to *chotdan long,* but has brown skin.

chotdan tanduki 2. Type of banana—longer than *chotdan long,* grows in small bunches. Used for cooking. Also **tanluki.**

chotge 1. Hand-feed, apply by dropper, applying any liquid to the mouth, eyes, nose, etc. by an eyedropper or cotton that has been soaked in the solution and is then squeezed. *Hu chotge i neni ni leche.* I hand-fed the baby with the milk. *I mediku ha chotge mata-hu ni amot.* The doctor squeezed medicine into my eyes.

Chu' Nickname for Jesus.

chubasko 2. Storm—out in open water, strong wind accompanied by heavy rain out at sea.

chucharita 2. Type of plant-alternanthera. Type of flower.

chuchuko' 2. Type of bird-demigretta sacra sacra, reef heron, plumed egret.

chuchumeku 2. Type of plant-dolichos lablab. Vine—same as cheribiya apaka'.

chuchurika 2. Type of bird-rhipidura rufifrons uraniae, rufous-fronted fantail. Also **chichirika.**

chuchurika 2. Type of plant-catharanthus roseus. Periwinkle.

chuda' 1. Pour (liquid) out, empty, spill. Cf. **Basiha.** Also **basia.** *Ha chuda' i neni na'-ña sup gi basu-ña.* The child spilled his soup from his cup. *Ma chuda' i hanom halom gi tanke.* They poured the water into the tank.

chuga 1. Stop, halt, put to a stop, make (something) end, quit. Cf. **Na'basta, na'para.** *Ha chuga i famagu'on ni manmumumu.* He stopped the children who were fighting.

chugo' 1. Feed (by hand), as in feeding a baby. *I nana ha chugo ' i neni ni i* *nenkanno'.* The mother fed the baby the food.

chugo' 2. Sap, juice, pus, semen. *Bula chigo'-ña i kahet.* The orange has lots of juice.

chugo' niyok 2. Coconut juice.

chuguangguang 2. Type of bird—flycatcher. Flycatcher.

chukan 1. Swing, cause to rock, cause to sway, cause to waver. *Hu chukan si Pedro gi siya.* I caused Pete to rock in the chair.

chukan 1. Wallow, roll around in something.

chule' 1. Take, bring, grab, snatch, grasp, clutch, seize. Cf. **Residi, aksepta.**

chule' magi 1. Hand over, bring here.

chuli'on 2. Portable, capable of being carried.

chulugaigai 2. Hop—on one foot, shuffle--on one foot. Cf. **Ka'dideng.**

Chumbai' Nickname for Jesus.

Chumen Nickname for Jesus.

chumenchulu 2. Type of fishing—with long nets. Cf. **Chenchulu.**

chumilong 2. Proper, becoming.

chuminea 2. Chimney, smoke stack. Also **chumineha, chiminea.**

chungat 1. Cut the belly open. *Hu chungat i babui nigap.* I cut the pig's belly open yesterday.

chungat 1. Rock—back and forth. Cf. **Chukan.** *Ha chuchungat i patgon.* She is rocking the baby.

chunge' 2. Gray hair, grizzled, white hair.

chunge' 2. Type of bird-phaethon lepturus dorotheae, white-tailed tropic bird.

chu'ot 1. Cause wound or sore to hurt from physical contact, hurt someone's feelings, aggravate. *Ha chu'ot i chetnot gi kannai-hu si Juan.* John hurt the wound in my hand.

chupa 1,2. Smoke cigarette; tobacco, cigarette. Cf. **Sigariyu.**

chupa 2. Type of plant-nicotiana tabacum. Tobacco.

chupón 2. Pacifier—for baby.

chupon 2. Pale, ghastly. Cf. **Boksion, chopon.**

chura 2. Ugly, unpleasant, disagreeable, contrary to beauty, not pretty. Cf. **Chatpa'go.**

churisos 2. Sausage, frankfurter, roll of salami, balogna, etc.

chuti 2. Type of plant-cerbera dilatata. A type of tree.

Conchita Nickname for Asuncion.

Da Nickname for Natividad.

dada'da' 2. Be blamed for, face consequences, debt. *Guahu dada'da' anai mayulang i kareta.* I was to be blamed when the car broke down.

dádagu [æ] 2. Go north, move north, northward movement. Cf. Lagu. *Dadagu si David gi gima'.* David went north to the house.

dádalak [æ] 1. Accompany, keep company, be with someone, tag along with. Cf. Dalalak.

dádalak [æ] 2. Tail of an animal. Cf. Dalalak. *Gaidadalak i ga'lagu.* The dog has a tail.

dádaña' [æ] 2. Sociable, companionable, affable.

dádangse [æ] 2. Sticker, one or that which sticks, adheres, or causes adhesion, sticky. *I danges lemmai dadangse.* Breadfruit gum is sticky.

dádangse [æ] 2. Type of plant-urena lobata. Aramina. Type of grass. Also dadangsen apaka', dadangsen machinga'.

daddao [æ] 2. Fierce, ferocious, vicious, mean—generally for animals with teeth, esp. dogs. Cf. Malamaña.

daddek [æ] 2. Coconut (young)—without any meat or water.

dado' 2. Malformed nose, cleft palate; describes manner of speech caused by malformed nose or cleft palate.

Dado' Nickname for Leonardo.

dafao 2. Type of plant-boerhaavia tetrandra.

dafe' Cf. Daffe', daife'.

daffe' 2. Weak , powerless, dull. Cf. Ñaño'. Also daife', dafe'.

dafflok [æ] 2. Be rich of (something), untrammeled, unhampered, have more than ample supply of something. Cf. Malulok, tunos, motgan, mutero', go'dan, dafflokgue. *Dafflok i patgon chumocho ais krim gi tenda.* The child had eaten his fill of ice cream at the store. *Dafflok yo' umegga' i feria.* I watched the celebration as much as I wanted to.

dafflokgue 1. Indulge (heartily), consume (too much), gorge. Cf. Dafflok. *Hu daflokgue chumocho*

meggai melon gi lancho. I consumed a lot of cantaloupes at the ranch.

dagan 2. Buttocks, hips, coitus (slang), rump.

dagga' [æ] 2. Inflame, redden with inflamation, cause suppuration, aggravate. *Dagga' i chetnot-hu nai inina ni atdao.* My sore was inflamed when the sun shone on it.

daggao 1. Throw, cast, fling, hurl, pitch, toss. Cf. Yotte, blanko, yute', foyang.

dagge' 2. Root crop—over-ripe, but not decayed, burning sensation caused by hot pepper.

dagge' 2. Type of fish-family siganidae. Rabbit fish. Second stage of growth between mañahak and sesyon. Cf. Mañahak, sesyon, hiteng.

daggua 2. Sunburned.

dagi [æ] 1. Lie, prevaricate, equivocate, fib, deny.

dagon agaga' 2. Yam (red).

dagon anakko' 2. Type of yam—very long. Considered one of the best types of yams.

dagon apaga 2. Yam (shoulder).

dagon a'paka' 2. Type of yam. White yam.

dagon halom tano' 2. Type of yam—wild yam, very bitter, not eaten.

dagon haya 2. Type of plant-dioscorea numularia. Yam, light in color, sweet taste.

dagon kunehu 2. Yam (rabbit).

dagon lila 2. Type of yam—purplish in color.

dagon Lukas 2. Type of yam.

dagon lulok 2. Type of yam—straight in shape.

dagu 2. Type of plant-dioscorea alata.

dai 2. Friend—when used in greeting.

daibang 2. Type of fish-family scombridae. Large tuna.

daibites 2. Diabetes.

Daidai Nickname for Soledad.

daife' 2. Weak, deficient in bodily vigor, not strong.

daigo' 2. Turnip—preserved. Cf. Daikon. Cf. Takuang.

daikon 2. Turnip, daikon—Japanese. Cf. Daigo'.

dais 2. Dice.

dakdak 1. Knock, rap, strike with a quick sharp blow. Cf. Adak, dakot.

dakngas 2. Bald-headed, bare. Cf. **Matfos.**

dakon 2. Liar, one addicted to lying or who knowingly utters falsehood. From *dagi'on.*

dakot 1. Knock, rap, strike with a quick sharp blow. Cf. **Adak, dakdak.**

dalai [æ] Too much, excessively. Exclamation. *Dalai enao.* That's too much. *E'kahat i dandan dalai na ina'gang.* Slow down the music, it's too loud.

dalak [æ] 1. Accompany, escort, follow. *Hu dalak i palao'an.* I accompanied the girl. Cf. **Dalalak.**

dalaki [æ] 1. Follow. Cf. **Dalalak.** *Pot fabot dalaki i direksion siha.* Please follow the directions.

dálalai [æ] 2. Slender, skinny, thin, slim.

dálalak [æ] 1. Alternate pronunciation for *dadalak.* Accompany, keep company, be with someone, tag along with. Cf. **Dadalak.**

dalalaki [æ] 1. Follow. Cf. **Dalaki.**

Dalen Nickname for Natividad.

dalle 1,2. Coitus, sexual intercourse—to have, (taboo). To win--over someone at game of skill or chance. Cf. **Baggai, sirek, kichi.** *Hu dalle hao dumama.* I beat you at checkers.

daloggai 2. Dent, dented, crumpled, caved in. Cf. **Maheffong, bulengngo'.**

dama 2. Checkers (game), play checkers.

dama di noche 2. Type of plant-cestrum nocturnum. Type of flower—emits sweet odor at night.

dáma'gas 2. Thumb, pincers, toe, claw of the crab.

Damenggo 2. Sunday.

Damenggon Ramos 2. Palm Sunday.

damla' 2. Cf. **Gamla'.**

dammot [æ] 2. Testicle, scrotum. Cf. **Dodole', dollan, bolabola.**

danche [æ] 1. Hit (a target), guess, guess correctly, get it right.

dandan 1,2. Play music, ring (bell). Cf. **Dilingdeng.** Music, phonograph, record player, sounds having rhythm and melody. Cf. **Musiku, Funografu.**

dandan kampana 2. Ringing of church bell. Cf. **Tohke.**

dandera 2. Musician, one who plays any musical instrument (f).

danderu 2. Musician, one who plays any musical instrument (m). Also **dandera** (f).

dánkolo 2. Big, large, great, huge. Cf. **Lamudong, tamong.**

dankolo na minagof Bliss, extreme happiness.

Dano' Cocos Island, a small island off the southern tip of Guam.

dansa 2. Dance, swinging, swaying, oscillation, vibration, fluctuation, wavering, undulation. Cf. **Baila.**

daña' [æ] 2. Combined, joined, be together, united, mingled, mix, compile, blend. *Hu na'daña i pan yan i mantikiya.* I put together the bread with the butter.

dañáo 2. Damaged, injured, spoiled, delicate—easily injured. *Dañao na fektos.* Damaged merchandise.

dañosu 2. Injurious, mischievous, detrimental, capable of harming or destroying something.

dañu 2. Harm, damage, injury, loss, pest.

danges [æ] 2. Candle, wax, gum.

danglon [æ] 2. Type of fish. Cowfish, trunkfish.

danglon [æ] 2. Type of bag.

dangnge' 2. Weak, weakling, feeble, frail, coward. Cf. **Pedde, dolle.**

dangse [æ] 1. Stick, cause to adhere, glue. *Ma dangse i ka'ka' gi basu.* They glued the crack of the glass.

dangse [æ] 1. Flatter, play up to.

dangson [æ] 2. Glutinous, sticky, resinous.

da'ok [æ] 2. Type of plant-calophyllum inophyllum. Palo-maria tree.

da'os 2. Defecate, have bowel movement, have diarrhea. Cf. **Masinek.** *Dumada'os yo'.* I am defecating, or I have diarrhea.

dasai 1. To give hair cut, shear, cut off (esp. hair), trim. Cf. **Laklak.** *Hu dasai i che'lu-hu nigap.* I gave my brother a haircut yesterday. *Hu dasai i flores gi uriyan guma'.* I trimmed the flowers around the house.

dasai adotfo 2. Type of haircut, crew cut, hair parted on one side.

dasai dakngas 2. Type of haircut—when head is completely shaved.

dasai kabayu Bangs, a hair style in which front hair is cut straight across the forehead.

dasai malachai 2. Type of haircut—when head is shaved. Cf. **Boyo'**.

dasai San Visente 2. Type of haircut. Extremely short on the sides and long on the top.

dasai tapbla 2. Type of haircut, flattop haircut.

de D—letter of the alphabet.

Dea' Nickname for Andrea.

debati 2. Debate, argument, dispute, quarrel. Cf. **Atgumento**.

debet 2. Haggard, debilitated, depressed by sickness. Cf. **Tufai**.

debet Rather than. *Debet di un mamaigo' maoleknña na un fanestutudia.* Rather than sleeping, it is better that you study.

debi Must, should, have to, ought to. Also **debidi**. *Debi un bisita si nana-mu gi espitat.* You must visit your mother at the hospital.

debidi Must, have to, ought to, should. Also **debi**. *Debidi un saga gi gima'.* You must stay at home, or You should stay at home.

debidít Division in arithmetic.

Dédedo Village in northern Guam.

dédeggo 2. Heel (of foot).

déde'on 2. Pincher, one who or that which pinches. Cf. **Chichiget**.

dedu 2. Measurement equal to the length of the second joint of the index finger.

definisión 2. Definition.

deggo 1. To tiptoe, to stand on toes. Cf. **Le'yok**.

deha 2. Squat, crouch, to sit down upon the heels.

dei 2. Friend (when used as direct address or in greetings). *Hafa dei.* Hello. *Hu tungo' dei na...*I know friend that. .. Also **dai**.

dekabuko' 2. Unsymmetrical, not round, lopsided, not perfectly round, but is supposed to be. (S) Also **todu echong**.

dekka' 1,2. Poke, pick (with pole or stick), nudge, pick at, pick nose, pick ears, pole, stick (used for picking). Cf. **Gaole, dossok**.

dekka' nifen 2. Toothpick.

dekkes 1. Cause to hit—one thing against another, cause to strike--one thing against another. *Hu dekkes i*

biyat. I caused a marble to hit another marble.

deklara 1. Declare, publicize, assert openly, affirm, announce, publish, proclaim, promulgate. Cf. **Proklama**.

deklarasión 2. Declaration, statement, deposition, testimony.

Delan Nickname for Adelia.

delegadu 2. Delegate, representative, proxy. Cf. **Representante**.

delekora 1. Syllabify, pronounce syllable by syllable.

deletrea 1. Spell, sound out the words.

dellan 2. Balance (oneself)—while walking, as on a rope or any extremely narrow edge. Also **dollan**.

demokrasia 2. Democracy.

denka 1. Nibble—food or bait, nip, peck, pick at, scratch off, scrape off. Cf. **Dekka'**. *I guihan ha denka i katnada.* The fish nibbled the bait. *Hu denka i pentura gi kareta.* I scraped off the paint on the car.

denke' 1,2. Flash light at, spot (with a light). (S) Flashlight. *Hu denke' i binadu.* I spotted the deer with a light.

denkot 1. Peck—strike with the beak, pick at one's food.

dentista 2. Dentist.

dentro Within. Used with *di. Bai hu gaige Guam dentro di kinse dies.* I will be in Guam within fifteen days.

dengdeng 2. Snail (large, land). Cf. **Akaleha'**.

dengha 2. Bow, bend over—with head lower than hips. Also **dengnga**. Cf. **Dilok, deha**.

dengnga 2. Bow, bend over. Also **dengha**.

dengua' 1,2. To phone, to cable, telephone, cablegram. (S) Cf. **Telefon, uailes**.

de'on 1. Pinch, tweak. Cf. **Chagga'**.

derepente 2. Suddenly, abruptly. Cf. **Gotpe**.

deres 2. Type of plant. Local name for a plant whose roots are used for poisoning fish.

des- Not, negative—usually used with Spanish loan words. Also **dis-**.

desabridu 2. Unsavory, insipid, tasteless, unpleasant to taste or smell, spoiled, sour.

desafte 1. Unroof (a house).

desagunáo 2. Disgust, aversion. *Nina'desagunao ni i malabida-ña.* He is disgusted with all the bad things that happened.

desaparehu 1. Unsaddle, unharness.

desapatta 1. Separate—one from another. Also **adespatta.**

desaprebáo 2. Disapproved, disliked. *Desaprebao i che'cho'-mu.* Your work was disapproved.

desaprueba 1. Disapprove, condemn, regard as wrong, pass unfavorable judgement upon.

desarekladu 2. Disorderly manner, disorderly way, untidy, disheveled, scattered around, messy way. Also **derechas, derechas kuetdas.**

desarekláo 2. Disarranged, disturbed the due arrangement of.

desareklo 2. Disorder, confusion, disarray, lack of order.

desatento 2. Disrespectful, irreverent, discourteous, inattentive (m). Also **desatenta** (f).

desatma 1. Disassemble, take apart, disarm.

desbela 1. Stay awake, lose sleep. Also **desbelu.**

desbeladu 2. Sleeplessness, insomnia, wakefulness.

desbeláo 2. Sleepless, stay awake all night, be awake all night. *Dumesbelao yo' gi painge.* I stayed up all last night.

desbelu 2. Stay awake. Also **desbela.**

desbira 1. Dislocate.

desbuetga 1. Deflower, despoil, to deprive of virginity, to conquer the maidenhead.

desde Since, from—used to connect phrases. Also **deste.** Cf. **Ginen.** *Desde nigap matto yo'.* I came yesterday (and am still here). *Desde nigap mamaigo' gue'.* He has been sleeping since yesterday. *Mamokkat yo' desde Susupe.* I walked from Susupe.

desde ki Ever since.

desde ngai'an Since when?

desempeña 1. Break lease.

desesperáo 2. Desperate, hopeless.

desfaborable 2. Ominous, unfavorable.

desfigura 2. Disfigure, deform, distort, deface.

desfiguradu 2. Disfiguration, disfigurement. Also **desfigurada.**

desfiguráo 2. Disfigured, deformed, defaced.

desfila 1. Pass by, as a parade.

desfonda 1. Break bottom, as in a boat.

desfonda 2. Bottomless, unfathomable, without bottom.

desganáo 2. Disgusted, disappointed, inattentive, apathetic, not interested, discouraged, disheartening, depressing, dispiriting. Cf. **Desgusto.**

desgrasia 2. Calamity, disaster, accident, misfortune. Cf. **Aksidente.**

desgrasiáo 2. Accident—be in an, involved in an accident. *Guaha desgrasiao pa'go.* Someone had an accident today.

desguas 2. Pole, fishing pole.

desguas 2. Snare—esp. used for catching chickens.

desgusta 1. Disgust, displease, discourage, dishearten.

desgusto 2. Disgusted, hatred, discouraged, quarrel. *Dumesgusto yo' ni tes-hu.* I was disgusted about my test. *Guaha desgusto entre siha.* There was a quarrel among themselves.

deshilachas 1. Remove strings or shreds from cloth. Also **desilachas, deslachas.** Cf. **Hilachas.**

desimát 2. Decimal.

désimu 2. Tenth, decimal.

deska 1. Flip (with fingertip), flick (with fingertip).

deskalentáo 2. Spoiled—esp. eggs.

deskansa 2. Rest, repose, sleep, slumber, relax, be dead. *Hu li'e' i dumeskansa na taotao.* I saw the man who rested.

deskanso 2. Rest, repose, sleep, slumber. *Anakko' i deskanso-ku gi gima'.* I had a long rest at the house.

deskaradu 2. Indecent, careless (m). Unclean, shameless, impudent, brazen. Also **deskarada** (f).

deskaráo 2. Indecent, shameless, unclean, careless.

deskareta 1. Hamstring, cut tendon on the rear leg of a four legged animal or two-legged creature. Unhook cow from bull cart. Cf. **Kadera.**

deskasa 1. Unload, liberate. Also **deskatga, deskata.**

deskata 1. Unload (weapon), liberate, set free. Also **deskasa.** Cf. **Deskatga.** *Hu deskata i paki.* I unloaded the

gun. *I patgon ha deskata i paluma.*
The child set the bird free.

deskatga 1. Unload, take the load from, remove the burden (cargo, freight) from. Cf. **Deskata.**

deskita 1. Retaliate, avenge, get revenge, take anger out on something. *Hu deskita i binibu-hu gi lamasa anai hu pañiti.* I took my anger out on the table when I hit it.

deskita 1. Recoup, regain losses by winning back.

deskonfiansa 2. Distrust, lack of confidence, mistrust, a feeling that appearances are not reliable.

deskonsuela 1. Discourage.

deskripsíon 2. Description.

deskuenta 1. Discount, withdraw, reduce or decrease the price.

deskuida 1. Neglect, be offguard, inattentive, careless. *Hu deskuida yo' ni patgon ya poddong gi banko.* I neglected the child and he fell off the bench.

deskuidáo 2. Careless, heedless, reckless, inadvertent, irresponsible. Cf. **Dehao.**

deskuidu 2. Carelessness, negligence, imprudence, inattention, disregard. Cf. **Dehao** (m), **Dehada** (f).

deskuluráo 2. Pale, ghostly, deathlike, fade (color).

deslachas Cf. **Deshilachas.**

desminuyi 1. Decimate, destroy a large portion of.

desmonte 1. Clear—a field of trees or stumps, cut down (a woods).

desmurón 2. Day dreaming, not paying attention, preoccupied mind.

desmurona 1. Destroy—by breaking into small pieces, to fragment.

desmuronu 2. Day dreamer, preoccupied mind, paying no attention (m). Also **desmurona** (f).

desnek 2. Appear unexpectedly.

desonesto 2. Immoral, indecent, dishonest.

desonra 1. Dishonor, disgrace, shame (f).

desonro 2. Dishonor, disgrace, shame (m).

despacha 1. Give (in exchange for), term used in purchasing situation. Cf. **Tulaika, bende.** *Despacha yo' un paketen sigariyu.* Give me a package of cigarettes.

despacha 1. Send away, dispatch. *Despacha i patgon para i gima'-ña.* Tell the child to go home.

desparadót 2. Trigger of a gun.

desparadu 2. Desperate, despair, desperado. Also **despirao.** *Desparadu na taotao.* He is a desperate man.

desparateru 2. Foul mouth, one who uses obscene language.

desparati 1. Separate, part, divide. Cf. **Sipara, adingu, dipatta, adespatta.**

desparati 2. Obscene words, dirty language.

despasio 2. Slow, soft (voice), diminished, decrease speed or volume. Cf. **E'kat.**

despega 1. Take off, remove, detach. Cf. **pega.**

despensa 1. Forgive, pardon, excuse, condone, grant forgiveness, exculpate. Cf. **Asi'i.**

despetdisia 1. Waste, squander, purposeful waste, ravage, pillage.

despetdisiáo 2. Wasteful, lavish, squandering.

despetdisio 2. Waste, useless expenditure, that which is waste. *Bula na despetdision nenkanno' gi gipot.* There was a lot of wasted food at the party.

despidi 1. Say good-bye, bid farewell. *Hu despidi si nana-hu.* I said good-bye to my mother.

despidida 2. Farewell, departure, dismissal.

despiráo 2. Desperate. Also **desesperao.**

desponi 1. Control, govern, manage, direct (by influence or counsel).

despongga 1. Cut off (point), break off (tip), prune. Cf. **Despunta.**

despresia 1. Ridicule, mock. Cf. **Botleha, despresio.**

despresiáo 2. Contemptuous, contemptible, disdainful, insolent, insulting.

despresiapble 2. Contemptible, worthless, insignificant, negligible.

despresio 2. Sarcasm, mockery, bitter remark. Cf. **Botleha.**

despribináo 2. Unprepared, unready, unexpectant. Cf. **Despribinidu.**

despribinidu 2. Unprepared, unaware, unready, unexpectant. Cf. **Despribinao.**

despues Then, later, afterward, hereafter, usually used to introduce a clause. Also **pues**. *Despues, estudia i leksion-mu.* Then, study your lesson. *Mamuda yo' despues humanao yo' asta i che'cho'-hu.* I dressed up, then I went to my job.

despues di After, (preposition), later. *Despues di guahu.* After me.

despuesto 2. Disposal, arrangement, ordering.

despunta 1. Cut off—point, break off--point, blunt, nip. Cf. **Despongga**.

deste ki Ever since. Also **desde ki**.

destempla 1. Distemper, to remove temper of a metal, put out of tune.

destempláo 2. Disarrangement, out of tune, not tasty.

destieru 1. Exile, relinquish, discard, cast off, abandon. Cf. **Destiladu**.

destiladu 1. Banish, exile, send away, deport. Cf. **Dipotta**.

destilipas 1. Eviscerate, remove the guts.

destináo 2. Destined.

destinasión 2. Destination.

destinu 2. Fate, destiny.

destotniyadót 2. Screw driver.

destronka 1. Truncate.

destrosa 1. Annihilate, destroy, wreck, demolish, ruin. Cf. **Disasi**.

destrosu 2. Disaster, wreck, destruction.

de'uda 2. Debt, liability.

di Spanish loan used in many constructions as part of a Spanish phrase. Also used as linker in constructions using non-Spanish phrases. *Basta di mama'tinas nenkanno'.* Stop preparing food. *Sigi hao di mama'baba fan ta'lo.* You are fooling around again. *Basta di mama'baba.* Stop fooling around.

dia 2. Day, period of 24 hours, day time, daylight. Cf. **Ha'ani**.

dia' See there, see here, take notice. *Dia' ga'-hu dukduk.* See my hermit crab. *Dia' na maolek patgon.* Take notice of the good child. *Dia' na poddong hao.* See there, you fell down.

dia dethuisio 2. Judgment day—at the end of the world. Also **dia di huisio**.

diablo 2. Devil, satan. Cf. **Aniti, satanas, hudas, maknganiti, dimonio**.

diablura 2. Foolishness, tomfoolery, devilment. From *diablo*.

diahlo [æ] No, no thanks. Also **dialu**.

dialekto 2. Dialect.

dialu [æ] No, no thanks, never mind. Also **diahlo, dihalu**.

diamante 2. Diamond.

diametro 2. Diameter.

diantre 2. Devil (expletive), gee, gosh. *Diantre, ti hu gacha' i sakke.* Devil, I didn't nab the thief. *Diantre na aguaguat taotao hao.* Devil, you naughty man. *Diantre na inaguaguat gue'.* Gosh, he is naughty.

di'ao 2. Base—used in a game, hide-and-seek (game). Also **di'u**.

di'ario 2. Daily, occurring each successive day, every day.

dias 2. Days. Cf. **Dia**.

dibana 1. Slice, cut (in slice). Cf. **Ribana**. *Hu dibana i pan.* I sliced the bread.

dibatde 2. Free, gratis, gratuitously, for nothing. Cf. **Grates**.

diberas 2. Swear, honest, certain, sure, declare or assert as true.

dibetsión 2. Entertainment, recreation, diversion.

dibettáo 2. Leisure, free from demands, at liberty.

dibette 1,2. To be at leisure, put (oneself) at ease, leisure, ease, freedom from business. *Para bai hu dibette yo' agupa'.* I will be at leisure tomorrow. *Bula lugat nai siña un dibette hao.* There are many places where you can be at leisure.

dibi 1,2. Owe, be in debt, due. Debt, credit. Cf. **Fiha**.

dibibiyon 2. Divisible.

dibidi 1. Divide, split evenly, sever, cause to be separate, share. Cf. **Patte, apatte, kompatte**.

dibiette 1. Liberate. Also **dibette**.

dibina 1. Guess—as in a guessing game. *Umadibina i dos.* The two played the guessing game.

dibina dibina Phrase used when beginning a guessing game.

dibinu 2. Diviner, fortune teller.

dibisión 2. Partition, dividing wall, subdivision, division. Also **dibusion**.

dibosión 2. Devotion, worship, adoration, prayer.

dibosionario 2. Devotionary, prayer book.

dibotsia 2. Divorce, dissolve marriage contract by legal authority.

dibotu 2. Devoted, dedicated, pious, religious, devout. Also **dibota** (f).

dibuetta 2. Round trip, returned from a trip, came back from traveling. *Para u dibuetta gue' magi ginen Guam.* He is going to make a round trip from Guam.

dibuhu 2. Crochet.

díchicheng 2. Tiny, small, minute, relatively little. Cf. **Chibe'**, dikike', po'yet.

dichosu 2. Faithful, loyal, devoted, dedicated, blessed, divine. Cf. **Dibotu.**

dichu The very, the said. Also **dicha.** *Gi dichu ora anai makama yo' estaba hao gi gipot.* The very hour when I was bed-ridden, you were at the party. *Pues dichu enao na tiempo.* At that very time.

dídide' 2. Few, a little, not many, not much. *Didide' ha' yo' un na'i.* You only gave me a few. *Didide' na taotao gi miteng.* (There were) few people at the meeting.

didinak 2. Parasite, sponger.

didok 2. Dark, deep, profound. *Didok na betde kulot-ña i kareta-mu.* Your car is dark green in color.

didok 2. Steep. *Didok na okso'.* A steep mountain.

dientes 2. Teeth—of comb or rake. Cf. **nifen.**

dies 2. Ten.

dies i sais 2. Sixteen.

dieta 1,2. Diet, be put on a diet. *I mediku ha dieta yo' asiga.* The doctor put me on a salt free diet.

difekto 2. Defect, flaw, fault, damage.

difende 1. Defend, protect, shield, guard, safeguard. Cf. **Guatdia.**

difensót 2. Defender, protector, guardian.

diferensia 2. Difference, variation, dissimilarity.

diferensiát 2. Differentiate, distinguish.

diferentes 2. Different, various, diverse, divergent, disparate.

difikuttát 2. Difficulty, hardship, rigor.

difina 1. Define.

difunto 2. Dead person, deceased, one who passed away, the late. Also **difunta** (f). Euphemistic for *matai. I difunto tata.* The late father. *Si difunto Jose.* The late Joseph.

diga 1,2. Raffle, cause to guess, bid. *Madiga i sidan gi feria.* The sedan was raffled at the fair. *Hu diga i patgon kande gi kannai-hu.* I let the child guess for the candy in my hand.

digeria 2. Falsehood, fraud. Also **dugeria.**

digeru 2. Cheater, swindler. Also **dugeru.**

digeruyi 1. Cheat, swindle. Also **dugeruyi.**

digueya 1. Behead, cut head off.

digula 2. Stuffed—from overeating, satiated--from eating. Cf. **Binaya'.**

diha' See—as in you see, guess, probably, maybe, reckon, imagine, think. *Diha' sa' bai hu deskansa.* Notice I will have to rest. *Diha', poddong hao, no.* See, you fell down, yes.

dihada 2. Careless, sloppy, slovenly. Cf. **Dihao, deskuidao, deskarada.**

diháo 2. Careless, sloppy, slovenly, one who misplaces things frequently. Also **dihada** (f). Cf. **Deskuidao.**

diháo 2. Short side at cock pit, the side designated for the cock against which odds are given.

díkike' 2. Small, little, diminutive, tiny, petite, wee. Cf. **Chibe', po'yet, dichicheng.**

diknidát 2. Dignity, nobility, worthiness, state of being honorable.

dikno 2. Dignified, majestic, noble, magnificent, honorable, glorious. Cf. **Maknifikante.**

diksinario 2. Dictionary. Also **diksionario.**

diksionario 2. Dictionary. Also **diksinario.**

dikta 1. Dictate, say aloud to be taken down in writing. *I ma'estro ha dikta ham noskuantos palabras para in tige' gi makinan mangge'.* The teacher dictated to us some words so we could write them on the typewriter.

Dikta Nickname for Benedicta.

dilenkuente 2. Delinquent.

diliba 1. Deliver, turn over, hand over.

dilihente 2. Diligent, quick, speedy.

dilikáo 2. Tender, delicate.

dílileng 1. Carry (by hand), handle—as on wash tub, brief case.

dilingdeng 1. Ring bell, rattle. Cf. **Dandan.**

dilisiosu 2. Delicious, exquisite, highly pleasing to the senses, taste, or mind. Cf. **Mannge'.**

diliti 1. Dissolve, melt, dilute. Also **diriti.** *I hanom ha diliti i asukat.* The water dissolved the sugar.

dilitrea 1. Trace, copy, spell out.

dilok 2. Bow, bend, prostrate, tilt. Cf. **Dengha, tekkon.** *Dumilok yo' para bai hu godde i sapatos-hu.* I bent down to tie my shoes.

dilok cha'ka 2. Somersault, somerset, upside down position, turn head over heels, turn upside down doing a cartwheel. Lit. Bent over rat. Cf. **Sakadatche'.**

dilubio 2. Deluge, flood, overflowing of land by water. Cf. **Milak.**

dimalas 2. Misfortune, mischance, adversity, bad luck.

dimanda 1. Demand, claim, require, exact.

dimandadót 2. Demander, demandant, the plaintiff in a real action. Cf. **Kasadot.**

dimasiáo 2. Superfluous, extravagant, overemphasized, too much.

dimimoria 1,2. Play, stage show, program, memorize.

dimonio 2. Demon, evil spirit, devil. Cf. **Aniti, maknganiti, hudas, diablo.**

dimu 2. Kneel, bend the knees.

dinagi [æ] **2.** Lie, untruthfulness, deception.

dinalak [æ] **2.** Type of sickness, swelling and inflammation of calf and legs. *Ti siña yo' mamokkat sa' dinalak yo'.* I cannot walk because of my swollen leg.

dinalalak 2. Imitation, following. Cf. **Dalalak.**

dinamita 1,2. To dynamite. Dynamite, TNT.

dinamu 2. Dynamo.

dinanche [æ] **2.** Correct, right, accurate, exact, precise.

dinaña' [æ] **2.** Mixture, blend. Cf. **Daña'.**

dinekko' 2. Seedling, that which has germinated. Cf. **Dokko'.**

dinekko' 2. Sprouting, growth, germimation. Cf. **Lina'chok.** *Manbunitu dinekko'-ñiha i tinanom.*

The sprouting of the plants was pretty.

dinida 2. Doubt, doubtfulness, feeling of uncertainty as to fact. Cf. **Duda.** *I dinida-ña na ti muna'hanao gue'.* His uncertainty caused him not to go.

dinigridu 2. Bruise, inflict a bruise, contusion. *Dankolo na dinigridu gi mata-hu.* There is a big bruise on my eye. *Ha na'dinigridu i adeng-hu anai ha gacha' gi gipot.* He inflicted a bruise on my foot when he stepped on it at the party.

dinimalas 2. Misfortune, bad luck. Cf. **Dimalas, disdicha.**

Ding Nickname for Leonardo.

dinga' 2. Twin, double, fork (of the tree), junction, crossroad.

dinga' chalan 2. Crossroad, junction, intersection.

dingu 1. Depart, leave behind, abandon, desert, forsake. Cf. **Abandona.**

Dios 2. God. Cf. **Asaina, Yu'us.**

dipatta 1. Depart with, separate from, isolate. Cf. **Adespatta, sipara, adingu, desparati.** *Hu dipatta yo' giya guiya.* I separated from him.

dipattemente 2. Department.

dipende 1. Depend on, trust, entrust, have faith, rely on. Cf. **Embatga, angokko.** *Dipende gi lugat ni para un saga.* It depends on the place where you would stay. *Hu dipende yo' gi tiningo'-hu.* I depend on my knowledge.

dipendensia 2. Dependence.

dipendiente 2. Dependent, subordinate, relying on something else for support. *Guaha tres na dipendiente-ku.* I have three dependents.

diploma 2. Diploma, certificate.

diplomátiku 2. Diplomat.

dipositon hanom 2. Reservoir (water).

dipósitu 2. Warehouse, depot, storage, supplyhouse, storehouse.

dipotsí Supposed. *Dipotsi para Guam yo'.* I was supposed to go to Guam. *Hu na'i si Andres ni guantes lao dipotsi para hagu.* I gave Andy the gloves, but they were supposed to be for you.

dipotta 1. Deport, depopulate, send away, exile, banish. Cf. **Destiladu.**

dipusita 1. Deposit, place, put, store.

direcha iskietda 2. Scattered—left and right. Formal way of saying *direchas kuetdas.*

direchas kuetdas Disorderly manner, disorderly way, untidy, disheveled, scaitered around, messy way. Also **direchas.** *Direchas kuetdas siha nai manggaige i kosas-hu.* My things were in a disorderly manner. *Direcha ha' nai un popo'lo i kosas-mu siha.* You have left your things scattered around.

direcho 2. Privilege, prerogative, right, a personal right.

direcho 2. Right side up, correct position, the state of being in the right manner. Cf. **Atderecho.**

direcho 2. Right—direction. Call given to a bull pulling a cart when turning right.

direktorio 2. Directory, book of instructions.

direktót 2. Director.

dirihi 1. Direct, lead, guide, conduct, administer. Cf. **Kondukta.**

diriti 2. Melt, liquefy. Also **diliti.**

diritiyon 2. Soluble, dissolvable.

diroga 1. Revoke, abolish, countermand, repeal, disapprove. Cf. **Richasa, rimati.** *Hu diroga i planu pot i gipot.* I revoked the plan for the party.

disasi 1. Demolish, disassemble, destroy, ruin, wreck, annihilate, take off (something). Cf. **Destrosa.**

disatende 1. Disregard, pay no attention to, slight.

disatma 1. Disarm, subdue.

disayunu 2. Breakfast. Cf. **Lisayunu.**

disdicha 2. Misfortune, misery, ill fortune.

disecha 1. Ignore, disregard, neglect, pay no heed to, pretend not to see.

disecha 2. Curse, to wish evil on another.

diseha 1. Wish, want, desire, hope, crave, covet. Cf. **Tanga.**

disehu 2. Desire, longing, craving. *I disehu taya' bali-ña.* The desire has no significance.

disembra 1. Replacing seed or plant that failed to survive.

disendensia 2. Descendents. Cf. **disendente.**

disendente 2. Descendant, an offspring (usually remote).

disente 2. Decent, appropriate, proper, clean, suitable. Cf. **Asientadu, gasgas.**

disentunadu 2. Inharmonious, out of tune. Cf. **Disentunao.** *Disentunadu i dandan-mu.* Your music is inharmonious.

disentunáo 2. Inharmonious, out of tune, out of harmony, sing off key. Cf. **Disentunadu.**

disetto 2. Desert, uninhabited, isolate, deserted. Also **disietto.**

disidi 1. Decide, resolve, settle, come to a conclusion, bring to a decision.

Disiembre 2. December. Cf. **Umayang.**

disietto 2. Desert, barren, arid region, sand dune.

disimula 1. Hide, conceal, keep secret, dissemble, secrete, make secret. Cf. **Na'na'.**

disiosu 2. Desirous, eager.

disiplina 2. Discipline, training, rule of conduct.

disípulu 2. The apostles, the disciples, follower, scholar. Cf. **Apostoles.**

disisión 2. Decision.

diskatga 1. Unload, take the load from, remove the burden (cargo, freight) from. Cf. **Deskata.**

diskriminasión 2. Discrimination, differentiation.

diskubre 1. Discover, reveal, explore, disclose, make plain or evident.

diskuti 1. Debate, discuss. *Hafa para un diskuti?* What are you going to discuss?

diskuti 1. Release, let go of. *Ha diskuti i binibu-ña.* He released his anger.

diso' 2. Lump (on head), weal, welt, pumpknot. Cf. **Kuku.**

diso' 2. Diesel, fuel.

dispara 1. Fire a gun. Cf. **Paki.**

disparati 2. Nonsense, blunder.

disparati 2. Bad language.

dispensa 1,2. Excuse, pardon, dispensation. Also **despensa.** *Dispensa yo'.* Excuse me.

dispensiya 2. Pantry. Cf. **Haichio'.**

dispusision 2. Disposition, decision.

distansia 2. Distance.

distengge 1. Distinguish, differentiate, tell apart, determine, discern.

distenggidu 2. Distinguished.

distraksión 2. Distraction, disturbance, agitation.

distrakto 1,2. Distract, divert, distraction.

distritu 2. District, region, precinct, tract (of land), territorial division.

Dita Nickname for Bernadita.

ditetmina 1. Determine, conclude, direct, designate.

ditetminasión 2. Determination, persistence, insistence.

ditieni 1. Delay, prolong, retard, slow, slacken, detain.

di'u 2. Base—used in a game, hide-and-seek (game). Also di'ao.

do'ak 2. Cataract (of the eye), white spot on pupil of eye, having one bad eye.

do'an 1,2. Carry (something)—on the shoulder with stick. Cf. Oddo'.

do'an 2. Mole—a congenital mark on the skin. Cf. *Lonnat.*

dobladura 2. Hem, as in a skirt or shirt sleeve. Also dopbladura.

dochon 2. Penetrate, pierce, stick in, thrust in, put in. *Hu na'dochon i haguha.* I made the needle penetrate.

doddak 2. Thimble—used to protect finger when sewing.

doddo 2. Type of fish-abudefduf sordidus. Damsel fishes.

doddo 2. Any of several damsel fishes of the family pomacentridae.

dódichan 2. Go west. Also lodichan.

do'do' 2. Fart, break wind, emit gas through the anus.

dódole' 2. Testicle, scrotum, penis, vagina, sexual organ. Cf. Dammot, bebe'.

dodole' 2. Part of bird from which tail feathers grow.

dofen 2. Type of fish-coryphaena hippurus. Dolphin.

doffe' 2. Missing tooth, chipped tooth, snaggle-toothed, chipped (blade).

do'gas 2. Small shell, sea shell.

dogga 2. Footwear (generic).

dohlan 2. Cyst, varicose veins.

dokdok 2. Type of plant-artocarpus mariannensis. Breadfruit—with seeds in the fruit.

dokko' 2. Sprout, shoot forth, germinate, grow. Cf. La'chok.

dokngos 2. Burned, scorched, crispy, dehydrated, dried from heat. Cf. Tostos, akong. *Dokngos i katne.* The meat is burned. *I kusineru ha*

na'dokngos i hineksa'. The cook scorched the rice.

dokto 2. Doctor, physician, surgeon, practitioner. Cf. Mediku, praktikante.

doktrina 1,2. Indoctrinate, give religious instruction. Also dottrina. Cf. Katisismo.

dollan 2. Testicle, global shape, a round object. Cf. Dammot, bolabola.

dollan 2. Balance. Also dellan.

dolle 2. Weak, weakling, feeble, frail. Cf. Pedde, dange'.

Dolot Nickname for Dorotea.

dómina 2. Domino.

domitorio 2. Dormitory. Also dotmitorio.

dommo' 1. Punch, sock, strike, hit with the fist. Cf. Pañiti, seku, tromponasu.

dondon 2. Freckle, spotted, dotted, speckled, pitted, tarnished, stained.

donesion 2. Donation. Cf. Ensimasion.

donne' 2. Type of plant-capsicum annuum. Hot pepper, bell pepper. Also done'.

donne' gollai 2. Type of plant-frutescens capsicum var grossum. Bell pepper. Red pepper whose unripe fruit is called green pepper or sweet pepper.

donne' i sisu 2. Budding breast.

donne' pika 2. Type of plant-capsicum. Chili pepper.

donne' sali 2. Type of plant-capsicum frutescens. Small pepper—very hot in taste.

donne' ti'ao 2. Pepper—larger than the regular *donne'.*

donseya 2. Virgin, maiden, maid servant.

donseyan nobia 2. Bridesmaid.

donseyu 2. Best man.

doña Mrs.—Title used only before Christian names of women, esp. when telling a story.

dongdong 1. Pierce repeatedly, hit repeatedly playing tops, stung by bees. *Hu dongdong i tolompon i amigu-hu.* I hit my friend's top repeatedly. *Ha dongdong yo' i sasata.* The bee stung me.

donggat 2. Type of fungus. White, tiny, and soft and is luminous, usually found in decayed matter which resembles mushroom, reflector, speck or point of light, as a single lantern in the distance.

donggat 2. Twinkling, twinkle of light, pin-point of light, sparkling blink of light, bright tiny light, phosphorescence. *Manli'e' yo' donggat gi halom tano'.* I saw a sparkling blink of light in the woods.

donggat 2. Type of insect-coleoptera lampyridae. Lightning bug, firefly.

dopbla 1. Bend, fold, strain, make tense. *Hu dopbla i lilok ni kannai-hu.* I bent the steel with my hand.

dopble 2. Double, twofold, two of a sort.

Dorang Nickname for Isidora.

Doreng Nickname for Dorotea.

dos 2. Two.

dos sientos 2. Two hundred.

dosse 2. Twelve.

dossok 1,2. Pierce, poke, pick (with pole or stick). Pole. Stick (used for picking). Cf. **Gaole, dekka'.**

dotgan 2. Penetrated. *Dotgan i bala gi liga.* The bullet penetrated the wall.

doti 1. Bestow, give. *Fanggagao ya un madoti ni mangguaguan na bendision.* Ask and you will be bestowed with the most precious gift.

doti 1,2. Inherit, inheritance, dowry. Inherited talent. *Ti madoti ni mañaina-ña.* There was no inheritance from his parents.

dotmiente 2. Beam, crossbeam.

dotmiladu 2. Drowsy, sleepy head.

dotmilón 2. Sleepy head, one who feels sleepy often.

dotmitorio 2. Dormitory.

dottrina 2. Catechism, catechizing, teaching, instructing (esp. in religion), doctrine. Also **luttrina, doktrina.**

dragón 2. Dragon.

draiba 1,2. Drive—by steering the course of a vehicle by mechanical means. Driver, operator. *Hu draiba i sidan asta i espitat.* I drove the sedan to the hospital. *I draiba ha na'despasio i kareta papa' gi ekso'.* The driver slowed the car down the hill. Cf. **Sugon.**

dreya 1,2. Dredge, excavate with or as with a dredge.

du'an 2. Wart, verruca, bud, a glandular excrescence or hardened protuberance on plants or animals. Cf. **Cho'le, du'an nanaso'.**

du'an nanaso' 2. Wart, verruca, a glandular excrescence of hardened protuberance which occurs on animals, caused from external stimuli. Cf. **Du'an.**

dubli 2. Double. Also **dopble.**

duda 2. Doubtful, dubious, equivocal, undetermined, problematical, questionable, doubt. *Duda na taotao si Juan.* John is a doubtful man.

dudok 1. Encircle—by making the two ends of something meet, such as the two arms, thumb and forefinger, two ends of a string. *Ha dudok i sintura-ña anai ha toktok gue'.* He encircled her waist when he embraced her. *Tatfoi i dalalai-ña i addeng-mu siña ha' hu dudok ni kannai-hu.* Your leg is so thin that I can encircle it with my hand.

Dudong Nickname for Pedro. Also **Dung.**

dudos 2. Showy, flirtatious.

dudosu 2. Distrust, dubious, questionable.

dudu 2. Container—small can, dipper (liquid).

duendes 2. Goblin, elf, ghost, spook, in the form of a dwarf. Cf. **Birak.**

dueñu 2. Owner, proprietor.

dugeria 2. Unfairness, falsehood, foul play, cheat, fraud, deceitfulness. Also **digiria.**

dugeru 2. Cheater, swindler, hoax (m). Also **dugera** (f), **digeru.**

dugeruyi 1. Cheat, swindle, defraud, hoax, beguile, befool, trick, outwit, hoodwink. Also **digeruyi.** *Un dugeruyi yo' gi huegu.* You cheated me in the game.

duka' 2. Imbecile, idiot, moron, feeble-minded. Cf. **Attamos.**

duko' 2. Imbecile, idiot, feeble-minded, moron. Cf. **Attamos.**

dukumento 2. Document, deed.

dúlalak 1. Chase, pursue, catch, put to flight, chase away, oust.

dulalas [æ] 2. Type of insect-odonata. Dragon fly.

dulili 2. Type of bird-pluvialis dominica fulva, Pacific golden plover. Type of bird-actitus hypoleucos. Common sandpiper. Type of bird-heteroscelus brevipes. Gray-tailed tattler. Type of bird-heteroscelus incanus. American wandering tattler. Type of bird-arenaria interpres. Turnstone. Type of bird-gallinago megala. Marsh snipe. Type of bird-crocethia alba. Sanderling. Type of bird-erolia acumimate. Sharp-tailed sandpiper.

dulok 1,2. Bore, stab, puncture, perforate, hypodermic needle, penetrate. *Ha dulok i emfetmera i kannai-hu.* The nurse gave me a shot in my arm. *I dilok dankolo.* The needle (thing that gives the shot) is big.

dumang 2. Tooth decay, decayed teeth, missing teeth.

dumeskarada 2. Flaunt, behave impudently.

Dung Nickname for Pedro. Also **Dudong.**

duplika 1. Duplicate.

dura 1. Delay, defer, put off, take up (time), time required. Also **dira.** Cf. **Taka'.** *Ha dura yo' i mediku dos oras gi espitat.* The doctor delayed me two hours at the hospital.

duranten During (preposition). *Duranten i gera bula manmatai.* During the war many died.

durao 2. Duration.

durapble 2. Durable, lasting, longstanding, abiding.

duru 2. Hard, fast, with pressure, vigorously, untiring. *Duru yo' macho'cho'.* I work hard. *Malagu yo' duru.* I ran fast.

dusena 2. Dozen, a group of twelve.

dutse 2. Type of plant—passion fruit.

dutse 2. Sweets.

duya' 2. Yaws, frambesia.

e E—letter.

e- Search for (something)—prefix. May be affixed to nouns or modifiers. Primary stress falls on *e-*. *Enenkanno' gi lancho.* Search for food at the ranch. *Ebunita palao'an para ga'chong-ta gi baila.* Search for pretty girls for our partners at the dance.

ébaba' 2. Low, short, extending upward, relatively little, below the normal height, too short. Cf. **Etigu, takpapa'.** *Ebaba' i haligen i gima'.* The post supporting the house is too short. *Ebaba' i ginaloppe-ña gi matka.* His

jump is short of the mark. *Ebaba' i tronkon hayu.* The tree is short.

ebang 2. Crooked, curve, bend, arch. Also **chebang.** Cf. **Echong.**

ebanghelio 2. Gospel. Also **banghelio.**

ebanghelista 2. Evangelist.

ebidensia 2. Evidence, proof, testimony. Also **ibidensia.**

echa 1. Bless, to give out blessing, as a parent or priest to his child. *Echa bendision i hadu-mu.* Give blessing to your godson. *I pale' ha echa i neni-hu.* The priest blessed my baby.

echan 2. Match, pit against, esp. in determining which cocks will be matched against each other to fight.

echo 2. Completed, finished, action done with regret, an action completed but regretted, used when one refers to an act, the completion of which he regrets. *Echo i magagu-mu esta.* Your clothes are ready. *Echo hu cho'gue i che'cho' sin i dispusision-mu.* I have completed the work without your consent. *Munga madiroga i che'cho' sa' esta echo munhayan.* Don't revoke the work because it has already been completed.

echong 2. Crooked, curve, bend, arch. Cf. **Ebang, ekklao.**

echóngñaña 1. Be at side of, to be at one's side.

edda' 2. Soil, dirt. Also **odda'.**

eddas 2. Stage, platform. Cf. **Satge.**

édipok 2. Type of fishing, fishing in a water hole in the reef with a fishing line.

editoriát 2. Editorial, leading article.

editót 2. Editor, author, journalist.

eduka 1. Educate, teach, develop and cultivate mentally or morally.

edukasión 2. Education.

efektibu 2. Effective, in operation, active, operative.

efektos 2. Merchandise. Also **fektos.**

efi F—letter.

éga'ga' Get busy, do something about whatever the situation may be. Lit. Hunt for animals. *Ega'ga' ya un na'gasgas hao.* Get yourself busy to clean yourself up.

égagao 2. Beg, live on charity, alms—ask for, ask--as a form of begging. Cf. **Gagao.**

egga' 1. Watch, observe (as spectator).

eggeng 2. Slant, slope, an inclined plane, lay or tilt on one side.

égigi 2. Type of bird-mycomola cardinalis saffordi, cardinal honey-eater.

egoismo 2. Egoism, selfishness.

egues 1. Scrape, scour, rub.

éguihan 1. Go fishing, go look for fish.

ehemplo 2. Example, parable.

ehetsisio 2. Exercise.

ehi 2. Axle (of a wagon).

éhinasso 1. Dull, stupid, lacking in brains. Lit. Looking for thought.

Éhipto 2. Egypt.

é'kahat 2. Slow, lingering. Also **e'kat.**

e'kat 2. Slow, slacken speed, reduce speed, take it easy. Cf. **Despasio.** *E'kat pinalala gi che'cho'-mu.* Slow down on your work.

ekglesia 2. Church. Cf. **Guma' Yu'us.**

ekgo' 2. Jealous (sexual), suspect of infidelity. Also **ugo'**. *Ekgo' gue' na lahi.* He is a jealous man. *Si Juan ekgo' na taotao.* John is a jealous person.

ekgu'i 1. Be jealous (sexual), be suspicious of infidelity, lust. Cf. **Ugo'.** *Hu ekgu'i i asagua-hu.* I am jealous of my spouse.

ekkes 1. Make a cross, mark with an X.

ekklao 2. Crooked, curved, bent, arched. Cf. **Ebang, echong.**

eklesiastiku 2. Ecclesiastic, belonging to the church.

ekonomia 2. Economy, thrifty management, saving, thrift.

ekpe 2. Impudence, sassy, back talker, one who answers back disrespectfully, one who responds impudently, to be saucy or sassy. *Ekpe i che'lu-hu lahi.* My brother is sassy.

ekpe' 2. Breaker, esp. of fragile things, slicer, cracker, one who breaks (fragile) things. *Ekpe' yo' mampos espeos.* I have a potential for breaking mirrors.

eksakatibu 2. Executive.

eksakto 2. Exact, marked by accuracy and thoroughness, precise and full, identical. Also **sakto.**

eksalente 2. Excellent, outstanding. Also **ekselente.**

eksamina 1. Examine, investigate, scrutinize, interrogate closely, try or test by question.

eksiste 2. Exist.

eksklamasión 2. Exclamation.

eksperensia 1,2. Experience, expert.

eksperensiáo 2. Experienced, expert.

ekspert 2. Expert, skillful. (G) Cf. **Meyeng.**

eksplika 1. Explain, expound, describe, relate, make clear. Cf. **Pula'.**

eksplikáo 2. Explicable, explainable, capable of explanation. Cf. **Eksplika.**

ekspotta 1. Export, ship overseas.

ekspresia 1. Express, utter. *Hu ekspresia i opinion-hu gi miteng.* I expressed my opinion at the meeting.

ekstende 1. Extend, lengthen, elongate, prolong, protract, expand, enlarge. Cf. **Umenta.**

ekstensión 2. Extension, act or state of extending.

eku 2. Echo.

ékulo' 1. Climb up, get on top of. Cf. **Feddos, kahulo'.**

ékungok 1. Listen to, hearken, give heed, yield to advice. Cf. **Hungok.** *Hu ekungok i rediu.* I listened to the radio.

elektrisidá 2. Electricity.

eli L—letter.

elifante 2. Elephant. Also alifante.

Elo' Nickname for Cornelio; Pedro.

embahadát 2. Embassy.

embahadót 2. Ambassador.

embarasos 2. Obstacle, junk, barricade, scrap, trivial objects, trifles, refuse, trash, litter. Cf. **Trompeson.**

embatga 1. Trust, depend, entrust, have faith. Also **batga.** Cf. **Dipende.** *Hu embatga yo' giya hagu.* I depended on you.

embatga 1. Claim—not owned by the claimant, take--something that is not truly owned by the claimant, purloin openly, steal openly--as opposed to covert stealing. *I patgon ha embatga i lapes ni ti iyo-ña.* The child claims the pencil that does not belong to him.

embatka 2. Embargo.

embes di Instead of. Also **enbes di, embes ki.** *Embes di un fanaitai chumachalek hao.* Instead of praying, you were laughing.

embeste 1. Challenge, attack, assail, invite defiantly to a contest of any kind.

embidia 2. Vengeful, envy. Cf. **Emmok, bengga.**

embidiosu 2. Hothead, easily angered, hot tempered, envious (m). Also **embidiosa** (f).

embilikeru 2. Nosey, annoying, curious, meddler, snooper (m). Also **embilikera** (f), **bilikeru.** *Embilikeru hao na patgon.* You are a nosey child.

embudu 2. Funnel.

embusteria 1. Brag, boast.

embusteru 2. Liar, deceitful, denial (m), backtalk. Also **embustera** (f).

embutiyi 1. Do inlaid work, do raised or embossed work.

emfetmera 2. Nurse, nursemaid. Also **emfetmeru** (m).

emfetmeria 2. Infirmary, nursing home, place for the care of the infirm or sick.

emi M—letter.

emigrante 2. Emigrant.

Émilin Nickname for Emelia.

emmok 1. Revenge, get even, hide (something) till it ripens. Cf. **Bengga, embidia.** *Hu emmok hao sa' un pañiti yo' nigap.* I avenge you because you hit me yesterday. *Hu emmok i chetda para u aga'.* I hid the banana for it to ripen.

empachu 2. Bored (from repetition), sickened (from repetition), satiated, fed up. Cf. **Singao, o'son, sosongte.** *Empachu i taotao chumocho mangga.* The person was satiated from eating mangoes. *I che'lu-hu lahi empachu ni nobia-ña.* My brother is fed up with his girl friend.

empanada 2. Meat pie; meat wrapped in dough and fried. Also **empañada.**

empañada 2. Meat pie. Also **empanada.**

empas 2. Even up, payment completed, atone.

empatma 1. Couple, patch, mend, splice, join together, sew up.

empe' 2. Piece, part (from a whole). Cf. **Pidasu.** *Empe' pan.* Piece of bread.

empe' buteya 2. Broken bottle, broken glass vessel.

empe' ridoma 2. Broken bottle, broken glass vessel, such as a vial. Cf. **Empe' buteya.** Also **empe' didoma.**

empeña 1. Lease, let by contract, pawn.

empeña 2. Mortgage.

empeñáo 2. Ardent, eager, jealous.

empeñosu 2. Eager, ardent, persistent, press earnestly, pertinacious, persevering, ambitious. Also **empeñosa.**

empeñu 2. Effort, with all one's power to achieve what is wanted. *Todu empeñu ha cho'gue i mediku para u satba i malangu.* The doctor tried everything to cure the sick one.

emperadót 2. Emperor (m). Also **emperadora** (f).

empeya 2. Chicken fat, oily or greasy meat of fowl or fish. *Manempeya ni yinemmok-ña.* It is so fat it is greasy.

empidi 1. Prohibit, forbid, prevent.

émpito 2. Temperament. *Baba empito-ña.* He has a bad temperament.

empitosu 2. Temperamental, impetuous. *Empitosu na taotao.* A temperamental person.

emplasta 1. Smear, blot out, smudge, daub, raze, plaster.

emplasta 2. To apply a poultice to, soak wound in liquid. Cf. **Plasta.**

emplasto 2. Poultice, soaking of wound in liquid.

emplea 1. Employ, hire, make use of the service of.

empleáo 2. Employee. Also **emplehao.**

empleháo 2. Employee. Also **empleao.**

emplehu 2. Employment, job, work. Also **empleo.**

empleo 2. Employment, job, work. Also **emplehu.**

en You—pl. pre-posed pronoun, used in transitive statements. *Kao en li'e' i taotao?* Did you see the man?

énague' There is (toward addressee), be right there, from *enao* plus *gue'.* Also **enaogue'.** *Enague' yo'.* I will be there. *Enague' si Juan.* There is John.

enamoráo 1. Enamored, in love, amorous, full of sexual passion, lustful. *Enamorao yo' as Maria.* I am in love with Maria.

enao That (demonstrative)—close to addressee.

enao guatu Over there—place next to the addressee.

enao ha' 2. That's all, that's it, all there is—the thing close to the addressee.

Enao ha' che'cho'-ña pa'go. That is all she has done today.

enao na That is why—something is done, that is the reason--talking to and about addressee. Also **taiguenao na.** *Enao na hu bisita hao gi espitat sa' malangu hao.* That is why I visited you at the hospital - because you were sick.

enao nai That is where, that is when, that is the time or place (where addressee is). *Enao nai para u guaha programa.* There (where you are) is the place where there is a program.

Encho' Nickname for Lorenzo.

encros 2. Criss-cross, zig-zag. *Hu na'encros i kareta.* I made the car go criss-cross.

endotsa 1. Endorse.

Eneru 2. January. Cf. **Tumaiguini.**

enfietno 2. Hell, abyss, inferno. Cf. **Sasalaguan.**

enhinieru 2. Engineer. Also **enyineria.**

eni N—letter.

enimigu 2. Enemy, foe, hostile force, adversary, opponent, challenger, competitor. Cf. **Kontrariu.**

enkahi 1,2. Lace, apply lace. Also **inkahi.**

enkantáo 2. Mysterious, magical, enchanted. *Munga umessalao guini sa' enkantao este na lugat.* Don't shout here, for this is an enchanted place.

enkaosa 2. Under investigation. *Si Juan ma'enkaosa sa' manaña.* John has been under investigation for assault.

enkasu If, in case. Also **akasu, sienkasu.**

enkatga 1. Commission (someone), order, entrust, to put in charge. *Ma enkatga yo' ni patgon na bai hu esgaihon guatu asta i gima'-ña.* They commissioned me to escort the child to his home.

enkatgáo 2. Caretaker, custodian. Cf. **Sobrekatgo.**

enkatgo 2. Caretaker, given responsibility, left to be in charge, the commission, the order. Cf. **Katgo, enkatgao.** *Hu na'enkatgo hao yanggen humanao yo'.* I will give you the responsibility when I leave. *Malangu i enkatgo pa'go.* The caretaker is sick now.

enkatmadura 2. Chancre, a wart that opens up and will not heal, venereal sore or ulcer.

enkattidu 1. Pickle, preserve food (by pickling).

enkebukáo 2. Argument, confusion, fuss, trouble, worry, inconvenience, troublesome, disagreement. Cf. **Plaito, yinaoyao, atborotu.** *Bula na enkebukao gi miteng.* There was a lot of disagreement at the meeting.

enkola 1. Bleach, whiten, blanch, make white or whiter, esp. in the sun.

enkotdio 2. Venereal disease, gonorrhea.

enlugat di Instead of, in place of. Cf. **Putno.** *Enlugat di manmapedde siha gi bola, manmangganna siha.* Instead of losing the ball game, they won it.

enmienda 1. Amend.

enmosa biaha 2. Type of plant-amaranthus tricolor. (?).

enpadrona 2. Census when everyone is called to a central location to be counted.

enredadót 2. Slanderer.

enredos 2. Slander, aspersion.

énsahi 2. Hurry, walk fast. *Nihi ta ensahi.* Let's hurry. *Hafa na ume'ensahi hao?* Why are you in a hurry?

ensahi 2. Hitch-hike. *Umensahi yo' asta Garapan.* I hitch-hiked to Garapan.

ensaiklopidia 2. Encyclopedia.

ensalada 2. Salad.

ensatta 1. String, draw through, thread, pass a thread through the eye of something, make a collection by stringing on a wire, thread, etc. to hold them together.

ensatto 2. A collection of (something) put together by stringing them on a wire, thread, etc. so as to hold them together, as a string of fish, shishkabob, string of beads. *Ensatton guihan.* String of fish. *Ensatton katne.* Shishkabob. *Ensatton pipitas.* String of seeds.

ensayu 2. Rehearsal, practice session. *Malak i ensayu yo'.* I went to choir practice.

ensenada 2. Cove, inlet, small bay.

ensima 1. To chip in (money), to put in money as shares, to have share. *Manensima yo' dies pesos para i gipot.* I chipped in ten dollars for the party. *Bai hu fanensima sinkuenta pesos para kabo'-hu.* I will put in fifty dollars as my share.

ensimasión 2. Donation.

énsinahyao Hurry up, walk fast—imperative when addressing a group of people. Cf. **Sahyao.**

éntalo' 2. Between, among, middle. *Entalo' i lepblo.* The middle of the book. *Tumohtohge yo' gi entalo' i dos tronkon hayu.* I am standing between the two trees.

éntalo' 2. Meddle. *Gof ya-ña umentalo' gi areklon dos umasagua.* He likes to meddle in the affairs of the two married people.

entalu'i 1. Interfere, meddle, interrupt, minding another's business. *Munga na un entalu'i i patgon gi huegu-ña.* Don't interfere with the child in his game.

enteru 2. Solid, not hollow; entire, all of.

entieru 2. Funeral, burial, entire, all of, whole. Also **enteru.** Cf. **Todu, puru.**

entinadu 2. Stepson. Entinada (f).

entonses Then, so, well then. Cf. **Pues.** *Entonses na munga hao.* Then, you don't want it.

entonses na Mean to say, one's intention, one's wish, what is being expected. *Entonses na munga hao humanao.* You mean to say that you aren't going. *Entonses na para un tattiyi yo'.* So you are going to follow me.

entot Piece of.

entrada 2. Entrance, entry, gateway, passageway.

entre Among, amid, amidst, between. *Guahu mas ñateng malagu gi entre hita na mangga'chong.* I am the slowest runner among our group.

entrega 1. Deliver, submit, yield, release, hand over.

entretanto Meanwhile, meantime, in the meantime, for the time being.

enyineria 2. Engineer.

éngelo' 2. Peep at, peek at, as through a crevice or small hole. Cf. **Ngelo', adu.** *Engelo' huyong gi bentana.* Peep out the window.

enggancha 2. Enlist.

enggansa 1. Engage, hire, secure the service of. Cf. **Ariendo, atkila.** *Hu enggansa si Antonio para u kahat i gima'-hu.* I engaged Tony to build my house.

enggañu 2. Imposition, trick, fraud, deception.

enggatsa 1. Inclose, encompass. Cf. **Uriyayi.**

enggranét 2. Piece, fragment, granule, portion.

enggratu 2. Ingrate, ungrateful person.

enggrudu 1,2. Glue, paste, mucilage.

engguente 2. Ointment, an unctuous substance applied to a wound or injured part.

énginge' 1. Sniff out, find source of odor by sniffing.

énginge' dagan 2. Brown nose, curry one's favor, flatter one's superior in hope of gaining favor.

Englatera 2. England.

Engles 2. English, language or people.

éngulo' 2. Look for hole, search for a hole. *Engulo' fan maddok panglao.* Search for some crab hole, please.

Epa' Nickname for Josepha.

épanglao 2. To hunt for crabs.

épapa' 2. Low. Also **ebaba'.**

epidemia 2. Epidemic.

eppok 1. Persuade, entice, urge. Cf. **Kombida, sohyo'.**

era Very—used with time expressions; pause particle used stylistically to fill space. *Era ayu na tiempo anai matto hao nai malangu gue'.* It was at that time when you came that he got sick. *Era hafa ilek-mu.* Now, what did you say?

eramienta 2. Equipment, tool. Also **ramienta.**

erensia 2. Heritage, inheritance. Also **rensia, irensia.**

eri R—letter.

eroplanu 2. Airplane. Cf. **Batkon aire.**

esek 2. Pass through, go by way of. Also **esgen, isek.**

esgaihon 1. Escort, watch over, accompany as an escort, lead the way for. Cf. **Pipet, akompaña, ga'chungi.** *Hu esgaihon i biha asta i siya-ña.* I escorted the old lady to her chair.

esgen 2. Go by way of. Also **sigen.** Cf. **Sumigen, umesgen, esek.** *Esgen i un banda.* Go by way of the one side.

esi S—letter.

ésinahyao 2. Hurry up, walk fast. Also **ensinahyao.** Cf. **sahyao.**

eskabeche 2. Type of food—fried fish cooked with vegetables.

eskama 2. Mark—indicating ability, esp. in chickens. A physical feature by which one may judge potential skill in animals, such as fighting cocks and hunting dogs.

eskama 2. Attitude.

eskandalisa 1. Scandalize.

eskándalu 2. Scandal, slander, gossip, defamatory talk.

eskapa 2. Escape, avoidance, evasion, elude. *Umeskapa gue' gi presu.* He escaped from prison.

eskapayi 1. Escape, avoid, evade, elude. *I patgon ha eskapayi i kareta gi chalan.* The child avoided the car on the road.

eskapulario 2. Medallion, medal—made of cloth. Cf. **Milaya.**

eskases 2. Scarcity, lack—esp. of food.

eskasu Rarely, seldom, scarce, not often. Cf. **Apenas, hassan.** *Eskasu ma'udai yo' gi boti.* I rarely ride in a boat.

eskatlatina 2. Scarlet fever.

eskerosu 2. Squeamish, queasy, fussy. Cf. **Chacha'.**

eskina 2. Corner (of building), outside corner.

esklabu 2. Slave, human being held in bondage.

eskoba 2. Broom, rake, brush.

eskoban nuhot 2. Broom—of coconut rib or leaf.

eskobeta 2. Whisk broom.

eskobiya 2. Type of plant-sida spp. A plant used for making brooms and medicine. Also **eskobiya adamelon, apaka', papago', sabana.**

eskomme 2. Corn—soaked in a mixture of lime and water in order to remove the hull.

eskopeta 2. Shotgun.

eskopplo 2. Chisel.

eskrepa' 2. Scraper, heavy equipment vehicle which scrapes.

eskribiente 2. Writer, clerk, accountant, one who writes, scribe, scribner.

eskritura 2. Writing, esp. sacred writings.

eskuela 2. Schoolhouse, school, institution for teaching children.

eskuelan pale' 2. Catechism, school for religious instruction. Cf. **Katisismo.**

eskuelan rai 2. Public school.

eskuelante 2. Student, scholar.

eskusa 2. Excuse, reason, pretense. *Un eskusa hao na malangu hao potno un hanao.* You pretended to be sick so that you won't go.

eslabón 2. Chain link.

esmeru 2. Zeal, eagerness.

espada 2. Sword, rapier, saber, scimitar. Cf. **Sapble.**

espada 2. Spade, a digging instrument.

espadas 2. Spades—card in the suit of.

espai 2. Spy, watch secretly. *Masodda' un espai giya Guam.* There was a spy found on Guam. *Umespai yo' gi .duranten i gera.* I was a spy during the war.

espanta 1. Threaten, menace, frighten, scare. Cf. **Fa'ñague, hongang, aminasa.**

espantahu 2. Scarecrow. Also **espanto.**

espantáo 2. Scared, frightened, menaced, threatened.

espanto 2. Threat, menace, scarecrow. Also **espantahu.** Cf. **Aminasu.**

españa 2. Burr, sandburr, sticker burr. Also **inifok, lason katu.**

España 2. Spain.

Españót 2. Spaniard, Spanish.

espedisión 2. Expedition.

espehos 2. Mirror, looking-glass. Also **espeos.**

espeki 1. Pry, raise or move, or pull (apart) with a pry.

espektadót 2. Spectator.

espeos 2. Mirror, looking-glass. Also **espehos.**

esperansa 2. Hope, expectation.

espesiát 2. Special, noteworthy, unique, distinguished by some unusual quality.

espesiatmente 2. Especially. Cf. **Kululo'ña.**

espia 1. Seek, search, look for. Also **espiha.**

espiga 2. Spoke—of a wheel, tassel--corn.

espiha 1. Seek, search, look for, locate. Also **espia.** Cf. **Aligao, buska, bando.**

espinasu 2. Backbone, spine, nape, the back of the neck to the tail bone.

espiniya 2. Shank.

espiritu 2. Spirit, ghost, proof—of liquor.

Espiritu Santo 2. Holy Spirit, Holy Ghost, third person of the Trinity.

espirituát 2. Spiritual.

espisifiku 2. Specific, precise, exact, definite, clearly stated.

espitát 2. Hospital. Also ospitat.

espiyu 2. Plane (carpenter's). Also supiyu.

esplika 1. Explain.

esplikayi 1. Interpret for, translate for. *Esplika* plus referential focus.

éspolon 2. Spur (of chicken).

espongha 2. Sponge, swell up.

esposu 2. Spouse, husband. Also esposa (f).

espót 2. Neat, dainty, fastidious, dressed-up, sharp in appearance. Cf. Bunitu, bunita.

espresa 1. Express, esp. by use of language.

espuelas 2. Riding spurs.

espuma 2. Foam, froth, scum. The residue that forms on top of a liquid during cooking. Is not edible.

éssalao 2. Shout, loud cry, outcry, a loud burst of voice, howl, clamor. *Umessalao yo' nigap.* I shouted yesterday. *A'gang na essalao.* The shout is loud.

essalaogue 1. Shout at, utter with a shout. *Si nana ha essalaogue i patgon-ña.* Mother shouted at her child.

essinahyao 2. Walking briskly. Also insinahyao.

éssitan 2. Joke, jest, witticism, something witty or sportive.

essitani 1. Joke, banter, make merry with. *Hu essitani si Juan gi eskuela.* I joked with John at school.

essok 2. Dried breadfruit, dried either in the sun or baked in an oven. *Umessok si nana-hu.* My mother baked some breadfruit.

essok somnak 2. Breadfruit—dried in the sun.

éssugon 1. Round up (animals), drive animals or fish into a corral or trap.

esta Okay, already, approve, ready. Cf. Listo. *Esta yo' munhayan.* I am already finished.

esta See you later, it's finished. Expression used when leaving someone after a conversation.

estaba Was, used to be, there was or were. *Estaba yo' gi gualo' anai umessalao hao.* I was at the farm when you shouted. *Estaba bula*

kareta gi pantalan. There used to be lots of cars at the pier.

estable 2. Stable.

establesi 1. Establish, set up, found, decree, ordain, start. Also establisa.

Estados Unidos 2. United States.

estadu 2. State, territory, condition.

estague' Here is, stating existence, show presence of something (object close to the speaker). Cf. Uhu. *Estague'.* Here it is. *Estague' i lepblo-mu.* Here is your book.

estaguiya Here is. Cf. estague'.

estaka 2. Stake, post, pole.

estampa 2. Stamp. Cf. Estampo'.

estampo' 1,2. Stamp, mark, distinguish, act of stamping, that which stamps.

estante 2. Counter, shelf, mantle. Cf. Taplita.

estaño 2. Tin, tin plating.

estáo 2. Situation, status, condition, state of being, position in a place.

estáo 2. Public land, government land.

estasión 2. Station, station house, stop-off, depot, post.

estasiones 2. Stations, station of the cross.

estatua 2. Statue, statuette.

este This (demonstrative). Cf. Ayu. *Hafa este?* What is this? *Guaguan este na lepblo.* This book is expensive.

este ha' This is all, this is it, all there is —the thing close to the speaker. *Este ha' iyo-ku.* This is all I've got.

este magi Over here (place next to the speaker).

este na This is why, this is the reason— talking about self. Also taiguini na. *Malangu yo' este na un fatto ya un bisita yo'.* I'm sick, that's why you should come and visit me.

este nai This is where, this is when, this is the time or place. *Este nai mambola hit nigap.* This is where we played ball yesterday.

estera si rai Once upon a time; way of beginning a story.

esterit 2. Sterile, barren, producing little or no crop.

estiba 1. Stockpile, store up.

estiende 1. Extend, enlarge.

estila 1. Distill—obtain by or as if by distillation.

estima 1. Esteem, appraise, set a value on, hold in high regard or prize.

estimasión 2. Estimation, esteem, valuation.

estira 1. Stretch, expand, strain.

estirante 1. Make taut, tighten or straighten, something that is slack, such as a rope.

estiyas 2. Splinter, splint, chip, small piece of metal or wood.

estola 2. Stole, a long loose garment worn by priests reaching to the feet, a vestment, consisting of a long narrow band worn around the neck.

estómagu 2. Stomach, belly, solar plexus. Cf. **Tuyan.**

estoria 2. Story, episode, occurrence, happening, event, tale. Cf. **Sinisedi, hemplo.**

estotba 1. Annoy, vex, irk, bother, hinder, disturb, irritate, molest, harrass, trouble. Cf. **Estraña.**

estotbo 2. Nuisance, hindrance, annoyance, vexation, burden, inconvenience. Cf. **Katgueti, inkombinensia, problema.**

estrabiyu 2. Superb, finishing touch. *Ha na'ye estrabiyu.* He put on the finishing touch.

estraña 1. Alienate, annoy, disturb, bother, trouble, irritate, harrass, irk, vex. Cf. **Estotba.**

estrañu 2. Strange, queer, unusual. Cf. **Sahnge.**

estrangheru 2. Stranger, foreigner, immigrant, alien, outsider. Also **estranghera** (f).

estrecho 2. Narrow.

estrena 1. Use (for first time), try (for first time). *Hu estrena i nuebu na sapatos-hu.* I tried out my new shoes.

estreyas 2. Star, sparkle, spark, asterisk. Cf. **Puti'on.**

estribu 2. Stirrup.

estrikto 2. Strict, unyielding, stern.

estroktura 2. Structure.

estropeha 1. Manhandle, treat rudely, quick shove, push roughly.

estudia 1. Study, acquire knowledge, apply the mind, educate oneself.

estudiante 2. Student, learner, scholar.

estudiayi 1. Make research, analyze. Cf. **Analisa.** *Hu estudiayi i mapa-hu.* I analyzed my map.

estudio 2. Lesson—that which is learned or taught, study, academic attainments. Cf. **Leksion.** *Hu estudia i estudio-hu.* I studied my lesson.

estudiosu 2. Studious.

estufáo 2. Pot roast. Also **adobu.**

estuleks 2. Type of game—dare base. Number of players may vary, but there are two teams, and the object of the game is to touch the opponent's base without being tagged by any player from the opposition. From 'steal eggs'.

esu Expression used when there is a doubt about a statement made. That, as in *esu es.* That is that.

etdichu 2. Exactly, unquestionably, definitely.

etdichu kichu That's right, that's just it, of course, quite so, as you say.

etgue 1,2. Wipe anus. Toilet paper, anything used to wipe anus.

étigu 2. Low, short—in height, below the normal height, too short, low elevation. Cf. **Ebaba'.**

etmana 2. Nun, sister, religious woman, anchorite. Also **hetmana.** Cf. **Madre.**

etmanu 2. Lay brother, friar, monk.

etmitanu 2. Hermit.

etnon 2. Assemblage, congregation, gathering, collection, combination, bringing together. Cf. **Rikohi, montohon.**

étokcha' 2. Fishing, spearfishing, skindiving. Cf. **Katokcha.** *Etokcha' fan guihan ya ta tunu.* Go spear some fish and we will barbeque.

etses 1,2. Grate. Grater, tool used for grating.

etsisio 2. Drill (soldiers), exercise.

ette 1. Touch (slightly), perceive by feeling, barely touch. Cf. **Pacha.** *Hu siente na ma'ette yo' gi halom tano'.* I felt that I was touched slightly in the forest. *Hu ette i ga'-mu ga'lagu.* I slightly touched your dog.

ette 1. Tear off—with teeth, rip off skin of fruit or meat from bone with teeth; peel--with teeth. *Hu ette i manha.* I peeled the green coconut with my teeth.

ette 1. Bunt—as in baseball, nudge, touch lightly.

étupak 2. To fish by line, bottom fishing.

Europa 2. Europe.

Europeo 2. European.

eyaf 2. Small louse, smaller stage of growth before becoming *hutu.*

eyak 1. Imitate, copy, mimic, follow as a pattern, model, or example. Cf. **Kopia.**

eyensia 2. Agency.

eyente 2. Agent.

eyok 2. Pain—from a thrust wound.

eyugue′ There is. Alternate form of *ayugue′.*

fa′- Pretend, change to, make believe, feign, sham (prefix usually used with transitive pronouns). Cf. **Kado′, pritende.** *Hu fa′guaha kareta-hu.* I pretended to have a car. *Ha fa′bunita gue′ i palao′an.* The woman pretended to be pretty. *Hu fa′bentana i petta.* I changed the door into a window.

fa′ i ninok Cause to wait. (Idiom.) From *nunok. I asagua-hu ha fa′ i ninok yo′.* My wife made me wait in some place.

fa′aila′ 1. Report on, prefer charge of misconduct against someone to a superior, tattle, tell on, blab. Cf. **Kehayi, keha, faila′.** *Hu fa′aila′ si Juan as nana-ña.* I reported on John to his mother.

fa′ande′ [æ] **1.** Wheedle, cajole, flatter, gain or get something by flattery or coaxing. Cf. **Fa′chada′.** *Hu fa′ande′ i amigu-hu drumaiba.* I coaxed my friend to drive.

fa′a′ñao [æ] **2.** Fearless.

fa′baba [æ] **1.** Fool, trick, deceive, dupe, betray. From *fa′* plus *baba.* Cf. **Trampasi.**

fa′babayon [æ] **2.** Gull, gullible, one who can easily be fooled, be tricked, be outwitted. Cf. **Fa′ga′ga′on.**

fábila di chispas 2. Talk too much, excessive talker. *Puru ha′ hao fabila di chispas.* You are all full of stories.

faborapble 2. Favorable, auspicious, well-disposed, propitious, advantageous.

faboresi 1. Contribute, give or supply in common with others, aid, assist. Cf. **Ayuda, asiste.** *I tenderu ha faboresi i taotao ni salape′.* The storekeeper contributed money to the man.

faboritu 2. Minion, favorite.

fabót 2. Favor, kindness, courtesy, grace, patronage.

fábrika 2. Manufacture, fabrication, factory. Cf. **Fakteria.**

fabrikan ais 2. Ice plant, manufacture of ice.

fábulas 2. Lie, fable. Cf. **Dagi.**

fa′buresi 1. Contribute, assist. Also faboresi.

fa′chada′ 1. Flatter, laud someone in order to obtain a favor; make a fool of someone. Cf. **Fa′ande′.** *Fa′chada′ si Jose ya un nina′i ni kareta.* Flatter Jose so that he will give you the car.

fa′chalani 1. Make a path. Cf. **Miche′.**

fache′ [æ] **2.** Mud, dirt, loam, mire, slime, bog, excess of liquid in a mixture, puddle.

fa′che′chu′i 1. Give one′s all, help, aid, assist, succor, be of service, give aid. Cf. **Asiste, faboresi, ayuda.**

facho′cho′ Work, toil, be industrious, be busily employed (imperative form). Cf. **Macho′cho′.** *Facho′cho′ gi lancho agupa′.* Work at the farm tomorrow.

fa′dagi [æ] **1.** Belie, create false impression, to use as excuse. *Hu fa′dagi i amigu-hu potno hu hanao gi gipot.* I used my friend as an excuse for not going to the party. *Si Paul ha fa′dagi si tata-ña nigap.* Paul used his father as an excuse yesterday.

fadang [æ] **2.** Type of plant—family cycadaceae. Cycad, federico palm.

fa′denne′ 1. Make sauce (hot), lit. make it like hot pepper. *Hu fa′denne′ i guihan.* I mixed the fish with hot sauce.

fa′et [æ] **2.** Salty.

fáfa′baba [æ] **2.** Swindler, rogue, deceiver, cheater, crook, trickery, cunning, faker, deceitfulness.

fáfacho′cho′ [æ] **2.** Worker, one who can work. Cf. **Facho′cho′, macho′cho′.**

fáfa′et [æ] **2.** Type of fish-lutjanus gibbus (family lutjanidae). Snappers.

fáfahan [æ] **2.** Buyer.

fáfakmata [æ] **2.** Light sleeper, one who can wake up easily. Cf. **Fakmata, makmata.**

fáfalagu [æ] **2.** Runner, one who or that which runs. Cf. **Falagu.**

fáfallot [æ] **2.** Lantern bearer.

fáfalu 2. The seed pod at the end of a banana stalk.

fáfamfok [æ] **2.** Weaver—of baskets or mats, one who crochets. Cf. **Tutufok, mamamfok.**

fáfa'na'gue [æ] 2. Teacher, educator, one who teaches, one who can teach. Cf. **Fa'na'gue.**

fáfanaitai [æ] 2. Reader, literate person, one who or that which can read, one who can recite a prayer. Cf. **Tataitai, fanaitai.**

fáfa'nu'i [æ] 2. Retriever. *I ga'-hu ga'lagu fafa'nu'i.* My dog is a retriever.

fáfañagu [æ] 2. Bearing young— capable of.

fáfa'ñagui [æ] 2. One who scares, bogey man, spook.

fáfa'pos [æ] 2. Transitory, fleeting.

fáfa'tinas [æ] 2. Maker, cooker, creator, inventor.

fáfatkilu [æ] 2. Silent (person), quiet, peaceful, not talkative.

fáfatna [æ] 2. The core of a boil.

fafatta 2. Pompous.

fáfatta [æ] 2. Absent, not present. Cf. **Fatta.** *Fafatta na ma'estro.* The teacher is usually absent.

fáfatta [æ] 2. Absent minded, not all there. Also **hafatta.** *Fafatta esta i amko'.* The old man is absent-minded.

fáfayi [æ] 2 Strongest part. Usually used with possessive suffix. *Metgot i fafayi-ña.* His strongest part is strong. *Agapa' fafayi-hu.* My right side is strong.

faga [æ] 2. Slightly sloping roof of house, which is poor for water runoff. Opposite of *koriente. I atof guma' senfaga.* The roof of the house is very slightly sloping.

fa'ga'ga'on [æ] 2. Gull, gullible, one who can easily be fooled, be tricked, be outwitted. Also **fa'ga'ga'yon.** Cf. **Fa'babayon.**

fágahot [æ] 2. An understanding person, one who comprehends things well.

fa'gas 2. Washer, cleanser, rinser, liquid used for washing.

fa'gasi 1. Wash, cleanse, wash away, make clean.

faggas [æ] 1. Punch, hit, smash, to hit by throwing something, destroy. *Ha faggas i katu ni acho'.* He hit the cat with a rock.

fago' [æ] 2. Type of plant-ochrosia oppositifolia. Type of tree.

fagot [æ] 2. Leader (wire for fishing line).

fagot [æ] 2. Leaf of *akgak* (pandanus) tree used for weaving mats and thatching roofs.

fagu [æ] 2. Leader—for fishing line. Also **fagot.** Cf. **Fo'i.**

fa'guaha 1. Pretend to have, put on airs.

Fagualo' 2. October. Cf. **Oktubre.**

faha 2. Waistband, cummerbund, cloth wrapped around the waist.

fa'hafa 1. Try to do or make something out of something. *Maseha un fa'hafa i, kareta-mu bibihu ha'.* No matter what you try to do with your car, it's still old.

fahan 1. Buy, purchase, bribe.

fa'hanom [æ] 1. Melt, cause to liquefy.

fahanon 2. For sale.

fahang 2. Type of bird-anous stolidus pileatus. Common noddy.

fa'hiyong 1. Despise, slander, castigate, exclude, debar.

fahna 2. Well liked, easily sold article, merchandise in great demand. Cf. **Fahan.**

fa'i 2. Type of plant-oryza sativa. Rice— when growing.

fai'a 2. Type of plant-tristiropsis obtusangula. Type of tree.

faichanak [æ] 1. Despise, disdain.

faidok 1. Pull out, draw out, root out, dig out. Cf. **Hali.** *Hu faidok i kamuti gi halom odda'.* I pulled out the sweet potato from the ground.

faila' 2. Notice, report, tell on.

failahyi 1. Betray, be untrue. Also **faila'yi.**

faila'muni 1. Estimate, calculate.

failek 1. Cause dizziness, dizziness— caused from something eaten. Cf. **Kalek, pina'lek.** *Ha failek yo' i amaska.* The chewing tobacco causes me to be dizzy.

failek 2. Word describing sour sensation on teeth after biting into a sour citrus fruit. Sour stomach.

faine 2. Sling, bandage used for sprained or broken arm. Cf. **A'fe.**

faininok 1. Put aside to ripen, cause to wait. *Hu faininok i asagua-hu.* I made my wife wait.

faiseknani 1. To accuse (falsely), to blame (someone) falsely, charge (someone) with, suspect. Also

faisekne. Cf. **Sokne, suspecha.** *Munga mafaiseknani i otro sa' hu tungo' na hagu.* Don't accuse others because I know you did it.

faisen 1. Ask, question, interrogate. Cf. **Abirigua, kuestiona.** *Hu faisen i ma'estro-mu.* I asked your teacher.

faisensini 1. Cut or remove meat from the bone.

faisini 1. Ask, request for permission, beg for. *Hu faisini hao as nana-mu para ta hanao para i mubi.* I asked your mother for you that we go to the movie.

fakcha' [æ] 2. Be lucky, be successful.

fakcha'i [æ] 1. Arrive (at propitious moment), discover, find. *Hu fakcha'i i amigu-hu gumigimen setbesa gi gima'-ña.* I found my friend drinking beer at his house. *Ha fakcha'i i tropan guihan gi saddok.* He found a school of fish in the river.

fakka' [æ] 2. Inner stem of red taro plant.

fakkai 1. Beat up, injure, harm, hurt.

fakkot [æ] 1. Delouse, to rid someone or animal of lice.

fakla' [æ] 2. Eater of raw food. Cf. **Tekcho'.** *Fakla' hamyo katne.* You are raw meat eaters.

fakla' [æ] 2. One who tells tales, tattle-tale. Cf. **Faila'.**

fakmata 2. Wake up, get up—from sleep (imperative form). *Sangani si Bob ya u fakmata.* Tell Bob to wake up.

fákmata [æ] 2. Light sleeper.

fakpe 2. Type of bird. Also **fakte.**

fakpo' 2. Finish, end, be over, stop, complete. *Para u fakpo' i miteng gi talo'ani.* The meeting will be over in the afternoon.

fakte 1. Catch rain water, tap (tree sap). *Hu fakte i ti'o' ni batde gi halom guma'.* I caught the leaking water with a bucket inside the house. *I bihu ha fakte i tiba-ña.* The old man tapped the sap from the coconut tree.

fakte 2. Type of bird-fregata minor minor, Pacific man-o-war, frigate bird. Cf. **Ga'ga' manglo'.**

fakteria 2. Factory, manufacture, fabrication. Cf. **Fabrika.**

fakto 2. Fact, actual, reality, actuality, exactly.

fala' 1. To eat raw food. Cf. **Tucho'.** *Hu fala' i tumates.* I ate the uncooked tomato. *Ha fala' i hima gi tasi.* He ate the raw clam at the ocean.

falaggue 1. Go and get, lay hold of, pick up. *Hu falaggue i kareta-hu giya Susupe.* I went to get my car at Susupe.

falagu 1. Run (imperative), move swiftly, hasten, go rapidly, elope, escape, flee. Cf. **Malagu.** *Falagu para i espitat.* Run to the hospital.

falaguaihon 1. Slip away, steal away, escape. Cf. **Laisen.** *Ha falaguaihon yo' i na'yan gi kannai-hu.* The dish slipped away from my hand. *Ha falaguaihon yo' i patgon gi gipot.* The child slipped away from me at the party.

falak [æ] 2. Go to, going to. Cf. **Malak.** *Falak i ofisina.* Go to the office.

fa'la'mon [æ] 1. Hoard, keep to oneself. *Ha fa'la'mon gue' ni atulai.* He hoarded all of the *atulai* to himself.

fa'lasuyi 1. Lasso for—make a; trap for--make a. Cf. **Lasu, lasuyi.**

falingu 2. Get lost (command), disappear (command). Cf. **Malingu.**

fallot 2. Lamp, kerosene lantern. Cf. **Kandet.**

falu 2. Game of marbles—tracks. A marble game in which two players take turns shooting at each other's marble. Probably comes from English follow.

falulon 1. Wrap, infold, cover by winding around or folding, enwrap, roll up. Cf. **Balutan, afuyot, royu.**

fama 1. Laud, praise highly, extol. Cf. **Tuna.**

fama'- [æ] Make, act like—imperative form. Combination of *fa'-* plus *man-* (indefinite object marker). *Fama'taotao ya un mafa'taotao.* Act like a man and you will be treated like one. *Fama'ma'gas sa' ma'gas hao ya un marespeta.* Act like a boss because you are the boss and you will be respected.

fama'ayan 2. Ricefield. Cf. **Fanfa'iyan.**

fama'gasiyan 2. Wash basin, sink, lavatory, lit. a place for washing.

famagu'on 2. Children, kids, infants, babies. Plural of *patgon*. Cf. **Neni, patgon.**

famahayan 2. Rice field, rice paddy. Also **fama'ayan**.

famai'che'cho' 1. Work hard, struggle, strive.

fa'maigu'i 1. Pretend to sleep, play possum.

famakiyan 2. Rifle range, place of shooting. Cf. **Paki**.

famaktiyan 2. A place where one puts the container for catching water or sap from tree. Cf. **Fakte**.

famalao'an 2. Females, women, ladies, girls, etc. Plural of *palao'an*.

fa'maleffa 1. Pretend to forget.

famáo 2. Admirable, praiseable, laudable, well known, famous.

fa'maolek 1. Fix, repair, make good.

famastuyan 2. Pasture land, meadow. Cf. **Pasto**.

famatkilu 2. Be silent, be quiet, hush, shut up. (Command form). Cf. **Silensio, pakaka', mamatkilu**. *Bai hu famatkilu gi eskuela.* I will be silent in school. *Famatkilu i pachot-mu.* Hush your mouth.

famfe' 1. Pick fruit, break fruit off a tree, pull tooth. Cf. **Tife'**.

famikayan 2. Cutting board, chopping block. Cf. **Pika**.

familia 2. Family, tribe, clan, folk, category of plants or animals.

famokkat 2. Walk (command). Cf. **Pokkat**. *Famokkat asta i eskuela.* Walk to school.

fa'montón 1. Accumulate, store up.

famosu 2. Famous.

famta' 2. Propagated, be produced by generation, or by seeds, cutting, etc. Become popular, famous. *Ma na'famta' i gima' padet pot i metgot para i pakyo.* The concrete house became popular for its capacity to withstand typhoons. *Famta' i rasan Chapanis giya Hawaii sa' layan famagu'on-ñiha.* The Japanese race propagates in Hawaii because they have lots of children.

fan [æ] Please, polite particle. *Maila' fan.* Please come. *Fatto agupa' fan.* Please come tomorrow. *Huchom fan i petta.* Please close the door. Also used figuratively in sense of daring someone. *Maila' fan.* I dare you to come.

fan- [æ] Imperative marker prefix, future indefinite object marker, plural subject marker. Cf. **Man-**. *I*

famagu'on para u fanpiknik giya Tatgua. The children are going for a picnic at Tatgua. *Fanhanao!* Go!

fan...an [æ] Place where—affixes which name a place devoted to some particular place where something exists. Suffix *-an* occurs as *-yan* following vowels. *Suni* 'taro'. *Fansuniyan* 'taro patch'. *O'mak* 'bathe'. *Fano'makan* 'bath tub, shower room'. *Fa'i* 'growing rice'. *Fanfa'iyan* 'rice field'.

fana' 1. Face, to face, withstand, stand up to look at someone sharply in the face. *Hu fana' i atdao anai uma'ason yo' gi inai.* I faced the sun when I was lying down on the sand. *Ha fana' kumontra i enemigu.* He stood up to fight his enemy.

fa'na'an [æ] 1. Nickname (someone), name (someone), call someone by a name other than his own. *Si Guelo' hu fa'na'an Labuchi.* I nicknamed Guelo', Labuchi.

fa'na'an [æ] Maybe, perhaps. *Fa'na'an hagu yuhi i hu li'e' gi painge.* Maybe you were the one that I saw last night.

fanachu'an 2. Quarry. Cf. **Acho'**.

fa'na'gue 1. Teach, educate, instruct, impart knowledge.

fa'na'guiyon 2. Docile, teachable, readily trainable, easily taught.

fanaitai 2. Say prayers, pray, read. *Hu na'fanaitai i patgon gi misa.* I made the child pray at the mass.

fanala'an 2. Drying space or place, clothes line. Cf. **Tala'**.

fananklayan 2. Anchorage, anchoring grounds or place.

fanapu'an 2. Footstool.

fanatan [æ] 2. Sight.

fanatukan 2. Hiding place, hideout, bomb shelter.

fandanggeru 2. Place for holding a *fandanggo*.

fandanggo 2. Wedding celebration, nuptial celebration, nuptial festivities.

fandeskansayan 2. Haven, rest space or place.

fanela 2. T-shirt. Also **franela**.

fanestilayan 2. Distillery.

fanetnon 2. Unite, join. Cf. **Etnon**.

fanfachi'an 2. Wallow, mud puddle.

fanfa'iyan 2. Rice field. Cf. **Fama'ayan.**

fanfa'pusan 2. Passageway, a place for passing through. Cf. **Ma'pos.**

fanhale' 2. Take root.

fanhalluman 2. A place for thinking, a retreat. Cf. **hallom.**

fanhaluman 2. Entrance, passage, inlet. Cf. **Halom.**

fanhasso [æ] 1. Think, conceive, imagine, fancy, realize, envision. Cf. **Hasso.**

fanhusgayan 2. Court of justice, place where justice is administered, judging place. Cf. **Kotte.**

fanigi 2. To distinguish one's self.

fanihen tasi 2. Type of fish-family dasyatidae. Manta ray, sting ray, leopard ray. Cf. **Hafula'.**

fanihen toyu 2. Bat—insect eating.

fanihi 2. Bat (mammal), fruit bat. *I fanihi gumupu ginen i tronkon hayu.* The bat flew from the tree.

fanlatu'an 2. Slippery.

fanlihengan 2. Shelter.

fanlugayan 2. Passageway, thoroughfare. Cf. **loffan.**

fanmaigu'an 2. Roost, sleeping place.

fanme'miyan 2. Place to urinate, urinal. Cf. **me'me'.**

fanoktan 2. Gutter (roof).

fano'la'an 2. Spitting place, bib (slavering), spittoon, cuspidor. Cf. **To'la'.**

fano'makan 2. Bathtub, shower room, swimming place.

fanomnagan 2. Dry season. Cf. **Fañomnagan.**

fano'pok 1. Lie down—on face. Imperative. Cf. **Oppop, o'pok.**

fanoppok 1. Persuade, entice. Cf. **Eppok.** *Fanoppok para ga'chong gi che'cho'.* Persuade people to help with the work.

fanpastuyan 2. Pasture, a place to tie a cow to graze.

fansagayan 2. Dwelling, place where one stays.

Fansen Nickanme for Estefania.

fansuluyan 2. Slippery place. Cf. **sulon.**

fantasia 2. Braggart, one who boasts.

fantasma 2. Fantasy, illusion, a figure that appears in a vision, phantom. Also **plantasma.**

fantupuyan 2. Sugar cane plantation. Cf. **Tupu.**

fanuchanan 2. Rainy season, wet season. Cf. **Fañata'an, tiempon uchan.**

fa'nu'i 1,2. Show, present to sight, manifest, demonstrate. Cf. **Fatta.**

fanyuti'an 2. Trash can, receptacle for dumping things.

fañagu 2. Bear (offspring), give birth. Cf. **Mafañagu.**

fa'ñague [æ] 1. Haunt, frighten, scare, threaten, menace. Cf. **Espanta, hongang, aminasa, huppa.**

fañe'lo 2. Be brothers—or sisters, be siblings. (Imperative form).

fañetnot 2. To wound, harm, damage.

fañomnagan 2. Dry season, hot season, summer. Cf. **Tiempon somnak.**

fañotdayan 2. Banana plantation.

fañotsot 2. Repent, be sorry for (imperative). *Fañotsot ni isao-mu ya munga mata'lo.* Feel sorry for your sin and never do it again.

fañudayan 2. Place for disposing of liquids, such as soapy water. Cf. **chuda'.**

fañugo' 2. Fester, suppurate.

fañupayan 2. Tobacco field, smoking area. Cf. **chupa.**

fangacha'an 2. Place to husk coconuts, device used in husking coconuts, usually a sharp pointed stick placed on end in the ground. Cf. **Kacha'.**

fangamutiyan 2. Potato field. Cf. **Kamuti.**

fanggacha'an [æ] 2. Footrest, stepping stone, something to step on.

fanggagao despensasión 1. Apologize, beg pardon, ask forgiveness.

fanggan 1. Pick fruit, pluck a fruit from tree or vine. Cf. **Tife'.** *Fanggan lemmai, Pedro.* Pedro, pick breadfruit.

fangganna 2. Triumph, victory, conquest.

fanggiminan 2. Drinking place, watering-hole, water fountain.

fanggoddiyan 2. A place to tie things, as a hitching post, a dock, etc.

fanggualu'an 2. Field for planting trees or vegetables.

fa'om 1,2. Clobber, defeat, knock down, beat, pound mercilessly. Cf. **Sapblasos.** Club, cudgel, bat, war club.

fa'otro 1. Disguise.

fa'pos 2. Go, leave, depart. (Imperative). Cf. **Hanao, ma'pos.**

Farallon de Pajaros   Farallon de Pajaros, the island farthest north of the Mariana Islands.

Fariseo 2.   Pharisee.

fa'sahnge   [æ] 2.   Exclude, isolate, set aside, segregate. Cf. **Na'sahnge**. *Hu fa'sahnge i patte-ña*. I set aside his share.

faset 2.   Easy, manageable, yielding, likely.

fasilidát 2.   Facility, resources, conveniences, appliances.

fastidia 1.   To annoy, bother, bore.

fastidio 2.   Boredom, disgust, nuisance, annoyance.

fastidiosu 2.   Fastidious, dainty, squeamish.

fasu 2.   Cheek, face. Cf. **Kara, maskaran mata.**

fata'chohnge 1.   Sit down on, sit in on a conversation, game, meeting, etc. *Fata'chohnge si Juan*. Sit on Juan. *Hu fata'chohnge i kombetsasion*. I sat in on the conversation.

fata'chong 2.   Sit down (command). Cf. **Mata'chong.**

fatani 1.   Placate, appease, concede grudgingly, give in, indifferent, unconcerned. Cf. **Hasnguni.**

fatches 2.   Fudges, pudges, hudges, term used in playing marbles. When the person shooting the marble moves his shooting hand toward the target before releasing his own marble.

fatda'   [æ] 1.   Eat meat—without bread, rice, or anything else. Applies to fish, poultry or meat.

fatiga 1.   Fatigue, fag, weary with exertion, exhaust the strength of.

fatigáo 2.   Fatigue, weariness, mental or physical exhaustion. Death throes. *Esta fatigagao*. He is already dying.

fa'tinas 1.   Cook, construct, create, invent, make, form, shape, build, fashion. Also **fattinas**. Cf. **Fotma, otganisa.**

fátkilu   [æ] 2.   Quiet, silent, not talkative, taciturn.

fatkiluyi 1.   Suppress, be secretive, not responding, withhold from talking back. *Hu fatkiluyi hao anai un a'agang yo'.* I remained quiet when you were calling me.

fatsea 1.   Adulterate, falsify.

fatso 2.   Broken (mechanically), out of order, cease to function, machinery rendered immobile or noisy usually due to lack of oil, false, unreal, not genuine, not keeping his words. *Fatso i makina*. The machine is broken. *Fatso i relos*. The watch is broken. *Fatso gue' kumontrata*. He made a false contract.

fatta 1.   Boast—by exposing something to view, display, exhibit, show off, boast, brag. *Ha fatta yo' si Jose ni kareta-ña*. Joseph showed off his car to me.

fatta 2.   Absent, missed. *I patgon fatta gi eskuela*. The child was absent from the school.

fatta 2.   Lacking, short. *Fatta yo' dos pesos*. I'm two dollars short.

fattáo 2.   Absentee, one who is lacking or missing (something). Cf. **Hafatta**. *Fattao si David na estudiante gi eskuela*. David is an absentee student at school. (Usually absent).

fattinas 1.   Cook, make. Also **fa'tinas**.

fattista 2.   Truant, one who stays away from business, schools, etc. without leave.

fatto 2.   Arrive (command), come to, show up, reach. Cf. **Matto**. *I ma'gas ha na'fatto i taotao*. The boss made the man come.

fattoigue 1.   Visit, pay visit to, go to see, drop by, drop in, arrive, haunt by a spirit. *Un fattoigue gue' gi gima'-ña*. You visited him at his home. *Ha fattoigue yo' si bihu-hu anai matai*. My grandfather haunted me when he died.

faya   [æ] 2.   Type of fish-thrissina baelama (family engraulidae). Anchovies.

fayao   [æ] 2.   Pestle, stick used in dancing by women. Cf. **Bailan fayao.**

fayao   [æ] 2.   Type of fish.

fayi   [æ] 2.   Crafty, sly, wily, learned, smart, wise.

fa'yi'os 1.   Deify. Cf. **Yu'us.**

Febreru 2.   February. Cf. **Maimo.**

fecha 2.   Date (noting time).

fechan mafañagu 2.   Date of birth.

fedda' 2.   Wide, broad, spacious, roomy. Cf. **Ancho.**

feddos 1.   Shinny, climb up (the tree), to climb up a tree or pole without branches or footholes. *Hu feddos i tronkon hayu*. I climbed up the tree.

federát 2.   Federal, federated, linked together.

federiku 2. Type of plant-cycas. Palm tree.

fegge' 2. Footprints. Cf. **Rastro.**

fehman 2. Serious, profound. Furious. Also **feman.**

fektos 2. Merchandise, goods, wares, groceries. Also **efektos.** Cf. **Benta.**

felís 2. Happy, lucky, merry. *Felis Paskua.* Happy Easter or Merry Christmas. *Felis Añu Nuebu.* Happy New Year.

felis bi'ahi Farewell, may you prosper.

felisidát 2. Happiness, joyousness, felicity.

felisita 1. Greet. Cf. **Saluda.**

felunia 2. Felony.

feman 2. Serious, deep, profound, sincere. Also **fehman.** *Feman i guinaiya-ña gi mañaina-ña.* His love is sincere for his parents.

fenso' 2. Seed (of pandanus), kernel—of pandanus seed.

feria 2. Fair, carnival—a big celebration where various games or activities are held.

fianiti 2. Type of plant-freycinetia mariannensis. A type of vine.

fiesta 2. Party, celebration, festival celebrating saint's day.

fiét 2. Loyal, true, faithful, sincere, cordial.

figan 2. Shine with intense heat, radiate heat and light, glow, hot.

figan 2. Fish eggs, eggs (fish). Cf. **Ña'ot.**

figes 1. Stamp, crush, impress.

figo' 2. Tough, tenacious, strong, stout, sturdy.

figura 2. Figure, model, emblem, type, sign. Cf. **Botto.**

figurín 2. Figurine.

figurín 2. Dress catalogue.

fiha 1. Buy on credit, purchase on credit. Also **fia.** *Hu fiha i kareta-hu gi as Tenorio.* I bought my car on credit from Tenorio.

fihadora 2. Debtor (f). Cf. **Fihadot.**

fihadót 2. Debtor, one who owes something on credit (m). Also **fiadot.** Cf. **Fifiha.**

fihu Often, frequent, often times, many times. Cf. **Sesso, taffo'.**

fila 2. Column, row, line.

filak 1,2. Braid, plait, tress, a long lock of hair, weave.

filisita 1. Congratulate, felicitate, salute, greet. *Hu filisita i manmagradua na estudiante.* I congratulated the graduating students.

filosifia 2. Philosophy.

filu 2. Blade—sharp edge.

fin 2. The end, outcome. *Hafa fin-ña?* What is the end of it? or What became of it?

fina'baba [æ] **2.** Trick, deception, fraud, cheat, imposition. Cf. **Dugeria.**

finaboresi 1. Oblige, gratify, render a favor to. Also **fina'boresi.**

fina'denne' 2. Sauce (hot), hot sauce made of pepper, onion, soy sauce, vinegar or lemon.

fina'ekso' 2. Mound, a man-made hill. Also **fina'okso'.**

finaila'iyi 2. Treason, trick.

finaisen 2. Question.

finakpo' [æ] **2.** End, conclusion, finish. *Ta a'asodda' gi finakpo' i miteng.* We will meet together at the end of the meeting. *Meggai na taotao gi finakpo' i gipot.* There were lots of people at the end of the party.

finakulu'an 2. Choke—on food or liquid. Also **fakulu'an.** *Finakulu'an yo' ni na'-hu.* My food choked me.

finalagu 2. Speed, running.

finalaguaihon 2. Slip, oversight, omission.

finalingu 2. Bankruptcy, loss.

finalisa 1. Finalize.

finalulon 2. Anything that is infolded or rolled up.

fina'maipe 2. Hot—something.

fina'mames [æ] **2.** Pastry (sweet), dessert, cake.

fina'maolek 2. Order, command, improvement.

finañagu 2. Offspring, the progeny of a plant or an animal, young, product, result.

fina'okso' 2. Hilly place, hilly shape, having the characteristics of a hill. Cf. **Okso'.** *Adahi sa' anakko' este na fina'okso'.* What do you know, this hilly place is long. *Fina'okso' na lugat anai gaige i gima'-mami.* Our house is located on the hilly place.

finatai [æ] **2.** Death.

fina'tinas 2. Prepared food.

fina'tinas 2. Action, act, deed, happened, done. Cf. **Aksion, fa'tinas.**

finatkilu 2. Silence, absence of sound.

finatto [æ] 2. Arrival. Cf. **Fatto.**

finayi [æ] 2. Dexterity, wisdom.

finedda' 2. Width. Cf. **Inancho.** *I
finedda' este na kuatto.* The width of
this room.

fine'na 2. First, first time, be first, Cf.
Primet, primeru, primera. *Hayi
fine'na magi?* Who was here first?
Guahu fine'na magi. I was here first.

finéne'na 2. First, be first, first of all,
former. Also **fine'nana.** Cf. **Fine'na.**

finette 2. Strength, power. Cf. **Fotte.**

finiho' 2. Words, commitment.

finilak 2. Basketwork, braided work.

fininot 2. Bundle. Cf. **Manu.**

fino' 2. Word, speak, language. *Ya-hu i
fino' Españot.* I like the Spanish
language.

fino'haya 2. Native words—of
Chamorro. Lit. words from the
south.

fino'lagu 2. Words—of foreign origin,
non-native words, esp. from Spanish.
Lit. words from the north.

finu 2. Smooth, frictionless, fine hair,
refined person, fine. Cf. **Mahlos.**
Finu che'cho'-ña i katpenteru. The
carpenter's work is accurate. *I neni
finu lassas-ña.* The baby has smooth
skin.

fioles 2. Type of plant-phaseolus sp.
Long bean, string beans.

fiom 2. Film, camera film.

fi'on 2. Near, beside, close to, next to. *I
siya gaige gi fi'on i lamasa.* The
chair is near the desk.

fisga 1,2. Spear, harpoon. Cf. **Tokcha',
lansa.**

fiskat 2. Attorney general.

fita' 1. Overpower, overcome. Cf.
Hulat, a'ñao.

fitma 1,2. Sign, convey, write,
signature. *Hu fitma i na'an-hu gi
papet.* I signed my name on the
paper.

fitmamento 2. Sky, arch of the heaven,
firmament.

fitme 2. Certain, sure, durable, lasting,
strong. Cf. **Metton, ma'ok.** *Fitme i
disision-mu.* Your decision is certain.
Fitme enao siha na magagu. Those
are durable clothes.

fiúm 2. Fume.

fiús 2. Fuse.

flamenko 2. Eggnog—mixture of eggs,
milk, sugar, and whisky. Cf. **Punche.**

flauta 2. Flute.

flautista 2. Flute player.

flecha 1,2. Shoot at—with bow or
slingshot, slingshot, bow, arrow.

fléksible 2. Flexible.

flema 2. Phlegm.

fleti 2. Freight, cost of freight.

flitada Cf. **Fritada.**

flohu 2. Lazy, loafer, idler, indolent,
slothful. Cf. **Gago'.**

flohu 2. Slack, not stretched tight.

floreru 2. Vase, vessels (with various
forms), florist, floral urn.

flores 2. Flower, blossom.

flores asusena 2. Type of plant—
polianthes tuberosa. Tuberose.

flores chichirika 2. Type of
plant-ipomoea aquatica. Type of
flower.

flores Krismas 2. Type of flower—
poinsettia.

flores kunanaf 2. Crawling vine.

flores mariposa 2. Type of
plant-bauhinia. Type of flower.

flores Mayu 2. Type of plant-plumeria
rubra. Plumeria.

flores rosa 2. Type of plant-hibiscus
rosa-sinensis, schizopetalus. Hibiscus,
rose.

flores rosát 1. Type of plant—rose.
Rose.

florisi 1. Decorate—with flowers.

flumoflores 2. Blooming, picking
flowers.

foffo 2. Snort, noisy expulsion of air
through both mouth and nose,
exhale (sharply), sign of anger. *Ha
na'foffo yo' i fette anai hu gimen.* It
made me snort when I drank the
liquor.

fofgo 2. Type of plant-ipomoea
hederacea. Type of vine—similar to
morning glory. Used for pasturing
and for medicinal purposes.

fo'fo' 2. Bubbling up, like a spring.

fofo'na 1. Go ahead, move forward. Cf.
Fo'na, sigi.

foge' 2. Type of fish-family scaridae.
Small parrot fish, becomes *lagua*
when fully grown.

foggera 2. Bonfire, camp fire, brush fire
for purpose of clearing a field.

foggon 2. Stove, barbecue pit.

foggon denke' 2. Electric stove, electric cookstove. Cf. **Foggon elektrisida.**

foggon elektrisida 2. Electric stove. Cf. **Foggon denke'.**

foggoneru 2. Stoker, fireman.

fohmo' 2. Type of fish-family pomacentridae. Damsel fishes. Also **fomho', fomo'.** Also includes members of family apogonidae.

fohmo' gadudok 2. Type of fish-amphiprion (family pomacentridae). Damsel fishes.

fohne 1,2. Smoke out (something), act of smoking out (something). Cf. **Pohne.**

fohyan 1. Fight off; debase, to say negative things about somebody.

fo'i 2. Leader—for fishing line. Cf. **Fagu.**

fokfok 2. Soft ground—that caves in when one walks on it, as in walking on the sand or swamp. Cf. **Luño'.**

fokos 2. Focus; center of origin.

fokse 1. Squeeze—pus out of a wound or boil, clean (intestines)--of an animal by squeezing out the interior contents, squeeze out something as in milking a cow, milk cow.

fokson 2. Gum, abcess of gums, inflammation (of gum), pyorrhea.

fo'na 2. Ahead, go on ahead or in front, be first. Cf. **Mo'na.** *Hu na'fo'na i biha gi fila.* I let the old lady be first in the line. *Bai hu na'fo'na hao gi me'na-hu.* I will let you be ahead of me. *Fo'na chumocho antes di guahu.* Eat first before me.

fo'naigue Precede, do something before someone else. *Ha fo'naigue yo' gi che'cho'.* He did the work ahead of me.

fondamento 2. Fundamental, essential, basic.

fondasión 2. Foundation, establishment.

fondo 1,2. Sink, submerge. Bottom, base, foundation. Cf. **San papa'.**

fondo 2. Balance (business), fund. Cf. **Balansa.**

fonksión 2. Function.

fonton 2. Hiccup.

fongfong 1. Pound (something against something), tamp, to pound one's head or fist against something. Cf. **Tongtong.**

fósforu 2. Phosphorus, match.

fotda 2. Worn blade, blade with a shallow cutting edge like a chisel. Opposite of *hatma*. *Fotda i filon machette.* The blade of the machete is worn.

fotge 1. Squeeze juice on, to apply citrus juice on something by squeezing. Cf. **Fugo'.** *Hu fotge i fina'denne' ni lemon.* I squeezed lemon juice into the hot sauce.

fotgon 2. Wet, watery, not dry, soaked, drenched. Cf. **Masmai.**

fotgonñaihon 2. Damp, slightly wet.

fotma 1. Form, make, shape, fashion, organize. Cf. **Fa'tinas, otganisa.**

fotmalidát 2. Formality, seriousness.

fotman 2. Foreman. Cf. **Kabesiyu.**

fotmasión 2. Formation, organization, manner in which a thing is formed.

fotmat 2. Formal, serious, earnest.

fotograferu 2. Photographer. Also **fotografera (f).** Cf. **Litratista.**

fotografia 2. Photography.

fotografu 2. Photograph, picture. Cf. **Litratu.**

fottalisa 2. Fecundity, fertility, fertilizer (inorganic).

fotte 2. Lusty, robust, powerful, strong —in taste, with power, lustful, energetic excessive. Cf. **Atdet.** *Fotte minames-ña i gimen-mu kafe.* Your coffee is excessively sweet. *Fotte kurente-ña i saddok.* The river current is strong. *Fotte bulacheru-ña.* He is an excessive drinker.

fotte 2. Sure, certain.

fottuna 2. Fortunate, wealthy, opulent, lucky, happy, auspicious, prosperous, fortune.

foyang 1. Throw against (something). (R) Also **foyong.** Cf. **Blanko, daggao, yute'.** *Hu foyang i kahon gi liga.* I threw the box against the wall. *Hu foyang i lepblo gi lamasa.* I hit the book against the table.

foyon 1. Press down. Cf. **Pannas.** *Foyon i lemmai.* Press down the breadfruit.

foyong 1. Throw down. Cf. **Blanko, foyang.** *Si Juan ha foyong yo' papa'.* Juan threw me down.

fragua 2. Forge, blacksmith shop.

franela 2. Inner shirt, T-shirt, undershirt, sweater. Also **fanela.**

frankamente 2. Frankly, openly.

franko 2. Frank, candid, outspoken, free, open, honest, truthful. Cf. **Magahet, sinseru, onesto, siguru.**

Franses [æ] 2. French.

Fransia 2. France.

frasa 2. Phrase.

fraskitu 2. Vial, cruet, flask, small bottle.

frasko 2. Flask.

frenu 2. Bit—part of a horse's bridle.

fresko 2. Fresh, cool, nonchalant, refrigerated, sassy. Also **freska** (f).

frigata 2. Frigate, sailing vessel.

frihón 2. Joker, jester, buffoon. Cf. **Frihonada.**

frihona 2. Joker, jester (f).

frihonada 2. Jesting, joking, pleasantry, jest, joke. Cf. **Frihon.** *Basta i frihonada.* Stop the joking. *Meggai na frihonada gi duranten i miteng.* There were a lot of jokes during the meeting.

frihonera 2. Joker. Also **frihon.** Cf. **Manggua'.**

frinkas 2. Real estate, land, property, asset. Also **finkas.**

fritada 2. Type of food—made from viscera of ruminating animals, swine, poultry. Also **flitada.**

fruta 2. Fruit (sweet), citrus fruit. Cf. **Gulusina.**

fueges 1. Beat up, overpower, punish, hurt, harm, injure. Cf. **Aña.**

fuera 2. Without, excluding, except, minus. Cf. **Sin.** *Todu Siña manhanao fuera si David.* Everyone can go except David. *Siña hao humanao lao fuera gue'.* You can go but not him.

fuera di Besides, outside of, aside from, except for. *Bula na taotao siha lumi'e' Hawaii fuera di hagu.* There are lots of people who have seen Hawaii besides you. *Fuera di Guam, Saipan mas dankolo na isla giya Marianas.* Except for Guam, Saipan is the largest island in the Marianas.

fuera sin buenas 2. Eleven points—in card game (tres siete).

fuetsa 2. Energy, power, strength, force, might. Cf. **Alimento, alentos, minetgot.**

fuetsáo 2. Required, obligatory. Also **afuetsao.**

fuetsudu 2. Muscular, having well-developed muscles (m). Also **fuetsuda** (f).

fueyes 2. Forge, furnace where metal is heated for shaping.

fugo' 1. Wring, squeeze.

fugu 2. Cold, chilly, freezing, icy, frigid. Cf. **Manengheng.**

fuhot 1. Bind—lightly, put a slender hoop around a barrel.

fulanu 2. Someone, Mr. So and So (m). Also **fulana** (f). Used for an imaginary person, such as John Doe. *Si fulanu sumangan na ginen mapresu hao.* Mr. So and So said that you were in prison before.

fulo' 1. Wrestle. Cf. **Umafulo'.**

fulot 2. Sensation or taste on tongue from eating unripe banana, tingling sensation from eating certain things.

funai 2. Type of fish-lutjanus kasmira (family lutjanidae). Snappers.

funas 1. Eradicate, erase, rub out, wipe out, put an end to, clear (of sin).

funda 2. Covering, case.

fundan alunan 2. Pillow case.

fundan katre 2. Sheet, bed sheet.

funhayan 2. Complete, finish, be done with it. *Funhayan gumimen pues ta hanao.* Finish drinking, then we will go.

funógrafu 2. Phonograph, record player, music. Cf. **Musiku, dandan.**

funot 1. Tighten up. Cf. **Fuñot.**

fuñot 1. Tighten up—as a bundle, squeeze, bind. *Hu fuñot i manohon siboyas.* I tightened up the bundle of onions. *Ma fuñot yo' gi halom kareta.* They squeezed me inside the car.

fusiños 2. Hoe—long handled with straight blade, used for weeding or clearing tall grass. Cf. **guassa.**

fuso' 1. Remove nut or coconut meat from shell.

futot 1. Block (pathway), barricade, set up roadblock.

fuyot 1. Sandwich in, wrap up, infold, cover by winding around or folding, roll up. Also **afuyot.** Cf. **Balutan, falulon.** *Hu fuyot i guihan ni titiyas.* I wrapped the fish with the tortilla.

ga'- [æ] Animal classifier, pet. *Dankolo i ga'-ña katu si Maria.* Maria's cat (her pet animal) is big.

ga'- [æ] Prefer, like—prefix showing strong desire. Cf. **Ga'ña.** *Ga'chotda hao.* You really like bananas. *Ga'bumola si Perez.* Perez loves to play ball. *Ga'salape' si Calvo.* Calvo loves money.

gabbe [æ] 1. Slash, cut (with one stroke), cut something hanging with one stroke (as a banana stalk), lop.

gacha' [æ] 1. Catch up with, detect. *Hu gacha' hao mo'na gi karera-ta.* I caught up with you in our race.

gachai 1,2. Ax, adze, split with ax.

ga'chong [æ] 2. Partner, associate, sharer, mate, companion, comrade, friend. Cf. **Amigu, kume'.**

gachu 2. Ear (cauliflower), ears that stick out or that have been twisted out of shape.

ga'chungi 1. Accompany, escort, chaperone. Cf. **Akompaña, esgaihon.** *Si Pete ha ga'chungi ham gi piknik.* Pete accompanied us on the picnic.

gada' [æ] 2. Young (fruit), immature (mind), not ripe, very young fruit or mind. *Gada' trabiha i tinekcha'-ña i mangga.* The fruit of the mango tree is still green. *Gada' trabiha ilu-ña i patgon.* The child's mind is still undeveloped.

gadao 2. Type of fish-(family serranidae). Groupers, sea basses.

gadao mama'te 2. Type of fish-epinephalus elongatus (serranidae). A species of grouper.

ga'das [æ] 2. Type of fish-cheilinus chlorurus (family labridae). Wrasse.

gaddai [æ] 2. Do in excess, too much, do something excessively. *Gaddai gue' chupa.* He smoked too many cigarettes. *Gaddai hao gumimen setbesa.* You drank too much beer.

gaddai bebe' 2. Womanizer, a man who has been with many women. (Taboo)

gaddai chili 2. Widow—who has had more than one husband. (Taboo)

gaddas [æ] 2. Type of fish. Also **ga'das.**

gadde' 1. Catch, entangle—with snare, lasso. *Manggade' yo' binadu gi halom tano'.* I caught a deer in the woods. *Ha gadde' i mannok gi lancho.* He caught the chicken at the ranch.

gaddo' [æ] 2. Wild yam, very thorny plant.

gaddo' [æ] 2. Search in bushes, search in woods, search out of bounds for something during a game. *Hu na'gaddo' i patgon anai hu panak i bola.* I let the child search for the ball in the bushes when I hit it.

gaddon 2. Entangled, complicated, involved (in a tangle), confused, intricate. Cf. **Ginaddon.**

gadi [æ] 2. (Type of) fishing, catch fish (at night using palm leaves or with long net), fishing (night). *Nihi ta fanggadi lamo'na.* Let's go fishing tonight. (Using palm leaves).

gafo' [æ] 2. Coconut—barely ripe on tree. Cf. **Pontan.**

gafo' [æ] 2. Type of plant-melastoma mariana. Palm tree.

gafos 2. Type of plant-medinilla rosea. (?).

ga'ga' 2. Animal, vermin, insect, beast, bug. Cf. **Animat.**

gaga 2. Type of fish-family exocoetidae (flyingfishes). Also **gahga.**

ga'ga' dikike' 2. Small insect—with jointed legs. Generic term.

ga'ga' karisu 2. Type of bird-acrocephalus luscinia syrinx, nightingale red-warbler.

ga'ga' manglo' 2. Type of bird-fregata minor minor, Pacific man-o-war, frigate bird. Cf. **Fakte.**

ga'ga' manglo' 2. Pin-wheel.

ga'ga' mutong 2. Type of insect-hemiptera pentatomidae. Stink bug.

ga'ga' sirenu 2. Cricket, gnat.

ga'ga' tasi 2. Sea dog, mariner, old salt.

gágaige [æ] 2. Exist, being. Cf. **Lala'la'.** *Gagaige ha' si nana-hu.* My mother is still living.

gagak 2. Shriek, scream, cry out. Cf. **Lossos.**

gágalak 2. Piles.

gagao 1. Request, ask for, ask, demand as due, claim. Cf. **Rekuesta.**

gagao asi'i 1. Apologize, beg pardon.

gaggao dálalai 2. Type of plant-mucuna gigantea. Wild bean. Cf. **Bayogu, gaye'.**

gago' [æ] 2. Lazy, loafer, idler, indolent, slothful, bum. Cf. **Floho.**

gagu 2. Type of plant-casuarina equisetifolia. Ironwood tree.

gahu 2. Node, cane joint or bamboo joint , sections—of citrus fruit. Also **gao.**

gai- Have something (prefix), possess, stative verb. Cf. **Guaha.** *Gaikareta yo'.* I have a car. *Gailitratu gue'.* He has a camera. *Gaisalape' siha.* They (two) have money. *Manggaisalape' siha.* They (pl.) have money.

gái'ase' 2. Have mercy, be merciful, have pity, have forgiveness. Also **gaima'ase', gaimina'ase'.** Cf. **Yo'ase'.** *Gai'ase' i ma'gas gi taotao-ña.* The boss is merciful to his people.

gáidifekto 2. Incorrect, faulty.

gáiganas 2. Having appetite, have desire for food. Cf. **Ganas.**

gaige Be present, here, opp. of absent, stative verb. *Gaige na pumepeska gi tasi.* He is fishing in the sea. *Gaige buente na ume'egga kachido'.* Maybe he is watching movies. *Gaige gue' gi eskuela.* He is at school.

gáihinasso 2. Sensible, reasonable.

gái'idat 2. Be of age, mature, meet the age requirement. Lit. Have age. Also **guaha idat.**

gái'iyo Have. *Gai'iyo yo' kareta.* I have a car.

gáilugat 2. Have time, spare time, opportunity, have place. *Gailugat yo' pumeska agupa'.* I have spare time to go fishing tomorrow. *Gailugat gue' giya Luta.* He has a place on Rota.

gáima'ase' 2. Have mercy, be merciful, have pity, have forgiveness. Also **gai'ase', gaimina'ase'.** Cf. **Yo'ase'.**

gáiminetgot 2. Have strength, having potential power.

gáisabot 2. Savory, delicious. Cf. **Mannge'.**

gá'isao [æ] **2.** Sinner, one who commits sin. *Hu li'e' i ga'isao na palao'an.* I saw the (female) sinner.

gáisensia 2. Common sense.

gáitaotao 2. Have a person, possesed by a spirit. *Metgot si Juan sa' gaitaotao.* Juan is strong because he is possessed by the evil spirit (*taotaomo'na*). *Gaitaotao si Rosa.* Rosa has a man. *Gaitaotao si Juan gi finakpo' lukao.* Juan had people at his house after the procession.

gake' 2. Selfish, stingy, niggardly, parsimonious, penurious, miserly. (R) Cf. **Meskinu, meskina, chattao.**

gakgao [æ] **2.** Beggar, mendicant. Cf. **Takgagao.**

gakma [æ] **1.** Good floater. From *gágama.* Cf. **Gama.**

gakna [æ] **2.** Winner, one who usually wins. From *gáganna.* Cf. **Gaknadot.**

gaknadót 2. Winner, one who usually wins, champion, hero. Cf. **Gakna.**

ga'kumuentos 2. Babbler, chatterbox, blabbermouth, talkative, garrulous, verbose. Lit. animal that talks. *Ga'kumuentos hao.* You are a blabbermouth.

gálabok 2. Lower bowel, rectum, sphincter.

galafati 1. Caulk.

galagala 1,2. Mastic, putty, sealing compound used for sealing gaskets or to stop leaks in boats, caulk.

ga'lagitu 2. Pup, puppy, a young dog.

ga'lagon machalek 2. Wild dog, fox.

ga'lagu 2. Dog, hound. Lit. animal from the north.

galaide' 2. Canoe, a log that is dug out.

galak 2. Type of plant-asplenium nidus. Type of bush.

galak dálalai 2. Type of plant-microsorum punctatum.

galak fedda' 2. Type of plant-asplenium nidus. Birdnest fern.

galamok [æ] **1.** Gulp, swallow whole. Also **galamokmok.** Cf. **Kalamot, kalamok.**

gálilek [æ] **2.** To roll (on the floor or ground), to lie down (on the floor or ground).

galón 2. Gallon.

galon [æ] **2.** Insignia—signifying rank of general, star--rank of general. Cf. **Gradu, raya.**

galoppe 2. To gallop—as a horse.

galuti 1,2. Hit—with a club or bat. Club, cudgel, bat, war club.

ga'ma [æ] **2.** Flexible, soft, easily yielding to pressure.

gama [æ] **2.** Float, be buoyant, be buoyed up. Cf. **Ma'ya.**

gá'maigo' [æ] **2.** Sleepyhead.

gamboleru 2. Gambler, one who gambles. Also **gambolera** (f).

gamla' [æ] **2.** The condition of a root plant which has slightly passed its harvesting period and has become crunchy and sweet. This stage precedes *dage'.*

gamson 2. Octopus.

gá'mumu 2. Fighter, one who fights a lot.

ganansia 2. Profit, gain.

ganas 2. Appetite. *Gai ganas yo'.* I have an appetite.

ganchiyu 2. Crochet. Cf. **Gansiyu.**

gancho 1,2. Gaff, hook. Cf. **Haguet.**

gani 2. Run aground, stall.

ganna 1. Win—something as in a raffle, defeat, overpower--someone, beat--an opponent, outmaneuver, earn. *Ta ganna siha gi pingpong.* We defeated them in pingpong.

gannadót 2. Champion, defender.

gansiyu 2. Crochet needle.

ganso 2. Goose.

ganta 2. Unit of measurement—equal to a gallon.

gante 2. Giant. Also **higante.**

ganye [æ] **1.** Claim, procure, acquire, gain, get, adopt by selection or preference.

ga'ña- [æ] **3.** Prefer, choose, like better. Alternate form of *ga'o-* and must be used with possessive pronouns. *Ga'ña-ku humugando bola.* I prefer to play ball.

ganggoche 2. Sack (burlap), typically large and of coarse material, as in rice or potato sack, burlap. Cf. **Kostat, kaban, piku.**

ganggosu 2. Chronic sore, an irritation or sore that will not go away.

ga'o- Prefer, choose, like better, choice, selection—used with possessive pronouns, hold in greater favor. Also **ga'ña-.** *Ga'o-ku lumi'e' Hawaii kinu Vietnam.* I prefer seeing Hawaii than Vietnam. *Ga'on-ñiha manhugando bola.* They like to play ball better.

gao 2. Node, joint of stalk of cane, bamboo, corn, etc. Section of orange or other citrus fruit. Also **gahu.**

gaode 1. Cross legs, cross feet. Also **agaode.**

gaogao díkike' 2. Type of plant-mucuna. Type of tree.

gaogao uchan 2. Type of plant, a bush.

gaole 1,2. Pick (with pole or stick), pull with hook or stick. Also **gualle.** Pole, stick (used for picking). Cf. **Dossok, dekka'.**

ga'om 1. Pick (bunch), break off (bunch), pick fruit by bunch, bend. *Ma ga'om i pigua' gi tronko.* They picked the betel nut from the tree by the bunch.

gaosali 2. Type of plant-bikkia mariannensis. A type of grass.

ga'otgan 2. Choked, stuck in throat, strangle, choke by food getting into windpipe. *Ga'otgan i ga'lagu ni na'-ña to'lang.* The dog choked on its bone.

ga'pet 2. Type of rope—used for climbing trees. A loop of rope or bark through which feet are placed to aid in climbing trees.

gapet atayaki 2. Type of plant-wikstroemia elliptica. (?).

gapgap 2. Type of plant-tacca leontopetaloides. Type of bush—used for starch and for medicine to treat heart trouble. Arrowroot.

gapi 1. Resemble—as son to father, take after. Used only in constructions with indefinite object marker. Cf. **Osge.** *I patgon mampos manggapi as tata-ña.* The child resembles his father very much.

gapi 1. To anger, to vex. Cf. **Guafi, guahi.**

ga'plaito 2. Fussy, making a fuss.

gapot 2. To pull (by the hair). *Magapot yo' nigap.* I was pulled by the hair yesterday.

gapotulu 2. Hair. Cf. **Pulu.**

garañón 2. Lustful, satyr, lascivious.

Gárapan 2. Name of a village on Saipan.

garapatas 2. Tick (insect).

garentia 1,2. Guarantee, give security.

garutasu 1. Beat up, punish, harm, hurt, injure. Cf. **Fueyes, aña, kastiga, galuti.**

gas [æ] **2.** Gasoline, gas, petrol, benzine, naphtha. Also **gasilina.**

gas [æ] **2.** Gas, vapor, air, steam, fume.

gasa 2. Gauze.

gaseta 2. Newspaper, journal, publication, periodical, gazette.

gasgas 2. Clean, neat, pure, unsoiled, decent, chaste. Cf. **Disente, asentadu.**

gasilina 2. Gasoline, gas, petrol, benzine, naphtha. Also **gas, gatsilina.**

gáso'so' [æ] **2.** Type of plant-colubrina asiatica. Type of bush—used for medicine.

gasta 1. Spend, wear out, waste, use up, expend. Cf. **Ginasta, usa, na'sietbe.** *Hu gasta i salape'-hu.* I spent my money. *Hu gasta i sapatos-hu.* I wore out my shoes. *Hu gasta i* *tiempo-ku gi gima'-mu.* I wasted my time at your house.

gastadora 2. Spendthrift. Cf. **Gastadot.**

gastadót 2. Spendthrift, spender, extravagance, lavish.

gastadu 2. Worn out, worn, used up, threadbare, worn to a thread.

gastáo 2. Consumable, capable of being consumed, worn out.

gasto 2. Expense, cost, expenditure, disbursement, consumption.

ga'sumalón 2. Bar-fly, a person who frequents bars.

gata'chongan 2. Arm chair.

gatbanso 2. Chick pea, garbanzo.

gatbesa 2. Decoration, ornament.

gatbo 2. Splendid, sublime, superb, grand, awe-inspiring, elegant, pretty, nice. Cf. **Tagalo', bunitu.**

gatcha' [æ] 1. Step on. *Ha gatcha' i sapatos-hu.* He stepped on my shoes.

gatdas 2. Type of fish-family labridae.

gatganta 2. Uvula—the pendent fleshy lobe in the middle of the posterior border of the soft palate.

gátgaras 1. Gargle, rinse mouth. *Hu gatgaras i pachot-hu anai munhayan hu gimen i amot.* I rinsed my mouth when I finished drinking the medicine.

gatgat 1. The sensation caused from tasting something too sweet, unpleasant feeling caused from something too sweet. Also the feeling when liquid or food goes into the windpipe. *Ha gatgat yo' i gimen-hu kafe.* My coffee which was too sweet caused some unpleasant feeling to me.

gatgat 2. Greedy, avaricious. Cf. **Hambiento.**

gatnadót 2. Winner. Also **gaknadót.**

ga'tot [æ] 2. Ridge, wheal, wale, a wale or raised growth resulting from tying a wire or string around a circumference thereby restricting growth (as when a wire has been tied around a young tree). Cf. **Ginetton.** Also, a mark left on body when belt or elastic is too tight.

ga'tot [æ] 2. Callous.

gatsilina 2. Gasoline. Cf. **Gasilina, gas.**

ga'uméssitan 2. Joker, jester.

gayadea 2. Type of plant-gaillardia. (?).

gaye' 2. Type of plant-macuna gigantes. Wild bean. Cf. **Bayogu, gaogao dalalai.**

gayera 2. Cockfight, cockpit. Cf. **Palitada, balentia.**

gayeru 2. Cockfighter (m). One who fights cocks.

gayetan 2. Type of plant-mucuna gigantes. (?) Cf. **Bayogu.**

gayi 2. Type of plant-entada pursaetha. A type of *bayogu.*

gayu 2. Rooster, cock.

ge G—letter.

ge'. A prefix forming the comparative degree for direction, when one is telling someone of a location. Cf. **Hat-.** *Ge'haya.* Move further east. *Ge'magi.* Move further here. *Ge'halom.* Move further in.

Ge' Nickname for Miguel.

géfmata 2. Sharp sighted, eagle eye, perceptive. From *gof* plus *mata.* Cf. **Akli'e'.**

géfpa'go 2. Pretty.

géfsaga 2. Wealthy, well off. Cf. **Gofsaga.**

geftao 2. Unselfish. Cf. **Goftao.**

gege 2. Type of plant-limnophila indica. (?).

gege sansoñan 2. Type of plant-limnophila fragrans. (?).

geha 1. Fan—woven from coconut leaves. Cf. **Goha, gueha, goia, gue'ha.**

ge'halom 2. Inner, go inside further, deeper inside, in group—belonging to the inner circle. Cf. **Halom, hattalom.**

ge'haya 2. South—move further, southward--move slightly. Cf. **Haya, hattaya.** *Ge'haya ya un espiha i pinaki-hu ni binadu.* Move further south and search for the deer which I have shot.

ge'hilo' 2. Further up, higher, upward—a little. Opposite of *ge'papa'.*

ge'hilu'i 1. Superimpose, put on top of. *Hu ge'hilu'i i katga-mu ni katga-ku.* I put my cargo on top of your cargo.

ge'hiyong 2. Outer, move out further, go further out. Cf. **Huyong, hattiyong.**

gé'kattan 2. East—move further, eastward--move slightly, easterly. Cf. **Kattan, hatkattan.** *Ge'kattan guihi sa' maolek yuhi na lugat para pumeska.* Move further east there because it is a good spot there for fishing.

gekmen 2. Drinker, glutton (for drink), one with a craving for a particular drink, one who snitches or drinks another person's drink.

gekmon 2. Larynx, Adam's apple.

gekmon 2. Gristle, cartilage. Also **getmon.**

gekpan 2. Jumper, one who jumps. Cf. **Geppan, goppe.**

gekpo 2. Flyer, capable of flying, flighty person.

gé'lagu 2. North—move further, northward--move slightly. Cf. **Lagu, hattagu.** *Ge'lagu asta i kanton halom tano'.* Move further north to the edge of the forest.

gé'lichan 2. West—move further, westward--move slightly, westerly. Cf. **Luchan, hattichan.** *Ge'lichan gi chalan siempre un sodda' i tenda.* Move further west on the road for you will surely find the store.

gelle'appan chotda 2. Cooked banana—green banana cooked in coconut milk. *Gelle'appan aga'* when made with ripe bananas. Also **gollai appan.**

gen Short form of *yanggen.*

gencha' 2. Give oneself away, expose (someone) inadvertantly, reveal the truth unwittingly.

Genge' Nickname for Miguel.

gé'papa' 2. Farther down, lower, downward. Opposite of *ge'hilo'.*

gé'papa'i 1. Put underneath.

geppan 2. Jumper, one who jumps. Also **gekpan.** Cf. **Goppe.**

gera 2. War, battle. Cf. **Bataya.**

gereru 2. Warrior.

geta' 2. Wooden Japanese slipper. Cf. **Suekos.**

getmon 2. Crunchy sound, cartilage. Pierce—solid object, cracking of bone when chewing. Also **gekmon.** *Hu hungok i getmon.* I heard the crunchy noise. *Getmon i tekcha' gi liga.* The spear pierced through the wall.

getpan 2. Bouncy, springy, capable of leaping or flying high, one who leaps or flies high.

gi At, at the, from (preposition). Used with locatives *fi'on, hilo',* etc. Cf. **Ginen.** *I ma'estra sumaga gi eskuela.* The teacher stayed at the school. *I gima' ma'estra gaige gi fi'on i*

eskuela. The teacher's house is near the school.

gi Short form of *ginen* 'from', or *giya* 'from'. *Gi Tamuning yo'.* I am from Tamuning.

gi guatu There—place, away from both speaker and addressee.

gi úttimo Eventually, ultimately, at the very end. Cf. **Alosuttimo, pot uttimo.**

gias 2. Graftage of vine, slip of vine—for planting.

gias kamuti 2. Shoot of sweet potato.

giga' 2. Loose, loose-jointed, lax, crack in seam, spread apart. *Giga' i nifen-hu.* My tooth is loose.

gigao 2. Fish trap, usually long, made from wire.

gigek 2. Cry out—in fear or pain.

gigek 2. Worm—intestinal.

gigon When (subordinator), as soon as. Cf. **Anai, nai.** *Gigon matto hao humanao gue'.* As soon as you came, he left. *Gigon makpo' i programa, mañocho ham.* When the program was over, we ate.

gigu 2. Go simultaneously, leave at the same time, at the same time. *Gigu ham matto yan i ma'estra gi klas.* We arrived simultaneously with the teacher in class. *Gigu siha munhayan.* They finished at the same time.

giha 1. To guide, to steer, point out the way to be taken. *Hu giha yo' gi puti'on anai abak yo' gi halom tano'.* I guided myself by the stars when I was lost in the woods.

giha 2. Gear—of a vehicle. Also **gia.**

gilagu [æ] **2.** Caucasian, foreigner. Lit. from the north (or west).

Gilita 2. Rotanese, one who speaks with a Rotanese accent.

gimen 1,2. Drink, imbibe, sip, lap, quaff.

gimen 2. Beverage, drink.

ginaddon [æ] **2.** Complication, problem, difficulty, hardship, vicissitude, confusion, entanglement. Cf. **Gaddon.**

ginagao [æ] **2.** Request, entreaty, petition, that which is asked for. Cf. **Gagao, pitision.**

ginago' [æ] **2.** Idleness, laziness.

ginanna [æ] **2.** Victory, gain, profit, acquisition. Cf. **Biktoria.**

ginasta [æ] 2. Waste, cost, expenditure, worn out. Cf. **Gasta.** *Ginasta gue' dies pesos ni sapatos-ña.* His shoes cost him ten dollars.

ginéfsaga 2. Tranquility, freedom from commotion, serenity, peacefulness, luxury.

ginen From, since. Cf. **Desde, gi.** *Matto i batkon aire ginen Guam.* The plane came from Guam. *Ginen ngai'an hao matto?* Since when did you come?

ginetton 2. Wrinkle—on the skin, imprint on the skin, impression on the skin caused by something tied or pressing against it, such as the elastic in socks or a watch band. Cf. **Ga'tot.**

ginigek 2. Have worms—intestinal.

gini'ot 2. Grip, grasp.

gini'ot 2. Electric shock.

ginipu 2. Blown away by wind. Cf. **Gupu.**

ginisa 2. Sauteed—in garlic and or onions. Cf. **Gisa.**

ginitos finiho' 2. Marriage agreement, marriage proposal, agreement of bride and groom's parents for marriage.

giñu 2. Type of fish-pranesus insularum (family atherinidae). Silversides.

girek 2. Greedy, ravenous, avaricious, covetous, having a keen appetite for food or drink. Cf. **Gulosu, padok.**

gisa 1. Sautee, fry onions or garlic quickly in a shallow pan and mix with meat or chicken. *Hu gisa i mannok gi la'uya.* I sauteed the chicken in the pot.

gitala 2. Guitar.

giya At, on, in, preposition used with place names and emphatic pronouns. *Sumaga yo' giya Honolulu giya Hawaii.* I stayed in Honolulu in Hawaii. *Para bai hu bola giya New York.* I will play ball in New York.

giya hamyo At your house. *Giya hami, siha, hita.* At our, their, our (inclusive) house.

glop 2. Light bulb.

gloria 2. Glory, thanksgiving, blessing, adoring praise, gratitude.

glorifika 1. Glorify, celebrate. Cf. **Silebra.**

glorifikáo 2. Glorified, glorifying.

gobietna 1. Govern, rule, regulate, restrain, determine, direct, control. Cf. **Manda.**

gobietnadót 2. Governor, one who governs. Also **gobetnadot.**

gobietno 2. Governor, government.

go'dan 2. Overindulge, overextend, overdo, have too much of something. Cf. **Dafflok, mutero', motgan, tuhos, dafflokgue, malulok.** *Go'dan hao gi chalek-mu.* You overdid your laguhter. *Go'dan i palao'an umestoria.* The woman was too much in telling stories.

goddas 2. Snare, lasso—tied to the end of a pole, to catch animals, esp. by the neck.

godde 1,2. Tie up, fasten, buckle. String, knot, hair band. Cf. **Tramoha, gramaderu.**

godden kabayu 2. Bowline (knot), any knot that will not slip or tighten up the loop on a post.

godden sapatos 2. Shoestring.

goddon 2. Be entrapped, be trapped (with a snare). *Goddon yo' gi lasu.* I was trapped in the lasso.

gof 2. Very, extremely (intensifier). Also **gos, ges, gef.** *Si Rosa gof malangu gi espitat.* Rosa was very sick at the hospital.

gofes 2. Lung.

gofgufan 2. Scaly.

gófha'an 2. Sunny day, good weather. Also **gefha'an.**

góflamen 2. Charitable, beneficent, liberal in judging others, lenient, likable, well-liked, agreeable, pleasing. Also **geflamen.** Cf. **Guaiyayon.**

gofli'e' 1. Like, befriend, love (platonic).

gofli'i'on 2. Amicable, friendly, benevolent, kind, warm-hearted, harmonious.

góflinan 2. Something in the eye, foreign matter in the eye, usually forcing one to shut the eye. Also **gineflinan.** *Goflinan mata-hu anai mangguaife i manglo'.* Something got into my eye when the wind blew.

gófsaga 2. Wealthy, rich, affluent, opulent, characterized by abundance. Cf. **Riku, miguinaha.**

goftao 2. Unselfish, selfless, having no regard for self, generous. Also **geftao.**

goggue 1. Save, rescue from danger, redeem, help, safeguard, protect, take care of, save from damnation.

goha 1. Fan. Cf. **Goia, geha.**

go'he 1. Hold, support, retain by force, grasp. (Rarely used). Cf. **Go'te, gu'ot, sustiene.**

gohe 2. To top and cast a shadow or protect, as a tall building or person that looms over another so as to shadow or protect.

goia 1,2. To fan, ventilate, aerate, cause air to blow upon. Fan, blower, instrument to cause air to blow upon. Cf. **Gueha, abaniku, bohao.** *Hu goia i guafi.* I fanned the fire.

goleta 2. Schooner.

gollai 2. Vegetable, (generic term).

gollai appan 2. Process of cooking something in liquid until the liquid evaporates. For example *gollai appan suni, gollai appan mendioka.*

gollai appan chotda 2. Cooked banana. Cf. **Gelle'appan.**

gollai chotda 2. Type of food—chicken or meat cooked with bananas and coconut milk.

gollai kalamasa 2. Tender shoots of pumpkin vine.

golondrina 2. Type of kite, fighting kite.

golondrina 2. Type of plant-euphorbia hirta. Type of grass—used in mixture for douching.

goma 2. Rubber, rubber band, innertube, tire.

gomgom 1. Jerk loose, loosen, pry loose. Cf. **Kamkam.**

go'naf 1,2. To scale, separate and come off in scales, shed scales, pare off. Scale—a thin coating, covering, film, or incrustation, fish scale.

gonggong 2. Grumble, growl, rumble, mumble, mutter in complaint, snarl in deep tones. *Bula siha manggonggong pot i takpapa' i suetdo.* Many of them grumbled about the low salary.

gonggong 2. Wasp—mud.

goppe 1. Jump over, leap over. Cf. **Agua', adanggua'.**

gopte 1. To celebrate, to dedicate, to commemorate.

gora 2. Cap. Cf. **Tuhong.**

gosa 1. Enjoy, have satisfaction. *Hu gosa i minagof-hu.* I enjoyed my happiness.

gosne 2. Molt, molting process referring to crustaceans as when a crab becomes soft after it sheds its shell. Cf. **Manggosña.** *Kuanto na ayuyu kinenne'-mu ni manggosne?* How many molted coconut crabs did you catch?

gosu 2. Hymn, a hymn sung at a novena but is in addition to the regular songs.

gota 2. Drop (of liquid). Cf. **To'he.**

go'te 1. Hold, support, retain by force, grasp. Cf. **Gu'ot, sustiene.**

gotgohu 2. Mite, animalcule, midge, arachnids. (Order acarina). Also **gotgo.** Cf. **Potgas.**

gotgoreta 2. A water container used by ancient Chamorros, made from a gourd.

gotgot 2. Tale bearer, gossiper, one who berates others, one who tells on others.

gotpe 2. Suddenly, abruptly, instantly. Cf. **Derepente.** *Gotpe matto i patgon magi.* The child instantly came here.

gotpeha 1. Sudden movement, to do something suddenly, raising of voice, as in anger. Also **gotpea.** *Gotpeha mo'na i mannok ya un konne'.* Rush to the chicken and catch it. *Cha'-mu gotpepeha yo' kumuentusi.* Don't raise up your voice when you talk to me.

graba 2. Grave, serious. Also **grabu, grabi.**

gradu 2. Grade, rank, status, degree of relationship.

graduha 1,2. Check temperature, take temperature, thermometer (medical).

graduha 2. Graduation, graduate, be graduated. Also **gradua.**

gramaderu 1,2. Secure, tie down, lash down, knot. Also **gramadera.** Cf. **Tramoha, godde.**

gramaderu 2. Type of plant-cynodon dactylon. (?).

gramátika Grammar.

granada 2. Type of plant-punica granatum. Pomegranate.

granu 2. Piece, part, a fragment, any single object or individual of a class or group.

granu matditu 2. Boil, a large festering of the skin, more severe than *pokpok.*

grasia 2. Grace, kindness.

grasias adios 2. Fortunately, luckily, good thing—it's a, thank God, good heavens, how fortunate.

grasiosu 2. Gracious, graceful, charming, delightful (m). Also grasiosa (f).

grates 1,2. Tip, aid, gratis, free. Cf. Dibatde.

gratifika Gratify, reward, repay, compensate, remunerate.

gratifikasión 2. Gratification, gratitude, reward, thanks. Cf. Agradesimiento.

gratu 2. Gratitude, gratefulness, thanks.

grifu 2. Faucet, tap.

griyos 2. Cricket. Also guriyos.

grupu 2. Group. Also gurupu.

guaddok 1. To dig, to investigate (slang), excavate. *Guaddok taddong i hoyu.* Dig the hole deep. *Sigi ha' hu guaddok i masakken kareta-hu.* I kept on investigating the theft of my car.

gua'deng 1. Cause to stumble, cause to trip. Cf. Tolleng. *Un gua'deng si Antonio gi chalan.* You tripped Tony on the road.

guafak 2. Mat—woven.

guafi 1. To anger, to vex. Cf. Gapi, guahi.

guafi 2. Fire, combustion, conflagration, burning mass of material.

gua'gua' 1. To cause regurgitation—by sticking finger down the throat. *I nana ha gua'gua' i patgon-ña.* The mother caused her baby to regurgitate (by sticking her finger down its throat).

guagua' [æ] 2. Basket—esp. for fish, fish basket.

guagua' tumalaya 2. Basket—for carrying fish when netting. Usually a woven basket attached to a strap that goes around the waist.

güagualo' 2. Good farmer, capable of farming.

guaguan [æ] 2. Expensive, costly.

gua'guas 1. Scrub—as in washing one's body. Cf. Guesgues.

guaguas 2. Type of fish-family leiognathidae. Soapys.

guaguat 1. Discipline, control. *Ti siña ma guaguat si Juan.* Juan cannot be disciplined.

güaguatu [æ] Hurry there. Cf. Guatu.

guaha [æ] 2. Have, there is, there exists. *Kao guaha chipa-mu.* Do you have a cigarette? *Guaha meggai na kareta giya Garapan.* There are many cars in Garapan. Cf. Gai.

guaha idát Be of age, mature, meet the age requirement, (generally used with the possessive pronouns). Lit. have age. Also gai idat.

guaha na biahi Sometimes, occasionally, now and then, once in a while, at times, at various times, every so often.

Guahan 2. Guam. Older spelling and current pronunciation.

gua'he 1. Remove fire from stove. Cf. Guahi.

guahi 1. To anger, vex, cause anger, angry at. Also gua'he. Cf. Guafi, gapi. *Ha guahi yo' i patgon ni fina'tinas-ña.* I was angry at the child for his act. Or The child angered me by his act. *Hu guahi i ma'estro-ku.* I angered my teacher.

guahi [æ] 1. To reduce heat by removing container of food from source of heat. Remove pot or food from stove.

guahi [æ] 1. To unearth, dig up.

guahlo' 2. Fail, not succeed.

guahne 1. Removal of feces from improper place. *Ha guahne i take' gi chalan.* He removed the feces from the road.

guahnom 2. Become watery, whey. Cf. Aguanon, huganom. Also guahnon.

guahof [æ] 1. To scratch the ground— as a chicken looking for food, to paw the earth--as a horse or bull. Cf. Guaddok. *I mannok mangguahof gi edda' para u fanespiha na'-ña.* The chicken scratched at the ground in search of its food.

guahu I (emphatic), me (emphatic).

gua'i 1. Transfer food from smaller to larger container for cooking.

guaife 1. Blow, force a current of air upon, puff.

guaifon 2. Windy, gusty, turbulent, stormy.

güailayi Just because. *Guailayi hao ha' mana'hanao, nina'gos banidosu hao.*

Just because you were sent away, you became very proud.

guaile 2. A pole with a hook on the end for picking fruit. Also **gaole**.

guaiya 1. Love, fond of, to like dearly.

guaiyayon [æ] 2. Lovable, desirable, likable, pleasing, agreeable. Cf. **Goflamen**. *Guaiyayon na neni enao*. That is a lovable baby.

guaka [æ] 2. Cow, cattle.

guakan Indian 2. Brahman—beef cattle.

guakkle 1. Empty contents from a hole, sack or other container.

guaknas 2. Type of fish-hepatus leucopareius (family acanthuridae).

guakse 1. Scrub, scour, scratch, eviscerate, turn inside out, rub vigorously, reach in and pull out something, as to turn a sock inside out. Cf. **Guesgues**. *Hu guakse i magagu-hu*. I scrubbed my clothes. *Hu guakse i tilipas-ña i mannok*. I reached in and pulled the guts from the chicken.

gualaf 2. Hunt crabs—at night during full moon or new moon.

gualafon 2. Full moon. *Maolek umepanglao anai gualafon i pilan*. It is good to go crabbing when it's full moon.

guali'ek 2. Small lizard—lives outdoors. Cf. **Achiak**.

gualo' 2. Farm, cultivate land, till soil, farming, husbandry, gardening, garden, produce crop, cultivation. Cf. **Fanggualu'an**.

Guam 2. The southernmost island of the Marianas chain. Pronounced Guahan.

-guan In spite of, a suffix denoting that something happened counter to one's intention or against one's wishes. *Palakse'* 'to slip'; *pinalakse'guan* 'slip of the tongue'. *Mafnot*'tight'; *Minafnotguan yo' ni ginedde-ku*. The thing that I tied became tight (but was supposed to remain loose). *Ha dangkolongguan yo' i cha'guan gi hatdin*. The grass in my garden grew big (without my being aware of it).

guantes 2. Glove, mitt, mitten, handwear.

guaña Really, truly, is it true? Used to address a third party to verify a statement just made by someone. Cf. **Agon**. *Guaña ilek-ña na para ta*

fanhanao? Really did he say we will go?

gua'ot 2. Stairs, stairway, steps, ladder.

guasa' 1. To sharpen, to make sharp.

guasa' 2. Type of fish-acanthurus metoprosophron (family acanthuridae). Surgeon fishes.

guasa' 2. Fish by poisoning.

guasang 2. Gill (of fish). Cf. **Atgayas**.

guasa'on 2. Sharpener (for metal tools), grindstone, whetstone.

guasguas 1. Scrape—for purpose of cleaning. Cf. **Kaleku**.

guasguas Used to form part of an idiom. *Hanao un guasguas hao*. I don't believe you. *Ombre un guasguas hao*. The heck with you.

guassan 1. Cut grass, cut or trim weeds in garden. To weed using Chamorro hoe. Cf. **Fusiños**. *Ha guassan i uriyan guma'-ña*. He cut the grass around his house. *Para u guassani yo' si Ton ni uriyan guma'*. Ton will cut the grass around the house for me.

guatde 2. Guard. *Dios di guatde*. God be your guard.

guatdia 1. Celebrate, observe a holiday, show regard for, do honor to. *Maguatdia i gipot Santa Maria nigap*. The blessed Virgin Mary's holy day was celebrated yesterday.

guatdia 1,2. Protect, defend, shield. Guard, patrolman, watcher. Cf. **Protehi, difende**.

guatu [æ] There—in that direction (away from speaker and addressee).

guatu guenao To there—direction toward the addressee.

guatu guihi To there—direction away from both speaker and addressee.

gue' He, she—intransitive subject pronouns, transitive subject pronouns with indefinite object; him, her, it (transitive object pronouns).

gue'gue' 1. Cause to vomit—usually by sticking finger down throat. Also **gua'gua'**.

gue'gue' 1. Pick teeth—with toothpick.

gue'gue' 1,2. Brush, duster, whisk, wisp, toothpick. Cf. **Brochas, guesgues**.

gue'ha 1,2. Fan—made from coconut fronds.

gueha 1,2. Fan, ventilate, aerate, blower, instrument to cause air to blow. (R) Also **gue'ha**. Cf. **Goia, abaniku, bohao**.

gueku 2. Hollow, empty, vacant within. Cf. **Baobao**.

guella 2. Grandmother. Also **guela'**.

guello 2. Grandfather. Also **guelo'**.

guelo' 2. Grandparent, ancestor, forebear, progenitor (m). Also **guela'** (f) (R). Also **guello** (G).

guenao There—in that place toward the addressee.

guenao guatu Over there—in the direction of the addressee.

guenggueng 2. Mutter, show vexation or anger by muttering under one's breath. *Kada matago' para u fanestudia gumenggueng*. Every time he was told to study he muttered under his breath.

gueru 2. Egg—spoiled, rotten egg, egg--unfertilized, sterile male.

guesgues 1,2. Brush, scrub, scrape, rub. Squeegee, scraper, brush. Cf. **Guakse, brochas**.

guesgues nifen 2. Toothbrush.

guetgueru 2. Throat. Also **gutgueru**.

gufan 2. Scaly skin. Also **gusan**.

gufgufan 2. Scaly skin. Also **gufan**.

gugan 1. Husk, remove kernel of corn or rice. To knock teeth out (slang).

gugat 2. Vein, muscle, tendon, artery, fishing line. Also **katgat**.

Guguan 2. Guguan, the third island north of Saipan.

guha 2. Asthma.

guha 2. Pant, gasp, breathless, out of breath, wheeze.

gui'eng 2. Nose.

guifi 1. Dream of, have a dream of. *Hu guifi iya Hawaii*. I dreamed of Hawaii. *Mangguifi yo' gi painge*. I dreamed last night. *Ha guifi si Maria*. He dreamed of Maria.

guihan 2. Fish—generic term.

guihan pabu 2. Type of fish-pterois sp. (Scorpaenidae). Turkey fish.

guihi There—place away from both speaker and addressee.

guihi guatu Over there—place away from both speaker and addressee.

guilen puenge 2. Type of fish-kyphosus vaigiensis (family kyphosidae). Rudder fishes.

guili 2. Type of fish-family kyphosidae. Rudder fish.

guinaddok [æ] **2.** Ditch, trench, moat.

guinaha [æ] **2.** Wealth, affluence, riches, large possessions esp. of worldly estate. Cf. **Rikesa**.

guinaife 2. Blown, ventilated. *Guinaife yo' ni manglo'*. I was blown by the wind.

guinaiya 2. Affection, love, fondness, desire.

guinassan [æ] **2.** Field, area cleared for planting. After crops begin growing, it then becomes *fanggualu'an*.

guini Here, in this place.

guini magi Over here (place in the direction of the speaker).

guinifi 2. Dream.

guiya He, she, it, (emphatic). Cf. **Ha, gue'**.

gulek 1,2. Grind, reduce to powder by friction, crush into small fragments, grinder, machine for grinding.

guleta 2. Small ship.

guliya 2. Gullet.

gulosu 2. Greedy, ravenous, eagerly desirous, having a keen appetite for food or drink. Cf. **Padok, girek, hambrento**.

gulusina 2. Fruit (sweet)—such as pineapple, watermelon, orange, guava, etc.

guma' 2. House, home, shelter, refuge, dwelling, dormitory, building.

guma' fañochuyan 2. Cafeteria, snack bar, dining place, restaurant, eating place.

guma' matansa 2. Slaughterhouse, house for killing, cleaning and processing meat, usually for larger animals.

guma' mela 2. Type of plant-hibiscus rosa-sinensis. (?).

guma' Yu'us 2. Church, chapel. Cf. **Ekglesia**.

gumága'chong [æ] **2.** Having an affair.

gunom 1. Squeeze—with arms or legs in fighting. *Ha gunom i kontrariu*. He squeezed the opponent.

gunos 1. Wean, accustom (a child or other young animal) to loss of mother's milk.

gunot 2. Coconut fibre—from trunk of coconut tree, used esp. for straining tuba and other liquids.

gu'ot 1. Hold, support, retain by force, grasp. Cf. **Go'te, sustiene, mantiene**.

gupallao [æ] 2. Carolinian—a native or inhabitant of the Caroline Islands. Also used to refer to Carolinians on Saipan. In Guam, is sometimes used as derogatory term for any rural Micronesian, including rural Guamanians.

gupo' 2. Skin fungus, ringworm—infested by.

gupot 2. Party, celebration, fiesta, festivity, holiday, feast.

gupu 2. Fly, move through the air, travel through the air. *Gumupu yo' gi batkon aire.* I flew by plane. *Gumupu i paharu.* The bird flew.

guriyos 2. Type of insect-orthoptera gryllidae. Male cricket.

gurobo' 2. Glove—baseball. (S) Cf. **Guantes, mitto'.**

gurupa 2. Win a hand but fail to make any points in tres siete (card game).

gurupos 2. Lice—found esp. on chickens.

gurupu 2. Group, cluster, aggregation, crowd, assemblage. Cf. **Katdumi, inetnon.**

gusan 2. Scaly skin, scaliness—of skin. Also **gufan.**

guse' 2. Hurry, fast, prompt, urge on, impel forward by force. Cf. **Chaddek, sahyao, alula.** *Guse' humanao guini giya Guam.* You had better leave Guam fast. *Guse' magi.* Hurry back.

guse' 2. Quick—to do something, impetuous. *Guse'kannai.* Grabber, quick handed. *Guse'pachot.* Backtalker, answers too fast.

guse'ña Might, sooner, more likely, better chance of, more probable, probably, earlier, prior, faster. *Guse'ña guahu mana'hanao para Hawaii.* I might be the one to be sent to Hawaii. *Guse'ña hagu hu li'e' gi painge.* It is more likely that you were the one I saw last night.

gusto 2. Relish, pleasure, taste, flavor (pleasing), lust, desire, joy. *Hu sosodda' gusto-ku yanggen manggaganna yo'.* I am finding my pleasure when I am winning. *Guaha gusto gi chipa.* The cigarette has taste.

gutai 1. Harvest—root crop at one time, picking fruit at one time. *Kanna' ha lachai si Juan gumutai i mangga.* Juan picked almost all of the mangoes at one time. *Hu gutai i dagu.* I harvested the yams at one time.

gutos 1. Break off—rubber band, string, etc., snap off--neck of chicken, root. *Hu gutos i aga'ga'-ña i mannok.* I broke off the neck of the chicken. *Hu gutos i goma.* I snapped the rubber band.

guyuria 2. Cookie—small, round, crispy, biscuit--small, sugar-coated.

ha [æ] He, she, pre-posed pronoun used in transitive non-focus statements. *Si Juan ha li'e' si Maria.* Juan saw Maria. *Ha galuti si Juan i ga'lagu.* Juan hit the dog.

ha [æ] Huh, what, indicating lack of comprehension. Yes, in rhetorical question. *Kao ya-mu ha?* You like it, yes?

ha- [æ] Usually, often (prefix). Primary stress on *ha-*. *Haguaha bisita gi gima'-ña.* He usually has a visitor at his house. *Hamayulang i kareta-hu gi chalan.* My car usually breaks down on the road.

ha' [æ] Very, really, still, alone, only (intensifier). *Mamaolek ha'.* Still fine. *Si Juan ha'.* Only John, John alone.

ha'a Yes. Alternate form of *hunggan, hu'u.*

há'abak [æ] 2. Lost—usually, gone astray--usually, often take something by mistake. Cf. **Abak.**

ha'anen apsinensia 2. Fast day.

ha'ani 2. Day, day light, day time. Cf. **Dia.**

habao [æ] 1. Snatch, grab, take or seize suddenly. Cf. **Hakot.**

habitasión 2. Habitation.

hábitu 2. Habit.

habon [æ] 2. Soap, detergent.

habon mama'gasi 2. Laundry soap.

habon umo'mak 2. Bath soap.

hábubu [æ] 2. Impetuous, given to anger. Cf. **Bubu.**

habuni 1. Wash (with soap), clean (with soap). *Hu habuni i kannai-hu.* I washed my hands with soap.

hache H—letter.

hachem [æ] 2. Sneeze, act of sneezing. Also **achom, hatcheng.**

hacheng [æ] 2. Black ant. Also **hateng, ateng.**

hacheru 2. Lumberjack, one who works in lumbering.

hachita 2. Hatchet, pickaxe. Also **acheta.**

hachón 2. Torch (usually used when fishing). Also **achon.**

hachuman 2. Type of fish-family carangidae. Type of mackerel—resembles *atulai,* but with smaller eyes. Also **achuman.**

hada 2. Goddaughter, godchild.

hadok [æ] 2. Dimple, indentation in flesh or skin. Describes human skin as well as that of fruits and vegetables.

hadu 2. Godson, godchild.

ha'ef 2. See a'ef.

hafa What, question word; also used in common greetings. *Hafa tatatmanu hao?* How are you? *Hafa este?* What is this? *Hafa ilek-mu?* What did you say?

hafa dai Hello (informal greeting). Also **hafa dei.**

hafa dei Hello (informal greeting). Also **hafa dai.**

hafa na klasi What kind. *Hafa na klasi ya-mu?* What kind do you like? *Hafa na klasi gimen-mu?* What kind is your drink? *Hafa na klasen kareta kareta-mu?* What kind of car is your car?

hafa taimanu How (question word).

háfalagu [æ] 2. Tendency to run away. From *malagu. Hafalagu este na patgon.* This child has a tendency to run away.

háfañagu [æ] 2. Fertile. Cf. **haffñak.**

háfatta [æ] 2. Absentee, one who is usually absent, absent minded, one who usually lacks something, usually has something missing. Also **fafatta.** Cf. **Fattao.** *Hu tungo' un hafatta na taotao.* I know an absent minded person.

ha'fe 1. Brace, put on splint, put on something. *Hu ha'fe i tronkon hayu ni mahlok.* I braced the tree that was broken.

hafkao [æ] 2. Silly, foolish, giddy.

hafkao [æ] Question word, stronger than *hafa.* From *hafa ha' hao. Hafkao bidada-mu guenao?* What in the world are you doing?

hafno' [æ] 2. Incoming tide. Also **hafnot.**

hafnot [æ] 2. Incoming tide, high tide. Also **hafno'.** Cf. **Bula.**

haffñak [æ] 2. DF Very *fertile (female), highly *reproductive (mammal), esp. human being. Cf. **Hafañagu.** hafot @1.

hafula' 2. Type of fish-family dasyatidae. Manta ray, sting ray, leopard ray, skate. Also **afula'.** Cf. **Fanihen tasi.**

hafye 1. Lay down a protecting cover upon which something is placed . *Hafye i nenkanno' gi hilo' unai.* Lay down a cover on the sand for the food.

hafyen katre 2. Bedcover, bedspread, quilt, coverlet. Cf. **Subrikama.**

hafyen lamasa 2. Tablecloth.

haga 2. Daughter. Cf. **Iha.**

haga' 2. Blood.

hagáf 2. Crab—generally found on rocks by the ocean and are very swift runners. Also **hagahaf.**

hagahaf 2. Rock crab—weak-shelled (crapsus tenuicrustatus, herbst).

hagamham 2. Leaf of coconut tree—dried.

hagan 2. Daughter of. *Hagan Tomas.* Thomas's daughter.

hagan hanom 2. Type of insect-coleoptera tytiscidae. Diving beetle.

hagas [æ] Long time ago, ago, gone, past, ages, awhile, since olden times. Cf. **Apmam.** *Hagas ha' gue' sumaga giya Hawaii.* He has been staying in Hawaii for a long time. *Hagas ha' para bai hu hanao para Hapon .* For a long time I have been planning to go to Japan.

hagasas 2. Dead branch—of coconut palm.

Hagatña Agaña, the capital of Guam.

haggan [æ] 2. Turtle, tortoise.

hagi 2. Type of fish-scomberoides santi-petri (family carangidae). Pompano or jack crevally.

hago' [æ] 1. Reach, attain. Cf. **Taka'.**

hago' [æ] 2. Sticky soil, soil type, becomes very hard and cracked when dry.

hagoe 2. Lake, lagoon, pond.

hagom 1. Cause to sag. Also **hugom.**

hagon 2. Leaf, foliage, frond.

hagon faha 2. Type of fish-oxymonacanthus longirostris (family monacanthidae). Filefishes.

hagong 1. Breathe, respire, inhale, exhale, draw breath.

hagu You (emphatic sing.). *Hagu gumanna i huegu.* You are the one who won the game.

hague' 2. Hand over. Also **hagu'i.** *Hague' magi.* Hand it here to me.

haguet [æ] 1,2. Hook, fish hook.

haguha 2. Needle (generic). Also **hagua.**

háguha [æ] 2. Asthmatic.

haguhan kannai 2. Needle—used for sewing by hand.

haguhan mákina 2. Needle—for sewing machine.

haguhan manlakse 2. Needle—sewing.

haguhi 2. Sandcrab. See **haguihi.**

hagu'i 1. Reach for. Cf. **hago'.**

hagui 2. Small. Cf. **Dikike'.**

haguihen aguas 2. Ghost crab—horn-eyed (ocypode ceracopthalma pallas).

haguihi 2. Ghost crab (ocypoda arenaria), sandcrab (generic). Also **haguhi.**

háguinafi [æ] 2. Excitable.

haha 1. Blow breath—in short puff, as if to moisten glass or to allow someone to smell breath.

háhatot See *kakatot.*

hahlon Cf. **Halon.**

ha'i 2. Forehead.

hai Who. Shortened form of *hayi.*

haichio' 2. Pantry, provision closet. (S)

ha'iguas 2. Shell (of a coconut).

ha'iguas 2. Skull—of head. *Mafak i ha'iguas ilu-ña si Juan.* Juan's skull was fractured.

haigue 2. Seedling—coconut, coconut plant--young, young coconut tree before it bears fruit.

ha'ilas 2. Famine, destitution, starvation, hunger, general scarcity of food. *Tiempon ha'ilas.* Time of famine.

haiteng 2. Type of fish-trachurops crumenophthalmus. Big eye scad, mature.

hakmang 2. Type of eel-gymnothorax meleagris (family muraenidae). Moray eel. Also echidna nebulosa and echidna zebra.

hakmang kulales 2. Type of eel-elaps (genus myrichthys).

hakmang lisayu 2. Type of eel-myrichthys maculosus (family ophichthidae). Snake eels.

hakmang pakpada 2. Type of eel (family muraenidae). Salt water eel.

hakmang palús 2. Type of eel-conger noordzieki (congridae). Salt water eel. Conger eel.

hakmang titugi Type of eel-echidna nebulosa (muraenidae). A type of moray eel that sometimes appears to be standing up. Cf. **Titugi, tohge.**

hakot [æ] 1. Snatch, grab, sieze or take suddenly, nab. Cf. **Habao.**

haku [æ] 2. Fingers (paralyzed), condition when the fingers are paralyzed in a half-closed position.

halacha [æ] Past time (recent), recently, previous, previously, some time ago. Cf. **Maloffan.** *Sesso pakyo giya Marianas gi halacha siha na tiempo.* There were often typhoons in the Marianas in the past times. *Gi halacha bula mansinagu na taotao.* Just recently many people had colds.

halahas 2. Jewelry. Also **alahas.**

ha'lak [æ] 1. To weed, uproot (weeds). Cf. **Bokbok, halle'.**

halak [æ] 2. Scarce, rarely.

halang 1. Cause to surrender, cause to have a feeling of defeat, cause to admit defeat, cause to give up, dread. *Ha halang yo' mamokkat hulo' gi ekso'.* Walking up the hill gets me. *Hu halang hao anai mumu hit.* I caused you to admit defeat when we fought.

hale' 1,2. Root (of a plant), source, origin. *I hale' matai.* The root is dead. *Espiha i hale' enao na sinangan.* Find the origin of that rumor.

hali 1. To harvest root crop.

hali'an 2. Stone—used for forming a fireplace for cooking. Fireplace. Also **alihan, halihan.**

haligi 2. Fence post, pillar, house post used for structural support. Cf. **Estaka.**

halla 1. Pull, haul, drag, tug, draw. Cf. **Sague'.**

halle' [æ] 1. Uproot, pull up root.

halli [æ] 2. Word used when driving a cow hitched to a bull cart, gidyap.

hallom [æ] 2. Surmise, presume, guess, think with uncertainty. Thoughts, suspicion. *Humallom yo' na mamaigo' gue'.* I presume that he is sleeping.

halom In, into, inside, enter. Cf. **Sanhalom**. Usually used with *gi*. *Humanao yo' gi halom i tenda*. I went inside the store. *Chule' halom*. Take it inside.

halom tano' 2. Woods, forest, jungle. (Lit. inside land).

halomgue 1. Go inside for. Also **kalomgue**. *Hu halomgue si Pedro gi gima'-ña*. I went in Pete's house to get him.

halon 1,2. Thread, string, twine, cord, thin rope. Also **hahlon**. *Halon fan i hagua*. Thread the needle, please. *Chuli'i yo' halon ya bai hu godde i ayuyu*. Get me a string so that I can tie the coconut-crab.

halu'on unai 2. Type of fish-family carcharhinidae. Sand shark.

halu'u 2. Type of fish-family carcharhinidae. Any of several sharks.

ham [æ] We—intransitive subject pronoun, exclusive, transitive subj. pron. with indefinite obj., us--transitive obj. pron., exclusive. *Manhanao ham asta i lancho*. We went up to the ranch. *Manmañule' ham lepblo*. We took books. *Un ofresi ham lapes*. You offered us pencils.

hámafak [æ] 2. Fragile, brittle, easily broken.

hámaleffa [æ] 2. Forgetful, one who easily forgets.

hámaniente [æ] 2. Sensitive, touchy, irritable, perceptive to presence of spirits.

hamás Never again. *Hamas ti bai kuentusi hao*. I'll never speak to you again.

hambiento 2. Avaricious. (G) Also **hambrento, ambiento**.

hambrento 2. Greedy, rapacious, avaricious, eagerly desirous. Also **hambiento, hambrenta** (f). Cf. **Padok, girek, gulosu**.

ha'me [æ] 1. Warm (something) by heat radiation, make warm, to cause something to wilt from heat. *Hu ha'me i kannai-hu gi guafi*. I warmed up my hands by the fire. *Hu ha'me i flores*. I made the flower wilt from the heat.

hami [æ] We, us (emphatic, exclusive). Cf. **Ham, in**.

hamlak 2. Type of plant-callicarpa candicans. Type of tree—from which a medicine is made for treatment of boils.

hámlangu [æ] 2. Sickly person, one who gets sick easily, one who gets sick often. From *hamalangu*.

hammon [æ] 2. Ham.

hamoktan 2. Type of fish-acanthurus guttatus (acanthuridae).

hamónika 2. Harmonica, mouth organ. Cf. **Bibek**.

hamottan 2. Type of fish-acanthurus guttatus (family acanthuridae). Surgeon fishes.

hamyo [æ] You—intransitive subj. pl. pron., transitive obj. pl. pron., emphatic pl. pron. *Manmanhungok hamyo buruka*. You heard noise. *Hu li'e' hamyo gi chalan*. I saw you on the road. *Hamyo sumodda' i patgon*. You were the ones who found the child.

hanao 2. Go, leave, depart. Cf. **Fa'pos**. *Humanao gue' nigap*. He went yesterday.

handa [æ] 1. To chase away dogs. Term used to chase dogs away.

handa [æ] 1,2. Flip card—facing upward, esp. in tres siete (card game).

hanhan [æ] 1. Threaten—with raised forefinger, to shake finger at someone as admonishment.

hankot 2. Type of fish-family hemiramphidae. Halfbeaks.

hannan [æ] 1,2. To feint, a mock punch in fighting or dueling.

hanom 2. Water, liquid. *Hanom fresko*. Fresh water. *Hanom ais*. Ice water. *Hanom uchan*. Rain water. *Hanom sinaga*. Collected rain water. *Hanom bo'bo'*. Spring water. *Hanom kloraks*. Chlorinated water.

hanom bo'bo' 2. Water from the spring.

hanom grifu 1. Tap water.

hanom ma'asen 2. Brine, pickling water.

hanom sinaga 2. Rain water, water—in water catchment.

hanom tika 2. Watery residue left after coconut milk is boiled to extract the coconut oil.

hanon 2. Burned, incinerated, conflagrated, consumed with fire. Cf. **Kumadu**. *Hanon kannai-hu*. My hand was burned.

hangai 1. Purpose—of being in a place, reason for being someplace. *Hafa hinangai-mu gi espitat?* What was your purpose for being at the hospital? *Hafa un hangai gi lancho-ku?* What was your reason for being at my ranch? *Guaha hinangai-hu gi gima'-mu.* There was a reason for being at your house.

hangon 2. Type of fish-naso lituratus (family acanthuridae). Surgeon fishes.

hao You—intransitive subj. sing. pron., transitive subj. sing. pron. with indefinite object, transitive obj. sing. pron. *Humanao hao.* You went. *Chumocho hao mansana.* You ate an apple.

ha'of 2. Chest (body), usually refers to interior of chest cavity. Cf. **Pecho.**

haohao 2. Bark—dog's.

Hapones 2. Japanese. Cf. **Chapanes.**

hara 2. Pitcher, jug, crock, jar.

hasa 1. Cause to drift, cause to blow away, be carried along by the current. (R) Also **asa.** *I manglo' ha hasa i gima'.* The wind blew the house away. *I korente ha hasa i boti gi tasi.* The current caused the boat to drift out to sea.

hasienda 2. Hacienda, house. Cf. **Guma'.**

hasmín 2. Type of plant-jasminum. Jasmine, ginger (edible).

hasngon 1. Deliberately, intentionally, intend, mean, purposely. *Hu hasngon ha' gumacha' addeng-mu.* I deliberately stepped on your foot. *Ha hasngon ha' ti umatan yo'.* He intended not to look at me.

hasngot 2. Type of plant-zingiber zerumbet. Ginger. Cf. **Hasmin.**

hasnguni 1. Overdo, do deliberately—as in anger, exaggerate, to carry too far. Cf. **Hasngon.** *Hu hasnguni hao ti guma'chungi un simana.* I deliberately refused to accompany you for a week. *Hu hasnguni gumacha i addeng-ña.* I kept stepping on his foot deliberately.

haspok 2. Full (from food), satiated, glutted, sated, filled (by pregnancy - slang). Cf. **Bula, hafnot.** *Haspok i neni ni leche.* The baby was filled up with milk. *Haspok yo' ni nenkanno'.* I was filled up with food .

hassan 2. Rarely, infrequent, rare, seldom, scarce, not often, scarcity, not abundant. Cf. **Apenas, eskasu.** *Hassan yo' matto gi gima'-ñiha.* I seldom go to their house. *Hassan gima' padet giya Marianas.* Cement block houses are scarce in the Marianas.

hasso [æ] **1.** Think, imagine, conceive, realize, envisage, remember. *Hu hasso i lepblo-ku gi halom sidan.* I remembered my book inside the sedan. *Hu hasso si nana-hu anai hu atan i litratu-ña.* I thought of my mother when I saw her picture.

hasta [æ] **2.** Pole. Cf. **Hastan bandera.** *Hastan denke'.* Pole with light.

hastan bandera 2. Flag pole.

hastan batberu 2. Barber pole.

hásupak [æ] **2.** Nuisance, one who visits others too often, thus making a nuisance of himself, a neighbor or friend who borrows things or eats other's food too often. Too forward in manners. Also **asupak.**

hat- [æ] Further, more, move further, a prefix forming the comparative degree for direction, similar to the English -er suffix form. Cf. **Ge'-.** *Hattichan.* Move further west. *Hatguatu.* Move further to there (away from speaker and addressee). *Hattilo'.* Move further up.

ha'tan 2. Type of fish-siganidae. Rabbit fish. Small *sesyon.*

hatcheng 2. Sneeze, act of sneezing. (R) Also **achom.**

hatdín 2. Garden.

hatdineru 2. Gardener, one who gardens.

hateng 2. Black ant. Cf. **Otdot.** Also **ateng, hacheng.**

hátkattan [æ] **2.** East—move further, eastward--move slightly, easterly. Cf. **Kattan, ge'kattan.** *Hatkattan para i fi'on-ña.* Move further east to his side.

hatma 2. Deep cutting blade—like a sharp machete. Opposite of *fotda.*

hatme 1. Attack, trespass, invade, penetrate, put on something, get inside. *Hu hatme i tano'-mu nigap.* I trespassed your land yesterday. *Hu hatme i chinina-hu ni nuebu.* I put on my shirt that was new. *I hanom ha hatme i magagu-hu.* The water penetrated my clothes.

hatopa 2. Type of plant-sporobolus virginicus. (?).

hatot [æ] 2. Type of fish-pitroscirtes mitratus (family blennidae). Mangrove hopper, scaleless blennies. Also **atot**.

hatpón 1,2. Harpoon, strike, catch or kill with or as with a harpoon, barbed spearlike missile.

hatsa 1. Lift, raise up, erect, hoist or raise with a tackle, promote, raise salary. Cf. **Kahat, sa'hang**.

hatsamiento 2. Raise, increase. Cf. **Subida**. *Guaha ta'lo hatsamienton suetdo*. There will be another raise in salary.

háttagu [æ] 2. North—move further, northward--move slightly, northerly. Cf. **Lagu, ge'lagu**. *Hattagu guenao asta i kanton kantit*. Move further north there to the edge of the cliff.

háttalom [æ] 2. Inside—move further, inward--move slightly, deeper--go in, go in further. Cf. **Halom, ge'halom**. *Hattalom gi gima'*. Move further inside the house.

háttaya [æ] 2. South—move further, southward--move slightly, southerly. Cf. **Haya, ge'haya**. *Hattaya gi plasa ya ayu na un hugando*. Move further south of the plaza and that's where you will play.

háttichan [æ] 2. West—move further, westward--move slightly, westerly. Cf. **Luchan, ge'lichan**. *Hattichan sa' bula kampo guihi*. Move further west because there is lots of space there.

háttiyong [æ] Out—move further, outward--move slightly, outside--move further. Cf. **Ge'hiyong, huyong**. *Hattiyong gi tasi guihi anai taddong*. Move further out to sea where it is deep.

haya 2. South (in Guam and Rota), east (in Saipan).

ha'yan 2. Type of fish-family scaridae. Parrot fishes.

hayi Who (question word). *Hayi na'an-mu?* What is your name? *Hayi enao?* Who is that?

hayi ha' 2. Whoever.

hayon lagu 2. Type of plant-serianthes nelsonii. (?).

hayon matutong 2. Firewood—for kitchen.

hayu 2. Stick, wood.

he G—letter of the alphabet. Also **ge**.

hechura 2. Dough, made from flour in preparation for baking.

hechura Form, figure, shape, image, outline. Cf. **Figura, butto**.

heddo 1. Tuck, pull up (in a fold or folds), roll up (shorten), shorten, tighten by drawing up or together in folds. Cf. **Limangga**. *Heddo i mangas chinina-mu*. Tuck up your shirt sleeve.

heddo 2. Shrivel, dry up, crumpled up.

heggao 2. Coconut husker. Also **hehgao**.

hehgao 2. Coconut husker—a pointed stick or piece of metal used for removing the husks from coconuts. Also **heggao**. Cf. **Kacha'**.

hekkua' Doubt, don't know, uncertainty of mind, lack of decision. *Hekkua'*. I don't know.

hektaria 2. Hectare, acre.

hemi 2. Measure, unit of measure from tip of index finger to tip of thumb.

hemmot 1. Cram, stuff, fill full, press, compress, jam tightly, pack in, overcrowd, crumple, wad. *Hu hemmot i papet siha gi halom katpeta-hu*. I stuffed the paper into the briefcase.

hemplo 2. Story, tale, episode, occurrence, happening, event. Cf. **Estoria, sinusedi**.

henerasión 2. Generation.

henerát 2. In general, general—as in the rank of armed forces. *Para u guaha miteng henerat gi eskuela*. There will be a general meeting at the school. *Matto i henerat*. The general came.

henio 2. Temperament, disposition, mood, humor. Also **henia** (f). Cf. *Mathenio*.

hentan 1. Get, obtain. *Hu hentan as Francisco*. I got it from Frank. *Manu nai un hentan enao?* Where did you get that? *Hinentan-hu gi bundak*. I got it in the forest.

hentra 1. Mention, make known, speak of, inform, discuss, refer to. Also **menta, mentra**. Cf. **Mensiona**. *Ta hentra i lini'e'-ta gi entre i mangga'chong*. We mentioned the thing we saw among friends.

hereria 2. Blacksmith's workshop.

hereru 2. Blacksmith.

Hesuitas 2. Jesuit. Also **Suitas**.

hetbana 2. Mend, patch—clothing.

hibiyas 2. Buckle. Also biyas.

hígadu 2. Liver.

higai 2. Woven palm leaves, roof of coconut palm, thatched roof. *Atof higai.* Roof of coconut palm. *Guma' higai.* Shack made of coconut palm.

higante 2. Giant, huge. Also gante.

higef 1. Surprise, catch (in the act), any criminal caught by surprise, capture secretly. *I polisia ha higef i sakke.* The police captured the thief in the act.

higef 1. Crush, squeeze. *Mahigef i chada'.* The egg was crushed.

higos 2. Type of plant-ficus cairica. Fig plant.

higu 2. Type of plant-ficus cairica. (?).

híhina 2. Poisoner—one who or that which poisons. Cf. Bibinenu, tatatse.

hihot 2. Near, close, almost, within, a little distance (in place or time). Usually followed by *gi. I palao'an hihot gi lahi.* The girl is close to the man. *Hihot yo' gi gima'.* I am near the house.

híkamas 2. Type of plant-pachyrrhizus erosus. Type of fruit—grows under the soil.

hikara 2. Type of plant-crescentia alata.

hila 1. Make strand from fiber for purpose of making rope. Cf. Hinila.

hila' guaka 2. Type of plant-nopalea cochinel. Cochineal cactus.

hilachas 2. Shreds—of cloth, small pieces of leftover cloth.

hila'gue [æ] 1. Stick tongue out as a gesture.

hilengga 2. Suppository. Also lilengga, lengga.

hilenggua i baka 2. Type of plant-euphorbia neriifolia. A type of flower.

hilitai 2. Lizard (large monitor lizard), iguana.

hilo' Cf. Hulo'.

hilon chotda 2. Basting thread.

hilu 2. String, twine, cord.

hima 2. Clam—various bivalve mollusks (venus mercenaria).

hina 1. Poison. Cf. Binenuyi, tatse.

hinafa [æ] 2. Thing, object. Cf. Hafa.

hinaga' [æ] 2. Dysentery. Cf. Masisinek haga'.

hinaga' [æ] 2. Leaves turning red in plant crops, and is considered a bad sign for harvesting crops. *Hinaga' i tinanom-hu mai'es.* The leaves of my corn are turning red.

hinagong [æ] 2. Breath, breathing, respiration.

hinagua 1. Rinse (in clean water), wash out. Also enhagua.

hinanao [æ] 2. Trip, voyage, journey, excursion, traveling. Cf. Biahi.

hinanom [æ] 2. Watery. Cf. Hanom.

hinanon [æ] 2. Scorched.

hinasa [æ] 2. Drifted away, blown away. Cf. Hasa.

hinasnguni 2. Malice, mischief. Cf. Hasngon.

hinasso [æ] 2. Thought, conception, imagination, cogitation, reflection, opinion, idea, memory, mind, intellect.

hinatme [æ] 2. Invasion, saturation. Cf. Hatme.

hinatme manglo' 2. Flatulence.

hinekka 2. Harvest, gathering.

hineksa' 2. Cooked rice.

hineksa' agaga' 2. Red rice, rice cooked with red coloring from the seed of the *achoti* . Usually served at parties.

hinemhom 2. Darkness, darkened.

hinemlo' 2. Recovery, restoration to health.

hineño' 2. Maltreatment, oppression.

hinengge 2. Belief, faith, creed, notion, inclination.

hiniebra 2. Gin.

hinigua 2. Disaster, calamity, storm, small typhoon. Cf. Ira.

hinila 2. Strand—of a rope.

hinilat 2. Overpowered, overcome, subdued. *Hinilat si Juan as Jose.* John was overpowered by Joseph. *Kao hinilat hao ni taotao?* Were you overpowered by the man?

hinilat maisa 2. Self-control.

hiniyong 2. Effect, consequence. Cf. Huyong.

hingao 2. Hairless (body), not bushy, not hairy, featherless. Cf. Dakngas.

hipokrisia 2. Hypocrisy, pretending to have a character (beliefs, principles, etc.) one does not possess.

hipokritu 2. Hypocrite, dissembler. Also hipokrita (f).

hirida 2. Wound, sore. Cf. Chetnot. Also irida.

hiridáo 2. Wounded. Cf. **Chetnudan.** Also **iridao.**

historia 2. History, a narrative of events. Also **istoria.**

historia sagrada 2. Bible history, sacred history. Cf. **Biblia.** Also **istoria sagrada.**

hit We—intransitive subj. pron., inclusive, transitive subj. pron. with indefinite obj., us--transitive obj. pron., inclusive. *Mañocho hit gi gipot.* We ate at the party. *Manggimen hit lemonada.* We drank lemonade. *Ha li'e' hit nigap.* He saw us yesterday.

hita We, us (emphatic, inclusive). *Hita fumahan i gima'.* We are the ones who bought the house.

hiteng 2. Type of fish-siganus punctatus (family siganidae). Rabbit fishes.

hiteng 2. Type of plant-hippobroma longiflora.

hiya' Again, temporarily, for a short while (idiomatic). *Munga hiya'.* Don't do it again. *Hayi na'an-mu hiya'?* What's your name again? *Fata'chong hiya'.* Sit down for a short while.

hiyok 2. Type of fish-family acanthuridae.

hoben 2. Young, immature, inexperienced. Youthfully fresh or vigorous in body, mind, or feeling.

hóbenes 2. Youngsters. Also **manhoben.**

hobensitu 2. Teen-ager, youth, adolescence (m). Also **hobensita** (f).

hobentút 2. Adolesence.

hoda 2. Type of plant-ficus tinctoria. Type of tree—used as medicine for treatment of sore throat.

hoe' Hello, call for someone.

hoflak 1. Lick, draw or pass the tongue over, lap.

hógadot 2. Gambler. Cf. **Gamboleru.**

hoggue 1. Carry—something in the arms. *Hu hoggue i neni nigap.* I carried the baby in my arms yesterday.

hokka 1. Collect, pick, infer, gather, assemble, pick up.

hokkok 2. No more, none, all gone, nothing, not one, not any, nothing at all, none at all. *Hokkok salape'-hu.* All my money is gone. *Hokkok kafe gi gima'.* There is no more coffee at the house.

hokse 1. Hold down, press down, pin down to prevent movement or being blown away. Cf. **Hoño'.**

Holandes 2. Dutch, Holland.

homhom 2. Dark, dim, obscure, dusky, gloomy, not light-colored, bleak.

homhom uchan 2. Rain clouds.

homlo' 2. Heal, revive, recover (from sickness). Cf. magong. *Homlo' yo' anai ma opera i chetnot-hu.* I recovered when my wound was operated on. *Homlo' i amigu-hu gi chetnot-ña.* My friend recovered from his sickness.

homme 1. Overshadow, hide, block (the view), break the natural course of light, vision, etc. *I mapagahes ha homme i tano'.* The clouds overshadowed the earth. *Hu homme i inatan-mu.* I blocked your vision.

homme 2. Awning, shade.

hommon 2. Lava rock, rock—large, lava.

homoráng 2. Homer, a home run, make a home run, hit a home run. (S)

hoño' 1. Press down, suppress, hold down, pin down to prevent movement or being blown away, pressure. Cf. **Hokse, yemme'.**

hongang 1. Scare, frighten, menace, threaten. Cf. **Aminasa, espanta, fa'ñague, huppa.** *Hu hongang i ga'lagu gi painge.* I scared the dog last night.

hongga 1. Audible, be heard. Cf. **Oppan.** *Hongga i essalao-hu asta i sengsong.* My shout was heard all the way to town.

hongge 1. Believe, trust, have faith or confidence, accept as true.

honggiyon 2. Believable.

honggo' 1. Cut off (bunch of bananas).

hopba 1. Lick, draw or pass tongue over, lap up—as the way a dog drinks water.

hoplat 2. Dirty, filthy. *Mampos hoplat na magagu.* The clothes are filthy.

hopyat 1. Rub, wash (by rubbing), scrub (with a cloth). Also **hotyat.**

hosgon 2. Jealous. Also **hosguan.**

hosguan 2. Jealous, wrathful, envious. Cf. **Kinahulo'guan.**

hosme 2. Attend, be present. *Humosme misa yo'.* I attended mass.

hota J—letter.

hotde 1. Scamper, ascend, mount. *Ha hotde i tronkon mangga.* He climbed the mango tree. *I ga'lagu ha hotde i otro ga'lagu.* The dog mounted the other dog.

hotkon 2. Pillar—a column to support a building, usually extending from ground to floor of building.

hotma 1,2. To mold, shape something. Mold—such as a jello mold or cake pan.

hotnaleru 2. Laborer, helper, day laborer.

hotnát 2. Labor, work, job, employment, manual labor, hard work.

hotne 1. Pierce, thread (needle), lace shoes.

hotno 1,2. Oven, barbecue, roast by oven or an underground pit, bake.

hotnon afok 2. Lime kiln.

hotyat 1. Scrub. Also **hopyat.**

houka 2. Type of plant-crescentia alata. (?) Cf. **Hikara.**

ho'ye 1. Accept, agree, promise, grant request. *Ho'ye yo' ni ginagao-hu.* Grant me my request.

hoyu 2. Hole, pit, fissure, concave. Cf. **Maddok.**

-hu My, mine (possessive). Also **-ku.** *Kao ya-mu i kareta-hu.* Do you like my car?

hu I—pre-posed pronoun used in transitive statements. Cf. **Guahu, yo'.** *Hu kanno' i mansana.* I ate the apple.

huba det poyu 2. Type of plant-portulaca quadrifida. (?).

huchom 1. Close, shut, cover. Cf. *Tampe. Si Pete ha huchom i petta.* Pete closed the door.

Hudas 2. Devil, Satan, Judas. Cf. **Diablo, aniti, satanas, maknganiti, dimonio.**

Hudios 2. Jew, Hebrew, Israelite, Judaist, rabbinist.

Huebes 2. Thursday.

huega 1. Play, perform, gamble. *Ta huega un huegu ta'lo.* We played one game again.

huegu 2. Game, sport, contest, recreation, program, performance, act, amusement. Cf. **Hugando.**

hues 2. Judge—the presiding magistrate in a court of justice, umpire, referee.

huetton olibas 2. Garden of Gesthemane, where Christ was betrayed by Judas.

hufot 1. Hang on to, keep—in the sense of saving money or food. *Hufot i salape'-mu.* Hang on to your money.

hugando 2. Play, amuse, toy with, perform, act, game, recreation, gamble. Cf. **Huegu.**

huganom 2. Whey, separation of liquids, as spoiled milk, oil and vinegar. After soupy food cools off, there is a separation of the upper lighter fluid from the lower heavier mass. Also **huguahnom, guahnom.**

hugeti 2. Toy, gewgaw, trinket, something to play with.

hugom 1. Cause to sag, cause to bend, lose firmness, resiliency or vigor. *Hu hugom i ramas kahet anai hu tife' i tinekcha'-ña.* I made the orange tree's branch sag down when I picked its fruit.

hugom 1. Squeeze—with arms or legs as in wrestling, give bear hug.

huguahnom 2. Whey. Cf. **Huganom.**

huguan Really, yes it is true. A contracted form of *hu'u guaña.* Cf. **Guaña.**

huguayon 2. Ambidextrous.

hugupao 2. Type of-fish-family acanthuridae. Surgeon fishes.

huisio 2. Judgment, decision, sentence, verdict. Cf. **Sentensia.**

hula 1. Swear, vow, take oath, pledge by oath, make a solemn promise. Used esp. in legal procedures. *Hu hula na bai hu hanao agupa' asta i gima'-mu.* I swear that I will go to your house tomorrow.

hula' 2. Tongue, tongue out, sticking tongue out.

hula'gue 1. Stick tongue out at someone, as a form of insult. Also **hilague.** Cf. **Hula'.**

hulat 1. Overpower, overcome, subdue. Cf. **A'ñao.**

hulo' Up, above, on top of, usually used with preposition *gi,* as in *gi hilo''*on top of', or *san,* as in *sanhilo''*on top of'.

hulof 1. To cover, to shelter, protect, to screen. Also **luhof.** Cf. **Liheng, atok.**

hulok 1. Break—by bending long objects.

hulos 1. Smooth out, rub (gently), pet by stroking.

hulu 2. Thunder.

humahnanao 2. Continuous, to keep going. Cf. **Hanao.** *Ha chule' i salape'-ña ya humahnanao ha'.* He took his money and he kept going.

humallom [æ] 2. Presume, suspect, suppose, assume, expect or assume with confidence. Cf. **Hallom.** *Humallom yo' na si Jose malangu.* I suspected that Joseph was sick.

humalom 2. Went inside. Cf. **Halom.** *Humalom yo' gi gima'.* I went inside the house.

humami [æ] We (exclusive) do something together. Cf. **Humita.** *Humami nu lumans.* We had lunch together.

humatcheng [æ] 2. Sneeze. Cf. **Hatcheng.** (R)

humita We do something together; *hita* plus *-um-*. *Bai hu hanao solamente humita.* I will go provided that we go together.

humitde 2. Humble, lowly, meek. Also **umitde.**

humomran 2. Make a homerun. (Homerun plus infix *-um-*).

humuyong 2. Discharge, go out from.

humuyongña 2. As a result, what it turned out to be. *Kumon hu na'i hao nu este humuyongña taya' yo'.* If I give you this, as a result I won't have any. *Humuyongña guahu ha' guini yanggen un dingu yo'.* As a result I would be here alone if you leave me.

hun Quotative marker. Used to distinguish a reported statement from a statement known to be fact. Usually follows the predicate. *Humanao gue' hun para i gipot.* He said he went to the party.

hunek 2. Type of plant-messerschmidia argentea. Type of tree.

hunek tasi 2. Type of plant-heliotropium ovalifolium.

hunta 2. Meeting, gathering, assembly. Cf. **Miteng.**

hunto 2. Ointment, salve, an ointment type of medicine. Cf. **Ingguente.**

hunggan 2. Yes—used to express affirmation, assent, or comfirmation in answer to a question, sure. Cf. **Hu'u.**

hungok 1. Hear, heed, be informed, perceive by the ear, gain knowledge. Cf. **Ekungok.** *Hu hungok i rediu.* I heard the radio. *Hu hungok na matai.* I heard that he died.

huppa 1. Frighten, scare, drive (away or into), force (out), threaten, menace. Cf. **Espanta, fa'ñague, hongang, aminasa.**

huramento 2. Pledge, vow, swear. *I huramento u macho'gue agupa'.* The pledge will be taken tomorrow.

husga 1. To judge, to pronounce judgement, to sit in judgement, to pass sentence.

hustisia 2. Justice, rightfulness, rectitude, integrity.

husto 2. Just, upright, fair, righteous.

huto' 1. Unfold, spread out.

huton dokdok 2. Seed of breadfruit.

hutu 2. Louse, lice (insect), seed— breadfruit.

hu'u Yes, okay, sure, yeah, of course. Cf. **Hunggan.**

huyong 2. Get out, outside, bring out, emerge. *Huyong gi gima'.* Go outside the house. *Humuyong i taotao gi gima'.* The person got out of the house. *Hu na'huyong i taotao gi gima'-hu.* I made the person get out of the house. *I patgon gaige gi hiyong i gima'.* The child is outside the house.

huyong Effect, outcome.

-i Referential focus marker. *Hu tugi'i si Maria ni katta.* I wrote the letter for Maria.

i The (definite article). Focus marking particle. Cf. **Ni.** *Hu chule' i lepblo.* I took the book.

i I—letter.

iba' 2. Puckered lips, puckering of lips —as when about to cry. Twisting of labia of vagina (slang). Cf. **Muyo'.**

Iba Nickname for Oliva.

ibba' 2. Type of plant-phyllanthus acidus. Type of tree—fruit grows on trunk or branches. Fruit has a sour taste that causes the lips to pucker up.

ibidensa 2. Evidence, proof, facts. Also **ebidensia.**

Icha' Nickname for Luisa.

idát 2. Age, number of years. Cf. **Años, sakkan.**

idea 2. Idea, notion, belief.

idolatria 2. Idolatry.

ídolu 2. Idol.

i'e' 2. Type of fish-family carangidae. Baby skipjack.

ifek 2. Type of tree. Also **ifet.**

ifet 2. Type of tree—intsia bijuga. A very hard and heavy wood resembling black walnut in color. Also **ifek.**

igi 1. Defeat, overcome, beat, vanquish, surpass, overpower. *Hu igi i amigu-hu gi tes.* I beat my friend on the test.

iha 2. Daughter. Cf. **Haga.**

ihu 2. Son. Cf. **Lahi.**

i'isao 2. Sinner, one who commits sin.

ika 2. Donation, gift—given to the family of a deceased person. The receiving of *ika* carries with it an obligation that the recipient will reciprocate to the donor at a later date.

ikak 1. Defeat, beat—in a race, finish first. *Ma'ikak yo' gi karera asta i eskuela.* They defeated me in the race to the school. *Hu ikak hao chumocho.* I beat you eating. (I finished first.).

iknora 1. Ignore.

iknoransia 2. Ignorance.

iknorante 2. Ignorant, illiterate, unlettered, untutored, unlearned.

Iku Nickname for Juan.

ilao 1. Look for, search. Cf. **Aligao, espiha.** *Hagas ha' ma'ilao hao.* You have been searched for a long time.

ilegát 2. Illegal.

ilehítimu 2. Illegitimate. Cf. **Bastatdo.**

ilék- 3. Say, said. From *alok. Ilek-ña si Rita na malangu hao.* Rita said that you were sick.

ilihi 2. Elect, designate for office by a majority or plurality vote, select, choose, appoint, pick out.

ilotes 1,2. Type of food. Sweet corn, boiled with coconut milk.

ilotes 2. Green corn, sweet corn as used for corn-on-the-cob.

imahen 2. Image, statue. Cf. **Estatua.**

imahina 1. Imagine. Cf. **Hasso.**

imahinasión 2. Imagination.

imbension 2. Invention.

imbenta 1. Invent, contrive something new, create.

imbentadót 2. Inventor. Also **imbentot.**

imbentibu 2. Inventive, creative.

imbentót 2. Inventor. Also **imbentadot.**

imbestiga 1. Investigate, probe, search, examine closely, inquire, scan, sift. Cf. **Abirigua.**

imbestigadót 1. Investigator, examiner, prober.

imbestigasión 2. Investigation, active effort to find out something.

imbita 1. Invite. Cf. **Kombida.**

imbitasión 2. Invitation. Cf. **Kombiti.**

imidiatamente 2. Immediately.

imigrante 2. Immigrant.

imitasión 2. Imitation.

impedimento 2. Impediment, obstruction, obstacle, hindrance (of marriage), barrier.

impeña 1. Mortgage, pledge. *Ma'impeña i kareta-ña ni banko.* His car was mortgaged by the bank.

imperio 2. Empire.

impetinente 2. Impertinent.

impetosu 2. Impetuous, furious, impulsive, or vehement in action or feeling, violent, short tempered (m). Also **empetosa** (f).

imposipble 2. Impossible, improbable, cannot be done.

impotente 2. Impotent.

impotta 1. Import, bring into a country from abroad.

impottante 2. Important, essential, necessary, vital. Cf. **Prisisu.**

imprenta 1. Imprint, impress, mark made by pressure, fix indelibly as in a memory.

impresa 1. Impress. Cf. **Imprenta.** *Ha impresa yo' i kuentos-ña.* His speech impressed me.

impresót 2. Compositor, printer.

imprudensia 2. Imprudent, heedless of consequences.

-in- Adjectivizer. An infix used to form modifiers from nominals, similar to English -ish. *Guaka* 'cow', *guinaka* 'cowish'. *A'paka'* 'white', *ina'paka'* 'whitish'. *Kahet* 'orange', *kinahet* 'orangeish'.

-in- Nominalizing infix. *Li'e'.* To see. *Lini'e'-ña.* The thing he saw.' *Na'i.* To give. *Nina'i.* Gift.

-in- Goal focus infix. *Lini'e' si Juan as Maria.* It was Juan that Maria saw.

in We—exclusive, pre-posed pronoun used in transitive statements.

ina 1. Illuminate, spot with light, shine on. *Hu ina i patgon ni denke'.* I shined the flashlight on the child.

ina Exclamation. Oh, wow. First syllable is usually pronounced with loudness and is prolonged. *Ina minaolek i gipot.* Oh, how good the party was.

Ina Nickname for Alfonsina.

Ina' Nickname for Rufina.

inabak [æ] 2. Misunderstanding, error, puzzled.

inábale' [æ] 2. Intercourse.

ináchago' [æ] 2. Distance.

ináchatli'e' [æ] 2. Hatred, hate, resentment, ruthlessness, the feeling of one who hates.

inadamelong 2. Sphere, globe.

inadayao 2. Arouse interest, become interested. *Inadayao i gobietno.* The governor became interested.

inadelanta 2. Improvement.

inádingan 2. Elocution, art or manner of speaking.

inádingu [æ] 2. Parting, fare-well, good-bye, withdrawal, departure. Cf. Dingu, despidida. *Na'triste i inadingu gi entre mangga'chong.* Parting causes sadness among friends.

inaflitu 2. Fried, a dish of anything fried. *Inafliton hineksa'.* Fried rice. *Inaflitu na mannok.* Fried chicken.

inagaga' [æ] 2. Reddish, containing red color.

ina'gang [æ] 2. Loudness, noise. *I ina'gang-ña kumuentos muna'ma'ilihi.* His loud way of talking was the cause of his being elected.

inagang [æ] 1. Call for, call to. Cf. Agang. *Inagang si Maria as Pete.* Pete called to Maria.

ina'go [æ] 2. Change, alteration. Cf. A'go.

inágofli'e' [æ] 2. Friendship, brotherhood, kindness, sympathy, association as friends, friendly relations. Cf. Gofli'e'.

inagradesi 2. Reward, recompense, gratitude.

inagua' [æ] 2. A long step, stride.

ináguaguat [æ] 2. General row or tussle, controversy, strife.

inakka' [æ] 1. Sting.

inákomprende 2. Concord, agreement.

inakpa'an 2. Food—from the day before.

inakpa'ña 2. Day after tomorrow. Also nakpa'ña.

inaksepta 1. Accepted, received. Cf. Rinisibi.

inale' [æ] 2. Misfortune, destruction, insult, make mistake. *Inale' ni bunitu-ña.* She was brought to ruin by his good looks.

inalula 2. Swiftness, hurriedness. Cf. Alula.

inamariyu 2. Yellowish, containing yellow color.

inamte [æ] 1. Cured. Cf. Amte.

inamte [æ] 2. Parson, clergyman.

inamuradu 2. Enamor, one who is enamored, inspire with ardent love, excite love (m). Also inamurada (f).

inanakko' 2. Length.

inancho [æ] 2. Width. Cf. Finedda'.

inaniti 2. Infernal, hellish, fiendish. Cf. Aniti.

inánokcha' [æ] 2. Report, account.

inangglo' [æ] 2. Dried, anything that is dried. *Inangglo' katne.* Dried meat. *Inangglo' guihan.* Dried fish. *Inangglo' magagu.* Dried clothes.

inaogarasión 2. Inauguration.

ina'paka' [æ] 2. Whitish, containing white color.

ina'paka'an 2. Whiteness, whitish.

inapigasa 2. Condition of having goose pimples.

inapmam [æ] 2. Stay so long, delayed so long. *Liame' na inapmam hao giya Rota.* Gosh, you certainly stayed a long time on Rota. *I inapmam-hu kuatro oras.* I was delayed four hours.

inapplacha' [æ] 2. Refuse, excrement, pollution.

inapu [æ] 2. Having ashes. *Inapu i nenkanno'.* The food has ashes in it.

inapu na kulót 2. Grayish, containing gray color.

inapulaihan 2. Moldy—cause to be, moldy--become. *Inapulaihan i pan.* The bread became moldy.

Inarajan Village in southern Guam. Pron. Inalahan.

inarekkla 2. Method, system, order, controlled.

Inas Nickname for Ignacio.

inasa [æ] 2. Blown away. Cf. **Hinasa**.

inasahan 2. Fruit—that ripens on tree before harvesting; ripe banana--still on the tree.

inasigayan 2. Salt—streak forming on the body from dried perspiration.

inasigura 2. Security, warranty, bail.

inasi'i 2. Pardon, forgiveness, absolution.

inasne [æ] 2. Pickled, something salted, treated, seasoned, or filled with salt.

inasút 2. Blueish, containing blue color.

inatan [æ] 2. Glance, something seen.

inátattiyi [æ] 2. Line, row, series.

inatborota 2. Insurrection, uprising, rebellion, disturbed, bothered. Cf. **Atborota**.

inatditi 2. Oppressed, depressed, made worse. *Inatditi ni baba-ña.* His badness was made worse.

ináttilong [æ] 2. Blackish, containing black color, blackness.

inatua 2. Refers to highest class in earlier Chamorro society.

inátungo' [æ] 2. Friendliness, pleasantness.

inayek [æ] 2. Choice, selection, option. Cf. **Sileksion**.

indefinitu 2. Indefinite.

independiente 2. Independent, self-supporting.

indiana 2. Cloth—with striped or checkered pattern.

indiferente 2. Indifferent, listless.

indika 1. Indicate, denote, show, manifest, designate.

indikasión 2. Indication, signifying, showing.

indirekto 2. Indirect, not straight.

indothensia 2. Indulgence, sufferance, tolerance, forbearance, compassion. Also indulensia.

indulensia 2. Indulgence. Also indothensia.

industria 2. Industry.

inechong 2. Wrong, fault, injustice. Cf. **Echong**.

inefresi 1. Offering, promise, proposal, proposition. Cf. **Ofresi**. *Inefresi i patgon as tata-ña bola.* The father offered the child a ball. *Maolek i inefresi-ña gi taotao siha.* His proposal to the people was good.

inenkanta 2. Fascination, attraction.

inenkatga 2. Arrangement, management, an order—as from restaurant or catalogue.

inentalu'i 2. Intermission, pause, interruption, interference. Cf. **Entalu'i**.

inesgaihon 2. Escorting, accompanying, haunted person—whose health may be affected or endangered. *Inesgaihon yo' gi halom tano' anai umugong yo'.* I was haunted in the woods when I moaned. *Inesgaihon gue' as tata-hu asta i misa.* He was escorted to the mass by my father. *Na'magof i inesgaihon-ña.* His escorting was pleasing.

inestila 2. Liquor—distilled from bananas or other sources. Cf. **Agi**, **aguayente**.

inestukon 2. Brine, pickling solution, something pickled. Cf. **Chigu'an**, **asnentukon**. *Ya-hu inestukon mañahak.* I like pickled mañahak. *Nihi ta fanmama'tinas inestukon.* Let's make some brine.

inetnon 2. Association, club, group, league, corporation, crowd. Cf. **Katdumi, gurupu, aliansa**.

ineyak 2. Education.

infeksión 2. Infection.

infelís 2. Unhappy, unfortunate.

infiét Doubting, sceptical, suspicious, unbelieving, free thinking, lacking faith.

infietno 2. Hell, abyss.

infin In case, in the event. At the end. *Infin ti humanao hao na'tutungo' yo'.* In case you don't go, let me know.

infotma 1. Inform, acquaint, apprise, notify.

infotmasión 2. Information, message. Cf. **Anunsia, notisia**.

inhuestisia 2. Injustice, oppression. Also inhustisia.

inhuria 1. Revile, reproach. Cf. **Kalumnia**.

ini This (demonstrative pronoun). Archaic form now mostly replaced by *este*. Cf. **este, guini**. *Hafa ini?* What is this? *Saga ini gi gima'-hu.* Stay here at my house.

ínifok 2. Type of plant-chrysopogon aciculatus. Type of grass, burr, stickerburr.

iniga 2. Caress.

inigas 2. Type of starch—made from tapioca or arrowroot. Cf. **ugas.**

inigo' 2. Envy, jealousy. Cf. **Ugo'.**

inigong 2. Moaning, lamentation, mourning.

iniho' 2. Thrift.

inina 2. Light, gleam, glimmer.

ininan atdao 2. Sunlight.

iningak 2. Sag, sink down, yield.

inkahi 1,2. Snag, become entangled, catch (by an obstruction), hook, lace trim, esp. on women's underclothes. Also **enkahi.**

inkilinatu 2. Leasehold, property held by lease.

inklinao 2. Inclination.

inkombinensia 2. Inconvenience, trouble, worry, disadvantage, fuss, annoyed with trifles.

inkombiniente 2. Inconvenient, troublesome.

inkurable 2. Incurable. Cf. **Tairemediu.**

inmottát 2. Immortal, imperishable, deathless, ever living.

inoru na kulot 2. Goldish, containing gold color.

inos 2. Capable of squeezing through a hole, to fit in a place. Exact size for fitting or squeezing into a hole or place, capable of being squeezed or fitted into a tight place. *Inos hao humalom gi maddok.* You squeezed inside the hole. *Hu na'inos i patgon halom gi kareta.* I squeezed the child into the car.

inosente 2. Innocent, not guilty, guileless, ignorant, naive, simple.

insensio 2. Frankincense, fragrant gum resin.

inseparable 2. Inseparable.

insigidas 2. Immediately, promptly, at once, hurry up, quick, right away, as soon as possible. Also **sigidas.** Cf. **Sayao, alula, alulayi, chaddek, apura.**

insima 1. Intensify, enhance—esp. feelings and emotions. *Si Maria ha insisima na maolek si Juan.* Maria enhanced the goodness of Juan.

insinahyao [æ] 2. Walking briskly. Also **essinahyao.**

insiste 1. Insist, urge, persist, demand—persistently. Cf. **Momye.** *Ma insiste na bai in kenne' siha.* They insisted that we take them.

inspekta 1,2. Inspect, inspector. Also **inspektot.** Cf. **Rikunosi.**

instituyi 1. Institute, begin something.

instrumento 2. Instrument.

insutta 1. Insult, mock, deride, ridicule, deceive, delude, defy. Cf. **Butleha.**

insutto 2. Insult, affront, gross indignity offered to another. Cf. **Despresio.**

intelihente 2. Intelligent, smart. Cf. **Malate'.**

intensión 2. Intention.

intensiona 1. Intend. *Hu intensiona mangge' katta.* I intended to write a letter.

ínteres 2. Interest, profit, commission, interested, concerned.

ínteres 2. Selfishness, interest, profit.

interesante 2. Interesting, pleasing, gratifying, attracting the curiosity, satisfying to the mind.

interesáo 2. Selfish, egotistic, egocentric, self-interested, self-centered, self-seeking. Cf. **Chattao, otguyosu.**

interesáo 2. Interested, attentive, mindful, concerned.

interinu 2. Intern.

interiót 2. Interior, interior government. Cf. **Intetno.**

intetno 2. Interior, internal. Cf. **Interiot.**

intétpiti 2. Interpreter, translator. Also **intetpriti.**

introdusi 1. Introduce, lead, bring in, insert.

introdusión 2. Introduction. Also **introduksion.**

inturompe 1. Interrupt, interfere with, intercept, disturb, cause a discontinuance, stop in the midst of. Cf. **Estotba.**

inutet 2. Paralysis, paralyzed, unfit, unserviceable.

ingglera 2. Row, a series of inanimate objects set in a row. Cf. **Lucha, fila.** *Kuanto ingglera un tanom?* How many rows did you plant?

ingguente 2. Ointment, salve. Cf. **Hunto.**

ingratu 2. Ungrateful, thankless.

ipe' 2. Cut open, split, notch, chip.

ira 2. Disaster, calamity, catastrophe, cataclysm, tumult, violent outburst, tempest. Cf. **Hinigua.**

irana 2. Toad. Cf. **Kairo', tot.**

irensia 2. Inheritance. Also **erensia, rensia.**

iresa 2. Eraser. Cf. **Misigomo'.**

irida 1. Will, give an inheritance.

irida 2. Wound, sore. Cf. **Chetnot.** Also hirida.

iridáo 2. Wounded, pregnant—before marriage. Also **hiridao.**

iridáo 2. Victim, dupe.

irideru 2. Heir. **Iridera** (f).

iriko' 2. Type of fish—small fish, often used as tuna bait. Obtained in dried form from Japan.

isa 2. Rainbow.

isa' An exclamation of surprise.

isague [æ] 1. Offend, transgress, cause to sin, cause to feel hurt or resentful. Cf. **Ofende.**

isao 2. Sin, offense, vice, crime, scandal, violation, guilt, guilty.

isao dankolo 2. Mortal sin. Lit. big sin. Cf. **Isao ma'gas.**

isao dikike' 2. Venial sin. Lit. small sin. Cf. **Isao ñalalang.**

isao ma'gas 2. Mortal sin.

isao ñalalang 2. Venial sin. Lit. light sin. Cf. **Isao dikike'.**

isao orihinat 2. Original sin.

isek 2. Pass through, go by way of. Also **esgen, esek.**

isisio 2. March—as in a formation. *Manisisio i milisianu.* The militia was marching.

isla 2. Island.

isleta 2. Small island.

istoria 2. History. Also **historia.**

Istoria Sagrada 2. Bible history. Also **Historia Sagrada.**

itak See **utak.**

Italia 2. Italy.

Italianu 2. Italian (m). Also **Italiana** (f).

itbana 2. Quilting seam.

iteng 1,2. Pick, break off, esp. from flowers, fruit, bananas, etc., banana bunch. Cf. **Tife'.** *Katgayi i bihu ni iteng chotda.* Carry the banana bunch for the old man. *Hu iteng i flores gi kanton chalan.* I picked the flower beside the road.

itmás Best, superlative. Cf. **Mas.** *Guam i itmas dankolo na isla giya Marianas.* Guam is the biggest island in the Marianas.

ito' 2. Type of fish-clarias batrachus (family clariidae). Fresh-water catfishes.

iya Article, used with geographical place names and with emphatic pronouns. *Dankolo iya Honolulu.*

Honolulu is big. *Taiguenao iya hagu.* That which is like you.

iya' By the way, incidentally. An expletive used to begin a new thought. Short form of *hiya'. Iya' para bai hu hanao agupa'.* By the way, I am going tomorrow.

Iyang Nickname for Juana.

iyo- 2. Belong to (something, someone) —used with possessive pronouns. *Iyo-ku este.* This is mine. *Hayi gai-iyo enao na tenda?* Who owns that store?

iyon 2. Belong to. Cf. **Iyo.** *Iyon Maria ayu na lepblo.* That book belongs to Mary.

iyon lahi 2. Belonging to males, penis.

iyon palao'an 2. Belonging to females, vagina, female sex organ. Cf. **Chada', bebe'.**

Julio 2. July. Cf. **Semo.** Pronounced hulio.

Junio 2. June. Cf. **Mananaf.** Pronounced hunio.

ka K—letter.

ka- Have something (prefix)—usually prefixed to a modifier. Stress falls on *ka-* in affixed form, there is. *Kao guaha kamaolek gi gima'-mu?* Do you have something good at your house? *Kalaña i magagu-hu.* I have some oil on my clothes. *Kafache' i chalan.* There is mud on the road.

kabales 2. Complete, brought to completion or perfection, finish, fully realized, intact. Cf. **Kumplidu.**

kabán 2. Burlap sack—one-hundred pound. Cf. **Kostat, ganggoche, piku.**

kabaña 2. Cottage, hut.

kabayeria 2. Cavalry.

kabayerisa 2. Stable.

kabayeros 2. Type of plant-caesalpinia pulcherrima. Pride-of-barbados.

kabayeru 2. Gentleman, horseman, knight, man of good family, man of good breeding, aristocrat. Also **kabayera** (f).

kabayeti 2. Cross-beam—of a house roof or ceiling.

kabayeti 2. Attic, place above the ceiling. Cf. **Kamaroti.**

kabayon katpenteru 2. Sawhorse.

kabayon tasi 2. Type of fish-hippocampus. Sea horse.

kabayu 2. Horse, pony.

kabayu 2. Trestle; a braced frame serving as a support, as for a table, sawhorse.

kabesa 2. Head—seat of the brain, brain, skull, mind. *Mahetok kabesan ilu-mu.* The skull of your head is hard.

kabesada 2. Stagger, totter, walk or stand unsteadily.

kabesiyu 2. Foreman, headman, leader. *Si Jose kabesiyon este na grupu.* Joe is the foreman of this group.

kabilosu 2. Brainy, smart, intelligent, brilliant, clever. Also **kabilosa** (f). Cf. **Tomtom, malate'.**

kabisera 2. Beam—for roof of a building.

kabisera 2. Yard (of a house), gable—of house, head of the table.

kábiyon 2. Mosquito net.

kabo' 2. Curve. From English through Japanese kaabo. (S)

kabo' 2. Share—of stock.

kabon Negro 2. Type of plant-arenga pinnata. Sugar palm.

kabosi Cf. **Akabosi.**

kabrón 2. Cuckold, one who permits too many liberties. Also **kabrona** (f).

kabu 2. Corporal, rank in the military service. Also **koporat.**

kacha' 1. Husk (coconut), husking; tool for husking.

kachang 2. Lackluster, colorless, describes the meat of betel nut when it is not firm and has a pale or dull color. Cf. **Changa.**

kachet 1. Dress up, put make-up on, apply cosmetics. Cf. **Katsa.**

káchido' 2. Movie, motion picture, cinema, theater. (S) Cf. **Mubi.**

kacho' 2. Type of fish-katsuwonus pelamis, gymnosarda nuda, white tuna, tuna.

kada [æ] Every time, each, each time.

kada dia Daily, every day, each day, day to day, one day after another. Cf. **Kada ha'ani.**

kada ha'ani Every day, daily, each day, day to day, one day after another. Cf. **Kada dia.**

kada ratu Frequently, usually, almost always, every time. *Kada ratu hu ngelo' i neni gi maigo'-ña.* I frequently peeked at the baby while he was sleeping.

kada sakkan Annual, each year, yearly.

kadabet 2. Clumsy, frail.

kadabet 2. Corpse, cadaver.

kádada' [æ] **2.** Short, brief, not long.

kádagan [æ] **2.** Type of plant-similar in taste to broccoli, used in cooking *eskabeche.*

kadena 2. Chain, bracelet, necklace.

kaderas 2. Hip. Cf. **Lommo.**

kaderas 2. Carcass.

kadidak 1,2. Tickle, titillate. Tickling.

kadidakon 2. Ticklish.

ká'dideng [æ] **2.** Hop, skip (with one leg), hopscotch—type of, limp.

kadidok 2. Sharp. Also **akadidok.**

kado' [æ] **2.** Pretend, feign, sham, make believe. Cf. **Pritende, fa'-.** *Kado' taigue yo'.* Pretend that I am not here.

kado' mama'maolek 2. Hypocrite, dissembler.

kaduka 2. Lunatic, demented, fool, idiot, crazy, (f). Cf. **Atmariao.** Cf. **Bruta, loka.**

kaduku 2. Lunatic, demented, fool, idiot, crazy, insane. Also **kaduka.** Cf. **Atmariao.**

kafé 2. Type of plant-coffea arabica. Coffee.

kafetera 2. Coffee pot.

kafetiria 2. Cafeteria.

kafo' [æ] **2.** Type of tree—pandanus, screw pine. Fruit bats feed on its fruit. Cf. **Akgak, pahong.**

kaguan 2. Decrease, lessening, shortening. *Kaguan i balen kareta-hu.* The worth of my car decreased.

kaguan 2. Gap, hole between two things through which one can see.

ka'guas [æ] **1.** Scratch, scrape—with claws or nails. Cf. **Kaku.** *I katu ha ka'guas i kannai-hu.* The cat scratched my hand.

kaha 2. Safe, steel box, chest—a place to put valuable things.

kahao 2. Type of fish-family leiognathidae. Soapys.

kahat 1. Lift, raise up, hoist or raise with a tackle, promote or raise salary, build house. Cf. **Hatsa, sa'ang.**

kahat [æ] **2.** Stalk, still-hunt, sneak, move furtively or slinkingly, creep, steal (so as to be unobserved). Cf. **Sikat.**

kahatgue [æ] 1. Stalk, still-hunt, sneak, move furtively or slinkingly, creep, steal (so as to be unobserved). Cf. **Kahat.**

kahaya 2. Saved, freed, helped, redeemed, rescued from danger. Cf. **Libre, ayuda.**

ka'he 2. Stuffed crab.

kaheru 2. Treasurer, cashier. Cf. **Tresurero.**

kahet 2. Type of plant-citrus aurantium. Orange. Also citrus sinensis, sweet orange.

kahet dankolo 2. Type of plant. A citrus fruit smaller than *kahet ma'gas.*

kahet dikike' 1. Type of plant-citrus reticulata. Tangerine.

kahet ma'gas 2. Type of plant-citrus grandis. Grapefruit. Literally ruler's orange.

kahida 2. Veranda, porch. Cf. **Baranda.**

kahita 2. Box, carton, case. Cf. **Kahon.**

kahlang [æ] 1. Hang—by suspending oneself from something, suspend, cling onto (something) in order to suspend oneself. Cf. **Kana'.** *Hu kahlang yo' gi ramas hayu.* I hung from the branch of a tree (by suspending).

kahlao 2. Type of plant-microsorum scolopendria. Type of bush—used for medicine.

kahna 2. Hex, heckle, wishing failure upon someone; sorcerer. *Kahna na taotao gue'.* He is a person who can hex. *I kahna-mu na ti hu danche i paluma.* Your heckling made me not hit the bird.

kahnayi 1. Hex, bewitch, cast a spell on.

kahon 2. Box, carton, case, drawer. Cf. **Kahita.**

kahon ais 2. Refrigerator, ice box. Also **ais boks.**

kahon balotu 2. Ballot box.

kahon limosna 2. Collection box, donation box—usually found in church.

kahulo' 2. Get up, climb up. Cf. **Feddos, ekilo'.** *Kumahulo' yo' gi tronkon hayu.* I climbed up the tree.

kahulo'gue 1. Climb on top of, get up on (something) for something. Cf. **Feddos, kahulo'.** *Hu kahulo'gue i ladera.* I climbed up the mountain.

Kai' Nickname for Francisca.

kaiako' 2. Gun powder, dynamite, TNT, explosive powder. (S) Cf. **Potbula.**

kaiha 2. Takes a long time, long way, long time. *Kaiha i batkon aire magi.* The plane won't get here for a long time. *Kaiha yo' matto gi karera-hu.* It's a long way to go to my destination. *Kaiha bula.* It takes a long time to fill up.

kaikai 1. Move from, cause to move. *Hu kaikai yo' gi siya.* I moved from the chair.

kaimán 2. Crocodile, alligator.

kairo' 2. Toad, frog. Also **kahero'.** (R) Cf. **Irana.**

kaiyio' 2. All clear—after bombardment. (S)

ka'ka' 2. Crack, crevice, fissure, fracture, cleft, break partially, open in chinks, become fissured, be fractured.

kákagong 2. Fontanel, an opening or soft spot on a baby's head.

káka'guas [æ] 2. Scratcher, capable of scratching, claws.

kakaguates 2. Type of plant-arachis hypogaea. Peanut.

kákahna [æ] 2. Witch doctor. Also **kakana.**

kakak [æ] 2. Hawk up—the sound heard when clearing the throat, as in hawking up phlegm. Also **katka.**

kaka'ka' [æ] 2. Type of fish-family lutjanidae. Snappers.

kákalamten [æ] 2. Able-bodied, capable of doing work. Cf. **Kalamten.**

kákale' [æ] 2. Stem—of fruit, flower, leaf, etc., vine. Cf. **Kakayu.**

kákalek [æ] 2. Bitter, sour, tart, acid.

kákalom 2. Come into, enter. *Mangakakalom siha gi sagua' Umatac.* They were coming into the Umatac channel.

kakalotes 2. Corn cob.

ka'ka'mata' [æ] 2. Cracked skin, cracked rubber as a result of rotting.

kákana [æ] 2. Witch doctor, witch crafter, one who performs witchcraft. (R) Also **kakahna.**

kakáo 2. Cacao, cocoa—a South American tree of the chocolate family.

kakaronde' 2. Hop—while spinning, like a playing top, skip around, not steady. Cf. **Kakaroti.** *Kakaronde' i* *tolompo-ku.* My top hopped while spinning.

kakaroño' 2. Blunted point of spinning top.

kakaroti 2. Hop—while spinning, like a playing top, fickle, rascal. Cf. **Kakaronde'.** *Kakaroti i tolompo-ku.* My top hopped while spinning. *Kakaroti hao, lai.* You are a rascal, friend.

kákatot [æ] 2. Itchy sensation in mouth from eating wild yams or other foods. Also **hahatot.**

kákattan 2. Go east, move east, eastward movement. Cf. **Kattan.** *Kao un sodda' i kareta-mu anai kakattan hao?* Did you find your car when you went east?

kákaya 2. Go south, move south, southward movement. Cf. **Haya.** *Kakaya si Maria para u fañule' flores.* Mary went south to get some flowers.

kákayu 2. Stem, midrib of a leaf. Cf. **Kakale'.**

kaki [æ] 2. Khaki.

kakkak [æ] 2. Type of bird-ixobrychus sinensis, Chinese least bitten.

kakko' 2. Looks, appearance, posture, position. (S)

kakno' [æ] 2. Eater, glutton—with a craving for a particular food, one who snitches or eats another person's food. *I hilitai kakno' chada'.* The lizard is a glutton for eggs. *Kakno' hao kande.* You are a glutton for candy.

káksaka Expletive. (Taboo) A very derogatory term, probably a corruption of a taboo English loanword.

kakte [æ] 2. Noisy person, cry-baby, one who makes noise often, one who cries at slight provocation.

kaku [æ] 1,2. To claw, tickle, scratch viciously. Cf. **Ka'guas.**

kalabasa 2. Long squash. Cf. **Kondot.**

kalabera 2. Skeleton, skull.

kalabosu 2. Jail, prison. Cf. **Presu.**

kalachucha 2. Type of plant-plumeria obtusifolia. Plumeria.

kálaguak 2. Side (portion of body), from hip bone to arm pit.

kalahi 2. Huge pot—shaped like a helmet, vat--used for cooking or mixing liquids in large quantities, frying pan. Also **kalai.**

kalái 2. Huge pot. Also **kalahi.**

ka'lak [æ] 2. Healthy looking, pleasing to the sight, attractive. *I asagua-hu ka'lak na palao'an.* My wife is a healthy looking, attractive woman.

kalakas [æ] 2. Revulsion—expression of distaste, dirty, uncleanliness, filthy. *Kalakas na inapplacha' lugat.* Yike, what a dirty place. *Mampos hao kalakas na patgon.* You are a very dirty child.

kalaktos 2. Sharp, keen, acute.

kalalang [æ] 2. Type of bird-numenius madagascariensis, long-billed curlew.

kalamái 2. Corn pudding—made with corn flour, coconut milk and sugar; coconut gelatin.

kalamasa [æ] 2. Type of plant-cucurbita moschata. Squash. Or, legenaria siceraria. Gourd, pumpkin, squash.

kalamelu 2. Caramel. Also **karamelu.**

kalamendo' 2. Type of plant-tamarindus indica. Tamarind. Also **kamalendo.**

kalamle 2. Cramped, convulsed, having spasms. *Kalamle i addeng-hu.* My foot cramped.

kalamot [æ] 1. Gulp, swallow whole. Also **galamokmok, kalamok.** Cf. **Galamok.**

kalamten [æ] 2. Start motion, set to action, move. *Hu na'kalamten i makina.* I turned on the engine. *Kalamten i malangu gi katre.* The patient moved on the bed.

kalamya 2. Dexterous, agile, nimble, quick. Cf. **Makalamya.**

kalankangi 1. Shake out, as salt, sugar, pepper, etc. on or into something. *Hu kalankangi i na'-hu didide' asiga.* I shook out a little salt on my food.

kálanke' [æ] 2. Little finger.

kalang [æ] 1. Hang. *Hu kalang i litratu gi liga.* I hung the picture on the wall.

kalang [æ] Like, such as. Also **kalan, kulang.** *Kalang gatbo este na flores.* This flower is like perfection.

kalang matai 2. Ghastly, deathlike.

kalapang 2. Bad starch—starch which leaves clothing spotted when used during ironing.

kalaskas [æ] 2. Rattle, crackling (of dry leaves), rustle—of dry grass or leaves, any rustling sound. Also **kaskas.**

kalaton [æ] 2. Rough (surface), scabrous, uneven surface, not smooth. Cf. *Bastos*.

kala'u [æ] 2. Messy, unkempt hair, untidy, disheveled, bedraggled, wrinkled (clothes). Cf. **Makalehlo**.

kalek [æ] 1. Cause dizziness, dizziness caused from taking lime with betel nut. *Ha kalek yo' i pigua'.* The betel nut made me dizzy. *Kinalek i patgon ni afok.* The lime made the child dizzy (as by chewing).

kaleku 1. Scrape, scrape surface, scratch surface—for purpose of cleaning. *I nana ha kaleku i hineksa' gi halom la'uya.* The mother scraped the rice from the bottom of the pot.

Kalen Nickname for Candido.

kalendario 2. Calendar.

kalentadu 2. Warm, tepid, of moderately high temperature.

kalentura 2. Fever, to have a fever.

kaleru 2. Container for lime used for mixing with betel nut.

kales 2. Chalice.

kalesa 2. Carriage, buggy.

kalesa 2. An obscene gesture using the middle finger pointing upward.

kalibre 2. Caliber.

kálile' [æ] 1. Petiole, stem of leaf.

kallo [æ] 2. Loose, lax, not tight or rigid, slacken. Also **kalu**.

kálulot 2. Finger (generic term), legs of crab.

kálulot talo' 2. Middle finger.

kalumnia 1. Assume, suppose, have in mind, take for granted. Slander. Cf. **Suponi, asuma**.

kama 2. Bed, cot, bedstead, resting place, sleeping place, bedridden, confined to bed while sick. Cf. **Katre**. *Mamahan yo' dos kama giya Guam.* I bought two beds on Guam. *Kumama yo' un simana.* I was sick in bed for one week.

kamachili 2. Type of plant-pithecellobium dulce.

káma'gas [æ] 2. Second in command, assistant to boss, lower level leader.

kámalen 2. Barn, a very large building for storage.

ka'mang 2. Type of plant-hibiscus abelmoschus. Also **ka'mang unai, ka'mang tiget**. Type of flower.

kamarera 2. Waitress, chambermaid, stewardess.

kamareru 2. Waiter, chamberlain, steward.

kamaroti 2. Attic, place above the ceiling. Cf. **Kamalen**.

kambrai 2. Type of cloth, chambray.

kameks 2. Comics, cartoon, comic strip.

kameyu 2. Camel, dromedary.

kámia 2. Type of flower. Ginger—white or red.

kamisita 2. Baby's undershirt.

kamisita 2. Half-slip—female undergarment.

kamisola 2. Petticoat, underskirt, slip.

kamkam [æ] 1. Jerk loose, loosen, pry loose. Cf. **Gomgom**.

kamma' 1,2. Cut with sickle. (S) Sickle—an agricultural implement consisting of a curved metal blade with a handle.

kampai' 2. Toast (in drinking), skoal, bottoms up. An exclamation pledging health in drinking. (Fr. Japanese). (S)

kampamento 2. Camp.

kampana 2. Bell.

kampanayon 2. Belfry, belltower.

kampaniya 2. Small bell. Cf. **Pandereta**.

kampañeru 2. Bell-ringer.

kampo 2. Space, room, area in which to work or stay. *Kao guaha kampo gi gima'-mu?* Is there room at your house?

kampo 2. Camp.

kampo' 1. Bombard, shelling—from heavy artillery. (S) *I batkon gera ha kampo' halom i tano'.* The battle ship bombarded the land.

kamten [æ] 2. Thief (polite), restless, nosey, active in a mischievous way. Cf. **Embilikeru**. *Kamten i neni gi maigo'-ña.* The baby was restless while he was sleeping. *Kamten hao na taotao.* You are a thief.

kamuten nanoffe 2. Type of plant-taeniophyllum mariannensis. (?).

kamuti 2. Type of plant-ipomoea batatas. Sweet potato.

kamyo 1,2. Grate (coconut). Coconut grater.

kana' [æ] 1,2. Hang, hang up, suspend. Cf. **Kalang**. Drooping, sagging. *Hu kana' i magagu siha gi talen manala'.* I hung up the clothes on the clothesline.

kana' fistula 2. Type of plant-cassia fistula. Golden shower.

kana' ha' Almost, nearly. Also kana', kanna' katna'.

kana' magagu 2. Clothes hanger.

kanario 2. Canary.

kanastra 2. Woven basket, esp. used for food container.

kandalu 1,2. Fasten (with a lock), lock in or out. Lock, padlock.

kandaroma 2. Type of plant-acacia farnesiana.

kande [æ] 2. Candy.

kandela 2. Candle.

kandelaria 2. Chandelier.

kandet 2. Lamp, flashlight, kerosene lamp. Cf. Fallot.

kandet gas 2. Gaslight, gas lantern.

kandidatu 2. Candidate, nominee, applicant, political contestant, aspirant.

kandidatura 2. Candidacy.

kandileru 2. Candle holder.

kanela 2. Type of spice—similar to cinnamon. Cinnamon.

kanifes 2. Thin, flimsy, not thick, sheer.

kaniya 2. Shin.

kankarakere' 2. Kick-the-can (game). (S)

kánkire' 2. Can opener. (S) Cf. Baban lata.

kankong [æ] 2. Type of plant-ipomoea aquatica.

kanna' [æ] Nearly, almost. Also kana', kanaha'. *Kanna' poddong yo' nigap gi tronkon hayu.* I nearly fell from the tree yesterday.

kannai 2. Hand, arm (up to shoulder), dial (of clock or watch).

kannat 2. Ditch, trench, pit, canal, channel.

kannat hanom 2. Rain gutter.

kanno' 1. Eat something, devour something, consume something, gnaw on something. Must always take an object. *Hafa kinanno'-mu?* What did you eat?

kannu'on 2. Coconut—having sweet husk while still green, edible, fit to be eaten as food. Combination of *kanno'* plus -on.

kanoa 2. Trough—for pig's food, feeding place of pigs.

kanoa 2. Canoe.

kanóniku 2. Register book, record book maintained by the church where all important data are kept, esp. records or birth dates.

kansadu 2. Tired, fatigued, exhausted, wearied, haggard, worn out. Barren, infertile, esp. worn out land. Cf. Pasadu, tufai.

kansela 1. Cancel, delete, render invalid.

kanselasión 2. Cancellation.

kanset 2. Cancer.

kansunsiyu 2. Shorts, undershorts. (R) Also katsunsiyu. Cf. Saromata'.

kanta 1,2. Hum, chant, sing. Song, chant. *Hu kanta i kanta.* I sang the song.

kantan Chamorrita 2. Folk song—Chamorro.

kántanes [æ] 2. Type of chicken—resembling bantam. Also kantones.

kántaru 2. Container (large can), such as garbage can, oil drum.

kanteha 1. Go around the edge.

kantidá 2. Plentiful, bountiful, many, lots of, bulk. *Kantida na taotao gi miteng.* There are many people at the meeting.

kantiku 2. Hymn.

kantina 2. Canteen, wine cellar, tavern, bar.

kantít 2. Cliff, bluff.

kanto 2. Edge, border, brim. *I kanto gi lamasa.* At the edge of the table. *Kanton tasi.* At the edge of the sea (sea-shore).

kanton langet 2. Horizon, limit of one's imagination.

kanton tasi 2. Seashore, beach. Cf. Chepchop tasi, chepchop unai.

kantones See kantanes.

kantora 2. Singer, vocalist (f).

kantores 2. Choir, chorus. Cf. Koru.

kantót 2. Singer, vocalist (m).

kanu 2. American (m). Short form for *Amerikanu.* Also kana (f).

kanya 1. Move—something from one place to another.

kányase' 2. Hairpin. (S) Cf. Chiget, atkiya.

kaña 2. Field (used for planting), garden.

kañada 2. Valley, gulch, canyon.

káñamu 2. Manila rope—made out of abaca.

kañón 2. Cannon, gun (heavy artillery), canyon.

kañonasu 2. Bombard—with artillery.

kañoneru 2. Artilleryman, gunner. Also kañonera (f).

kañutu 2. Gun barrel.

kangga 2. Top rack of a *batangga* (sled) used for carrying fragile items.

kanggrena 2. Gangrenous, gangrene.

kánghelon 2. Horn (of animal), gore, antler.

kao Question marker (general). *Kao para un hanao?* Are you going? *Kao bula i tasi pa'go?* Is it a high tide now? *Kao guaha gima'-mu?* Do you have a house? *Kao guaha nai malak Hawaii hao?* Have you been to Hawaii?

kaohao 2. Storage chest, box, esp. for safekeeping of possessions.

kaosa 2. Court case, lawsuit, a situation involving a problem.

kaosadót 2. Plaintiff, the one who takes someone to court.

kaotiba 2. Be captured, be charmed, be fascinated.

kaotibu 2. Captive.

kapa 2. Cape, cloak, wrap, mantel, overdress, shawl.

kapa de la raina 2. Type of plant-clitoreaternatea. A type of vine.

kapás 2. Capable, able, fitted for, suited for, capacious, competent.

kapasidát 2. Capacity, ability. Cf. Abilidat.

kapát 2. Reduced work load, out of work. *Yanggen kapat che'cho'-mu espiha yo'.* When you are out of work, look for me.

kapble 1,2. Cablegram, telegram, send or receive message by cablegram.

kapitalisa 1. Capitalize.

kapitan 2. Captain.

kapitani 1. Command, lead, command for, lead to. *Ha kapitani i batko.* He commanded the ship.

kapitát 2. Capitol, capital.

kapítulu 2. Chapter.

kapiya 2. Chapel, shrine.

káporat [æ] 2. Bodily, corporeal.

kappon 1,2. Castrate, capon, eunuch.

kaprichosu 2. Capricious, whimsical, changeable, fickle.

kaprichu 2. Caprice, unrestricted choice, free will.

kápsulas [æ] 2. Pill. Also katsulas.

kapua 2. Type of plant-polyscias fruticosa. A type of flower.

kapuchinu 2. Capuchin, Franciscan friar.

kápurat [æ] 2. Foreman, boss.

kaputi 2. One fails to win a point in tres siete (card game).

kaputón 2. Raincoat, slicker, poncho. Cf. Pancho.

kapuyo' 2. Bud (of plant), flower bud.

kara 2. Face. Cf. Fasu, maskaran fasu.

kara' 2. Broke, bankrupt, destitute. (S)

kara' 2. Bullet shell, shell casing. (S) Cf. Kaskara.

karabáo 2. Water buffalo, carabao.

karahu 2. Mild expletive, heck, baloney, phooey. Lit. 'My eye.'

karái 2. Turtle shell, stiff plastic, plexiglass.

karakót 2. Type of shell—genus cyprea.

karamanset Euphemism for *karahu.*

karamba 2. Great scott, gosh, golly, for crying out loud.

karambot 2. Gee whiz, by golly, darn it, heck (interj.). Cf. Karanchot.

karanchot 2. Darn it, heck, by golly (interj.). Cf. Karambot.

karate' 1,2. Karate, type of Japanese judo.

karera 2. Race, a contest of speed as in running, walking, rowing, etc. Cf. Acha'ikak.

karera 2. Journey, voyage, trip, travel. Cf. Rumbo.

kareta 2. Vehicle, car, automobile, bull cart. Cf. Tumobet, sahyan.

karetada 2. Cartload.

karetan chíchechek 2. Legendary vehicle that makes a squeaking noise. Is said to go out at night, and is considered haunted. Is often referred to in stories of the *taotaomo'na.* Is also responsible for the cracks and fissures on the flat rocks by the seashore.

karetatibu 2. Industrious, active. *Hayi mas karetatibu komo ti si Pedro?* Who is the most industrious if not Pedro?

karetiya 2. Wheelbarrow, shopping cart, spool.

karetiyan hilu 2. Spool of thread.

karetón 2. Wagon.

karí 2. Curry.

karidát 2. Charity, alms.

kariñosu 2. Affectionate, loving (m). Also **kariñosa** (f).

kariñu 1,2. Caress, petting, fondness, affection, tenderness. *I nana ha kariñu i neni-ña.* The mother caressed her baby. *Ha kariñu i palao'an.* He petted the woman.

karisu 2. Type of plant-phragmites karka. Bamboo—swamp type. Cf. **Pi'ao.**

karít 2. Rut, track of wheel, groove.

karitatibu 2. Charitable.

kariteru 2. Rascal, rogue, one who drives a *kareta.* Also **karitera** (f).

karitét 2. Spool of thread—large.

karu 2. Flat car—a platform railroad car for freight.

kas [æ] 2. Cash.

kasa 1. Cock (firearm), cover a bet. *Na'siguru na un kasa i paki antes de un fanapunta.* Be sure to cock the gun before you aim it. *Ha kasa si Pedro i aposta-ku.* Pedro covered my bet.

kasadules 2. Chaser (in hunting), one who chases the animal to an open area to be shot by the hunter—usually a dog.

kasamiento 2. Marriage, married, wedding. Cf. **Akkamo'.** *Gaige yo' gi kasamiento na estao.* I am in the marriage state.

kasáo 2. Married person, spouse, married, not single.

kasao 2. Cry, bawl, sob, moan, weep, whimper, wail, to cry out-with a loud, full sound. Cf. **Tanges, kati.** *Kumasao i patgon sa' ma'amot ni kande.* The child bawled because the candy was taken from him.

kaserola 2. Sauce pan, frying pan.

kasi About, approximately, nearly, almost, probably, maybe, perhaps, more or less. *Kasi un año esta ti umali'e' hit.* About a year since we saw each other. *Kasi si David humanao nigap asta i espitat.* Probably David went to the hospital yesterday.

kasinu 2. Type of card game.

kasiyas 2. Coop, chicken coop, brooding place for birds.

kaskahu 2. Gravel—coarse, coral, crushed stone, pebble. Also **kaskao.**

káskara 2. Shell (bullet), shell—of animal, crab, etc., casing of ammunition. Cf. **Kara', karakot.**

kaskaran chada' 2. Egg shell. Cf. **Lassas chada'.**

kaskas [æ] 2. Rustle, soft sounds, rustling. *Kaskas i hagon siha anai mangguaife i manglo'.* The leaves rustled when the wind blew.

kasko 2. Empty, nothing, broke, used esp. referring to money when gambling. Cf. **Hokkok.**

kasoe 2. Type of plant-anacardium occidentale. Cashew tree, cashew nut.

kaspa 2. Crispy, snapped off easily. Also **paska.**

kaspa 2. Dandruff, skin peeling off caused from dryness, as in sunburn.

kassas [æ] 1. Scratch, as when one itches.

kasse [æ] 1. Tease, vex, harass, irritate by petty requests, or by jests and raillery. *Hu kasse i ga'lagu.* I teased the dog.

kastaneta 2. Castanet.

kastiga 1. Punish, force to labor. Cf. **Fueges, aña, galuti.**

kastigáo 2. Punishable, liable to punishment, prisoner.

kastigu 2. Punishment. Cf. **Pena.**

Kastilianu 2. Castilian (m). Also **Kastiliana** (f).

kastiyu 2. Castle, fort.

kastom 2. Costume.

kasu 2. Case, matter, event, point.

kasualidát 2. Casualty.

kasungái 2. Large staple—used for joining heavy pieces of lumber.

kat 2. Cot. Cf. **kama.**

katálagu 2. Catalogue.

katan See **kattan.**

Katbario 2. Calvary, place of the cross, suffering, tribulation.

katbon 2. Charcoal, coal.

katboneru 2. Collier, charcoal vendor (m). Also **katbonera** (f).

katbonkulu 2. Carbuncle.

katbureta 2. Carburetor.

katderón 2. Large kettle, calderon.

katderu 2. Tub, large pan.

katdes 2. Type of plant-moringa oleifera. (?) Cf. **Maronggai.**

105

katdinát 2. Cardinal.

katdiritu 2. Kettle—small, small pot.

katdiyu 2. Food concoction made with sauteed onions seasoned with vinegar and salt.

katdumen abeas 2. Swarm of bees.

katdumi 2. Crowd, group, school (of fish), flock. Cf. **Gurupu, inetnon, aliansa.**

katen chiba 2. Bleat.

katga 1,2. Carry, transfer, haul, transport. Cf. **Loffan.**

katgaderu 2. Sinker—used on fishing line, one or that which is capable of carrying, carrier.

katgadót 2. Loader, stevedore, carrier, mover. Cf. **Katgadu.**

katgadu 2. Overloaded. Carrier, one who does the carrying, one who carries a load, porter.

katgamento 2. Loading—cargo. *Duranten i katgamento mumalangu si Antonio.* While loading the cargo, Tony became sick.

katgat 2. Fishing line—nylon. Also **gugat.**

katgo 2. Commission, charge, order, burden. *Mana'i yo' katgo-ku gi gima'.* I was given a responsibility at home.

katgueti 2. Annoyance, culpable—permitting others to do wrong, permissive--overly. Also **atkagueti.** Cf. **Estotbo.**

kati 2. Sob, scream, shout, weep, outcry, cry. Cf. **Tanges.**

katigurát 2. Category.

katisismo 2. Catechism book, a manual for catechizing, esp. for religious instruction.

katiyi 1. Cry for, weep for, call for. Cf. **Tangse.** *Katiyi i guaka ya u fanmatto.* Call for the cattle so they will come.

katkat 2. Clear throat. Cf. **Kokkok.** *Basta kumatkat.* Stop clearing your throat. Also **kakak.**

katkula 1. Calculate, estimate, compute.

katkulasión 2. Calculation, estimate. Cf. **Katkulu.**

katkulu 2. Calculation, estimate. Cf. **Katkulasion.**

katma 2. Calm, no breeze, not breezy.

katna 2. Good bait, bait which fish are especially attracted to.

katna 2. Good fishing. *Gof katna gi painge.* Good fishing last night.

katna' ** Almost, nearly. Also **kana', kanna', kana ha'.

katnada 2. Bait, lure.

katnadayi 1. Set out bait for, set out lure for. *Hu katnadayi i guihan ni satdinas siha.* I set out bait for the fish with sardines.

katne 2. Meat, flesh, (esp. refers to mammal's flesh).

katnen babui 2. Pork.

katnen guaka 2. Beef.

katnen kinilu 2. Mutton.

katnen notte 2. Corned beef.

kátokcha' [æ] 2. Fishing—by spear, fish--catch by spear. (R) Cf. **Tokcha'.** *Kumakatokcha' yo' nigap.* I was spear fishing yesterday.

Katóliku 2. Catholic.

Katolisismo 2. Catholicism.

katot [æ] 2. Type of plant-claoxylon marianum. A type of tree. Cf. **Panao.**

katot [æ] 2. Sensation in mouth caused by eating certain foods. Also **kakatot.**

katotse 2. Fourteen.

katpenteria 2. Carpentry.

katpenteru 2. Carpenter.

katpeta 2. Wallet, briefcase, suitcase. Cf. **Balakbak.**

katre 2. Bed, cot.

katsa 1. Dress up, put make-up on, apply cosmetics. Cf. **Kachet.**

katsada 2. Road—gravel, street. Cf. **Chalan kaskao.**

katset 2. Prison, jail.

kátsulas 2. Pill, tablet (medicine). Also **kapsulas.**

katsulas 2. Cartridge shell—the brass shell portion of a bullet or artillery shell. Cf. **Kara'.**

katsunes 2. Pants, trousers, underwear (f), panties.

katsunesitu 2. Type of fish-family carcharhinidae. Baby shark.

katsunsiyu 2. Undershorts (for males).

katta 2. Letter, correspondence, a written or printed communication of a direct or personal nature, mail.

kattan 2. East (in Guam and Rota), north (in Saipan). Also **katan.**

kattan balaha 2. Cards (playing).

kattayi 1. Write letter (to someone). Cf. **Katta, tuge'.** *Hu kattayi hao sesso.* I often write to you.

kattiya 2. Primer, elementary text.

kattón 2. Carton, cardboard box, packing case, paper box.

kattuchu 2. Clip of bullets, bundle. *Mamahan yo' un kattuchon bala.* I bought a clip of bullets. *Guaha un kattuchon siboyas tetehnan.* There is one bundle of onions left.

kattuchu 2. Stringer, to put on a stringer—as to put fish on a stringer.

katu [æ] **2.** Cat, kitten.

katupat 2. Woven container used for cooking rice, a box-like container woven from coconut leaves, into which rice is placed, then submerged in boiling water for cooking.

katupat 2. Slingshot, as the one used by David.

katurai 2. Type of plant-sesbania grandiflora. Type of tree—both flowers and pods are edible and serve as a laxative.

ka'u [æ] **2.** Bean pole—usually three poles forming a tripod.

kayada 2. Silent, quiet, calm, slackening —of wind or rain.

kayada 2. Slackening. Cf. **Kallo.**

kayáo 2. Subside, calm down. *Yanggen kayao i manglo' ta fanhanao.* When the wind subsides, we will go.

kayi 1,2. Path, street, trail, road, alley. Cf. **Kayon.**

kayon 1,2. Path, street, trail, road, alley. Cf. **Kayi.**

kayos 2. Callus.

kayu 2. Word used to address a person with same name. For example, Juan addressing another Juan may use *kayu* as form of direct address.

ke Well, so, in such wise, in that case. *Ke, munga mafaisen siha.* Well, don't ask them. *Ke, facho'cho' ya un gaisalape'.* So, work and you will have some money.

ke- Try to do (something). *Hu kedanche i bola ni panak.* I tried to hit the ball with the bat. *Ma na'kehalom i ga'lagu gi gima'.* They tried to make the dog go inside the house. *Hu na'kesaga i che'lu-hu lahi gi gima'.* I tried to make my brother stay at the house.

kebra 2. Calamity, disaster, to go wrong, bankrupt. Cf. **Sala'.** *I pakyo ha na'kebra i kosecha-ku.* The typhoon brought disaster to my harvest. *Kebra todu i planu-hu.* All my plans went wrong. *Manhungok yo' ni kebra.* I heard about the disaster.

kebranta 1. Overwork, cause to labor too much, overdo.

kechap 2. Soy sauce, catsup.

kéchule' 1. Try to take. Cf. **Chule'.**

kédanche 1. Try to hit, try to guess.

kedanchiyi 2. Figure out—a riddle or puzzle.

kedera 1. Hamstring, cut ligaments (so as to cripple animal). (R) Cf. *Deskareta.*

keha 2. Report, charge of misconduct against (one) to a superior, complaint, sue. Cf. **Fa'aila', kehayi.** *Kumeha i patgon gi ma'estro pot i bidan Jose.* The child reported what Joe did to the teacher.

kéhatsa 1. Lift—try to, about to raise. Cf. **Hatsa.**

kehayi 1. Report on, perfer charge of misconduct against (one) to a superior, tattle, tell on, blab, sue, complain. Cf. **Fa'aila', keha.** *Ha kehayi yo' gi ma'estro anai malagu yo' gi eskuela.* He reported me to the teacher when I ran away from school. *Ha kehayi i patgon.* He complained about the child.

kek 2. Cake. Cf. **Broas.**

keke Begin to, start to, about to (do something), try to. Auxiliary used in constructions with specific objects. Cf. **Kumeke, mangeke, ke-.** A reduplicated form of *ke-.* *Hafa kumeke'ilek-ña?* What is he trying to say? *Hafa un kekecho'gue?* What are you about to do? *Hu keketuge' i katta.* I'm starting to write the letter *Kumekemaolek.* It's getting good. *Pa'go hu keketutuhon i che'cho'-hu.* I'm beginning to start my work now.

kélachai 1. Finish—try to, about to finish, about to take all. Cf. **Lachai.**

kélaguen 2. Type of food. Dish made of fish, chicken, venison or beef, salt, red pepper, and lemon juice.

kéli'e' 1. See—try to, about to see. Cf. **Li'e'.**

ken sabe Doubtful, I doubt it.

kepes 2. Nightcap, cap.

késangan 1. Say—try to, about to say. Cf. Sangan.

kesnudu 2. Nude, naked (m). Also kesnuda (f).

kesu 2. Cheese.

ketu 2. Keep still, be quiet, shut up. Quiet. Also kietu.

kétungo' 1. Know—try to, about to know. Cf. Tungo'.

ke'yao 2. Limp (when walking), loose-jointed (when walking).

kéyute' 1. Throw away—try to. Cf. Yute'.

ki ora What time.

ki sabes None of one's business. Ki sabes hao nu enao. That is none of your business.

kiba' 2. Puckered (lips), downturned lips to show dislike. Also iba'. Si Maria ha kiba'i si Juan. Maria stuck her lips out at John to show her dislike.

kichala 2. Spoon. Also kuchala.

kicharón 2. Spoon—large and used in cooking, ladle. Also kucharon.

kichi 1. Coitus, sexual intercourse— have, (taboo). Cf. Sirek, baggai, dalle.

kichu 2. Type of fish-family of acanthuridae (convict tang). Acanthurus triostegus.

kietu 2. Keep still, don't move, be quiet. Also ketu.

kifan 1. Dislocate jaw bone, pop jaw— out of joint.

kifan 2. Aggravate, worsen, increase inflammation in, make more severe. (R). Kifan i atadok-hu anai tineñak ni ramas. My eye was inflamed when a branch poked it. Kifan i chetnot gi kannai-hu. My sore got worse on my hand.

kihadas 2. Jaw. Also kriadas, kiadas.

Kika' Nickname for Francisca.

kikanyio' 2. Machine gun. (S)

Kiko' Nickname for Francisco.

kílili 1. To hand-carry, drift away—by current, carry along. Hu kilili i litratu-hu anai pumasehu yo'. I hand-carried my camera when I went strolling along. I koriente ha kilili i boti. The current carried the boat away (caused it to drift).

Kilisyanu 2. Christian, Catholic.

kilites 2. Type of plant-chenopodium album. Type of bush—edible.

kilites 2. Type of plant-amaranthus. Type of bush. Also kilites apaka'.

kilok See kilulok.

kilu 2. Always last. Guiya kilu. He is always last.

kilu 2. Kilogram, kilowatt.

kilu 2. Type of plant-thespesia populnea. (?) Cf. Banalu.

kílulok 2. Revolve, roll in a circle, turn around (as on an axis), spin. Cf. Likuko', liliko'.

kílulok 2. Type of plant-thespesia populnea. Also kilok.

kilumetro 2. Kilometer.

kilu'os 2. Cross, crucifix, the cross of Jesus. Cf. Krusifio.

kimadu 2. Scorched, burned without being inflamed, become scorched, become burned. Kimadu i hineksa' gi feggon. The rice was scorched on the stove.

kimasón 2. Fire, conflagration, blazing, burned, scorched, singed, consumed by fire, be on fire. Also kumason. Cf. Kimadu. Kimason i gima'. The house burned down. Hu li'e' i kimason gi siuda. I saw the conflagation in the city.

kime' 2. Mongol-eyed person, a person with slant eyes. Cf. Batchigo'.

Kin Nickname for Joaquin.

kinahet na kulot 2. Orangeish, containing orange color. Kahet plus -in-. (R)

kinahulo' 2. Score, points—number of, record of points made by competitors. Cf. Tantos.

kinahulo' 2. Growing up, waking up.

kinahulo' atdao 2. Sunrise, dawn, the break of day.

kinahulo'guan 2. Sudden rise, be angry suddenly, out of one's mind suddenly. Cf. Hosguan. Kinahulo'guan i malangu ni kalentura-ña. The patient's fever suddenly rose (not being aware of it). Kinahulo'guan hao fan. You became out of your mind. Kinahulo'guan i saddok. The river rose suddenly.

kinalamten [æ] 2. Motion, state of moving, progress, improvement. Cf. Progresu, adelanto.

kinamyo [æ] 2. Grated coconut.

kinanno' [æ] 1. Eaten up, consumed. Kinanno' i nenkanno' ni ga'lagu. The food was eaten up by the dog.

kinasse [æ] 2. Sarcastic, bitter, sarcasm. Cf. **Botlehu.**

Kindo' Nickname for Joaquin.

kinekuyong tasi 2. Ebb tide, receding tide. Cf. **Huyong.**

kinentento 2. Contentment. Cf. **Kontentamento.**

kinibatde 2. Horror, fear, terror, fright. Cf. **Mina'a'añao.**

kinientos 2. Five hundred.

kinilak 2. Watery, as in diarrhea, diarrhea, diarrhoetic. *Kinilak i neni.* The baby has diarrhea.

kinilís 2. Eclipse—of sun or moon. Farmers sometimes attribute poor or defective harvest to this. *Kinilis i pilan gi painge.* There was an eclipse of the moon last night.

kinilot di rosa 2. Pinkish, containing pink color. (R)

kinilu 2. Sheep, lamb.

kinké 2. Lamp, kerosene lamp.

kinke 2. Kink, kinky—a short and often tight twist of hair. Cf. **Mulatu, mulata.**

Kinkeng Nickname for Joaquin—used for small boys.

kinse 2. Fifteen.

kinto 2. Fifth.

kinto Short form of *kon todu. Chule' enao i chinina kinto i katsunes.* Bring that shirt and also the pants.

kinu Than. (*-ña...kinu*) in comparative constructions, more. *Maolekña si Pedro kinu guiya.* Pedro is better than he. *Dankoloña este na ga'lagu kinu ayu guatu.* This dog is bigger than that one.

kiosko 2. Kiosk, small pavillion, book stand.

kiridu 2. Favorite (child), bosom child, favorite, darling, sweetheart, lover (m). Also **kirida** (f).

kisabes Don't know. *Kisabes gue'.* He doesn't know.

kísami 2. Ceiling.

Kita' Nickname for Maria.

kitan 2. Cross-eyed, cock-eyed, floating eye. A person whose eyes do not focus in the same direction.

kitánlaña' 2. Cock-eyed, slightly crazy person. A derogatory term. (Taboo).

kiya 2. Keel, a timber or metal extending along the center of the bottom of the vessel.

klaba 1. Pin against, pin down, hold down, nail down, crucify.

klabu 2. Clef—in music to indicate the pitch of the written notes.

klaridát 2. Clarity, clearness.

klarifika 1. Clarify, make clear. Cf. **Na'klaru.**

klaru 2. Clear, true, doubtless, faultless, free of impurities, clean, purified, clarified, no doubt.

klaruyi 1. Clarify, certify, testify, give evidence of, manifest, reveal, signify, tell clearly, frank. *Hu klaruyi sumangani si nana-hu ni bida-hu.* I clarified to my mother what I had done.

klas [æ] 2. Class—as in school.

klasi 2. Type, kind, class, sort, variety, nature, character. *Hafa na klasi ya-mu.* What kind do you like? *Este na klasi malago'-hu.* This is the kind I wanted.

klasifika 1. Classify, categorize, catalogue.

klasifikáo 2. Classificable, classified, that which may be classified.

klasifikasión 2. Classification, arrangement.

klema 2. Climate. Also **klima.**

klemensia 2. Mercy, clemency.

klemente 2. Merciful.

kleptomania 2. Kleptomania.

klima 2. Climate, condition (referring to soil). Also **klema. Maipe i klima giya Marianas.** The climate is hot in the Marianas. *Maolek klima-ña este na odda'.* The condition of this soil is rich.

Ko' Nickname for Francisco.

kobra 1. Pin down—as in fighting, hold down, to fasten securely. *Ha kobra kontra i satge.* He pinned him against the floor.

kocha 2. Slipper, light shoe easily slipped on (usually for indoor use), sandal, slip-on, house shoe. Also **kotcha.**

kocha 2. Cork. Also **kotcha.**

koche 2. Carriage, coach.

koche 2. Chase pigs away.

koche' 2. Long hair—of a man's head.

kocheru 2. Chauffeur, coachman.

kódigu 2. Code, any system of principles or rules.

kodu 2. Arm muscle, arm wrestle. Cf. **Makodu.**

kohu 2. Crippled, crooked leg, lame, one-legged. Cf. **Changko, ke'yao.**

kokañao 2. Weak-hearted, weak spirit, coward, chicken-hearted.

kokas 2. Tangled (by twisting), entangled. Cf. **Matahlek.** *I guaka ha na'kokas i tali-ña.* The cow entangled its rope.

kokkok 2. Clear throat. Also **kakak.**

kókkolo' 2. Go up, go north, opp. of *totonok. Kokkolo' yo' gi lancho nigap.* I went up to the ranch yesterday. *Kokkolo' yo' gi ladera.* I went up to the mountain.

ko'ko' 1. Harvest (corn).

ko'ko' 2. Type of bird-rallus owstoni, Guam rail.

kokoti 1. Do (something) repeatedly, do (something) without stopping. *Ha kokoti yo' i sasata umakka'.* The bee stung me repeatedly. *Ha kokoti umaña i ga'lagu.* He repeatedly beat the dog.

kola 2. Glue, train—of dress.

kóladot 2. Strainer, sieve. Also **kuladot.**

ko'lao 1,2. Take food—to someone at work or in hospital. Food--taken to someone at work or in hospital. *Hu ko'lao i emfetmera.* I took food to the nurse. *I sindalu ha kanno' i ke'lao.* The soldier ate the food that was brought to him.

kolayi 1. Put train on a dress.

kolehio 2. College. Also **kolehu.**

kolehu 2. College. Also **kolehio.**

koleksión 2. Collection, donation.

kolektót 2. Collector.

kolepbla 2. Snake.

kólera 2. Cholera.

koleru 2. Ballot box, collection, container placed where donation is solicited in the church, box—usually found in church. (S)

koleta 2. Butt (of a firearm).

kollat 1,2. To fence, corral, pen, fence, barricade.

kollat cha'guan 2. Hedge, fence of shrubbery.

kololo'ña Especially, specially. Cf. **Espesiatmente.** *Mannge' sumaga giya Hawaii kololo'ña yanggen meggai salape'-mu.* It is fun to stay in Hawaii, especially when you have lots of money. Also **kulolo'ña.**

kolumna 2. Column. Cf. **Fila, lucha.** *I primet kolumna.* The first column.

koma 2. Comma.

komanda 1. Command, order with authority. Cf. **Dimanda, otden, tago'.** *Hu komanda i ga'-hu ga'lagu na u falagu.* I commanded my pet dog to run.

komanda 2. Commander.

kombalacheru 2. Swapper, barterer, exchanger (m). Also **kombalachera** (f).

kombalachi 2. Fuss, argument, confusion, disagreement, trouble, racket. Cf. **Yinaoyao.**

kombateru 2. Troublemaker, fighter, combatant, bruiser, pugilist.

kombati 2. Fight, argument. *Ti ya-hu kumombati yan amigu-hu.* I don't want to fight with my friend.

kombenensia 2. Convenience, comfort, utility, profit.

kombeniente 2. Convenient, useful, profitable, suitable.

kombense 1. Convince, persuade, influence, satisfy by proof, bring by argument to belief beyond doubt.

kombension 2. Convention, formal assembly of representatives or delegates for action on particular matters.

kombento 2. Convent.

kombetsa 2. Converse, talk, speak. Cf. **Kuentos.**

kombetsasión 2. Conversation.

kombida 1. Invite. Cf. **Sohyo', eppok.**

kombidáo 2. Guest—invited, inviting, capable of being invited.

kombieni 2. Proper, right thing to do. Also **kombeni.** *Kombieni na u matattiyi i planu.* It is proper to follow the plan.

kombiette 1. Convert, change over.

kombiti 2. Guest.

kometi 1. Commit. *Ha kometi un dankolo na isao.* He commited one big sin.

kometsiante 2. Merchant, trader, dealer, storekeeper.

kometsio 2. Commerce, trade, business, bargain.

komeya 2. Comedy.

komidiante 2. Comedian.

komísina 2. Commissioner. Also **komisiona.**

komiti 2. Committee.

kommat 2. Toaster (for tortillas), griddle, flat metal used for toasting bread, tortillas, pancakes, etc.

kommon 2. Toilet, restroom.

kómoda 2. Commode, bureau, chest of drawers. Cf. **Tanso'**.

kómodu 2. Useful, handy.

komon If, in case. (R) Also **komu**. From *komu mohon*. Cf. **Yanggen**. *Komon un tungo' siha kuentusi*. If you know them, speak to them.

kómotgan 2. Receive communion—in church. *Si pale' ha na'komotgan i malangu*. The priest let the sick person receive communion.

komotgatorio 2. Communion rail, place for receiving holy communion in the church.

kompaile 2. Alternate form of *kompaire* used with third person possessive pronoun. *Kompaile-ña si Juan*. Juan is his compadre.

kompaire 2. Godfather, term of address used between fathers and godfathers, or mother to a godfather. Also **pari**.

kompania 2. Company, firm, companion, corporation, associate.

kompañeru 2. Gang, partner, friend, escort, member of a group. Also **kompañera** (f).

kompara 1. Compare, contrast, make a comparison. Also **akompara**.

komparasión 2. Comparison, contrasting.

kompás 2. Tempo, rhythm, beat of music. *Bibu i kompas gi kanta*. The tempo was fast in the song.

kompás 2. Compass (mariner's), a device for determining directions by means of a magnetic needle.

kompatte 1. Divide, share, cause to separate. Also **patte**. Cf. **Dibidi**.

kompetensia 1. Compete, competition, challenge. Cf. **Cha'igi**.

kompetente 2. Competent, able, capable, qualified, suitable, fitted, proficient, efficient, sufficient. (S) Cf. **Kapas**.

kompetidót 2. Competitor, one who competes.

kompiti 1. Compete, engage in a contest. *Hu kompiti hao gi huegu*. I competed with you in the game.

kompitisión 2. Competition. Cf. **Kompetensia, cha'igi**.

komplasi 1. Placate, pacify, soothe, reconcile, conciliate.

kompletamente 2. Completely.

kompletu 2. Completed, finished. Cf. **Munhayan**.

komplikáo 2. Complicated, difficult.

komplimenta 1. Compliment, congratulate.

komplimentu 2. Wedding party—held the night before the wedding, compliment, fulfilment, completion.

komplisi 2. Accomplice, accessory.

kompradót 2. Purchaser, buyer.

kompremeti 2. Compromise.

komprende 1. Understand, comprehend, know, learn.

komprendiyon 2. Understandable, comprehensible.

kompromisu 2. Compromise, agreement.

komu In case, if, such as, as, when— usually used to connect phrases or clauses, like, since, provided that. Cf. **Yanggen**. Also **komon**. *Komu humanao yo' para Hawaii bai hu bisita iya Waikiki*. If I go to Hawaii I will visit Waikiki.

komunidá 2. Community. Also **komunidat**.

komuñón 2. Holy communion.

kon With (prep.), in conjunction with, by, provided that. Usually used with Spanish loans. *Kon sigi gi hinanao-mu*. Keep on with your journey. *Kon patte i guinaha-mu yan hami*. Share your wealth with us. *Sangani yo' kon tiempo*. Tell us ahead of time. *Kon petmisu*. With permission.

konbetsión 2. Conversion—to Christian faith.

koncha 2. Sea shell—generic term. Cf. **Karakot**.

kondena 1. Condemn, penalize.

kondenasión 2. Condemnation, damnation.

kondensa 2. Condenser.

kondisión 2. Condition, disposition.

kondót 2. Type of plant-benincasa hispida. Large squash. Winter squash.

kondukta 1. Direct, lead, guide, conduct. Cf. **Dirihi**.

kondukta 1,2. Conduct, behavior. Cf. **Maneha**.

koneo 2. Rabbit. Also konehu.

kónfesat 1. Confess, have confessed. *Hu konfesat i isao-hu todu.* I confessed all my sins. *Kumonfesat yo' as pale'.* I confessed to the priest.

konfesión 2. Confession.

konfesonario 2. Confessional.

konfesores 2. Confessors, shrivers, advisers—spiritual, pl. for *Konfesot.*

konfesót 2. Confessor, one who confesses.

konfia 1. Confide.

konfiansa 2. Confidence, trust, reliance, assurance, aplomb, self-possession. *Taya' konfiansa-ña giya guiya.* He doesn't have any confidence in himself.

konfirensia 2. Conference.

konfitma 1. Confirm (in Catholic church), administer confirmation to.

konfitmasión 2. Confirmation.

konfotma 1. Conform, adjust to fit, agree, accept. *I publiku ma konfotma i mahatsan i apas i hanom.* The public conformed to the increase of the water tax. *I estudiante siha ma konfotma i lain i eskuela.* The students conformed to the school rules.

konfotme 2. Agree, concur, coincide, conform. *I amigu-hu konfotme na bai in hanao asta i lanchon-mami.* My friend agreed that we will go to our ranch.

konfradia 2. Sisterhood, confraternity of the Christian Mothers Society -*I Nanan Kilisyanu.*

konfronta 2. Confront. Cf. **Afana'.**

konkista 1. Acquire, conquer.

kónkore' 2. Concrete, cement. (R) Cf. **Patdet, simento.**

konkrit 2. Concrete. Cf. **Patdet, simento.**

konkurahi 2. Angry, becoming angry.

konne' 1. Catch, take (someone), bring (someone), capture, adopt. *Ha konne' i guihan.* He caught the fish. *Konne' i patgon para i eskuela.* Take the child to the school. *Hu konne' i amigu-hu para i programa.* I took my friend to the program. *Konne' i neni para patgon-mu.* Adopt the baby for your own. *Hu konne' i mannok ni kannai-hu.* I seized the chicken with my hand.

konosidu 2. Known, recognizable, detectable. *Konosidu na umisao hao.* It is recognizable that you committed a sin. Also **kunisidu.**

konsagra 1. Transform, consecrate.

konsagrasión 2. Transubstantiation, consecration.

konseha 1. To advise, counsel, give advice to, recommend (a course of action) to. Also **akonseha.**

konseheru 2. Adviser, counselor, a counsel. Also **akonseheru.**

konsensia 2. Conscience, mind.

konsentimento 2. Consent, liberty, freedom. Also **konsentimiento.**

konsetba 1,2. Preserve food in sugar, conserves, preserves, as a jam or sweetmeat.

konsidera 1. Consider, think over, contemplate, give a thought to.

konsideradu 2. Considerate, thoughtful, unselfish. Also **konsiderao, konsiderayon.**

konsiderasión 2. Consideration.

konsiente 1. Consent, permit, allow, give permission for. Cf. **Petmiti.** Also **konsente.** *Ha konsiente yo' si nana umegga' movie.* Mother consented for me to see a movie.

konsigi 1. Continue, keep on. *Hu konsigi i hinanao-hu.* I continued my journey.

konsilio 2. Council, legislature.

konsiste 1. Consist of, include, contain, involve. *I gobietno ha konsisiste meggai na depattamento.* The government consists of various departments.

konsiste Depending on, according to. Cf. **Dipende.** *Konsiste gi as nana-hu kao bai hu fatto pat ahe'.* It depends on my mother whether I will come or not.

konsoladót 2. Sympathizer, soother, alleviator, reliever, condoler.

konsoladu 2. Consolation, comfort, sympathy. Cf. **Konsolasion.**

konsolasión 2. Consolation, comfort, sympathy. Cf. **Konsoladu.**

konstraksion 2. Construction.

konsuela 1. Enliven, cheer up, , condole, sympathize, make rejoice, raise the spirits of, be in (such) spirits, be or become cheerful.

konsuelu 2. Consolation, cheer, happiness, gaiety, mirth, that which cheers or gladdens. Cf. **Minagof, konsolasion, konsoladu.** *Ha na'gaikonsuelu yo' si tata-hu.* My father gave me consolation.

konsuma 1. Consume, deplete, expend by use, use up. Cf. **Lachai.** *Makonsuma bulan nenkanno' gi gipot.* There was lots of food being consumed at the party. *Hu konsuma tres chada' gi sentada-hu.* I consumed three eggs at my meal.

konsutta 1. Consult, seek counsel from, ask advice of, seek the opinion of.

kontadót 2. Accountant, bookkeeper, auditor, comptroller, inspector of accounts, examiner of business accounts.

kontahiosu 2. Contagious.

kontat ki As long as. Also **kuentat ki.**

kontempla 1. Contemplate, observe, watch.

kontentamento 2. Contentment, content, ease, satisfaction.

kontento 2. Content, satisfied, appeased the desire of. Cf. **Satisfecho.**

kontesta 1. Reply, answer. *Si Jeff ha kontesta i katta-mu.* Jéff replied to your letter.

kontestasión 2. Reply, answer, response. Cf. **Kontesta.**

kontiempo 2. Ahead of time, beforehand, previous to, prior to. *Sangani yo' kontiempo hafa planu-mu.* Tell me ahead of time what your plan is.

kontinensia 2. Continent (land).

kontinua 1. Continue, last, endure, abide, persist. Cf. **Masigi.**

kontinuasión 2. Continuation, continuance.

kontodu Including, included, so does, too, also. Also **kon todu.** *Humanao si Jose kontodu si Juan.* Joseph left and so did John. *Malingu i lepblo-ku kontodu i lapes-hu.* My book was lost and so was my pencil. *Humanao yo' yan i lalahi kontodu si Joe.* I went with the boys, including Joe .

kontra 1. Challenge, compete with, be against (someone). *Hu kontra i lahi.* I challenged the man.

kontra Against, attached to. *Mata'chong yo' kontra i liga.* I sat against the wall.

kontra tiempo Against time. *Inalulula yo' ya hu kokontra i tiempo.* I'm in a hurry against time.

kontrabando 1. Contraband—traffic of, smuggle, bring secretly, take secretly, illegal goods. Cf. **Na'lifet.**

kontradiksión 2. Violation, transgression, breach, infringement, act not in keeping with the law, contradiction. Also **kontradision.**

kontradisi 1. Contradict, oppose, contravene, counteract, violate.

kontrapesa 2. Counterweight, weight that balances another weight.

kontrariu 2. Enemy, foe, hostile force, competitor, challenger, adversary, opponent. Cf. **Enemigu.**

kontrata 1,2. To bargain, make contract, make deal, make agreement. Contract, bargain, agreement, deal.

kontratamiento 2. Agreement, a deal.

kontratista 2. Contractor.

kontribusión 2. Contribution, tax.

kongresisto Congressman.

kongresu 2. Congress.

ko'operasión 2. Cooperation.

ko'operatibu 2. Co-operative, co-operating.

kopa 2. Goblet.

kopa di oru 2. Type of flower. Cup of gold.

kopas 2. Hearts—card in the suit of.

kopbla 1,2. Dun. The demand of payment of credits, dues, funds, etc.

kopble 2. Money. Cf. **Salape'.**

kopble 2. Copper, red metal.

kopia 1,2. Copy, imitate, mimic, follow as a pattern, model, or example. Cf. **Eyak.**

kóporat 2. Corporal, a rank in the armed forces. Also **kabu.**

koranko' 2. Crank—a device used to turn the crank shaft when batteries are dead. (S)

korasón 2. Heart, darling, sweetheart, lover; core.

Korason di Santa Maria 2. Type of plant-caladium bicolor. A type of flower.

koredót 2. Corridor, gallery around a patio.

koreha 2. Motherhood, religious organization for older women who are married, an organization similar to Christian Mothers. Also **korea.**

koreha 2. Belt, strap worn by the members of the Christian Mothers. Also **korea.**

113

korehas 1,2. Spank (with a belt). Belt, strap, fan belt. Also **koreas.** Cf. **Sinturon.**

korehong 2. Crayon, pointed stick of colored clay. (R)

koresponde 1. Correspond, write letters to, communicate with by exchange of letters.

koresponde 2. Correspond, be similar, correlate, be equivalent.

korespondensia 2. Correspondence.

kori 2. Having a weak hand of the suit being played (tres siete game).

kori 2. Saleable, marketable goods, a business establishment that sells a lot of merchandise.

koriente 2. Current, flowing of liquid or electricity, running, fluent.

koriente 2. Steep sloping roof of a house. Opposite of *faga*.

korona 1,2. Crown, wreath.

koronét 2. Colonel, a rank in the armed forces.

kórorot 1. Call chicken, summon chickens. *Hu kororot i mannok.* I called the chickens.

koru 2. Choir, chorus. Cf. **Kantores.**

kosa ki So that. Cf. **Noseha ki.** *Na'i yo' lapes kosa ki siña yo' mangge' gi eskuela.* Give me a pencil so that I can write at school.

kosas 2. Thing (inanimate), implement, tool.

kosecha 1,2. To harvest, gather in, reap. Harvest, crop, yield of crop.

kossos 2. Filthy, smutty, muddy, dirty. Also **kosos.** Cf. **Akong, maskara.**

kosta 2. Cost, expense, rate, fare, charge, face value, market price. Cf. **Gasto, presiu.**

kosta 2. Coast, shore, seaside, bank, seashore, brink, brim, beach.

kostat 2. Sack, bag, typically large and of coarse material. Also **small sack.** Cf. **Ganggoche.** *Kostat papet* 'paper bag.'

kostura 2. Seam, where two pieces of cloth are joined together.

kosturera 2. Seamstress.

kostureru 2. Tailor.

kot 2. Coat, jacket.

kotbata 2. Necktie, cravat, scarf, neckerchief.

kotcha 2. Cork, stopper, stopcock. Also **kocha.**

kotcha 2. Slipper. Also **kocha.**

kotchetes 2. Snap, a fastening which closes or locks with a click (usually used for clothes).

kotchon 2. Mattress, cushion.

kotderu 2. Lamb—as used in scriptures.

kotdét 2. Fishing line. Cf. **Tupak.**

kotdisia 2. Courtesy.

kotdón 2. Line, rope, belt.

Kotdon di San Fransisco 2. Type of plant-lycopodium phlegmaria. A type of flower.

kotdura 2. Wisdom, good judgement. (S)

kotma 1. Hold—such as headlock, wrist lock, etc., so as to prevent movement, clamp, tie down, pin down, pin against. (S)

kotneta 2. Horn (musical), cornet, trumpet.

kotniyos 2. Canine tooth, bicuspid, tusk, dog tooth, fang.

kotpos 2. Shrine—religious.

kottadu 2. Curdle, change into curd, coagulate, thicken.

kotte 1,2. To try, to put one to trial, court, trial, the hearing in a trial.

kottesia 2. Genuflect, bow—in respect.

kottidu 2. Pickle, preserve food (by pickling). Also **enkattidu.**

kottot 2. Basket—woven of akgak, bag--woven. Cf. **Tisage'.**

krakas [æ] **2.** Cracker, biscuit—hard or crisp. Cf. **Biskuchu.**

kreadót 2. Creator. Cf. **Fafa'tinas.** *Humanao para u fana' i kreadot-ña.* He went to meet his creator.

kréditu 2. Credit, esteem, merit, honor.

kredu 2. Creed, belief.

kresiente 2. Crescent—used when referring to the moon.

kresta 2. Comb (chicken), clitoris (slang), crest.

kresta i rosa 2. Type of chicken—resembling crest-wyandott varieties.

krestan gayu 2. Type of plant-celosia argentea. Cocks comb—type of flower.

krestát 2. Crystal, glass.

kret 2. Ruthless, pitiless, cruel, harsh. Also **kruet.**

kriadas 2. Jaw, jawbone. (R) Also **kihadas.**

kriadu 2. Create. Cf. **Fa'tinas.**

kriadu 2. Servant. *Kriada* (f). Cf. **Muchachu.**

kriansa 2. Treatment—manner of, way of treating a person, breeding, training. *Maolek kriansa-ku giya guiya.* My treatment of him was good.

kriminát 2. Criminal.

krisidu 2. Huge, great, large, gigantic, giant, vast, enormous (m), robust. Also **krisida** (f).

Krismas 2. Christmas.

kristát 2. Crystal (dinner ware). Also **okristat.**

Kristianu 2. Christian (m). Also **Kristiana** (f).

Kristo 2. Christ.

kritisisa 1. Criticize, reproach.

kruet 2. Cruel. Also **kret.** Cf. **Malamaña, sakat, tai'ase'.** *Mampos kruet na taotao.* He's a very cruel man.

kruetdát 2. Cruelty.

krusa 1. Cross over, pass over.

krusifika 1. To crucify, put to death upon the cross.

krusifio 2. Crucifix, cross. Cf. **Kilu'os.**

kuadra 1. Square a house by using a carpenter's square or by measurement. *Ha kuakuadra i gima'-hu.* He is squaring my house.

kuadra Prepare—for an action, posture--ready to do something, get ready, set to go, fixed in position ready to act. *Hu kuadra yo' para mumu.* I prepared myself for a fight.

kuadrante 2. Square (carpenter's), quadrant.

kuadráo 2. Square.

kuadron bentana 2. Window sash, window frame.

kuadru 2. Frame, picture frame.

kualidát 2. Quality, feature, characteristic, grade, trait.

kualifika 1. Qualify, fit, make competent, make capable.

kualifikáo 2. Qualified, competent, eligible, fit, capable, able, proficient, skillful.

kualifikasión 2. Qualification, fitness, capacity, efficiency, skill.

kualitai 2. Type of plant-callicarpa candicans. (?).

kuando So many, so much. Also **kuanto, kuantas.** *Kuando beses chetnudan lao ti mamasga.* Many times he had an injury but he never learned his lesson.

kuanto How many. How much. Usually followed by *na. Kuanto bi'ahi?* How many times? *Kuanto bali-ña?* How much does it cost? *Kuanto na chada' kinanno'-mu?* How many eggs did you eat?

kuanto antes Ahead. *Hu pripara i che'cho'-hu kuanto antes.* I prepared my work ahead of time. *Kuanto antes na hu chocho'gue este para hagu ya taya' hafa ilelek-mu.* I have been doing this for you many times before and you didn't say anything.

kuantos How long, used with time expressions. *Kuantos tiempo?* How long? *Kuantos años hao?* How old are you?

kuarenta 2. Forty.

kuarenta i unu 2. Forty-one.

kuarentena 1,2. Quarantine.

kuaresma 2. Lent, time of fasting.

kuastaria Especially, particularly. Also **kuat estaria.** *Kuastaria ya sumaonao hao gi huegu siempre mas bumunitu i programa.* Especially, if you join the play, the program will surely be nice.

kuat estaria See **kuasteria.**

kuates 2. Egg—double yolk, double yolk.

kuatkiera See **kuatkuera.**

kuatkiet See **kuatkuet.**

kuatkuera Whatever—it may be, whichever--it may be, in any way, anyone within a group. Also **kuatkuet, kuatkiera.** *Kuatkuera giya hamyo siña dumalak yo'.* Any one of you can follow me.

kuatkuét Any, no matter. Also **kuatkiet.** Cf. **Kuatkuera.** *Kuatkuet manera.* Any manner, Any way. *Kuatkuet ora.* Any time, any hour. *Kuatkuet lugat.* Any place. *Kuatkuet na taotao.* No matter what person.

kuatro 2. Four.

kuatro sientos 2. Four hundred.

kuatta 2. Measure—by means of hand spread. *Na'i-yo' tres kuatta na halon.* Give me three hand spreads of string.

kuatta 2. Whip, slim leather instrument made from cow's tail used for spanking.

kuatta 2. Fourth—as in one-fourth, three-fourths. *Un kuatta patte.* One-fourth part.

kuattasu 2. To whip—as with a belt. To beat with a whip. *Adahi ha' na hu kuattasu hao.* Look out or I will whip you.

kuattét 2. Quarters, barracks.

kuatto 2. Room.

kuatto 2. Fourth.

kuba 2. Type of chicken—resembling black Sumatra, Cuban breed. Also kiuba.

Kubanu 2. Cuba, Cuban.

kubatde 2. Coward, destitute of courage, easily scared, not brave, timid.

kubietta 2. Deck (of ship).

kubietto 2. Silverware, small items which are easy to handle.

kubietto 2. Covered with, many. Cf. Abundansia. *Kubietto i chandia gi gualo'.* The watermelons were abundant at the farm.

kubransa [æ] 2. Bill—due for payment.

kubre 1. Help (someone) out, cover (a bet), travel over, pass through. *Hu kubre hao gi nisisidat-mu.* I helped you with your needs. *Ha kubre todu iya Guam.* He traveled all over Guam.

kubu 2. Digging tool—with straight, sharp blade and long heavy handle. Used for digging large holes, such as those needed for planting banana trees.

kuchala 2. Spoon. Also kichala.

kucharita 2. Teaspoon, small spoon.

kucharón 2. Ladle. Also kicharon.

kuchinada 2. Dirtiness, dirty trick, dishonesty, deceitfulness.

kuchinu 2. Dirty, filthy, foul, nasty, squalid. Also kuchina (f). Cf. Applacha'.

kudisio 2. Greedy, asking for things one already has, greed, acquisitiveness (m). Also kudisia (f).

kuenta 1. Include, enclose, inclose. Cf. Saonao.

kuenta 1. Substitute for. *Hanao kuenta-ku.* Go and substitute for me.

kuenta 2. Account, balance statement, reckoning of charged purchases and credits rendered periodically; behalf.

kuentan 2. Substitution for, replacement for, stand in, alternative for, in place of. Cf. Kuentayi.

Kuentan Thomas yo'. I am Tommy's replacement.

kuentas 2. Mathematics, arithmetic, solve mathematically, do mathematical problem. Cf. Arofmetika.

kuentat ki As long as, so long as. Also kontat ki. *Kuentat ki hagu drumadraiba trankikilu ha' yo'.* So long as you are driving, I am tranquil.

kuentayi 1. Substitute (for someone), replace someone. Cf. Tulaika, a'go, kuentan. *Hu kuentayi hao gi bola.* I substituted for you in the ball game.

kuentos 2. Talk, speak, converse, utter, chat. Cf. Kombetsa.

kuentusi 1. Talk to, speak to, converse with, utter.

kueru 2. Leather, leather skin—as of a cow, hide, rawhide.

kuestión 2. Question, query, puzzle, problem, point in dispute.

kuestiona 1. To question, interrogate, inquire, ask, to quiz. Cf. Faisen, abirigua.

kuetdas 2. Mainspring—of watch, phonograph, wind-up toy, etc.

kuetdasi 1. To wind—as a clock or watch.

kuetes 2. Firecracker.

kuetpo 2. Body, muscular appearance, figure.

kueyon chinina 2. Collar—of shirt or blouse.

kueyu 2. Neck, the back side, nape. Cf. Tongho.

kuidáo 2. Watch out, careful, be careful of.

kuikuentos 1. Orator. Cf. kuentos.

kuka 1. Incite, advise, counsel.

kuka' 2. Cra y, insane. Shortened form of *kaduka.*

kuku 2. Lump (on the head), pumpknot, weal, welt, a swelling on the head, usually from a blow. (S) Cf. Diso'.

Kuku Nickname for Juan.

kukunitos 2. Beetle.

kukuracha 2. Cockroach.

kula 1. Filter, strain, sift. *Hu kula i kafe.* I strained the coffee.

kula 1. Scrutinize, examine carefully.

Kula Nickname for Escolastica.

kúladot 2. Strainer, filter. Also koladot. Cf. Kula.

kulakong [æ] 2. Scorched, dirty. Dirt, filth—accumulated over a period of time, such as cobwebs, algae, mold; anything dirty, such as discharges from the body. Also **lakulakong**.

kulakong talanga 2. Ear wax.

kulales 2. Eggs—attached to a female body, fish eggs, egg of lobsters, fish, crabs.

kulales 2. Beads.

kulales Type of plant-adenanthera pavonina. Type of vine.

kulales halom tano' 2. Type of plant-abrus precatorius.

kulanda [æ] 2. Colander, a bowl-shaped sieve or strainer.

kulang Looks like, seems like, similar. Also **kalang**. *Kulang lepblo-ku enao.* That looks like my book.

Kulas Nickname for Nicolas.

kuleka 2. Setting hen, brood hen.

kulo' 2. Trumpet shell.

kulót 2. Color, chroma, hue.

kulot apu 2. Gray (color).

kulot chikolati 2. Brown (color). Also **chokolati**.

kulot di rosa 2. Pink (color).

kulot kahet 2. Orange (color).

kulot lila 2. Purple (color).

kulot salape' 2. Silvery, containing silver color.

kulu 2. Last. *Kulu yo' gi fila.* I was last in the line.

kululo'ña Especially. Also **kololo'ña**.

kumadu 2. Scorched, burned without being inflamed, become scorched, become burned. Also **kimadu**. *Kumadu i hineksa' gi feggon.* The rice was scorched on the stove.

kumahulo' 2. Ascend, go up.

kumaire 2. Godmother, term of address used between mothers and godmothers, or a father to a godmother. Also **male'** (short form).

kumasón 2. Fire, conflagration, burned, scorched, singed, blazing, comsumed by fire, be on fire. Also **kimason**. Cf. **Kumadu**. *Kumason i gima'.* The house burned down. *Hu li'e' i kimason gi siuda.* I saw the conflagration in the city.

kume' 2. Friend, gang, partner, buddy, pal. (S) Cf. **Amigu, ga'chong**.

kumeke Begin to, start to, about to, try to. Auxiliary used in constructions with indefinite objects and with defective verbs. Cf. **Mangeke, keke**. *Kumeke macho'cho' yo'.* I'm about to begin to work. *Kumeke mangge' gue'.* He is about to start to write. *Hafa kumeke ilek-ña?* What does it mean?, What is he trying to say?

kumekematai 2. Dying, perishing, death —approaching, near one's end, departing from the present life. Cf. **Kumematai, matai**. *Kumekematai i sasata gi halom i taru.* The bee is dying inside the jar.

kumematai 2. Die—about to, perish--about to. Cf. **Matai**. *Kumematai i guaka gi pastai.* The cow was about to die in the pasture.

kumida 2. Meal, eating, eating time, time for eating. *I gima'-hu nai para u guaha kumida.* It is at my house where the eating will take place. *Esta oran kumida.* It is time to eat.

kumotgatorio 2. Communion rail—in church.

kumple 1. Complete, accomplish, done with, fulfill, comply, carry out. *Hu kumple i che'cho'-hu.* I am done with my work. *Otro na sakkan bai hu kumple sinkuenta años.* Next year I will have completed my fifty years.

kumple años 2. Birthday, anniversary. Cf. **Anitbetsariu**.

kumplidu 2. Complete, brought to completion or perfection, fully realized, concluded. Cf. **Kabales**.

kumuleka 2. Hatching. Cf. **Kuleka**.

kuna 2. Baby crib, cradle. Also **kunao**.

kúnanaf 2. Crawl—on belly or hands and knees, creep, move with the body close to the ground. Cf. **Toru**.

kunao 2. Crib—for a baby. Also **kuna**.

kunisidu Known. Also **konosidu**.

kunitos 2. Small insect, gnat.

kuña 2. Brother-in-law—short form for *kuñadu* or *kuñao*.

kuña 2. Cotter pin, used esp. on axles of the bull carts.

kuñada 2. Sister-in-law.

kuñadu 2. Brother-in-law. Also **kuñao, kuña, ñao**.

kuñáo 2. Brother-in-law. Cf. **Kuñadu**.

kungkung 2. Word for penis—used for little boys.

kuota 2. Quota, allotment.

kura 2. Parish priest, the priest who presides over the parish.

kurahi 2. Temper tantrum, anger. *Basta kumarahi.* That's enough temper tantrum.

kurihi 1. Correct, rectify. Cf. **Rektifika.**

kurihi 1. Lead, show the way, guide.

kuriosu 2. Curious, inquisitive (m). Also **kiriosu.**

kusina 2. Kitchen, cuisine, cooking apartment.

kusineru 2. Cook, one who prepares food for eating, chef.

kusio' 2. Air-raid, outbreak of war. (S)

kúsion 2. Cushion, pad, stuff of spongy material. Cf. **Kotchon.**

kustiyas 2. Rib.

kustrafas 2. Gristle, tendon.

kustumbre 2. Habit, custom, tradition. Cf. **Bisiu, usu.**

kutba 2. Curve. Cf. **Kabo'.**

kuttiba 1. Cultivate, educate, enrich, till, bestow labor upon land in raising crops.

kuttina 2. Drapery, curtain.

kuttura 2. Culture.

kutturát 2. Cultural.

kuyontura 2. Joint, where two bones are joined, chink, fissure.

la 2. Whoa, word used to tell a water buffalo to stop. Cf. **Cho.**

La' Nickname for Nicolas.

la- [æ] More (slightly), a little bit (more)—comparative degree marker (prefix). *Lamaolek siniente-ku.* I feel slightly better. *Labunitu i gima'-mu anai un penta.* Your house became prettier when you painted it.

lá'ancho [æ] **2.** Wider, broader, cause to be wider. Cf. **Ancho, lafedda'.** *Hu na'la'ancho i chalan.* I made the road a little wider.

lá'apmam [æ] For some time, for quite some time. *Esta la'apman yo' guini giya Guam.* I have been here on Guam for quite sometime already.

labada 2. Clothes—to be laundered.

labadót 2. Sink, lavatory.

labadu 1. Laundry, dirty clothes.

labana 2. Cigar, chewing tobacco.

labandera 2. Laundress, laundry work—woman who takes in laundry.

labanderu 2. Laundryman—man who takes in laundry.

labaniyu 2. Swelling around feet or ankles.

labatorio 1. Douche.

labatorio 2. Laboratory, lab, testing place, experimental room.

labbet 2. Violin, fiddle.

labbon 1. Trim, clip, lop off, cut off evenly. *Hu labbon i gapotilu-ña i patgon.* I trimmed the child's hair.

labbon 2. Type of chicken—with no tail, bob-tail, a tail that has been clipped.

labios 2. Lips, lip.

lachai [æ] **1.** Dispose of all, consume, finish off. Usually followed by an action word. *Hu lachai kumanno' i na'-mu.* I ate all your food. *Malachai i pigas siha manmabende gi tenda.* All the rice at the store was sold out.

lácheddek [æ] **2.** Giddyap, hurry up. A combination of prefix *la-* and *chaddek.*

lachi [æ] **2.** Error, wrong, mistake, incorrect, guilty. *Lachi si Juan.* John was wrong.

la'chok [æ] **2.** Sprout, shoot forth, germinate, grow. Cf. **Dokko'.** *Hu li'e' i la'chok na flores.* I saw the flower sprout.

ládagu 2. Go north, move north, northward movement. Also **dadagu.** Cf. **Lagu.** *Ladagu yo' nigap anai ha agang yo' si Kiko'.* I went north yesterday when Kiko' called me.

ladda [æ] **2.** Type of plant-morinda citrifolia. Type of tree—used for medicine. Also **lahda.**

ladera 2. Cliff, precipice.

ladriyu 2. Brick, paving material made by molding clay into blocks.

ladrón 2. Thief, robber—one who robs. Cf. **Sakke, chekle'.**

láfedda' [æ] **2.** Wiser, broader. Cf. **Fedda', la'ancho, ancho.**

lagabista 2. Binoculars, spyglass, small telescope. Also **latgabista.** Cf. **Teleskopio.**

lagansát 2. Type of plant-barringtonia racemosa. A type of grass.

lagas [æ] **1,2.** Skid, rub against, slide, slip, rub something against something. Cf. **Lalacha'.** *Hu lagas i addeng-hu gi inai.* I rubbed my feet on the sand. *Lumagas yo' gi gua'ot.* I slipped on the steps.

lage'- Further—a little (bit), more--a little (bit), a combination of two prefixes, *la-* 'a little (bit)', and *ge'-* 'further or more'. Cf. **Lahat-.**

Lage'fe'na gi fila. Move further up the line.

laggua 2. Type of fish-family scaridae. Parrot fish.

lago' 2. Tear—a saline fluid secreted by the lachrymal gland.

lago' [æ] 2. Melt, liquefy, soften—cause to change from a solid to a liquid state, usually by heat; fuse, cause to vanish.

lagon 2. Type of plant-merremia peltata. A type of grass.

lagon tasi 2. Type of plant-ipomoea littoralis. A type of grass.

lagu 2. North (in Guam and Rota), west (in Saipan).

lagu 2. Type of fish-gaterin diagrammus. (Family plectorhynchidae) sweetlips.

lagua' 2. Net—scoop, hand net.

lagua' [æ] 1. Step over.

lagua' [æ] 2. Omit. Cf. **Omiti.**

láguaha [æ] Have plenty, several. From *la-* plus *guaha*. *Yanggen laguaha yo', siña hu na'i hao mas.* If I had more, I could give you more.

laguaná 2. Type of plant-annona muricata. Soursop. Has a spiny skin and filled with a soft white juicy pulp.

laguas 2. Long, skinny, long and slender—refers to plants or animals.

laguet [æ] 1. Catch with a hook. Alternate form of *haguet.*

laguna 2. Lagoon.

lagunde 2. Type of plant-vitex negundo. (?).

láguse' [æ] 2. Hurry, hurried, fast, quick. Cf. **Guse', sahyao, alula.**

lahát- [æ] Denotes comparative degree (distance). *Lahattaya.* Farther south. Cf. **Haya.** *Lahattichan.* Farther west. Cf. **Luchan.** *Lahattilo'.* Farther up, higher. Cf. **Hulo'.** *Lahattalom.* Farther in. Cf. **Halom.** *Lahatfe'na.* Farther front. Cf. **Mo'na.** *Lahattatte.* Farther back. Cf. **Tatte.** Further—a little, more--a little, further--a little bit, more--a little bit, a combination of two prefixes, *la-* a little (bit), and *hat-* further or more. Cf. **Lage'-.**

lahen [æ] 2. Son of, man of. Cf. **Lahi, ihu.** *Lahen Jose si David.* David is the son of Joseph.

lahi 2. Man, male, boy. Also used in direct address among friends in the same way that *lai* is used.

lahu 2. Go, walk. Cf. **hanao.**

lahyan Plenty, many, a bunch of, a lot of, a whole lot of, full of. Also **layan.** Cf. **Meggai, bula.**

lahyao [æ] 2. Hurry up—imperative; walk faster. Also **sahyao.**

lai 2. Friend, man—when used in direct address or in greeting. *Hafa lai.* Hello, friend.

lai Short form of *lahi.*

lai [æ] 2. Law, jurisprudence, code.

laiguan 2. Type of fish-chelon vaigiensis (family mugilidae). Mullets.

lailai 2. Motion (irregular), swaying, an irregular movement, such as that of palms in the breeze, rocking. (S) *Lumailai i ramas anai umakalaye' yo'.* The branch shook when I swung from it. *Lumailai i lamasa anai hu totpe.* The table teetered when I bumped into it. *Lumailai i kareta anai matto gi baranka na lugat.* The car vibrated up and down when it came to a rocky place.

lailai 2. Wander, roam aimlessly. *Lumalailai i taotao sin bida.* The man is wandering around without purpose.

lailai 2. Loiter, hang around wasting time. *Basta di lumailai, espiha che'cho'-mu.* Stop loitering around, go look for some work.

laime 1,2. Trick, defraud, deceive by cunning or artifice. Trick, ruse, artifice, wile, feint.

laisen 1. Avoid, fail to meet someone, fail to notice, fail to recognize, abstain from, keep away from, shun. Cf. **Álaisen.** *Ha laisen i enemigu-ña.* He avoided his enemy. *I binadu ha laisen i ga'lagu.* The deer avoided the dog.

lakkao [æ] 2. Climber, one who climbs trees expertly. Also **lekkao.**

laklak [æ] 1. Haircut—give, cut off (esp. hair); shear, or trim with shears, such as hedges or grass. (R) Cf. **Dasai.**

laknos [æ] 1. Take out. *Hu laknos sinko pesos para i gipot.* I took out five dollars for the party. *Hu laknos i yabi gi halom i betsa-ku.* I took the key out of my pocket. *Hu laknos i* *salape' gi pottamuneda.* I took out the money from the purse.

laknos [æ] 1. Put forth, present. *Guaha papet ti ha laknos.* There was a paper he did not put forth.

lakngayao 2. Type of plant-acrosticum aurem. Mangrove fern.

lakse 1. Sew, stitch.

lakse' [æ] 2. Capable of sliding with very little friction, sliding smoothly, such as a ski, boat or sled; slippery, slick. Cf. **lasge', palakse'.**

láksese' [æ] 1. Ejaculate, utter suddenly.

lakte' [æ] 2. Type of rock, volcanic rock.

laktos 2. Thorn, sharp, pointed rock or coral.

lakulakong [æ] 2. Dirty, filthy, soiled with dirt. (S). Also **kulakong.** Cf. **Kossos, akong.**

lakulakong [æ] 2. Phlegm.

la'la' 2. Alive, vivacious, full of life, lusty, robust, healthy, vigorous. Cf. **Brabu.** *La'la' na tinanom.* It is a healthy plant. *La'la' i guihan ni matokcha'.* The fish was alive that was speared.

la'la' [æ] 1. Peel off—dead skin, skin back (foreskin).

lálacha' [æ] 2. Skid, slide, lie on, fall on, roll on. Cf. **Lagas.** *Lumalacha' i patgon gi fache'.* The child slid in the mud.

lalacha' mamati 2. Type of fish-thalassoma trilobata (family labridae).

lála'et [æ] 2. Gall bladder.

lalahi 2. Males, men, boys, kids, etc.

lalai 1. Sing, chant. Cf. **Kanta.** *Nihi ta fanlalai.* Let's all sing.

lálakse [æ] 2. Seamstress, tailor, mender—one who can sew, mend or stitch.

lála'la' [æ] 2. Live, alive, exist, living. Cf. **Gagaige.** *Lala'la' ha' i ga'ga' trabiha.* The animal is still alive. *Lala'la' ha' i kareta anai poddong gi kantit.* The motor was still running when the car fell off the cliff.

lála'la' [æ] 2. Something that causes peeling of the skin, such as clorox or lime.

lalalo' 2. Mad, enraged, anger.

Lalan Nickname for Isidora.

lalanyok 2. Type of plant-xylocarpus granatum. (Carapa moluccensis). A type of tree.

lalangha 2. Type of plant-citrus grandis. Pomelo, a variety of grapefruit, very bitter and sour. Also **lalanga.**

lalanghita 2. Type of plant-citrus reticulata. Tangerine.

lálangu [æ] 2. Unconscious, not conscious, faint, fall in a swoon. Cf. **Tisu, mamaitaguan.**

lalatde 1. Scold, chide, reprove, reprimand.

lalatdiyon 2. Guilty, reprehensible, deserving of being scolded.

lálima [æ] 1. File a little more. *La-* plus *lima.*

lalo' 2. Fly, housefly.

lalo' guaka 2. Type of fly—family Tabanidae. Horsefly, any type of fly that lives around horses, cattle, etc.

lalo' lagu 2. Type of fly—family Casterophilidae or Oestridae. Botfly, large fly resembling bumblebee.

lámagong [æ] 2. Recuperate, to get better from injury or illness. Cf. **Magong.**

lámahgong [æ] 2. Calmer, more peaceful. Cf. **Mahgong.**

lamahu 2. Type of plant-rhus taitensis. (?).

lamas [æ] 2. Rot, decay, become decomposed, putrefy, rotten.

lamasa [æ] 2. Desk, table.

lame' [æ] Mild expletive. Also **liame'.** *Lame' dei na inande' hao.* Gosh, you certainly are a flirt.

lamen 2. Harm, hurt, wound, injure, punish. Cf. **Fueges, kastiga, galuti, aña.** *Munga mana'lamen i patgon.* Don't harm the child. *Ha na'lamen yo' si Juan.* John hurt me.

lamentásion 2. Lamentation.

lámina 2. Icon, holy portrait, representation in painting of some sacred personage. Also **lapina.**

lamitá 2. Half, half-and-half—part of anything approximately equal to the remainder. Cf. **Media, empe'.** *Na'i yo' lamita.* Give me half. *Lamita sopbla gi boteya pa'go.* There is half left in the bottle now.

lámlalam 2. Very shiny. Cf. **Lamlam.**

lamlam 2. Glare, shiny, polished, glossy, radiant, bright, lightning, luster. Cf. **Mañila'.**

lammok [æ] **2.** Stink, reek, be malodorous, emit a strong offensive smell. Cf. **Mutong**. *Lammok i matai cha'ka gi chalan.* The dead rat on the road stunk.

la'mok [æ] **1.** Open up, skin back (foreskin), turn inside-out; to turn everything out for purpose of orderly rearrangement. Cf. **Baleng**. *I lancheru ha la'mok i lassas binadu.* The farmer skinned the deer.

la'mon [æ] **2.** Up to (someone), be responsible for. *Guahu la'mon ni che'cho'-hu.* My work is up to me. *Hagu la'mon.* It is up to you. *Hagu la'mon nu guahu.* I leave myself up to you.

la'mon [æ] **2.** Know—a place, be familiar with--a place. *La'mon yo' giya Saipan.* I am very familar with Saipan.

lámo'na [æ] **2.** Tonight, this evening, this night, after dark to midnight.

lamot 2. Type of seaweed. Also **lumot**.

lámpara 2. Globe—lamp, the glass part of a lantern which protects the flame from the wind. Cf. **Tubu**.

lampasu 1,2. Rub, wipe—as with a mop; mop.

lampuayi 2. Type of plant-dodonaea viscosa. (?).

lámudong [æ] **2.** Bigger, larger, taller, greater, became bigger, became larger, became greater. *Lamudong i tinanom-hu flores.* The flowers that I transplanted grew bigger.

lana 2. Wool.

lanan [æ] Cf. **Lannan**.

lancheria 2. Farm, ranch, husbandry, farming, agriculture, gardening.

lancheru 2. Rancher—a herdsman employed on a ranch or rancho, the owner of a ranch, farmer. Also **lanchera**. Cf. **Sumentereru**.

lancho [æ] **2.** Ranch, farm.

lanchon grande 2. Makeshift house, temporary house.

laniya 2. Flannel (cloth), cotton—used for underwear, infants' wear, etc., outing flannel. Type of cloth.

lanka 2. Jackfruit. Also **nanka**.

lannan [æ] **2.** Snore, be sound asleep. *Lannan si Jose gi maigo'-ña.* Joseph snored in his sleep. *Lannan hao gi painge.* You snored last night.

lansa 1,2. Spear, lance (used on land). Cf. **Tokcha', fisga**.

lansadera 2. Bobbin—of sewing machine.

lanse 2. Type of fish-family apogonidae. Cardinal fish.

lanseta 2. Large needle, lancet.

lanta'as 2. Type of plant-cajanus cajan. Pigeon peas.

laña 2. Oil (generic).

laña' [æ] Expletive to express feelings ranging from mild surprise to complete disgust. Taboo word in mixed society, now used much more freely by younger generation. Still used by some males in a comdemnatory manner to indicate having had sexual intercourse with a female.

lañan niyok 2. Coconut oil.

lañayon 2. Spoiled fruit—caused by impact from falling down from tree; capable of being oiled.

langak [æ] **1.** Strong enough—to do something, withstand, can carry, able to lift up. Cf. **Sungon**. *Ha langak yo' i patgon humatsa.* The child was strong enough to lift me. *I sapatos-hu ha langak sumungon yo' kasi dos meses ta'lo.* My shoes can last me maybe two more months. *Ha langak sumungon todu i piniti-ña.* He can withstand all of his suffering.

langat [æ] **2.** Rough water, big wave—that is not breaking. *Goflangat i tasi despues di i pakyo.* The waves were big after the typhoon.

langet 2. Heaven, sky, the outer space.

lángiti 2. Type of plant-bleekeria mariannensis. A type of tree.

langle 2. Railing, bannister, guard rail, any rail used for support, protection, or to block a passageway.

langnga' [æ] **2.** Gape, hold mouth agape. Cf. **Angla'a'**. *Basta di lumangnga'.* Stop holding your mouth open.

langsan 2. Type of plant-lansium domesticum. Also **langasat**. A type of tree.

langse [æ] **1,2.** Set fishing net in position, closing net, bring together as the two ends of a net or seine so as to trap fish. Also **lanse**. *I peskadores ma langse i chenchulu tres bi'ahi.* The fishermen set the fishing net in position three times.

lao   But, yet. Also lu. *Puno' lao debidi un kanno'.* Kill it, but you must eat it.

lao'an 2.   Effeminate person. From *palao'an.*

laolao 2.   Shake, vibrate, quiver, totter, tremble. Also naonao. *Laolao yo' anai ha go'te yo' i elektrisida.* I shook when I received the electric shock.

la'on 2.   Wander, roam, ramble, wander about aimlessly. Also la'ong. Cf. Laoya. *La'on na lahi.* He is a wandering man. *I la'on taibali.* The roamer has no value.

la'on 2.   Person who knows his way around a place by virtue of his having traveled, traveler.

la'on 2.   Sea urchin—diadema.

la'ong 2.   See la'on.

laoya 2.   Sauntered, strolled, loiter, walk around, stroll around, wandered about idly. Cf. La'on. *Lumaoya yo' gi siuda.* I strolled in the city.

lapbla 1.   Cut curves, zigzag cut, scallop, slap—causing cut lip. *Bunitu malapbla-ña i magagu-mu.* Your dress has a nice zig-zag cut. *Ha lapbla i papet siha.* He zig-zag cut the papers.

lapes 2.   Pencil, any of various objects suggesting a pencil.

lápida 2.   Tombstone, grave marker.

lápina 2.   Statue (R). Cf. Lamina.

laputa 2.   Whore, prostitute; also used as expletive. Also puta.

laraina 2.   Queen. Also raraina.

las   [æ] Particle—used in telling time (same as *alas*). *Las kuatro,* Four o'clock, or *Alas kuatro,* Four o'clock. *La una* One o'clock, or *Ala una,* One o'clock.

lasa   [æ] 1.   Massage, rub, as in massaging.

lasaga 2.   Type of plant-lepturus repens. Creeping vines on the beach.

lasarinu 2.   Leper. Also nasarinu.

lasge'   [æ] 2.   Slippery, slick, lubricated, lubricious. Also lakse'.

lasgue   [æ] 1.   Whittle, sharpen, make pointed, cut into pieces or slices, shape by cutting, as sharpening a pencil. *Hu lasgue i hayu.* I carved the wood. *I estudiante ha lasgue i lapes-ña.* The student sharpened his pencil.

laso'   [æ] 2.   Penis, testicle. Cf. balaso'.

laso' katu 2.   Type of plant-cenchrus echinatus, type of grass—having burr-like seed pod.

lasret 2.   Type of plant-pangium edule. (?).

lassas 1,2.   Skin, peel, epidermis, bark, peeling, crust, rind. *Hu lassas i mangga.* I peeled the mango.

lassas átadok 2.   Eyelid. Cf. babali.

lassas chada' 2.   Egg shell. Cf. Kaskaran chada'.

lassas ulu 2.   Scalp.

lastek   [æ] 2.   Elastic.

lástima 2.   Waste, of no use or purpose. *Lastima i tinanom-hu gi gualo' sa' manyinamak ni pakyo.* My crops were of no use because the typhoon destroyed them.

lasu 1,2.   Trap—using rope, catch with a lasso, lariat, lasso.

lat-   [æ] Short form for *lahat-.* Cf. Lahat-.

lata 2.   Can (container).

latan ganta 2.   Can, container—equal to a gallon.

latdon 2.   Full of flies, covered with flies. *Latdon i kuatto.* The room was filled with flies.

latek   [æ] 2.   Crispy residue of coconut milk after oil is cooked out.

latga 2.   Greedy, spendthrift.

latgabista 2.   Binoculars. Also lagabista.

latgeru 2.   Shaft, part of a bull cart, the shafts or poles that attach to the harness of a bull or horse.

latigasu 2.   Lash, spanking, whipping, belting, scourge, whip, hurt. Also latigu.

látigu   [æ] 2.   Spanking, whipping, belting. Also latigasu. *Fotte i latigu-ña si tata-hu.* My father's spanking is hard.

Latinu 2.   Latin, Roman language, classical language.

latiria 2.   Canned goods, cans of merchandise, esp. meat and fish. Food—canned. Cf. Lata.

lato'   [æ] Heck, darn. Mild expletive.

láttanao   [æ] Get away, move away, move out, get out. From *lahattanao.* Cf. Lahat-. *Lattanao guini.* Get away from here.

latte   [æ] 2.   A large stone carving presumed to be made by the Chamorro people in pre-historical times. Latte sites have been found on all of the larger islands of the Marianas.

latte' [æ] 2. Scab, a crust over the sore, wound, etc.

latto' [æ] 2. Healing. Cf. **Magong**. *Esta latto' chetnot-ña*. His wound is healing.

la'uya 2. Pan, pot. Cf. **Satten**.

la'uyan kaddo 2. Sauce pan.

la'uyan manaflitu 2. Frying pan, skillet. Cf. **Kalahi**.

la'yak [æ] 2. Sail. Also **layak**.

layak [æ] 2. Mast, sails. Also **la'yak**.

la'yao [æ] 2. Stroll idly. Cf. **Laoya**.

lá'yiyi Especially, really. Cf. **Espesiatmente, kololo'ña**. *Ya-hu pastet la'yiyi yanggen lemon*. I like pie, especially if it is lemon.

layo' [æ] 2. Hurt feelings. *Hu na'layo' si Maria*. I hurt Maria's feelings.

le' 1. See, short form of *li'e'*. *Hu le' hao anai chumachalek*. I saw you when you were laughing.

le'an 2. Sharp- eyed, keen-sighted, eagle-eye, clairvoyant.

lebbok 2. Muddy, cause to be muddy; cloudy—of liquid.

leche 1,2. Add coconut milk to cooking food. Milk, cream, lactage, sperm. *Hu leche i fina'tinas-hu*. I added coconut milk to my cooking. *Gumigimen yo' leche kada oga'an*. I drink milk every morning.

leche 2. Expression similar to the English words gee, golly, gosh, etc. Considered taboo by older speakers.

lechen niyok 2. Coconut milk.

lechera 2. Full of milk, dairy, milking cow, big breasted (slang). *Lechera i ga'-hu guaka*. My cow has lots of milk.

lechon 2. Litter—of pigs, pig--young, piglet, suckling pig.

legua 2. League—measurement, about three miles.

lehgua' 1. Stir, agitate. Also **legua'**. Cf. **Batte, chalehgua'**.

lehnge 1. To shield, to screen, to furnish shade, to protect by shielding with something or with one's body. (R). Cf. **Choffe**.

lehngon 2. Shade, shady. Also **lengon, lenghon**.

lekkao 2. Climber. Also **lakkao**.

leklek 1. Guide, bring, direct. *Hu leklek i patgon guatu asta as nana-ña*. I guided the child there to his mother. *Leklek magi i taotao siha*. Direct the people here.

leklok 1,2. Masturbate, perform masturbation.

lekngai 2. Stiff neck.

leksión 2. Lesson, something which is learned or taught. Cf. **Estudio**.

lektura 2. Lecture, formal discourse on any subject.

lela' Nickname for Manuela.

le'le' 1. Act of kidding, act of fooling, to joke with. *Basta di lume'le'*. Stop kidding. *Ombre un le'le' hao*. You must be kidding.

lemasa 2. Type of plant-artocarpus integra, champeden. (?).

lemlem 1. Fail to recognize what one is used to seeing, surprise (from changes). *Iya Guam ha lemlem yo' pot i matulaika-ña*. Guam surprised me because of its changes.

lemlem taotao 2. Twilight, sunset.

lemmai 2. Type of plant-artocarpus altilis. Breadfruit without seeds.

lemmok Cf. **Lommok**.

lemon 2. Type of plant-citrus aurantifolia. Lime.

lemon China 2. Type of plant-triphasia trifolia. Type of bush.

lemon reat 2. Type of plant-citrus limon. Lemon.

lemonada 2. Lemonade.

lemonayas 2. To put lights on at night in the front of the house so as to provide light for travelers on the road.

lempiesa 1,2. Clean, sweep, cleanliness, put in order, health inspection. Cf. **Balle, gasgas**. *Brabu yo' manlempiesa*. I work hard cleaning. *Hu lempiesa i uriyan guma'*. I cleaned around the house.

lenderu 2. Boundary, border.

lente 2. Lens.

lenteha Franchesa 2. Type of plant-cajanus cajan. French bean.

lengga 2. Suppository, lubricate anus for aid in defecation. Cf. **Hilengga, lilengga**.

lenggua 2. Tongue. Cf. **Hula'**.

lenggua i baka 2. Type of plant-opuntia or nopalea cochinelifera, or euphorbia neriifolia. Cactus.

lengguahi 2. Language, dialect, speech.

lepblo 2. Book, notebook, article—in periodical, magazine.

lepra 2. Leper.

leprosu 2. Leprosy. Cf. **Nasarinu.**

lesso' 2. Type of fish—slightly larger than *mañahak.*

lessok 2. Type of fish-holocentrus unipunctatus (family holocentridae). Squirrel fishes.

leston 2. Ribbon.

leston 2. Type of plant-ophioglossum pendulum. Type of flower.

leston puyitos 2. Type of plant-codiaeum variegatum.

letke 1. Give abundantly, excess, get rid of. (R) Cf. **Alatgayi.** *Ha letke bumende i produkto-ña siha.* He got rid of all of his produce by selling it. *Hu letke manna'i kosas-hu.* I gave away too many of my things. *Basta maletke nenkanno' i patgon.* Don't give the child too much food.

letke 1. Dodge, avoid. Cf. **Suhayi, eskapayi.** *Letke i fache'.* Get away from the mud. *Ha letke yo' gi gipot.* She avoided me at the party.

letra 2. Letter (of alphabet).

leyeslatura 2. Legislature—a body of persons in a state invested with power to make, alter, and repeal laws.

le'yok 2. Stand (on toes), tiptoe (R). Cf. **Deggo.**

le'yok 2. Rough, uneven surface.

le'yok 2. Water hole—in reef, hole--in the road.

Lia' Nickname for Emelia or Maria.

liame' [æ] Mild expletive. Also **lame'.**

libadura 2. Yeast, leaven, ferment.

liberasión 2. Liberation, deliverance.

libetta 2. Liberate, disengage, be on leave, be on vacation.

libettáo 2. Leisure, free from demands, at liberty. Cf. **Dibettao.**

libettát 2. Liberty, freedom.

libette 1. To give leisure, relax, liberate, set free. Cf. **Dibiette.** *I famagu'on ma libette siha gi plasa.* The children relaxed at the plaza.

libianu 2. Easy, effortless, not laborious, not burdensome, easily done, requiring no great effort.

libra 2. Pound (weight). Cf. **Piku.**

libre 2. Saved, made safe, safeguarded, rescued, delivered from danger. Cf. **Liheng.**

licheng 1,2. Raise (with pulley), lower (with pulley); pulley, tackle (for pulling), crane.

li'e' 1. See, look, behold, perceive, watch.

lienso 2. Linen. Also **linu.**

li'e'on 1. Visible, can be seen. *Li'e'* plus *-on* (abilitative suffix).

lifet 2. Slink away, creep away.

liga Wall. Also **luga.**

Liga di Nasión League of Nations.

ligalisa 1. Legalize.

ligas 2. Garter.

ligát 2. Legal, lawful, legitimate.

liheng 2. Saved, safeguarded, rescued, sheltered, shelter, refuge, made safe. *Lumiheng gue' gi kareta anai uchan.* He sheltered himself in the car when it rained.

lihítimu 2. Legitimate, lawful, legalized, admissible, justifiable.

líkoko' 2. Revolve, roll in a circle, turn around (as on an axis), spin. Also **liliko'.** Cf. **Kilolok.**

likoku'i 1. Circumscribe, encircle, go around completely. Also **liliku'i.**

likót 2. Liquor.

lilengga 1,2. Lubricate anus, syringe, suppository—all used as a form of aid in defecation. Also **hilengga.**

liles 1. To father, to procreate, be a male progenitor. *Hu liles i patgon.* I fathered the child.

líliko' 2. Revolve, spin, roll in a circle. Also **likoko'.** Cf. **Kilolok.**

líli'of 2. Diver. Cf. **Buseru.**

lílogru 2. Odds maker, one who determines the odds in gambling, esp. at cock fights.

lima 1,2. File, rub smooth or cut off with a file.

limangga 1. Tuck, pull up (in a fold or folds), roll up (shorten), shorten, tighten by drawing up or together in folds. Cf. **Heddo.** *Ya-hu na hu limangga i manggas chinina-hu.* I like to tuck up my shirt sleeve.

limbo 2. Limbo.

limenda 1. Mend (clothes), patch (tire), repair shoes. Cf. **Patche.** *I sapateru ha limenda i sapatos-hu.* The shoemaker patched my shoes.

limosna 1,2. Donate (money), contribute (money). Alms, gift, present in the form of money.

limosneru 2. Moocher, beggar.

linachi [æ] **2.** Mistake, error, falsity, fallacy, wrongness, wrongdoing. Cf. **Lachi.**

lina'chok [æ] **2.** Sprouting, growth, germination. Cf. **Dinekko'.** *Ha rega i lina'chok i simiya.* He sprinkled the sprouting seedlings.

linahyan [æ] **2.** Group, crowd, assemblage, gathering, group of, place in a group. Also **linayan, lina'yan.** Cf. **Gurupu, inetnon, katdumi.** *Maolek ha' linahyan-ña gi miteng.* It was quite a crowd at the meeting. *Maigo' yo' gi halom linahyan taotao.* I fell asleep in the middle of the group of people.

linakse [æ] **2.** Seam, clothes—ready made, edge of cloth or dress.

lina'la' [æ] **2.** Life, existence, living being. *Debi u maprotehi i lina'la' i taotao.* The life of the people must be protected.

linalalo' 2. Anger, vexation. Cf. **Binibu.**

lina'mon [æ] **2.** Experience, skill. Cf. **La'mon.**

linangitan 2. Heavenly, sublime, resembling heaven. Also **linanghitan.**

linao 2. Earthquake.

linatga [æ] **2.** Avarice.

linekka' 2. Altitude, height, elevation.

linihan 2. Panic, fright, fear, thing feared. *I linihan-hu kanna' pumuno' yo'.* My fear almost got me killed.

linila 2. Purplish, containing purple color.

linimutan 2. Mold (covered with), moldy, that which is covered with mold.

linipa 2. Fraud, deceit.

liniti 2. Mortar, mixture.

lintek 2. Filipino (slang).

linu 2. Linen, a cloth made from flax. Also **lienso.**

liña 2. Line—as on paper. Cf. **Raya.** *Dalalaki i liña.* Follow the line.

Ling Nickname for Dolores.

li'of 2. Dive, submerge.

lión 2. Lion.

lipa 1. Side with—in argument, favor, cover up for someone. *Hu lipa si Pedro.* I sided with Pedro.

lipa 2. Give vent to one's anger, let off steam. *Hu dommo' i lamasa pot para bai hu lipa i binibu-hu.* I hit the table in order to let off steam.

lipes 2. Petticoat, underskirt, slip (underwear). (R) Also **lupes a'paka'.**

lirio 2. Type of flower. Lily.

lirio di palu 2. Type of plant-agave vivipara.

lisayu 2. Rosary, necklace, string of beads used in counting prayers, the prayers of the rosary.

lisayunu 2. Breakfast—formal, morning meal. (R) Also **disayunu.** Cf. **Na'oga'an, amotsa.**

lisensia 1,2. License, permit, authorize; license, permission, condescension, allowance.

lista 2. List, index.

listo 2. Quick, alert, brisk, prompt, apt, ready. Cf. **Esta.**

litania 2. Litany. Also **litanias.**

litanias 2. Litany.

liti 1. Mix, stir (liquid), dilute, mix something with liquid. *Hu liti i gimen-hu kafe.* I stirred my coffee. *Hu liti i asukat yan i leche gi gimen-hu.* I mixed the sugar with the milk in my drink.

lítiku 2. Polio, infantile paralysis (poliomyelitis). Also refers to any type of paralysis, and especially to a rare disease-amyotropic lateral sclerosis-which has a high degree of incidence in Guam. Also refers to parkinsonian dementia.

litira 1. Dismiss, permit to leave an assignment, release someone. *I ma'gas ha litira i famagu'on.* The boss dismissed the children.

litirada 2. End of working period, quitting time. *Esta oran litirada.* It's quitting time.

litratista 2. Photography, photographer. Cf. **Fotograferu.**

litratu 1,2. Take a picture; camera, picture. Cf. **Pinenta.**

liyang 2. Cave (natural), cavern. Cf. **Bokugo', bokungo'.**

liyanggua 2. Small cave. Cf. **Liyang.**

lobu 2. Wolf, large doglike carnivorous mammals of the genus canes.

lobu 2. Balloon, bulb. Cf. **Abubu.**

loddo' 2. Fat, obese, husky, muscular, stout, thick—esp. a long object such as a root plant.

lódichan 2. Go west, move west, westward movement. Also **dodichan.** Cf. **Luchan.** *Lodichan siha sesso.* They often went west.

lódigao 2. Type of plant-clerodendruin inerme.

lodosong 2. Type of plant-entada. Type of vine.

lodosong tasi 2. Type of plant-canavalia microcarpa. Type of vine.

loffan 1. Transfer, haul, transport, carry. Cf. **Katga.**

logan 2. Type of plant-nephelium. (?).

logra 1. Acquire, win by conquest.

logra 2. Indulge.

logru 1,2. Give odds (gambling), give chance. Cf. **Yeba.**

loka 2. Lunacy, mental unsoundness, crazy, stupid. Also **loku** (m). Cf. **Kaduku, bruta, atmariao.**

lokka' 2. Tall, high, lofty.

lokklok 2. Boiled, bubbling (from heat). Cf. **Bulokbok.**

lokklok haga' 2. Hives, a kind of skin rash.

lokkue' Also, too.

loku 2. Lunacy, crazy, stupid, mental unsoundness. Also **loka** (f). Cf. **Brutu, kaduku, atmariao, tarugu.**

Lola Nickname for Dolores.

Lole' Nickname for Dolores.

lo'lo' 2. Cough, hack.

lolokklok 2. Boiling sound, bubbling, gurgling. Cf. **Bulokbok.**

lolu 2. Dull, unintelligent, slow of understanding.

loma 2. Ridge, top of a long hill, mound.

lommok 1,2. Pound, pestle, beat, pulverize, make into pulp by beating, strike heavily or repeatedly with fist, pounder, pulverizer, smasher. Cf. **Tutu.**

lomu 2. Hip, loin, haunch. Cf. **Kaderas.**

lonnat 2. Mole, birthmark, dots.

Loria Holy Saturday, the day after Good Friday; spanking day.

loru 2. Parrot (bird).

losa 2. Porcelain.

loskuantos Several, couple of. Also **noskuantos.**

lossos 2. Hoarse, grating (voice), harsh (voice), snoring, wheeze. Cf. **Lonan.**

lotge 2. Fill up, carry water in a container. *Hu lotge i basu-hu ni setbesa.* I filled up my cup with beer. *Ha lotge yo' setbesa.* He filled me up with beer. *Hanao fanlotge hanom.* Go fetch water.

lotgon 2. Fall—into a hole or pit.

lotsa 2. Nit, egg (of louse).

lottot 2. Full of lice, full of ticks. Cf. **Mehto.**

lo'u 2. Type of seaweed, usually found in shallow water, greenish-brown and grows in bunches.

lu Alternate form of *lao.*

lu'an 2. Frightened. Also **luhan.**

lu'ao 2. Type of bird-sula leucogaster plotus, brown booby.

lubradu 2. Cloudy. Also **nupbladu.**

lucha 2. Row, column, line. Cf. **Fila.**

luchan 2. West (in Guam and Rota), south (in Saipan). *Ma'pos gue' luchan.* He went west.

luga 2. Wall, partition, the upright enclosing parts of a building or a room.

luga' 1. Spit out (mouthful), to spew or spray out of mouth by blowing, such as a mouthful of chewed coconut meat after juice is gone. Cf. **Bohbo, boyok.**

luga' 1,2. Apply pomade or shampoo, shampoo, pomade, oil—for hair, hair dressing of an oily or liquid type.

luga' haga' 2. Blood blister, a darkening of skin caused from pinching or mashing, such as a finger mashed by a blow from a hammer. Cf. **Dinigridu.**

lugát 2. Place, area, location, residential area, region, locality, spot, site.

lugát 2. Spare time, extra time, time to kill. *Taya' lugat-hu.* I don't have any spare time now.

luhan 2. Frightened, scared, terrified, horrified, fear. Also **lu'an.** Cf. **Susto, manghang.**

luhuriosu 2. Playboy, one who seeks worldly pleasures, hedonist. *Luhuriosu na taotao.* The man is a playboy.

lukao 2. Procession, usually a church procession, wandering around. *Lumukao yo'.* I was at the procession. *Humanao gue' para i likao.* He went to the procession.

lulai 2. Type of fishing, moonlight night fishing on the reef with a fishing line or with a pole and a line.

lulo' 2. Lift head—so as to display the front neck. Cf. **Ngaha'.**

lulok 2. Steel, metal, iron, nail.

luluhot 2. Type of plant-maytenus thompsonii. Type of vine.

luluki 1. Nail, fasten.

lumámagof [æ] 1. Relieve, free from pain. Cf. **Magof.**

lumámaolek [æ] 1. Improve, make better.

lumámeggai [æ] 1. Increase—in number, enlarge, enhance.

Lumamlam 2. September. Cf. **Septiembre.**

lumayak [æ] 2. Sail, be moved by a sail. *Lumalayak i boti.* The boat is sailing. *Hu na'layak i boti.* I sailed the boat.

lumbang 2. Type of plant-aleurites moluccana. (?).

lumos 1. Drown, suffocate. Cf. **Ñokñok, matmos.**

lumot 2. Moss, lichen, type of seaweed, green vegetation covering still water.

lumot katdeniyu 2. Green moss covering still water, a type of algae.

Lumuhu 2. April. Cf. **Abrit.**

lumulai 2. Type of fishing—go fishing on a moonlit night on the reef with a fishing line or a pole and a line.

lunátiku 2. Lunatic.

Lunes 2. Monday.

luño' 1. Insert—something in a pliable substance, such as mud or dough; cause to sink in. *Hu luño' i estaka gi fache'.* I inserted the stake in the mud.

luño' 2. Soft ground, that caves in when one walks on it, as in walking on the sand or swamp. Cf. **Fokfok.**

lupes 2. Skirt, petticoat.

lupes a'paka' 2. Half slip—ladies undergarment.

lupok 1. To dip water in bucket—or other comparable vessel, get water in bucket. *In lipok i hanom gi tipo'.* We dipped water in the well.

lupok 2. Deep hole—in the ground, crevasse. Cf. **Maddok.**

luseru 2. Star—north, star--morning. Cf. **Puti'on chatanmak.**

lusong 2. Mortar.

lusu 1. Release, untie, slacken, loosen. Cf. **Na'kallo.** *Hu lusu i lasu gi*

aga'ga' i guaka. I released the lasso on the cow's neck.

Luta 2. Rota—the southernmost island in the Marianas District, just north of Guam.

lutu 2. Mourning, sorrow, grief, mourning dress, dress up in black (when a husband or wife dies).

ma They—pre-posed pronoun used in transitive statements.

ma- Passive marker, used as prefix usually with verbs. *Ma'espiha si Jose nigap.* Joseph was looked for yesterday. *Mahuchom i petta.* The door was closed. *Mali' e' gue'.* He was seen.

ma- Verbalizing prefix. *Macho'cho yo'.* I worked. *Mata'chong yo'.* I sat down.

ma'agoddai 2. Excited, angered, fighting (mad). Also **ma'goddai.** *I palao'an ha na'ma'agoddai si Badu.* The girl made Badu excited (or angry).

ma'akgak [æ] 2. Cut on foot, cut on sole of foot by a sharp object, such as a broken glass, slash by a sharp object on the sole of foot.

ma'aksom [æ] 2. Sour, acid, acidulous, tart.

ma'ankla 2. To anchor.

ma'a'ñao 2. Afraid, scared, frightened, terrified, be threatened, be menaced. Also **ma'a'añao.**

ma'arimata 2. Last church bell before mass begins. *Ma'arimata i kampana.* The last church bell rang.

ma'ase' 2. Mercy, merciful, pity, forgiveness, sympathy. *Ma'ase' i lahi.* The man has mercy. *I ma'estro ma'ase' ni patgon.* The teacher had sympathy for the child. *Hu respeta i mina'ase'.* I respect forgiveness.

ma'asen [æ] 2. Salty, saline, briny, brackish.

ma'asne 2. Salted.

ma'atde [æ] 2. Need to defecate.

mabakbak [æ] 2. Low cut, something that is cut low, such as the neck or back of a dress.

mabende 2. Sold. *Mabende i kareta-hu.* My car was sold.

mabira 2. Overturned, capsized, inverted, reversed, turn around. Cf. **Bira, puha.** *Mabira i batko.* The boat was turned around.

mabotda 2. Embroidery. Cf. **Botda.**

machaba' 2. Cut lip—by hitting chin against something. *Machaba' i patgon gi lamasa.* The child cut his lip on the table.

machachalani 2. Instructed.

machaflakos 2. Wrinkled skin—used in teasing someone about getting old. *Todu machaflakos hao.* You're getting wrinkled.

machakchak [æ] 2. Break of dawn, dawning. Cf. **Pa'go manana.**

machakchak kattan 2. Dawn, daybreak.

machalapon [æ] 2. Scattered, spread.

machalehgua' 2. Divulged, diffused, spread about. Cf. **Lehgua'.**

machalek 2. Wild (animals), untamed, not domesticated, an evasive person who is skillful in avoiding people he prefers not to see; barbaric.

machalonchon 2. Messed up, in a state of disarray. Also **machalonchom.** *Machalonchon i magagu-hu.* My clothes were messed up.

machatatan [æ] 2. Hated, hateful.

macheng [æ] 2. Monkey, ape. Cf. **Saro'.**

macheng [æ] 2. Type of fish-any member of the families platychephalidae, bleniidae, and goriidae. Whitish mangrove hoppers, and other small fish.

maches 2. Match, matches.

machette. 2. Machete.

machetten anakko' 2. Long machete.

machetten matadót 2. Cleaver, a butcher's cleaver.

macho'cho' 2. Work, labor, toil, drudge, employed—be busy, be industrious, be diligent.

machom 2. Become closed, become impassable, become covered with vines, trees, bushes, etc., stopped up. *Machom i chalan para i saddok.* The road to the river became impassable.

machom 2. Unaggressive male, effeminate man. Cf. **Mamflorita.**

machora 2. Sterile (f), not capable of reproducing.

machuda' 1. Overflow.

madakngas 2. Shave head, make bald.

maddok 2. Hole, pit, cavity, a hollow place. Cf. **Ngulo', hoyu.** *Hu na'maddok i papet.* I made a hole in my paper. *Humalom i cha'ka gi*

maddok hayu. The rat went inside the hole of the tree.

maddok atgoya 2. Hole in which a nose ring of a carabao is inserted.

maddok gui'eng 2. Nostril.

maddok tátaotao 2. Pores—of the human skin.

maddok yabi 2. Keyhole.

madea 2. Coil of rope, ball of yarn, ball of twine, bundle of rope. Also **madeha.** (S) Cf. **Mandeha.**

madeha 2. Coil of rope, coil of yarn, bundle of rope. Also **madea.**

maderas 2. Lumber—for house construction.

madoya 2. Fried banana—ripe and dipped in flour before frying.

madre 2. Nun, mother (church). (S) Cf. **etmana, mongha.**

madre superiora 2. Mother superior.

madúlalak 2. Expulsion, expelled from.

madulok dagan 2. Anus. Also **maddok dagan.**

ma'empon 2. Need to urinate.

ma'estro 2. Teacher, instructor (m). Also **ma'estra** (f).

ma'etdot 2. Numb, be numbed, make numb.

mafa'baba [æ] 2. Be cheated, be fooled, be tricked, be defrauded.

mafa'boreresi 2. Favorite, minion, bosom child.

mafa'ga'ga' [æ] 2. Be treated as an animal (fig.).

mafama 2. Be well-known, be well-liked, illustrious (of deeds or acts, famous), be praised. Cf. **Matuna.**

mafañagu 2. Born, brought into existence by or as by birth, birthday. *Mafañagu yo' giya Saipan.* I was born in Saipan. *Pa'go mafañagu-hu.* Today is my birthday.

maffak 2. Shatter, burst, break into fragments, crack (on the head). *Maffak i basu anai poddong gi lamasa.* The cup was broken when it fell off the table.

maffong 2. Sleeping soundly, sound asleep.

mafgo' 2. Bent, fractured, squeezed. Cf. **Fugo'.**

mafla 2. Muffler (of engine). Cf. **Mafura.**

mafnas 2. Faded, lose color, wiped out.

mafnot 2. Tight, full. Also **mafñot**.

mafñot [æ] 2. Tight. Also **mafnot**.

mafondo 2. Sink, subside, become submerged, swallowed up, go down as to be partly covered. Cf. **Fondo**. *Mafondo i batko.* The ship sank. *Mafondo i addeng-hu gi fache'.* My feet sank in the mud.

mafongfong 1. Pug-nose, short nose. *Manosge i patgon gi as nana-ña mafongfong.* The child takes after her mother's pug-nose.

mafte' 2. Nicked (blade), broken tooth, a nick in the sharp edge of a cutting tool. Cf. **Doffe', tengteng, chebbang**.

máfura 2. Muffler (of engine). (S) Also **mafla**.

mafute' 2. Type of fish-family lutjanidae. Snappers.

maga 2. Early, before its proper time. Cf. **Taftaf**. *Maga i ichan.* The rain came early.

maga'an 2. Awake—wide. (R) Cf. **Makmata**.

magagu 2. Clothes, dress, shirt, yardage. Cf. **Bestidu**.

maga'haga 2. First lady, in old Chamorro society the wife of the highest ranking male. Lit. daughter of the chief. Also **asaguan maga'lahi**.

magahet 2. Honest, truthful, frank, true, sincere, indeed, authentic, genuine. Cf. **Franko, sinseru, onesto, siguru**. *Magahet yo' na hu espiha hao gi eskuela.* I am truthful that I looked for you at school. *Magahet na maolek hao bumola.* Indeed, you are a good ball player.

maga'lahi 2. Ruler, the highest rank of a state, as president, governor, mayor, magistrate, chief, chieftain.

maga'om 2. Have sex appeal.

magap 2. Yawn, evaporate.

ma'gas 2. Boss, master, superior, foreman, manager, be master. Cf. **Amu**.

ma'gasi 1. Govern, rule, dominate.

magéfatan 2. Screened, looked over carefully.

magéftungo' 2. Popular, well known.

magen This side of. Fr. *magi. I pilan gaige gi magen i atdao.* The moon is on this side of the sun. *I kareta-hu magen i kareta-mu.* My car is on this side of your car.

maggem [æ] 2. Damp, wilted, humid, limp from moisture, soft hearted. Cf. **Umidu, malayu**.

maggem [æ] 2. Silent, cautious.

magguak 2. Roomy, big, large quantity.

magi Here, (toward or in the direction of the speaker). *Chule' magi.* Bring it here. *Espiha guini magi.* Look for it over here.

magof [æ] 2. Happy, gay, glad, delight.

magófatan 2. Liked, beloved, favorite.

magofli'e' 2. Beloved, dear.

magomgom 2. Contusion, internal injury. *Magomgom i sanhalom-ña.* He has internal injuries.

magong 2. Healed, recovered. Cf. **Lato'**. *Magong i chetnot gi addeng-hu.* The wound on my foot is healed.

maguan 2. Type of dish.

maguro' 2. Type of fish-neothunnus albacora macropterus. Yellow fin tuna.

magutos i finiho' 2. Last word involving marriage discussion among family members; betrothal. Last details are decided upon at this time.

mahadera 2. Hussy, tricky gal. Cf. **Tulisan, pikara, petbetsa**.

mahaderu 2. Rascal, rogue, scoundrel, tricky fellow, knave, villain. Cf. **Tulisan, pikaru, petbetso**.

máhadok 2. Dimple. Cf. **Hadok**.

mahaga' 2. Be in heat, menstruating. Cf. **Haga'**.

mahagga' 2. Bleed. Cf. **Haga'**. *Mahahagga' i taotao.* The man is bleeding.

mahagga' gui'eng 2. Nose bleed.

mahalang 2. Yearn, feel an earnest desire, lonely.

mahañas [æ] 2. Deflated, shrinkage through loss of air or liquid.

mahange' [æ] 2. Rancid, stale, not fresh, spoiled food.

mahatot [æ] 2. Disagreeable, aloof, strong personality, difficult to overcome. *Mahatot na kontrariu.* The opponent is tough.

mahatot [æ] 2. Bitter feeling, bitter taste, bitter.

mahayo' 2. Well trained—especially for heavy farm work. Also **mahayu**.

mahayu Strong, hardy, indefatigable. Cf. **Metgot**. Also **mahayo'**.

maheddo 2. Shrunk, contracted, cause to shrink, cause to contract.

maheffong 2. Dented, dull point, flat nose, crumbled, cave in. Cf. **Bulengngo', daloggai.** *Hu na'maheffong i lapes-mu.* I caused your pencil to have a dull point. *Maheffong i kareta-ña nigap.* His car was dented yesterday. *Maheffong i gui'eng-mu.* You have a flat nose.

mahegat 2. Muscular, strong. Cf. **Fuetsudu.**

mahetok 2. Obdurate, hard, firm, hardened in feeling, stubborn. Cf. **Sugat.**

mahgef [æ] 2. Tired (physically), become tired, weary, made tired by doing something for too long. Cf. **Yafai.**

mahgong 2. Calm, peaceful. *Todu esta manmahgong.* Everything is peaceful.

mahlok 2. Fractured, broken—by bending, twisting, etc., wrinkled starched clothes. *Mahlok i haguha.* The needle was broken. *Mahlok i maprensan magagu-hu.* My pressed clothes were wrinkled.

mahlos 2. Smooth, frictionless, not rough, become smooth. Cf. **Finu.**

mahñao 2. Refrain (from an action), postpone, change of decision, return to former state, cancel. *Mahñao gue' gi biahi-ña para Hawaii.* He canceled his trip to Hawaii.

mahngang [æ] 2. Startled, stupefied, stunned, frightened suddenly, start or move suddenly, as in surprise, fear, etc. Also **manghang.** *Mahngang yo' anai un pacha i apaga-hu.* I was startled when you touched me on the shoulder.

mahngok 2. Public, celebrated, well known. Cf. **Hungok.**

ma'ho 2. Thirsty. Also **ma'o.**

maholok hayu 2. Type of plant-geniostoma micranthum. (?).

maholok layu 2. Type of plant-timonius nitidus. (?).

mahongang 2. Lobster, langouste, be scared. Cf. **Hongang.**

mai'agas 2. Type of plant-cassytha filiformis. A parasitic vine. Type of vine.

mai'ana 2. Type of plant-iresine. Bleeding heart.

ma'i'eng 1. Peel—first layer of husk from ripe coconut with one's fingers.

mai'es 2. Type of plant-zea mays. Also **ma'es.** Corn.

maigo' 2. Sleep, slumber, hibernate, spin so quickly and smoothly that its motion is imperceptible.

maigo' lalo' 2. Type of plant-phyllanthus amarus. Type of grass.

maigo'ñaihon 2. Nap.

mai'imot 2. Stingy, tight with money.

maila' 1. Come, hand over. *Maila'.* Come (to me). *Maila' i salape'.* Hand over the money.

Maimo 2. February. Cf. **Febreru.**

ma'i'ot 2. Narrow, acute, not wide or broad.

maipe 2. Hot, fiery, suggesting heat. *Maipe na ha'ani.* It's a hot day.

mairastra 2. Stepmother. Also **mairasta.**

maisa Alone, oneself, self (reflexive). *Guiya na maisa humanao.* He went by himself.

makabebi 2. Cripple, lame—physically disabled in the leg or foot. Cf. **Chanko.**

makachichi 2. Wrinkled skin.

makahnayi 1. Be bewitched. Cf. **kahnayi.**

makaka [æ] 2. Itch, sexual climax (slang), feel itchy.

makalamya 2. Dexterous, agile, active, nimble, quick. Cf. **Kalamya.**

makalaton [æ] 2. Rough.

makalehlo 2. Wrinkle, crease, pucker, slight fold, wrinkled skin.

makana' [æ] 2. Hang. Cf. **Kana'.**

mákaro' 2. Type of fish-euthynnus affinis yaito. Tuna.

makaroni 2. Macaroni.

mákina 2. Engine, machine.

makinan chachak 2. Sawmill, electric saw.

makinan manlakse 2. Sewing machine.

makinan mañotda 2. Welding machine.

makinan mangge' 2. Typewriter.

makineria 2. Machinery.

makinista 2. Mechanic, machinist.

makkat [æ] 2. Difficult, hard, not easy, hard to do, make, or carry out. Cf. **Chatsaga, mappot.**

makkat [æ] 2. Heavy, weighty, ponderous, cumbrous, cumbersome.

Makmamao 2. May. Cf. **Mayu**

makmata 2. Waken, wake up.

makna huegu 2. Type of plant-dioscorea bulbifera. (?) Yam.

maknitu 2. Magnet, magnetic. Cf. **Aseru.**

makño' 2. Sink in, be sunk in. *Makño' yo' gi fache'.* I sank in the mud.

maknganiti 2. Devil, satan. (R) Also **manganiti.** Cf. **Aniti, hudas, satanas, diablo, dimonio.**

makodu 2. Hand wrestle. Cf. **Kodu.** *Kao ya-mu makodu?* Do you want to hand wrestle?

Makpe' 2. Marpe—a point on the north end of Saipan.

makpo' 2. Finished, terminated, over, come to an end, adjourn.

makpong 2. Type of sickness—esp. among children, bed-wetting.

maktan 2. Gutter, down spout, channel for carrying away water.

maktingan 2. Deep water outside the reef. Also **mattinan.**

maktos 2. Snap, as in string, rubber band, etc., break off. *Maktos i tali.* The rope snapped.

makupa 2. Type of plant-eugenia javanica, or e. malaccensis. A type of tree.

makuttinayi 2. Be curtained. *Makuttinayi i petta.* The door has a curtain on it.

mala 2. Bad, evil. *Todu enao mala bida-ña.* All those are his wrong doings. *Hu suspecha na mala intension-ña.* I suspected his evil intentions.

malachai [æ] **2.** Exhausted, used up.

mala'et [æ] **2.** Bitter, caustic, acrimonious, distasteful.

malaganas 2. No appetite. Cf. **Taiganas.**

malago' [æ] **2.** Want, desire, wish for, long for, will, need. *Malago' gue' humanao.* He wants to go. *I minalago'-ña para humanao.* He wants to go.

malagradesidu 2. Thankless, ungrateful, merciless. Also **malagradesida** (f).

malagu 2. Run, take flight, make off rapidly, gallop, dash, spurt. Cf. **Falagu.**

malahechura 2. Disfigured.

ma'lak [æ] **2.** Brilliant, sparkling, glittering, radiant, bright, luminous.

malak [æ] **2.** Go to, depart for, usually used as past form or infinitive. Cf. **Hanao.** *Malago' yo' malak Honolulu.* I want to go to Honolulu. *Malak Honolulu yo'.* I went to Honolulu.

malakara 2. Sourface.

malakes [æ] **2.** Penis (slang).

malaknos [æ] **2.** Bulge.

malaktos 2. Stern, severe, serious look. *Malaktos mata-ña i profesot.* The professor's face is very stern. *I lahi ti siña ha dingu i asagua-ña na maisa sa' mampos malaktos inigo'-ña.* The man cannot leave his wife alone because of his severe jealousy.

malakuenta 2. Hold responsible. *Munga yo' malakuenta.* I don't want to be held responsible.

malamaña 2. Cruel, merciless, fierce, savage. Cf. **Daddao.**

malaña' [æ] **2.** Dissolute, a worthless person. A derogatory term considered taboo in polite society. Penis (slang).

malangon pulan 2. Menstrual period. Cf. **Rumekkla.**

malangu 2. Sick, ill, not well.

malas 2. Points from one through nine in tres siete (card game).

malasa [æ] **2.** Massaged, to be rubbed down.

malassas 2. Bruise, be skinned, be peeled, be scabbed.

malate' 2. Smart, intelligent, clever, alert. Cf. **Tomtom, menhalom, kabilosu, intelihente.** *Malate' i abugao.* The lawyer is smart.

malatte' 2. Be scabbed, be peeled (of sore scab), removal of a scab. *Malatte' i chetnot-hu.* My sore was scabbed.

malayu 2. Wilted, dry (leaves), showing lack of fluid. Cf. **Maggem.**

maleffa 2. Forget, neglect, be unable to recall. Also **malefa.** *Maleffa yo' ni lepblo.* I forgot the book. *Maleffa i patgon ni lepblo.* The child forgot the book.

maleta 2. Baggage, suitcase, luggage, trunk (for clothes).

malinao 2. Calm water, still water, as the ocean, sea, lake.

malinek ulu 2. Headache.

malingu 2. Lost, disappeared, vanished, missing, deficit. *I malingu na taotao.* The lost man. *Ha na'falingu i ga'lagu.* He lost the dog.

malinguñaihon 2. Doze off. Cf. **malingu.**

malisia 2. Malice, malevolence, ill will, malignity, grudge.

malisiosu 2. Malicious, evil-minded, slanderous.

malle' 2. Short form for *kumaire.*

maloffan 2. Transported, toted, hauled, transferred, carried from one place to another. Cf. **Loffan.** *Maloffan i fektos siha ginen i batko asta i tenda.* The merchandise was carried away from the ship to the store.

maloffan Past time, recently, previous, some time ago, previously. Cf. **Halacha.** *Maloffan esta i tiempo anai para u fatto magi.* The time is past already when he would be here. *Tres dias maloffan ti hu li'e' hao.* I haven't seen you for three days. Or, Three days have passed since I saw you.

maloffan Exceedingly, surpassingly, superlatively, notably, excessively, extremely, amazingly, preeminently, immeasurably. *Maloffan yo' yayas.* I am excessively tired. *Maloffan i patgon aguaguat.* The child is immeasurably naughty. *Maloffan hao tonto.* You are extremely foolish.

maloria 2. Be punished, be spanked. Cf. **Loria.** *Siempre maloria hao.* You are going to be spanked.

malulasa [æ] **2.** Smooth. Cf. **Mahlos.**

malulok 2. Gorged, glutted, satiated, filled to repletion, be rich of (something), untrammeled, unhampered, have more than ample supply of something. Cf. **Dafflok, tuhos, mutero', go'dan, dafflokgue.** *Malulok yo' gumimen kok gi gipot.* I had as much coke as I wanted to drink at the party. *Si Pete malulok chumocho mangga.* Pete had eaten his fill of mangoes.

malumoradu 2. Bad humor.

malumót 2. Sickening odor, contagiousness.

mama' 1. Chew betel nut—mixed with lime, pepper leaf and tobacco. Cf. **Mama'on.**

mama' 2. False alarm, to err in keeping appointment or responding to a call.

mama'- [æ] Change into, become, turn into (prefix). Cf. **Fa'-.** *Mama'kaddo i batatas.* The potatoes became liquid.

Mama'hanom i asukat. The sugar turned into a liquid.

mama'ais 2. Freeze, frozen.

mama'baba [æ] 2. Fool around, goof around, act silly, not being serious, be bad, became bad.

mama'che'cho' 2. Struggle, to put forth great effort, scuffle.

mama'chigo' 2. Sore—infected, containing pus, abscess. Cf. **Chugo'.**

mamadót 2. Baby bottle—with nipple.

mama'gas 2. Type of fish-family priacanthidae. Big eyes.

mama'gasiyan 2. Washbasin.

mámaguantes [æ] 2. Boxer, one who fights or boxes.

mamahlao 2. Ashamed, be ashamed, shamefaced, bashful, shy, embarrassed. Also **mamalao.**

mámahna 2. Calf, the fleshy hind part of the leg below the knee. Also **mamanha.**

mamaila' 2. Come, get here, arrive, show up. Cf. **Matto, maila'.** *Mamaila' si Jose gi gima'.* Jose came to the house.

mamaila'ña na mes 2. Month after next, two months later. (R) Cf. **Otroña na mes.**

mamaila'ña na sakkan 2. Year after next, two years later. (R) Cf. **Otroña na sakkan.**

mamaila'ña na simana 2. Week after next, two weeks later. (R) Cf. **Otroña na simana.**

mámaisa 2. Single, sole, solitary, isolated.

mamaisen 2. Ask for—something, ask for (permission). *Mamaisen yo' infotmasion pot Hawaii.* I asked for information about Hawaii.

mamaisen saina 2. Ask the bride's parents for hand in marriage.

mamaitaguan 2. Weakened, enfeebled, debilitated, loss of energy, unconscious, faint. Also **mama' i taguan.** Cf. **Tisu, lalangu.**

mámakanno' [æ] 2. Edible, fit to be eaten as food.

mama'lahi 2. Manly, courageous.

mamalao 2. Ashamed, be ashamed, shamefaced, bashful, shy. Also **mamahlao.**

mamale' 2. Priests, pastors, preachers, ministers—plural for *pale.*

mama'loma 2. Resembling a ridge. Cf. **Loma.**

mama'ma'gas [æ] 2. Stuck-up, conceited, self-opinionated, pretending to be a boss, arrogant.

mamamaila' na mes 2. Coming month. Cf. **Otro na mes.**

mamamaila' na sakkan 2. Coming year. Cf. **Otro na sakkan.**

mamamaila' na simana Coming week. Cf. **Otro na simana.**

mámamfok [æ] 2. Weaver—of mats or baskets. Cf. **Tutufok, fafamfok.**

mámanha [æ] 2. Calf. Also **mamana.**

mamantieni 2. Impounded.

mama'on 2. Betel nut—mixed with lime, pepper leaf, tobacco, etc. Cf. **Mama'.** *Bula mama'on giya Luta.* There are lots of betel nut with its ingredients in Rota.

mámatago' [æ] 2. Inferior, subordinate.

mama'tatte [æ] 2. Straggle, lag behind.

mama'te 2. Low tide, becoming low tide, shallow water. Cf. **Ma'te.**

mamatek 2. Buck, kick up hind quarters esp. of four legged animals. Cf. **patek.**

mamatkilu 2. Being quiet, hush, silence, silent. Cf. **Pakaka', fatkilu.** *Mamatkilu i estudiante gi klas.* The student was quiet in class. *Mamatkilu si Juan anai humalom i ma'estro gi klas.* John was silent when the teacher went inside the class.

máma'udai [æ] 2. Rider.

máma'ya [æ] 2. Superficial, not thorough, indecisive, wandering mind.

máma'ya [æ] 2. Navigable, bouyant.

mambula 2. Pregnant. Cf. **Mapotge'.**

mambula 2. Swollen, filled.

Mame' Nickname for Carmen, used for younger women.

mameddos 2. Climbed up, got up. Cf. **Feddos.**

mames [æ] 2. Sweet, kind, sugary taste.

mamfe' 2. To pick (fruit). Also **manfe'.** Cf. **Tife'.**

mamflores 2. Bloom, produce, yield (blossom), flourish.

mamflorita 2. Hermaphrodite, homosexual, effiminate male. Bi-sexual goat.

mamfok 2. Weave, plait. Cf. **Tufok.**

mamfong 2. Count—prefixed form of *tufong.* Variant of *manufong.* Cf. **Tufong.**

-mami Our, ours, us—possessive, exclusive. *Karetan-mami este.* This is our car.

mamokkat 2. Walk, roam, stroll, rove. Cf. **Pokkat.**

mamo'lo 1. Put, place. *Po'lo* plus *man-.*

mamo'lo 2. Perfunctory, done carelessly with purpose of getting rid of duty.

mamo'lo 2. Ceases to reproduce, unable to reproduce anymore.

mamopble 2. Poor (pl), needy. Cf. **Popble.**

mámpo'lo [æ] 2. Customary place, proper place, usual place. *Po'lo gi anai mampo'lo.* Put it in its usual place.

mampos [æ] Very, extreme, exceeding great, greatest, of the highest degree. Cf. **Sen, gof.**

mamta' 2. Increasing.

mamuda 2. Dressed up, dolled up, change clothes.

mamuga' 2. Split widely open, fart (slang). Cf. **Puga'.**

mamulan 2. Type of fish-family carangidae. Large skipjack, from 15 to 100 pounds or more.

mamulan 2. Keep vigil, watch over, keep guard; watch for while hunting at night. *Mamulan yo' gi espitat gi painge.* I kept vigil at the hospital last night.

mamuti 2. Painful joints, aching muscles, sore muscles.

man 2. Type of plant-dicranopteris linearis. (?).

man- [æ] Plural subject marker used in intransitive statements. Occurs as *fan-* in future tense. *Mañaga ham giya Tamuning.* We stayed in Tamuning. *Para in fañaga gi tihon-mami giya Guam.* We are going to stay at our uncle's on Guam.

man- [æ] Indefinite object marker. May occur with plural subject marker *man-,* occurs as *fan-* in future tense. *Ya-hu manespiha sidan-hu giya Guam.* I like to look for a sedan for my own on Guam. *Yan-ñiha na u fandraiba kareta.* They like to drive a car.

mana'- [æ] It is made—combination of passive voice and causative used with class 2 words. *Mana'maigo' i neni gi kuna.* The baby was made to sleep in the crib. *Guahu mana'taitai ni gaseta.* I was the one who was made to read the newspaper.

manachang 2. Bashful, shy. Cf. **Mamahlao.** Refers to lower class of people in earlier Chamorro society.

manada 2. Plenty, lots of, surfeit, herd. *Mutero' i bulacheru manadan setbesa.* The drunkard had too much beer.

manadahi [æ] **2.** Hoard, collect and store.

maná'echan [æ] **2.** Matching area—at cockpit, where owners of the cocks meet to decide which cocks are to be paired off for fighting.

managaga' [æ] **2.** Blush. Cf. **agaga'.**

mana'huyong 2. Created, order, directive. *Mana'huyong i taotao ginen i taya'.* Man was created from nothing. *Mana'huyong tinago' na taya' taotao siña pumeska binadu.* The order was given out that nobody was allowed to hunt deer.

manai- None, not have (plural). Comb. of *man-* plus *tai-.* Cf. **Tai.** *Manaihanom ham gi lancho.* We don't have any water at the ranch.

manakihom 2. Frugal, thrifty, parsimonious.

Manan Nickname for Hermana.

manana [æ] **2.** Daylight, daytime, light —of day.

manana [æ] **2.** A clearing, clear, features are easily distinguished, clear-headed.

Mananaf 2. June. Cf. **Junio.**

mana'payon 2. Customary, habitual. *Mana'payon mahoggue i neni.* They caused the baby to want to be carried habitually.

manatma 2. Headstrong, stubborn.

mancha 2. Stain, spot, discolored with foreign matter. Cf. **Chatko, pekas.**

manda 1. Command, rule. Cf. **Gobietna, nombra.**

mandagi [æ] **2.** Lie, denial, deceit.

mando 2. Authority—position of, assuming responsibility. *Guahu pa'go mando gi gima'.* I am now the authority at the house. *Hayi mando gi che'cho'-miyu?* Who is the authority at your work?

mandolina 2. Mandolin.

manea 1. Manage, operate, supervise, guide, control, direct, conduct, boss, lead, regulate, head. Cf. **Kondukta, dirihi, mando.**

maneha 2. Manage. Also **manea.**

manehyok 2. Severe pain. Also **maneyok.**

manempeya 2. Fat, greasy.

manempluma 2. Grow feathers, moult, having new feathers, renewed courage (slang).

manengheng 2. Cold, frigid, chilled, gelid. Cf. **Fugu.**

manera 2. Manner, way, mode, style, fashion, method. Cf. **Pusision.**

maneska 2. Liquor, alcoholic drink, beverage—alcoholic.

manespiga 2. Tasseling (corn), have tassel, bear tassel.

maneyok 2. Severe pain. Also **manehyok.** Cf. **Puti.**

manha 2. Green coconut, with tender meat. Also **manna.**

manhale' 2. Grow root, sprout root. *Manhale' i niyok.* The coconut grows roots.

manhoben 2. Youngsters, young people.

manhufa 2. To stretch out both arms.

manifesta 1. Manifest, show. Also **manifiesta.**

manifestasión 2. Manifestation, showing, exhibition, unfoldment.

manifesto 2. Manifest—list of cargo, manifesto.

manila' 2. Flame, illuminated, lighted. *Manila' i kandet.* The light was on.

mániya 2. Manager.

manka 2. One armed, amputated arm, amputee—arm (f). Cf. **Ma'tot.**

manko 2. Crippled, one armed, amputated, pruned, amputee—arm, cut off, bow-legged (m). Also **manka** (f). Cf. **Ma'tot.** *I duranten i gera anai manko i kannai-hu.* It was during the war when my hand was amputated.

mankuetnas 2. Cuff link.

manman [æ] **2.** Sluggish, slow moving, markedly slow in movement, slow. Cf. **Ñama'.**

manman [æ] **2.** Astonished, surprised, amazed, astounded, stare blankly, perplexed.

manna 2. Green coconut. Also **manha.**

mannai Plural of *tai*.

mannok 2. Chicken, poultry. (Generic term).

mannge' 2. Delicious, exquisite, highly pleasing to the senses, taste, or mind. Cf. **Dilisiosu**.

manó 2. Bundle—of things tied together, things tied together, bunch--of things tied together, such as onions, beans, wood, etc. (R) Also **manohu**.

manohu 1,2. Bundle, bind, fasten, tie on, sheaf. Also **mano**. Cf. **Fuñot, godde**.

manokcha' 2. Sprout, bring forth fruit.

manosge 2. Resemble. Cf. **Gapi**.

mansana 2. Apple.

mansanan paotake' Type of plant.

mansanita 2. Type of plant-muntingia calabura. Parsma berry. Very sweet with many seeds, about the size of a cherry.

mansaniya 2. Type of plant-chrysanthemum morifolium. Chrysanthemum. Cf. **Yetban Santa Maria**.

manso 2. Tame, docile, timid, harmless, domesticated.

manta 2. Cloth—coarse cotton, unbleached muslin.

manteles 2. Tablecloth, white tablecloth used for special occasions.

mantensión 2. Supplies, provisions, food, subsistence, act of providing.

mantieni 1. Hold, seize, grasp, receive and keep in the hand. Cf. **Sustieni, go'te, gu'ot**.

mantika 2. Lard, fat, lardy, fatty, greasy, oily, grease.

mantikan leche 2. Cream, oily part of milk.

mantikiya 2. Butter.

mantiya 2. Mantilla, head shawl.

manu 2. Millstone, roller, the smaller of the two pieces of stone used for grinding corn, rice, etc.

manu Which, whichever—interrogative. *Manu mas ya-mu na lugat?* Which place do you like the best?

manu nai Where (question word), used with verbs. Cf. **Mangge**. *Manu nai sumasaga hao?* Where are you staying?

manugong 2. Moan, groan, lament. Cf. **Ugong**.

manugong 2. Take off (with high speed), dash, rush, bolt, start forth. Cf. **Tugong**.

Manúng Nickname for Manuel.

manungo' 2. Literate, knowledgeable.

maña 2. Custom, habit, tradition. Cf. **Kustombre, bisio**.

mañada' 2. Lay (egg). Cf. **Chada'**. *Mañada' i mannok*. The chicken laid eggs.

mañagu 2. Give birth, bear a child. Cf. **Mafañagu**. *Mañagu yo'*. I gave birth.

mañague' 2. Death quiver, convulsion, convulsive quivering, usually indicating approaching death, twitching of body. *Mañague' i lahi-hu anai tres meses i idat-ña*. My son had a convulsion when he was three months old.

mañahak 2. Type of fish-family siganidae. Rabbit fish.

mañaina 2. Parents, elders (pl). Cf. **Saina**.

máñaña' [æ] 2. Soft, tender, lenient, easily yielding to physical pressure, gentle, yielding.

mañeha 2. Move backwards.

mañe'lo 2. Siblings, brothers, sisters. Plural for *che'lo*.

mañetnot 2. Infected—with sores.

mañila' 2. Inflame, light up, glare, burst into flame, become inflamed, blaze, lightning. Cf. **Lamlam**. *Mañila' i gima'*. The house is in flames. *Ma'lak na mañila'*. It is a brilliant glare. *Mañila' i chetnot-hu*. My wound is inflamed.

mañini 2. Pregnant. Cf. **Mapotge, sini**.

mañokñok 2. Sunk, submerged. Cf. **Makño', mafondo**.

mañom [æ] 2. Cold, flu, runny nose. *Mañom yo'*. I have a cold.

mañongsong 2. Clogged up, plugged up. Cf. **Songsong**. *Mañongson yo' maddok*. I plugged up the hole.

mañostieni 2. Cling, hang on to, hold on to, clasp, grip, brace. Cf. **Sostieni**.

mañotsot 2. Reformed, repented.

mañufa' 2. Rooting (pig), fall on face. Cf. **Sufa'**.

mañugo' 2. Suppurate, fester, orgasm, generate pus or juice, ejaculate, ooze.

mañusu 2. Budding, have buds.

Mang Nickname for Herman.

ma'ngak 2. Tilt, lose balance, teeter, rock. Cf. **Aso'.**

manganiti 2. Devil, satan. Also **maknganiti.**

mangeke- Begin to, start to, about to (do something), try to. Auxiliary used in plural constructions with indefinite objects. Cf. **Keke, kumeke.** *Mangekeñangu hit.* We are about to swim. *Hafa mangeke'ilek-ñiha?* What are they trying to say?

mangfong 2. Reckon, count, compute. Also **mamfong.**

mangga 2. Mango (fruit).

manggai Plural of *gai.*

manggas 2. Sleeve.

mangge Where (question word). Used with nouns or stative constructions. Cf. **Manu nai.** *Mangge i kareta?* Where is the car?

mangge' 2. Write, inscribe, transcribe, jot down, typewrite. Cf. **Tuge'.**

manggo 1,2. Steering wheel.

manggosne 2. Molt—crustaceans. Also **manggosña.**

manggosña 2. Molt, molting process referring to crustaceans as when a crab becomes soft after it sheds its shell. (R) Also **manggosne.**

manggua' 2. Cartoon, funny act, humorous, joker, jester. (S)

mangguetna 1. To harness a runaway cow behind a water buffalo in order to bring it back to its proper place. Also used when referring to dragging a child by force.

manghang [æ] **2.** Startled, frightened suddenly and, usually, not seriously, shocked, scared. (R) Also **mahngang.** Cf. **Luhan, susto.**

Mangilao Village in central Guam.

mangle [æ] **2.** Type of plant-rhizophora. Or bruguiere. Mangrove tree.

mangle [æ] **2.** Moocher, sponger, beggar. (G)

mangle hembra 2. Type of plant-rhizophora mucronata. Mangrove tree.

mangle machu 2. Type of plant-bruguiera gymnorrhiza.

manglo' 2. Air, wind, draft, current of air. Cf. **Aire.**

mango' [æ] **2.** Type of plant-curcuma longa. Turmeric, ginger.

mangto' 2. Powdery, pulverulent, consisting of dust or fine powder, crumbly. *Hu na'mangto' ngumangas i na'-hu ni nifen-hu.* I pulverized my food with my teeth by chewing.

ma'o 2. Thirsty. Also **ma'ho.**

ma'ok [æ] **2.** Durable, lasting, strong. Cf. **Fitme.**

maolek 2. Good, fine, well.

maolekña Better, to the contrary, rather, much better, much more. *Maolekña na un facho'cho' kinu un bulachu.* It is better that you work than for you to get drunk. *Maolekña bai hu hanao para Saipan.* I had better go to Saipan.

mapa 2. Map, chart.

mapagahes 2. Cloud.

mapannas [æ] **2.** Be flattened, make flat, be squashed, be flattened out. Cf. **Pannas.**

mapao 2. Quiet down, cool off, become cool. *Mapao i buruka.* The noise quieted down.

ma'pe' 2. Split, broken, cracked.

ma'pe' espehos 2. Piece of glass, broken glass. Cf. **Empe' espehos.**

mapedde 2. Defeated, be beaten, lose a contest with an opponent. Cf. **Pedde.** *Mapedde i taotao gi aposta-ña.* The man lost in his bet.

mapetsigi 2. Persecuted, to suffer persecution, pursued.

mapga' 2. Split—of something forked, spread widely apart. *Mapga' yo' anai sulon yo' gi gua'ot.* I did the split when I fell down the stairs. *Hu na'mapga' i dinga' hayu.* I spread the fork of the branch so wide that it split.

mapga' 2. Dislocation of pelvic bones.

mapgao 2. Scattered (flock, group, etc.), dispersed. Also **mapuao.** Cf. **Pugao.** *Mapgao i inetnon fanihi gi ladera.* The flock of bats scattered on the mountain.

mapola 2. Type of plant-hibiscus mutabilis. A type of flower. Hibiscus.

ma'pong 2. Point (broken), broken point, chipped point. *Ma'pong i lapes-hu gi duranten i eksaminasion.* The point of my pencil broke off during the examination.

ma'pong 2. A nervous condition, often associated with frequent urinating.

ma'pos 2. Past, past form for go, leave, depart, went. *Ma'pos na simana.* Last week. *Ma'pos para Hawaii.* He went to Hawaii.

ma'pos na mes 2. Last month.

ma'pos na sakkan 2. Last year.

ma'pos na simana 2. Last week.

ma'posña 2. Before last, two (something) ago. *Ma'posña na simana.* Two weeks ago.

ma'posña na mes 2. Month before last.

ma'posña na sakkan 2. Year before last.

ma'posña na simana 2. Week before last.

mapotge' 2. Pregnant, gravid, being with young, conceive, conception.

mappa 2. Become disjoined, separated, detached. Cf. **Tupa.** *Mappa i ligan guma'.* The wall became detached from the house. *Mappa i tampen lepblo.* The cover of the book came off.

mappla' 2. Loose, become loosened. *Mappla' i ga'lagu gi magodde-ña.* The dog got loose from its rope.

mappot [æ] 2. Difficult, hard, not easy, hard to do, make, or carry out. Cf. **Chatsaga, makkat.**

mapta' 2. Burst, crack open, rupture, split. *Mapta' i chinina-hu.* My shirt split open. *Mapta' i balutan.* The bundle burst, or The baby was born.

mapta' 2. Breaking of wave on the shore. Opposite of *risapa.*

mapula' 2. Interpretation, explanation, translation. Cf. **Pula'.**

mapulakes [æ] 1. Be fooled, deluded. *Mapulakes hao.* You are being fooled.

mapulakes [æ] 2. Hatched—as an egg. *I deskalentao na chada' ti siña mapulakes.* The spoiled egg cannot be hatched.

mapuñao 2. Type of plant-aglaia mariannensis. Type of tree.

marabiya 2. Type of plant-mirabilis jalapa. A type of flower.

marasón 2. Marathon, long race.

Marianas 2. Named after the queen of Spain, Mary Ann. It constitutes one of the main districts in Micronesia, called the Marianas District.

Marikita Nickname for Maria (diminutive).

marimata 2. Mass bell, last bell for mass or for prayer at the church,

commencing of mass or church prayers, the ringing of the last bell.

marineru 2. Crew.

marinon mantikiya 2. Navy steward. Lit. butter sailor, a term used for men who served as stewards for the U.S. Navy. Cf. **bayineru.**

marinu 2. Marine, marine corps, sailor.

maronggai 2. Type of plant-moringa oleifera. Type of tree.

maru 2. Box kite.

mas 2. Most (superlative), beyond. *I mas bunita na palao'an.* The prettiest girl.

mas di More than. Cf. **Mas ki.** *Guaguan-ña i lepblo-ku mas di i lepblo-mu.* My book is more expensive than your book.

mas ki More than. Cf. **Mas di.** *Metgot-ña i kabayu mas ki i ga'lagu.* The horse is stronger than the dog. *Bai hu na'i hao mas ki i malago'-mu.* I will give you more than you need.

masa 2. Ripe, cooked. *Ya-hu i masa na papaya.* I like ripe papaya.

masahalom [æ] 2. Perspire, sweat, perspiration. Lit. *masa* 'ripe' *halom* 'inside'.

masahegat 2. Muscular. Also **masegat.** Cf. **Fotte, metgot.**

masakada 2. Brave woman.

masangan 1. Said—it is, mentioned--it was. *Masangan na humanao hao asta Amerika.* It was said that you went to America.

masea Either. (G) Also **maseha.**

masegat 2. Muscular, strong, powerful, vigorous, firm body. Also **masahegat.** Cf. **Masisu.**

maseha Either, whether, even, even though, regardless, on the contrary, be that as it may, short form for *maskeseha.*(R) Also **masea.** *Maseha manu giya siha, todu manmaolek.* Any one of them, they are all good. *Na'mabakuna hao maseha ti ya-mu.* Let yourself be vaccinated, even though you don't like it. *Maseha baratu pat guaguan na kareta.* Either an expensive or cheap car. *Maseha kuanto.* Any amount, quantity, number, etc.

maseha hayi Anyone, anybody, no matter who. *Maseha hayi un sodda' guenao gi gima', konne' magi.* Anyone you find there at home, bring him here.

maseha manu   Anywhere, anyplace, no matter where. *Maseha manu malago'-mu nai ta asodda', maolek ha' para guahu.* Anywhere you want us to meet, it is all right with me.

maseha ngai'an   Anytime, anyday, no matter when. *Maseha ngai'an fafatto ya un bisita yo'.* Anytime, come and visit me.

maseha taimanu   Anyway, anyhow. *Maseha taimanu malago'-mu.* Anyway you want it to be.

maseta 2.   Flowerpot.

masga 2.   Repent, have contrition for, be sorry for.

masge' 2.   Slip away, get away, become free from entanglement. (R) Also **maske'**. *Masge' yo' gi magodde-ku.* I slipped away from my bonds.

masiksik 2.   Type of plant-wedelia biflora. A type of grass. Also **masiksik chungi**.

masiksik hembra 2.   Type of plant-triumfetta procumbens. A type of grass.

masiksik lahi 2.   Type of plant-triumfetta semitriloba. A type of grass.

masinek 2.   Defecate, have bowel movement. Cf. **Da'os.**

masisinek haga' 2.   Bloody feces, dysentery. *Nina'ye si Joaquin masisinek haga'.* Joaquin has dysentery.

masisu 2.   Muscular, flesh, solid, strong, fleshy, not hollow, having its interior filled with matter, not mushy. Cf. **Masegat, maso'.** *Masisu i katne ni finahan-hu gi tenda.* The meat that I bought from the store was fleshy.

máskara 2.   Filthy, smutty, muddy, dirty. Cf. **Kossos, akong.**

máskara 2.   Form (of face), face (figure), dirty face, filthy face. *Bunita maskaran mata-ña.* Her face looked pretty.

máskara 2.   Mask—to cover face or eyes.

maskaran mata 2.   Face shape, facial feature. Cf. **Kara, fasu.** *Bunita maskaran matan Maria.* Maria has a nice face shape.

maske' 2.   Slip away. Also **masge'**. *Maske' i magagu gi malakse-ña.* The material slipped away during my sewing.

maskeseha   Although, even though, though, even if, for all that, despite

the fact that, even, supposing. Cf. **Sikiera.** Also **Maskesea, Maseha.** *Maskeseha ti un tungo' i taotao ayuda ha'.* Although you don't know the man, help him.

masko' 2.   Face mask—catcher's, mask--protecting the face of a catcher in baseball. (S) Cf. **Tampen mata.**

masmai 2.   Wet, soaked, drenched, watery, not dry. Also **masmas**. Cf. **Fotgon.**

masmas 2.   Wet, damp, moist. Also **masmai**.

maso' 2.   Muscular, full of muscle. Cf. **Masisu, masegat.** *Maso' hao na taotao.* You are a muscular person.

maso' 2.   Healed, healed wound. Cf. **Paladan.**

masoksok 2.   Lean, meager, skinny, thin, spare, lank, gaunt, rawboned, scrawny. Cf. **Soksok.**

ma'son 2.   Coconut—barely ripe, ripe coconut with green husk.

masón 2.   Mason, a fraternity organization; concrete mason.

masotka 2.   Ear of corn. Also **hotka**.

masotta 2.   Be released, be saved.

massa' 2.   Nauseated, sickened, repulsed, uneasy, afraid. *Ha na'massa' yo' i haga'.* The blood made me nauseated.

masu 2.   Hammer—sledge, a large heavy hammer.

masu 2.   Type of insect-orthoptera mantidae. Praying mantis.

masubi 1.   Increase, enlarge, enhance.

mata 2.   Eye, eyeball, face. Cf. **Atadok.**

mata 2.   Hole for planting. *Matan chotda.* Place where banana is planted.

mata' 2.   Raw, uncooked.

mata'chong 2.   Sit, be seated. *Mata'chong yo' gi siya.* I sat on the chair.

mata'chong pannas 2.   Cross feet or legs while sitting, to sit flat on floor with legs extended straight out, pratfall, fall on buttocks.

mataderu 2.   Butcher, slaughterer, one who slays animals or cuts animals into pieces (m). Also **matadera** (f).

matadót 2.   Slaughterer. Cf. **Pekno'.**

matahlek [æ] 2.   Entangled, crooked, twisted. Also **matalek, natahlek.**

matai 2. Dead, corpse, die. *Matai i ga'-hu ga'lagu nigap.* My pet dog died yesterday. *I matai mahafot gi simenteyu.* The corpse was buried at the cemetery.

matañalang 2. Famine, die of hunger.

matala' 2. Outgoing person, self-confident person.

matalek [æ] 2. Entangled, tangled (by twisting). Also **matahlek.** Cf. **Kokas.** *Matalek i guaka gi magodde-ña.* The cow was entangled in its tether.

matan achiak 2. Slanted eyes, eyes—slanted.

matan hagon 2. Type of fish-morotaxis grandoculis (family lutjanidae). Snappers.

matan hanom 2. Spring, a source of water.

matan katu 2. Cat eyes, blue eyes.

matan lahi 2. Boy's face.

matan lalalo' 2. Frown.

matan neni 2. Baby face.

matansa 2. Slaughterhouse.

matáo 2. Higher class, overseers in pre-Spanish Chamorro society. Cf. **Matua.**

mata'pang 2. Snob, snobbish, discourteous, rude, uncivil; brackish. *Mata'pang si Gregorio na taotao.* Greg is a snobbish person. *Mata'pang este na hanom.* This water is brackish.

mata'pang 2. Uninteresting, bland (taste), dreary.

Mata'pang Name of Chamorro chief who killed Father Sanvitores.

matarabiran tano' 2. Dizziness, spinning of the earth.

matatnga [æ] 2. Strong—personality, fearless. Cf. **Taima'a'ñao.**

matbas 2. Type of plant-abutilon. Type of bush.

matcha 2. March, parade, walk with regular and measured tread, drill (marching).

matdisi 1. Curse, denounce, maledict, doom, swear, wish calamity on, imprecate evil upon.

matdisión 2. Under spell, act of casting evil spell.

matditu 2. Savage, untamed, not domesticated, cruel, fierce, ferocious, cursed, condemned, wicked.

ma'te 2. Low tide. *Ma'te i tasi.* The sea is at low tide.

ma'teng 2. Break, break off, to break at a joint. Cf. **Matgan, ma'tot.** *Ma'teng i sinturon-ña.* His belt broke. *Ma'teng i tinekcha'-ña i papaya.* The papaya fruit broke off from the tree. *Ma'teng i dilileng-ña i balakbak.* The handle of the suitcase broke.

materialisa 1. Cause to materialize, become a realized fact, appear as a material form. *Ha na'materialisa i idea-ña anai ha cho'gue.* He made his idea materialize when he did it.

matfet 2. Ivory.

matfos 2. Balding, getting bald—but not completely. Cf. **Dakngas.**

matgan 2. Come off, pop off, come out, as a fruit falling off a tree, a button from a shirt, a handle off a suitcase. Cf. **Ma'teng.** *Matgan i batunes gi chinina-hu.* The button popped off my shirt. *Matgan i nifen-hu.* My tooth came out. Contracted form of *matugan.* Cf. **Tugan.**

matgua' 2. Term used in game of batu when the stick is knocked down.

mathenio 2. Ill-tempered, testy, touchy, snappish, moody, ill-humored. Cf. **Henio.**

matiriát 2. Material, textile fabrics, building materials, timber, fabric.

matitek 2. Split—esp. cloth, torn.

matka 1,2. Mark, engrave, put a mark upon, impress, earmark. *Hu matka i na'an-hu gi aniyu-hu.* I engraved my name on my ring.

matkadót 2. Engraver, etcher, sculptor.

matko 2. Mark (coin).

matkrusidu 2. Egg—soft boiled. (R) Also **matkusidu.**

matkusidu 2. Egg—soft boiled. Also **matkrusidu.**

matlina 2. Godmother, godparent.

matmo 2. Heavy rain, downpour. *Matmo na uchan nigap.* It rained heavily yesterday.

matmo 2. Plenty of, lots of, many. Cf. **bula. Matmo taotao gi gipot.** There were many people at the party.

matmos 2. Drown, be drowned.

matmot 2. Marble—stone.

matohleng 2. Be tripped—in walking, running, etc., stumbled, caused to lose one's footing. Cf. **Matompo'.**

matokngaihon 2. Drowsy, half-asleep, heavy-eyed, nodding. Cf. **Matuhokñaihon.**

matomba 2. Fall down, be fallen, fall over, cease to be erect. Cf. **Mappa.**

matompo' 2. Stumbled, tripped—in walking, running, etc. Cf. **Matohleng.** *Matompo' si Bob gi painge.* Bob stumbled last night.

ma'tot 2. Amputated, cut off, pruned, missing, maim. Cf. **Manko.**

matraba 2. Tangled up, esp. with a rope, entangled.

matraka 2. Rattle.

matrimoniu 2. Matrimony, marriage, wedlock, married state.

matrís 2. Matrix, womb.

Matso 2. March (month). Cf. **Umakalaf.**

Mattes 2. Tuesday.

mattet 2. Martyr, martyrdom.

mattetsio 2. Abuse, curse.

mattinan 2. Deep water—just outside the reef. Also **maktingan.**

mattirio 2. Punishment, suffering, torture, torment. Cf. **Kastigu.**

mattiyu 2. Hammer.

matto 2. Arrive, come, reach destination. Cf. **Maila'.**

mattrata 1. Maltreat, ill-treat, ill-use, molest, mistreat, do wrong to, treat badly.

mattratu 2. Maltreatment, ill-treatment, molestation.

matua 2. Noble, magnanimous, lofty, highborn, person possessing high qualities.

matua 2. Archaic form referring to higher class in pre-Spanish Chamorro society. Cf. **Matao.**

matuba 2. Notches in trunk of coconut tree to facilitate climbing. Cf. **Tuba.**

matuhok 2. Sleepy, drowsy, half asleep.

matuhokñaihon 2. Be drowsy, become sleepy for a while.

matulaihon 2. Stagger, walk unsteadily, stumbling, hobbling, staggering.

matulongtong 2. Bumpy, jolting. *I barankan i chalan muna'matulongtong yo'.* The bumpy condition of the road caused me to be jolted. *Matulongtong yo' gi kareta.* I was jolted in the car.

matuna 2. Be praised, be lauded, be complemented, extolled. Cf. **Mafama.**

ma'udai 2. Ride, be carried—on the back of an animal, be borne in or on a vehicle. Cf. **Ankas.**

Maug 2. Maug, the eighth island north of Saipan. Pronounced ma'ok.

ma'ya 2. Float, be floated. Cf. **Gama.** *Mama'ya ha' i hinasso-ku.* My thoughts are wandering.

maya' [æ] 2. Blurry, blurred, become blurred, obscured. *Maya' i inatan-hu.* My eyesight is blurred. *Maya' i tano'.* The world is obscured.

mayabok 1. Soil, make dirty.

mayamak [æ] 2. Break down, go to pieces, collapse, fall down. Cf. **Yamak.**

mayao 2. Shade tree, tree with many leaves and branches.

mayaye' 2. Weakened (person). Cf. **Patot, debet.**

mayengyong 2. Quake, shake. Cf. **Yengyong.**

mayidoma 2. Stewardess, hostess, person in charge of a household or a big party. Cf. **Mayotdomu.**

mayoria 2. Majority.

mayót 2. Mayor, major—a commissioned officer next in rank above a captain, main, superior.

mayotdomu 2. Major domo, head of an organization, chief.

mayotmente 2. Especially, mainly, chiefly, particularly, mostly, primarily.

Mayu 2. May. Cf. **Makmamao.**

mayulang 2. Broken, inoperable. *Mayulang i makinan boti.* The outboard motor is broken.

mayute' 2. Outcast.

mecha 2. Wick, filament, mantle, tinder, combustible material used to start a fire.

mechio' 2. Sharp shooter, bulls-eye, esp. in marble game. (S)

media 2. Half, one of two equal parts of anything.

medianu 2. Medium, average, middle state, moderation, temperateness, regular.

médiku 2. Doctor, physician, surgeon. Cf. **Dokto.**

mediu 2. Half, measure of half.

mediu di For the sake of. *Mediu di hagu.* For your sake.

mediu dia 2. Half day, from morning till noon.

mefgo' Cf. **Mesgo'.**

mefno' 2. Talkative, loquacious, wordy.

meggai 2. Many, plenty, lots of, much, full of. Cf. **Bula, lahyan.**

meggai na biahi Many times.

meggaiña More, greater in number, quantity, or extent. *Meggaiña iyo-ku ki iyo-mu.* I have more than you have.

mehga′ 2. Bloody. Also **mihaga′.**

mehna 2. Catch—big, lots of luck in hunting. Cf. **Menha.**

méhnalom 2. Wise, sage, intelligent. From *mi-* plus *hinalom.* Also **menhalom.**

mehto 2. Lousy, infested with lice. Also **metto.** Cf. **Mihitu.**

me′i 1. Urinate on, to discharge urine on. Cf. **Me′mi′i.**

Meksikana 2. Mexican (f).

Meksikanu 2. Mexican (m).

Méksiku 2. Mexico.

Melang Nickname for Emelia.

melindres 2. Type of plant-lagerstroemia. A type of flower.

melodia 2. Melody.

melon 2. Cantaloupe, muskmelon (generic term).

melon 2. Type of plant-cucumis melo. Melon.

me′me′ 2. Urinate, urine.

memmang 2. Auntie—nickname.

memorias 2. Remembrance, capacity of recalling or recognizing previous experiences, memoriam.

memos 2. Penny, cent. Also **sentimos.**

me′nan In front of. Cf. **Mo′na.** *Gaige gi me′nan i siya i sapatos.* The shoes are in front of the chair.

me′nan Yu′us Honesty, honest, before God. *Me′nan Yu′us, ti ume′essitan yo′.* Honestly, I′m not kidding.

mendioka 2. Type of plant-manihot esculenta. Tapioca, manioc, cassava.

menha 2. Catch a lot—hunting or fishing. Also **mehna.** *Pumeska yo′ nigap ya menha yo′.* I went fishing yesterday and I caught a lot. *Menha si Jose fanihi anai humanao mamaki gi ma′pos na simana.* Joseph caught a lot of fruit bats when he went hunting last week.

ménhalom 2. Smart, intelligent, sharp, bright. Also **menalom, mehnalom.** Cf. **Tomtom, malate′, kabilosu.** *Menhalom hao.* You are intelligent.

mennong 2. Pubic region, extending down from navel, sex organ.

menos 2. Less, smaller, not so great, much less. *Mas menos na′-hu kinu na′-mu.* I have much less food than you do.

menót 2. Miniature, minor, extremely small, young; minority.

menót di idát 2. Minor, person under legal age, youngster, teen-ager.

mensiona 1. Mention, refer to, discuss casually. Cf. **Hentra, mentra.**

menta Cf. **Mentra.**

mento′ 2. Host, hostess, person having charge of a party or fiesta.

mentra 1. Mention. Also **mientra, menta.**

menggua 2. Lessened, become less, reduced in quantity, become fewer. *Hafa na menggua i pine′lo-ku.* Why did the things I put there become less. *Hayi muna′menggua i chipa-hu.* Who caused my cigarettes to become fewer. *Gofadahi na umenggua i pine′lo-ku.* Be careful that the things I put there don′t become lessened.

meppa′ 2. Fruitful, fertile (for reproduction), prolific, productive. *Meppa′ na tronkon mangga este.* This is a fruitful mango tree.

mepplo 2. Hairy, hirsute. Cf. **Batbudu, mipilu.**

merienda 2. Snack—afternoon. Also **mirenda.**

méritu 2. Merit, chance, hope.

Merizo Village in southern Guam. Pron. malesso′.

mes 2. Month—calendar month, lunar month, solar month, menstral cycle.

mesge′ 2. Unafraid.

mesgo′ 2. Juicy, have lots of juice. From *mi-* plus *chugo′.*

meskinu 2. Stingy, selfish, niggardly, parsimonious, penurious, miser, (m). Also **meskina** (f). Cf. **Chattao, gake′.**

meskla 1,2. Mix, mixture. *Ma meskla i lemonada.* They mixed the lemonade. *Dinanche i mesklan-ñiha ni lemonada.* Their mixture of the lemonade was perfect.

meskla 2. Cement mixture.

meskláo 2. A person of uncertain mixed racial extraction, half-breed. Cf. **Mestisu.**

mesngon 2. Durable, able to endure, lasting, enduring, not wearing out.

mespe′ 2. Rich, lots of money. From *misalape′*.

mestisa 2. Mestizo, half-breed, a person of mixed blood (f); Blouse—formal, esp. used by elder women for religious or formal ceremonies.

mestisu 2. Half-breed, hybrid (m). Also **mestisa** (f).

metát 2. Metal.

metati 2. Millstone. Cf. **Mitati**.

metgot 2. Strong, stout, sturdy, stalwart, tough, tenacious, powerful, solid.

meti 2. Merit, right, privilege. *Ti meti hao na un ma′erensia.* You don't deserve your inheritence.

metkáo 2. Market—public, grocery store.

Metkoles 2. Wednesday.

metro 2. Meter.

metton 2. Certain, definite, absolute, sure, attached to, true. *Metton yo′ gi fino′-hu.* I am certain of my word. *Metton yo′ gi nobia-hu.* I am attached to my girlfriend.

meyas 2. Socks, stockings.

meyeng 2. Good at, expert, skillful, masterly, professional, proficient, winner. (S)

meyu 2. Penny, smallest denomination of Spanish coin.

mi- To have lots of (prefix), many, plenty. *Misapatos si Jose.* Joseph has lots of shoes. *Mifamagu′on gue′.* She has lots of children.

mi′acho′ 2. Rocky, having lots of rocks.

miche′ 1. Make a path—in marble game, path or groove made by a player to guide the marble to the target. (S) Cf. **Fa′chalani**.

miche′ 2. Poor, needy.

midi 1. Measure (something), mark the bounds or limits of, determine or lay out in measuring, take or make a measurement.

midida 2. Measuring tool, system of measure, any device used for measuring, measurement.

miembro 2. Member, part, bodily part or organ. Also **membro**.

mientra 1. Mention, speak of, make known, inform, refer to, discuss. Also **mentra, menta**. Cf. **Hentra, mensiona**. *Hu mientra na malangu*

gue′ gi painge. I mentioned that he was sick last night.

mientras While, meanwhile, in the mean time, used to connect clauses or phrases. Also **mentras**. *Bai hu chupa mientras hu nanangga hao.* I will smoke while I am waiting for you.

miét 2. Honey, syrup. Cf. **Anibat**.

miganchio′ 2. Eyeglass wearer, one who wears eyeglasses, a person with poor eyesight. Also **miganche′**. (S)

míguinaha 2. Wealthy, rich, affluent, opulent, ample, lots of wealth.

míhinallom 2. Intelligent. Also **menhallom**.

míhinilat 2. Efficient, powerful.

míhitu 2. Lousy, infested with lice. Cf. **Mehto**.

míkulot 2. Colorful, gaudy.

mílachi 2. Wrongful, injurious.

milagro 2. Miracle.

milagrosu 2. Miraculous, one who is capable of performing miracles (m). Also **milagrosa** (f). *Milagrosu hao na taotao.* You are a miraculous person.

milak 2. Flood, deluge, inundation, overflow, flowing. Cf. **Dilubiu**. *Milak i hanom gi tanke.* The water overflowed from the tank. *Milak i saddok.* The river flooded. *Milak i lago′-ña.* Her fears flowed.

milaya 2. Medal, medallion. Cf. **Eskapulario**.

Milen Nickname for Carmen.

milisia 2. Militia.

milisianu 2. Militia.

militát 2. Military, armed forces, body of soldiers.

Mimo′ Nickname for Maximo.

Min Nickname for Carmen.

mina 2. Mine, quarry, subterranean passage.

mina′ The reason. Also **muna′**. *Este mina′ hu sangani hao.* This is why I told you. *Ayu muna′ hu sangani hao.* That is why I told you. *Mina′ ti hu na′ma′agang hao sa′ pine′lo-ku na ti un fatto ha′.* The reason I didn't have someone call you is that I thought you would not come anyway.

mina′- Ordinal marker, prefix used to make ordinal numbers from cardinal. *Dos.* Two. *I mina′dos.* The second.

Dosse. Twelve. *I mina'dosse.* The twelfth.

mina'a'ñao 2. Horror, fear, terror, fright. Cf. **Kinubatde.**

mina'ase' 2. Forgiveness, pardon, remission, mercy, disposition to pardon, pity. Cf. **Ma'ase'.**

minachom atdao [æ] 2. Sunset.

minafak [æ] 2. Bankruptcy, cracked.

minagagu 2. Clothe, put clothes on, get dressed. *Minagagu ya ta hanao.* Get dressed and we will leave.

minagahet 2. Truth, fact, realism, reality, frankness.

mina'gas [æ] 2. Radiance, brightness, luster. Cf. **Mina'lak.**

minaggem [æ] 2. Peace.

minagof [æ] 2. Happiness, pleasure, cheer, gaiety, mirth, joy, fun, that which gladdens. Cf. **Konsuelu.**

minahalang 2. Loneliness, solitariness, disconsolateness, forlornness, deprivation of companionship.

mina'ho [æ] 2. Thirst. Cf. **Ma'o.**

minakkat [æ] 2. Weight. Cf. **Pesada.** *Kuanto minakkat-mu?* What is your weight?

minalago' [æ] 2. Ambition.

mina'lak [æ] 2. Glare, brilliance, splendor, luster, brightness. Cf. **Ma'lak, mina'gas.**

minalangu 2. Sickness, illness, state of being sick. Cf. **Malangu.**

minaleffa 2. Oblivion, blotted from memory. Cf. **Maleffa.**

minalulok 2. Freedom, softness. Cf. **Malulok.**

minames [æ] 2. Likeableness, sugary, sweet. Cf. **Mames.**

minampos [æ] 2. Excess, superfluity. Cf. **Mampos.**

minanggao pulan [æ] 2. Rising of the moon.

mina'ok [æ] 2. Duration, endurance, lasting. Cf. **Ma'ok.** *I mina'ok este na materiat sinko años na garentia.* The duration of this material is five years guaranteed.

minaolek 2. Integrity.

minappot [æ] 2. Difficulty. Cf. **Difikuttat, mappot.**

minatai [æ] 2. Death.

minatatnga [æ] 2. Valor, bravery. Cf. **Matatnga.**

minattrata 2. Maltreatment, oppression.

minayulang 2. Demolition, destruction. Cf. **Mayulang.**

mineddong 2. Size, dimensions, measurement. *Maolek esta mineddong-ñiha i tinanom-hu siha para u fanmatransplanta.* The size of my plants is good for transplanting already.

minesngon 2. Forbearance, indulgence, endurance. *Maolek minesngon-mu malagu.* Your endurance in running is good.

minetgot 2. Power, energy, strength, might, force, stamina. Cf. **Nina'siña, fuetsa.**

mineyas 2. Put socks on.

minidiyi 2. Limitation, confinement. Cf. **Midi.**

minigu'an 2. Condition of having matter in the eyes. Cf. **Mugo'.**

ministét Prerequisite, necessary, have to, must. *Ministet un lachaddek sinu madingu hit gi gipot.* You have to hurry or you will be late for the party. *Ministet un maigo' sa' esta hao matuhok.* You have to sleep because you are already sleepy.

ministro 2. Minister, protestant clergyman.

minito' 2. Intention, purpose.

minito' See muto'.

minuteru 2. Minute hand—on watch or clock.

minutu 2. Minute. Also minutos (pl).

miña 2. To have lots of, have more than ample supply of something. Cf. **Dafflok, malulok.**

mípilu 2. Hairy, fibrous, stringy. Cf. **Mepplo, batbudu.**

mira 2. Myrrh, aromatic gum resin.

mirenda 2. Snack, light meal. Also merienda.

miresi 1. Receive, deserve. Cf. **Risibi.**

mirón 2. Inattentive, one who usually gets distracted from his work. *Miron hao mampos gi che'cho'-mu.* You are very inattentive to your work.

misa 2. Mass, the commemorative sacrifice of the Catholic church.

misan ánimas 2. Requiem, mass for deceased person, mass for the souls.

misan gayu 2. Midnight mass—on Easter Sunday, Christmas, and New Year's Eve. Lit. rooster's mass.

misan kantada 2. High mass.

misan mo'na 2. Mass—early, first mass when there is no midnight mass offered, but more masses are to follow. Cf. **Misan gayu, misan tatalo'puengi.**

misan risada 2. Low mass.

misan talo' 2. Mass—middle, the second mass offered out of three masses.

misan tátalo'puengi 2. Mass—midnight. Cf. **Misan gayu, misan mo'na.**

misan tatte 2. Mass—late, the last mass offered of the day.

misát 2. Missal, prayer book for Catholic church.

misen 2. Full of liquid, abundant liquid, root crops—big and plentiiful. *Misen i tasi.* High tide. *Misen sisu-ña i baka.* The cow's udder contains lots of milk. *Misen sensen-ñiha i kamuti-ta.* Our sweet potato crops are big and plentiful.

miserable 2. Miserable, disconsolate, comfortless, cheerless.

misería 2. Misery, poverty.

misioneru 2. Missionary.

misirikotdia 2. For mercy sake, goodness gracious, for goodness sake.

mismo Personally, really, very, by oneself, emphasizer. *Guahu mismo sumangani hao ni lugat.* I personally was the one who told you about the place. *Hagu mismo pumacha i guafi.* You are the very one who touched the fire.

miso' 2. Bean paste—from soy beans.

misterio 2. Mystery, enigma, conundrum, profound secret, riddle, puzzle.

mit 2. One thousand.

mit leguas 2. Type of plant-telosma cordata. (?).

mitati 2. Millstone, a flat stone use for grinding corn, rice, etc. The base against which *manu* is rolled. Also **metati.**

miteng 2. Meeting, assembly, gathering, convention. Cf. **Hunta.**

mítitanos 2. Wise, prudent, learned. Cf. **Titanos.**

mítituka' 2. Thorny, having lots of thorns.

mitto' 2. Mitt (baseball). (S) Cf. **Guantes, gurobo'.**

mí'unai 2. Sandy, having lots of sand.

miyas 2. Mile, knot (nautical).

miyón 2. Million.

miyonario 2. Millionaire (m). Also **miyonaria** (f).

-miyu Your, yours (possessive pl.). *Na'-miyu enao.* That is your food.

mobimiento 2. Movement, motion, maneuver. Also **mobimento.**

mocha 1. Cut off ear, to cut off part or all of the ear of a person or animal. *Hu mocha talanga-ña i ga'-hu babui.* I cut the ear off my pig.

moda 2. Fashion, conventional custom of dress, mode. *Nuebu na moda ayu na chinina.* That is a new fashion of dress.

moddong 2. Size, depth. *Kuanto mineddong sapatos-mu?* What size are your shoes?

moddong 2. Boat, ship.

modelu 2. Model, pattern, example, facsimile, design—an example for imitation.

moderasión 2. Moderation.

moderatu 2. Moderate, temperate, mild, tolerant, compassionate.

modesto 2. Modest, unpretentious, unobtrusive, unpretending.

modetno 2. Modern, existing in the present age.

modoru 2. Stupid, illiterate, coarse person, retarded. **Modora** (f) . Also **mudoru.**

modu 2. Mode, manner, way, mood. Cf. **Manera.**

mofa 2. Ridicule. Cf. **Mofeha.** *Enao na kuentos para mofa ha'.* Those kinds of words are for ridicule.

mofeha 1. Mock, deride, ridicule, laugh at, tease, insult, taunt, make fun of, curse, defy, make a fool of. Also **mofea.** Cf. **Kasse, chatge, botleha.**

mohmo 1,2. Chew for (feeding), to chew food for baby-feeding, mouth-to-mouth feeding, sediment, dregs, remnant—of the betel nut which is thrown away after chewing. Also **momo.** Cf. **Amme, bagasu.** *Hu mohmo i patgon.* I fed the child (using one's mouth to guide food to someone's mouth).

mohón 2. Landmark, boundary marker.

mohon Wish feeling, expressing desire, want, a structure word expressing something contrary to fact. *Sumaga mohon gi gima' si Frank asta ki manmatto-hit.* I wish Frank would stay at home until we arrive.

Sumaga yo' mohon giya Agaña. I hope we can stay in Agaña. Or, I'm looking forward to the chance to stay in Agaña.

mokmok 1. Gargle, wash the throat with a liquid held in the mouth.

molestia 1. Molest, trouble, annoy, bother, harass, pester.

momento 2. Moment, instant. Cf. **Ratu.**

mommo' 2. Short-eared owl.

momye 1. Scold, insult—harshly or severely. *I palao'an ha momye si Maria sa' sinangañaihon ni mandagi.* The girl insulted Maria sharply for her telling lies. *I ma'estro ha momye ham sa' ti manmanestudia ham.* The teacher scolded us for not studying.

mo'na 2. Front, be first, in front of, forward. *Gaige gue' gi mo'na.* He is at the front. *Mo'na hao matto gi che'cho.* You came first to work.

monasterio 2. Monastery, priests' friary.

monchón 2. Plentiful, many. Also **monton.** Cf. **Bula, meggai.** *Monchon taotao gi gipot gi painge.* There were plenty of people at the party last night.

moneda 2. Coins. Cf. **Salape'.**

monhayan 2. Finish, complete. Also **munhayan.**

monhe 2. Monk.

monte 2. Type of card game. A dealer places two different cards up so the opponent may choose one of the cards for him to bet on, then the dealer gets the card that is left unchosen. The deck of cards is turned upwards and the cards are dealt one by one. Whoever's card is paired first wins the hand.

montesiyu 2. Shrubbery, bush.

montohon 2. Bundle, collection, congregation, gathering, assemblage. (R) Also **monton.** Cf. **Rikohi, etnon, monton.**

montón 2. Bundle, cluster. Also **montohon.**

monton 2. Heap, pile. Cf. **Amontona.** *Ha na'monton i kamuti.* He heaped up the sweet potatoes.

monumento 2. Monument, shrine, statue, gravestone.

monggos 2. Type of plant-phaseolus mungo. Mung bean.

monggos ayuke' 2. Type of plant-phaseolus angularis. **Ayuke'** beans.

monggos paluma 2. Type of plant-cleome viscosa. Smaller variety of *monggos.*

mongha 2. Nun.

mongmong 2. Hollow sounding—such as a drum, heartbeat, ripe melon.

Mongmong Village in central Guam linked with Toto and Maite.

morón 2. Moron, feeble minded. Also **moro.**

moru 2. Pagan, person with no religion, homeless person. (R) Also refers to the Moros of the Philippines.

moru 2. Concealing something unlicensed, such as a gun or car, illegal.

moseria 2. Employed. Cf. **Mosu.** *Gaige gi moseria.* Serving as a *mosu.*

mosión 2. Motion, proposal, movement.

moskas 2. Carpenter's fitting, system of fitting pieces of wood together without using nails.

mostasa 2. Type of plant-brassica juncea. Mustard plant, mustard.

mostra 1,2. Exhibit, display, sample—to be copied.

mosu 2. Servant, an employee who is employed on a 24 hour basis and is treated as one of the family. Also **mosa** (f).

motas 2. Defect in sewing, weak stitching, caused from imbalance of two threads on sewing machine.

motgan 2. Have too much fun, good time, have access, have available, have surplus, overindulge, overdo. (S) Cf. **Dafflok, mutero', go'dan, dafflokgue, tuhos, malulok.** *Motgan hao gi gipot.* You had too much fun at the party. *Motgan ham setbesa.* We had access to all the beer we wanted.

motibu 2. Motive, reason.

motmot 2. Full, crowded, full up, containing all that can be held. *Motmot taotao gi kotte.* The court house was full of people.

motón 2. Block and tackle, a combination pulley and chain or rope to lift heavy things.

motosaikot 2. Motorcycle. Cf. **Otobai'.**

motsiyas 2. Stuffed neck of chicken. After chicken is killed by stretching the neck, the cavity left by pulling the bones apart is stuffed with vegetables before boiling.

mottát 2. Mortal, human being, living soul.

motu 2. Motor.

moyeha 2. Gizzard, the second (posterior) stomach of birds, having thick walls and horny lining for grinding food.

moyong 2. Grindstone, millstone.

-mu Your, yours (possessive sing).

mubét 2. Level (carpenter's). Also **nubet, nebet.**

mubi 2. Movie, motion picture, cinema. Cf. **Kachido'.**

muchachu 2. Servant, person employed in domestic duties, person in the service of another (m). Also **muchacha** (f).

muchumas Especially. *Señores muchumas este i taotao distritu numiru dos.* Men, especially those people of district number two.

muda 2. Clothing—nice, clothes--Sunday, change clothes--fresh and clean.

mudista 2. Dressmaker.

muebi 1. Move, budge, change place.

muestra 2. Sample.

mueyi 2. Elasticity, spring—a metal spring or device that recovers its original shape when released after being distorted. *Metgot mueyi-ña i trak.* The spring of the truck is strong.

mugo' 2. Matter (from eyes), a purulent substance that secretes from the eyes.

mukos 2. Mucus, mucous, snot.

mula 2. Mule, hybrid of jackass and mare.

mulata 2. Permanent wave, curly hair.

mulatu 2. Curly hair, curl, tress of hair, ringlet, lovelock, curlicue, wavy hair, curling of leaves (m). Also **mulata** (f). Cf. **Kinke.**

mulidu 2. Bruise. Cf. **Dinigridu.**

mulinu 1,2. Grind, reduce to powder by friction, grinder, grindstone. *Ha mulinu i mai'es.* He grinds the corn. *Makkat mabira i mulinu.* The grinder is hard to turn.

mumahetok 2. Hardened, solidified, become hard. Cf. **Mahetok.**

mumamahlao 2. Become ashamed, become embarrassed, become

bashful, become humiliated, be put to shame, be abashed by guilt.

mumáñaña' [æ] **2.** Softened, became tender, weakened, dampened. Cf. **Mañaña'.**

mumaolek 2. Become good, become well. Cf. **Maolek.**

mumaya' [æ] **2.** Become blurred, become obscured, hazy, become indistinct to the sight. Cf. **Maya'.**

mumon linahyan 2. Revolution, uprising.

mumu 2. Combat, battle, argue, fight, quarrel. *Mumu yo' nigap.* I fought yesterday. *Kao un li'e' i mimu?* Did you see the fight?

mumutong 2. Type of plant-ageratum conyzoides. Or hyptis capitata. Type of bush.

mumutong palao'an 2. Type of plant-cassia tora. Or hyptis. Type of bush—used for medicine.

mumutong sapble 2. Type of plant-cassia occidentalis. Type of bush—used for medicine.

muna' The reason. See **mina'.** A combined form of *-um-* plus *na'-.*

muna'- Cause, make, causative prefix— with actor focus affix. Cf. **Na'-, nina'-.** *Si Juan muna'gasgas i lamasa.* John is the one who cleaned the table.

mundonggo 2. First stomach of cow, rumen, reticulum. Used for making *fritadas,* tripe.

munhayan 2. Finish (already), complete. Also **munayan, monhayan.** *Munhayan yo' ni lepblo.* I finished the book. *Hu na'funhayan tumaitai i lepblo.* I finished (made myself finish) reading the book.

munidensia 2. Vital organs—located in the thoracic part of the interior of the body, consisting of heart, lungs, liver, etc.

munisipát 2. Municipality.

munon pachot 2. Bicker, quarrel.

muñeka 2. Doll, puppet.

muñeru 2. Cry-baby (m), timid, grouchy, cranky, hard to please. Also **muñera** (f).

munga 2. Not—in an either-or situation. No, when declining something offered, don't (imperative). Cf. **Cha'-mu, ahe'.** *Kao para un hanao pat munga hao?* Are you going or not? *Munga humanao gi gima'.* Don't leave the house.

muraya 2. Rampart, surrounding wall.

murena 2. Type of complexion, tea-colored, neither dark nor white complexion.

musigomo' 2. Rubber, eraser. (S) Cf. Goma, iresa.

músika 2. Music. Cf. Dandan.

músiku 2. Band, orchestra.

muta' 2. Vomit, throw up, regurgitate, cast up from the stomach, upchuck, belch forth.

mutero' 2. Have too much fun, good time, have access, have available. (S). Cf. Dafflok, dafflokgue, motgan, go'dan, tuhos, malulok. *Mutero' i bulacheru manadan setbesa.* The drunkard had too much beer. *Mutero' hao giya Hawaii.* You had too much fun in Hawaii.

muto' 1. Desire, feeling disposition. *Komon nina'ye ni minito'-ña taya' siña ta cho'gue.* If he is of that disposition, we can't do anything.

mutong 2. Stink, malodorous, smell bad. Cf. Lammok. *Mutong gue'.* He stinks.

mutta 2. Fine, penalty, payment of fine, sum paid by way of settlement.

muttiplika 1. Multiply, increase by large quantity.

muttiplikát 2. Multiplication.

muyo' 2. Puckered lips, protruded lips —when angry or displeased; pout. Cf. Iba', kiba'.

muyu'i 1. Sneer, show contempt by facial expression. Cf. Muyo'.

na Linking particle, used to connect a noun with its modifier. *I dankolo na tatotao.* The big man.

ná'- [æ] One who does something. Derived from causative prefix *na'-* plus primary stress.

na' [æ] Food classifier, edibles— classifier for. *Ha kanno' i na'-hu.* He ate my food. *Ha kanno' i na'-hu guihan.* He ate my fish.

na'- [æ] Causative prefix, cause, make (someone do something), let (someone do something). Used with class 1 and class 2 words. Cf. Muna'-, nina'-. *Na'fakmata si Juan sa' esta oran eskuela.* Make John wake up because it is time for school. *Na'gasgas i lamasa.* Clean the table. *Hu na'draiba si Pete ni kareta.* I let Pete drive the car.

na' oga'an 2. Meal—morning, breakfast. Cf. Amotsa.

na' talo'ani 2. Dinner, main meal of the day, lunch. Cf. Amotsa.

na'ádanche [æ] 1. Correct, set right, straighten out, make right, fit together properly.

na'adespatta 2. Take apart, separate, disconnect, disunite, split, divorce, disengage. Cf. Sipara. *I makinista ha na'adespatta i makinan butdosa.* The mechanic took the bulldozer's engine apart.

na'adotgan 2. Pierce through, stick through, run through.

na'afa'maolek 1. Reconcile, atone, expiate.

na'ágaole 1. Cross legs.

na'ágihilu'i 1. Head up, lay on top of each other. Also na'agitilu'i, na'age'hilu'i.

na'ágitilu'i 1. Heap up, lay on top of each other. Also na'agihilu'i.

na'ahustáo 2. Adjust, set right, put in order. Cf. Na'tunas.

na'an 2. Name.

na'anakko' 2. Lengthen, elongate, extend, cause (something) to be long. Cf. Na'apmam.

na'ancho 2. Widen, broaden, cause to be wide. Cf. Ancho, na'lafedda', fedda'.

na'annok [æ] 1. View—bring into, reveal, unwrap or uncover, expose.

na'ápalo'po' [æ] 1. Stack up, pile up in a stack.

na'áplacha' [æ] 1. Mar.

na'apmam 2. Prolong, lengthen—time, sustain.

na'apo' [æ] 1. Support, offer hand for support. Cf. Apo'.

na'asgon 1. Dirty, make impure, fog up.

na'atarantáo 1. Disunite, set at variance. Cf. Atarantao.

na'atborutáo 1. Demoralize. Corrupt. Cf. Atborutao.

na'atok [æ] 1. Hide, conceal, secrete, make secret. Cf. Na'na', disimula.

na'ayao [æ] 2. Lend, grant (something) to another for temporary use, opposite of borrow. Lit. Cause to borrow. *Hu na'ayao si Pedro ni salape'.* I lent the money to Pedro.

nabaha 2. Razor, pocketknife, small knife. Cf. Hinabaha.

na'balansa 1. Balance debt.

nabegadót 2. Navigator.

na'beste 1. Garnish, adorn. Cf. Beste.

Nabidát 2. Christmas. Cf. Pasgua. *Felis Nabidat.* Merry Christmas.

na'boka 1. Feed. Cf. Boka.

ná'brabu [æ] 2. Strengthening, enlivening.

na'bubu 1. Anger, vex, infuriate. Cf. Bubu.

ná'bubu [æ] 2. Antagonist, unpleasant person, one who antagonizes.

na'bula 1. Replenish. Cf. Bula.

ná'chaddek [æ] 2. Expediter, one who hurrys things.

na'chaddek [æ] 1. Hurry, hustle. Cf. Chaddek, alula.

na'chalek 2. Cause to laugh. *Hu na'chalek i ma'estro-ku.* I made my teacher laugh.

ná'chalek [æ] 2. Funny, humorous, laughable. *Na'chalek hao na taotao.* You are a funny man.

ná'chatsaga [æ] 2. Pest, one who bothers people, nuisance.

na'chatsaga [æ] 1. Annoy, bother.

na'chetnudan 1. Wound, injure, hurt, impregnate.

na'chetton 1. Connect, join, bring together.

ná'chetton [æ] 2. Connector; anything that joins two things together.

na'chilong 1. Equalize, arrange proportionately. Cf. Chilong.

nada mas Nothing else. Cf. taya'.

na'dankolo 1. Exaggerate.

ná'daña' [æ] 2. Mixer, match-maker, one who brings things together.

na'daña' [æ] 1. Cause to mingle, combine, mix, blend, integrate.

na'dengha 1. Turn upside down, cause to bend over. Cf. Dengha. .

Nadet Nickname for Bernadita.

na'dilok 1. Cause to lower head. Cf. Dilok.

na'dinanche [æ] 1. Correct, rectify, set right. Cf. Rektifika, kurihi.

Nado' Nickname for Bernardo.

na'dochon 1. Knock in, drive in. Cf. Dochon.

na'echong 1. Bend, make crooked.

na'empas 1. Pay up, even up, give satisfaction. *Hu na'empas i dibi-hu gi banko.* I paid up my debt at the bank.

na'éntalo' 1. Set in between.

na'espongha 1. Inflate, swell, to cause swelling. Cf. Espongha.

ná'espongha [æ] 2. Yeast, something that causes swelling.

na'etnon 2. Collect, gather, group, convene, bring toether into one aggregate. Cf. Na'montohon.

ná'fache' [æ] 2. Liquid—added to something.

na'fache' [æ] 1. Smear. Cf. Fache'.

ná'failek [æ] 2. Sour, bitter.

na'fakpo' 1. Close—an agreement, close a sale, finalize. Cf. Makpo'.

na'falingu 1. Destroy, annihilate. Cf. Malingu.

ná'falingu [æ] 2. Anything that causes someone to be lost. *Ná'falingu i chichirika.* The chichirika bird causes one to get lost.

na'faloffan 1. Produce, create, transmit. Cf. Maloffan.

na'famadesi 1. Harm, hurt, injure, cause physical pain to. Cf. Na'lamen, padesi.

na'fa'na'an [æ] 1. Denominate, name someone to do something, call upon.

na'fañila' 2. Cause to burn, light up, cause to be brilliant. *Hu na'fañila i danges anai matto yo' gi gima'.* I lighted up the candle when I came home.

na'fañotsot 1. Reform, regret, cause to repent.

ná'fañotsot [æ] 2. Regrettable, lamentable, sorrowful, woeful, dreadful. Cf. Fañotsot. *Na'fañotsot humanao asta Guam yanggen batko ha' na transpottasion.* It is regrettable to go to Guam if the ship is the only transportation available.

na'fata'chong 1. Set, support, sustain. Cf. Mata'chong.

na'fitme 1. Strengthen, insure. Cf. Fitme.

na'flohu 1. Slacken. *Na'flohu fan i tali.* Slacken the rope, please.

na'fófo'na 1. Send ahead, send on in advance. Cf. Na'fo'na.

na'fo'na 1. Precede, advance, prefer. Cf. Mo'na.

na'fotgon 1. Dampen, moisten. Cf. Fotgon.

naftan 2. Grave, sepulcher, tomb, burial place.

naga 2. Flooded, covered with water.

na'gai- 1. Cause to have. Cf. **Na'-** and **gai-**. *Hu na'gaihanom i babui.* I watered the pigs.

na'gáisabot 1. Flavor, season with flavoring.

na'gálilek [æ] 2. Cause to roll, to roll a cylindrical object.

na'gao 2. Ripe coconut—without juice. Water has been fully absorbed.

nagase' 2. Sink, lavatory. Also **nangase'**. (S) Cf. **Labadot**.

na'gasgas 1. Clean, purify. Cf. **Gasgas**.

na'gatbo 1. Beautify, embellish. Cf. **Gatbo**.

na'getmon 2. Chew audibly, crunch. *Hu na'getmon i karot anai hu akka'.* I crunched the carrot when I bit it. *Ha na'getmon i kinanno'-ña ni mangga.* He crunched into the mango while eating it.

nagong [æ] 2. Shelter. Also **ñagong**.

ná'guaha [æ] 2. Supplier, one who usually supplies things when needed. One who brings out things into existence, one who makes something exist. Cf. **Guaha**.

na'gupu 1. Swing, brandish, wave something. Cf. **Gupu**.

na'hallom [æ] 1. Imagine, fancy, take a liking to.

na'halom 1. Insert.

na'hanao 1. Disconnect, detach, direct. Cf. **Hanao**.

na'haspok 1. Satiate, fill up (one's stomach). Cf. **Haspok**.

na'hasso [æ] 2. Cause to think, conceive, imagine, realize, envisage, remind. *Hu na'hasso si Juan na u chule' i lepblo-ña gi eskuela.* I reminded John to get his book at school.

na'ha'yan 1. Put down—with words, tell off, put someone in his place verbally. *Si Juan ha na'ha'yan i banidosu na taotao.* Juan put the conceited man in his place.

na'homlo' 1. Heal, cause to be healthy.

ná'homlo' [æ] 2. Healer, curer, one who heals. Cf. **A'amte**.

nahong [æ] 2. Enough, sufficient, satisfied. Cf. **Basta**. *Nahong yo' esta setbesa.* I had enough beer already. *Kao nahong salape'-mu para i rediu?* Do you have enough money for the radio?

na'huyong 1. Invent, devise, find out; beget, create. Cf. **Huyong**.

na'huyungi 1. Furnish, supply, equip. Cf. **Huyong**.

na'i 1. Give, deliver, provide, donate, bestow without a return, grant, distribute. (Comb. of *na'* 'cause' and *-i* 'referential focus particle'). *Hu na'i i patgon ga'-ña ga'lagu.* I gave the boy a pet dog.

nai Where (relative), when (relative). *I gima' amigu-hu nai sumaga yo'.* It was my friend's house where I stayed. *Mananaitai-yo' estoria nai hu li'e' i aksidente.* I was reading a story when I saw the accident. Also linking particle used with question words *manu* and *ngai'an*. *Manu nai sumasaga hao?* Where do you live? *Ngai'an nai humanao hao?* When did you go?

na'i patte Impart, give a share, give notice.

na'i prenda Post bail, to be responsible.

naile 2. Tall and slender.

na'kádada' [æ] 1. Abridge, shorten.

na'káfache' [æ] 1. Bespatter with mud. Cf. **Fache'**.

na'kahulo' 1. Raise up, haul up. Cf. **Kahulo'**.

na'kalamten [æ] 1. Stir up, move, set in motion. Cf. **Kalamten**.

na'kallo 1. Loosen, slacken. Cf. **Lusu**, **kallo**.

na'kapát 1. Make room.

na'kayada 1. Mitigate, alleviate. Cf. **Kayada**.

na'kemaigo' 1. Lull, soothe to sleep.

na'késiña 1. Endeavor, try.

na'kílulok 1. Spin, set into spinning motion, as a top.

na'klaru 1. Clarify, make clear. Cf. **Klarifika**.

nakpa'ña 2. Day after tomorrow. Also **inakpa'ña**. Cf. **Agupa'ña**.

na'lá'anakko' [æ] 1. Lengthen, add to length.

na'lábaratu [æ] 1. Put on sale, lower the price. Cf. **Baratu**.

na'lachi [æ] 1. Mislead.

na'lage'- Make a little bit further, make a little more, a triple combination of prefixes *na'-* 'make', *la-* 'a little (bit)', and *ge'-* 'further or more'. Cf. **Na'lahat-**. *Na'lage'hilo' i amot gi* *estante.* Put the medicine a little bit further up on the shelf.

na'lago' [æ] 1. Melt, cause to liquefy.

na'lagu 1. Cook, boil, set upon the fire.

na'lahat- [æ] Make a little bit further, make a little bit more, a triple combination of prefixes *na-* 'make', *la-* 'a little (bit), and *hat-* 'further or more'. Also na'lat-. Cf. Na'lage'-. *Na'lahatmagi i kannai-mu ya bai hu go'te.* Bring your hand a little bit closer so that I can hold it.

na'lákallo [æ] 1. Loosen more, make looser. Cf. Kallo.

na'la'la' 1. Turn on, make alive, plant, make grow. *Na'la'la' i kandet.* Turn on the light.

na'lámafnot [æ] 2. Tighten, make tight, take up the slack.

na'lámaolek [æ] 1. Improve, insure, to give one credit.

na'lamen 2. Harm, injure, hurt, cause physical pain to. Cf. Na'famadesi, na'chetnudan. *Hu na'lamen i taotao.* I hurt the man.

ná'lamen [æ] 2. Harmful, injurious. Cf. Na'tailayi. *Na'lamen gue' na taotao yanggen lalalo'.* He is a harmful person when he is angry.

na'lámoddong [æ] 1. Deepen, enlarge. Cf. Moddong.

na'lástima 1. Waste. Cf. Lastima.

na'lat- [æ] See na'lahat-.

na'latfe'na 1. Improve, prosper, thrive. Cf. Mo'na.

na'layo' [æ] 1. Insult, embitter, incite. Cf. Layo'.

na'libre 1. Save, spare, forgive—of sins, liberate. Cf. Libre, ridima.

na'lifet 1. Smuggle, contraband—traffic of, import without paying customs duties. *I biha ha na'lifet i pigua' asta Saipan.* The old woman smuggled the betel nut to Saipan.

na'liheng 2. Rescue, make safe, deliver from danger, protect, defend, guard, provide shelter. *Hu na'liheng i lahi gi gima'.* I rescued the man at my house.

na'lo [æ] 2. Return—to its original state. Also na'na'lo. *Numa'lo i pakyo'.* The typhoon returned. *Na'lo guatu gi gima'-mu sa' ninanangga hao as nana-mu.* Return to your home because your mother is waiting for you.

na'ma'aksom [æ] 1. Make sour. Cf. Ma'aksom.

ná'ma'a'ñao [æ] 2. Monster, ghost, evil spirit, horror, monstrous, frightful, horrible, horrid, dreadful. Cf. Fafa'ñague, e'espanta.

na'ma'ase' 2. Be merciful, have compassion.

ná'ma'ase' [æ] 2. Miserable, pitiful, wretched.

na'mafnas 1. Wipe out, blot out, eradicate, extinguish, erase, delete, eliminate. Cf. Funas. One who or that which erases, one who or that which causes to fade away.

ná'mafnas [æ] 2. Clorox, bleach, any bleaching agent.

na'magof [æ] 1. Gladden, enliven, satisfy, amuse. Cf. Magof.

ná'magong [æ] 2. Healer, curer, a restorer of good health or condition.

na'mahlos 1. Smoothe, polish. Cf. Mahlos.

ná'mahlos [æ] 2. Steam iron, steamroller, anything used for making things smooth.

na'mahñao 1. Recall, call back, revoke.

na'maipe 1. Heat, warm up. Cf. Maipe.

na'makatga 1. Load on, put goods to be transported, to ship.

ná'malago' [æ] 2. Desirable, be desired, appetizing, worth having. Cf. Malago'. *Na'malago' makanno' i mansana ni agaga'-ña.* The apple is desirable to be eaten for its redness.

na'malago' [æ] 2. Desirous, yearning, wishful, voracious, passionate, ardent.

ná'malangu 2. Sickening, nauseating.

na'mamahlao 2. Ashamed—cause (someone) to be, embarrass, shame--put to, humiliate. *Hu na'mamahlao i lahi.* I shamed the man.

ná'mamahlao [æ] 2. Embarrassing, bashful, shameful, humiliating. *Na'mamahlao bumulachu gi chalan.* It is shameful to be drunk on the road.

na'manana [æ] 1. Explain, make clear, make a clearing with a bulldozer.

na'mancha 1. Stain, desecrate. Cf. Mancha.

ná'manman [æ] 2. Sublime, awe-inspiring, incredible, unbelievable, exciting. *Na'manman hao na a'atte.* You are an incredible magician.

na'manso 1. Tame, calm down. Cf. **Manso.**

na'máñaña' 1. Soften, move the heart.

na'mangto' 2. Pulverize, reduce to powder or dust.

na'maolek 2. Repair, fix, mend, good condition—put in, adjust, make good, turn to good account.

ná'maolek [æ] 2. Repairman, fixer, one who or that which makes good. Cf. **Maolek.**

na'mapao 1. Cool off, refresh. Cf. **Mapao.**

na'masa 1. Make ready, place (food) in vinegar, cook.

na'ma'se' 2. Pitiful, destitute, pathetic. *Na'ma'se' i patgon sa' matai i nana-ña.* The child is pitiful because his mother died.

ná'masinek 2. Laxative, cathartic.

ná'massa' [æ] 2. Nauseous, loathesome, odious, offensive.

na'matatnga [æ] 1. Inspire, encourage.

na'matunu 1. Barbeque, cause to burn.

na'matungo' 1. Publicize, make known, propagate, promulgate, spread word of, bring to public. Cf. **Pupblika.**

na'maya [æ] 1. Cause to blur, make obscure, cause to obscure. *Hu na'maya' inatan-ña si Jose anai hu ina ni denke'.* I caused Jose's eyes to blur when I shined the flashlight.

ná'moda [æ] 2. Fad, passing fancy.

na'montohon 2. Gather, collect, group, convene, bring together into one aggregate. Also **na'monton.** Cf. **Na'etnon.**

na'monton 2. Collect, gather. Also **na'montohon.**

na'na' 1. Hide, conceal, secrete, make secret. Cf. **Na'atok.**

nana 2. Mother, a female parent.

nana 2. Type of plant-pterocarpus indicus. (?).

nanagu 2. Type of plant-alyxia torresiana. A type of tree.

na'nahong [æ] 1. Supply, provide.

nána'huyong [æ] 2. Creator, the one who caused things to be.

nánalao 2. My goodness, goodness gracious, a mild expletive. *Nanalao si Maria sa' humanao.* My goodness, Maria left.

nána'libre [æ] 2. Savior.

na'na'lo [æ] 1. Return (something) borrowed—usually something other than money. *I estudiante ha na'na'lo i inayao-ña gi amigu-ña.* The student returned that which he borrowed to his friend.

Nanan Kilisyanu 2. Christian Mother, religious organization for married women.

nanasu 2. Type of plant-scaevola taccada. Fan flower.

nanasu 2. Type of plant-geniostona micranthum. A type of tree.

nane' 2. Shoals, sandbank, shallow stretch of water.

nani [æ] 2. Goat call, word used for calling goats.

nanka 2. Type of plant-artocarpus heterophyllus. Jackfruit. Also **lanka.**

nanu 2. Dwarf, a diminutive human being.

nangga [æ] 1. Wait, stay for, await, wait for. *Si Linda ha nangga i bus gi estasion.* Linda waited for the bus at the station.

nangu [æ] 2. Swim. Also **ñangu.**

nao'ao 2. Clear (liquid), transparent (liquid), capable of being seen through.

naofragu 2. Shipwrecked person.

naonao 2. Quiver—jelly-like, shake like jelly or fat flesh. Also **laolao.**

ná'o'son [æ] 2. Boring, tiring, wearied, exhausting.

napa 2. Type of grass-napier grass.

na'para 1. Halt, stop, put to a stop, cause to stop.

na'parañaihon 1. Suspend, delay.

na'parehu 1. Assimilate, arrange.

na'payon 2. Accustom, cause to be used to. *Ha na'payon yo' si nana-hu manaitai kada dia.* My mother made me accustomed to reciting a prayer daily.

na'piniti 1. Sadden, make sad. Cf. **Piniti.**

nappa' [æ] 2. Type of plant-brassica. Chinese cabbage.

napu 2. Wave, rough water, surf.

nasa 2. Fish trap—portable, movable fish trap, usually made from chicken wire and wooden posts, sometimes made of bamboo strips.

na'sahnge 2. Change appearance, minus. Also **na'sangi.**

nasan panglao 2. Crab trap—for land crabs. Cf. **Okudon panglao.**

na'sangi 2. Change appearance, look strange, cause to change, set aside. Also **na'sahnge.** Cf. **Fa'sangi.** *Un na'sangi posision-ña i kareta-mu anai un penta.* You made your car look strange when you painted it.

na'saonao 1. Include. *Na'saonao gue'.* Include him.

Nasarét 2. Nazareth.

nasarinu 2. Leprosy, leper. Also **lasarinu.**

Nasarinu 2. Nazarene.

na'satisfecho 1. Satisfy.

na'sénbula 1. Fill, flood. Cf. **Bula.**

na'setbe 2. Use. Also **na'sietbe.**

na'sietbe 2. Use, employ, utilize, spend, expend. Also **na'setbe.** Cf. **Aplika, gasta, usa.** *Ha na'sietbe i lapes.* He used the pencil.

na'sikat 2. Pre-trial of cockfighting—just to see whether they will fight. Cf. **Sikat.**

ná'siña [æ] 2. Mighty.

na'siñayon 2. Feasible, practicable.

nasión 2. Nation, folk.

nasionát 2. Nationality, national.

na'suha 1. Remove, set aside, exclude, eliminate, separate, minus. Cf. **Remotke, remoeba.**

natahlek [æ] 2. Crooked, winding, curved, bending. Also **matahlek.**

na'táibali 1. Avoid, annul.

na'taiguenao Do like that, make it like that. (Close to addressee). *Na'taiguenao i kareta-hu i kareta-mu.* Make my car look like your car.

na'taiguihi Do like that, make it like that. (Away from speaker and addressee). *Na'taiguihi kulot-ña guatu.* Make its color like that there.

na'táilayi 2. Be cruel, make bad, bad—cause to be, cause (someone) to do evil. Cf. **Tailayi.**

ná'tailayi [æ] 2. Harmful, injurious. Cf. **Na'lamen.** *Si Jose na'tailayi na taotao.* Joseph is a harmful person.

na'talo'ani 1. Dine, eat lunch.

ná'tanga [æ] 2. Deafening, make deaf, deprive of the power of hearing.

natas See **ñatas.**

nátata [æ] 2. Shallow, not deep, shoal, become shallow.

na'tatnon [æ] 1. Distract, divert someone's attention.

na'tatte 1. Hesitate, hang back.

natdo 2. Type of plant-zephyranthes rosea. Type of flower.

Natibidát 2. Nativity, Christmas.

natibu 2. Native, indigenous.

na'tosta 1. Toast, make crispy.

na'tunas 1. Unbend, unharness, relax, correct, straighten. Cf. **Tunas.**

na'tunok 1. Lower, let down, digest. Cf. **Tunok.**

na'tungo' 1. Reveal, make known. Cf. **Tungo'.**

na'tungo'ñaihon 1. Insinuate, hint, suggest indirectly.

naturát 2. Naturally, natural.

naya Yet, for a while, for a second, for a minute, for a moment. Cf. **Ñaihon.** *Cha'-mu humahanao naya.* Don't leave yet. *Nangga naya.* Wait for a while.

na'yan 1,2. Serve (food), put, place food on the dish or water in the cup. Dish, plate, cup, eating container. *Hu na'yan i kaddo gi tasa.* I fill the cup with soup. *Ha na'yan i palao'an i katne gi platu.* The woman served the meat in the plate.

na'yan 2. Food or gifts from a party or novena.

na'yan mata' 2. Unprepared food—given in lieu of a party.

na'yan me'me' 2. Urinal.

na'ye 1. Contaminate, pollute, taint, defile, add in, put in. *Ma na'ye abonu gi hatdin.* They put fertilizer in the garden. *I malangu ha na'ye yo' ni sinagu-ña.* The patient contaminated me with his cold.

na'yommok 1. Fatten, feed. Cf. **Yommok.**

ná'yommok [æ] 2. Anything causing one to be fat.

Ne' Nickname for Manuel.

nebenu 2. Ninth.

nebét 2. Level—carpenter's. Also **nubet.**

negosiante 2. Negotiator, mediator, arbitrator.

negosio 2. Negotiation, bargain, agreement to arbitrate. *Mannegosio i emplehao siha yan i emplehon-ñiha.* The employees negotiated with their employer.

negro 2. Negro, black complexion. Also **negra** (f). Cf. **Bakuko', nekglo.**

nehong 2. Stoop, hunch over, duck under. *Numehong yo' gi petta.* I stooped over at the door.

nekglo 2. Negro, black complexion. Cf. **Bakuko', negro.**

Nelong Nickname for Cornelio.

nena 2. Beloved, dear.

nena' 2. Pig's call. Cf. **Bu.**

Nena' 2. Pet name for Anna or Magdalena.

Nenan Nickname for Magdalena.

neni 2. Baby, infant, child, kid. Cf. **Patgon.**

nénkanno' 2. Food, aliment, nutriment, nourishment, sustenance.

nenggue 2. Wait. Older form for *nangga.*

nesio 2. Perverse, obstinate, foolish. Cf. **Aguaguat.**

nétbios 2. Nervous.

nette 2. Type of plant-miscanthus floridulus. Sword grass.

ni Which (relative), who (relative). Contracted form of *nu* plus *i. I kareta ni poddong gi saddok iyo-ku.* The car which fell in the river is mine. *I taotao ni tata-hu.* The man who is my father. Particle marking indefinite or distributive object. *Hu taitai i lepblo.* I read the book. *Manaitai yo' ni lepblo.* I read of the book. Always used with definite objects in constructions using class 2 verbs. *Malago' yo' ni lepblo.* I want the book. Not even. *Ni si Jose.* Not even Jose. Used for marking instrumental phrases. *Hu ipe' i mansana ni se'se'-hu.* I cut the apple with my knife. Used for marking non-focused elements in a clause. *Si Pedro ha na'hatsayi si Maria ni lamasa para i patgon.* Pedro caused Maria to lift the table for the child.

ni' Alternate form of particle *ni,* the contracted form of *nu* plus *i.*

ni hafa Nothing, none, nought, nil, naught, all gone. *Ni hafa ti un na'saga yo'.* There is nothing you can do to make me stay. *Ni hafa ya-hu guini.* There is nothing I like here.

ni hayi Nobody, no one, not a one, never a one. *Ni hayi tumungo' yo' giya Guam.* Nobody knows me on Guam.

ni kuanto Nowise, in no manner or degree. *Ni kuanto minetgot-mu ti un hulat yo'.* No matter how strong you are you won't beat me.

ni manu Nowhere, not anywhere, at no place. *Ni manu hao guatu esta.* There is nowhere for you to go already.

ni ngai'an Never, not possible, not ever. *Ni ngai'an ti un fa'maolek.* You will never fix it. *Ni ngai'an.* Never. (decision made not to do).

ni taimanu No matter, nowise, no way, by no means, not by a long shot, in no respect. *Ni taimanu ti un tungo'.* There is no way that you can know.

ni unu 2. Nobody, no one.

Nia' Nickname for Estefania.

nichu 2. Niche.

niebi 2. Snow.

niega 1. Deny. Cf. **Puni.**

nieta 2. Granddaughter.

nietkot 2. Type of plant-suriana maritima. And pemphis acidula. Similar to *fofgo.* Type of vine.

nietu 2. Grandson.

nifen 2. Tooth, teeth.

nigap 2. Yesterday.

nigapña 2. Day before yesterday.

nigas 2. Type of tree-pemphis acidula.

nigritos 2. Black race, negrito, negro, people of very dark or black skin.

nihi Let's (do something)—used with future verb and 1st person plural pronouns. *Nihi ta falagu.* Let's run. *Nihi ta fanhanao.* Let's all go.

nika 2. Type of plant-dioscorea esculenta. Variety fasciculate. Type of yam. Cf. **Gaddo'.**

nikan asumsion Type of yam—hairy. Hairy root with thorny vines. Cf. **Gaddo', nika.**

nikan simarón 2. Type of plant-dioscorea esculenta. (?).

nina 2. Godmother—short form. Also **matlina.**

nina'- Cause to. *Na'-* plus goal focus infix *-in-. Nina'maleffa hao ni estudiu-mu ni kontrata-ta.* Your study caused you to forget about our agreement. *Nina'pokpok mata-ña anai inakka' ni sasata.* Your eye was caused to swell when the bee stung it.

nina'halom 2. Income; that which is caused to be in.

nina'huyong 2. Creation, work.

nina'i [æ] 2. Gift, present, donation, a thing that is given away. Cf. **Chinchule', rigalu.**

nina'libre 2. One who is saved, one who is set free.

nina'maolek 2. Improvement.

Ninan Nickname for Catalina.

nina'siña 2. Power, strength, might, force, energy, stamina. Cf. **Fuetsa, minetgot, alimento, alentos.**

nina'ye [æ] 2. Contaminated, polluted, tainted, defiled, stained, soiled, or corrupted by contact.

nina'ye masisinik 2. Diarrhea, have diarrhea.

ninu 2. Godfather—short form. Also **patlinu.**

Niñu 2. Baby Jesus.

nipa 2. Type of plant-nipa. A palm that grows by the rivers, very good for making thatch.

nira' 2. Leek, scallion, onion—flat-leaf. (S) Cf. **Siboyas.**

nisisario 2. Necessary, needful, essential.

nisisidát 2. Necessity, need.

nisisita 1. Need, require, want, necessary.

nisisitáo 2. Needy, necessitous, poor, destitute, in need.

niyok 2. Coconut—tree or fruit.

niyok 2. Type of plant-cocos nucifera. Coconut palm.

niyok kannu'on 2. Coconut—having sweet husk, milk, etc. while still green.

no Yes, in rhetorical question. *Ya-mu no humanao para Hawaii?* You like to go to Hawaii, yes? *Un espiha gue', no?* You looked for him, yes?

nobena 2. Novena, devotion.

nobenta 2. Ninety.

nobenta i unu 2. Ninety-one.

nobia 2. Sweetheart, girlfriend, lover, loved one, bride.

nobidát 2. Novelty, news.

Nobiembre 2. November. Cf. **Sumongsong.**

nobilidát 2. Nobility, royalty.

nobiu 2. Sweetheart, fiance, groom, bridegroom, suitor.

nochebuena 2. Evening, eve, Christmas eve.

noches 2. Evening, night, but used only in a phrase, such as, *buenas noches,* good night, or good evening.

nokieru Dislike. Also **nukeru.**

nombra 1. Command, force, rule, appoint. Cf. **Manda.**

nombrayon 2. Eligible, legally qualified.

nones 2. Odd (not even), not divisible by two, not a pair.

nonnak 2. Type of plant-hernandia sonora. Jack-in-the-box tree. Has very soft wood.

nopble 2. Noble, highborn.

nosa' 2. Type of bird-zosterops c. Conspicillata, bridled white-eye (green).

noseha ki Might, in case. Also **nosea ki.** *Ta nangganñaihon noseha ki u bira gue' magi ta'lo.* We will wait for a while in case he turns back again.

noskuantos 2. Several, couple of, few, some, more than two or three (but not many). Also **unos kuantos, los kuantos.** *Noskuantos granu ha' tinekcha'-hu na guihan.* I speared a few fish.

nosnos 2. Squid, cuttlefish. Decapod cephalopod. Also **nosngos.**

nota 1. Note, record, set (down) in writing, make a special mention of.

notifika 1. Notify. Cf. **Infotma.**

notifikasión 2. Notification.

notisia 2. Notice, message, information, announcement. Cf. **Infotmasion, anunsia.**

notte 2. North. Cf. **Lagu.**

nu Particle, used to mark non-focus elements of a construction. Usually occurs as *ni* which is a contracted form of *nu* plus *i*. Always occurs as *nu* when preceding pronouns. *Ti hiningok hao nu guiya.* He didn't hear you. *Kao hagu pinacha nu siha?* Were you the one who was touched by them?

nu Pause particle used to fill space during pause in speaking.

nubét 2. Level (carpenter's)—a device for establishing a horizontal line, vertical line, or diagonal line. Also **mubet, nebet.**

nubiyitu 2. Young steer, young male ox.

nubiyu 2. Ox, steer—castrated bull.

nubladu 2. Cloudy. Also **nupbladu.**

nudu A knot, any type of knot including knot on a tree or knot tied with rope. Also **ñudu.**

nuebi 2. Nine.

nuebu 2. New, modern, strange, unfamiliar, fresh.

nufo' 2. Type of fish-family scorpaenidae. Stone fish, scorpion fish. Highly poisonous if dorsal spines penetrate the skin.

nufo' pabu 2. Type of fish-pterois antennata (family scorpaenidae). Scorpion fish.

nuhong 2. Shady, shaded, shadowy, abounding in shade. Cf. **Lehngong**.

nuhot 2. Stem—coconut leaf, midrib--coconut leaf.

nukeru Eschew, care for none, want no part of it, dislike, have no desire. Also **nokieru**. *Nukeru bumaila*. I have no desire to dance.

nulu 2. Null, void.

numa'lo [æ] **2.** Revive, do again, return. Cf. **Ta'lo**. *Numa'lo i pakyo*. The typhoon returned.

númiru 2. Number.

nunka Never, not ever, at no time—not in any degree, way, or condition. Cf. **Taya'**. *Nunka yo' nai mandagi*. I have never lied. *Nunka si Rosa na fatta gi eskuela*. Rosa is never absent from school.

nunok 1. Make ripen, conceal fruit for ripening.

nunu 2. Type of plant-ficus prolixa. Type of tree. Banyan tree.

nupbladu 2. Cloudy, cloudy weather. Also **lubradu, nubladu**.

nupi 2. Type of vine—formerly used for lashing in building houses.

nutrát 2. Neutral, unbiased.

-ña His, her, its, hers (possessive). *Si Pete patgon-ña*. Pete is his child.

-ña More, better, comparative degree, usually used with *kinu* in comparative statements. *Maolekña kareta-hu kinu kareta-mu*. My car is better than your car. *Meggaiña salape'-hu kinu hagu*. I have more money than you.

-ña...ki Comparative construction. Used in place of *ña...kinu*. *Maolekña kareta-hu ki kareta-mu*. My car is better than your car.

ñaba' [æ] **2.** Relaxed, pliable, flexible, easily bent. Cf. **Ñaohan**.

ñáfula [æ] **2.** Flabby, weak in appearance. Cf. **Ñaba'**.

ñagong [æ] **2.** Shelter—from the rain. (S) Also **nagong**. *Bai hu ñagong gi kareta*. I will shelter myself from the

rain in the car. *Ñumagong yo' nigap*. I sheltered myself from the rain yesterday. *Ñagong gi gima'*. Shelter yourself from the rain in the house. *Hu na'ñagong i amigu-hu gi gima'*. I sheltered my friend from the rain at the house.

ñáhlalang [æ] **2.** Light (in weight), easy. Also **ñalalang**.

-ñaihon Awhile, for a while, for a moment, a short time, short moment (suffix). *Saganñaihon asta ki matto yo'*. Stay for a while until I come back. *Sugo'ñaihon gi gima' gi birada-mu*. Stop by at the house for a while on your way back.

-ñaihon Little bit. *Ballenñaihon*. Sweep a little bit.

ñaka' [æ] **1.** Hang (to death), suspend by the neck until dead.

ñálalang [æ] **2.** Light (in weight), easy, not heavy. Also **ñahlalang**.

ñalang 2. Hungry, feeling hunger, marked by lack of food.

ñama' [æ] **2.** Sluggish, slow poke, slow, slow moving, markedly slow in movement, weak, deficient in bodily vigor. Cf. **Manman**.

ñamñam [æ] **2.** Chew, sound of chewing, eat. Cf. **Ngangas**. *Fanñamñam papaya*. Eat the papaya.

ñamu Mosquito.

ña'ña' 1. Mix—grated coconut meat with raw fish, shrimp, or meat. (R) *Hu ña'ña' i guihan*. I mixed fish with the coconut meat.

ñañak 2. Type of rock-pumice. A very light weight stone found in the Marianas.

ñañas 2. Weary, fatigued, exhausted, tired (physically), done in, worn out, prostrate, haggard, all in. (R) Also **yayas**.

ñaño' [æ] **1.** Cause to sniff, cause to smell, put something close to a person's nose, thereby causing him to smell it.

ñaño' [æ] **2.** Dull, not sharp. Cf. **Dafe'**.

ñanggo 2. Hip, haunch, loins.

ñangnang [æ] **2.** Talkative, entertaining.

ñangñang [æ] **2.** Cute baby, cooing, smiling. *Ñangñang na patgon*. A cute baby.

ñangon [æ] **1,2.** Whisper, soft voice, talk with constricted vocal cords, speak covertly esp. in conspiracy or criticism. Soft utterance, volume—soft, speech without voice.

ñangu [æ] 2. Swim. Also **nangu**. *I maolek na ñangu*. The good swim. *Ñumangu yo' asta i mama'te*. I swam to the reef.

ñao 2. Brother-in-law. Short form for *kuñadu*. Also **kuña**.

ñaohan 2. Flabby, loose, less tense, slacken. Cf. **Ñaba'**. *Ñaohan tataotao-mu*. Your body is flabby. *Ñaohan i tali*. The rope is slack.

ña'ot [æ] 2. Crab—when carrying eggs. Stage when crabs are carrying eggs on them. Cf. **Mangulales**. *Manña'ot i panglao siha*. The crabs have eggs on them.

ña'ot [æ] 2. Crab eggs, fish eggs. Cf. **Figan**.

ñatas 2. Scum, skimmings, which forms on the surface of any soupy food or liquid. Also **natas**.

ñateng [æ] 2. Slow, not hasty, slow-witted.

ñedok 2. Adolescent male, changing voice—in adolescent male.

ñega 1. Deny, nullify, contradict, break contract. Cf. **Puni**. *Mañega i ginagao-ta*. Our request was denied. *Ha ñega i kontrata*. He cancelled the contract.

ñehngon 2. Shaded area—where soil is fresh and moist.

ñehom 2. Lurk, to duck, bob down, evade. Also **ñehong**. *Ñumehom yo' gi tatten i acho'*. I ducked behind the rock.

ñehong See **ñehom**.

-ñiha Their, theirs. *Bunitu i karetan-ñiha*. Their car is pretty.

Ñiñu 2. Baby Jesus. (R) Also **Niñu**.

ñohmon 2. Watery soil—almost muddy, one's feet will sink in 3 to 4 inches when walking over it.

ñokñok 1. Submerge, immerse, cause to submerge. Cf. **Lumos, supok**.

ñongñong 2. Talkative, entertaining, gabby. Also **ñangñang**.

ñora Expression used when kissing a woman's hand when performing *nginge'*. From *señora*.

ñot Expression used when kissing a man's hand in performing *nginge'*. From *señot*. Also used when answering an older male's call.

ñotak 2. Type of eel-lycodontis picta. Lycodontis picta—grayish white brown covered with very fine dots. (R) Cf. **Hakmang**.

ñudu 2. Hollow, not solid—having a cavity within a solid substance, knot--in wood.

ñufo' 2. Type of fish-family scorpaenidae. Scorpion fish, stone fish. Also **nufo'**.

ñukot 1. Strangle, choke, stifle, suffocated by choking.

ñuña 1. Flatter, pacify by stroking or petting; boost one's morale.

ngaha Don't know, don't understand. (R).

ngaha' [æ] 2. Look up, with head tilted back.

ngai'an When (question word). Usually followed by *nai. Ngai'an nai mafañagu hao?* When were you born?

nga'nga' 2. Open mouthed—while staring blankly, look up with mouth open, gape.

nganga' 2. Duck (fowl).

nganga' 2. Type of plant-lumnitzera littorea. A type of flower. *Flores nganga'*.

nganga' palao 2. Type of bird-anas oustaleti, marianas mallard.

ngangas 1. Chew, masticate, grind with the teeth.

ngangas [æ] 2. Balding. Cf. **Dakngas**.

ngasan 2. Straw, anything made of straw, such as hat, bag, slippers.

ngatnan 2. Leftover food—used for slop or for feeding animals. Cf. **Ankanno'**.

ngayu [æ] 2. Collect firewood. *Ngumayu yo'*. I collected firewood.

nge'lo' 2. Peeping tom, one who peeks surreptitiously at things, voyeur.

ngelo' 1. Peep at, peek at, as through a crevice or small hole. Cf. **Adu, engelo'**.

nget 2. Type of plant-allophylus timorensis. (?).

nginge' 1. Sniff, smell (something), kissing back part of a person's right hand upon meeting as a sign of respect.

ngisot 2. Shorten, short in length, make short, make tight. *Hu na'ngisot i tali-ña i guaka*. I shortened the cow's rope. *Ngisot i magagu-ña i* *palao'an.* The woman's dress was short.

ngofngof 2. Blow (the nose), blow nose.

ngokngok 2. Unclear speech, sometimes a temporary condition resulting from accident.

ngulo' 2. Hole, crack, porous, capable of being seen through, as porous cloth, slit, aperture.

o O—letter.

o Oh, so, (expression).

o- Search for (something)—prefix. Alternate form of *e-*. *Opanglao.* Look for crabs.

oba' 2. Fever blister—at corner of the mouth. Cf. **Pakpak.**

obehas 2. Sheep. Cf. **Kinilu.**

obidiente 2. Obedient, amenable, submissive to restraint, control, or command. Cf. **Osgon.**

obispo 2. Bishop.

obra 1. Design, scheme, outline, sketch, work. *Hu obra i gima'-hu.* I designed my house. *Mañule' hao obran guma'.* You took on the job of building a house.

obra 2. Free to act. *Obra i patgon manestudia gi gima' sa' guiya ha' na maisa.* The child was free to study in the house for he was by himself.

Ocha' Nickname for Rosa.

ochenta 2. Eighty.

ochenta i unu 2. Eighty-one.

ocho 2. Eight.

odda 2. Type of fish-ctenochaetus striatus (family acanthuridae). Surgeon fish.

odda' 2. Soil, ground, dirt. Also **edda'.**

odda' sabana 2. Clay.

oddas 1,2. Support, bear the weight or stress of, sustain (a load). Footstool.

oddo 2. Smudge, smudge pot, fumigation, fire to smoke mosquitos out, smoke out, mosquito coil. Cf. **Senko'.** *Ti guinaiya i eddo ni ñamu.* The mosquitos dislike the smoke from the fire.

oddo' 2. Carry—on head. Also **otdo'.**

ó'duko' 2. Crazy, foolish. Cf. **Kaduku.**

ofende 1. Offend, transgress, to sin, cause to feel hurt or resentful. Cf. **Isagui.**

ofensa 2. Offense—as to commit an offense.

ofisiát 2. Officer, official.

ofisina 2. Office, administration, administrative department, clerical department.

ofisiu 2. Job, post, official position, employment, work, career, occupation.

ofresi 1. Offer, propose, proffer, bid (as a price), make an offer of.

ofresimiento 2. Offer, offering, promise. *Bula ofresimiento-mu giya siha lao taya' un kukumple.* You made lots of promises to them, but you have never accomplished any of them.

ogga'an 2. Morning, dawn.

oggan 2. Stuck on, run aground, stranded, to land on accidentally. *Oggan i batko gi mama'te.* The ship was stuck on the reef. *I papaloti oggan gi tronkon hayu.* The kite was stuck in the tree.

oha 2. Solid covering for doorway or window.

óhala Thankful, how thankful or grateful one may be. Also **o'la'.** *Ohala ya i la'la' ta'lo' si nana-hu.* How thankful I would be to have my mother living again.

ohales 1,2. Buttonhole, make buttonhole. Also **uales, ales.**

ohan bentana 2. Shutter—for window, solid covering for window.

ohan potta 2. Door. Cf. **Oha.**

ohas 2. Leaf, page, sheet of paper.

ohlo' 2. Stooped person, usually among older people; slouchy posture.

oia' 2. Shooter, taw, in a marble game. (S) Cf. **Bakulu.**

okasión 2. Occasion.

ókkodon panglao 2. Crab trap—for land crabs.

ókkodu 2. Snare, trap, anything by which one is entangled, rat trap.

okra 2. Type of plant-hibiscus esculentus. Okra. A type of vegetable.

okso' 2. Hill, heap, mound, a raised bank, knoll, hilly. Cf. **Bokka'.**

oktaba 2. Octave.

oktabu 2. Eighth.

okte 1. Give abundantly. Cf. na'i.

Oktubre 2. October. Cf. **Fagualo'.**

okupa 1. Occupy, employ, be busy, keep engaged, dwell in (as a tenant).

okupante 2. Occupant.

okupáo 2. Occupied.

okupasión 2. Occupation, occupancy, profession, career, trade, employment.

o'la' Oh how—exclamation usually followed by *mohon*. Also **ohala**. *O'la' mohon ya hohoben ha' yo'.* Oh how I wish i were young.

Oleai 2. Oleai, one of the villages on Saipan, north of Chalan Kanoa, recently named San Jose.

olibas 2. Olives.

ólios 2. Unction, extreme unction.

Olo' Nickname—for Pedro. Also **Elo'**.

o'mak 2. Take a shower, swim, bathe. *Umo'mak i patgon gi saddok.* The child swam in the river.

ombo' 1. Carry, pickaback, carry piggyback, astraddle, as when babies are carried on the backs of their mothers. (S) Cf. **Uke'**.

ombre Please, usually has a connotation that the addressee has already been asked or warned before. Cf. **Me'nan**. *Ombre nihi.* Please let's go. *Ombre munga ma'estotba i amko'.* Please (I told you once) don't annoy the old man.

ombres Even though, furthermore, as well, similarly, besides, also, too. *Ombres hagu ti ya-mu gamson kuastaria yo'.* Even you don't like octopus, least of all me. *Ombres tataya' salape'-hu sigi ha' yo' un ayao.* Even though I'm running out of money, you continue to borrow from me.

omiti 1. Omit, leave out, not include.

omlat 2. Fit, fit into. Also **ulat**. *Omlat i aniyu gi kalulot-hu.* The ring fit my finger. *Omlat yo' gi sapatos-hu.* I fit into my shoes.

ómumu 2. Type of plant-pisonia grandis. A type of tree.

-on Abilitative suffix, capable of. *-yon* following vowels. *Guasa',* sharpen. *I guasa'on,* something capable of being sharpened. *Kannu'on este na fruta.* This fruit is edible. *Taitayon ayu na lepblo.* That book is readable.

onesto 2. Honest, truthful, frank, sincere. Also **onesta** (f). Cf. **Franko, sinseru, magahet, siguru**.

Onin Nickname for Antonia.

onno' 2. Covering, blanket, linen. Cf. **Sabanas**.

onra 1,2. Honor, fame, credit, good name, homage, reverence, deference, obeisance.

onse 1. Put on harness, to yoke.

onse 2. Eleven.

ongngo' 2. Flat nose, noseless, speak through the nose, nasal speech. *Ongngo' na gui'eng.* A flat nose. *I taotao ongngo' kumuentos.* The person spoke through his nose.

o'o' 2. Drink (soup).

o'o' 2. Crow (of rooster).

kaddo 1, 2. Boil—type of cooking meat or soup, sauce, broth, soup. *Ma gimen i kaddo.* They drank the broth.

opbliga 1. Oblige, bind by an obligation, bring or place under moral or legal duty or constraint. Cf. **Afuetsas**. *Ta opbliga i patgon humanao asta i eskuela.* We obliged the child to go to school.

opbligáo 2. Obligated, compulsory, bound, restricted, forced. Cf. **Afuetsas**. *Opbligao i mañaina na u na'fanhanao i famagu'on-ñiha maneskuela.* The parents are obligated to send their children to be educated.

opbligasión 2. Obligation, duty, responsibility, commitment. Cf. **Responsibilidat**.

opela 2. Opal.

opera 1. Operate, perform an operation.

operasión 2. Operation.

ophetu 2. Object.

o'pok 1. Lie down—with face down. Cf. **Oppop**.

opottunidát 2. Opportunity.

oppan 2. Audible, resound, can be heard, be heard. Cf. **Hongga**. *Oppan i bos-hu gi halom kuatto.* My voice was heard inside the room.

oppe 1. Reply, answer, respond.

oppop 2. Lie down on stomach, recline on stomach, lying face down. *Hu na'oppop i patgon.* I laid the baby face down. *Umoppop i patgon anai madulok gi espitat.* The child lay down on his stomach when he was given a shot at the hospital.

ora 1,2. Time. Hour, time. *Hu ora i buseru anai lumi'of asta i fondo.* I timed the diver when he dived to the bottom. *Hayi guaha ora-ña?* Who has the time?

orario 2. Hour hand—on watch or clock.

orasión 2. Oration, prayer time.

Ordot Village in central Guam. Pron. otdot.

oriente 2. Orient, the east. Countries east of the Mediterranean or eastern Asiatic countries; eastern, oriental.

orihinát 2. Original, that which is the source or origin (of something).

oropa 1. Cover up, conceal, hide by covering. (R) Cf. **Tampe.**

oros 2. Diamonds—card in the suit of.

oru 2. Gold.

osge 1. Mind, pay attention to, give heed to, be obedient to.

osge 1. Resemble, look like, take after. Cf. **Gapi, parehu.** *Si Pedro ha osge si tata-ña.* Pete takes after his father.

osgon 2. Amenable, submissive, dutiful, obedient. Cf. **Obidiente.**

osiosu 2. Leisure, ease, freedom from occupation, idle, lazy.

osngan 1. Carry (something)—by putting a stick over one's shoulder. Cf. **Pingga.**

o'son 2. Bored, tired, exhaust one's patience. Cf. **Sosongte, singao, impachu.** *O'son yo' humungok i kanta-mu.* I am bored listening to your song.

ospitát 2. Hospital, clinic, infirmary, sick bay, dispensary. Also **espitat.**

óssitan 2. Joke. Also **essitan.**

óstia 2. Eucharist—before or after consecration, sacrament.

osu 2. Bear, bruin, ursus.

otden 1. Command, give an order to, order, direct, instruct, prescribe. Cf. **Komanda.**

otdena 1. Ordain, enact, predestine, introduce into the office of the Christian ministry.

otdinariu 2. Ordinary, usual, normal, common.

otdo' 1. Carry (something) on the head. Also **oddo'.** Cf. **Do'an.**

otdon 2. Pimple, sty—in the eye.

otdot 2. Ant, pismire. Cf. **Hateng.**

otdot agaga' 2. Red ant.

otdot áttilong 2. Black ant.

otdot díkike' 2. Type of ant—especially fond of sweets.

otdot sakkan 2. Ant—small black.

otganisa 1. Organize, form, make, shape. Cf. **Fa'tinas, fotma.**

otguyosu 2. Self-opinionated, selfish, stuck-up, avaricious, greedy. Also **atguyosu.** Cf. **Chattao, interesao.**

otobái' 2. Motorcycle, motorscooter. (S) Also **motosaikot.**

otpos 2. Ashes—from burned tobacco, butt--from cigarette or cigar.

otro 2. Other, else, different, additional, another. *Kao guaha otro ta'lo?* Is there another one? *Hafa otro?* What else is there? *I otro na lahi.* The other man.

otro na mes 2. Next month, coming month. Also **otro mes.** Cf. **Mamamaila' na mes.**

otro na sakkan 2. Next year. Also **otro sakkan.** Cf. **Mamamaila' na sakkan.**

otro na simana 2. Next week. Also **otro simana.** Cf. **Mamamaila' na simana.**

otroña na mes 2. Month after next. Also **otroña mes.** Cf. **Mamaila'ña na mes.**

otroña na sakkan 2. Year after next. Also **otroña sakkan.** Cf. **Mamaila'ña na sakkan.**

otroña na simana Week after next. Also **otroña simana.** Cf. **Mamaila'ña na simana.**

otto 1,2. Bump, bang, thump, poke, butt, jolt, jostle. Cf. **Toyo', totpos.**

ottot 2. Type of plant-discocalyx megacarpa. A type of tree.

pabu 2. Turkey.

pacha [æ] 1. Touch, be in contact, perceive by feeling. Cf. **Ette.**

pachakati 2. Small—in growth, weak, underdeveloped in stature.

pachang [æ] 2. Weakling, milksop, cry-baby, sissy, an unmanly man.

pachinko' 2. Spear gun (local made)—used for spear fishing. (S) Cf. **Paken tokcha'.**

pachodak 2. Type of plant-luffa cylindrica. (?).

pachot 2. Mouth.

pachuchang 2. Neat, nice—speaking of girls, pretty, a manner of walking with noticeable hip movement.

padakdak [æ] 2. Lie, deceit, denial.

padarao' 2. Long machete, long knife. (S)

padda' [æ] 1,2. Clap, slap, pat. Banana leaf or sheet of non-adhering paper used in patting out tortillas. Cf. **Pampan.**

paddet 2. Concrete, hard cement. Also **patdet.** Cf. **Simento.**

paderón 2. Crag, cliff, esp. bordering the sea.

padesi 1. Suffer, bear, be forced to endure.

padok [æ] **2.** Greedy, covetous, ravenous, eagerly desirious, having a keen appetite for food or drink. Cf. **Gulosu, girek.**

padong [æ] **2.** Smegma—the secretion of a sebaceous gland, specif. the cheesy matter that collects between the glands penis and the foreskin or around the clitoris and labia minora.

padrón 2. Pattern.

pagadót 2. Paymaster. *Mangge i pagadot?* Where is the paymaster?

pagagu 2. Type of plant-malachra capitata. (?).

pagamento 2. Payday.

paganu 2. Pagan, heathen.

pa'gang 2. Type of clam. Larger than *tapon.* Also **pahgang.**

pagat 1. Preach to, exhort, proclaim the gospel, deliver a sermon, advise. Cf. **Petdika.** *I pale' ha pagat i taotao siha.* The priest preached to the people.

pa'go Now, today.

pago' [æ] **1.** Irritate skin, to cause skin irritation, to kid by giving false information. *Ha pago' i kannai-hu i diso'.* The diesel irritated my hands.

pa'go gi egga'an Morning—this.

pa'go manana 2. Day break, morning twilight, dawn—the first appearance of light in the morning. Cf. **Machakchak.**

pa'go na simana Week—this.

pa'go yan ayu Now and then, sometimes, once in a while.

pagu 2. Type of plant-hibiscus tiliaceus.

paguan 2. Scent—give off, odor, aroma, smell. *Paguan i fina'tinas-mu.* Your cooking gives off an odor.

paha 2. Spinning smoothly. *Paha i tolompo-ña.* His top spins smoothly.

paharita 2. Small bird (generic). Birdie. Also **paharitu.**

pahariya 2. Spleen.

páharu 2. Bird (generic term).

pahgang 2. Type of clam. Also **pa'gang.**

páhina 2. Page (of paper).

pahlo 2. Mast, pole, antenna. Also **palu.**

pahngon 1. Arouse, wake, wake up. Also **pangon.** Cf. **Ya'ho.** *I buruka ha pahngon yo'.* The noise woke me up. *Hu pahngon i patgon para sumena.* I woke up the child for dinner.

pahong 2. Type of tree-pandanus, screw pine—bears edible fruit. Cf. **Kafo', akgak.**

pahya' [æ] **2.** Garbled speech, mumbled or unclear speech, one who does not speak clearly, unclear reception of speaker's voice on radio, refers to a particular kind of speech impediment where the speaker substitutes the sound represented by t for the sound represented by y. Also **paya'.** *Pahya' i fino'-mu gi telefon.* Your talk on the phone was garbled.

pai 2. Pie.

Pai' Nickname for Josepha.

pa'iket 2. Gambling—usually cards or dice. *Si Andres ya-ña puma'iket.* Andy likes gambling.

paine 1,2. Comb.

painen basula 2. Rake—an instrument used for gathering trash or leaves around the yard.

paineta 2. Comb—ornamental, big comb.

painge 2. Last night.

paipai 2. Type of tree—hardwood, very useful for building materials.

pairastro 2. Stepfather. (S) Also **pairasto.** (G)

paire 2. Champion, breeder—best.

paireha 1. To father, sire, beget, procreate, coitus, esp. animals.

paisanu 2. Countryman, fellow citizen.

pákaka' 2. Silent, hush, be quiet. Cf. **Mamatkilu.** Also **pahkaka'.** *Pakaka' guenao.* Be quiet there. *Pumakaka' yo' nigap gi eskuela.* I was silent at school yesterday.

pakao [æ] **2.** Type of plant-caesalpinia major. A woody climber with spiny stems. Wait-a-bit.

pakcha [æ] **2.** Toucher, thief, one who has light fingers. From *papacha.*

paken fisga 2. Spear gun—used in Guam.

paken goma [æ] **2.** Slingshot.

paken tokcha' 2. Spear gun (commercial type). Cf. **Pachinko'.**

pa'kes 1. Scrape, chip, peel away, pry loose. (R) *Hu pa'kes i acho'.* I pried the rocks. *Ha pa'kes i kayos.* He peeled away the callus.

paketi 1,2. Parcel, pack, package—small.

paki [æ] **1,2.** Shoot, fire (a gun). Rifle, pistol, fire-arm (small).

pakiáo 2. Work fast, work contract, fast job, cash payment in full. Cf. **Apretao.** *Ma pakiao i che'cho' nigap.* They finished the job fast yesterday. *Cho'cho' pakiao enao.* That is a fast job.

Pakitu Nickname for Francisco.

pakke' [æ] **2.** Arching, bending, as in the forming an arch, curved—as eyelash or buttock.

pakko' 2. Blister from heat, burn—from a fire or burning charcoal. Also **panko'.**

pakngas [æ] **1.** Split (with an ax). Cf. **Gachai.**

pakpak 2. Blistered, exploded, pop, burst forth with sudden violence and noise, explosion, blister, clap (hands), clatter, boom. *Pakpak i kannai-hu anai humugando yo' boleng.* My hand blistered when I went bowling. *Kao un hungok i pakpak?* Did you hear the explosion? *Hu na'pakpak i kannai-hu.* I clapped my hands.

paksiú 1,2. Type of food—pork or fish cooked in lard, water, and vinegar plus additional seasoning. *Ha paksiu i mannok.* She made a chicken soup with vinegar. *Pumaksiu i palao'an guihan.* The woman made some fish soup with vinegar.

paktek [æ] **2.** Kicker—as a dangerous horse.

pakto 2. magic power, possessed by magic power.

pakyo 2. Typhoon, storm, tropical cyclone. Cf. **Papakyo.**

pala 1,2. To shovel, to spade. Shovel, spade.

palabra 2. Word, language.

palacha' 1,2. Tease; teaser, troublesome, troublemaker. Cf. **Akacha, achaka.**

paladan [æ] **2.** Scar, wheal, wound mark. Cf. **Maso'.**

páladat [æ] **2.** Palate, roof of the mouth.

palaga' 2. Slip, fall by a loss of footing, balance, support, etc. Cf. **Sulon.** *Palaga' i kareta gi kantit.* The car fell off the cliff.

palaga hilitai 2. Type of plant-desmodium umbellatum. A type of grass.

palai [æ] **1.** Smear, rub—with grease, to grease, spread greasy material, ointment. *Hu palai i kannai-ña ni mantika.* He smeared his hand with fat.

palai'i 2. Type of plant-chrysopogon aciculatus. (?).

palakñaihon 2. Hold and throw down, as in wrestling. Also **panakñaihon.**

palakpak 2. Cracking noise such as thunder, shotgun; chatterbox, babble, one who talks a lot. Cf. **pakpak.**

palakpak 2. Chatter, run off at the mouth.

palakse' [æ] **2.** Slippery (surface).

palakse' [æ] **2.** Type of fish-family labridae. Wrasses. Name for several of the longer and thicker members of the wrasse family. Also for family scaridae, small parrot fish.

palanggana 2. Washpan, washtub.

palangpang 2. Loud noise, fall down (noisely). *Palangpang makina-ña i kareta-hu.* My car has a loud noise. *Palangpang yo' papa' gi gua'ot.* I fell noisily down the stairs.

palao'an 2. Female, woman. Cf. **Famala'oan.** *Hu li'e' i palao'an.* I saw the woman. *I palao'an na katu.* The female cat.

palapala 2. Shack, hut, shanty, roof extending from house to provide shelter from sun and rain, pavillion.

palapala 2. Frame for vine type vegetables with sticks criss-crossing across top. Used esp. for bitter melon.

palapan hilitai 2. Type of plant-callicarpa candicans. (?).

palappa [æ] **2.** Flapping noise, rustling sound, flapped, flopped, splashing. *Pumalappa i guihan gi fi'on i boti.* The fish flopped near the boat. *I gayu pumalappa anai gumupu asta i ramas.* The rooster flapped when it flew to the branch. *Pumalappa i hagon hayu.* The leaves were rustling.

pa'las 1. Dupe, swindle, deceive, hoax, take advantage of the credulity of a person. Cf. **Fa'chada'.**

palaspas [æ] 2. Splash. *Palaspas i guihan gi halom hanom.* The fish splashed in the water.

palasyo 2. Palace, castle, governor's house.

Palau 2. Islands of Palau district in Micronesia.

pale' 2. Priest, minister, parson, pastor, preacher, ordained in ministry.

paleta 2. Trowel, agitator—in washing machine.

paleta 2. Palette, painter's palette.

paletan hineksa' 2. Rice scoop—made of wood.

palitada 2. Fight, battle, cockfight, combat. Cf. **Gayera**.

palitiya 2. Trapezius muscle, loin—that part of a human being or quadruped on either side of the spinal column between the hip bone and the shoulder. Shoulder blade.

palitu 1,2. Use chopsticks. Chopstick, stick (for stick dance), match stick.

paliyu 2. Tobacco twist, unit of tobacco.

palo'po' 1. Fall on—something or someone, to lie down on something or someone.

palos 2. Type of fish-strongylura gigantea (family belonidae). Needle fishes.

palu 2. Mast, pole. Also **pahlo**.

palu Some, some more. *Na'i si Pete palu ni na'-mu.* Give Pete some of your food. *Guaha palu famagu'on gi plasa.* There are some children at the plaza.

palu maria 2. Type of plant-calophyllum inophyllum. (?).

paluma 2. Bird, dove, pigeon, slang for penis.

paluman kunao 2. Type of bird-gallicolumba xanthonura, ground dove—reddish-brown. It is said to be the female for *apaka'.* Also **paluman agaga', paluman fache', paluman somnak**.

paluman kutbata 2. Type of bird-gallixolumba xanthonura, white-throated ground dove. Also **apaka', paluman kunao**.

paluman sinisa 2. Type of bird-streptopelia bitorquata dusumieri, Philippine turtle dove. Also **paluman apu, paluman odda'**.

palumat 2. Dove cote, pigeon roost, bird house.

pampan 1,2. Pat repeatedly, pat gently, as a baby, dog, or tortilla dough. Cf. **Pada'**.

pan 2. Bread.

pan mames 2. Bun, sweet bread.

pan royu 2. Bread—twisted, toasted.

panaderia 2. Bakery.

panaderu 2. Baker, one who bakes bread, pastry, etc. (m). Also **panadera** (f).

panaguan 2. Type of chicken—a rooster, black in color.

panak [æ] 1,2. Hit—something with a bat or flat sided object, slam, bang, shut noisily. Bat, instrument for hitting.

panak lalo' 2. Fly swatter. Cf. **Puno' lalo'**.

panak tenes 2. Tennis racket.

panakñaihon See **palakñaihon**.

panandera 2. Sow—used for breeding. Also **parandela**.

panao 2. Type of tree—hard wood, good for lumber.

pancho 2. Raincoat, slicker, poncho. Cf. **Kaputon**.

panda 2. Swayback.

pandereta 2. Little bell, tambourine. Cf. **Kampaniya**.

panelón 2. Veil, shawl that is also used to cover the head. Bigger than *pañu*.

paneta 2. Deck—movable (boat), removable floorboard of a boat.

paniti 1. Punch, hit with the fist, strike with the fist, sock. Cf. **Dommo', seku tromponasu**.

panket 2. Pancake, slang for vagina.

panko' 2. Flat tire, empty. (S)

panko' 2. Blister from heat. See **pakko'**.

pannas [æ] 1. Smash flat, flatten, cause to flatten.

panocha 2. Taffy, cooled thick syrup—like sugar daddy candy.

pansa 2. Rumen, stomach, protuding belly of pregnant woman.

pansaimada 2. Sweet roll with butter on top.

pantalán 2. Wharf, pier, dock, quay, landing for boats.

pantaya 2. Lampshade.

pantek [æ] 2. Handslap—a consequence of losing a kind of game.

pantes [æ] 2. Panties, women's underpants.

pañales 2. Diaper, infant's breechcloth. Cf. Sade'.

pañelu 2. Scarf, shawl, shoulder wrap. (S) Also pañuelu.

pañolón 2. Shawl, mantilla.

pañot [æ] 1. Swallow, gulp down, consume. Cf. Pañot ales.

pañot ales 1. Swallow (without chewing), gulp down (without chewing). Cf. Pañot. *I malangu ha pañot ales i petduras.* The patient gulped down the pill.

pañu 2. Handkerchief, scarf.

pañuelu 2. Scarf. Also pañelu.

pangela 1,2. To strap the yoke against the neck of the bull, strap used to hold the yoke in place against the neck of the bull.

panggengge' 2. Fool around. *Basta pumanggengge'.* Don't fool around.

panglao 2. Crab (generic term).

panglao oros 2. Type of crab-carpilius maculatus. Golden crab.

panglao tunas 2. Type of crab-cardisoma (gecarcinidae). Land crab.

pangon 1. To wake (someone) up, rouse (someone)—from sleep, awaken.Cf. Ya'ho. *Despasio sa' un pangon i neni.* Take it easy because you might wake up the baby.

pangpang 2. Explode, blast, explosion, concussion, shattering sound.

pao 2. Odor, smell, scent, aroma. *Pao binadu.* Deer scent. *Pao paopao.* Perfume odor. *Pao gas.* Odor of gas.

paode'do' 2. Type of plant-hedyotis sp. A type of vine, medicinal.

paokeke 2. Type of plant-clitorea ternatea. (?).

paola 2. Stuffed, given more than one wants or can take.

paomata' [æ] 2. Fishy smell, fleshy odor, such as blood, raw meat, raw egg, etc. Lit. raw or uncooked smell.

paopao 2. Perfume, fragrant, sweet smell.

paosa 2. Slowpoke, slothful, sluggish, moving at a slow speed.

paosadang [æ] 2. Urine odor, smell of urine.

paotake' [æ] 2. Type of plant-typhonium cuspidatum. (?).

paotake' [æ] 2. Odor of feces, feces odor.

papa 2. Pope, the holy father. Also santo papa.

papa' Down, below, bottom, southward, downward, beneath.

pápada 2. Jowl, flesh of the lower face, fleshy, meaty.

pápago' [æ] 2. Irritant—of skin, anything that causes skin irritation, kidder, to kid someone by giving them false information or promise. *Papago' i diso'.* The diesel is an irritant. *Papago' hao.* You are a kidder.

pápago' [æ] 2. Type of plant-pseudelophantopus spicatus. (?).

papago' halom tano' 2. Type of plant-elephantopus mollis.

pápakes 2. Fingernail, toenail, claw, talon, hoof.

papakyo 2. Stormy, typhoon condition. Cf. Pakyo.

papaloti 2. Kite.

pápangpang [æ] 2. Type of lobster-(family scylarridae). Slipper lobster.

papao 2. Type of plant-colocasia esculenta. Wild taro.

papaya 2. Papaya.

papet 2. Paper.

papet aseru 2. Sandpaper.

papet etgue 2. Toilet paper, or tissue. Cf. Chirigame'.

pappa 1. Strip off—bark of a tree, to skin--an animal, to peel off, to rip off. *Mapappa i lassas-hu.* My skin peeled off. *Hu pappa i lassas i hayu.* I peeled off the bark of the tree.

pappa [æ] 2. Wing.

para 2. Stop, quit, enough (command). Cf. Basta. *Para.* Stop (whatever you are doing).

para [æ] To, towards (directional). Cf. Asta. *Para i tenda.* To the store.

para [æ] Future tense marker, intention. Cf. Siempre. Para hu hanao asta i gipot. I will go to the party.

para [æ] For, on account of. *Hu cho'gue enao para hagu.* I did that for you.

para hafa What for. Cf. Pot hafa. *Para hafa i tapbleru gi gima'-mu?* What is the sign for at your house? '

para hafa Never mind, forget it. *Para hafa este.* Never mind this. *Para hafa i che'cho'-mu.* Forget about your work.

para ke Indifferent, no desire. Also **para kehi.**

para kehi Indifferent, no desire, forget about (something), have no concern, don't care at all. (R) Also **para ke.** *Para kehi yo' ni na'-mu sa' ti ya-hu.* I have no desire for your food because I don't like it.

para mo'na Henceforth, from now on, for or in the future. *Para mo'na siempre bula na uchan.* Henceforth, there will be plenty of rain. *Para mo'na maolek mannanom gollai.* Henceforth it is good to plant vegetables.

parábola 2. Parable, biblical story or fable.

parada 1,2. Bet, wager. Stake (gambling), the pot in gambling. Cf. **Aposta.**

paradisu 2. Paradise, Eden.

parafu 2. Paragraph, clause.

para'isu 2. Type of plant-melia azedarach. A type of flower.

paralítiku 2. Paralytic, paralysis, palsy.

parandela 2. Sow—used for breeding. Also **panandera.**

parasiút 2. Parachute. (G) Also **rakka'.**

parehu 2. Same, equal, alike, similar, identical. Cf. **Achaigua.** *Parehu gradon-mami yan guiya.* My grade is the same as his. *Parehu i lepblon-mami.* Our books are the same.

pares 2. Pair, divisible by two.

pares 2. Placenta, afterbirth.

pares 2. Gallop, trot, move by leaps.

pari 2. Short form for *kumpaire.*

parientes 2. Relative, a person connected with another by blood or marriage, kinsman, kinswoman. Also **parentes.**

Paro' Nickname for Ampara.

parókia 2. Parochial.

paroku 2. Curate—of a parish.

pas 2. Peace, quiet, silent.

pasabara 2. Type of game—same as game of jacks.

pasada 2. Aisle, walkway.

pasaderu 2. Passage, crossway, path.

pasadu 2. Barren, sterile, unfertile, used up soil, worn out land, flat—beer, coke, or any carbonated drink, boring--from repetition, loss of flavor. Cf. **Kansadu.**

pasadura 2. Lane.

pasaheru 2. Passenger.

pasamanu 2. Bannister, hand rail for stairs.

pasáo Past, after—used for telling time. *Tres minutos pasao las dosse.* Three minutes past twelve o'clock.

pasapotte 2. Passport.

pasas 2. Raisins.

pasehu 2. Wander around, tour, stroll. Also **paseo.** *Pumasehu yo' gi halom siuda.* I strolled in the city. *Hu na'pasehu si nana-hu asta Guam.* I let my mother tour Guam.

pasensia 2. Patient, lenient, yielding.

pasgua 2. Easter, Christmas. Also **Paskua.**

pasiadora 2. Traveler, tourist, adventurer, sightseer, wanderer (f) . Cf. **Pasehu.**

pasiadót 2. Traveler, tourist, adventurer, sightseer, wanderer (m) . Cf. **Pasehu.**

pasiando 2. Traveling, roving, roaming, rambling. *Mampos ya-ña i sotteru i pasiando.* The young man likes traveling very much.

pasiensia 2. Patience, patient. *Na'pasiensia i korason-mu.* Let your heart be patient.

pasífiku 2. Pacific, peaceful, peaceful state, peace.

pasión 2. Passion, deep feeling or excitement.

paska 2. Brittle, easily broken or snapped.

pasmo 2. Pneumonia, type of sickness the symptoms of which are chilling and stiff joints. Often associated with sudden chilling from cold water or air.

pasmo 2. Faded (color), partially cooked starch foods, such as potatoes, yams, rice, when an insufficient amount of water has been used.

pasmo 2. Fade, lose color, pale, lose brightness, become dull.

pastahi 2. Pasture, grazing land— fenced. Also **pastai.**

pastet 2. Pie, turnover—meat filled.

pasto 1,2. Pasture, graze, feed on growing grass, put cattle or flocks to graze. *Si Jose ha pasto i guaka gi sabaneta.* Joseph put the cow to graze in the plain. *La'la' i pasto gi halom kollat.* The pasture is green inside the fence.

pastót 2. Herder, shepherd.

pasturisa 1. Pasteurize. Also **pasterisa.**

pasu 2. Urn.

pasu 2. Story, narrative, biography, autobiography, novel.

pasu 2. Pace, footstep, step.

pat 2. Pair, couplet, match, twosome. Cf. **Pares.** *Guaha ga'-hu un pat paluma.* I have a pair of birds (a male and a female). *Mamahan yo' dos pat sapatos.* I bought two pairs of shoes.

pat [æ] Or—a co-ordinating particle that marks an alternative. *Hunggan pat ahe'.* Yes or no.

patang [æ] 2. Blockade. Also **pattang.**

patas 2. Foot, limb, leg—of animal.

patas ga'ga' 2. Paw, foot of an animal with claws.

patche 1. Mend, patch up, punch, hit (slang). Cf. **Limenda.**

patdet 1,2. Cement, concrete. Also **paddet.**

patek 1. Kick, strike with foot.

patente 2. Patent, evident, open for public perusal. *I pale' ha na'patente i Santisimu.* The priest put the Eucharist out in the open.

patgon 2. Child, infant, kid, baby. Cf. **Neni, famagu'on.**

patgon hugupao 2. Type of fish-naso sp. (Acanthuridae). Small surgeon fish.

patgon kabayu 2. Colt, pony.

patgon katu 2. Kitten, kitty.

patgon tátaga' 2. Type of fish-naso unicornis (acanthuride). Also called **guasa.** Small surgeon fish.

patiu 2. Patio.

patlinu 2. Godfather, godparent.

patma 2. Palm (of the hand).

patma 2. Palm (of coconut), blessed Palm Sunday.

patma 2. Cigarette—hand rolled.

patmada 1. Slap, strike with the open hand.

patnitos 1,2. Heart—coconut palm, cut heart out of coconut palm. Also **patmitos.**

patot [æ] 2. Weakened (person).

patriatka 2. Patriarch.

patriotiku 2. Patriotism, love of one's country.

patrón 2. Patron, protector.

pattang [æ] 1. Block, interfere with, blockade. Also **patang.** Cf. **Taggam.**

patte 1,2. Share, divide, apportion. Part, portion.

pattera 2. Midwife, obstetrician, woman assisting in childbirth.

patteru 2. Obstetrician, a doctor assisting in childbirth (m).

pattida 2. Party (political), share, dividend, portion, part, ration. Cf. **Rasion.**

pattikulát 2. Particular, fastidious, squeamish, hard to please.

patto 2. Birth, delivery, labor, parturition. *Maolek patto-ña i puetka.* The delivery of the sow was good.

patuleku 2. Bow-legged (m), pigeon-toed. Also **patuleka** (f).

paya'ya' [æ] 2. Soaring, gliding, float in the air at random. *Pumaya'ya' i papet gi aire anai guinaife ni manglo'.* The paper floated in the air when the wind blew it.

paya'ya' [æ] 2. Type of bird-puffinus tenuirostrio. Short-tailed shearwater.

paya'ya' [æ] 2. Type of bird-puffinus iherminieri dichrous. Dusky shearwater.

payesyes 2. Type of bird-swiftlet. Lives around caves and come out at sundown. Also **paye'ye'.**

paye'ye' Cf. **Payesyes.**

payon 2. Accustomed, habitual, usual, customary, used to. *Payon yo' chumocho hineksa'.* I am accustomed to eating rice.

payon duendes 2. Type of plant-mushroom.

payu 2. Umbrella, parasol.

payuni 1. Accustom, be accustomed, habituate, familiarize, make familiar by use, acquainted, know well. Also **apayuni.** *Hu payuni este esta i kareta-hu.* I became accustomed already to my car.

pe P—letter.

Pechang Nickname for Priscilla.

pechao 2. Dart, zoom, dash (away), a quick movement, flirt. Cf. **Chispas.**

pecho 2. Chest, mainly the fleshy part of the chest. Cf. **Ha'of.**

pechuda 2. Big breast (f), busty, referring to a woman with a large breast. Cf. **Lechera.**

pechudu 2. Big chest (m); chesty (person).

pedde 2. Weak, weakling, feeble, frail. Also **petde.** Cf. **Dangnge', dolle.**

pega 1. Place, put, stick on. *I polisia ha pega i tapbleru gi kanton chalan.* The policeman placed the traffic sign on the side of the road.

pega ni duru 2. Spanking, hard whipping.

pegge' 2. Type of fish-generic term for small fish. (S)

peha 2. Compress—hot or cold, applied to a sore or bruise.

pekadót 2. Sinner.

pekas 2. Spotted, freckle, mildew. Cf. **Chatko, mancha, pento, pellon.**

pekka' 2. Dignity.

pekke 1. Peg, tuck in, fasten, keep fixed, insert. (S) *Hu pekke i chinina-hu.* I tucked in my shirt.

pekno' 2. Murderous, murderer, capable of killing, homocidal.

pellon 2. Spotted—usually refers to pigs. Cf. **Pento.**

peludu 2. Hairy, wooly. Cf. **Mepplo.**

pena 2. Punishment, penalty. Cf. **Kastigu.**

pena 2. To haunt, visit habitually as a supposed spirit or ghost. *Munga macho'gue ti maolek sa' un na'pena si tata-mu.* Don't do something bad or you will cause your father to haunt.

penche' 1,2. Pliers, hold with pliers. (S)

pendehu 2. Rascal, rogue, mischievous. Also **pendeha** (f). Cf. **Mahaderu, pikaru.**

pendiente 2. Permanent, immovable. Also **prendiente.**

pendiks 2. Appendicitis.

penka 2. Coconut shoot—just before it opens up.

pennga' 2. Custom, way of doing things, a person's custom. Also **pengnga'.**

pennga' 2. Big, used in comparing size of material things. *Pennga'ña este kinu ayu.* This one is bigger than that one.

pensét 2. Paintbrush.

pensiana 2. Louver, as in a window. Also **petsiana.**

penta 1. Paint, color, cover with coloring matter, draw, design. Cf. **Yunga'.**

pentan labios 2. Lipstick. Also **bene'.**

Pentekostes 2. Pentecost, seventh Sunday after Easter, the descent of the Holy Spirit on the apostles.

pento 2. Spotted, pinto, marked with spots. Cf. **Pellon.**

pentot 2. Painter, artist.

pentura 2. Paint, coloring, the dried film of paint.

pengnga' 2. Custom. Also **pennga'.**

pengua 2. Type of plant-macaranga thompsonii. (?).

Pepe Nickname for Jose.

pépeska 2. Fisherman, hunter. Also **pipeska.**

peras 2. Pear.

peredika 1. Annoy, bother. *Munga pineredika nu este na problema.* Don't let this problem bother you.

peregrinu 2. Pilgrim. Also **piligrinu.**

perfekto 2. Perfect, exactly. Also **prifekto.**

periodiku 2. Periodic, again and again at regular intervals.

péritu 2. Appraise, put value on.

pes 1. Impose diet, prohibit eating—of certain foods. A restrictive diet, usually prescribed by a herb doctor, to aid in curing an ailment. (S) Cf. **Dieta.** *Mapes yo' chumocho gamson.* I was prohibited to eat octopus. *I mediku ha pes yo' chumocho ma'asen.* The doctor prohibited me to eat salty food.

pesa 1. Weigh, hoist.

pesada 2. Weight. Cf. **Minakkat.** *Kuanto pesada-mu?* What is your weight?

pesadiya 2. Nightmare, bad dream. Also **pesatdiya, pisadiya.**

pesadót 2. Scale, weighing machine, balance.

pesadumbre 2. Grief, sorrow.

pesatdiya 2. Nightmare. Also **pesadiya.**

peska 1. To fish, catch fish, hunt. Cf. **Pumeska.** *Hanao ya un peska guihan.* Go and catch fish.

peskadores 2. Fishermen, hunters.

peskadót 2. Fisherman, hunter.

pesson 2. Scraper, heavy equipment vehicle which scrapes, steam roller.

peste 2. Plague, pest, epidemic, scourge.

pesu 2. Dollar, peso, unit of money.

petbetso 2. Rascal, rogue, tricky fellow, jocular, scoundrel, knave, villain. Also **petbetsa.** Cf. **Pikaru.** *Petbetso si*

Juan na patgon. John is a roguish boy.

petde See **pedde.**

pétdidu 2. Loss.

petdidu 2. Lost, strayed.

petdigón 2. Pellet—as in shotgun shells. Also **pidigon.**

petdika 1. Insist, persist, urge, demand, press earnestly. (R) Cf. **Insiste.**

petdón 2. Forgiveness, pardon.

pétduras 2. Pill. Also **petdulas, pitduras.**

pethudika 2. Prejudiced.

pethuisiu 2. Harm, loss.

petlas 2. Pearl, some types of jewelry, such as pearl necklace, earrings.

petmamente 2. Permanent, durable, impermeable, steady, lasting, enduring.Also **petmanente.**

petmanente 2. Permanent. Also **petmamente.**

petmisu 2. Permission, permit, authorization.

petmiti 1. Permit, consent, allow, give permission for. Cf. **Konsiente.** *Ha petmiti yo' i ma'estra lumasgue i lapes-hu.* The teacher permitted me to sharpen my pencil.

petna 2. Thigh. Also **pietna.**

petno 2. Bolt—usually threaded for a nut. Also **petno basante.**

petroliu 2. Petroleum, kerosene.

petsan 2. Rush violently, dash, squirt, dart, zoom, flash. Cf. **Besbes.** *Petsan i ga'lagu huyong gi petta.* The dog rushed violently out through the door. *Petsan i hanom gi grifu.* The water squirted out of the faucet.

petsiana 2. Louver. Also **ponsiana.**

petsigi 1. Persist, continue, pursue, esp. with intent to harm someone. *Lalalo' nu guahu ya ha petsigi yo' para u na'lamen yo'.* He was mad at me and he continued to find a way to harm me.

petsona 2. Person.

pettanesi 2. Pertinent, to the point.

pi'ai 2. Foot (measurement). (R) Also **pie.**

pianu 2. Piano, musical instrument.

pi'ao 2. Type of plant-bambusa arundinacea. Bamboo (general).

pi'ao lahi 2. Thorny bamboo. Also **pi'ao tituka'.**

pi'ao palao'an 2. Type of plant-bambusa arundinacea. Bamboo—smooth.

pi'ao tituka 2. Type of plant-bambusa blumeana. Bamboo—thorny. Also **pi'ao lahi.**

pichipichi 2. Talkative, garrulous.

pichura 2. Big breast. Also **pechuda.**

pidasitu 2. Small portion, tiny part, little bit of, particle. *Hu na'i i patgon un pidasitu gi kande.* I gave the child a tiny portion of candy.

pidasu 2. Piece, part, hunk, crumb. Cf. **Empe'.**

piderecho 2. Wall stud, prop, support for wall construction.

pidigón 2. Pellet. Also **petdigon.**

pie 2. Foot (measurement).

piesa 2. Scattered (in large numbers), many of something covering an area or spread out. *Piesa ha' guihan i halom tasi.* Fish are all over the sea. *Piesa taotao gi kanton tasi giya Waikiki.* In Waikiki there are people all over the beach.

piesan magagu 2. Bolt—of cloth.

piesan metát 2. Metal sheet. Also **teppang.**

pietna 2. Thigh, upper part of leg of any two-legged animal, refers only to the back legs of a four-legged animal. Also **petna.** Cf. **Chachaga'.**

piga' 2. Type of plant-alocasia indica. Taro—acrid, not edible.

piga' palayi 2. Type of plant-crinum asiaticum. Type of taro.

pigo' 2. Sediment, deposit, dregs, suds, left over after evaporation or filtering process.

pika 1. Mince, chop, cut into slices, cut by striking esp. repeatedly with a sharp instrument. Cf. **Taktak.** *Hu pika i ensalada.* I chopped up the salad.

pika 1,2. Burn (with hot pepper). Hot (spicy). *I denne' ha pika i pachot-hu.* The pepper burned my mouth. *Pika na donne'.* It is a hot pepper. *Pika i na'-hu.* My food is spicy hot.

pikadót 2. Sinner.

píkaru 2. Rascal, rogue, tricky fellow, jocular, scoundrel, knave, villain. Also **pikara** (f). Cf. **Petbetso.** *Pikaru hao.* You are a rascal.

pikatdiha 2. Villainy, roguery, knavery, villain, mischievous, bad deed, perverse. Also **pikatdia.** *Bula na pikatdiha gi puenge.* There are lots of mischievous deeds at night.

piké 2. Pique, type of cloth material.

piknik 2. Picnic. *Pumipiknik siha.* They went on a picnic.

piku 2. Gunny sack, sack which holds 200 pounds or more.

piku 2. Beak, bill (of a bird), or of some other animal, as a turtle.

piku 2. Pick (tool), hoe. Cf. **Sakapiku.**

piku Little more, over, a little bit over, plus some small amount. Fr. Span. poko. *Tres pesos i piku.* Three dollars and some cents. *Dos libras i piku.* A little over two pounds.

pikue 2. Type of plant-averrhoa bilimbi. (?).

pila 2. Basin—for holy water by the front door of a church.

pilapat 2. Pile—of grass or wood in preparation for burning or hauling.

Pileng Nickname for Jose.

pili'ao 2. Welt, weal, wheal.

piligrinu 2. Pilgrim, wanderer. Also **piligrina** (f). Also **peregrinu.**

piligro 2. Peril, danger, jeopardy, risky, dangerous, perilous. *Piligro drumaiba gi puenge.* It is dangerous to drive at night.

piligrosu 2. Dangerous, hazardous, precarious, perilous, risky.

pilon dulili 2. Type of chicken—similar to Plymouth rock. Also **boremos.**

pilong 2. Great chief, most influentual person in a community, champion. (S)

pilota 2. Dumpling—made from flour of *fadang* or wheat.

pilotu 2. Pilot, guide.

pimentos 2. Sweet pepper, pimento.

pimienta 2. Pepper, Spanish pepper.

Pin Nickname for Jose.

pinadesi 2. Agony, pangs of death, suffering, pain, misery.

pinagat 2. Sermon, preaching, gospel, advice, counsel.

pinalakse' [æ] 2. Fluent, voluble, smooth talker.

pinalakse'guan 2. Slip of tongue, to slip away against one's intentions or plans. *Pinalakse'guan yo' ni fino'-hu.* My word slipped out from my mouth (unintentionally).

pinalala 2. Rush, hurry, dash, hasten. *Pinalala i estudiante asta i eskuela.* The student rushed to school.

pinalao'anan 2. Effeminate man, male person with feminine characteristics.

pina'lek [æ] 2. Cause dizziness, dizziness—caused from something eaten, sour stomach. *Pina'lek i patgon ni amot.* The child got dizzy from the medicine.

pinat Too much, excess of, a lot of, plenty of, lots of, mostly. *Pinat asukat i gimen-mu kafe.* There is too much sugar in your coffee. *Pinat i restaurant yo' nai gumimen.* I drink mostly at the restaurant.

pinatokso' 2. Hilly.

pinatu [æ] 2. Swollen scrotum, swollen testicles—temporary.

pinayon [æ] 2. Experience, skill. Cf. **Payon.**

pinayongguan 2. Habitual. *Pinayongguan mama'baba.* He is habitually foolish.

pincho 2. Tweezers, pincers. Cf. **Tinasa.**

pineddong atdao 2. Sundown. Also **pineddong somnak.**

pineddong somnak 2. Sundown. Also **pineddong atdao.**

pinekkat 2. Walk, stroll. Cf. **Pokkat.**

pineksai 2. Propagation. Cf. **Poksai.**

pinekso' 2. Feces—hard.

pine'lo 2. Thing—that is placed, object--which has been placed. *Masa i pine'lo-ku mangga.* The mango which I placed was ripe. *Machule' i pine'lo-ku.* The object that I put aside was taken.

pine'lo Presumption, presume, assume, assumption, thought, presuming (opinion), usually used with possessive type pronouns. *Pine'lo-ku na hagu humanao asta Guam.* I thought you were the one who left for Guam. *Pine'lo-mu na ume'essitan yo'.* You presumed I was joking.

pinenta 1. Picture, design, painting, drawing. Cf. **Litratu.**

pinepble 2. Poverty. Cf. **Popble.**

pinetsigi 2. Persecution, pursuit. Cf. **Petsigi.**

pínigan 2. Cinder, ember, charcoal, a glowing fragment of coal, metal, etc.

pinini 2. Refusal, rejection. Cf. **Puni.**

pinino' maisa' 2. Suicide, person who commits suicide.

pinipon 2. Group of, bunch of. Also **pupon.** *Pinipon otdot.* Ant hill.

pinitensia 2. Penance, atonement.

piniti 2. Sad, grief, anguish, pain, sorrow, mourn. Cf. **Triste.** *Piniti yo'* *anai humanao hao.* I was sad when you left.

pinitiyi 1. Grieve for, lament. Cf. **Piniti.**

pinitiyiyi 2. Sympathizing, grateful.

Pinke' Nickname for Jose—used for small boys.

Pinkile' Nickname for Jose.

pinu 2. Type of tree—pine. Fir tree.

piña 2. Type of plant-ananas comosus. Pineapple.

Ping Nickname for Jose.

pingga 1. Carry (something)—by using a stick on the shoulder of two or more people. Cf. **Osngan.**

pión 2. Checker, the round object used in the game of checkers; disc or any object used to cover numbers in bingo game. *Malingu un pion.* One of the checkers is lost.

pi'os 2. Type of fish-family mugilidae. Mullet, notably slender.

pipa 2. Large barrel.

pípenta 2. Painter.

pípeska 2. Fisherman, hunter. Also **pepeska.**

pipet 1. Lead (by the hand), guide (by the hand). Cf. **Esgaihon.** *Hu pipet i bachet gi chalan.* I led the blind person by the hand on the road.

pípino' 2. Assassin, killer, murderer.

pipinu 2. Type of plant-cucumis sativus. Cucumber, type of melon.

pipitas 2. Seed, nut. Cf. **Simiya.**

pipong 2. Ridge (of roof), peak of roof. Also **pupong.**

pirada 2. Nonsense, nuisance.

pirata 2. Pirate.

pire' 2. Harelip, a congenitally divided lip, like that of a hare, or this deformity. Cf. **A'pe'.**

pisadiya 2. Sleep walking, somnambulism, nightmare. Also **pesadiya.**

pisagon 2. Frequent urge to urinate, having difficulty in urinating.

pisao 2. Fishing pole.

pisara 2. Blackboard, writing board.

pistola 2. Pistol, revolver. Cf. **Rubetbet.**

piston 2. Piston, movable disk or cylinder.

pisu 1,2. Put in (a floor). Floor, platform. Cf. **Satge.**

pitduras 2. Pill. Also **petduras, petdulas.**

Piti Village in central Guam.

pitisión 2. Petition, entreaty, solemn request. Cf. **Ginagao.**

pítuma 2. Stick—used in *batu* game, target when pitching coins, marbles, horseshoes, or stones. Also **tangganu.**

plaito 2. Fuss, trouble, quarrel, worry, inconvenience, troublesomeness, disadvantage. Cf. **Atborotu, enkebukao, yinaoyao.**

plaka 2. Record (phonograph), reel, a strip of motion picture film, wound on a spool.

planas 2. Plains.

planasos 1. Beat up, wallop, knock down, smack, hit, slug, spank, whip. Cf. **Yagai, sapblasos, saolak.**

plancha 2. Sheet metal, tin.

planeha 1. Plan, form a plan. Also **planea.**

planeta 2. Planet.

planta 1. Set up, set, fix in position. Cf. **Pripara, sahyan.** *Hu planta i lamasa.* I set the table. *Ha planta i lasu.* He set the trap.

planta i lamasa 1. Set the table.

plantasma 2. Ghost, spectre, phantom. *Manli'e' yo' plantasma gi painge.* I saw a ghost last night.

plantet 2. Plant nursery.

plantiyas 2. Mold, model, form, template. *Fama'tinas plantiyas para i satge.* Make a form for the foundation.

plantiyas 2. Inner sole of shoe or slipper.

planu 2. Plan, design, plot, scheme, project.

plasa 2. Plaza, field, court.

plasan batkon aire 2. Airport, airstrip, airfield, terminal.

plasta 1. Bandage, to apply a poultice to, to soak wound in liquid. Cf. **Emplasta.**

plastek [æ] 2. Plastic, plasticity.

plasu 1. Engagement period, the length of time set by the parents between announcement of engagement and wedding. *Hu plasu si Juan un añu.* I gave Juan a year's time of engagement.

plasu 2. Excuse—false, make believe story, episode, meaningless story, story making. (S) Also **eskusa.** *Ya-hu i plasu-ña nigap.* I liked his false excuse yesterday. *Basta i plasu-mu* *guenao.* Stop your make-believe story there.

plata 2. Silver, silver (as a form of money). Cf. **Salape', kopble.**

platea 1. Silver plate, cover with silver. *Hu platea i na'yan siha.* I silver-plated the dishes.

plateru 2. Silversmith.

platitos 2. Type of plant-polyscias scutellaria. A type of flower.

platitu 2. Saucer, plate—small, usually used to mix hot sauce.

platón 2. Platter, large plate—having oval shape.

platu 2. Plate, dish.

pleges 2. Pleat. *Prensan maolek i pleges.* Press the pleat well.

plegu 2. Page, sheet—of paper.

pliegu Cf. *Plegu.*

plimenta 2. Pepper (ground), the fruit of the piper nigrum species. Also **primienta.**

plinata na kulot 2. Silvery, containing silver color. (R) Also **kulot salape'.**

plomisu 2. Made of lead, leaden.

plomu 2. Lead, sinker—used on fishing net or line.

plomuyi 1. Put sinker on—fishing line, put weights on a fishing net or line. *Hu plomuyi i talaya-hu.* I put sinkers on my throwing net.

pluma 2. Fountain pen, ball point pen.

poblekanu 2. Poor people—biblical. Also **publikanu.**

po'dak Adolescent female, protruding, sprouting, budding, refers especially to developing breasts or buttocks.

po'dang 2. Buttocks—having big.

poddak 1,2. Depimple, squeeze pimple. Also **potdak.** Cf. **Fokse.**

poddong 2. Fall down, drop, collapse, flunk, stumble and fall, cease to be erect, fail in school grades. Cf. **Basnak.**

pohne 1,2. To smoke out—someone or something, act of smoking out—someone or something. (S) Cf. **Fohne.**

pokka' 1. Shatter, crack open, abortion.

pokkat 2. Pace, step, footstep, gait. Cf. **Mamokkat.**

pokpok 2. Swelling, bulge, boil—on skin. Cf. **Bokka', bocha.**

poksai 1. Paddle, propel, row. Cf. Tulos. *Hu poksai i galaide asta i*

mama'te. I paddled the canoe to the reef.

poksai 1. Raise, nurture, breed. *Hu poksai i ga'-hu gi pastai.* I raised my pet cattle at the pasture.

pokse' 2. Type of plant—fiber tree (type of hibiscus).

pokse' 2. Fibre—from *pagu* tree, used for tying and lashing things together.

poksen Cf. **Poksion.**

poksión 2. Stink, smell bad, malodorous, anything that becomes spoiled or begins to stink from soaking in liquid too long. (R) Also **poksen.**

pokto 1. Cause jilting. Also **potto.**

polainas 2. Legging—wrapping legs with a strip of cloth, as a Japanese soldier's uniform.

polisia 1,2. Guard, patrol. Police, constabulary.

polista 2. Working age.

polítiku 2. Political, of or pertaining to politics.

po'lo 1. Place, set, arrange, establish, put, invest. Cf. **Dipusita, sa'ang.**

po'lo ya Let, well then, leave it up to. Cf. **Pues po'lo.** *Po'lo ya guahu bai hu hanao para Guam.* Let me be the one to go to Guam.

po'lonñaihon 1. Delay, detain, hold up, set aside for a while.

pon Contracted form of *para un*, future marker plus pronoun.

ponedera 2. Brood hen. Also **punidera.**

ponne 1,2. To lure—coconut crabs by smearing coconut meat on a tree or similar object so that odor will attract the crabs, bait--for coconut crab, stale coconut meat. *Hu ponne i sabana gi painge.* I smeared coconut as a lure at the field last night. *Fama'tinas ponne.* Make a lure for coconut crab.

ponsiana 2. Louver. (R) Also **petsiana, pensiana.**

pontan 2. Coconut—ripe, usually refers to that which has fallen from the tree. Cf. **Gafo'.**

pongga 1. Top—placement of, marble--placed in position to be struck. *Hu pongga i tolompo-ku.* I placed my top in the striking zone to be hit.

pongle 1. To cage, to confine, to box in, to jail.

pongpong 2. Scum, any solid-like substance floating on top of liquid, dirty matter on surface of liquid, such as dust or soot. Not fungus. Cf. **Poppo**. *Pinengpungi i na'-hu kalamai.* There are particles on my corn pudding.

popble 2. Poor, needy, indigent, impoverished, scanty, inadequate, barren, sterile.

poppo 2. Scum, powder substance from a decayed plant, dropping—termites, dirty substance on top of liquid such as dust, or soot. Not fungus. Also **popo**. Cf. **Pongpong**.

populasión 2. Population

poresu For that reason. Also **potesu**. *Poresu na taiguenao lina'la'-hu gi tano'.* For that is the reason for my living in the world.

pos Then. Alternate form of *pues*.

posa 1. Pose—as for a picture.

posa 1,2. Handcuff.

posipble 2. Possible, can be done, probably. *Posipble macho'gue.* It is possible to be worked out.

postisu 2. Prosthesis. The addition to the human body of some artificial part, as a leg, eye, or tooth; wig. *Maolekña yanggen un na'setbe i postisu-mu.* It is better if you use your artificial limb.

postisu 2. Artificial.

postre 2. Pastry. *Nahong ha' yo' ni postre na ogga'an.* Pastry is enough for me in the morning.

postura 2. Posture, pose of a model or figure. *Pumostura yo' nigap.* I posed yesterday.

posturayi Pose for. (S) Cf. **Pumos**. *Hu posturayi i litratu.* I posed for the picture.

pot Because, on account of, for the sake of, about, of. Cf. **Ni, nu.** *Humanao yo' para i espitat pot malangu yo'.* I went to the hospital because I was sick. *Hu cho'gue pot hagu.* I did it on account of you.

pot By—as in measurement. *Dos pot dos.* Two by two. *Sinko pot dosse.* Five by twelve.

pot ayu For that (away from speaker and addressee). *Pot ayu i chinago'-ña na cha'-mu humahanao.* Because of the long distance, you shouldn't go.

pot enao For that (to addressee). *Pot enao na rason na ya-hu hao.* For that reason I like you.

pot este For this. *Pot este i minaolek-ña na bai hu konsidera gue'.* For this goodness of his, I will consider him.

pot fabot Please.

pot fin 2. Finally, at last.

pot hafa Why, for what, what for. Cf. **Sa' hafa.** *Pot hafa na ti matto hao nigap?* Why didn't you come yesterday?

pot i hemplo For example, instance serving for illustration.

pot i siñat 2. Sign of cross, make a sign of a cross. Also **pot siñat**.

pot ke motibu 2. Why, what is your reason. *Pot ke motibu na ti matto hao?* Why didn't you come?

pot uttimo Eventually, ultimately, at the very end. Cf. **Alosuttimo, gi uttimo**.

potbos 2. Powder, talcum powder, dust, a medicinal, cosmetic, or other preparation in the form of fine particles.

pótbula 2. Gun powder. Cf. **Kaiako'**.

potbusi 1. To powder, apply cosmetic powder, sprinkle with powder, use cosmetic powder.

potdak See **poddak**.

potfia 1. Persist, persevere, be steadfast, maintain one's efforts, unyielding, pursue relentlessly. Also **potfiha**. *Hu potfia kumefahan i kareta.* I persisted in trying to buy the car.

potga 1,2. Purge, purgative, cathartic—taken usually for worms, laxative.

potgada 2. Inch, one-twelfth of a foot.

potgadas 2. Inches.

potgas 2. Mite, animalcule midge, arachnids (order acarina). Cf. **Gutgohu**.

potgas 2. Flea.

potgatoriu 2. Purgatory.

potgue 1. Pluck (feathers), remove hair by plucking, remove stickerburr off clothes, or the like.

potkeria 2. Filth, filthy act or word, worthless object, junk.

potlilu 2. Decayed, rotten, easily broken or torn. *Potlilu i hayon i gima'.* The wood of the building was rotten.

potne 1. Burn, destroy by fire. Also **pohne**. (S) Also **songge**.

potno Instead of, in place of. Cf.
Enlugat di. *Potno bai hu kahulo' gi
ta'chong-hu, na'i yo' fan magi ni
chipa.* Instead of my getting up from
my seat, please give me the
cigarette.

pótpopot 2. Type of plant-peperomia
pellucida. A type of grass.

potpot 2. Thick, dense, having or being
of relatively great depth or extent
from one surface to its opposite, not
thin.

potpot palao'an 2. Type of
plant-peperomia spp. (?).

potsan 2. Protruding, sticking out.

potseras 2. Bracelet, arm ring.

potso 2. Sharpshooter—in playing
marbles, good shooter, marksman.

potso 2. Heartbeat, pulse.

potsuelu 2. Cup. Also **pusuelu.**

potta 2. Door, entrance, passageway.

pottamuneda 2. Purse, wallet.

potto 1. Cause jilting—from one's lover,
pull seedling--from its place, uproot
seedling, take someone's sweetheart
away, dig up seedling. (S) Also **pokto.**

potu 2. Rice cake, rice pudding.

poya 2. Hen (young).

po'yet 2. Midget, diminutive, extremely
small in size. Cf. **Che'che', chibe',
dichicheng.**

poyu 2. Cock (young).

praktika 1. Practice, apply, put into
application, exercise. *Hu praktika
umusa i tiningo'-hu gi che'cho'-hu.* I
applied my knowledge in my work.

praktikante 2. Practitioner, doctor,
physician. Cf. **Mediku, dokto.**

praktikát 2. Practical.

praktiku 2. Skilled, experienced.

predika 1. Predict, forecast, foretell the
future. *Hu predika na para u maolek
i tiempo pa'go.* I predict that there
will be fair weather today.

predikamento 2. Predicament, crisis,
problem—serious, dilemma.

preferable 2. Preferable, to be
preferred.

premisias 2. Premises.

premiu 2. Prize, reward, award.

prenda 1,2. Give gift to sweetheart as a
sign of engagement. Gift (to
sweetheart), token.

prende 1. Fasten, clasp, pleat, attach,
hold something together by sewing

up. *Prende i litratu kontra i liga.*
Fasten the picture against the wall.

prendiente 2. Permanent, immovable,
stationary. Also **pendiente.** Cf.
Petmamente.

prensa 1,2. Iron (clothes), smooth with
an iron. Iron. Cf. **Asienta.**

preparáo 2. Prepared, ready for. *Esta
yo' preparao.* I am prepared.

preparasión 2. Preparation.

presa 2. Press—as a printing press.

presemida 2. Unfriendly, discourteous,
arrogant. Also **presemidu.** Cf.
Mata'pang.

presenta 1. Present, perform, act,
introduce, give.

presente 2. Present, present time, the
time being, the way it stands now.

presidente 2. President, chief executive,
head of government.

presiosu 2. Precious, valuable, of high
value, dear, of great value.

presiu 2. Price, value.

presonidu 2. Arrogant person, proud.

presta 1. Borrow—for consumption
purposes with an intention of paying
back, opposite of lend. Cf. **Ayao.** *Hu
presta un boteyan sirasime' gi
bisinu.* I borrowed a bottle of salad
oil from the neighbor.

presu 2. Prison, jail, dungeon. Cf.
Kalabosu, tribunat.

presuneru 2. Prisoner (m). Also
presunera (f).

pretendiente 2. Suitor, bachelor who is
courting and seeking the hand of a
fiancee.

pretina 2. Waistband—of trousers or
skirt.

pribeni 1. Provide, furnish. Also
pribiene. *Hu pribeniyi i lahi-hu
magagu yan lepblo para umeskuela.*
I provided clothes and books for my
son to go to school.

pribensión 2. Provisions, supplies. Also
probension.

pribi 1. Prohibit, restrict, forbid, hinder,
deny, disallow. Also **pruibi.**

pribidu 2. Prohibited, restricted, off
limits, not allowed, forbidden. Also
pruibidu.

pribilehu 2. Privilege, right or
immunity granted as a peculiar
advantage or favor, personal right.

prifekto 2. Perfect, exactly, precisely, accurately, in an exact manner. Also perfekto.

priferi 2. Prefer.

prikura 1. Preserve in, persist in, put more effort, hurry, remain fixed in. Also prokura. Cf. Usuni, potfiha. *Hu prikura i che'cho'-hu.* I persevered in my work.

prima 2. Cousin (f). Used also as form of direct address.

primerisa 2. First born, primogeniture.

primeru 2. First (m), best, first time. Also primera (f). Cf. Primet, fine'na. *I primeru na premiu, boti.* The first prize is a boat. *Guahu i primeru na makinista.* I am the best mechanic.

primét 2. First, first time. Cf. Primeru, primera, fine'na. *Este na guihan i primet na kinenne'-hu.* This is the first fish I have caught.

primienta 2. Pepper. Also plimenta.

primu 2. Cousin (m).

prinemeti 2. Vow, assurance, oath, pledge, promise. Cf. Prometi, promesa.

prinsesa 2. Princess.

prinsipát 2. Main, primary, principal, chief, leading, first.

prinsipát 2. Capital—monetary, the principal of an investment.

prinsipatmente 2. Principally, mainly.

prinsipi 2. Prince.

prinsipiu 2. First, origin, commencement, beginning.

pripara 1. Prepare, make ready.

prisión 2. Prison. Also presu.

prisisu 2. Urgent, necessary, essential, indispensable, inevitable, vital. Cf. Nisisario, impottante.

pritende 1. Pretend, feign, sham, make believe. Cf. Kado', fa'-. *Hu pritende na kabayu yo'.* I pretended to be a horse.

pritoliu 2. Petroleum, kerosene. (R) Also petroliu.

proa 2. Bow, front part of boat. *Falak mo'na gi proa.* Go to the bow.

probecho 2. Benefit. *Gai probecho hao.* You have some benefit.

probechosu 2. Benefiting, benefited, benefacting. *Probechosu i konggresu i resolusion-ña para i pupbliku.* The congress' resolution is benefiting to the public.

probensia 2. Province.

probensión 2. Provisions, supplies. Also pribension

probidu 2. Forbidden, prohibit. Also pruibidu.

problema 2. Problem, question proposed for solution. Cf. Estotbo, katgueti, inkombinensia.

produkto 2. Product, produce, yield.

produsi 1. Produce.

prófesias 2. Prophecy.

profesót 2. Professor, professional, instructor, teacher (m). Also professora (f).

profeta. 2. Wise man, prophet, seer, one who phophesies future events.

profisiente 2. Proficient, adept, versed. (S) Cf. Kapas.

programa 2. Program, drama, performance, proclamation.

progresu 2. Progress, improvement, advancement. Cf. Adelanto, kinalamten.

prohibi 1. Ban, prohibit, forbid.

prohibisión 2. Prohibition, forbiddance, restriction.

próhimu 2. Fellow, fellow man, comrade, neighbor, companion.

proklama 1. Proclaim, declare, publicize, assert openly, announce, publish. Cf. Deklara.

prokura 1. Procure. See prikura.

promesa 1,2. Pledge, promise, vow.

prometi 1. Promise, pledge, vow, assure, guarantee. Cf. Prinemeti, promesa.

promisu 1. Promise. Also prometi.

prononsasión 2. Pronunciation.

pronunsia 1. Pronounce, articulate.

propela 2. Propeller.

propiedát 2. Property, real estate, estate, dominions, claim.

propiu 2. Proper, specific, exact, particular. Cf. Pattikulat, espisifiku, eksakto.

proponi 1. Resolve, prepare. Cf. Pripara.

proposisión 2. Proposition.

própositu 2. Purposely, aim, intent. *Ti ya-hu pumeska propositu yanggen napu i tasi.* I don't like to fish especially when the water is rough.

propotsión 2. Proportion.

protehi 1. Protect, defend, guard, shield. Cf. Guatdia, difende.

proteksión 2. Protection.

protektót 2. Protector, defender, guardian.

protesta 1,2. Protest, renounce, remonstrate. Protest, renunciation, remonstration.

protestante 2. Protestant.

protestasión 2. Protestation.

prueba 1,2. Prove, proof. Also **preba.**

pruebasión 2. Proof, evidence. *Un pruebasion para bai hu sangan pot este.* I will tell one piece of evidence about this.

pruibi 1. Prohibit, forbid. Also **pribi.**

pruibidu 2. Prohibited, restricted. Also **pribidu.**

puchu 2. Pouch, sack, receptacle, container, small bag. (S) Also **kostat.**

puchu 2. Economical, thrifty.

pudeng 2. Pudding, rennet custard.

pudera Wish, hope, should have. Also **pudiera.** Cf. **Mohon.** *Pudera u uchan pa'go.* I wish it would rain today. *Pudera un fahan meggai nu enao sa' baratu.* I wish you had bought a lot because they are cheap.

pudét 2. Have authority, be capable, be able, power.

pudiera See **pudera.**

pudos 2. Hemorrhoid, tag-along, one who follows people all the time (slang).

puedi Maybe, perhaps (contrary to fact), hope to, wish to, chance of. *Puedi mangganna yo' premiu.* Perhaps I may win a prize. *Puedi humanao yo' agupa' asta Guam.* There is a chance of my going to Guam tomorrow.

puengi 2. Night.

pues Then, afterward, hereafter. Also **despues.**

pues po'lo Well then. Cf. **Po'lo ya.**

puesto 2. Territory, place, private property.

puetka 2. Sow (with litter), female pig.

puetkasita 2. Young pig, shoat, gilt, shote (f).

puetto 2. Harbor, channel, port.

puga' 1. Open (wide)—with force, spread apart--anything joined together, rip widely open. *Ta puga' i dama'gas i ayuyu.* We ripped open the claws of the coconut crab.

pugao 1. Cause to scatter, to scatter a group, flock, herd, school of fish, etc.

Hu pugao i inetnon fanihi gi halom tano'. I scattered the group of bats in the woods.

pugas 2. Uncooked rice.

pugi 1,2. To lure, entice. Decoy, lure.

pugua' 2. Type of plant-areca catechu. Betel nut palm.

pugua' China 2. Type of plant-veitchia merrillii. Manila palm, white betel.

pugua' machena 2. Type of plant-davallia solida. A type of bush.

puha 1,2. Capsize, turn over. Cf. **Alenken.** Mound.

puhot 1. To press—into a ball by pressing palms of hands together, as in making a rice ball, snowball, etc. Cf. **Afuyot.** *Hu puhot i inai ni kannai-hu.* I pressed the sand into a ball with my hands.

pula' 1. Untie, unwrap, unfold, unravel, translate. *Hu pula' i sapatos-hu.* I took off my shoes. *Ha pula' gue' si Maria.* Maria got undressed. *Hu pula' i estoria.* I translated the story.

pulakes [æ] **1.** Peel, unwrap, open up. *Hu pulakes i masa na chada'.* I peeled the hard-boiled egg.

pulakes [æ] Used in idiomatic expression. *Ombre un pulakes hao.* Oh, you are cracking me up.

pulan 1. Watch over, keep guard, guard. *Hu pulan i oru.* I watched over the gold.

pulan 2. Moon, eye of cateye shell.

pulan 2. Type of fish-megalops cyprinoides. (Family elopidae) tarpons

pulattat [æ] **2.** Type of bird-gallinula chloropus guami. Gallinule.

pulattat [æ] **2.** Type of bird-fulica atra atra. Common coot.

pulattat [æ] **2.** Type of bird-squatorola squatarola. Black-bellied plover.

pulon ga'ga' 2. Fur, hair of animals.

pulon tengho 2. Mane.

pulonnon 2. Type of fish-family balistidae. Trigger fish.

pulonnon attilong 2. Type of fish-family balistidae. Black trigger fish.

pulonnon lagu 2. Type of fish-rhinecanthus rectangulus. (Family balistidae). Trigger fish.

pulonnon sasadu 2. Type of fish-balistoides viridescens (family balistidae). Type of fish-pseudobalistes flavomarginatus (family balistidae). Trigger fish.

pulos 2. Type of fish-strongylura gigantea (belonidae). Needlefish.

pulu 2. Feather, hair.

pumada 2. Pomade.

pumalu [æ] 2. Some, things—other. Cf. **Palu.**

pumara 2. Pause, stop for a moment.

pumaya'ya' [æ] 2. Adrift, floating at random.

pumeska 1. Go fishing, hunting. *Pumeska yo' guihan.* I went fishing. *Mameska ham giya Susupe.* We went fishing at Susupe.

pumós 2. Pose. (G).

punche 2. Mixed drink—whiskey, milk, sugar stirred, similar to egg-nog mixed with whiskey. Cf. **Flamenko.**

puni 1. Deny, contradict, gainsay. Cf. **Ñega.** *Ma puni na ti ma li'e' i sakke.* They denied that they saw the thief.

punidera 2. Hen (chicken).

puno' 1. Kill, murder, slay, assassinate, shut off, turn off, extinguish, execute. Cf. **Digueya.** *Hu puno' i kandet.* I turned off the light. *Ta puno' i guaka.* We killed the cow.

puno' guafi 2. Fire extinguisher. Cf. **Puno' kimason.**

puno' kimasón 2. Fire extinguisher. Cf. **Puno' guafi.**

puno' lalo' 2. Fly swatter, insect spray, fly killer. Cf. **Panak lalo'.**

punot 2. Husk of coconut, coconut husk.

punsón 2. Punch, counter-sink. *Umechong i punson anai hu acha ni mattiyu.* The punch was crooked when I hit it with a hammer.

punta 2. Point, end—of long object, peak, fore.

puntada 2. Stitch.

punto 2. Period, decimal point.

punto 2. Point, unit of scoring, etc., mark, score.

punto 2. Point, motive, objective, cause, reason, substance, end towards which effort is directed.

punu'on 2. Guilty, deserving of punishment or scolding. Cf. **Puno', lalatdiyon.**

puñát 2. Dagger, hunting knife.

puñeta Expletive (mild), term of mild abuse when used in addressing someone.

puñu 2. Handful. *Ma na'i yo' un puñu na kande.* They gave me a handful of candy.

pupblika 1. Publicize, propagate, make known, promulgate, spread word of, bring to public, advertise. Cf. **Na'matungo'.**

pupbliku 2. Public, the general body of mankind, or of a nation, state, or community.

pupon 2. Group of, bunch of, gathering of. Also **pinipon.** *Tumohge i katu gi halom pupon otdot.* The cat stood in a group of ants. *Guaha pupon sasata gi uriyan guma'.* There is a bunch of bees around the house.

pupong 2. Ridge (of a roof), peak of roof. Also **pipong.**

pupuenge 2. Evening.

pupulon aniti 2. Type of plant-piper guahamensis.

pupulu 2. Type of plant-piper betel.

purifika 1. Purify.

puru All, entirely, wholly. Cf. **Todu, entieru.** *Puru lapes este.* These are all pencils. *Puru Amerikanu siha.* They are all Americans.

pusada 2. Curve—in road. Cf. **Birada.**

pusisión 2. Position, location, job, occupation. *Hafa na pusision malago'-mu?* What position do you want? *Gaige yo' guini na pusision.* I'm at this location.

puspus 1,2. Coitus, sexual intercourse—to have (taboo). Cf. **Dalle, sirek, kichi, baggai.**

puspus 2. Corn—ground and toasted, and cooked in chicken or beef broth.

pusuelo 2. Cup. Cf. **Tasa.**

puta 2. Whore, prostitute. Cf. **laputa.**

puta' 1. Split, cleave, burst.

putahi 2. Serving, helping, a portion of food.

puten matan Saipan 2. Trachoma. Cf. **Bayila'.**

puteng 2. Type of plant-barringtonia asiatica. A type of tree, used for poisoning fish.

puti 2. Hurt, pain, ache.

puti tainobiu 2. Type of flower. Bougainvillaea.

puti'on 2. Star. Cf. **Estreyas.**

puti'on chatanmak 2. Star—north, star--morning. Cf. **Luseru.**

putot 2. Mortar and pestle, used to pound herbs into pulp.

pútpitu 2. Pulpit, turret. *Na'gasgas i putpitu.* Clean the pulpit.

puyitos 2. Chick, baby chicken.

rabanos 2. Turnip.

rabia 2. Rabies, hydrophobia.

radis [æ] 2. Type of plant-raphanus raphanistrum, radish.

rai 2. King.

rai Expression used in tres siete to let your partner know that you have the ace of the suit playing.

raina 2. Queen.

raino 2. Kingdom, state.

rakka' 1,2. Parachute, descend by means of a parachute. (S) Cf. **Parasiut.**

rakkio' 2. Onion—pickled.

ramas 2. Branch, twig, bough.

ramenta 2. Hand tools. Also **heramienta, ramienta.**

ramienta 2. Equipment, tool, device, instrument, cutlery. Also **eramienta.** Cf. **Instrumento.**

ramiyeti 2. Bouquet, bunch of flowers.

ransio 2. Rancid, stale-smelling, strong-smelling.

raoel 2. Type of plant-pangium edule. A type of fruit.

raraina 2. Queen. Also **laraina.**

rasa 2. Race (breed), brood, nationality, folk, geneaology.

rasimu 2. Stalk of fruit, stem of fruit.

rasion 2. Ration, share, portion, part. Cf. **Pattida.**

rasón 2. Reason, ground, cause.

rasonapble 2. Reasonable, agreeable to reason, rational, just, having the faculty of reason.

raspa 2. Brush against—slightly, to hit just on edge of or near target, to side-swipe. *Raspa i bala gi binadu anai hu paki.* The bullet just grazed the deer when I shot it.

raspada 1. Brush against. Also **raskat.**

rastreha 1. Track, track down, follow—by tracking, pursue by following footmarks. Also **lastreha, rastrea.**

rastro 2. Footprint, track, rut (of a wheel), vortex, wake (of a ship). Also lastro. Cf. **Fegge'.**

rasu 2. Solid color, any color that is solid as opposed to designed, satin.

rata 2. Low throw, low pitch, grounder, grounded throw, roll (something) on the ground, esp. by throwing.

ratu Short time, little while. *Nangga fan un ratu.* Wait please for a little while.

raya 1,2. Line, rule, underline, to scratch or mark a smooth surface. Line—as on ruled paper, a line on the road to mark lanes, stripe, as in rank in service.

rayaó 2. Striped, streaked, anything having the appearance of having stripes.

rebolusión 2. Revolution, revolving.

rebotbida 2. Ricochet.

redán 2. Arena where the cocks fight. Also **rueda.**

réditu 2. Revenue, taxes, customs, etc. for the general income of a government. (R)

rediu 2. Radio.

re'enggancha 1. Reenlist.

refran 2. Adage, saying.

rega 1. Sow, spread seeds upon the earth for growth, sprinkle, scatter (drops or particles). Also **riega.** Cf. **Biba.**

regalu 2. Regality, present, donation, gift. Cf. **Chinchule', nina'i.** *Hu na'i ni regalu si Maria.* I gave the gift to Maria.

regla 2. Ruler, measuring stick.

regong 2. Type of chicken—resembling dark Cornish. Also **reguhong.** From Leghorn.

regulát 2. Regular, moderate, temperate, average, normal, typical.

regulatmente 2. Customary, usual, ordinary.

rehas 2. Railing, rail fence, lattice, grating, grid.

rehistra 1. Register, enroll, enlist.

rehistrasión 2. Registration, registry, enrollment, enlistment. Cf. **Rekohida.**

rekla 2. Menstruate, menstruation. Cf. **Rumekla.** *Nina'ye hao ni rekla-mu.* You have your menstruation (period). (Lit. you are contaminated with your period.)

rekomenda 1. Recommend, commend.

rekomendasión 2. Recommendation.

rekompensa 1,2. Recompense.

rektifika 1. Rectify, set right. Cf. **Kurihi.**

rekto 2. Strict, rigorous, disciplining, tyrannical, dictatorial, despotic.

relós 2. Watch, (something which measures time), clock, wristwatch.

remedia 1. To remedy, revive, relieve, aid, redress, restore.

remediu 2. Remedy, cure, change. Cf. **Empeñu.**

remoebi 1. Remove, change location. Cf. **Remotke, na'suha.**

remolacha 2. Type of plant-beta vulgaris. (?).

rempesa 1. Arrange things, clean house, put things in order. *Si nana-hu ha rempesa i halom guma'.* My mother cleaned the house inside.

rempua 1. Budge, move. Cf. **Aranka.** Also **rempuha.** *Hu rempua i lamasa gi gima'.* I moved the table in the house.

rempuha 1. Move. Also **rempua.**

renkón 2. Corner, edge. *Espiha i sapatos-hu gi renkon.* Look for my shoes in the corner.

renkonera 2. Whatnot, a triangular shelf that fits in a corner.

rénsia 2. Heritage, inheritance, patrimony, birthright. Also **erensia.**

renueba 1. Renew, revise, review. Cf. **Ribisa, ripasa.**

renunsia 1. Renounce, refuse, decline, reject, deny, decline to submit to or undergo. Cf. **Re'usa.**

replika 2. Replica, reply.

repot 2. Physical condition—caused by mental depression and physical exhaustion. A person who is described by this may be said to be in a daze. The symptoms are very similar to those of palsy. It may signify the beginning of paralysis. Epilepsy. Cf. **Debet, tufai.**

reprende 1. Reprimand, scold.

representa 1. Represent, symbolize, stand for, fill place of. *Hu representa i mangga'chong-hu gi miteng.* I represented my partners at the meeting.

reputasión 2. Reputation.

resiste 1. Resist, contradict, disagree, quarrel, dispute. Cf. **Aguaguatte.**

reskata 1. Rescue, help out—as paying debt for. *Hu reskata si Antonio anai para u mapresiu.* I bailed Tony out when he was about to go to jail. *Hayi rumeskata hao anai hinasa hao?* Who rescued you when you were drifting?

resolusión 2. Resolution.

respeta 1. Respect, honor, esteem, admire. *Hu respeta i mañaina.* I respect the parents.

respetáo 2. Polite, respectful. *Respetao si Jose na patgon.* Joseph is a polite child.

respetayon 2. Respectful, polite, respectable, honorable, attentive, courteous, gentlemanly, mannerly. Cf. **Respetao.**

respetu 2. Respect, veneration, reverence. *Hu fa'na'gue i patgon respetu.* I taught the child respect.

responde 1. Be saucy, sass, respond, talk back, reply, be insolent. (S) Also **oppe.**

respondo 2. Response, sass, back-talk, reply, answer.

responsabilidát 2. Responsibility.

responsapble 2. Responsible, be responsible for, answer for, account for.

resta 1. Subtract (mathematics).

restát 2. Subtraction.

resureksión 2. Resurrection, rebirth, new birth, rising again from the dead.

resutta 2. Result, consequence, effect.

retatdo 2. Retarded. Also **retatda** (f).

reuma 2. Rheumatism. Also **riuma.**

re'usa 1. Refuse, decline, decline to accept, reject, deny, decline to submit to or undergo, renounce. Cf. **Renunsia.**

reyes 2. Kings—as in Bible, three wise men.

rialisa 1. Realize.

riát 2. Dime, ten cents.

ribaha 1. Reduce, bring down to a smaller size, amount, number. Turn down—volume. *Hu ribaha i finalagu-ña i kareta gi chalan.* I reduced the speed of the car on the road.

ribana 1,2. Slice, cut (in slices), (R). Cf. **Dibana.**

ribát 2. Rival, competitor.

ribentasón 2. Reef. Also **rubentason.**

riberensia 1. Revere, reverence, console, soothe. Cf. **Uga.**

ribet 2. Rivet. Also **rimacha.**

ribisa 1. Revise, renew, review, re-examine, make anew. Cf. **Renueba.**

richasa 1. Abolish, repeal approval, countermand, revoke. Cf. **Diroga, rimati.**

ridima 1. Redeem, rescue from bondage. (S)

ridondeha 1. Encircle, go around, go a roundabout way, circulate, make a complete revolution. Also **aridondeha.**

ridondo 2. Round, circular. Also **aridondo.**

ridu 2. Noise. Also **ruidu.**

riega 1. Sow, sprinkle. Also **rega.**

riesgo 2. Risky.

rifa 1,2. Raffle, lottery. *Ma rifa i kareta gi plasa.* They raffled the car at the plaza. *Umegga' yo' rifa.* I watched a raffle.

rifa 2. Freezer, deep freeze, reefer. *Guaguan na rifa enao.* That is an expensive freezer.

riferi 1. Refer, allude.

riflekta 2. Reflector.

rifotma 1. Reform, make better, correct.

rifotmatoriu 2. Reformatory.

rifresko 2. Refresh, freshen up, replenish, renovate.

rikesa 2. Wealth, affluence, riches. Cf. **Guinaha.**

rikohi 1. Gather, collect, assemble, convene, congregate, bring together. Also **rikoi.** Cf. **Etnon, montohon.**

rikohida 2. Enrollment, enlistment, registration, registry, entry. Cf. **Rehistrasion.**

rikonisa 1. Acknowledge.

rikonosi 1. Investigate, search, inquire, examine closely, scan, sift, probe, reconnoiter. Cf. **Imbestiga.**

rikonosimento 2. Inspection, sanitation inspection.

riku 1. Rich, wealthy, affluent, opulent. Cf. **Gofsaga, miguinaha.**

rikuesta 1. Request, solicit, ask, entreat, make application, supplicate, implore.

rikuetdo 2. Token, souvenir, remembrance, collection, keepsake.

rilihión 2. Religion. Also **rilihon.**

rilihiosu 2. Religious (m). Also **rilihiosa** (f).

rilihón 2. Religion. Also **rilihion.**

rimacha 1. Rivet.

rimachi 2. Rivet. (S)

rimata 1. Kick out, chase away, put to flight, cause to depart by threatening or molesting, to finish, to completely destroy or ruin.

rimati 1. Abolish, revoke, repeal approval, countermand. (R) Cf. **Richasa, diroga, rimata.**

rimiti 1. Remit.

rimotke 1. Remove, dump, get rid of, throw away. Cf. **Remoebe, na'suha, rimati.**

rimulinu 2. Tornado, whirl, twirl, whirlwind, waterspout *(rimulinu i tasi).*

rimulinu 2. Cowlick, crown (of the head), a place on the head where the hair grows in a whirl pattern.

rinaya [æ] 1. Etch, engrave—by using acid.

rinefresko 2. Refreshment.

rinibaha 2. Reduction, state of being reduced, shortening, depression, diminution. *I rinibaha-ña ni presiu gofbaratu.* His reduction of the price was very cheap.

rinisibi 2. Receipt, acceptance.

rinkón 2. Corner, edge.

rinola 2. Chamber pot.

riñón 2. Kidney.

ripara 1. Notice, be aware, take notice, be cognizant, observe, check on.

ripasa 1. Weeding, weed out (grass), remove weeds from a cultivated area.

ripiti 1. Repeat, say again.

ripotte 1,2. Report, notify, make known, announcement. (G)

ripoyu 2. Cabbage, head cabbage.

ripresta 1. Answer, respond. *Ha ripresta i katta-ku.* She answered my letter.

risáin 2. Resign. Also **resikna.**

risaka 1. Cut tuba—at improper time during middle of the day in order to try to get more. *Hu risaka i tiba.* I cut the tuba.

risaki 2. Receding wave—from the shore. Used to describe the receding movement of a wave on the shore. Opposite of *mapta'. Korente i risaken i napu.* The receding of the waves caused a current to occur. *Ha halla ham i risaki.* The receding wave dragged us back out.

riseta 1. Listen to heartbeat with stethoscope, medical check-up.

risetba 1.   Reserve, make a reservation.

risibi 1.   Receive, accept. Cf. Miresi.

risibu 2.   Receipt, invoice.

risidensia 2.   Residence, the place where one actually has his home.

risiembra 2.   Replace seed or plant that failed to survive. Also disembra.

risikna 1.   Resign, withdraw.

ritachi 2.   Ricochet.

ritasos 2.   Shred, piece, fragment, remnant.

ritira 1.   Dismiss, return (something), retire, retreat, chase away, withdraw. Also litira. *Ma ritira yo' gi che'cho'.* They dismissed me at work. *I ma'estro ha ritira i ga'lagu gi eskuela.* The teacher chased the dog away from school.

ritirada 2.   Dismissal, adjournment, liberty to depart, permission to go, return, way back. Also litirada.

ritiráo 2.   Retired. *Esta yo' ritirao.* I am retired.

ritiru 2.   Retirement.

ritumbo 2.   Vibration (caused by loud noise), oscillation, echo, resonance.

riuma 2.   Rheumatism. Also ruma, reuma.

rodo' 2.   Type of chicken—Rhode Island red.

Roma 2.   Rome.

rora' 2.   Roller, a heavy vehicle used to smooth or harden the surface of the ground. (S)

rosa 2.   Type of flower—hibiscus. Cf. flores rosa.

rosát 2.   Type of flower-rose.

roseli 2.   Type of plant-hibiscus sabdariffa. (?).

roskas 2.   Type of bread—toasted until it becomes crisp. Sometimes twisted like a roll. Also rosko.

rosko   See roskas.

Rota 2.   Rota island. Cf. Luta.

royon tali 2.   Coil of rope.

royu 1,2.   Roll up, enwrap, roll, scroll. Cf. Falulon, afuyot, balutan.

rubentasón 2.   Reef—deep outer part. Deep water--beyond the reef. Also ribentason.

rubetbet 2.   Pistol, revolver. Cf. Pistola, paki.

rueda 2.   Wheel, tire, rim, cockpit.

ruidu 2.   Roar, thunder, loud noise. Also ridu.

rula 2.   Ruler—measuring stick. Also sase'.

ruma 2.   Rheumatism. (R) Also mamuten tataotao.

rumbo 2.   Journey, voyage, trip, travel. Cf. Karera.

rumekla 2.   Menstruate. *Rumekla i palao'an.* The woman menstruated.

rumót 2.   Rumor, current story.

Rusia 2.   Russia.

sa' [æ]   Because, because of, on account of, due to the fact. *Humahanao yo' para Saipan sa' mañasaga siha i mañaina-hu.* I am going to Saipan because my parents are living (there).

sa' hafa   Why. Cf. Pot hafa. *Sa' hafa na ti ya-mu yo'?* Why don't you like me?

sa'ang [æ] 1.   Put—something on something, place--something on something, usually used when one is placing something out of the way for protection. (R) Also sa'hang. Cf. Po'lo. *Hu sa'ang i ilu-hu gi hilo' i alunan.* I put my head on the pillow. *Hu sa'ang i amot gi hilo' i tapblita.* I put the medicine on top of the shelf.

Sábalu 2.   Saturday.

sabana 2.   Mountain, hilly area, plain— usually covered with swordgrass.

sábanas 2.   Blanket, lining, spread, padding, bed sheet. Cf. Onno'.

sabaneta 2.   Plain, small field, prairie, meadow, savana, treeless place or country.

sabate' 1.   Kick. (S) Also patek.

sábio 2.   Clairvoyant, perspicacious, clairvoyance, perspicacity.

sabót 2.   Taste of, flavor. *Sabot ripoyu este na nappa'.* This Chinese cabbage tastes like cabbage. *Sabot kahet este.* This has an orange flavor.

sa'dang [æ] 1.   Straddle, astraddle, with one leg on each side, in a straddling position. Has strong sexual connotations.

sadda' 1.   Lift up, lift from the bottom something that is hanging, such as curtains or a skirt, for the purpose of seeing what is beneath. *Ha sadda' i kuttina.* He lifted the curtain.

sadde 1.   Hold on lap, place on thighs, place on lap. Also satde'. *Kada dia i nana ha sadde i neni-ña.* Every day the mother holds the baby on her lap.

saddok 2. River, stream, brook.

sade' 1,2. Put diaper on, wear a loin cloth. Diaper, loin cloth, sanitary napkin. Cf. **Pañales.** *I nana ha sade' i neni.* The mother diapered the baby. *Fotgon i sade'-ña i neni.* The diaper of the baby is wet.

sade'gani 2. Shack, hut, cabin.

sade'guani 2. Typhoon shelter. Usually an A-frame construction with lower part of the roof buried underground. Also **sade'gani.**

saffe 1,2. To dust, brush. Duster, brush.

safo' 2. Safe, protected.

safu 1. Take off (hat), remove, doff. (R)

saga 2. Stay, stop by, rest, dwell, remain, address, place. *I polisia ha na'saga i kareta siha gi chalan.* The policeman detained the cars on the road. *Bunitu na saga este.* This is a beautiful place.

ságamai [æ] **2.** Gnat.

sagámilon 2. Type of fish-family holocentridae. General name for several types of squirrel fish and soldier fish.

sagan 2. Place for (something). From *saga. Sagan chumocho.* Eating place, cafeteria, restaurant, dining room. *Sagan gumimen.* Drinking place. *Sagan mama'gasi.* Laundry.

sagan apu 2. Ash tray, place for ashes.

sagan basula 2. Trash can, dump, garbage can, waste basket, place for trash.

sagan mama'tinas 2. Kitchen, cooking place. Cf. **Kusina.**

sagan otpos 2. Ash tray. Cf. **Sagan apu.**

sagayi 1. Colonize, settle, inhabit. Cf. **Saga.**

sage' [æ] **2.** Painful, pain, affect with pain, burning sensation.

saggue' 1. Pull, haul, drag, tug, draw. Cf. **Halla.** *Ha saggue' i kannai-ña anai magu'ot gi painge.* She pulled her hand away swiftly when it was held last night.

sagradu 2. Sacred, holy, consecrated, sanctified, blessed, purified. Cf. **Santo.**

sagu 2. Bad cold, runny nose, influenza, epidemic.

sagu 2. Type of plant-maranta arundinacea. (?).

sagu 2. Season for—fishing, crabs, hunting, etc. Usually refers to the time when a large group of fish is making a run. *Esta sagon laiguan pa'go na mes.* It's the season for mullet this month.

sagua' 2. Channel, inlet—of water, canal, narrow passage of water breaking the reef barrier.

saguale' 2. Thatched house, usually made with *karisu.*

saguan 2. Help—in fighting, to join someone's side in a fight. *Sumaguan si Jose anai mumu ham yan si Juan.* Jose helped Juan when he was fighting.

saguat 2. Tenacious, persistent.

saguat 2. Insolent, shameless.

sague' 1. Help, aid, assist, succour, promote, support, be of use, avail, profit, do good to, remedy, deliver. Used esp. in prayers. *Si Jesukristo ha sague' i taotao siha gi tano'.* Jesus saved his people on earth.

saha 1. Whittle, slice, as if peeling a skin. Cf. **Lasgue, sahi.**

sahagu 2. Deep water.

sa'hang [æ] **1.** Put, place, shelve, perch. Also **sa'ang.**

sahguan [æ] **1,2.** Put in, place in, container. *Hu sahguan i lapes gi kahita.* I put the pencil in the box.

sahguani [æ] **1.** Put in (something) for, place in (something) for. Cf. **Sini.** *Masahguani i tasa-hu setbesa.* My cup was filled with beer. *Hu sahguani hao ni gas gi galon.* I filled the gallon (container) with gas for you.

sahi 2. Waxing—of the moon.

sahnge [æ] **2.** Strange, unusual, peculiar, abnormal. *Sahnge i chinina-ña.* His shirt is peculiar.

sahsa 1. Brush away. Cf. **Sassa.**

sahuma 1. Inhale vapor—usually for asthma or to clear nasal passages.

sahyan 1. Set table, put the food on the table. Cf. **Planta.** *Sahyan i sentada.* Put the food on the table.

sahyan 2. Automobile, small vehicle, jeep, sedan, car. Cf. **Kareta, tumobet.**

sahyao 2. Speedy, quick, fast, speed, hurried, hurry. Also **sayao.** Cf. **Guse', chaddek, alula, insigidas.**

saibok 1,2. Boil starchy food, starchy food—boiled, such as taro, bananas, breadfruit.

saigón 2. Type of chicken—red pyle game. Also **siamo'**.

saina 2. Lord, father, master, parents, supreme being.

Saipan 2. Saipan, the second largest island of the Marianas chain. Pronounced sa'ipan.

sais 2. Six.

saisio Call given by odds-maker at cockfight to indicate the cock against which odds are being given. Also **saisiot**, a form of English 'this side short'.

saka 1. Liberate, free.

sakadatche' 2. Somersault, somerset, turn head over heels, upside down position. (S) Cf. **Dilok cha'ka.** *Hu tungo' sumakadatche'.* I know how to somersault. *Bunitu gue' sumakadatche'.* He somersaults beautifully.

sakafakteru 2. Braggart, one who publicized the favors he did for others. (R) Also **sakafatteru**.

sakapiku 2. Pick (tool). Cf. **Piku.**

sakat 2. Sadistic, cruel, merciless, desposed to give pain to others, one that likes to hurt others. (S) Cf. **Malamaña.**

sakati 2. Hay, forage.

sakkan 2. Year, season—for planting or harvesting. Cf. **Año, idat.**

sakke [æ] **1,2.** Steal, rob. Thief, robber, stealer, burglar. Cf. **Chekle', ladron.** *Ha sakke i kareta-hu.* He stole my car. *Hu tungo' i sakke.* I knew the thief.

sakman [æ] **2.** Large canoe—from Polynesia or Papua, no outrigger, capable of carrying over 100 people.

sakmoneten acho' 2. Type of fish-parupeneus trifasciatus (family mullidae). Goatfishes. Also **satmonete acho'.**

sakmoneten le'ao 2. Type of fish-upeneus vittatus (family mullidae). Goatfish.

sakmoneten maninen 2. Type of fish-mulloidichthys auriflamma (family mullidae). Goatfish.

sakmoneti 2. Type of fish-(family mullidae). Goatfishes. (R) Also **satmoneti.**

sakne [æ] **2.** Tattle-tale, gossiper.

sakngan [æ] **2.** Mentionable, gossiper, talkative person.

sakramento 2. Sacrament.

sakrestan 2. Sacristan, one in charge of sacristy.

sakrifisia 1. Sacrifice, make a sacrifice or offering, offer up.

sakrifisiu 2. Sacrifice, relinquishment, offering.

sakrilehu 2. Sacrilege, commiting an act by stealing sacred things or desecrating that which is sacred. Also **sakrilehiu.**

sakristia 2. Sacrìsty, vestry.

saksak 2. Type of fish-family holocentridae. Squirrel fish.

saksak fetda Type of fish-holocentrus tierra (holocentridae).

saksak sumulo' 2. Type of fish-family holocentridae. Snapper, squirrel fish.

saku 2. Coat, jacket, suit, overcoat.

sakudi 1. Spank, whip. Cf. **Saolak, ba'ba'.**

sakutassu 1. Spank, whip. Cf. **sakudi.**

sala 2. Living room, sitting room, hall.

sala' 2. Late, far gone, incurable. Cf. **Kebra.** *Esta hao sala'.* You are already late. *Sala' i chetnot, ti siña mana'homlo.* The disease is too far gone to be cured.

salamanka 1,2. Outwit, outmaneuver, trick, fool, get the better of by superior ingenuity or cleverness. Trick, snare, trickster. Cf. **Laime, fa'baba.**

salamanka 2. Tripped, fall down as one loses his balance, stumbled, be thrown off balance, somersault. *Sumalamanka i patgon anai poddong gi gua'ot.* The child fell down the stairs head over heels.

salang 2. Type of mollusk—genus limax. Slug--land, any of numerous terrestrial pulmonate gastropods related to land snails, but entirely lacking of shell, slug--salt water, having its shell rudimentary and buried in the mantle. (R) Also **tagula.**

salape' 2. Money, currency, silver (as a form of money). Cf. **Kopble, plata.**

salasa 2. Shallow water—just outside the reef. (R)

sali 2. Type of bird-aplonis opacus guami, Micronesia starling, all black.

sali 2. Black people. Cf. **Bakuko'.**

salibao 1. Whack at, swat at, wave away, slap at. (R) Also **yalibao, yabbao.** *Hu salibao i lalo' ni* *kannai-hu.* I slapped at the fly with my hand.

salida 2.   Wave action—lull in wave action near channel or rocky shore.

saligai 2.   Type of fish-gnathodentex aureolineatus (family lutjanidae). Snappers.

saligao 2.   Centipede.

salinas 2.   Saltern, a place where salt is made. *Sumalinas i amko' gi kanton tasi.* The old man made some salt at the edge of the sea. *Dankolo i salinas-ña i amko'.* The old man's salt-making plant is big.

salón 2.   Salon, saloon, bar.

saluda 1.   Salute, bow, greet, welcome, give respect, show respect.

saludu 2.   Salute, respect, greeting, bow, salutation, address of welcome.

salungai 2.   School (fish), whales—school of, be in abundance. (S) Also *pupon.*

salút 2.   Health, condition of health.

Samaritanu 2.   Samaritan, a native or inhabitant of Samaria.

sambo 2.   Knock-kneed, a person whose knees are turned in, pigeon-toed.

sampagita 2.   Type of plant-jasminum sambac. A type of flower. Also **sampakita.**

sampakita   See **sampagita.**

san   [æ] 2.   Saint (m). Cf. **Santo.**

san-   [æ]   Directional prefix—used with locatives. *Gasgas sanhalom-mu.* Your inside is clean. Or You are an honest person. *Gaige i sapatos gi sanpapa' i lamasa.* The shoes are under the table. *Hu fa'maolek i sankattan na bentana gi gima'.* I fixed the east-side window of the house.

San Ignasio 2.   Type of insect-coleoptera buprestidae. Beetle—wood boring.

San Roque 2.   San Roque, a village located at the northern part of Saipan.

sanban 2.   Type of plant-donaxarundiformis. (?).

sancho 2.   Hoop.

sandalias 2.   Sandal, slipper, open shoe, lounging shoe.

sanhalom   [æ]   Inside, interior, internal, in, into. Cf. **Halom.**

sanhilo'   Above (preposition), on top of. Usually used with preposition *gi,* as in *gi sanhilo'* 'on top of'. Cf. **Hulo'.**

sanhiyong   Outside, the external, the outer part, exterior of. Usually used

with the preposition *gi,* as in *gi sanhiyong* 'the outer parts.' Cf. **Huyong.**

sankarón 2.   Boney, boney parts of an animal such as chicken wings, back, etc., meat scraps—of fish or meat, gristle.

sanlagu   [æ]   Continental United States.

santa 2.   Saint (f).

santa' 2.   Comical, funny, humorous person, funny man.

Santa Ana 2.   Type of plant-jatropha multifida. A type of grass.

Santa Madre i Eklesia 2.   Christ, curia romana, the body of congregation through which the Pope governs the Roman Catholic Church; Holy Mother.

Santa Rita   Village in central Guam.

santán 2.   Type of plant—jatropha multifida. Another name for Santa Ana.

santatte   [æ]   Back side of, back of, behind. *Saga gi santatte gi fila.* Stay at the back of the line.

santifika 2.   Sanctify, make holy or sacred.

Santisima Trinidát 2.   Holy Trinity.

santisimu 2.   Monstrance, vessel in which the consecrate host is exposed to receive the veneration of the faithful.

santo 2.   Holy, saint (m).

Santo Papa 2.   Pope.

santolón 2.   Pious, holy person, saint, religious person, devotee (m). Cf. **Santos, sinantosan.**

santolona 2.   Pious, holy person, saint, religious person, devotee (f). Cf. **Santos, sinantosan.**

santos 2.   Saints. Cf. **Santolon, sinantosan.**

santos olios 2.   Holy oil, extreme unction —the sacrament administered by a priest to one in danger of death. Cf. **Bi'atiku.**

santót 2.   Type of plant-sandoricum koetjape. A type of tree.

sanye'ye' 2.   Spider, small spider. Cf. **Apayuhak.**

sangan 1.   Say, tell (something), speak, utter. *Hu sangan i estoria.* I told the story.

sangani 1.   Say, tell (something), speak, utter. Cf. **Sangan, kuentos, kuentusi.**

Hu sangani si Pete ni estoria. I told the story to Pete.

sanganiyi 1. Interpret, explain, translate, tell for. *Hu saganiyi si Pete ni estoria.* I told the story for Pete.

sángganu 2. Loafer, unindustrious person, dissolute, licentious.

sanggra 1. Tap (blood), drain, let blood, bleed (something). *Masanggra i malangu.* The blood was drained from the patient.

saoara' 2. Type of fish-istiophorus genus. Sailfish, having teeth, scales, and a very large dorsal fin. Also swordfish.

saolak 1. Spank, whip. Cf. **Ba'ba'**, **kastiga, sakudi**.

saonao 2. Involve, be involved, included, join, participate. *Sumaonao yo' gi inetnon.* I joined in the group. *Sumaonao gue' gi piknik.* He was included at the picnic. *Sumaonao siha gi aksidente.* They were involved in the accident.

saosao 1. Wipe, rub lightly with a cloth.

saosao magagu 2. Ironing cloth, damp cloth used to dampen fabric before ironing it.

sapateru 2. Shoemaker, one who makes shoes.

sapatiya 2. Small shoes, slippers.

sapatos 2. Shoes, boots.

sapblasos 1. Beat up, wallop, knock down, hit, smack, slug, vanquish, torture, spank, whip. Cf. **Yagai, planasos, saolak, baketa', fa'om**.

sapble 2. Sword, rapier, saber, scimitar. Cf. **Espada**.

sa'pet 1. Exhaust, overwork, overtask, laborious, cause to suffer. *Mampos sa'pet i estudiu gi kolehu.* Study is very laborious in college. *Masa'pet gue' fehman gi tiempon gera.* He was made to suffer severely during the war.

sapisapi [æ] 2. Type of kite.

sapo' 2. Seedling—of leafy plant, such as young vegetable plant, young tobacco plant, or young weeds.

sappe [æ] Go away, scat—when addressing a cat.

saragati 1. Clobber, beat mercilessly, defeat overwhelmingly. (S)

saragati 2. A useless rascal, an unworthy person. Also **saragatte**.

saragatte 2. Rogue, rascal, witty person, sly. Cf. **pikaru**. Also **saragati**.

saranggola 2. Type of kite, fighting kite.

sarento 2. Sergeant, a rank in the armed forces, police force, etc.

sarento 2. Athlete's foot, type of fungus, ringworm of the foot.

Sariguan 2. Sariguan, the second island north of Saipan.

saro' 2. Monkey, ape, chimpanzee. (S) Cf. **Macheng**.

saromata' 2. Panties, underpants (women). (S) Cf. **Pantes, katsunsiyu**.

sárukang 2. Swivel, turning link in a chain. (S)

sasa' [æ] 2. Spread apart, open up legs by spreading apart.

sasalaguan 2. Hell—the place or state of punishment for the wicked after death. Cf. **Infietno**.

sasata [æ] 2. Bee, (generic term).

sásatba [æ] 2. Savior.

sase' 2. Ruler (for measurement), measuring stick. (S) Also **rula**.

sasetdoti 2. Student priest.

sásime' 2. Sashimi, sliced fish—raw.

sasngat [æ] 2. Type of bird-megpodius laperousei, Micronesian.

sassa 1. Brush away (with hand), to clean or clear a spot by slow, gentle movement of hand or object, to dust, to clear away. *Hu sassa i petbos gi lepblo.* I cleared away the dust on the book.

sassa 1,2. Type of food, liver—preparing, chopped liver. (R) Cf. **Satsa**. *Sassa enao i higadu.* Prepare the liver by chopping it and frying it with chopped onions. *Kao ya-mu sassa?* Do you like chopped liver?

sassa 2. Type of fish.

sastre 2. Tailor, seamstress.

sata Type of fish-ctenochaetus striatus (acanthuridae). Called *oda'* in Rota.

satan apaka' dadalak-ña Type of fish-acanthurus glaucpareius (acanthuridae). Similar to *sata*, but has a white tail.

satanás 2. Devil, satan. Cf. **Diablo, aniti, hudas, maknganiti**.

satba 1. Save, make safe, rescue or deliver from danger, safeguard.

satbabida 2. Life jacket, life buoy, lifesaver.

satbadót 2. Savior, rescuer, redeemer, deliverer, freer, protector.

satbahi 2. Rascal, savage, wild.

satbasión 2. Salvation.

satbayones 2. Athlete's foot, sore on the foot caused by a ringworm.

satdinas 2. Sardine.

satén 2. Satin. Cf. **Rasu.**

satge 1,2. Install a floor. Floor, platform. Cf. **Pisu.**

satisfecho 2. Satisfied, contented, appeased the desire of. Cf. **Kontento.**

satmón 2. Type of fish-salmo salar (family salmonidae). Salmon.

satmoneti See **sakmoneti.**

satmuera 2. Salted fish, salted meat.

satna 2. Rash, having sores all over the body.

satnot 1,2. Hit on shin-bone. Shin, front part of lower leg.

satpa 1. Burn, parch the ground, squander.

satpe 1. Sow, sprinkle, slang for go ahead, o.k. *Hu satpe i simiyan melon gi tirenu.* I sowed the melon seeds in the field. *Hu satpe i tinanom ni hanom kada dia.* I sprinkled the plant with water daily.

satpon 2. Blowing rain—into a house or shelter, spray. *Satpon i ichan halom gi gima'.* The rain is blowing inside the house.

satpuyidos 2. Skin rash, accompanied by itchiness of the skin.

satsa 2. Sauce, catsup, gravy. (G).

sattea 1. Sort, place in order here and there as in planting seeds.

satten 2. Pot, pan. Cf. **La'uya.**

sayafi 2. Type of plant-melochia. (?).

sayáihagon 2. Type of plant-nervilia aragoana. A type of grass, terrestrial orchid.

se C—letter of the alphabet. Also **che.**

seba 1. Give abundantly, raise abundantly, give lots of goodies, fatten up. *Ma seba i neni leche.* They gave the baby a lot of milk.

sebu 2. Fat, grease, lard, tallow, adipose tissue.

seda 2. Type of plant-morus alba. Silk tree, silk, type of cloth.

sedi 1. Allow, let, approve of, sanction, concede, permit, consent. Cf. **Konsiente.**

sédulas 2. I.D. card, credentials, identity book.

segondariu 2. Second hand—on watch or clock.

seha 2. Back off, back up, go backward, back down. *Seha fan.* Back up please. *Hu na'seha i kareta.* I backed up the car. *Sumeha i mannok gi lasu.* The chicken backed away from the lasso.

sehas 2. Eyebrow, brow.

sekpapa'i 1. Undermine, indirect interrogation.

seku 1,2. Sock, punch, hit with the fist, strike with the fist. Cf. **Pañiti, dommo', tromponasu.**

seladura 2. Lock. Also **seradura.**

seluloit 2. Celluloid, plexiglass. (G).

Semo 2. July. Cf. **Julio.**

sen Extremely, very, greatly, (intensifier). *Sen bunitu i programa.* The program is extremely beautiful. *Sen magof yo' na umasodda' hit.* I am extremely glad that we met.

sena 2. Dinner, supper. Cf. **Na' pupuenge.**

senadót 2. Senator.

senadu 2. Senate—upper branch of the bicameral legislature.

senko Mosquito coil. (S) Also **puno' ñamu.**

senko' 2. Mosquito coil. Cf. **Oddo.**

señala 1. Earmark, designate.

sensen 2. Meat, flesh, any kind of meat. Cf. **Katne.**

sensét 2. Chisel.

sensia 2. Character, sense, denoting quality or character of a person. *Baba sensia-ña yanggen bumulachu gue'.* His character is bad when he becomes drunk.

sensiyu 2. Coins (money), loose change.

sensiyu 2. Easy going, affable, carefree. *Si Jose sumen sensiyu na taotao.* Joe is a very easy going man.

sensiyu 2. Only one, single.

sensiyu 2. Without undershirt or slip.

sensiyu 2. Chaste, pure. *Sensiyu i hinasso-ña.* His thoughts are pure.

senso 1,2. Censor, take a census. Censorship, census, censer.

sensoru 2. Censor, faultfinder, adverse critic, an official empowered to examine written or printed matter, motion pictures, etc., in order to forbid publication if objectionable.

sensura 1. Censor, examine, expurgate, inspect, review, oversee. (S) Cf. **Eksamina.**

sensuradót 2. Censor, one who takes census. (S)

sentabu 2. Cent, one hundredth.

sentada 2. Meal, banquet, snack, dinner table, meal-time.

sentensia 2. Sentence, statement, speech.

sentensia 2. Judgment, decision, penalty, sentence. Cf. **Huisio**.

sentensiadót 2. Referee, one who determines the winner, as in boxing or cockfight.

sentidu 2. Sensitive, susceptible, touchy. Also **sientidu**.

sentidu 2. Temple—on side of the head.

sentimento 2. Sentiment. Cf. **sentimiento**.

sentimiento 2. Regret, sorrow, sentiment, feeling. Also **sentimento**.

séntimos 2. Cent, penny. Also **memos**.

sentinát 2. Sentinel.

sentro 2. Center, core, middle, nucleus. Cf. **Talo'**.

señas 1. Wink, twinkle, raise the eyebrows as a signal, give signal. Cf. **Achetgue**.

señát 2. Sign, signal, symptom.

señora 2. Madam, lady, Mrs.

señorita 2. Lady—young, miss, woman (single).

señoritu 2. Gentleman—young, man (single), mister, bachelor.

señót 2. Sir, mister, gentleman.

se'pe 1. Snack, eat a quick snack.

Septembre 2. September. Cf. **lumamlam**.

séptimu 2. Seventh.

seputkro 2. Sepulcher.

seputtura 2. Cemetery, burial ground. Cf. **Simenteyu**.

será Maybe, perhaps. Cf. **Buente**. *Sera ti matto hao gi gipot.* Maybe you were not at the party.

sera 1. Accept, agree to, take willingly, accede to, consent, allow. Also **siera**. *Bai hu sera i planu yanggen ya-hu.* I will accept the plan if I like it.

sera 2. Bees-wax.

seradura 2. Padlock, lock. Also **aseradura, seladura**. Cf. **Andaba**.

seremonias 2. Ceremony, ritual, solemnity, ceremonial.

serenata 2. Serenade, evening music in the air.

seroroidu 2. Celluloid, plexiglass, stiff plastic. (S) Cf. **Karai, seluloit**.

seru 2. Zero, naught, nothing.

se'se' 1,2. Cut (with a knife). Knife.

sese 2. Type of plant-microsorum scolopendria. Cf. **Galak, kahlao**.

se'se' kubetto 2. Knife (table). Also **se'se' kubietto**.

sesgáo 2. Diagonal line.

sesion 2. Session, sitting of court, council, legislature, etc.

sesonyan 2. Swamp, marsh, bog. Also **sosonyan, sosomyan**.

sesse 1. Delouse.

sesso Often, frequent, often times, many times. Cf. **Fihu, taffo'**. *Sesso yo' humanao para i lancho.* I often go to the ranch.

sessuyi 1. Often, frequent, often times, many times. *Ha sessuyi pumasehu giya Hawaii.* He often toured Hawaii.

sesyon 2. Type of fish-siganus spinus (family siganidae). Rabbit fish.

setbe 1. Serve, labor as a servant, render services. Also **sietbe**. Cf. **Usa**.

setbente 2. Servant. Also **sitbiente**.

setbesa 2. Beer.

setbeyeta 2. Napkin.

setbisiu 2. Service, benefit, military duty, organization, and its performance, facilitating service.

setlas Type of plant-citrus grandis. Pomelo.

setmon 2. Sermon, a lecture of one's conduct or duty, homily.

setpiente 2. Serpent. Also **setpente**.

setro 2. Sceptre.

settifika 1. Certify, attest, approve, register a letter.

settifikasión 2. Certification.

settifiku 2. Certificate, document, diploma.

se'yon 2. Weakened back—by hauling something heavy, having a weak back, strained back. *Se'yon yo'.* My back is weakened. *Se'yon yo' anai hu hatsa i makkat na katga.* I have a weak back from lifting the heavy cargo.

seyu 2. Stamp—postage, seal, stamp. Cf. **Estampo'**.

si Article, used with proper names, but not used for direct address. *Si Jose, si Maria, si Yu'us.*

si Yu'us ma'ase' 2. Thank you, (literal translation - God have mercy).

siakasu Perhaps, in case.

siamo' 2. Type of chicken—resembling red pyle game. (S)

sibada 2. Barley, millet.

sibilisa 1. Civilize, educate, inform of civilized ways.

sibilisáo 2. Civilized, informed of civilized ways.

sibilisasión 2. Civilization, race or national culture, degree of cultivation, state of refinement.

sibít 2. Civilian, non-military person, private person.

siboyas 2. Type of plant-allium cepa. Onion (generic).

siboyas halomtano' 2. Type of plant-calanthe, bulbophyllum, luisia, etc. Orchid.

sibu 2. Metal liner for hub of wagon wheel.

sibukáo 2. Type of plant-caesalpinia sappan. A kind of tree.

sidán 2. Sedan, car, automobile, vehicle.

siembra 2. Sowing, sown field. *I siembra siha mandankolo.* The sowing was big.

siempre Surely, certainly, definitely. Future marker indicating strong determination. Cf. **Teneki.** *Siempre malate' yo' yanggen sigi yo' umeskuela.* I am sure to be smart if I continue attending school. *Siempre matai i flores sa' anglo' i edda'.* The flower will die because the soil is dry. *Siempre bai hu hanao para i eskuela agupa'.* I am sure to go to the school tomorrow.

siemprebiba 2. Type of plant-commelina diffusa. Spider wort. A type of grass.

sien 2. Hundred. Cf. **Siento.** *Manbende i sumentereru sien libras na produkto.* The farmer sold one hundred pounds of produce.

sien mit 2. One hundred thousand.

sienkasu If, in case. Also **akasu, enkasu.** *Pot sienkasu ti matto yo', hanao ha' na maisa.* In case I don't come, you go by yourself.

siente 1. Feel, perceive by sensation, grope, sense.

siento 2. One hundred. Cf. **Sien.**

siento i unu 2. One-hundred one.

si'eng 1. Crowd in, elbow one's way in a crowd, squeeze together—to let someone sit down. *Si'eng hao.* Push yourself in.

sierá See sera.

siesta 2. Nap—afternoon, take a nap, sleep, rest.

sietbe 1. Serve, act as a servant, work for, be in the service of. (R). Also setbe. *Hu sietbe i ma'gas-hu dos años.* I served my boss for two years.

sietbo 2. Servant, serf—of God. Used only in prayers. *Sietbon Yu'us.* God's servant.

siete 2. Seven.

sigariyu 2. Cigarette. Cf. **Chupa.**

sigen 2. Go by way of. Also **esgen.** Cf. **Sumigen, umesgen.** *Sigen papa'.* Take the lower route.

sigi 2. Go on, advance, continue, forward. *Sigi mo'na.* Move on, onward, go forward. *Sigi tatte.* Retreat, move back. *Sigi magi.* Come here. *Sigi halom.* Get in, go in or into.

sigi mo'na 2. Advance, go ahead.

sigidas Hurry, move quickly, in double-quick time, move with rapidity, fast, quick. Also **insigidas.** Cf. **Chaddek, listo.** *Sigidas magi.* Hurry over here. *Sigidas humanao asta i eskuela.* Hurry up and go to school.

sigidiyas 2. Type of plant-psophocarpus tetragonolobus. Wing bean.

sigidu 2. Successive, consecutive, successively, rounds. *Dies sigidu kinenne'-ña na guihan.* He caught ten fish successively.

sigiente 2. Following, succeeding, successive, sequential, that is now to follow. *Menha hao gi sigiente puenge.* You caught a great number of fish on the following night. *Mumalangu yo' gi sigiente dia.* I became sick the following day.

sigilu 2. In succession. Also **sigidu.** *Tres bi'ahi sigilu.* Three times in succession.

sigún Depends upon, according to. *Sigun gi fino' nana-mu siña hun hao humugando.* According to your mother's statement, she said that you can play.

sigunda 2. Second—measurement of time.

sigundayi 1. Second—a motion, support a statement which is delivered, assist, aid, remedy.

sigundayi 1. Sing alto, play alto part of a song.

sigundo 2. Second.

sigundon Second from, next to—refers to age. *Guahu i sigundon i mas amko' na patgon.* I was the second oldest child.

siguramente 2. Certainly.

sigurida 2. Certainty, security.

siguridát 2. Assurance, insurance, security, safety, certitude, certainty, confidence, self-reliance.

siguru 2. Sure, certain, positive, cocksure, authentic, definite. Cf. **Onesto, sinseru, franko.**

siha They—intransitive subject pronoun, transitive object pronoun, emphatic pronoun. *Manhugando siha bola.* They played ball. *Hu espiha siha gi bola.* I looked for them at the ball game. *Siha manmangganna.* They were the ones who won.

siha Plural marker for countable nouns. *Manmanaitai i taotao siha.* The people prayed.

sihek 2. Type of bird-halcyon cinnamomina. Micronesian kingfisher, blue and rust.

sihek 2. Type of fish-scolpsis cancellatus (family lutjanidae). Snappers. Also includes members of the families apigonidae, holocentridae.

sihok 1. Stab, pierce—with a pointed weapon, thrust (a knife, etc.). (R) Also **si'ok.** Cf. **Tokcha'.**

si'i 2. Type of tool, for preparing weaving materials, usually made of metal sheet, cut out in a triangular shape with sharp edges.

sikat 2. Creep, stalk, still-hunt, move furtively or slinkingly, sneak, steal (so as to be unobserved). Cf. **Kahat.** *Sumikat yo' halom asta i kuatto-ku.* I creeped into my room.

sikat 2. Nod, nodding, act of nodding, make a downward motion of the head involuntarily because of drowsiness.

sikat 2. Preparing cocks to fight in the arena. The cocks are held, allowed to peck at each other, then are placed on the ground and held by the tail feathers while they begin to scratch, raise the neck feathers and bob their heads up and down.

sikera At least. Also **sikiera.** Cf. **Maskeseha, maseha.** *Sikera un po'luyi yo' dos granon melon.* At least you should leave me two pieces of cantaloupe.

sikiera At least. Also **sikera.** Cf. **Maskeseha, kidera.**

siklo 2. Century, period (of time), epoch.

siknifika 1. Signify, symbolize, indicate, manifest.

siknifikante 2. Significant, significative.

siknifikasión 2. Signification, significance.

sikno 2. Signal.

sikretu 2. Secret, detective.

sikumstansia 2. Circumstance, situation, position, state, predicament, condition. Cf. **Situasion.**

sílaba 2. Syllable.

silebra 1. Celebrate, glorify, praise, honor, be glad.

silebrasión 2. Celebration, glorification. Cf. **Glorifika.**

sileksion 2. Selection, choice. Cf. **Inayek.**

silensio 2. Silence, quiet, hush, be silent, shut up, hold your tongue. Cf. **Pakaka', famatkilu.**

silindro 2. Cylinder.

silisiu 2. Vestment—priests'.

silok 2. Visit excessively, visit someone else often enough to become a nuisance, mooch food, to eat someone else's food, refers to birds that eat freshly sown seeds, bothersome. *E'kat sumilok giya hami.* Don't visit our house often.

simana 2. Week.

simana santa 2. Holy week.

símbalu 2. Cymbal.

símbulu 2. Symbol.

simenterera 2. Farmer, peasant, one who works on the farm (f).

simentereru 2. Farmer, peasant (m). Also **sumenterera** (f). Cf. **Lancheru.**

simenteyu 2. Cemetery, burial ground, churchyard. Also **simenteyu.** Cf. **Seputtura.**

simento 2. Cement. Cf. **Padet.**

simetrikát 2. Symmetrical.

simiento 2. Foundation, cement.

siminariu 2. Seminarian, one who studies for priesthood.

simiya 2. Seed, progeny, seedling, bud, any propagative portion of a plant. Cf. **Pipitas.**

simpeng 2. Brand new, new (article). (S)

sin 2. Without, except, not, excluding, bare. Cf. **Fuera.** *Ti siña hao humanao sin guahu.* You can't go without me.

sin 2. Tin, corrugated metal used for roofing, roof, zinc.

sin enao Notwithstanding, regardless.

sin laso' 2. Without pants, partly naked male person without any clothes on from the waist down. (S)

sin magagu 2. Naked, without clothes.

sin parát 2. Incessantly, without stopping, persistently.

Sina Nickname for Andersina.

sinagoga 2. Synagogue.

sinagu [æ] 2. A person suffering from influenza, one who has influenza. Cf. **Sahgo.**

sinague' [æ] 2. Protection, guard.

sinahguan 2. Contents. Cf. **sahguan.**

sinahi [æ] 2. New moon.

Sinajaña Village in central Guam. Pron. Sinahaña.

sinamomu 2. Type of plant-lawsonia intermis. A type of flower.

sinantusan 2. Saint, holy person, believer, pietist, religious. Cf. **Santos, santolon.**

sinangan [æ] 2. Statement, speech, recitation, narrative, quotation, passage from some author or speaker, story. Cf. **Sangan.** *Mandagi enao na sinangan.* That which was said was false. *I sinangan i manprofeta.* The words of the wise men.

sinaolak 2. Spanking, whipping.

Sinapalu 2. Name for a place on Rota where the airfield is located.

sina'pet [æ] 2. Exhaustion, toilsome, torture, agony of mind or body. *I sina'pet-mu ni patgon muna'malangu gue'.* Your exhausting the child made him sick.

sinasalaguan 2. Fiendish, hellish. Cf. **Sasalaguan.**

sindalu 2. Soldier, warrior.

sindogga 2. Barefoot, go barefoot. (Lit. without shoes). *Sumindogga yo' asta i tasi.* I went barefoot to the sea.

sinembatgo Nevertheless, still, yet. *Ya-hu manestudia lao sinembatgo bai hu egga' kachido'.* I'd like to study, but nevertheless I will watch the movie.

sine'se' 2. Thrust, stab.

sine'so' 2. Copra, coconut meat (ripe)—taken from its shell.

sinetnan 2. Boiled food (starchy)—such as taro, yam, and breadfruit.

sinetsot 2. Repentance.

sini 1. Place in, put into. Cf. **Sahguan, siniyi, sahguani.** *Hu sini i kafe gi halom basu.* I put the coffee in the cup.

siniabi 2. Gentleness, mildness, meekness. Cf. **Su'abi.**

sinibi 2. Improvement. Cf. **Subi.**

siniente 2. Touch, perception. Cf. **Siente.**

sinikretu 2. Secrecy.

sinilo' 2. Lose temper, fly off the handle, become extremely angry, pain—a worsening, sickness--a worsening, aggravated, made worse. Cf. **Taohan.** *Sinilo' i chetnot-hu.* My sore became worse. *Sinilo' si Juan anai mana'bubu gi huego.* Juan lost his temper when he was made angry at the game. *Sinilo' i nana anai i famagu'on-ña sigi manburuka.* The mother lost her temper when her children continued to make noise.

sininbatgo No choice, face whatever consequence arises, no alternative, never mind. *Sininbatgo ta konne' gue' maseha esta maggai gi kareta.* No alternative for us but to take him though the car was filled already. *Sininbatgo bai hu facho'cho' ha'.* No choice but to work.

sinisa 1. Ash Wednesday, ash colored, gray.

sinisa 2. Type of chicken—resembling gray Andalusian.

sinisedi 2. Incident, occurrence, event, happening, phenomenon, something that occurs. Cf. **Susedi.**

sinisu 2. Shoot (of a plant), offshoot, scion, bud (of plant).

siniyi 1. Fill, put in, place in. Cf. **Sini, sahguan.** *Hu siniyi i basu.* I put something in the cup.

sinko 2. Five.

sinkuenta 2. Fifty.

sinkuenta i unu 2. Fifty-one.

sinó Otherwise, else, or. *Rega hanom i flores sino siempre matai.* Sprinkle the flower with water; otherwise it will die. *Suette na ha li'e' i patgon gi tasi sino siña ha' matmos.* It is lucky that he saw the child at the sea; otherwise he might have drowned.

sinónimu 2. Synonym.

sinseramente 2. Sincerity, frankness, seriousness.

sinseru 2. Sincere, unadulterated, serious, wholehearted, heartfelt, unfeigned. Cf. **Franko, magahet.**

sinta 2. Edging, border.

sintas 2. Strip—wooden, such as in wood work.

sintura 2. Waist, waistline, bodice.

sinturón 2. Belt, strap. Cf. **Korehas.**

siña 2. Can, be able, may, might, probable. *Siña yo' humanao.* I can go.

siña buente Maybe, possible, perhaps. Cf. **Buente, kasi.**

siña ha' Maybe, perhaps, it's possible.

siñala 1. Mark, to mark a place such as where something is to be planted or attached. *Hanao ha' sa' esta hu siñala i lugat.* Go ahead (and do it) because I have already marked the place.

siñát 2. Sign, mark, token, omen, symptom. *Siñat para maolek na ha'ani pa'go sa' fresko i tiempo.* It is a sign of a good day today because the weather is cool.

singao 1. Surfeit, sick from repetition, satiate, cause to be fed up. Cf. **Impachu, o'son, sosongte.** *Ha singao yo' i kek.* I am sick of cake.

Singgapót 2. Singapore. Also **Singgapoa.**

siobo' 2. Even up, tie game, draw match, equal in contest, come out even. (S) Cf. **Parehu, tapbla.** *Siobo' hit pa'go.* We are even up now.

sióganai' 2. No way, no method, too bad, can't be helped, nothing can be done about it, irrelevant. (S) *Sioganai' amigu sa' ti makombida hao para i gipot.* Too bad friend because you weren't invited to the party.

si'ok 1. Stab. Also **siok, sihok.**

siok 1. Stab, pierce. Also **sihok, si'ok.**

sipara 1. Separate, part, divide. Cf. **Depatta, adingu, adespatta.**

siparáo 2. Separated, parted, separable, divided.

siparasión 2. Separation.

sipu 1. Corner, move it into a corner when fighting or chasing something.

sirásime' 2. Oil (for frying), salad oil, cooking oil. (S) Cf. **Asaite.**

sirek 1,2. Coitus, sexual intercourse—have. (Taboo). Cf. **Baggai, dalle, kichi.**

Sirena 2. Mermaid, a woman's body and a fish's tail—a fabled marine creature.

sirenu 2. Cold, damp air, esp. at night. *Fotte na sirenu gi paigne.* The humid air was extremely cold last night. *Ha na'sinagu yo' i sirenu.* The cold humidity caused me to have a cold.

siriales 2. Cereal.

siruanu 2. Herb doctor, quack doctor, witch doctor, (m). Also **siruana** (f). Cf. **Suruhana.** *Konne' i lahi-mu para i siruana.* Take your son to a herb doctor.

sis Because. Alternate form of *sa'.* *Ñateng i boti sis katgadu.* The boat is slow because it is loaded. *Sis ilelek-ta ha'.* Because we have been saying that.

sisenta 2. Sixty.

sisenta i unu 2. Sixty-one.

sisi 1. Rip, split, tear off, saw. Cf. **Titek.** *Hu sisi i papet ya hu yute' gi sagan basula.* I tore the paper and I threw it in the trashcan. *Ta sisi i hayon i liga.* We split the lumber for the wall.

sísi'ok 2. Type of fish-family holocentridae. Squirrel fish.

sisitan 2. Aggravate (sore or wound), to make worse a sore or wound. Cf. **Tinaohan.**

Siska Nickname for Francisca.

siso' 2. See-saw, teeter-totter. Cf. **Balansa.**

sistema 1,2. System, arrangement, systematize, orderly, method.

sita 1. Cite, summon, send for, serve with a writ.

sítara 2. Sitar, a musical instrument from India.

sitasión 2. Citation, summons, official call or notice.

sitbiente 2. Servant, person employed in domestic duties, person in the service of another. Also **setbente**.

sitenta 2. Seventy.

sitenta i unu 2. Seventy-one.

sitio 2. Site, place, lot (of land), location. Cf. **Tano'**.

sítkulu 2. Circle.

sitron 2. Type of plant-citrus medica. Pomelo. Cf. **Setlas**.

situasión 2. Situation, circumstance, predicament, condition. Cf. **Sikumstansia**.

siudá 2. City, metropolis, town. Also **siudat**.

siudadanu 2. Citizen, citizenship, resident of a state.

siudát 2. City, town. Also **siuda**.

siya 2. Seat, chair. Cf. **Ta'chong**.

siyan kabayu 2. Saddle.

siyan machukan 2. Rocking chair.

skerosu See **askerosu**.

skuiyi 2. Type of brush—made from coconut husk, used for scrubbing or polishing.

slait 2. Slide, sliding board. Cf. **Soberidai'**.

soberidai' 2. Slide, sliding board as found on playground. (S) Also **slait**.

sobre 2. Envelope.

sodáliti 2. Sodality, religious organization for young women.

sodda' 1. Find, come upon, gain the use of. *Hu sodda' i haggan mañañada' gi inai.* I found the turtle laying eggs in the sand.

sofá 2. Sofa, divan.

sogra 2. Mother-in-law. Also **suegra, sugra**.

sogro 2. Father-in-law. Also **suegro, sugro**.

sohgon 2. Drenched—from perspiration or rain, soaked. *Sohgon yo' ni masahalom.* I am drenched with perspiration.

sohgue 1. Empty water out of something, bail, dip out. Also **so'gue**. *I bomba ha sohgue i hanom gi halom boti.* The pump drained the water out of the boat.

sohmok 1. Squeeze in tightly (into a hole), cram tightly (into a hole), shove (into a hole), pack (into a hole), stuff (into a hole).

so'hon See **so'on**.

sohon See **so'on**.

sohyo' 1. Influence, convince, invite, persuade. Also **soyok**. Cf. **Kombida, eppok**.

sokka 1. Hold down, pin against, clamp.

sokkai 1. Snag (cloth), rip—by being caught on something, tear off--by being caught on something. *Masokkai i katsunes-hu gi halom tano'.* My pants ripped off in the forest. *I alamlen tituka' ha sokkai i katsunes-hu.* The barbed wire snagged my pants.

sokkok 1. To elbow, nudge, jog, jostle, jolt, poke (with the elbow), kick (with the knee), thrust. Cf. **Toyo'**.

sokkos 2. Dirty. Cf. **Applacha'**.

sokkos 2. Breech birth.

sokne 1. Accuse, charge (someone) with, suspect. Cf. **Suspecha, faiseknani, kalomña**.

soksok 2. Tuberculosis, consumption, TB, skinny. Cf. **Tibi**.

solamente 2. Except, provided that, unless, only, alone. Cf. **Solu**. *Bai hu hanao solamente humita.* I will go provided that you go with me. *Guahu ha' solamente gumimen i amot.* I was the only one who drank the medicine.

solemne 2. Solemn, formal, serious, somber.

solisita 2. Solicit, ask, invite, request, plea, try to obtain by asking for.

solu 2. Alone, unless, only. *Guahu solu.* I am alone. *Ti bai hu hanao solu matto hao.* I won't go unless you come.

sombra 2. Shade—of a tree, shade from the sun.

somnak 2. Sunshine, sunlight, ray (from the sun).

son 2. Tone, music, song, chant. Cf. **Musiku, kanta**.

songge 1. Burn, lighted, set on fire, ignite. Cf. **Totnge**. *Hu songge i paliton maches.* I burned the match stick.

songgiyon 2. Inflammable, combustible.

songsong 1,2. Plug up, close up (hole). Stopper, plug.

songsong 2. Town, village. Name of principal village on Rota.

so'on 2. Staggering, stumbling, jerking, about to stop, about to fall, growling (of dog), barking (of dog)—when after a prey. Also **sohon, so'hon**.

So'on i kareta-ña anai hokkok gas. His car sputtered to a stop when it ran out of gas. *Mana'so'on i binadu ni ga'lagu.* The deer staggered from exhaustion and the dog was growling for the kill.

sopas 1,2. Mixing (of liquid with solid). Mixture (of liquid and solid), soup. *Hu sopas i biskuchu yan i leche.* I mixed the biscuit with the milk. *Ha kanno' i patgon todu i sopas-ña.* The child ate all his soup.

sopbla 2. Remains, left over, remainder. Cf. **Tetehnan.**

soppla 1,2. Suck in (as in smoking), suck —as through a straw, suck noodles, soup, or other liquid. *I bihu ha soppla i chigalu-ña.* The old man puffed his cigar.

sopplo 2. Remainder, leftover, taking opponent's checkers because he did not make a jump during his turn.

sorohu 2. Sliding bar to lock door.

sosiát 2. Social.

so'so' 1. Scrape—coconut meat from its shell, make copra, pry loose, scrape (with thrusting motion)--as scraping a pancake from the griddle.

sosomyan 2. See **sesonyan.** Also **sosonyan.**

sosongte 1. Tired, bored, fed up with. (R) Cf. **O'son, singao, empachu.** *Ha sosongte yo' i dandan-mu humungok.* I am fed up with listening to your music.

sosse 1. Mend. Also **sotse.**

sota 2. Jack (cards).

sotadót 2. One who holds the fighting cock during *sikat.*

sotda 1. Weld, unite metallic parts by heating, hammering, or compressing.

sotdadura 2. Welding equipment.

sotfa 2. Note (music), tune, melody, written notes of music.

sotgan 2. Proliferation, prolific. (R) Cf. **Hafñak.**

sotne 1. Cook (by boiling), to boil, usually refers to starchy food.

sotse 1. Mend, sew, stitch, darn. Cf. **Lakse.**

sotsot 2. Contrite, repentant. *Fañotsot ni isao-mu.* Repent of your sins.

sotta 1. Release, set free, make free, let go. Cf. **Ri'asi.**

sottayi 1. Slacken for, loosen, enervate, release for. *I peskadot ha sottayi i*

guihan ni kotdet anai hinalla. The fisherman slackened the fishing line for the fish when it pulled. *Sottayi yo' mas hilu.* Slacken more string for me.

sottera 2. Bachelorette, single woman, puberty.

sotteritu 2. Teen-ager (m). *Sotterita* (f).

sotteru 2. Bachelor, single man.

soyok 1. See **sohyo'.**

su'abi 2. Suave, sophisticated, curteous, refined, urbane, cultured (person).

su'anu 2. Calm, even tempered, cool-headed.

subes In fact, even though. *Subes taya' salape'-hu ya un gagagao yo'.* Even though I have no money, you are asking me.

subetbia 2. Brave, courage, stubborn, daring (f). Cf. **Baliente.**

subetbiu 2. Brave, courageous, haughty, daring (m). Also **subetbia** (f). Cf. **Baliente.**

subi 1. Raise in salary, upgrade in rank, promote in rank. Also **subre.** *Masubi i suetdo-ku.* My salary was raised.

subida 2. Promotion, advancement in position, increase. Also **subidu.**

subida 2. Receding of wave.

subida 2. Approach, draw near.

subre 2. Pay raise.

subrekama 2. Bed sheet, quilt, bedspread. Cf. **Hafyen katre.**

subrekatgo 2. Supercargo, cargo chief, caretaker, custodian, one who is in charge of cargo. Cf. **Enkatgao.**

subrenaturát 2. Unnatural.

subres An expletive calling attention to a negative or unfortunate situation. *Subres ti mamaolek si tata-mu, ya sigi hao ha' pumasehu.* Look, your father is not well, and you still go out running around. *Subres ti ya-hu hao, ya un fafaisen yo'.* Look, I don't like you, and you keep asking me.

subrina 2. Niece.

subrinu 2. Nephew.

suegro See **sogro.**

suekos 2. Wooden Japanese slipper, resembling geta'. Cf. **Geta'.**

suelas 2. Shoe sole.

suena 2. Popular, become popular by name, character, or work that one performs.

suena 2. Audible, easily perceived noise when everything else is quiet.

suetdo Wage, salary, stipend, fee, recompense for service rendered. Cf. **Apas.**

suette 2. Lucky, luck, good fortune.

suetto 2. Free, unbound.

sufa' 1. Rush at, charge at—with head lowered, grovel, root--as pig. Cf. **Totpe, tugong.** *I babui ha sufa' i sini.* The pig rooted up the taro.

sufan 1. Pare, peel, cut away by slicing the peeling. *Hu sufan i mangga.* I peeled the mango.

sufisiente 2. Sufficient, enough, adequate, competent.

sufoka 1. Suffocate.

sugat 2. Hard, solid, firm, tough. Cf. **Mahetok.**

sugo' 2. Stop by, stop for a while, moment, a few minutes. Visit briefly, drop in on.

sugon 1. Steer, guide, drive.

sugon 1. Drive away, chase away. *Sugon i ga'lagu.* Chase the dog away.

suha 2. Move away, scram, step aside, get away, get off. *Suha guenao.* Get away from there.

suhayi 1. Avoid, dodge, evade, keep out of the way, keep away from, keep clear of. *Hu suhayi i bulacheru.* I evaded the drunkard.

suheta 1. Subdue, control, subjugate, overpower, cool off (anger). *Hu suheta si tata-hu anai bulachu.* I subdued my father when he was drunk. *Suheta pachot-mu.* Control your mouth.

suhetu 2. Subject, theme.

suhu 1,2. Dip water (with container). Water container. *Ha suhu i hanom ni didu.* He got some water with the water container. *Mafondo i sihu gi tanken hanom.* The water container sank in the water tank.

Suitas 2. Jesuit, religious order of Jesuits. Also **Hesuitas.**

sukato' 2. Skirt. (S) Also **lupes.**

suki 2. Venereal (disease), syphilis, gonorrhea, lymphogranuloma.

sukori 1. Succor, help, assist, aid. (G) Also **sukoru.**

sukoru 1. Succor, help, aid. Also **sukori.**

sukos 2. Snout, mouth. *Huchom sikos-mu.* Shut your mouth. (Impolite.)

sukos babui 2. Mouth—of pig.

suleras 2. Joist, beam, stud, scantling—any of small timbers ranged parallelwise from wall to wall, to support the floor, or to support the laths or furring strips of a ceiling. Cf. **Haligi.**

sulitario 2. Type of card game.

sulo' 2. Type of fishing, torch-fishing, hunting (with light), fishing or hunting with a lighted torch or flashlight. *Maolek i silu' yanggen homhom i puenge.* The torch-fishing is good when the night is dark.

sulon 2. Slip, slide. Cf. **Palaga'.** *Sulon yo' papa' gi ekso'.* I slid down the hill.

suma 1. Add, combining together. *Hu suma i dibi-hu.* I combined my debts together.

suma 1. Figure out—in arithmetic, make arithmetic calculations.

sumagágayi 2. Occupant, one who occupies a place. Cf. **Saga.**

sumai 1. Soak, saturate, drench, impregnate with liquid.

sumai Expression used in tres siete telling the dealer to give each player ten cards straight when four people are playing.

sumak 2. Type of plant-tarenna sambucina, randia cochinchinensis. A type of grass.

sumak ladda 2. Type of plant-tarenna sambucina or timonius nitidus. A type of tree.

suman 2. Type of food—made from rice and coconut milk. After rice is cooked in coconut milk, it is wrapped in banana leaf and steamed. Usually served as a dessert.

sumaria 2. Summary.

sumát 2. Addition—in arithmetic.

sume' 2. Leak, leakage. Cf. **Tu'o'.** *Sume' i batde.* The bucket leaks. *Hu na'sume' i batde.* I made the bucket leak. *Guaha dankolo na sume' gi batde.* There is a big leak in the bucket.

sumen See **sen.** *Sen* plus infix *-um-.* *Sumen bunita i palao'an.* The girl became very pretty.

sumigen 2. Go by way of. Also **umesgen.**

sumísiha 2. Simultaneous, together. Cf. **Siha.**

Sumongsong 2. November. Cf. Nobiembre.

sumugo' 2. Conceive (child).

suncho 2. Hoop, metal band on cask or barrel.

sunen agaga' 2. Type of taro—reddish in color. Grows on dry or swampy land.

sunen Hapón 2. Type of taro—introduced by the Japanese.

sunen Honolulu 2. Type of plant-xanthosoma violacea. Taro.

sunen sisonyan 2. Type of taro—grows in swampy area.

suni 2. Type of plant-colocasia esculenta. Taro (generic).

sunidu 2. Audible, sound which can be heard. Cf. Suena.

sungon 1. Tolerate, endure, sustain, bear, tolerate with patience, withstand, last, strong enough. Cf. Aguanta. *Ma sungon i maipen somnak gi plasa.* They tolerated the heat of the sun at the plaza. *Ha sungon i puten tiyan-ña gi gima'.* He endured his stomach ache at home.

sungon ha' Accept something, face the fact. *Sungon ha' sa' ti maguaiya hao.* Accept it, because you are not liked.

su'ok 1. Persuade, induce, prevail upon, lure. Cf. Eppok.

su'on 1. Push, shove, thrust, propel, encourage, raise the spirit of. Build up fire by adding new wood. Cf. Chonnek.

supi 2. Foul ball, chipped ball, indirect hit, glance off.

supiriót 2. Superior, superior being, sovereign, Mother Superior.

supiriót Deluxe.

supiyu 2. Plane (carpenter's), paring tool.

suplenta 1. Supplant.

suplika 1. Supply, furnish with what is lacking, provide with what is requisite. (R)

suplika 1. Supplicate, entreat. *Hu suplika hao na un na'i yo' ni nisisidat-hu salape'.* I entreat you to lend me the money that I need.

supmarinu 2. Submarine. Cf. Bapot lumi'of.

supok 1. Submerge, immerse, sink, plunge into anything that surrounds

or covers, esp. into a fluid. Cf. Ñokñok, lumos.

suponi 1. Suppose, assume. Cf. Asuma. *Hu suponi na un tungo' i planu.* I suppose you knew my plan.

supotta 1. Support—financial or legal.

surón 2. Sack—of dried cattle hides used for carrying beef. Hide of cattle made into a sack.

suruhana 2. Herb doctor (f). *Suruhanu (m). Also* siruana, siruhana.

susedi 1. Experienced, happened to, tried. *Hu susedi mamuno' dos na paharu gi un tiru ha'.* I experienced killing two birds with one shot. *Ginen hu susedi gumimen setbesa.* I experienced drinking beer.

susiadét 2. Occurrence, happening. *Hafa susiadet-mu?* What happened to you?

suspecha 1. Suspect, distrust. Cf. Sokne, faiseknani.

suspechadóra 2. Suspicious person (f).

suspechadót 2. Suspicious person (m).

suspecháo 2. Suspicious, questionable.

suspecho 2. Suspicion, an instance of suspecting.

suspechosu 2. Suspect, be suspicious, suspected, questionable. Also suspechosa (f). *Suspechosu hao mampos na taotao.* You are a suspicious person.

suspende 1. Suspend, dismiss, expel, put off.

suspiros 2. Gasp (air), sigh, gasping for breath while sobbing. Cf. Kasao.

sustansia 2. Definition, explanation, meaning, nutrition, substance, sustenance.

sustieni 1. Hold, sieze, grasp, sustain, support, brace, receive and keep in the hand. Cf. Mantieni, gu'ot, go'te.

susto 2. Terrified, horrified, fear, shock, frightened, scared. Cf. Luhan, manhang.

susu 1,2. Suck, suckle. Breast, breast feeding. *I patgon ha susu i sisun nana-ña.* The child fed on his mother's breast. *Dankolo na susu i sisu-ña i guaka.* The teats of the cow are big.

Susupe 2. Susupe, a village on Saipan near Chalan Kanoa.

sut 2. South. Used especially in describing direction typhoon is coming from.

sutana 2. Robe, loose outer garment worn by females.

sutana 2. Robe, vestment, dress of ecclesiastical vestment, cassock—black outer robe of a priest, frock.

sutko 1. Plow a row, heap up small branches or leaves for burning.

-ta Our, ours, us (possessive, inclusive). *Bunitu i kareta-ta.* Our car is pretty.

ta We (inclusive), pre-posed pronoun used in transitive statements.

ta'an 1. Threaten—by gesture of a fist doubled up as though to sock someone. (S) Cf. **Hannan.**

taba' 1,2. Measure, unit of measure, a distance of any finger tip to the thumb's tip. (R) Cf. **Hemi.**

tabinákulu 2. Tabernacle. Also **tabitnakulu.**

tablón 2. Plank, thick board. Also **tapblon.**

tacha 1. Criticize, blame, find fault with, reprove, reprimand. (R)

tachi 1. Tag (someone)—with an object, as in a game, counter--in argument, counter attack with a better point in argument, give counter example.

ta'chong 2. Seat, chair, bench. Cf. **Mata'chong.**

ta'chong pannas Sitting cross-legged on the floor, sitting on the floor.

tachu [æ] 2. Raise up, erect, hoist, stand up, upright, straight. Cf. **Tohge, tunas.**

tachuelas 2. Heel taps, taps for shoes, tack, small nail. Also **atachuelas.** Cf. **Chapeta.**

taddong 2. Deep, profound, serious. Also **tahdong.**

taffo' [æ] 2. Brash, tactless, insensitive to etiquette. Also **tafo'.** *Taffo' gue' matto gi gima'-mami.* He was tactless in coming to our house.

tafo' 2. Tactless. Cf. **taffo'.**

taftaf 2. Early.

tafye 1. Thresh, remove husk from grain by threshing.

taga' 1. Hack, chop.

Taga' 2. Taga—legendary hero.

tagafen saddok 2. Type of fish-lutjanus argentimaculatus (family lutjanidae). Snappers.

tagafi 2. Type of fish-lutjanus bohar (family lutjanidae). Red snapper.

tagahlo' 2. Superb, splendid. Also **tagalo'.**

tagalo' 2. Superb, sublime, grand, splendid, awe inspiring. Also **tagahlo'.** Cf. **Gatbo.**

Tagalu 2. Filipino.

tage'te' 2. Type of plant-ficus tinctoria. A type of tree.

tagga' [æ] 2. Flush, become blotched. *Nina'tagga' i patgon ni kalentura-ña.* The child is flushed from fever.

taggam [æ] 1. Block, interfere with, blockade. *Hu taggam i lahi.* I blocked the man. Cf. **Pattang.**

tago' 1. Command, send on errand, be a messenger.

tagong 2. Shell—of crustacean family which protects the main body, usually that part where the eyes are located. Also **tahgong.**

tagu'a 2. Type of plant-lagenaria siceraria. Gourd.

tágula 2. Land slug. Cf. **Salang.**

tagu'on 2. Obediant, trustworthy, dependable.

taha 1. Estimate, calculate.

ta'hafkao 2. Hocus-pocus, mumbo jumbo, puzzling act, wierd thing, strange, queer. *Ta'hafkao siha finono'-mu.* You are talking a bunch of hocus-pocus. *Ta'hafkao bidada-mu.* You have been up to something. *Ta'hafkao un na'kekehaftaimanu hao.* Something you are trying to do to yourself doesn't make any sense at all.

tahdong 2. Deep, serious, profound—that which is very far below the surface. Also **taddong.** *Tahdong i tasi gi hiyong i mama'te.* The sea is deep outside the reef. *Tahdong i hinasosso-ña pa'go.* His thinking is profound now.

tahgue [æ] 1. Substitute, take one's place.

tahlang [æ] 1. Weigh (using the hand), estimate weight—by using one's body esp. with the hand or hands. Also **talang.** Cf. **Tanteha.**

tahlek 2. Twist.

táhtaotao 2. Body, shape, form, figure, bodily nature, physical shape. Also **tataotao.** *Bunitu tahtaotao-mu.* Your body is nice. *Dankolo tahtaotao-ña i patgon.* The child's body is big.

tahu 1. Fishing—or catching crabs with a flashlight during the night.

tahu 2. Cut, cutting, slice, operation, incision.

tahu 2. Coconut—grated and rotting, used for coconut crab lure.

tai- None, not have (prefix). *Taisalape' yo'.* I don't have any money.

taia' 2. Tire—of a vehicle, rubber tire.

tái'achaigua 2. Matchless, incomparable, peerless. Cf. **Tai'atparehu.**

tai'ai 1. Put out to dry, hang clothes to dry, dry up, make dry, dry. Cf. **Tala'.**

tái'ase' 2. Cruel, savage, fierce, brutal, no pity, merciless. *Tai'ase' i patgon gi che'lu-ña.* The boy was cruel to his brother.

tái'atparehu 2. Matchless, incomparable, peerless. Also **taiparehu.** Cf. **Tai'achaigua.**

táibali 2. Worthless, useless, waste, destitute of wealth.

táibisio 2. Virtuous, without habits.

taiche' 2. Immeasurable, immense, vast, limitless. Also **taichi.** *Taiche' i minaolek-mu nu guahu.* Your kindness to me has no limit.

táichetnot 2. Uninjured, free from defect, ailment, wound, etc.

táichilong 2. Matchless, peerless.

táidinakon 2. Truthful. Cf. **Dakon.**

tái'eksperensia 2. Inexperienced, unskilled.

táifinakpo' 2. Endless, infinity, infiniteness, infinitude. Cf. **Taihinekkok, taiuttimo.**

táifinatai 2. Imperishable, immortal, indestructible. Cf. **Matai.**

táiga'chong 2. Lonely, solitary, friendless, odd, eccentric.

taiganas 2. Lacking appetite, having no desire for food. Cf. **Tumaiganas.**

táiguailayi 2. Unfit, useless, in vain.

táigue 2. Absent, not present, inattentive, disappear. *Taigue i siya.* The chair has disappeared. *Taigue i taotao.* The man is absent.

táigueku 2. Solid, not hollow.

taiguenao That is the way (something is done), that is how, that is why, that is the reason—talking to and about addressee. Cf. **Enao na.** *Taiguenao kulot-ña i kareta-hu i kareta-mu.* That color on your car is the same as that color on my car. *Taiguenao un cho'gue yanggen mafaisen hao.* That is the way to do it when you are asked.

taigúi Short form for *taiguihi.* Cf. **Ayu na.**

taiguihi That is the way (something is done), that is how, that is why, that is the reason—talking about a third person or persons. Cf. **Taigui, ayu na.** *Taiguihi un cho'gue.* That's the way you do it.

taiguini This is how, this is the way (something is done), this is why, this is the reason—talking about self. Cf. **Este na.** *Taiguini matuge'-ña.* This is how it should be written.

táiha'ani 2. Inanimate, lifeless, dead. Cf. **Ha'ani.**

táihinadahi 2. Reckless, careless, heedless. Also **tai'inadahi.**

táihinasso 2. Ignorant. Cf. **Hasso.**

táihinekkok 2. Endless, infinity, infiniteness, boundlessness. Cf. **Taifinakpo', taiuttimo.**

tái'inadahi 2. Recklessness, carelessness. Also **taihinadahi.**

tái'inangokko 2. Independent, not supported by others. Cf. **Angokko.**

tái'ine'son 2. Patient, forebearing. Cf. **O'son.**

tái'interes 2. Impartial, fair, without interest.

tái'isao 2. Innocent, guiltless.

táikinalamten 2. Immovable, fixed, unchanging.

táilayi 2. Rude, selfish, cruel, unfriendly, unpropitious, not kind, cause to harm.

táima'a'ñao 2. Fearless. Also **táima'ñao.** Cf. **Matatnga.**

táimancha 2. Unstained, without blemish.

taimanu [æ] How (question word). Also used with *hafa* with same meaning. *Hafa taimanu?* How to do it? *Taimanu mafattinas-ña i ahu?* How do you make ahu?

táiminagof 2. Sad, full of grief. Cf. **Triste.**

táiminaolek 2. Sterile, barren, producing little or no crop.

táininangga 2. Hopeless, desperate.

táiparehu 2. Unique, incomparable, matchless, incommensurable, cannot be compared with anything else. Cf. **Tai'atparehu.**

táipresiu 2. Priceless, invaluable.

táipunta 2. Obtuse, dull.

táiremediu 2.   Incurable, incorrigible.

táirespetu 2.   Impudent, disrespectful.

táisabot 2.   Tasteless, bland.

táisaga 2.   Indigent, destitute, needy.

táisalape' 2.   Poor, without money.

táisentidu 2.   Idiot, fool.

táisetbe 2.   Rudeness, forwardness.

taitai 1.   Read.

táitiningo' 2.   Simpleton, devoid of knowledge.

táiuttimo 2.   Infiniteness, infinity, endlessness. Cf. **Taifinakpo', taihinekkok.**

tak- [æ]   Comparative prefix, used with location and direction words, the degree indicated by *tak-* is less than that indicated by *ya-*. Cf. **Ya-.** *Takfe'na i dinagao-mu ni bola.* You have thrown the ball way up front. *Takhiyong hao gi tasi gi boti-mu.* You are far out on the sea in your boat.

taka' [æ] 1.   Reach, gain, achieve, attain. Cf. **Hago'.** *Hu taka' i kisami.* I reached the ceiling.

taka' [æ] 1.   Time required, last, delay, take up (time), put off, defer, endure. Cf. **Dura, sungon.** *Hu taka' ti humagong un minutu.* I lasted one minute without breathing. *Tinaka' una ora i klas-hu pa'go.* My class takes up one hour today.

take' 2.   Feces, droppings, manure, excrement, dung, muck.

take' biha 2.   Type of plant-cassia alate. Candle bush. Used for treating ringworm.

take' ga'ga' 2.   Manure.

take' lulok 2.   Rust.

take' uchan 2.   Type of plant—a type of algae that grows on the ground during the wet season. Lit. Feces of the rain.

takfia   See takfiha.

takfiha   Guess size, estimate. Also **takfia.** *Takfiha dinankolo-ña i tronkon hayu.* Guess how big the tree is. *Takfihayi yo' ni yinemmok-ña i palao'an.* Guess how fat the woman is for me.

tákgagao [æ] 2.   Beggar, mendicant, pauper. Cf. **Gakgao.**

takka' [æ] 1.   Grope, search blindly, reach for, frisk, search a person. *Ha takka' gi halom kahon para i antihos-ña.* He groped inside the

box for his glasses. *Ha takka' i hinasso-ña.* He searched for his thoughts.

tákkalom [æ]   Too far inside, intensive. Cf. **halom.**

tákkilo' [æ]   Eminent, high, in a high place.

táklalo' [æ] 2.   Harsh, stern, rigid. *Taklalo' si tata-hu.* My father is stern.

tákleffa [æ] 2.   Forgetful.

takme [æ] 2.   Bed wetter, one who frequently urinates in bed.

takme [æ] 2.   Contagious.

takong 2.   Heel (of shoes).

takos 1.   Sock, punch, hit with a fist. Cf. **Pañiti, dommo'.**

takpangi 1.   Baptize, christen.

tákpapa' [æ] 2.   Low, humble, abject.

tákpapa' [æ] 2.   Snake, reptile.

taktak 1.   Mince, chop, cut up into slices, cut by striking repeatedly with a sharp instrument. Cf. **Pika.**

taktak 2.   Pecking (sound). Cf. **Talaktak.**

taktamudu 2.   Dumb, stupid. See **tattamudu.**

takuán 2.   Turnip—preserved. Cf. **Daigo'.**

takurí 2.   Kettle, used esp. for boiling water for tea or coffee. Cf. **Charera.**

tala' 1.   Dry, dry up, expose, make dry, lay open, spread over.

talak- [æ]   To face certain direction. *Talakpapa'.* Face downward, look down from above. *Talaklichan.* Face westward. *Talakhiyong.* Face outside, look out from inside.

talaktak 2.   Rattle, tapping, clicking, clacking, clink, clatter. Also **taktak.** A sound made by double clacking, as a pencil inside an empty box when shaken, sound made when pounding.

talanga [æ] 2.   Ear.

talangan hayu 2.   Type of fungus, dark brownish and quite slippery when wet, usually attaches to decayed wood and looks just like the ear of people. Often found on dead tree trunks.

talangan hulu 2.   Roll of thunder, bolt of lightning. After a storm, disorders of thickets or woods are attributed to it.

talapia 2.   Type of fish—fresh water, originally imported from the Philippines. Also **tilapia.**

talapos 2. Rag, shred, tatter, a waste piece of cloth torn or cut off.

talaya 2. Net, circular or throwing net used for fishing.

talayan mañahak 2. Throw net—very fine mesh, used for catching small fish inside the reef.

talayan ti'ao 2. Throw net—with small holes, small lead sinkers.

talayeru 2. Fisherman—throwing net, one who fishes with a throwing net. Also **talayera** (f).

tala'yok [æ] **2.** Hop—on two feet.

talen manala' 2. Clothesline.

talen moddong 2. Sea cucumber—long, rope-like in appearance. Long rope.

talento 2. Talent, ability, knowledge, mentality, mind, brain, brainy, smart, intelligent. Cf. **Tomtom, intelihente, malate'.**

tali 2. Rope, twine.

talisai 2. Type of plant-terminalia catappa. A type of tree, bears nuts. Indian almond.

talisai ganu 2. Type of plant-terminalia litoralis. (?).

ta'lo [æ] **2.** Repeat, again, re-. Cf. **Agonta'lo, agon-.** *Hu ta'lo rumipiti i palabra.* I repeated the word again. *Fata'chong ta'lo.* Sit down again. *Chule' ta'lo.* Regain, recover, etc. *Establesi ta'lo.* Re-establish. *Fatto ta'lo.* Come back again.

talo' [æ] **2.** Center, central point of anything. Cf. **Sentro.**

talo'ani 2. Afternoon, noon.

Talofofo Village in southern Guam. Pron. talo'fo'fo'.

talonan 1,2. Kill, overpower. The corpse as a result from fighting (usually refers to cockfighting). Dead cock after cockfight.

tálulo' [æ] **2.** Bullseye, right on the spot.

ta'luyi 1. Add more to, increase in quantity or number. *Hu ta'luyi numa'i hao mas guihan.* I increased giving more fish to you.

tama' 2. Bearing (ball), marbles (playing). (S)

tamanege' 2. Onion—round bulb. Also **tamanenge'.**

tamanes hateng 2. Type of plant-carinta herbacea. (?).

tambo' 2. Unit of measurement—approximately 1, 000 sq. meters. (S)

tambot 2. Drum.

tamong 2. Big, large, huge. (R) Cf. **Dankolo.**

tampat 2. Type of fish-bothus mancus. (Bothidae) flounder, flatfish.

tampe 1,2. Cover up, put lid on. Cover, lid, binding (for books). Cf. **Huchom.** *Hu tampe i guihan ni talaya-mu.* I covered up the fish with your throwing net. *Malingu i tampe.* The lid is lost.

tampen katre 2. Bed cover.

tampen lamasa 2. Tablecloth.

tampen mata 2. Face mask—such as a catcher's mask. Cf. **Masko'.**

tampoku By no means, not in the least, in no condition, in no way, not even, not so much as. *Ti ya-hu mapedde gi huegu tampoku hao.* I don't want to lose in the game, and neither do you. *Tampoku un chachatao pot enao ha' na baban kareta.* In no condition should you be selfish about that junk car.

tamtam [æ] **1.** Test, try out, sip, taste. Cf. **Taña', chagi.**

Tamuning Village and commercial center in central Guam.

tamyao [æ] **1,2.** Juggle, juggling. Also **tangyao.**

tan [æ] **2.** Madam, used as term of respect to address older women or older female relative along with the first name. A short form for *tian*. *Humanao si tan Maria asta Guam.* Madam Mary went to Guam. *Si tan Martha este.* This is Madam Martha.

Tanan Nickname for Juliana.

Tanapag 2. A village located south of San Roque on Saipan. Pron. tanapak.

tancho' [æ] **1.** Select, nominate, point, elect. Cf. **Apunta.**

tandan 2. Rooster—young.

tane' 1. Detain, prevent doing, distracting, keep from doing something, detaining. *Hu tane' i amigu-hu gi gima'-hu.* I detained my friend at my house. *Ha tane' yo' i che'cho'-hu gi eskuela.* My work at school detained me.

tánkala 2. Watery batter—condition of batter when too much water is added.

tánkala 2. Porous, permeable (by water, air, etc.).

tankat 1,2. Cage, a place of confinement, put in a small cage. Used only for small animals, such as birds. *Humalon i paluma gi tankat.* The bird went into the cage. *Ha tankat i gayu nigap.* He caged the rooster yesterday.

tankat gayu 2. Cage for rooster, esp. at cockpits.

tanke 2. Tank, drum (can), large cylindrical can.

tanken 2. Can for, drum for, tank for. *Tanken basula.* Trash can. *Tanken gasilina.* Gasoline drum. *Tanken hanom.* Water tank.

tanko 2. Tank, a heavily armored combat vehicle. (S)

tanme See **tatme.**

tano' 2. World, earth, land, soil, ground. Cf. **Sitio.**

tano' maipe 2. Tropics, tropical land.

tano' manengheng 2. Cold region, cold place.

tanom 1. Plant—seeds or seedlings. Cf. **Tatme.**

tanores 2. Altar boy.

tanso' 2. Clothes closet, wardrobe—usually portable. (S) Cf. **Aparadot, kumuda.**

tanteha 1. Weigh (by lifting), estimate weight by using one's body, esp. with the hand or hands. (R) Also **tantea.** Cf. **Tahlang.** *Hu tanteha i minakkat-mu.* I weighed your weight by lifting you up.

tanto 2. Poker chips, chips—used to keep track of points in a game, total, sum. Also **tantos** (plural form).

tanto Including, even. *Tanto hagu mana'halom gi lista.* Even you are included on the list. *Tanto guiya.* Including him, even he is included, he is also included, he is included too, so is he.

tantos 2. Score, point—number of, record of points made by competitors. Cf. **Kinahulo'.**

tantos di So much of, so many times, so much time, often, repeatedly. Also **tanto di.** *Tantos di ti un atan i pinekkat-mu enao muna'matomba hao.* You were not watching your step often, that was why you fell down. *Tantos di hu espiha hao asta ki guma'chong hit.* I looked for you often until we became partners.

taña' [æ] 1. Taste, sip, try out, test. Cf. **Tamtam, chagi.**

tanga 1. Wish for, long for, hope for, crave, want, set one's heart upon. To wish for something that is unlikely to happen. *Hu tanga lumi'e' Hapon.* I wish to see Japan. *Un tanga chumule' pues un yute'.* You took it with desire, then you discarded it.

tangantangan 2. Type of plant-leucaena leucocephala. A large bush that proliferates on many of the high islands in Micronesia. Good for cattle feed and fuel.

tanges 2. Cry, weep, sob. Cf. **Kati.** *Akgang na tanges.* It is a loud cry. *Akgang i tanges.* The cry is loud. *Tumatanges gue'.* She is crying.

tángganu 2. Stick—used in *batu* game or horseshoes. Also **pituma.** Type of game--contestants try to throw rings onto a vertical stick.

tangison 2. Type of fish-cheilinus undulatus (family labridae). Large wrasse, markings under the eyes suggest that it is crying. Cf. **Tanges.**

tangnga [æ] 2. Deaf, having hearing problem.

tangse 1. Cry for, weep for. Cf. **Katiyi.**

tangsong [æ] 2. High pitched voice. *Tangsong i kati-ña i patgon.* The child's cry was high pitched.

tangyao 1,2. Juggle, perform juggling. Juggling, act of juggling. (R) Also **tamyao.** *Hu tangyao i dos bola gi aire.* I juggled the two balls in the air. *I patgon maolek gi tangyao.* The child is good in juggling.

taoase' 2. Scrub brush, brush—for washing clothes. (S) Also **brochas magagu.**

taohan 2. Aggravate, worsen (the wound), increase inflammation in, heighten in pain. Cf. **Sinilo'.** *Tumaohan i chetnot-hu.* My wound became aggravated.

taotagues 2. Many people of a place. Also **taotaguiyes.** *Ayu siha na taotagues iya sanhaya manmetgot.* Those people from down south are strong.

taotaguiyes 2. Many people of a place, plural of *taotao.* Also **taotagues.**

taotao 2. Human being, person, people, man, guy, folk.

taotao guma' 2. Host, man of the house.

taotao isla 2. People from the other islands of Micronesia.

taotaomo'na 2. Ghost, demon, disembodied soul. Specter. Lit. 'People of before.' Cf. **Birak.**

tap [æ] **2.** Tub, vat, cask. Cf. **Taraí', kalai.**

ta'pang 1. Rinse—salt water by using fresh water, rinse (urine), douche. *I nana ha ta'pang i patgon-ña taftaf gi ega'an.* The mother rinsed the urine off the child early in the morning. *Hu ta'pang i magagu-hu anai matto yo' ginen pumeska.* I rinsed my clothes with fresh water when I came from fishing.

tapbla 2. Board (wood), lumber.

tapbla 2. Draw, even; no winner, as in cockfight or boxing match.

tapbleru 2. Post, traffic sign, signboard, guidepost.

tapblita 2. Shelf, cupboard, hob, mantel, banquette, counter. Cf. **Estante.**

tapblón 2. Plank, thick board.

tapes 1,2. Put on apron, protect dress with an apron. Apron.

taplong 2. Repeat, reiterate.

tapon [æ] **2.** Oyster, any of a genus ostrea or family ostreidae. Any of the marine bivalve mollusks. Clam.

tappe' [æ] **2.** Cap—with bill, helmet--with brim, pith helmet.

tappe' [æ] **2.** Trough, a feeding trough made from hollowed log.

tarabira 1. Turn over again. From *ta'lon bumira.*

tarabira 2. Turn—the opposite direction.

taraha 2. Thread—metal.

taráí' 2. Tub, vat, cask. (S) Cf. **Tap, kalahi.**

tarakitiyu 2. Type of fish-family carangidae. Skipjack, slightly larger than *i'e',* but smaller than *tarakitu.*

tarakitu 2. Type of fish-caranx ignobilis (family carangidae). Skipjack.

tararanas 2. Spiderweb. Also **tararañas.**

tararañas 2. Spider web, cobweb. Also **tararanas.**

tareha 1,2. Assign responsibility, give one a portion of a task to be completed, a portion of a task that is to be completed. (R) Also **tarea.** *Hu tareha i famagu'on che'cho'-ñiha.* I gave the children their task to do. *Si nana-hu ha tareha yo' manbali gi gima'.* My mother gave me a job of sweeping the house.

tareha 2. Chore, assignment.

taru 2. Jar, jug, flask, mug, earthen jar with broad mouth.

tarugu 2. Stupid, stubborn, dunce, mischievous, blockhead. Also **taruga** (f).

tarugu 2. Peg, the strong wooden peg that rests on a beam and supports the rafters of a thatched roof.

tasa 1. Figure out, value, put price on value. *Hu tasa baratu i amko' anai mamahan guihan.* I gave the old man a cheap price when he bought some fish. *Ti guaguan hu tasa hao ni chipa.* I didn't price you high on the cigarettes.

tasa 2. Cup, saucer. Cf. **Pusuelu.**

tasahos 1,2. Slice, chop, cut, esp. meat or clothes, sliced meat, chunk, cloth that has been torn into pieces. Also **tasaos.** *Dankolo tasahos-mu ni katne.* You sliced a big chunk of meat. *Manu nai siña mañule' yo' tasahos magagu para talapos?* Where can I find torn pieces of clothes for rags?

tasi 2. Sea, ocean, beach.

tasme 1. Sharpen—to a point.

tasón 2. Mixing bowl, bowl.

tasyan 2. Mist, caused by surf or heavy waves. (S)

tat- Short form for *taya'* when used as first member of negative compound words. *Tatsiguru kao hu fatto gi Matso.* I doubt whether I'll come in March. *Tattaiguini che'cho'-mu.* You have never done it like this.

tat komu Such as.

tata 2. Father, dad, papa, daddy, male parent.

tátaga' [æ] **2.** Type of fish-naso unicornus (family acanthuridae). Unicorn fishes.

tátaga' [æ] **2.** Slicer, chopper, cutter, one who is capable of cutting.

tataga' halu'u 2. Type of fish-family acanthuridae. Surgeon fish.

tátago' [æ] **2.** Commander, foreman, magistrate, governor.

tátaitai [æ] **2.** Reader, literate person, one who or that which can read. Cf. **Fafanaitai, fanaitai, taitai.**

tátalo' 2. Back, backside—of person or animal.

tátalo' puenge [æ] 2. Midnight, middle of the night.

tátancho' [æ] 2. Forefinger, index finger. Cf. **Tancho'**.

tátaotao 2. Human body. Also **tahtaotao**.

tataranieta 2. Granddaughter (great, great).

tataranietu 2. Grandson (great, great).

tatatmanu Greeting word, but cannot be used by itself, only in a phrase, such as *Hafa tatatmanu hao?* How are you?

tátatse [æ] 2. Poisoner—one who or that which poisons. Cf. **Hihina, bibinenu**.

tátatte 2. Progeny, offspring, descendant.

tatde ti Almost always, usually, always. Contracted form of *taya' nai di* plus *ti*. Without negative particle *ti* the meaning is 'never'. Also **tatke ti, tatnai ti**. *Tatde ti hagu mas tataftaf guatu asta i che'cho'*. You are usually the earliest one there to work. *Tatde hagu mas tataftaf guatu asta i che'cho'*. You are never the earliest one there to work.

tatdes 2. Afternoon, but used only in a phrase, such as, *Buenas tatdes* 'Good afternoon.' Cf. **Talo'ani**.

tatfiét So much of, so great, it is so.... Cf. **Tatfoi**. *Tatfiet i mina'lak-ña i atdao, ha na'maya' yo'*. So great was the brilliance of the sun, it blurred my vision.

tatfoi So much of, so great, it is so... Cf. **Tatfiet**. *Tatfoi i pinalala-ña asta malagu*. He was so much in a rush that he ran. *Tatfoi i hinaspok-hu gi gima' asta ti hu lachai i na'-hu*. I was so full at home that I didn't finish my food. *Tatfoi i mina'o-ku gi tasi asta pumakpak i labios-hu*. I was so thirsty at sea that my lips cracked.

Tatgua 2. Name of a place on Rota.

tatheta 2. Name card.

tatke 1. Defecate on. Cf. **Masinek**. *I patgon ha tatke i katsunes-ña*. The child defecated in his pants.

tatkomu Such as, for example.

tatme 1. Plant—seeds or seedlings. Also **tanme**. Cf. **Tanom**. *Hu tatme i flores gi uriyan guma'*. I planted flowers around the house.

tatme 1. Contaminate, pollute, cause to spread by contact, as a contagious disease, polluter. Also **tanme**.

tatnai Never, none, to no degree. Cf. **Taya' nai**. *Tatnai hu li'e' iya America*. I've never seen America.

tatnai ti Almost always, usually, always, contracted form of *taya' nai di* plus *ti*. Without negative particle *ti* the meaning is 'never'. Also **tatne ti**. Cf. **Tatde ti**. *Tatnai ti hagu mas burukento*. You are almost always the noisiest one.

tatne 1. Bury. Cf. **Hafot**.

tatneru 2. Calf—male. Cf. **Be', turiyu**.

tatnon [æ] 2. Dawdler, poke, one who gets distracted easily, carried away easily.

tatos 2. Bet, wager. Cf. **Aposta**. *Hafa tatos-mu?* What is your bet?

tatse 1. Kill (by poison), infect, impregnate with poison. Cf. **Hina**.

tattamudu 2. Dumb, stupid, slow-witted, feather-brained, dull, stutterer, stammerer (m). Also **tattamuda**(f), **taktamudu**.

tatte 2. Back of, behind, rear, follow, backward, ensue. *Hu na'tatte si Jose as Maria*. I made Joseph follow Maria. *Tumatte si Jose as Maria*. Joseph followed Maria. *Sigi tatte gi kuatto*. Go back to the room. *Sigi tatte*. Go to the rear.

tattiyi 1. Follow, pursue, chase, trail. Cf. **Tatte**.

tatu 1,2. Tattoo.

taya' Nothing, never, none, naught, zero. Cf. **Nunka, hokkok**. *Taya' salape'-hu*. I don't have any money. *Taya' hao nai manbisita gi espitat*. You have never visited the hospital.

taya' nai Never, none at all, to no degree. Cf. **Tatnai**. *Taya' nai un hasso i totno-mu*. You never thought of your turn.

ta'yok [æ] 2. Jump, hop, skip.

táyuyot 1. Implore, pray to, beg, ask for, cry to, beseech, call upon in urgent supplication. *Tayuyot i saina ya u guaha pas gi tano'*. Implore the Lord so that there will be peace in the world.

tayuyuti 1. Pray for. *Para bai hu tayuyuti hao*. I will pray for you.

te T—letter.

tebbot 2. Container, an earthenware container.

tébiu 2. Warm liquid, slightly hot. Also **tibiu.** Cf. **Ha'me.**

techa 2. One who leads prayers, prayer director. Cf. **Tucha.**

techo 2. Roof, ceiling. Cf. **Atof.**

teha 2. Tile, shingle—for roofing.

tehnan 2. Leftover, what else, remaining, left. *Hafa tehnan hao?* What else have you? *Hafa tehnan?* What is left?

te'i 2. Sprinkle (of water), scattered shower. Also **tette.** *Teti'i i ichan.* It's sprinkling rain.

tekcha' 2. Fruitful, prolific, fertile.

tekcho' 2. Predatory, predacious, carnivorous, carnivore, cannibal, eater of raw flesh. Cf. **Fakla'.** *Tekcho' i ga'lagu binadu.* The dog is a deer eater. *I taotao tekcho' chada'.* The man is a raw egg eater.

tekken 2. Gill net, fish net.

tekkeng 2. Rod—used in construction, such as a reinforcing steel. (S) Cf. **Bariya.**

tekkon 2. Bow, bend head and body down. Cf. **Ñehom.**

tekla 2. Key (piano), typewriter key.

tekla 2. Piano key.

telebikbik 2. Television (G).

telefón 1,2. Call by telephone, communicate by telephone, speak on a telephone. Telephone, phone.

telefon alaihai 2. Gossip, by the grapevine. *Hiningok-mu ha' enao gi telefon alaihai.* You just heard that by the grapevine.

telegrama 2. Telegram, dispatch.

teles 2. Drunk, drunken, intoxicated, inebriated, tipsy, tight. (R) Cf. **bulachu.**

teleskopiu 2. Telescope, viewer, binoculars, spyglass. Cf. **Lagabista.**

temos 2. Thermos bottle. (R) Also **tetmosa.**

templa 1. Adjust, tune (engine), mix, blend. *Hu templa i gimen-hu kafe.* I mixed my coffee.

templada 2. Adjustment, mixture, tuning, blending.

templáo 2. Mixable, tuned-up, tunable, anything that is capable of being mixed or tuned. *Esta templao i gitala.* The guitar has already been tuned up.

templo 2. Temple.

témpura' 2. Tempura—deep fried fish or shrimp that has been dipped in batter of flour and starch. (S) Also **totta.**

ten 2. Tent. (G).

tenda 2. Store, market.

tenderu 2. Clerk—sales, storekeeper (m). Also **tendera** (f).

tenedót 2. Bookmaker, one who keeps track of the betting on one of the cocks at cockfights.

tenedot di libro 2. Accountant, bookkeeper.

téneki Surely, certainly, definitely, must. From Spanish tener que. Also **tieneki.** *Teneki u ma li'e' hao gi* They will surely see you at the party. *Teneki hu saolak hao.* I'm going to spank you for sure.

tenhos 2. Impatient, impatience, jealous. (R)

Tenhos 2. August. Cf. **Agosto.**

ténidot 2. Fork.

tenidot basula 2. Pitchfork.

tenta 1. Tempt, seduce, entice.

tentago' 2. Servant, attendant, messenger.

tentanchinu 2. Type of plant-cestrum diurnum. A type of tree.

tentasión 2. Temptation.

Tente' Nickname for Vicente.

tento' 2. Tent, canvas supported by poles, canvas.

tenga Usually, often, most of the time. *Tenga, un sangan na ti ya-mu guihan.* Usually you say that you dislike fish. *Hafa na ti un kanno' i satmon lao tenga un mensiona na gof ya-mu.* Why didn't you eat the salmom, since you usually mention that you like it very much.

tengguang 1,2. Food (carried as supplies), provisions (food), box lunch, to take food to be eaten, as a lunch, picnic supper.

tengteng 1. Nick (blade), chip, put a nick in the blade of a tool, break off —esp. hard or brittle substance. (R) Cf. **Doffe', mafte'.** *Ma tengteng i se'se'.* They nicked the blade of the knife.

te'ok 2. Thick (liquid), thick consistency, strong (coffee, tea). *Te'ok na kaddo.* It is a thick soup. *I palao'an hu na'te'ok i kaddo-ña.* The woman made her soup thicker.

teppang 2. Metal sheet. (S) Also **piesan metat.**

teripble 2. Terrible.

teritoriát 2. Territorial.

teritoriu 2. Territory, domain, land.

terudang 2. Hand grenade, bomb—incendiary. (S)

tesgue 1. Cheat, deceive, defraud, dupe, trick. Cf. **Fa'baba.**

tesna 2. Charcoal dust, be covered with charcoal dust, soot.

tesoreria 2. Treasury. Also **tresurat.**

tesoru 2. Treasure.

tesson 2. Fire stick (partly burned), charred stick, ember, partly burned fire stick, brand, firebrand.

testamento 2. Testament.

testigu 2. Witness, testifier, attestor, deponent, one who gives testimony.

testiguyi 1. Testify, attest.

testimoniu 2. Testimony, attestation, act of testifying.

te'te' 1. Drain pus, to puncture an infection for purpose of draining. Cf. **Tucha.**

Tete' Nickname for Margarita, Vicente.

tétenan 2. Left over, remains, remainder, unfinished. Also **tetehnan, tetenhan.** Cf. **Sopbla.** *Este ha' tetenan gi salape'-hu.* This is all that was left over of my money. *Hayi tetenan ti mafatto?* Who remains missing? (Who else did not come?)

tetenhan 2. Remainder, left-over, left. Also **tetenan.**

tétmenu 2. Time, period, alloted time, a period of time alloted, as for a visa, contract, etc. *Bai hu na'i hao tres meses na tetmenu.* I will grant you a three month period. *I tetmenu-mu fatta un añu.* Your alloted time is one more year.

tetmina 1. Terminate, limit or bound.

tétmomentro 2. Thermometer.

tetmosa 2. Thermos. Also **temos.**

tetno 2. Pair, couplet, match, couple, same, of like kind (sort, degree). Cf. **Pat, parehu.**

tetno Matching blouse and skirt of mestisa dress.

tets 2. Target, as in a game of marbles or batu, in which contestants throw marbles, coins, discs at a target. Also used at times to refer to a base in games.

tetseru 2. Third.

tetsét 2. Third.

tette 2. Sprinkle, misty, overspread (with drops or particles of water), scattered shower. Also **teti.** Cf. **Te'i.** *Tette i ichan anai humanao yo' para i eskuela.* There was a sprinkle of rain when I went to school. *Hu na'tette i hanom anai hu rega i flores.* I sprinkled the water when I watered the plant.

ti Not (negative marker).

ti annok 2. Invisible, concealed.

ti apmam 2. Momentary, short duration, not for long, short while, a while, soon.

ti atanon 2. Horrid, dreadful, hideous.

ti chumá'igi Tie game, even-score, deuce game, no competition, no contest. *Ti chuma'igi hit gi tes nigap.* We had an even-score on the test yesterday.

ti chuma'on 2. Incorrigible.

ti fina'baba 2. Allegiance, fidelity to cause.

ti gobietnayon 2. Unruly, ungovernable.

ti guáilayi Don't, not necessary. *Ti guailayi malak i tasi.* Don't go to the ocean. *Ti guailayi si Jose mana'egga' mubi.* Don't let Joe see the movie. *Ti guailayi un hugando ni salape'.* It is not necessary to gamble with money.

ti guaiyayon 2. Hateful, repugnant.

ti kabales 2. Imperfect, incomplete.

ti kahulo' 2. Fail, fall short, deficient.

ti komprendiyon 2. Incoherent, incomprehensible.

ti kontento 2. Discontented, envious.

ti mamafnas 2. Indelible.

ti manieniente 2. Numb, torpid. Cf. **Ma'etdot.**

ti ma'ok 2. Transitory, fleeting.

ti mappot 2. Simple, easy, not difficult. Cf. **Ñalalang.**

ti masa 2. Raw, uncooked.

ti naturát 2. Abnormal, not natural.

ti sungunon 2. Overbearing, domineering. Cf. **sungon.**

ti'ao 2. Type of fish-upeneus vittatus (family mullidae). Goatfishes.

tibi 2. Tuberculosis, TB, tubercular, consumptive. Cf. **Soksok.**

tíbiu 2. Tepid, warm. Also **tebiu.**

tiempo 2. Weather, time, length of time.

tiempon somnak 2. Dry season, summer, sultry condition. Cf. **Fanomnagan.**

tiempon uchan 2. Wet season, rainy season. Cf. **Fanuchanan, fañata'an.**

tieneki Then, surely, definitely, certainly. Cf. **Siempre.** (Fr. Sp. tener que). Also **teneke.** *Tieneki, ti bumola yo' sa' appleng i kannai-hu.* I surely won't play ball because my hand is sprained. *Tieneki, ma li'e' hao gi gipot.* Surely they will see you at the party.

tienta 1. Tempt, persuade, lead into evil, endeavor to lead into evil.

tieras 2. Scissors. Also **tiheras.**

tieras pugua' 2. Special type of scissors for cutting betel nut. Also **tiheras pugua'.**

tife' 1. Pick, break off, esp. the fruit from trees, vines, etc., pull (a tooth). Cf. **Iteng, tugan.**

tiges 1. Smash, crush, mash, stamp, crumble, step on. Cf. **Yamak.**

tígiri 2. Tiger.

tigre 2. Type of plant-sansevieria sp. (?).

tiguang- 2. Fellow man, brotherhood, neighborhood. (Used with possessive pronouns). *Bai hu sungon i tiguang-hu.* I will bear my fellow man.

tiha 2. Aunt. Also **tia.**

tiheras 2. Scissors, cross-beam. Also **tieras.**

tihu 2. Uncle. Also **tiu.**

tika 1. Make coconut oil, to make oil from the coconut by boiling grated coconut meat and filtering the oil.

tika 2. Coconut oil—before it has been separated.

Tika Nickname for Francisca.

tiket 2. Ticket, citation.

Tiku Nickname for Francisco.

tilapia 2. Kind of fish. Fresh water fish. Also **talapia.**

tilentines 2. Trinkets, such as shells, beads, sequins used for ornamenting hair or clothes. Also **tirentines.**

tilingteng 1,2. Clink, ding, tinkle, jingle. Cf. **Tingteng.** *Tilingteng i buteya siha gi halom i kahon.* The bottles clinked inside the box.

tilipas 2. Intestines, entrails.

tilipas 2. Hose, garden hose.

Tima' Nickname for Thomas.

Timo' Nickname for Maximo.

timón 1,2. Steer (with a rudder), guide (with a rudder). Rudder. Cf. **Sugon, draiba.**

timoneru 2. Steerer, the guide, driver.

tina 2. Barrel (small), keg. Cf. **Bariles.**

Tina Nickname for Asuncion.

tinacho' [æ] 2. Type of sickness, believed to be caused by being stared at while eating. (R)

tinaddong [æ] 2. Depth. *Tres pie tinaddong-ña i maddok.* The depth of the hole is three feet.

tinaga' [æ] 2. Cut—by heavy object. Cf. **Chinachak.**

tinaha [æ] 2. Crock, a container made of clay.

tinaha [æ] 2. Unit of measurement (bushel), 12 *gantas.*

tinaichi 2. Eternity.

tináifondo 2. Hell, abyss.

tinaitai 2. Tree—bent by wind and still attached to the land. Also **lamasa.**

tinaitai 2. Prayer, reading.

tinake' [æ] 2. Tarnished, rusted.

tinaktak [æ] 2. Type of food—a meat dish in which the meat is chopped into small pieces; the process of chopping or mincing meat. Cf. **taktak.**

tinane' [æ] 2. Busy, become busy, need to go to the toilet, occupied time, preoccupied. *Tuminane' i amigu-hu gi gima'-ñiha.* My friend was busy at their house. *Despensa hun gue' ya u tinane'.* He asked to be excused for he needs to go to the toilet.

tinanom [æ] 2. Plant, as in the garden.

tinanga [æ] 2. Craving, desire, longing.

tinangnga [æ] 2. Deafness.

tinaohan 2. Aggravate (wound or sore), inflamation. Also **tinao'an.** Cf. **Sisitan.**

tinasa [æ] 2. Pliers, tongs, pincers, tweezers, forceps.

tinatme [æ] 2. Contaminated.

tináyuyot [æ] 2. Prayer. Cf. **Tayuyot.**

tinekcha' 2. Fruit (on a plant), puncture. *Tinekcha' i kalulot-hu ni haguha.* My finger was punctured by the needle. *Dankolo i tinekcha' chandia.* The fruit of the watermelon is big.

tinemba 2. Depression, low spirits.

tinemtom 2. Wisdom. Cf. **Tomtom.**

Tinian 2. Tinian, the island immediately south of Saipan in the Marianas District. (Pronounced tini'an).

tinienta 1. Tempted.

tinifok 2. Webbing, woven or braided work.

tinilada 2. Ton. Also **tonelada.**

tinilaika 2. Alteration, mutation, variation.

tinina 2. Praise, blessing.

tininas 2. Honesty.

tininu 2. Piles, hemorrhoids.

tiningo' 2. Knowledge, learning, enlightenment. Cf. **Tungo'. Takhilo'** i tiningo'-ña. His knowledge is great.

tinitu 2. Shelled rice, pounded coffee.

tinta 2. Ink.

tinteru 2. Ink maker, ink well.

Tinung Nickname for Faustino.

tingteng 2. Clink, ding, tinkle, jingle. *Tingteng i sensiyu gi betsa-ku.* The loose change jingled in my pocket. *Tingteng i basu anai ma'otto gi lamasa.* The cup clinked when it hit the table.

tiot All. From *todu i* as in *todu i tiempo. Tiot tiempo machocho'cho' yo'.* I work all the time.

tiot tiempo Forever, all the time.

tira 1. Pitch (underhand), throw (underhand), as horseshoes, or when skipping a flat rock on the surface of water, toss, toss up. *Hu tira duru i bola.* I threw the ball hard (by an underhand pitch.)

tirante 2. Strap, suspender.

tiratira 2. Thick syrup—for making candy.

tirayi 1. Throw to, throw for, sic—used as command to a dog.

tirentines See **tilentines.**

tirenu 2. Field, tract, terrain.

tiru 2. Sound of gun shot, round of shots. *Mamaki yo' un tiru.* I fired one shot. *Hu hungok i tiru anai un paki i binadu.* I heard the sound of shot when you shot the deer.

tisage' 2. Hand bag (made from weaving), woven bag. (R) Cf. **Kottot, balakbak.**

tison chili 2. Erection—of penis. Also lalalo' chili.

tisu 2. Erect, stiff, straight, rigid, tense, taut. *Tumisu i abuchuelas anai mapo'lo gi halom kahon ais.* The

string bean was stiff when it was placed in the refrigerator.

tisu 2. Unconscious, fainted, not conscious, fall in a swoon, knocked out. Cf. **Lalangu, mamaitaguan.**

Titan Nickname for Teresita.

títanos 2. Brain.

titek 1. Tear off, rip. Cf. **Sisi.**

títenta 2. Dying agent, stainer, painter. (S) Cf. **Pepenta, tutumu.**

titeng 1. Carry—by 2 people using both hands as in carrying a stretcher. Also **titen.**

títienta 2. Tempter, enticer, capable of enticing.

títimu 2. Type of plant-jussiaea suffruticosa. A type of grass.

títimu 2. Type of plant-eclipta alba. A type of grass.

títires 2. Buffoon, oaf.

titiyas 2. Tortillas.

títokcha' 2. Bee stinger.

Titu Nickname for Jacinto.

títufok 2. Weaver—of mats or baskets. Cf. **Mamamfok.**

títuge' 2. Writer, penman, calligrapher, calligraphist.

títuge' Author.

títugi 2. Type of eel-gymnothorax pictus (family muraenidae). Moray eels. Cf. **Hakmang, ñotak.**

títuka' 2. Thorn, usually comes from trees, bushes, or vines; barb.

títula 2. Title, inscription, heading, caption, position, style, appellation, rank. Cf. **Pusision, gradu.**

títumu 2. Dyer, stainer, one who dyes. Cf. **Titenta.**

to'a 2. Mature (fruit), mature mind, fruit—ready for picking. *To'a esta iteng-ña i chetda.* The bunch of bananas is ready for picking. *I sotteru to'a esta hinasso-ña.* The bachelor's mind has already been developed.

to'chong 1. Connect by tying.

to'chong 2. Type of knot, slip knot, flat knot, reef knot.

todábia See **trabiha.**

todu All, everything, entire. Cf. **Puru, enteru.**

todu esta Everything, already.

todu i dos Both.

todu i lugat 2. Everywhere, in every place, places, all over, in all throughout the world.

todu i tiempo 2. All the time, every time.

to'he 1. Drop (liquid), give a drop of liquid. Also **to'i.** Cf. **Gota.** *To'he tres gota.* Add three drops.

tohge 2. Stand up, erect. Also **toge.** *Tohge tunas.* Stand up straight. *Tumohge yo' gi hilo' i siya.* I stood up on the chair.

tohke 2. Chime, stroke of the hour, ring of the bell.

tohlai See **tollai.**

tohne 1,2. To brace, support so as to give firmness, support with a brace. Also **tone.** Brace, strut, prop, stanchion. *Hu tohne i bentana sa' mayulang.* I braced the window because it was broken. *Ha tohne gue' gi lamasa.* He braced himself against the table.

to'i 1. Drop liquid. See **to'he.**

toka 2. Be caught, be trapped, be snared, be hit. *Toka i paluma anai hu paki.* I hit the bird when I shot it.

tokante As long as, so far as. Cf. **Kontat ki.** *Tokante ki ti hu li'e'.* As long as I don't see it.

tokcha' 1,2. Spear, stab, pierce. Spear, lance. Cf. **Lansa, fisga.**

tokche 1. Extend, splice, connect, make longer. Also **totche.**

tokpong 2. Handle (of tool).

tokpong eskoba 2. Broom handle.

tokpong lampasu 2. Mop handle.

tokpungi 1. Make handle for. Cf. **Tokpong.** *Hu tokpungi i machette.* I made a handle for the machete.

toktok 1. Hug, embrace, hold fast.

toktok 2. Cluck—as when the hen calls for her chicks.

toktugák 2. Cackle, cackling, sound of a hen, esp. after laying.

to'la' 2. Saliva, spittle, spit, sputum.

to'la'i 1. Spit at. *Ha to'la'i i ga'lagu.* He spit at the dog.

to'lang 2. Bone, skeleton.

to'lang satnot 2. Shin bone.

toleti 2. Oarlock.

tollai 2. Bridge. Also **tohlai.**

tolleng 1. Cause to stumble, to trip—by catching foot on something. Also **tohleng.** Cf. **Gua'deng.** *Ha tolleng yo' i acho'.* The rock caused me to trip. *Matolleng siha gi inai.* They were tripped in the sand.

tolleng 1. Fool, trick, hoax, dupe.

tomba 1. Knock down.

tommo 2. Knee, elbow.

tommon kannai 2. Elbow, lit. knee of the hand. Cf. **Tommon kodu.**

tommon kodu 2. Elbow, lit. knee of the arm. Cf. **Tommon kannai.**

tompo' 1. To trip, cause to stumble, stub one's toe. Cf. **Tolleng.** *Hu tompo' i ma'estro ni addeng-hu.* I tripped the teacher with my foot.

tomtom 2. Smart, intelligent, clever, brilliant. Cf. **Malate', kabilosu, menhalom.**

tomu 2. Tome, volume.

ton 2. Mister, sir—used as respect when addressing an old man. Cf. **Tun.**

Ton Nickname for Antonio. Also **Tong.**

Tona' Nickname for Antonia.

tonada 2. Accent—as a foreign accent when speaking.

tonelada 2. Ton (2000 lbs.). Also **tinilada.**

tonnas 2. Stick—larger than *balas.*

tonteria 2. Stupidity, nonsense, folly, silly action, blunder, foolish pranks.

tonto 2. Foolish, fool, nonsense, silly (m). Also **tonta** (f).

tonu 2. Tune, tone.

Tong Nickname for Antonio. Also **Ton.**

tongho 2. Nape—of neck, neck--the back side. Cf. **Kueyu.**

tongtong 1. Pound, beat, batter, bang against, strike heavily or repeatedly with fist. Cf. **Tutu, fongfong.**

toreru 2. Bullfighter.

toreti 2. Steer, ox (young).

tori 2. Tower. *Bula tori giya America.* There are lots of towers in America.

toriyu 2. Type of fish-cowfish. A small fish with hard plates with two frontal spines resembling horns.

toriyu 2. Steer, young bull—not ready for breeding. Also **toreti.**

toron binadu 2. Stag, the male deer, buck.

toropela 2. Propeller. (R)

toropidu 1,2. Torpedo. (R)

toru 2. Bull, buck.

toru 2. To crawl—on hands and knees. (R) *Tumoru i patgon gi satge.* The child crawled on the floor.

toru 2. Spider shell, seashell.

tosta 1,2. Toast, scorch, parch, dry up, dried from heat, cooked to a crisp.

Hu tosta i pan gi halom hotno. I toasted the bread in the oven.

tostos 2. Burned, crispy, dehydrated, dried from heat, toasted, overcooked to a crisp. Cf. **Akong.**

tot 2. Toad. Cf. **Kairo'.**

totbos 1. Bump against, collide with. Cf. **Totpe.**

totche 1. Dunk, dip—something into liquid. *Ha totche i pan gi leche.* He dunked the bread in the milk.

totche 2. Protein, food such as meat, fish, crab, or egg.

totche See **tokche.**

totda 2. Roof of vehicle.

totko 2. Idiot, fool, utterly senseless person, blockhead.

totmento 2. Torment, anguish, torture, pain.

totniyu 1,2. Screw, turn (as a screw). Screw, bolt—a pin or rod, esp. of steel, to fasten or hold something in place, often having a head at one end and a screw thread on the other, nut--used on a bolt or screw for tightening or holding something. *Hu totniyu i banko kontra i satge.* I screwed the bench down on the floor. *Mana'mafnot i totniyu gi petta.* The nut was tightened on the door.

totno 2. Turn, be on duty, alternate order, as 'It's my turn now.' *Totno-hu agupa'.* Tomorrow is my turn. *Tumotno yo' gi Sabalu.* I was on duty Saturday.

totnge 1. Ignite (a fire). Cf. **Songge.**

to'to 2. Lie down on back, recline on back. *Hu na'to'to i patgon.* I laid the baby down on its back.

to'to' 1. Pick (leaves by hand). Also **toto.** *I bihu ha to'to' i hagon chupa.* The old man picked the tobacco leaves.

toto 1. Tear off leaf, break (branch off tree). Also **to'to'.**

Toto 2. Name of village in Guam.

tótonok 2. Go down. Cf. **Tunok.** *Bai hu totonok asta i gima'-mu.* I will go down to your house.

totot 2. Type of bird-philinopus roseicapillus, Marianas fruit dove.

totot 2. Cluck—as when the hen calls for her chicks. Also **tottok, tuktuk.**

totpe 1. Bump (against), collide with, strike, knock, or thump. Cf. **Totbos.**

totpidu 2. Torpedo. Also **toropidu.**

totta 2. Porch floor—of cement. Cf. **Satge.**

totta 2. Deep fried fish or shrimp that has been dipped in batter. Also **tempura'.**

tottok See **totot.**

toyo' 1. Poke, nudge, jog, jostle, jolt. Cf. **Sokkok.** *Ha toyo' i mata-hu ni tommo-ña.* He poked my face with his elbow. *Hu toyo' i amigu-hu gi tatalo'-ña.* I nudged my friend in his back.

traba 1. To tie, bond, twist (rope), entangle.

trabadót 2. Industrious, energetic. Cf. **Brabu, butmuchachu.**

trabadót 2. Rope maker, one who makes ropes.

trabahadót 2. Industrious, energetic. Also **trabadot.** Cf. **Brabu, butmuchachu.**

trabiha Yet, still, not yet, still unfinished. Also **trabia, todabia.** *Ti munhahayan yo' trabiha.* I am not finished yet. *Kao trabiha ti humahanao hao?* Didn't you leave yet?

trabisañu 2. Transom, a transverse in a structure, the horizontal bar of a cross, gallow, etc. Also **atrabisañu.** *Gaige i tihong-hu na masasa'ang gi trabisaño.* My hat was put on top of the crossbeam.

trabuka 1. Mess, disarrange, dishevel, make a mess, disorder.

tradisionát 2. Traditional.

tragón 2. Greedy, avaricious.

trahi 2. Looks, appearance, suit—of clothes for men. *Applacha' trahi-ña gi gipot.* His clothes were dirty at the party.

trahoma 2. Trachoma.

traianggo' 2. Triangle. (R) Also **trianggulu.**

traiangula 2. Triangular.

traidót 2. Traitor, unfaithful, treacherous.

traiduti 1. Betray, trick, attack from the rear, break faith with, ambush. Cf. **Trampasi, fa'baba, dugeruyi.** *Hu traiduti i binadu anai hu paki.* I ambushed the deer when I shot it.

traisión 2. Ambush, betrayal, fraud, deception, treason, treachery.

trak 2. Truck, vehicle.

trak guafi 2. Fire truck.

trak kimasón 2. Fire truck. Also trak guafi.

tramoha 1. Tie down, lash down, knot, secure. Cf. Gramaderu, godde.

trampas 2. Trick, stratagem, artifice, ruse, wile.

trampasi 1. Trick, defraud, cheat, dupe, swindle, double cross, deceiveby cunning or artifice. Cf. Fa'baba, traiduti.

tramposu 2. Swindler, rogue, crook, cheating, tricking.

tranka 1,2. Cage, bar—to prevent children from going out a door of house, enclosure, gate, gateway, entrance of fence.

trankilu 2. Tranquil, peaceful life, calm, undisturbed.

transferi 1. Transfer, transport, convey from one place to another. Also trasfieri.

translada 1. Translate, decode, turn from one language into another, interpret. Also transulada.

transplanta 1. Transplant, replant, plant in a new place.

transpotta 1. Transport, transfer, convey from one place to another. Also traspotta.

transpottasión 2. Transportation.

trapát 2. Canvas. Cf. Brin.

trapichi 2. Sugar mill, the device used to squeeze the sap of the sugar cane.

tras Besides, moreover. Na'saonao yo' bumola tras iyo-ku i bola. Let me join the ball (game), besides, the ball is mine.

trasfieri See transferi.

traskila 1. Shave (sideburn), trim lower part of haircut all around.

trasoras Occasionally. Also asolas.

traspotta See transpotta.

trastes 2. Material, equipment, device, implement, tool.

trastes guma' 2. Domestic.

trastes halom guma' 2. Furniture.

trata 2. Treat, act toward, behave toward. Trata yo' komu taotao. Treat me as a human being.

tratos 1,2. Bargain, make a deal, contract. deal. Si Juan ha tratos yo' ni ga'-ña guaka. John gave me a bargain on his cow. Guaha tratos-hu

giya Guam. I have a bargain on Guam.

trela 2. Trailer—a highway vehicle designed to be hauled, esp. by an automotive vehicle.

trenchera 2. Trench.

trensiyas 2. Rickrack.

trenta 2. Thirty. Also trienta.

tres 2. Three.

tres siete 2. Card game (Chamorro), similar to hearts, lit. three sevens.

tresse 2. Thirteen.

tresurát 2. Treasury.

tresureru 2. Treasurer. Cf. Kaheru.

triánggulu See traianggo'.

tribu 2. Tribute.

tribunát 2. Prison, jail, place for criminals while serving their sentences. Cf. Kalabosu, presu.

trienta 2. Thirty. Also trenta.

trienta i unu 2. Thirty-one.

trigu 2. Kind of plant—wheat. Cf. Fa'i.

Trinidát 2. Trinity, triune God, threefold unity, the trinity in unity.

triniste 2. Sadness, melancholy, unhappiness, despondency, cheerlessness, deprivation of joy.

tripulasión 2. Tripling—in large numbers.

triste 2. Sad, full of grief, gloomy, sorrowful, downcast, grievous. Triste yo' pot hagu. I was sad because of you.

troki 1,2. Exchange, trade off, swap, change for another.

trompada 1. Sock, punch—in the face, slap--in the face. Cf. Trompunasu, seku.

trompesón 2. Junk, waste, refuse, scrap, discard as worthless. Cf. Embarasu.

trompón 2. Fist, the clenched hand.

trompunasu 1,2. Sock, punch, hit with the fist. Cf. Seku, pañiti, dommo'.

tronko 1. Punch, sock. Cf. Pañiti, dommo', seku, trompunasu.

tronko 2. Trunk, stem, tree.

tronko 2. Head of family, head of household.

tronkon agalonde 2. Type of plant-vitex negundo. (?).

tronkon boforeng 2. Type of plant-acacia kauaiensis, acacia koaia. (?).

tronkon gaogao 2. Type of plant-erythina corallodendron. (?).

tronkon gaogao uchan 2. Type of plant-phyllanthus marianus. (?).

tronkon hayu 2. Tree.

tronkon mames 2. Type of plant-albizia lebbeck. Type of tree.

tronkon papaya 2. Type of plant-carica papaya. Papaya.

tronkon pugua' Type of tree—betel.

tronkon sósigi 2. Type of plant-acacia kauaiensis, acacia koaia.

tronu 2. Throne.

tropa 2. Troop, army.

troson lamlam 2. Thunderbolt, bolt of lightning. Cf. **Talangan hulu.**

trosu 2. Chunk, a short, thick fragment, as of wood, meat, metal, etc., timber, section of cut wood, log, solid whole mass. *Troson hayu.* Timber. *Troson lulok.* A chunk of metal, steel, or any metallic materials. *Troson sensen.* A chunk of meat or fish.

trosu 2. Type of food—pot roast.

trukos 1. Punch (in the face), sock (in the face), hit (in the face).Cf. **Pañiti, dommo', seku.**

trumosu 2. Logging, to cut logs.

tu'aya 2. Towel, wash cloth. Also **tuaya.**

tuba 2. Bud of coconut tree, juice which is tapped from bud of coconut tree which ferments very quickly. Beverage from sap of coconut tree. Coconut sap, toddy, notch put in a tree to ease climbing.

tuban chá'ka 2. Type of plant-corchorus aestuans. Wild jute.

tubatuba 2. Type of plant-jatropha curcas. Physic nut.

tubon ilektrik 2. Light bulb. Cf. **glop.**

tubon pi'ao 2. Reed pipe, bamboo pipe.

tubu 2. Lamp globe, the glass part of a lantern which protects the flame from the wind, drain pipe, duct. Cf. **Fala'.**

tucha 1. Puncture, pierce, to lead or start a prayer. *Hu tucha i manha ya hu gimen.* I punctured the green coconut and drank it. *Si pale' ha tucha i lisayu gi gima' Yu'us.* The priest led the rosary in the church.

tucho' 1. To eat raw meat, or fleshy foods such as eggs, eat cooked food without any manners, eat savagely. Cf. **Fala'.** *I katu ha tucho' i cha'ka.* The cat ate the rat. *Hu tucho' i tininon guihan.* I ate ravenously the barbequed fish.

tuchu 1. Catch—a prey, as a cat catching a mouse. Also **atuchuchu, tucho'.**

tufai 2. Haggard, worn out, depressed by old age. (R) Cf. **Debet.**

tufok 1. Weave. Cf. **Mamfok.** *I palao'an ha tufok i kanastra.* The woman wove the basket.

tufong 1. Count. Cf. **Mamfong.**

tufungon 2. Countable, can be counted. From *tufong* plus -on.

tugan 1. Break off, pick from tree.

tugap 2. Burp, belch, eruct.

tuge' 1. Write, tabulate. *Hu tuge' i katta.* I wrote the letter.

tugi'i 1. Write to (someone), write for (someone). *Hu tugi'i si Maria ni katta.* I wrote the letter to Maria.

tugong 1. Rush, charge at. Cf. **Sufa'.** *Ha tugong yo' i ga'lagu.* The dog charged at me.

tugot 1. Crush—with fingers, as to crush a flea or louse.

tugua' 1. Scythe—to cut with, to mow with a scythe.

tugua' 1. Strike down, throw down, hit down, as in batu (game).

tuho' 2. Drip, leak. Also **tu'o'.**

tuhong 2. Hat, sombrero, cap.

tuhong tappe' 2. Helmet, hat.

tuhos 2. Have too much fun, good time, have access, over-joy, have available, have surplus, overindulge, overdo. Cf. **Dafflok, mutero' , motgan, go'dan, dafflokgue, malulok.** *Ya-hu na un tuhos gi bi'ahi-mu.* I want you to have a good time on your trip.

tuka 1. Start, commence, begin. Cf. **Tutuhon.** *Hu tuka i kombetsasion.* I started the conversation.

tukadót 2. Dressing table, boudoir.

tuktuk See **totot.**

tulaika 1. Exchange, trade, replace, substitute. Cf. **Despacha, a'go, kuentayi.**

tulaikayon 2. Exchangeable. Cf. **Tulaika.**

tulanoche 2. Night—all, evening--all.

tuleti 1. To row, to propel with two oars.

tulisán 2. Devilish, rascal, hussy, scoundrel, rogue, tricky person, fool, moron. Cf. **Mahadera, petbetsa.**

tulompo 2. Spinning top, play with a top. *Tumulompo yo' yan i che'lu-hu.* I played spinning tops with my brother. *Dankolo i tolompo-ku.* My spinning top is big.

tulondron 2. Congeal.

tulongtong 1. Pound—as in hammering or washing clothes, pound against, as in a car going over a bumpy road. *Hu tulongtong i magagu-hu gi bateha.* I pounded my clothes on the washboard. *Un tulongtong i ilu-ña anai mumu-hamyo.* You pounded his head when you fought (together).

tulos 1,2. Propel boat—by using a pole. Cf. **Poksai.** Pole--for poling a boat, oar.

tumachon pulu Bristle, as when an animal's hair bristles when excited.

tumachu [æ] **2.** Upright, vertical.

tumáiganas 2. Become nauseated, no appetite, become sick at stomach. Cf. *Taiganas.*

tumaiguenao 2. Become like that—close to the listener. *Tumaiguenao kulot-ña i magagu-hu anai fotgon.* The color of my clothes became like that when they were wet.

tumaiguihi 2. Become like that—away from listener and speaker. *Tumaiguihi hao siempre chunge'-mu i biu-hu.* Your hair will probably become as white as that of my grandfather.

tumaiguini 2. Become like this. *Tumaiguini i lassas-ña anai matunu gi guafi.* His skin became like this when he was burned in the fire.

Tumaiguini 2. January. Cf. **Eneru.**

tuma'lo [æ] **2.** Return, restore to original size, shape, or condition. Cf. **Na'lo.**

tumátatte 2. Subsequently, later.

tumates 2. Type of plant-solanum lycopersicum. Tomato.

tumates aga'ga' 2. Tonsils.

tumates aniti 2. Type of plant-desmodium gangeticum. Tomato.

tumates cha'ka 2. Type of plant-physalis angulata. Ground cherry.

tumates kaputi 2. Type of plant-physalis lanceifolia. Cherry tomato. Also **tumates halom tano'.**

tumates ubas 2. Type of plant-solanum lycopersicum. Cherry tomato.

tumaya' 1,2. Dispense with, do without. Cf. **Taya'.**

tumobet 2. Automobile, car, sedan, vehicle. Cf. **Kareta, sahyan.**

tumo'la' 2. Spit out, expectorate, eject. *Tumo'la' i patgon gi hilo' odda'.* The child spit on the ground.

tumu 1,2. Coloring, dye. Cf. **Titenta.**

tumunok 2. Descend.

tun 2. Mister, sir—used as respect when addressing an elderly male. Distinct from *Ton* in speech of some Chamorros; *Ton* is more formal.

tuna 1. Laud, extol, praise highly, compliment. Cf. **Fama.**

tuna 2. Type of fish-katsuwonus pelamis. Tuna.

tunada 2. Tune, tone, sound; dialect.

tunante 2. Disrespectful, rogue, lewd person.

tunas 2. Straight, erect, upright. Cf. **Tachu.**

tunayon 2. Praiseworthy, laudable, admirable.

túniku 2. Garment, habit.

tuninos 2. Porpoise, dolphin.

tunok 2. Get down, let down. *Tunok papa' gi tronkon hayu.* Get down from the tree. *Tumunok yo' ginen i katre.* I got down from the bed.

tunu 1. Burn, barbecue, scald, broil.

tungo' 1. Know, be acquainted with, have knowledge of, recognize, distinguish, have knowledge.

tungu'on 2. Comprehensible, perceptible, understandable, intelligible, knowable.

tu'o' 2. Drip, leak, trickle, fall in or form drops, spot with rain, pour drop by drop. (R) Also *tuho'.* Cf. **Sume'.** *Tu'o' i atof i kusina.* The kitchen's roof leaked. *Guaha tu'o' gi atof gima'-mu.* There is a leak in the roof of your house.

tupa 1. Tear off, knock down, rip, rend, split, cleave, rive, pry, peel off. Cf. **Chapak.**

tupak 1,2. Catch fish—with a pole and line or lines. Fishing line, pole--with fishing line. Cf. **Kotdet.**

tupo' 2. Well, a pit sunk into the earth to reach a supply of water.

tupon ayuyu 2. Type of plant-elatostema calcarea. A type of grass that grows in rocky area.

tupon nette 2. Type of plant-miscanthus floridulus. A type of grass.

tupu 2. Type of plant-saccharum officinarum. Sugar cane.

turiyu 2. Young bull.

turoru 1. Cradle (in one's arms), rock (in one's arms), swing—as in a hammock or playground swing, rock to sleep.

tutát 1,2. Sum up, add, total, sum, gross amount.

tutno 1. Turn—on a lathe, shape by turning on a lathe. *Hu tutno i rehas.* I shaped the rails on a lathe.

tutong 1. Pound, grind—such as corn, rice, wheat or coffee, pounder.

tutu 1. Pound, strike heavily or repeatedly with fist, beat, pulverize, make into pulp by beating. Cf. **Lommok, tongtong.**

tutuhon 1. Start, commence, begin, set out. Cf. **Tuka.**

tutuni Contracted form of *tutuhuni.* Cf. **Tutuhon.**

tuyan 2. Stomach, belly, abdomen. Cf. **Estomagu.**

u Future marker—third person. *Para u hanao agupa'.* He will go tomorrow. *Para u fanhanao agupa'.* They will go tomorrow.

u U—letter.

uahu 2. Type of fish-acanthocybium solandri (family scombridae). Wahoo, type of tuna.

uaia' 2. Wire, cable, metallic thread. Cf. **Alamle.**

uailes 1,2. To cable, to phone, telephone, cablegram. Cf. **Telefon, dengua'.** *Kao guaha uailes-mu?* Do you have a wireless?

uales See **ohales, uhales.**

uaragume' 2. Bad man, as in children's games. Also refers to Indians in game of cowboys and Indians. (S)

ubas 2. Type of plant-vitis vinifera. Grape.

uchan 2. Rain.

uchon 2. Groan, grunt—as when lifting a heavy object or moving bowels.

uda 2. Dumb, mute, speechless, destitute of the power of speech. (f).

udai 2. Means of transportation. Cf. **Ma'udai.** *Hafa para udai-mu?* What will be your means of transportation?

udu 2. Dumb, mute, speechless, destitute of the power of speech. (m). Also **uda** (f).

ufa 2. Type of plant-heritiera littoralis. A type of tree.

uga 1. Caress, flatter, wheedle, cajole, soothe, bestow caresses upon. Cf. **Reberensia.**

ugas 1,2. Making of starch, starch, any starchy substance that may be used for food, medicine, clothing, etc. *Hu ugas i mendioka.* I made starch from tapioca.

uges 2. Pretty, pleasant to look at.

ugo' 1. Be jealous (sexual), be suspicious (infidelity), desire (sexual), envy. Cf. **Ekgu'i.** *Hu ugo' i asagua-hu.* I am jealous of my spouse.

ugong 2. Moan, groan, lament, mourn, utter in lamentation.

ugot 1. Massage (with the feet)—usually by walking on the body. Cf. **Lasa, yettek.**

uha' 1. Pry open.

uha' 2. Gag, retch, heave with nausea.

uhales 1,2. Make buttonhole. Also **uales.** Buttonhole.

uhang [æ] 2. Shrimp.

uhang tasi 2. Type of shrimp-enoplometopus antillensis. Salt water shrimp.

uhi Alternate form of *yuhi.*

uho' 1. Use sparingly, use economically.

uhu Here, take it—expression used to attract (someone's) attention when giving something. Cf. **Estague'.** *Uhu.* Here it is. *Uhu i na'-mu.* Here is your food.

uke' 1. Carry piggyback, carry (something) on the shoulders. Cf. **Uma, ombo'.** *Ma uke' i katgan-ñiha ginen i gualo' asta i sengsong.* They carried their loads from the farm to the village.

ulat 2. Fit, fit into. Also **omlat.**

uli 2. Oilcloth.

ulo' 2. Worm, germ, bacteria, caterpillar, maggot.

ulo' ababang 2. Caterpillar.

ulon matiyu na halu'u 2. Type of shark-sphyrnalewinii (sphyrnidae). Hammerhead shark.

ulu 2. Head.

-um- Verbalizer, to become (something), used with regular class 2 words to form predicates. Infinitive marker. *Mumahetok i titiyas.* The tortilla became hard. (From *mahetok*). *Mumaolek i estudiante.* The student became good. (From *maolek). Umestudiante i patgon.* The child became a student. *Gumupu i paluma.* The bird flew. (from *gupu).*

-um- Actor focus affix. Used with class 1 and 2 words. *Si Pete tumokcha' i guihan.* Pete is the one who speared the fish. *I estudiante umestudia.* The student is the one who studied.

umá Reciprocal marker—with verbalizing affix -*um-*. Cf. **A-**. *Umatungo' i dos.* The two of them know each other.

uma 1. Carry, tote, bear. General term for carrying on the shoulder. Cf. **Uke'.** *Hu uma un kostat pugas asta i gima'.* I carried a sack of rice to the house.

umá'abale' [æ] 2. Commiting adultery.

umá'ande' [æ] 2. Flirting, showing off. Cf. **Ande'.**

uma'ápaniti 2. Boxing, fighting. Cf. **paniti.**

umáchetton [æ] 2. Closely connected —with each other, stuck together.

umáchuli [æ] 2. Look alike, resemble —each other.

umádespatta [æ] 2. Asunder, separate.

umáfa'baba [æ] 2. Cheat—each other.

umáfulo' [æ] 2. Wrestle (with someone), wrestle with each other, with one another. Use prefix *man*-with the base *afulo'* to form plural statement or interrogative. *Umafulo' i dos patgon.* The two children wrestled one another. *Manafulo' i manchampion siha.* All the champions wrestled one another.

umagonias 2. Be in the last throes of death.

umákkamo' [æ] 2. Get married, wed, marry. *Umakkamo' yo' yan i Amerikana.* I married (with) the American girl.

umanidát 2. Humanity, humane.

umang 2. Hermit crab—land. (Paguridae). Cf. **Umang duk.**

umang duk 2. Hermit crab—small. Cf. **Umang.**

umang maknganiti 2. Hermit crab— land (coenobita rugosa), red and hairy on its shell, also brownish and spotted on the larger pincher.

umang Yu'us 2. Hermit crab—land (coenobita rugosa), smooth pinkish

shell and the best kind of its species for food.

umásagua [æ] 2. Marry, wed, take spouse.

umásodda' [æ] 1. Encounter.

Umatac Village in southern Guam. Pron. umatak.

Umátalaf 2. March. Cf. **Matso.**

umatang 2. Type of fish-kuhlia rupestris (family kuhlidae). Black bass.

umátungo' [æ] 2. Agree, to know each other.

umá'uyu [æ] 2. Have intercourse, coitus. Cf. **uyu.**

umaya [æ] 2. Fit, suitable, appropriate. Cf. **Apropositu, aya.**

Umayangan 2. December. Cf. **Desiembre.**

umáyute' [æ] 2. Divorce, dissolve a marriage contract.

Umbai' Nickname for Jesus.

umé'gagao 2. Beg, ask alms.

umenta 1. Add on to. *Ha umenta kuatto gi gima'-ña.* He added a room to his house.

umenta See aomenta.

umentalo' 2. Interfere, come between.

umesgen 2. Go by way of, take a certain route. Also **sumigen.** *Umesgen i sanhilo' yo'.* I went the upper way. *Umesgen i tasi gue' para Susupe.* He went by the sea to Susupe.

umeskuela 2. School—attend, school--to go. Cf. **Eskuela.**

umespongha 2. Swell up—from absorption like a sponge. *Umespongha i pigas anai masumai gi hanom.* The rice swelled up when it absorbed the water.

umidát 2. Humility.

úmidu 2. Moisture, moist, damp, humid. Cf. **Makgem.**

umitde 2. Humble, meek. Also **humitde.**

umiya 1. Humiliate, humble one's self.

umok 2. Type of plant-digitaria spp. Or eleusine indica. (?).

umugong 2. Groan, lament.

un A, an, one (indefinite article). *Na'i yo' un lapes.* Give me a pencil. *Na'ayao gue' un pesu.* Lend him one dollar.

un You (sing.), pre-posed pronoun used in transitive statements. *Kao un li'e' i palao'an?* Did you see the woman?

un bi'ahi   Once.

un miyón 2.   One million.

un momento 2.   A moment, awhile, briefly, shortly. Cf. **Unratu.**

una 2.   One (telling time). Cf. **Un.** *Ala una pa'go.* It is one o'clock now.

unai 2.   Sand.

unbanda 2.   Beside, on the side, next to, side—one. Cf. **Banda, uriya.**

Uncha'   Nickname for Anunciacion.

unibetsiha 2.   University. Also **unibetsia, unibetsidat.**

unifotme 2.   Uniform.

úniku 2.   Sole, only, unique, rare, singular.

unmanada 2.   Plenty, lots of, many, full of. Cf. **Meggai, bula.** Also **manada.** *Unmanada na taotao gumuaiya manegga' afulo'.* There are plenty of people who like to watch wrestling.

unos kuantos 2.   Several, couple of, few, some, more than two or three (but not many). Also **noskuantos.**

unratu 2.   Moment, instant. Cf. **Momento.** Un plus *ratu. Nangga unratu.* Wait for a moment. *Unratu ha' sumaga i lahi.* The man stayed only for a moment.

unu 2.   One.

ungak 1.   Knock off balance, cause to tilt. Cf. **Ma'ngak.** *Yanggen un ungak siempre u poddong.* If you knock him off balance he will fall.

u'os 1.   To strike (match), to start fire, ignite. (S)

u'os 1.   Peel—with teeth, tear off with teeth when eating such things as sugar cane, green coconut.

upiñón 2.   Opinion.

upong 1.   Break (point), cut off (point).

upos 1.   Pass, go beyond, surpass, transcend, exceed.

uranggutanu 2.   Orangutan.

urinola 2.   Bedpan. Also **ninola.**

uriya 2.   Nearby, in proximity, vicinity, surrounding, environment, locality, neighborhood, neighboring. Also **oriya.** *Espiha i patgon sa' gaige ha' gi uriya.* Look for the child because he is somewhere nearby.

uriya   Nearby, edge, proximity. *Gaige ha' guini gi uriya.* It is somewhere nearby here.

uriyan tasi 2.   Coast, seaside, seacoast, seashore.

uriyayi 1.   Surround, approach nearby, encompass, encircle. *Hu uriyayi kumollat i lenderu.* I encircled the boundary by putting up a fence. *I patgon ha uriyayi i kabayu.* The child came close to the horse.

usa 1.   Use, employ, utilize, spend, use up, waste. Cf. **Gasta, na'setbe.** *Hu usa i payu-mu nigap.* I used your umbrella yesterday.

usáo 2.   Used, second-hand, usable.

usea   Or else. *Cho'gue este usea munga humanao.* Do this or else don't go.

usu 2.   Custom, habit. Cf. **Kustumbre, bisiu.**

usuni 1.   Persevere in, persist in, put more effort, remain fixed in. Cf. **Prikura, potfiha.** *Hu usuni lumi'of asta i fondo gi tasi.* I persisted in trying to dive to the bottom of the ocean.

utak 2.   Bird—legendary. Is said to come out at night, and is heard only by a few people, esp. when an unmarried girl is pregnant. Also **itak.**

utas 2.   Conserve, use sparingly. Cf. **Ma'ok.** *Hu na'utas i papet-hu yanggen mangge' yo'.* I conserve my papers when I write.

utdón 2.   Noodle.

utot 1.   Cut, sever, gash, incise, chop, amputate.

uttimamente 2.   Ultimately, eventually. Cf. **Alosuttimo.**

uttimo 2.   Ultimate, extreme, farthest, last, final terms, final.

uttimon i tano' 2.   Doomsday.

uyu 1.   Do (something). *Ha uyu i kutbata-hu anai munhayan ha godde i kutbata-ña.* When he finished tying his tie, he did it to mine.

uyu   A word used when someone can't think of the proper word.

ya   And, so—as used to connect relative clauses or phrases, or phrases of a cause-effect relationship. Cf. **Yan.** *Humanao yo' asta i lancho ya hu na'chocho i mannok siha.* I went to the ranch and I fed the chickens. *Gumimen yo' setbesa ya bulachu yo'.* I drank beer and I was drunk.

ya-   [æ] 3.   Like, be attracted towards, have a liking for, wish for, enjoy. (Must use with one of the possessive pronouns.) *Ya-ña sumaga gi kanton tasi.* He likes to stay at the beach.

Ya-hu mansana. I like apples.
Yan-ñiha hao. They like you.

ya- [æ] Superlative prefix—used only with location and direction words with reduplication of final syllable of stem. Cf. **Tak-. Yaguatutu.** Furthest away. *Ya-* plus *guatu.*

yá'balak [æ] 2. Worn out, tattered, decrepit, crumpled.

yabbao [æ] 1. Swat at, whack at, wave away, clear path by chopping bushes, mow, chop down trees. Cf. **Salibao.** *Hu yabbao i ñamu gi kanton talanga-hu.* I swatted at the mosquito next to my ear. *Ma yabbao i halom tano'.* They cleared the forest.

yabi 2. Key.

yafai 2. Exhausted (physically), weakened, enfeebled, become tired. Cf. **Mahgef.**

yafyaf [æ] 2. Skin disease—white spots form on the skin. Tinea versicolor.

yagai 1. Spank, whip, beat up, wallop, knock down, overpower, slug, hit. Cf. **Saolak, planasos, sapblasos.** *Mayagai i patgon anai umaguaguat gi gima'.* The child was spanked when he was naughty at the house. *Ma yagai i lahi anai ha kasi siha.* They hurt the man when he teased them.

yaggen [æ] Cf. **Yanggen.**

yaguátutu Farthest away. Also **takguatu.** Cf. **Chagugo'.**

yahálolom Way inside, farthest inside, way in, farthest in. Also **takhalom, takkalom.**

yaháyaya 2. Way south, farthest south. Also **takhaya, takkaya.**

ya'ho 1. Arouse, awake, wake up. Cf. **Pangon.** *Hu ya'ho i estudiante gi eskuela.* I woke up the student at school.

yahúlulo' Way up, farthest up. Also **takhilo', takkilo'.**

yahúyoyong Way outside, farthest outside, way out, farthest out. Also **takhiyong, takkiyong.**

yaka' [æ] 1. Knead, work or press into a mass as dough, usually with the hands. Cf. **Batte, yinaka'.**

yakáttatan 2. Way east, farthest east. Also **takkattan.**

yalágugu 2. Way north, farthest north. Also **taklagu.**

yalaka' [æ] 1. Mix up, stir, to make batter, rearrange by stirring up. *Hu yalaka' i ensalada.* I mixed the salad.

yalibao 1. Whack at, swat at. Also **salibao, yabbao.**

yalúchachan 2. Way west, farthest west. Also **taklichan.**

yama 1. Mention, bring up, state, speak of, call attention to. Cf. **Mensiona, menta, mentra.**

yama 1. Object, oppose, disapprove, offer a reason or argument in opposition. Cf. **Kontra.**

yamágigi 2. Closest, nearest to here. Also **takmagi.**

yamak [æ] 1. Break, destroy, impair, disable. Cf. **Yulang, tiges.**

yamao 2. Favorite side of cock pit, the side designated for the cock that is favored to win.

yamó'nana 2. Way front, farthest front. Also **takfe'na.**

yan [æ] And, as used to connect words or independent clauses or phrases. Cf. **Ya.** *Si Juan yan guahu umo'mak gi tasi.* John and I swam in the ocean. *Gumimen yo' kok yan bumaila yo' gi gipot.* I drank coke and I danced at the party.

yanken 2. Type of game. Also **yanken po.** Similar to American game scissors-paper-rock, played by pounding fist into palm of opposite hand.

yantas 2. Iron rim—used to hold wooden wheel.

yanto 2. Trouble. *Si Maria ha dagi si Jesus, humuyong dankolo na yanto.* Maria lied to Jesus, there followed big trouble.

yanu 2. Flat land, plain, not hilly.

yanggen [æ] If, when, (usually used to connect clauses or phrases). Cf. **Anggen.** *Yanggen guaha salape'-hu bai hu famahan kareta.* If I had money, I would buy the car. *Yanggen ha apasi yo' bai hu fahan i kareta.* When he pays me I will buy the car.

yaoyao 2. Disturbance, fuss, unsettlement, interruption of the peace and quiet of, agitating with noise. Also **yinaoyao.** *Hayi tumutuhon i yaoyao?* Who started the disturbance?

yapápapa' 2. Way down, farthest down. Also **takpapa'.**

yatáttiti 2. Way back, farthest back. Also **taktatte.**

yatdas 2. Yard (measurement); fabric, yardage.

yaya [æ] **1.** Tear (to pieces), break (into pieces), shatter, smash. Cf. **Yamak.**

yayaguak [æ] **2.** Type of bird-collocalis inexpectata bartschi, edible nest swiftlet.

yayas [æ] **2.** Weary, tired, fatigued, exhausted, worn out, done in, prostrate, haggard, all in. Also **ñañas.**

yeba 1. Share bet, give odds—in betting. Cf. **Logro.**

yekte' 2. Rubbish, anything discarded or thrown away, trash.

yello 2. Jello, gelatin.

yema 2. Egg yolk.

yemme' 1. Press against with fingers, squeeze between fingers. Cf. **Hoño'.**

yenao Old form for *enao.*

yenereta 2. Generator.

yengyong 1. Shake, vibrate.

yeografia 2. Geography.

yeográfiku Geographic.

yeometria 2. Geometry.

yesta Old form for *esta.*

yesu 2. Chalk.

yetban Santa Maria 2. Type of plant-Indian chrysanthemum. False camolile. Cf. **Mansaniya.**

yetbas babui 2. Type of plant-blechum brownei. A type of grass.

yetbas bihu 2. Type of plant-ramalina farinacea. Lichen.

yetbas buena 2. Type of plant-mentha arvensis. A type of grass. Also **yetba buena.**

yetbas Santa Maria 2. Type of plant-artemisia vulgaris. A type of grass.

ye'te' 1. Massage, using tips of fingers. Different from *lasa.*

yetna 2. Daughter-in-law.

yetno 2. Son-in-law.

yettek 1. Massage—with the hands or fingers, massage by gentle pounding. Cf. **Lasa, ugot.**

-yi Suffix. Alternate form of *-i.*

Yigo Village in northern Guam. Pron. yigu.

yílulok 1. Wad, rub, roll (between two things), as between the two hands. *Hu yilulok i papet ya hu yute' gi sagan basula.* I wadded the paper

up and I threw it in the trash can. *Hu yilulok i pomada gi kannai-hu.* I rubbed the pomade in between my hands.

yinabbao [æ] **2.** Field—for farming, cleaning. Cf. **yabbao.**

yinaka' [æ] **2.** Dough, soft mass of moistened flour or meal, thick enough to knead or roll, as in making bread, biscuits, etc., batter. Cf. **Yaka'.**

yinalaka' [æ] **2.** Batter, a mixture of flour and liquid.

yinaoyao 2. Fuss, trouble, argument, confusion, disagreement, troublesome. Cf. **Kombalachi, plaito, inkombinensia, atborotu, enkebukao.** *Ti ya-hu na u guaha yinaoyao gi entre hita na mangga'chong.* I don't like to have troubles among us friends.

yini Old form for *ini.*

yinite' 2. Divorce—without legal procedures, leave wife.

yini'usan 2. Godlike, of or pertaining to God. Cf. **Yu'us.**

yini'usan 2. Solemn, devout.

yip 2. Jeep.

yippa 1,2. To zip up, close by zipping, zipper.

yo' I—intransitive subject pronoun, transitive subj. pron. with indefinite object, me (transitive object pronoun). *Chumocho yo'.* I ate. *Chumocho yo' kahet.* I ate an orange. *Un pacha yo'.* You touched me.

yo'ase' 2. Merciful person, forgiving person. Cf. **Gai'ase', gaima'ase'.**

yódahi 2. Thrifty, economical, one who knows how to take care of his possessions.

yogga' 2. Type of plant-elaeocarpus joga. A type of tree.

yoggua 1. Punish, be punished, torture, sentence, scourge—subject to a penalty for an offense, punish (by burning), torture (by burning), be punished in hell.

yokyok 1. Shake, cause to shake. *Ha yokyok i nana i patgon-ña.* The mother shook her child.

yokyok 2. Fire—made from rubbing sticks together, flint--used in starting a fire.

yómahlao 2.   Shy, bashful, shamefaced, timid, modest, demure, unobtrusive, timorous. Also **yomalao**.

yommok 2.   Fat, fleshy, plump, stocky, obese, stout, corpulent, portly. Cf. **Chebot**.

yomsan 2.   Fleshy, plump, stocky, stout, well built. Cf. **Yommok, chebot**.

-yon   Abilitative suffix. Alternate form of *-on* following vowels. Cf. **-on**.

Yoña   Village in central Guam. Pronounced yo'ña.

yore' 2.   Slipper, Japanese slipper.

yotte 1.   Throw, cast, fling, hurl, pitch, toss, sling. Cf. **Blanko, daggao**.

yu   Short form for *yuhi*.

yu   Y—letter.

yudo' 1,2.   Judo.

yugi 1.   To strike (match), to start fire, ignite. (S) *Hu yugi i maches anai hu songge i chipa-hu*. I struck the match when I lighted my cigarette.

yugu 2.   Yoke—the v-shaped frame placed over neck of bull when harnessed to a cart.

yuhi   That, refers to something away from both speaker and listener. *Ya-hu yuhi na lepblo guatu*. I like that book there.

yuka'   Alternate form for *achokka'*.

yulang 1.   Annihilate, destroy, wreck, break. Cf. **Yamak**.

yuma 1.   Use, make use of.

yunke 2.   Anvil.

yunga' 1,2.   To draw (pictures), paint, drawing, painting, picture. (S) Cf. **Penta**.

yute' 1.   Throw away, dump, drop down, cast away, discard. Cf. **Blanko, dagao, foyang**.

Yu'us 2.   God, the supreme being. Cf. **Saina**.

ENGLISH-CHAMORRO FINDER LIST

a: *a, un.*
abandon: *abandona, dingu.*
abandoned: *abandonáo.*
abbreviate: *abríbiet.*
abbreviation: *abrebiasión.*
abdomen: *tuyan.*
abhor: *chatli'e'.*
abide: *kontinua.*
abilitative suffix: *-on, -yon.*
ability: *abilidát.*
abject: *tákpapa'.*
able: *kapás, kompetente.*
  able-bodied: *kákalamten.*
  be able: *siña.*
abnormal: *ti naturát.*
abolish: *diroga, richasa, rimati.*
abominate: *chatli'e'.*
abortion: *pokka'.*
about: *kasi, pot.*
  about to: *kumeke.*
  about to (do something): *keke,*
    mangeke-.
above: *hulo'.*
  above (preposition): *sanhilo'.*
abridge: *na'kádada'.*
abruptly: *derepente, gotpe.*
abscess: *mama'chigo'.*
absent: *fáfatta, fatta, táigue.*
  absent-minded: *fáfatta, háfatta.*
absentee: *fattáo, háfatta.*
absolute: *apsolutu, metton.*
absolutely: *apsolutamente.*
absolution: *apsolusión, inasi'i.*
absorb: *chinepchop, chopchop.*
abstain
  abstain from: *laisen.*
abstinence: *apstinensia.*
abundance: *abundansia.*
abundant: *abundante.*
abuse: *abusu, mattetsio.*
abyss: *enfietno, infietno, tináifondo.*
academic: *akadémiku.*
academy: *akademia.*
accelerate: *atisa.*
accent: *tonada.*
accept: *aksepta, ho'ye, risibi, sera.*
acceptance: *akseptasión.*
acceptancy: *akseptasión.*
accepted: *inaksepta.*
access
  have access: *mutero', tuhos.*
accident: *aksidente, desgrasiáo,*
  desgrasia.

accompaniment: *akompañamento.*
accompany: *akompaña, dádalak, dalak,*
  ga'chungi.
accomplice: *komplisi.*
accomplish: *kumple.*
according
  according to: *konsiste.*
accordjon: *akotdión, atmoniku.*
account: *kuenta.*
  on account of: *pot.*
accountant: *akaontan, eskribiente,*
  kontadót, tenedot di libro.
accumulate: *fa'montón.*
accurate: *dinanche.*
accurately: *prifekto.*
accuse: *akusa, sokne.*
  to accuse (falsely): *faiseknani.*
accused: *akusáo.*
accuser: *akusadót.*
accustom: *na'payon, payuni.*
accustomed: *payon.*
  be accustomed: *ápayuni, payuni.*
  become accustomed: *akostombra.*
ace: *as.*
ache: *puti.*
achieve: *taka'.*
aching
  aching muscles: *mamuti.*
acid: *ásidu.*
acidulous: *ma'aksom.*
acknowledge: *rikonisa.*
acquaint: *átungo'.*
acquaintance: *átungo'.*
acquainted
  be acquainted with: *tungo'.*
acquire: *ganye, konkista, logra.*
acquisitiveness
  acquisitiveness (m): *kudisio.*
acre: *hektaria.*
act: *akto, bida, fina'tinas, huegu,*
  hugando.
  act like: *fama'-.*
action: *aksión, fina'tinas.*
  set to action: *kalamten.*
active: *aktibu, karetatibu, makalamya.*
actor: *akta.*
  actor focus affix: *-um-.*
actual: *akto.*
acute: *kalaktos.*
adage: *refran.*
adapt: *adapta.*
add: *suma, tutát.*
  add in: *na'ye.*
  add more to: *ta'luyi.*

add on to: *umenta.*
add to: *añadi.*
addict: *adiktáo.*
addition: *sumát.*
additional: *otro.*
address: *saga.*
adept: *profisiente.*
adequate: *sufisiente.*
adhere: *chetton.*
adipose tissue: *sebu.*
adjacent: *checho, chehcho.*
adjectivizer: *-in-.*
adjourn: *makpo'.*
adjournment: *ritirada.*
adjust: *ahusta, na'ahustáo, na'maolek, templa.*
adjustment: *templada.*
administer: *dirihi.*
administration: *atministrasión, ofisina.*
administrator: *atministradót.*
admirable: *atmirapble, famáo.*
admiral: *atmirante.*
admire: *respeta.*
admit: *atmiti.*
admonish: *atmonesta.*
adolescence: *adulisensia, hobentút.*
adolescence (m): *hobensitu.*
adolescent
adolescent female: *po'dak.*
adolescent male: *ñedok.*
adopt: *adapta, adopta, adotta, konne'.*
adorate: *adora.*
adoration: *adorasión.*
adore: *adora.*
adorn: *adotna, beste, na'beste.*
adornment: *adotno.*
adrift: *pumaya'ya'.*
adult: *amko'.*
adulterer: *adotteru.*
adulteress: *adottera.*
adulterous
adulterous (man): *adotteru.*
adulterous (woman): *adottera.*
adultery: *adutteria.*
advance: *abansa, adilanta, atbansa, na'fo'na, sigi mo'na.*
advance pay: *abanse.*
advanced: *adilantáo.*
advancement: *adilanto, progresu.*
advantage: *adilanto, bentaha.*
advent: *atbiento.*
adventurer: *biaheru, pasiadót, pasiadora.*

adversary: *enimigu, kontrariu.*
adversity: *dimalas.*
advertise: *pupblika.*
advice: *pinagat.*
advise: *abisa, akonseha, chalani, kuka, pagat.*
to advise: *konseha.*
adviser: *á'akonseha, akonseheru, konseheru.*
adze: *gachai.*
aerate: *bohao, goia.*
afar: *chago'.*
affable: *chihet.*
affect: *afekta.*
affection: *guinaiya.*
affectionate: *kariñosu.*
affirm: *afitma.*
affluence: *guinaha, rikesa.*
affluent: *gófsaga, míguinaha, riku.*
affront: *insutto.*
afraid: *ma'a'ñao, massa'.*
after: *despues di, pasáo.*
afterbirth: *pares.*
afternoon: *talo'ani, tatdes.*
afterward: *despues, pues.*
again: *agon-, hiya', ta'lo.*
say again: *ripiti.*
against: *kontra.*
be against (someone): *kontra.*
age: *años, idát.*
be of age: *gái'idat, guaha idát.*
aged: *amko', bihu.*
agency: *ahensia, eyensia.*
agenda: *ayenda.*
agent: *ahente, eyente.*
agent (m): *benteru.*
aggravate: *aguanta, chu'ot, kifan, taohan.*
aggravate (sore or wound): *sisitan, tinaohan.*
aggravated: *sinilo'.*
agile: *kalamya, makalamya.*
agitate: *chalehgua', lehgua'.*
agitator: *paleta.*
ago: *apmam, hagas.*
agony: *agonias, pinadesi.*
agree: *akomprende, aprueba, ho'ye, konfotme, umátungo'.*
agreeable: *agradapble, atendidu.*
agreement: *inákomprende, kompromisu, kontrata, kontratamiento.*
agriculture: *agrikuttura.*
Agrihan: *Agrihan.*

aground
  run aground: *oggan.*

ahead: *fo'na, kuanto antes.*
  ahead of time: *kontiempo.*
  send ahead: *na'fófo'na.*

aid: *á'ayuda, akudi, aosiliu, apasigua, ayuda, ayudante, fa'che'chu'i, faboresi, grates, sague'.*
  give aid: *asiste.*

aim: *apunta, propósitu.*

aimless: *botdo.*

air: *aire, manglo'.*
  air out: *aire.*
  air-raid: *kusio'.*

airfield: *plasan batkon aire.*

airplane: *batkon aire, eroplanu.*

airport: *plasan batkon aire.*

airstrip: *plasan batkon aire.*

aisle: *pasada.*

ajar: *atbuetto.*

alabaster: *alabastro.*

Alamagan: *Alamagan.*

alangilang: *alangilang.*

alarm: *abisa, abisu.*

albino
  albino (person): *atbinu.*

album: *albom.*

alcohol: *atkahót.*

alcoholic
  alcoholic drink: *maneska.*

alert: *aktibu, listo, malate'.*

Alfonsina
  nickname for Alfonsina: *Ina.*

alien: *estrangheru.*

alienate: *estraña.*

alike: *achaigua.*

aliment: *nénkanno'.*

alive: *lála'la', la'la'.*

all: *puru, tiot, todu.*
  all right: *buenu.*
  all the time: *todu i tiempo.*

allege: *afitma.*

allegiance: *ti fina'baba.*

allergic: *cha'ot.*

alleviate: *alibia, na'kayada.*

alliance: *aliansa.*

alligator: *kaimán.*

allotment: *kuota.*

allow: *atmiti, konsiente, petmiti, sedi.*

allowance: *lisensia.*

allude: *riferi.*

almond
  Indian almond: *talisai.*

almost: *hihot, kana' ha', kanna', kasi, katna'.*

alms: *égagao, karidát, limosna.*

alone: *ha', maisa, solamente, solu.*

alphabet: *atfabetu.*

already: *esta.*

also: *lokkue'.*

altar: *attat.*
  altar boy: *tanores.*

alteration: *ina'go, tinilaika.*

alternate: *átahgue.*

although: *áchokka', maskeseha.*

altitude: *attura, linekka'.*

alto
  sing alto: *sigundayi.*

aluminum: *aluminom.*

always
  almost always: *tatde ti.*

amazed: *manman.*

ambassador: *ambasadót, embahadót.*

ambidextrous: *huguayon.*

ambition: *minalago'.*

ambitious: *empeñosu.*

ambulance: *ámbulan.*

ambush: *traisión.*

ameliorate: *adilanta.*

amen: *amen.*

amenable: *obidiente, osgon.*

amend: *amenda, enmienda.*

American
  American (m): *kanu, Amerikanu.*
  American wandering tattler: *dulili.*

amicable: *gofli'i'on.*

amid: *entre.*

amidst: *entre.*

among: *éntalo', entre.*

amorous: *enamoráo.*

amour: *águaiya.*

ample: *míguinaha.*

amplify: *aomenta.*

amputate: *utot.*

amputated: *ma'tot, manko.*
  amputated arm: *manka.*

amputee: *manka.*

amuse: *hugando, na'magof.*

amusement: *huegu.*

an: *un.*

analyze: *analisa, estudiayi.*

Anatahan: *Anatahan.*

anatto: *achoti.*

ancestor: *guelo'.*

anchor: *ankla.*
  to anchor: *ma'ankla.*

anchorage: *fananklayan.*
anchovies: *faya.*
ancient: *amko', ansianu, antigon, antigu.*
and: *ya, yan.*
angel: *anghet.*
angels: *ángheles.*
anger: *binibu, cháthinallom, kurahi, lalalo', linalalo', na'bubu.*
  sign of anger: *foffo.*
  to anger: *gapi, guafi, guahi.*
angered: *ma'agoddai.*
angry: *bubu, konkurahi.*
  angry person: *bíburas.*
  be angry suddenly: *kinahulo'guan.*
anguish: *piniti, totmento.*
animal: *animát, ga'ga'.*
  animal classifier: *ga'-.*
annihilate: *destrosa, disasi, na'falingu, yulang.*
anniversary: *anibetsariu, kumple años.*
announce: *agangñaihon, anunsia, bandoñaihon.*
announcement: *anunsiu, notisia, ripotte.*
annoy: *atborota, estotba, estraña, molestia, na'chatsaga, peredika.*
  to annoy: *fastidia.*
annoyance: *estotbo, katgueti.*
annual: *kada sakkan.*
annul: *anula, na'táibali.*
another: *otro.*
answer: *kontesta, kontestasión, oppe, ripresta.*
ant: *otdot, otdot sakkan.*
  black ant: *ateng, hacheng, hateng, otdot áttilong.*
  red ant: *otdot agaga'.*
  type of ant: *otdot díkike'.*
antagonist: *antagonista, ná'bubu.*
antenna: *pahlo.*
anti-Christ: *antikristo.*
anticipant: *antisipante.*
anticipate: *antisipa.*
anticipation: *antisipasión.*
antler: *kánghelon.*
anus: *madulok dagan.*
anvil: *yunke.*
anxious: *ansias.*
any: *kuatkuét.*
anybody: *maseha hayi.*
anyday: *maseha ngai'an.*
anyhow: *maseha taimanu.*
anyone: *maseha hayi.*

anyplace: *maseha manu.*
anytime: *maseha ngai'an.*
anyway: *maseha taimanu.*
anywhere: *maseha manu.*
apart
  take apart: *na'adespatta.*
apathetic: *desgánao.*
ape: *macheng, saro'.*
aperture: *abettura, atbettura, atbietto, ngulo'.*
apologize: *fanggagao despensasión, gagao asi'i.*
apostles
  the apostles: *apóstoles, disípulu.*
apostolic: *apostóliku.*
apparatus: *aparatos.*
apparel: *chinina.*
apparent: *annok.*
appeal: *apela.*
appear
  appear unexpectedly: *desnek.*
appearance: *atanon, kakko', trahi.*
appease: *fatani.*
appellation: *títula.*
appendicitis: *pendiks.*
appetite: *ganas.*
  having appetite: *gáiganas.*
  lacking appetite: *taiganas.*
  no appetite: *malaganas, tumáiganas.*
appetizing: *ná'malago'.*
applaud: *aplasu.*
applause: *aplasu.*
apple: *mansana.*
applicable: *aplikáo, aplikapble.*
applicant: *kandidatu.*
application: *aplikasión.*
apply: *praktika.*
  apply by dropper: *chotge.*
  apply for: *aplika.*
appoint: *apunta, asikna, nombra.*
apportion: *patte.*
appraise: *estima, péritu.*
appreciate: *agradesi.*
apprehend: *aprehende, aresta.*
apprise: *átungo', infotma.*
approach: *subida.*
  approach nearby: *uriyayi.*
approbation: *apruebasión.*
appropriate: *apropósitu, asientadu, aya, umaya.*
approval: *aplasu, apruebasión, buen.*
approve: *aprueba, esta, settifika.*
  approve of: *sedi.*

approved: *aprebáo.*

approximately: *kasi.*

April: *Abrít, Lumuhu.*

apron: *tapes.*
   put on apron: *tapes.*

Arab: *Arabia.*

Arabian: *Arabia.*

aramina: *dádangse.*

arch: *atkos, ebang, echong.*

archangels: *atkángheles.*

arched: *ekklao.*

arching: *pakke'.*

ardent: *empeñosu.*

area: *lugát.*

argue: *mumu.*

argument: *agumento, atgumento, debati, enkebukáo, kombalachi, kombati, yinaoyao.*

arid: *angglo'.*

arithmetic: *aresmetika, arofmetika, kuentas.*

ark: *atka.*

arm: *brasu.*
   arm (up to shoulder): *kannai.*
   arm's length: *bara.*
   one-armed: *manka, manko.*

armaments: *atma.*

armpit: *afa'fa'.*

arms: *atma.*

army: *tropa.*

aroma: *paguan, pao.*

around
   all around: *aridedót.*
   go around: *ridondeha.*

arouse: *pahngon, ya'ho.*

arrange: *arekla, na'parehu, po'lo.*
   arrange things: *rempesa.*

arrangement: *inenkatga.*

arrest: *aresta.*

arrested: *arestáo.*

arrival: *finatto.*

arrive: *mamaila', matto.*
   arrive (at propitious moment): *fakcha'i.*
   arrive (command): *fatto.*

arrogant: *mama'ma'gas.*

arrow: *flecha.*

arrowroot: *arurú, gapgap.*

article: *áttikulu, as, iya, si.*

articulate: *pronunsia.*

artifice: *atte, laime, trampas.*

artificial: *postisu.*

artilleryman: *kañoneru.*

artist: *attisa.*

as: *achá-, komu.*
   as long as: *kontat ki, kuentat ki, tokante.*
   as soon as: *gigon.*

ascend: *hotde, kumahulo'.*

ascension
   Ascension of Christ: *asensión.*

ash: *apu.*
   ash tray: *sagan apu, sagan otpos.*
   Ash Wednesday: *sinisa.*
   ash-colored: *sinisa.*

ashamed: *mamahlao, mamalao, na'mamahlao.*
   become ashamed: *mumamahlao.*

ashes: *otpos.*
   having ashes: *inapu.*

aside
   aside from: *fuera di.*
   set aside: *na'suha.*

ask: *égagao, faisen, faisini, rikuesta, solisita.*
   ask for: *gagao, mamaisen, táyuyot.*

asleep
   sound asleep: *maffong.*

aspirin: *aspirina.*

assassin: *pípino'.*

assault: *ataka.*

assemblage: *etnon, linahyan, montohon.*

assemble: *assemble, atma, atmayi, hokka, rikohi.*

assembled: *atmao.*

assembly: *assemble, hunta, miteng.*

assert: *afitma.*

assign: *asikna.*

assimilate: *na'parehu.*

assist: *akudi, aosiliu, apasigua, asiste, ayuda, fa'buresi, fa'che'chu'i, faboresi, sague'.*

assistance: *asistensia.*

assistant: *á'ayuda, asistente, ayudante.*

associate: *ga'chong.*

association: *asosiasión, inetnon.*

assume: *asuma, humallom, kalumnia, suponi.*

assumption: *binanidosu.*

assurance: *konfiansa, prinemeti, siguridát.*

assure: *asigura, prometi.*

assured: *asiguráo.*

asterisk: *estreyas.*

asthma: *guha.*
   asthma attack: *ataken guha.*

asthmatic: *háguha.*
astonished: *manman.*
astounded: *manman.*
astraddle: *ombo', sa'dang.*
astray
  gone astray: *atsadu.*
astronomy: *astronomia.*
Asuncion: *Asunsión.*
asunder: *umádespatta.*
at: *gi, giya.*
  at least: *anto'asi, sikiera.*
athlete's foot: *sarento, satbayones.*
atone: *empas, na'afa'maolek.*
atonement: *pinitensia.*
attach: *atani.*
attached
  attached to: *chechet, kontra, metton.*
attack: *aplakáo, ataki, hatme.*
attacker: *atakeru.*
attain: *hago', taka'.*
attempt: *chagi.*
attend: *atende, hosme.*
attendant: *tentago'.*
attention: *atensión.*
  pay attention: *atende, atituyi.*
attentive: *atendidu, atento, respetayon.*
attest: *settifika, testiguyi.*
attestation: *testimoniu.*
attestor: *testigu.*
attic: *kabayeti, kamaroti.*
attire: *chinina.*
attitude: *eskama.*
attorney: *abugáo, abugadu.*
  attorney general: *fiskat.*
attracted
  be attracted towards: *ya-.*
attractive: *ka'lak.*
attrition: *atrisión.*
auction: *atmoneda.*
audible: *hongga, oppan, suena, sunidu.*
audience: *aodensia.*
auditor: *aoditót, kontadót.*
auditorium: *aoditoriu.*
auger
  auger bit: *baró.*
augment: *aomenta.*
August: *Agosto, Tenhos.*
aunt: *tiha.*
auntie: *memmang.*
aurora: *chakchak manana.*
auspicious: *faborapble, fottuna.*
austere: *addet, atdet.*
authentic: *magahet, siguru.*

author: *títuge'.*
authority: *aotoridát, aturidát, mando.*
  have authority: *pudét.*
authorization: *aotorisasión.*
authorize: *aotorisa, aturisa, lisensia.*
automobile: *kareta, sahyan, sidán,*
  tumobet.
available
  have available: *mutero'.*
avarice: *linatga.*
avaricious: *ambiento, chattao, gatgat,*
  hambiento, hambrento, otguyosu,
  tragón.
avenge: *bengga, deskita.*
avenger: *benggadót.*
average: *medianu, regulát.*
aversion: *desagunáo.*
avocado: *alagatapeha', alageta.*
avoid: *eskapayi, laisen, letke, na'táibali,*
  suhayi.
await: *nangga.*
awake: *maga'an, ya'ho.*
  stay awake: *desbela, desbelu.*
awaken: *pangon.*
award: *premiu.*
awe
  awe-inspiring: *gatbo, ná'manman,*
  tagalo'.
awhile: *-ñaihon, un momento.*
awl: *alesna.*
awning: *homme.*
ax: *gachai.*
axle
  axle (of a wagon): *ehi.*
azure: *asút.*
b: *be.*
babble: *palakpak.*
babbler: *ga'kumuentos.*
babies: *famagu'on.*
baby: *neni, patgon.*
  baby face: *matan neni.*
  baby sitter: *chichigua.*
  baby walker: *anadót, andadót.*
bachelor: *señoritu, sotteru.*
bachelorette: *sottera.*
back: *tátalo'.*
  back of: *santatte, tatte.*
  back off: *seha.*
  back side of: *santatte.*
  back up: *ato', seha.*
  small of the back: *átayo'.*
  way back: *yatáttiti.*
  weakened back: *se'yon.*
backbone: *espinasu.*

backtalk: *embusteru.*
backward: *tatte.*
backwards
  move backwards: *mañeha.*
bacteria: *ulo'.*
bad: *baba, mala, na'táilayi.*
  be bad: *mama'baba.*
  became bad: *mama'baba.*
  make bad: *na'táilayi.*
badge: *bach.*
bag: *ala, kostat, kottot.*
  handbag (made from weaving):
    tisage'.
  type of bag: *danglon.*
  woven bag: *tisage'.*
baggage: *maleta.*
  small baggage: *balakbak.*
bail: *sohgue.*
bait: *katnada, ponne.*
  good bait: *katna.*
  set out bait for: *katnadayi.*
bake: *hotno.*
baker: *panaderu.*
bakery: *panaderia.*
balance: *ábalansa, achá'ungak, balansa,*
  balansa, balanse, dollan.
  balance (business): *fondo.*
  balance (oneself): *dellan.*
  balance debt: *na'balansa.*
  balance statement: *kuenta.*
balanced
  balanced (upright): *belu.*
balcony: *batkón.*
bald: *boyo'.*
  bald-headed: *dakngas.*
balding: *matfos, ngangas.*
ball: *bola.*
  ball game: *bola.*
  make ball: *afuyot.*
ballerina: *bailarina.*
balloon: *abubu, lobu.*
ballot: *balotu, botu.*
  ballot box: *kahon balotu, koleru.*
balsam apple: *atmagosu.*
bamboo: *karisu, pi'ao palao'an, pi'ao*
  tituka.
  bamboo (general): *pi'ao.*
  bamboo container: *bahdot, bongbong.*
  bamboo pipe: *chigando' pi'ao, tubon*
    pi'ao.
  thorny bamboo: *pi'ao lahi.*
ban: *prohibi.*
banana: *chotdan dama.*
  banana plantation: *fañotdayan.*
  cooked banana: *gelle'appan chotda,*
    gollai appan chotda.

fried banana: *madoya.*
green banana: *chotda.*
kind of banana-similar to Taiwan
  banana: *aga' guahú.*
  ripe banana: *aga', inasahan.*
  short banana: *chotdan Manila.*
  type of banana: *chotdan bunita,*
    chotdan gálayan, chotdan guahú,
    chotdan halom tano', chotdan
    lakatán, chotdan long, chotdan
    pahong, chotdan paladang, chotdan
    tanduki, chotdan Makáo.
band: *músiku.*
  band together: *átugan.*
  band together against: *agululumi,*
    asaguani.
  hair band: *godde.*
bandage: *be'i, bendas, plasta.*
bandit: *bandoleru.*
bang: *otto.*
  bang against: *tongtong.*
bangs: *dasai kabayu.*
banish: *destiladu.*
banjo: *bandulina, banyo.*
bank: *banko.*
banker: *bankera, bankeru.*
bankrupt: *kara', kebra.*
bankruptcy: *finalingu, minafak.*
bannister: *langle, pasamanu.*
banquet: *sentada.*
banquette: *tapblita.*
bantam
  bantam (chicken): *kántanes.*
banter: *essitani.*
banyan
  banyan tree: *nunu.*
baptism: *baotismo.*
baptismal gown: *bata'.*
Baptist: *baotista.*
baptize: *takpangi.*
baptizer: *baotista.*
bar: *salón, tranka.*
  bar-fly: *ga'sumalón.*
barb: *títuka'.*
barbaric: *machalek.*
barbecue: *hotno, na'matunu, tunu.*
  barbecue pit: *foggon.*
barber
  barber (m): *batberu.*
  barber pole: *hastan batberu.*
  barber shop: *batberia.*
bare: *sin.*
barefoot: *sindogga.*
barely: *chat-, chatta'.*

bargain: *kontrata, negosio, tratos.*
 to bargain: *kontrata.*
barge: *batsa.*
bark: *haohao, lassas.*
barking
 barking (of dog): *so'on.*
barley: *sibada.*
barn: *kámalen.*
barometer: *barometro.*
barracks: *kuattét.*
barracuda: *alu.*
 type of barracuda: *alon laiguan.*
barrel: *baliles, bariles.*
 large barrel: *pipa.*
 small barrel: *tina.*
barren: *cha ttano', kansadu, pasadu,
 táiminaolek.*
barricade: *futot.*
barrier: *impedimento.*
barrow: *andas.*
barterer: *kombalacheru.*
basalt
 basalt rock: *alutong.*
base: *bes, di'ao, di'u, fondo.*
baseball: *bola.*
basement: *budega.*
bashful: *mamahlao, mamalao,
 manachang, ná'mamahlao,
 yómahlao.*
 become bashful: *mumamahlao.*
basic: *fondamento.*
basil
 sweet basil: *atbahakat.*
basin: *pila.*
basket: *ala, che'op, guagua', guagua'
 tumalaya, kottot.*
 woven basket: *kanastra.*
basketwork: *finilak.*
bass
 bass voice: *bahu.*
bastard: *bastatdo.*
bat: *fanihen toyu, panak.*
 bat (mammal): *fanihi.*
 fruit bat: *fanihi.*
bathe: *o'mak.*
bathroom: *baño.*
bathtub: *fano'makan.*
battalion: *batayón.*
batter: *tongtong, yinaka', yinalaka'.*
 cake batter: *binatte.*
battery: *bateria.*
battle: *bataya, batiya, gera, mumu,
 palitada.*
battleship: *batkon gera.*

bawl: *kasao.*
bay: *báhia, bakana.*
bayonet: *bayineta.*
be
 be numbed: *ma'etdot.*
 be present: *gaige.*
 be quiet: *ketu.*
beach: *kanton tasi, tasi.*
beads: *kulales.*
beak: *piku.*
beaker: *buteya.*
beam: *dotmiente, kabisera, suleras.*
bean
 bean paste: *miso'.*
 bean pole: *ka'u.*
 French bean: *lenteha Franchesa.*
 long bean: *fioles.*
 sea bean: *akankang kalaton.*
 wild bean: *bayogon dikike', gaggao
  dálalai, gaye'.*
 wing bean: *sigidiyas.*
beans
 ayuke' beans: *monggos ayuke'*
 beans (generic): *abuchuelas.*
 green beans: *abuchuelas.*
bear: *osu, padesi, sungon.*
 bear (offspring): *fañagu.*
beard: *batbas.*
bearded
 bearded person: *batbon.*
bearing
 bearing (ball): *tama'.*
 bearing young: *fáfañagu.*
beast: *ga'ga'.*
beat: *acha, ganna, igi, ikak, lommok,
 tongtong, tutu.*
 beat mercilessly: *saragati.*
 beat up: *aña, fakkai, fueges,
  garutasu, planasos, sapblasos, yagai.*
 to beat up: *baketa.*
beaten
 be beaten: *mapedde.*
beatified: *biatu.*
beatitude: *biátiku.*
beautification: *adotno.*
beautify: *adotna, na'gatbo.*
because: *pot, sa', sis.*
 because of: *sa'.*
beche-de-mer: *balate'.*
beckon: *agang, agangñaihon, alof.*
become: *mama'-.*
 become like that: *tumaiguenao,
  tumaiguihi.*
 become like this: *tumaiguini.*
 to become (something): *-um-.*

bed: *kama, katre.*
  bed sheet: *sábanas.*
  bed wetter: *takme.*
  bed-wetting: *makpong.*
bedbug: *chenche.*
bedcover: *hafyen katre, tampen katre.*
bedpan: *urinola.*
bedridden: *kama.*
bedroom: *apusento.*
bedspread: *hafyen katre, subrekama.*
bedstead: *kama.*
bee: *abeha, sasata.*
beef: *katnen guaka.*
beer: *setbesa.*
beeswax: *sera.*
beet
  garden beet: *asetga.*
beetle: *kukunitos, San Ignasio.*
  diving beetle: *hagan hanom.*
befool: *dugeruyi.*
before: *antes di.*
  before last: *ma'posña.*
beforehand: *antes di, kontiempo.*
beg: *égagao, táyuyot, umé'gagao.*
beget: *na'huyong, paireha.*
beggar: *gakgao, limosneru, tákgagao.*
begin: *tuka, tutuhon.*
  begin to: *keke, kumeke, mangeke-.*
beginning: *prinsipiu.*
behalf: *kuenta.*
behavior: *aksión, kondukta.*
behead: *digueya.*
behind: *santatte, tatte.*
being: *gágaige.*
belch: *tugap.*
belfry: *kampanayon.*
belie: *fa'dagi.*
belief: *hinengge.*
believable: *honggiyon.*
believe: *hongge.*
bell: *kampana.*
  bell-ringer: *kampañeru.*
  little bell: *pandereta.*
  small bell: *kampaniya.*
belly: *estómagu, tuyan.*
belong
  belong to: *iyon.*
  belong to (something: *iyo-.*
beloved: *magófatan, magofli'e', nena.*
below: *papa'.*
belt: *koreha, korehas, kotdón, sinturón.*
belting: *latigasu.*
bench: *banko, ta'chong.*

bend: *dilok, dopbla, ebang, echong, ga'om, na'echong.*
  bend (of road): *birada.*
  bend down: *baha', baha'.*
  bend over: *aso', dengha.*
  cause to bend: *hugom.*
bending: *pakke'.*
beneath: *papa'.*
benediction: *benediksión.*
benefaction: *benefisiu.*
benefactor: *benifaktót.*
beneficent: *góflamen.*
benefit: *benefisiu, bentaha, probecho, setbisiu.*
benefiting: *probechosu.*
benevolence: *binebolensia.*
benign: *benikno.*
bent: *aso', ekklao, mafgo'.*
beriberi: *berebere'.*
berry
  type of berry: *adotse.*
beseech: *táyuyot.*
beside: *fi'on, unbanda.*
besides: *fuera di, tras.*
best: *itmás, primeru.*
  best man: *donseyu.*
bestow: *doti.*
bet: *aposta, parada, tatos.*
betel
  betel nut: *mama'on.*
  betel nut palm: *pugua'.*
  betel pepper: *pupulu.*
  betel tree: *tronkon pugua'.*
  chew betel nut: *amme, mama'.*
  white betel: *pugua' China.*
Bethlehem: *Bilen.*
betray: *fa'baba, failahyi, traiduti.*
betrayal: *traisión.*
betrothal: *magutos i finiho'.*
better: *-ña, buenecho, maolekña.*
  better not: *cha'-, chacha'-.*
between: *éntalo'.*
beverage: *gimen, maneska.*
  beverage (alcoholic): *bíberes.*
beware: *adahi.*
bewitch: *atgimat, kahnayi.*
bewitched
  be bewitched: *makahnayi.*
beyond: *mas.*
bias: *baias.*
bib: *baberu.*
  bib (slavering): *fano'la'an.*
Bible: *bíblia.*
  Bible history: *historia sagrada.*

biblical: *bibliku.*

bicep: *cha'ka.*

bicker: *munon pachot.*

bicuspid: *kotniyos.*

bicycle: *bisikleta.*

bid: *atmoneda, diga.*

big: *dánkolo, pennga', tamong.*
  big eye: *mama'gas.*
  big-bellied: *barigón, barigona.*

bigger: *lámudong.*

bill: *kubransa.*
  bill (of a bird): *piku.*

billards: *biyát.*

bind: *fuñot, fuhot, manohu.*

binding
  binding (for books): *tampe.*

binoculars: *lagabista, latgabista.*

bird: *paluma, utak.*
  bird (generic term): *páharu.*
  bird house: *palumat.*
  small bird (generic): *paharita.*
  type of bird: *chuguangguang, fakpe.*
  type of bird-acrocephalus luscinia
    syrinx: *ga'ga' karisu.*
  type of bird-actitus hypoleucos: *dulili.*
  type of bird-anas oustaleti: *nganga'
    palao.*
  type of bird-anous stolidus pileatus:
    fahang.
  type of bird-aplonis opacus guami:
    sali.
  type of bird-arenaria interpres: *dulili.*
  type of bird-collocalis inexpectata
    bartschi: *yayaguak.*
  type of bird-corus kubaryi: *aga.*
  type of bird-coturnix chinensis liteata:
    bengbeng.
  type of bird-crocethia alba: *dulili.*
  type of bird-demigretta sacra sacra:
    chuchuko'.
  type of bird-erolia acumimate: *dulili.*
  type of bird-fregata minor minor:
    fakte, ga'ga' manglo'.
  type of bird-fulica atra atra: *pulattat.*
  type of bird-gallicolumba xanthonura:
    apaka', paluman kunao.
  type of bird-gallinago megala: *dulili.*
  type of bird-gallinula chloropus guami:
    pulattat.
  type of bird-gallixolumba xanthonura:
    paluman kutbata.
  type of bird-halcyon cinnamomina:
    sihek.
  type of bird-heteroscelus brevipes:
    dulili.
  type of bird-heteroscelus incanus:
    dulili.

  type of bird-ixobrychus sinensis:
    kakkak.
  type of bird-megpodius laperousei:
    sasngat.
  type of bird-mycomola cardinalis
    saffordi: *égigi.*
  type of bird-myiagra oceanica
    freycineta: *chaguangguan.*
  type of bird-numenius
    madagascariensis: *kalalang.*
  type of bird-phaethon lepturus
    dorotheae: *chunge'.*
  type of bird-philinopus roseicapillus:
    totot.
  type of bird-pluvialis dominica fulva:
    dulili.
  type of bird-puffinus iherminieri
    dichrous: *paya'ya'.*
  type of bird-puffinus tenuirostrio:
    paya'ya'.
  type of bird-rallus owstoni: *ko'ko'.*
  type of bird-rhipdura rufifrons uraniae:
    chuchurika.
  type of bird-squatorola squatarola:
    pulattat.
  type of bird-streptopelia bitorquata
    dusumieri: *paluman sinisa.*
  type of bird-sula leucogaster plotus:
    lu'ao.
  type of bird-swiftlet: *payesyes.*
  type of bird-zosterops c.: *nosa'.*

birdie: *paharita.*

birdlime: *afok.*

birdnest fern: *galak fedda'.*

birth: *patto.*
  breech birth: *sokkos.*
  give birth: *fañagu, mañagu.*

birthday: *kumple años, mafañagu.*

birthmark: *lonnat.*

birthright: *rénsia.*

biscuit: *biskuchu, guyuria, krakas.*

bishop: *obispo.*

bit: *frenu.*
  a little bit (at a time): *adumídide'.*
  little bit of: *pidasitu.*

bite: *akka'.*

bitten: *kakkak.*

bitter: *kákalek, kinasse, mahatot,
  mala'et, ná'failek.*

blab: *fa'aila', kehayi.*

blabbermouth: *ga'kumuentos.*

black: *áttilong.*
  black bass: *umatang.*
  black people: *sali.*
  black race: *nigritos.*

blackboard: *pisara.*

blackeye: *bocha, botcha.*

blackish: *ináttilong.*

blackness: *ináttilong.*

blacksmith: *hereru.*
blacksmith shop: *fragua.*

bladder: *bíhiga.*

blade: *blet, filu.*
worn blade: *fotda.*

blame: *achaka, tacha.*
to blame (someone) falsely: *faiseknani.*

blamed: *akusáo.*
be blamed for: *dada'da'.*

blanch: *enkola.*

bland: *táisabot.*
bland (taste): *mata'pang.*

blanket: *onno', sábanas.*

blaspheme
blaspheme at: *chatfinu'i.*

blasphemy: *chátfino', chinatpachot.*

blast: *pangpang.*

bleach: *enkola, ná'mafnas.*

bleak: *cháta'an, homhom.*

bleat: *katen chiba.*

bleed: *mahagga'.*
bleed (something): *sanggra.*

blend: *dinaña', templa.*

blenny: *hatot.*

bless: *bendisi, echa.*

blessed: *bendisión, biatu, sagradu.*

blessedness: *bienabenturansa.*

blessing: *bendisión, tinina.*

blind: *bachet.*

blindfold: *bendas.*

blink: *chalamlam, chibaleng.*

bliss: *dankolo na minagof.*

blister: *pakpak.*
blister from heat: *pakko', panko'.*
fever blister: *oba'.*

blistered: *pakpak.*

bloated: *binila.*

block: *pattang, taggam.*
block (pathway): *futot.*
block (the view): *homme.*
block and tackle: *motón.*

blockade: *patang, pattang, taggam.*

blonde: *betmehu, blandina.*

blood: *haga'.*
blood blister: *luga' haga'.*

bloody: *mehga'.*

bloom: *mamflores.*

blooming: *flumoflores.*

blossom: *flores.*

blot
blot out: *emplasta, na'mafnas.*

blotch: *burón.*

blouse: *blusa, mestisa.*

blow: *guaife.*
blow (the nose): *ngofngof.*
cause to blow away: *asa, hasa.*

blower: *bohao, goia.*

blow-fish: *buteti.*
spotted blow-fish: *buteten pento.*

blowing: *belemba.*

blown: *guinaife.*
blown away: *hinasa, inasa.*

blue: *asút.*

blueish: *inasút.*

bluing
bluing agent: *anít.*

blunder: *disparati.*

blunt: *despunta.*

blur
cause to blur: *na'maya'.*

blurred: *maya'.*
become blurred: *mumaya'.*

blurry: *asgon, maya'.*

blush: *managaga'.*

boar: *balaku.*
young boar: *balakiyu.*

board
board (wood): *tapbla.*
cutting board: *famikayan.*
thick board: *tapblón.*

boast: *embusteria, fatta.*

boastfulness: *banidát.*

boat: *boti, moddong.*
sail boat: *boten layak.*
sailing boat: *batkon layak.*

bob-tail: *labbon.*

bobbin: *lansadera.*

body: *kuetpo, táhtaotao.*
body guard: *á'adahi.*
human body: *tátaotao.*

bog: *ataska, fache', sesonyan.*

bogey man: *fáfa'ñagui.*

boil: *chankocha, granu matditu, na'lagu, pokpok.*
boil starchy food: *saibok.*
to boil: *sotne.*

boiled: *lokklok.*

boiled food
boiled food (starchy): *sinetnan.*

boiling
boiling sound: *lolokklok.*

bold: *atrebidu, bátbaru.*

bolt: *manugong, petno, piesan magagu, totniyu.*

bomb: *bákudang, bam, terudang.*
bombard: *bam, bomba, kañonasu, kampo'.*
bombardment: *bombatdea.*
bone: *to'lang.*
  ankle bone: *bayogu.*
boney: *sankarón.*
bonfire: *foggera.*
bonito: *bunitu, tuna.*
booby
  brown booby: *lu'ao.*
book: *lepblo.*
bookkeeper: *kontadót, tenedot di libro.*
bookmaker: *tenedót.*
boom: *pakpak.*
booth: *buf.*
boots: *botas, sapatos.*
boozer: *butlacheru.*
border: *kanto, lenderu, sinta.*
bordering: *checho.*
bore: *dulok, fastidia.*
  bore into: *barena.*
bored: *o'son, sosongte.*
  bored (from repetition): *empachu.*
boredom: *fastidio.*
boring: *ná'o'son, pasadu.*
born: *mafañagu.*
  first born: *primerisa.*
Borneo: *Botneo.*
borrow: *ayao, presta.*
boss: *amu, bosong, kápurat, ma'gas.*
botany: *botana.*
botfly: *lalo' lagu.*
both: *ambos, todu i dos.*
bother: *atborota, estotba, estraña, fastidia, molestia, na'chatsaga, peredika.*
bothersome: *silok.*
bottle: *buteya.*
  baby bottle: *mamadót.*
  bottle (half gallon): *buteyón.*
  bottle opener: *baban boteya.*
  broken bottle: *empe' buteya.*
bottom: *fondo, papa'.*
bottomless: *desfonda.*
boudoir: *tukadót.*
bougainvillaea: *puti tainobiu.*
bough: *ramas.*
bouncy: *chalaochao, getpan.*
bound: *opbligáo.*
boundary: *chi-, lenderu.*
  boundary line: *checho.*
bouquet: *ramiyeti.*

bouyant: *máma'ya.*
bow: *atkos, dengha, dengnga, dilok, flecha, kottesia, proa, saluda, tekkon.*
  bow-legged: *chanko.*
  bow-legged (m): *manko, patuleku.*
bowel
  lower bowel: *gálabok.*
bowl: *tasón.*
  mixing bowl: *tasón.*
bowline
  bowline (knot): *godden kabayu.*
box: *ápaniti, kahita, kahon, kaohao.*
  to box in: *pongle.*
boxer: *mámaguantes.*
boxing: *uma'ápaniti.*
boy: *lahi.*
boys: *lalahi.*
brace: *ha'fe, mañostieni, tohne.*
  brace and bit: *broka.*
  to brace: *tohne.*
bracelet: *kadena, potseras.*
brackish: *mata'pang.*
brag: *embusteria, fatta.*
braggart: *balenten pachot, fantasia, sakafakteru.*
bragging: *banidát.*
Brahman: *guakan Indian.*
braid: *akeyo', filak.*
brain: *kabesa, títanos.*
  brain (slang): *ábuni.*
brainless: *bruta.*
brainy: *kabilosu.*
branch: *ramas.*
  dead branch: *hagasas.*
brand: *tesson.*
  brand new: *simpeng.*
branding iron: *batkadót.*
brandish: *na'gupu.*
brash: *adilantáo, taffo'.*
brass: *bronse.*
brassiere: *brusia.*
brave: *baliente, subetbia, subetbiu.*
  brave woman: *masakada.*
bravery: *minatatnga.*
bread: *pan, pan royu.*
  type of bread: *roskas.*
breadfruit: *dokdok, essok somnak, lemmai.*
  dried breadfruit: *essok.*
break: *hulok, ma'teng, yamak, yulang.*
  break (branch off tree): *toto.*
  break (into pieces): *yaya.*
  break (point): *upong.*
  break away: *ádespatta.*
  break bottom: *desfonda.*

break down: *mayamak.*
break off: *chebbang, despunta, gutos, iteng, ma'teng, tife', tugan.*
break off (bunch): *ga'om.*
break off (tip): *despongga.*
break partially: *ka'ka'.*
breaker: *ekpe'.*
breakfast: *amotsa, disayunu, lisayunu, na' oga'an.*
breakfast time: *amotsát.*
breast: *susu.*
big breast: *pichura.*
big breast (f): *pechuda.*
big-breasted (slang): *lechera.*
breast feeding: *susu.*
budding breast: *donne' i sisu.*
breath: *alientos, hinagong.*
blow breath: *haha.*
breathe: *hagong.*
breathless: *guha.*
breed: *poksai.*
breeder: *paire.*
brew: *batte.*
bribe: *fahan.*
brick: *ladriyu.*
bride: *nobia.*
bridegroom: *nobiu.*
bridesmaid: *donseyan nobia.*
bridge: *tollai.*
bridle: *bossat.*
bridled white-eye
bridled white-eye (green bird): *nosa'.*
brief: *kádada'.*
briefcase: *katpeta.*
bright: *lamlam, ma'lak.*
brightness: *mina'gas, mina'lak.*
brilliance: *mina'lak.*
brilliant: *kabilosu, ma'lak, tomtom.*
Brillo: *brilu.*
brim: *kanto.*
brine: *chigu'an, hanom ma'asen, inestukon.*
briney: *asnentukon.*
bring: *chule', leklek.*
bring (someone): *konne'.*
bring here: *chule' magi.*
bring up: *yama.*
brisk: *listo.*
briskness: *chinaddek.*
bristle: *tumachon pulu.*
brittle: *hámafak, paska.*
broad: *fedda'.*
broadbill
broadbill bird: *chaguangguan.*

broadcast: *anunsia.*
broaden: *aomenta, na'ancho.*
broader: *lá'ancho, láfedda'.*
broil: *tunu.*
broke: *kara', kasko.*
broken: *ma'pe', mahlok, mayulang.*
broken (mechanically): *fatso.*
broken bottle: *empe' ridoma.*
broken point: *ma'pong.*
bronze: *bronse.*
brood hen: *kuleka.*
brook: *saddok.*
broom: *eskoba, eskoban nuhot.*
broom handle: *tokpong eskoba.*
whisk broom: *eskobeta.*
broth: *atuli, kaddo.*
brother: *che'lu.*
brother-in-law: *ñao, kuñáo, kuña, kuñadu.*
lay brother: *etmanu.*
brotherhood: *afañe'los, inágofli'e', tiguang-.*
brothers: *mañe'lo.*
be brothers: *fañe'lo.*
brow: *sehas.*
brown
brown (color): *kulot chikolati.*
brown nose: *énginge' dagan.*
brown-nose: *ámama.*
brownish: *chinikulati na kulot.*
bruise: *dinigridu, malassas.*
brush: *balle, brochas, eskoba, gue'gue', guesgues, guesgues, saffe, saffe, taoase'.*
brush (something): *brochas.*
brush against: *raspa, raspada.*
brush away: *sahsa.*
brush away (with hand): *sassa.*
clothes brush: *brochas magagu.*
type of brush: *skuiyi.*
brutal: *tái'ase'.*
brute: *brutu.*
bubble: *bu'o'.*
bubbling
bubbling (from heat): *lokklok.*
bubbling sound: *bulokbok.*
bubbling up: *fo'fo'.*
buck: *mamatek, toron binadu, toru.*
bucket: *batde.*
buckle: *biyas, godde, hibiyas.*
bud: *du'an, simiya.*
bud (of plant): *kapuyo', sinisu.*
bud of coconut tree: *tuba.*
to bud: *binga.*
budding: *mañusu, po'dak.*

buddy: *abok, amiga, amigu.*
budge: *aranka, muebi, rempua.*
  not budge: *chetta' kalalamten.*
buffalo
  water buffalo: *karabáo.*
buffer: *bafa.*
buffoon: *frihón, títires.*
bug: *ga'ga'.*
buggy: *kalesa.*
build: *fa'tinas.*
  build house: *kahat.*
building: *guma'.*
built
  well built: *buenaplanta, yomsan.*
bulb
  light bulb: *glop.*
bulge: *malaknos, pokpok.*
bulk: *botto, kantidá.*
bull: *toru.*
  young bull: *toriyu, turiyu.*
bulldozer: *butdosa.*
bullet: *bala.*
bullfighter: *toreru.*
bull's-eye: *mechio', tálulo'.*
bum: *gago'.*
bumblebee: *abeha.*
bump: *bokka', otto.*
  bump against: *totbos, totpe.*
bumper: *bampa.*
bumpy: *baranka, matulongtong.*
bun: *pan mames.*
bunch: *manó.*
  a bunch of: *lahyan, pinipon, pupon.*
  banana bunch: *iteng.*
bundle: *balutan, fininot, kattuchu,*
  manó, manohu, montón, montohon.
bungle: *che'cho' baba.*
bunt: *ette.*
buoy: *balisa, boya.*
  life buoy: *satbabida.*
buoyant: *máma'ya.*
  be buoyant: *gama.*
buoyed
  be buoyed up: *gama.*
burden: *estotbo, katgo.*
bureau: *kómoda.*
burglar: *sakke.*
burial: *entieru.*
burlap: *ganggoche.*
burn: *pakko', potne, songge, tunu.*
  burn (with hot pepper): *pika.*
  cause to burn: *na'fañila', na'matunu.*
burned: *dokngos, hanon, kimasón,*
  kumasón, tostos.

burning
  burning off hair: *chamosga.*
burp: *tugap.*
burr: *ínifok, españa.*
burro: *buru.*
burst: *maffak, mapta', puta'.*
bury: *hafot, tatne.*
bus: *bas.*
bush: *montesiyu.*
  candle bush: *take' biha.*
  type of bush: *kahlao, kilites, kilites,*
    lemon China, matbas, mumutong,
    mumutong palao'an, mumutong
    sapble.
bushy: *chomchom.*
business: *bisnes, kometsio.*
busty: *pechuda.*
busy: *tinane'.*
  get busy: *éga'ga'.*
but: *ada lao, lao.*
butcher: *mataderu.*
butt: *otpos, otto.*
  butt (of a firearm): *koleta.*
butter: *mantikiya.*
butterfly: *ababang.*
buttocks: *dagan, po'dang.*
button: *batunes.*
buttonhole: *ohales, uhales.*
buy: *bona, fahan.*
  buy on credit: *fiha.*
buyer: *fáfahan, kompradót.*
buzz: *bengbeng, bilengbeng.*
  buzz at: *bengbingi, bilengbingi.*
by
  by no means: *tampoku.*
  by the way: *iya'.*
c: *che, se.*
cabbage: *ripoyu.*
cabin: *sade'gani.*
cabinet: *aparadót.*
cable: *uaia'.*
  to cable: *uailes.*
cablegram: *kapble, uailes.*
cacao: *kakáo.*
cackle: *toktugák.*
cackling: *toktugák.*
cactus: *lenggua i baka.*
  cochineal cactus: *hila' guaka.*
cadaver: *kadabet.*
cafeteria: *guma' fañochuyan, kafetiria.*
cage: *tankat, tranka.*
  to cage: *pongle.*
cajole: *fa'ande', uga.*

cake: *fina'mames*.
  sponge cake: *broas, brohas*.
calamity: *desgrasia, hinigua, ira, kebra*.
calculate: *faila'muni, katkula, taha*.
calculation: *katkulasión, katkulu*.
calendar: *kalendario*.
calf: *be', mámahna, mámanha, tatneru*.
  calf (f): *bakiya*.
caliber: *kalibre*.
call: *agangi*.
  call (someone): *agang*.
  call chicken: *kórorot*.
  call for: *katiyi*.
  call to: *inagang*.
callous: *ga'tot*.
callus: *kayos*.
calm: *katma, kayada, mahgong, su'anu, trankilu*.
  calm down: *kayáo, na'manso*.
calmer: *lámahgong*.
Calvary: *Katbario*.
camel: *kameyu*.
camera: *litratu*.
camp: *kampamento, kampo*.
can: *latan ganta, siña*.
  can (container): *lata*.
  can for: *tanken*.
  can opener: *abrilata, baban lata, kánkire'*.
canal: *kannat*.
canary: *kanario*.
cancel: *kansela*.
cancellation: *kanselasión*.
cancer: *kanset*.
candelabra: *arañas*.
candid: *franko*.
candidacy: *kandidatura*.
candidate: *kandidatu*.
candle: *danges, kandela*.
  candle bush: *akapuku*.
  candle holder: *kandileru*.
candy: *kande*.
cane: *bákulu, baston*.
canned
  canned goods: *latiria*.
cannibal: *tekcho'*.
cannon: *kañón*.
canoe: *galaide', kanoa*.
  large canoe: *sakman*.
cantaloupe: *melon*.
canteen: *kantina*.
canvas: *brin, trapát*.
canyon: *kañón*.

cap: *gora, kepes, tappe', tuhong*.
capable: *kapás, kompetente*.
  capable of: *-on*.
capacity: *kapasidát*.
cape: *kapa*.
caper
  wild caper: *atkaparas*.
capital: *kapitát, prinsipát*.
capitalize: *kapitalisa*.
capitol: *kapitát*.
capon: *kappon*.
caprice: *kaprichu*.
capricious: *kaprichosu*.
capsize: *alenken, puha*.
capsized: *mabira*.
captain: *kapitan*.
captive: *kaotibu*.
capture: *konne'*.
captured
  be captured: *kaotiba*.
Capuchin: *kapuchinu*.
car: *kareta, sidán, tumobet*.
  flat car (for freight): *bagón*.
caramel: *kalamelu*.
carbuncle: *katbonkulu*.
carburetor: *katbureta*.
carcass: *kaderas*.
card
  card game (Chamorro): *tres siete*.
  type of card game: *balahan sakke, kasinu, monte, sulitario*.
cardboard
  cardboard box: *kattón*.
cardinal: *katdinát*.
  cardinal fish: *lanse*.
cards
  cards (playing): *balaha, kattan balaha*.
care
  take care of: *adahi*.
career: *ofisiu*.
carefree: *sensiyu*.
careful: *adahi, kuidáo*.
careless: *arebatáo, bronka, bronko, deskaráo, deskuidáo, diháo, dihada, táihinadahi*.
  careless (m): *deskaradu*.
carelessness: *deskuidu, tái'inadahi*.
caress: *iniga, kariñu, uga*.
caretaker: *á'adahi, enkatgáo, enkatgo, subrekatgo*.
cargo
  cargo chief: *subrekatgo*.
carnival: *feria*.

carnivore: *tekcho'.*

carnivorous: *tekcho'.*

Carolinian: *gupallao.*

carpenter: *katpenteru.*

carpentry: *katpenteria.*

carpet: *atfombra.*

carriage: *kalesa, koche.*

carried
  be carried: *ma'udai.*

carrier: *katgadu.*

carry: *afa'fa'i, chanka', hoggue, katga, loffan, oddo', ombo', titeng, uma.*
  can carry: *langak.*
  carry (by hand): *dílileng.*
  carry (in woven basket): *alayi.*
  carry (something): *apaga, do'an, osngan, pingga.*
  carry (something) on the head: *otdo'.*
  carry (something) under the arm: *apecheng.*
  carry along: *kílili.*
  carry each other: *átiteng.*
  carry for: *atiteng.*
  carry on shoulder: *apagayi.*
  carry piggyback: *uke'.*

cart
  bull cart: *kareta.*

cartilage: *gekmon.*

cartload: *karetada.*

carton: *kahita, kahon, kattón.*

cartoon: *manggua'.*

cartridge
  cartridge shell: *katsulas.*

case: *kahita, kahon, kasu.*
  court case: *kaosa.*
  in case: *akasu.*

cash: *kas.*

cashew
  cashew nut: *kasoe.*
  cashew tree: *kasoe.*

cashier: *kaheru.*

casing
  shell casing: *kara'.*

casket: *ata'út.*

cassava: *mendioka.*

cassock: *sutana.*

cast: *blanko, daggao, yotte.*
  cast away: *yute'.*

castanet: *kastaneta.*

castigate: *fa'hiyong.*

Castilian
  Castilian (m): *Kastilianu.*

castle: *kastiyu, palasyo.*

castor bean: *agaliya.*

castrate: *kappon.*

casualty: *kasualidát.*

cat: *katu.*

catalogue: *katálagu.*
  dress catalogue: *figurín.*

cataract
  cataract (of the eye): *do'ak.*

catastrophe: *ira.*

catch: *chahlao, chalao, dúlalak, gadde', konne', mehna, tuchu.*
  catch (in the act): *higef.*
  catch a lot: *menha.*
  catch fish: *tupak.*
  catch rain water: *fakte.*
  catch up with: *gacha'.*

catechism: *dottrina, eskuelan pale'.*
  catechism book: *katisismo.*

category: *katigurát.*

caterpillar: *ulo', ulo' ababang.*

cateye
  cateye shell: *alileng.*
  eye of cateye shell: *pulan.*

catfish: *ito'.*

cathartic: *ná'masinek, potga.*

Catholic: *Katóliku, Kilisyanu.*

Catholicism: *Katolisismo.*

catsup: *kechap, satsa.*

cattle: *guaka.*

Caucasian: *gilagu.*

caught
  be caught: *toka.*

caulk: *galafati, galagala.*

causative
  causative prefix: *muna'-, na'-.*

cause: *muna'-, na'-, rasón.*
  cause to: *nina'-.*

caustic: *mala'et.*

cautious: *maggem.*

cavalry: *kabayeria.*

cave: *bókugo'.*
  cave (natural): *liyang.*
  man-made cave: *bókungo'.*
  small cave: *liyanggua.*

cavern: *liyang.*

cavity: *betmehu, maddok.*

ceiling: *kísami, techo.*

celebrate: *glorifika, guatdia, silebra.*
  to celebrate: *gopte.*

celebrated: *mahngok.*

celebration: *fiesta, gupot, silebrasión.*

celery: *apiu.*

cellar: *budega.*
  wine cellar: *kantina.*

celluloid: *seluloit, seroroidu.*

cement: *patdet, simento, simiento.*
  cement mixture: *meskla.*
  hard cement: *paddet.*
cemetery: *seputtura, simenteyu.*
censer: *senso.*
censor: *senso, sensoru, sensura,*
  sensuradót.
censorship: *senso.*
census: *senso.*
  census when everyone is called to a
  central location to be counted:
  enpadrona.
  take a census: *senso.*
cent: *memos, séntimos, sentabu.*
center: *sentro, talo'.*
centipede: *saligao.*
century: *siklo.*
cereal: *siriales.*
ceremony: *seremonias.*
certain: *diberas, fitme, fotte, metton,*
  siguru.
certainly: *siempre, siguramente, téneki.*
certainty: *siguridát, sigurida.*
certificate: *settifiku.*
certification: *settifikasión.*
certify: *klaruyi, settifika.*
certitude: *siguridát.*
chain: *kadena.*
  chain link: *eslabón.*
chair: *siya, ta'chong.*
  arm chair: *gata'chongan.*
  rocking chair: *siyan machukan.*
Chalan Kanoa
  Chalan Kanoa (slang): *Charanka'.*
chalice: *kales.*
chalk: *chak, yesu.*
challenge: *champa, chanda, embeste,*
  kompetensia, kontra.
challenger: *enimigu, kontrariu.*
chamber pot: *rinola.*
chamberlain: *kamareru.*
chambermaid: *kamarera.*
chambray: *kambrai.*
Chamorro
  young Chamorro (female):
  Chamorrita.
  young Chamorro (male): *Chamorritu.*
champion: *gannadót, paire, pilong.*
chance: *chansa.*
  chance of: *puedi.*
  one who chances: *chanseru.*
chanceful: *chansa.*
chancre: *enkatmadura.*
chandelier: *kandelaria.*

change: *a'go, ina'go, remediu.*
  change appearance: *na'sahnge,*
  na'sangi.
  change into: *mama'-.*
  change over: *kombiette.*
  change to: *fa'-.*
changeable: *a'guyon, bariapble.*
channel: *kannat, puetto, sagua'.*
chant: *kanta, kanta, lalai.*
chapel: *guma' Yu'us, kapiya.*
chaperone: *ga'chungi.*
chapter: *kapítulu.*
character: *sensia.*
charcoal: *katbon, pínigan.*
  charcoal dust: *tesna.*
  charcoal vendor (m): *katboneru.*
charge
  charge (someone) with: *sokne.*
  charge at: *sufa', tugong.*
charitable: *góflamen, karitatibu.*
charity: *karidát.*
charmed
  be charmed: *kaotiba.*
charred
  charred stick: *tesson.*
chart: *mapa.*
chase: *dúlalak, tattiyi.*
  chase away: *rimata, ritira, sugon.*
  to chase away dogs: *handa.*
chaser
  chaser (in hunting): *kasadules.*
chaste: *gasgas, sensiyu.*
chat: *kuentos.*
chatter: *palakpak.*
chatterbox: *ga'kumuentos, palakpak.*
chauffeur: *kocheru.*
cheap: *baratu.*
cheat: *digeruyi, dugeruyi, tesgue,*
  umáfa'baba.
cheated
  be cheated: *mafa'baba.*
cheater: *chapuseru, digeru, dugeru,*
  fáfa'baba.
check: *chek.*
  check on: *ripara.*
  medical check-up: *riseta.*
checker: *pión.*
checkers
  checkers (game): *dama.*
cheek: *fasu.*
cheer: *konsuelu, minagof.*
  cheer up: *konsuela.*
cheerlessness: *triniste.*
cheese: *kesu.*

chef: *kusineru.*
cherish: *agradesi.*
chest: *ba'út, kaha, pecho.*
  big chest (m): *pechudu.*
  chest (body): *ha'of.*
  storage chest: *kaohao.*
chesty
  chesty (person): *pechudu.*
chew: *ñamñam, ngangas.*
  chew audibly: *na'getmon.*
  chew for (feeding): *mohmo.*
chewing tobacco: *amme.*
chick: *puyitos.*
  chick pea: *gatbanso.*
chicken: *mannok.*
  chicken coop: *kasiyas.*
  type of chicken: *balaskes, bankas,*
  bulaskes, buremos, kántanes, kresta i
  rosa, kuba, labbon, panaguan, pilon
  dulili, regong, rodo', saigón, siamo',
  sinisa.
chide: *lalatde.*
chief: *atkadi.*
  great chief: *pilong.*
child: *patgon.*
children: *famagu'on.*
chilled: *manengheng.*
chilly: *fugu.*
chime: *tohke.*
chimney: *chiminea, chuminea.*
chimpanzee: *saro'.*
chin: *achai, babas.*
China: *China.*
Chinese
  Chinese (f): *China.*
  Chinese (m): *Chinu.*
  Chinese cabbage: *nappa'.*
chink: *kuyontura.*
chip: *chebbang, estiyas, ipe', pa'kes,*
  tengteng.
  chip in: *atmiñudu.*
  to chip in (money): *ensima.*
chipped
  chipped (blade): *doffe'.*
  chipped ball: *supi.*
chips: *tanto.*
chisel: *asuela, eskopplo, sensét.*
chocolate: *chikulati, chokolati.*
choice: *ga'o-, inayek, sileksion.*
choir: *kantores, koru.*
choke: *ñukot, finakulu'an.*
choked: *ga'otgan.*
cholera: *kólera.*
choose: *ayek, ga'ña-, ga'o-.*

choosy: *chacha', cha'tan.*
chop: *chaba, pika, taga', taktak,*
  tasahos, utot.
  chop off: *chebbang.*
chopper: *tátaga'.*
chopping block: *famikayan.*
chopstick: *palitu.*
chopsticks
  use chopsticks: *palitu.*
chore: *tareha.*
chorus: *kantores.*
Christ: *Kristo, Santa Madre i Ekglesia.*
christen: *takpangi.*
christening: *baotismo.*
Christian: *Kilisyanu.*
  Christian (m): *Kristianu.*
  Christian Mother: *Nanan Kilisyanu.*
Christmas: *pasgua, Krismas, Nabidát,*
  Natibidát.
  Christmas Eve: *bespiran nochebuena,*
  nochebuena.
chroma: *kulót.*
chrysanthemum: *mansaniya.*
  Indian chrysanthemum: *yetban Santa*
  Maria.
chubby: *chebot.*
chuckle: *chakka', chekchek.*
chunk: *tasahos, trosu.*
church: *ekglesia, guma' Yu'us.*
  first church bell: *atba.*
churchyard: *simenteyu.*
cigar: *chigalu, labana.*
cigarette: *chupa, patma, sigariyu.*
cinder: *pínigan.*
cinnamon: *kanela.*
circle: *sítkulu.*
circular: *adamelong, aridondo, ridondo.*
circulate: *ridondeha.*
circumscribe: *likoku'i.*
circumstance: *sikumstansia, situasión.*
citation: *sitasión, tiket.*
cite: *sita.*
citizen: *siudadanu.*
citizenship: *siudadanu.*
citrus
  citrus fruit: *fruta.*
city: *siudá, siudát.*
civilian: *sibít.*
civilization: *sibilisasión.*
civilize: *sibilisa.*
civilized: *sibilisáo.*
clack: *alapika.*
clacking: *talaktak.*

claim: *apudera, dimanda, embatga, gagao, ganye.*

clairvoyance: *sábio.*

clairvoyant: *le'an, sábio.*

clam: *hima, tapon.*
  type of clam: *pa'gang, pahgang.*

clamor: *éssalao.*

clamp: *kotma, sokka.*

clan: *familia.*

clap: *padda'.*
  clap (hands): *pakpak.*

clarified: *klaru.*

clarify: *aklara, klarifika, klaruyi, na'klaru.*

clarity: *klaridát.*

clash: *ápannak, átotpe.*

clasp: *mañostieni, prende.*

class: *klas, klasi.*

classificable: *klasifikáo.*

classification: *klasifikasión.*

classified: *klasifikáo.*

classify: *klasifika.*

clatter: *pakpak, talaktak.*

clause: *parafu.*

claw: *pápakes.*
  claw of the crab: *dáma'gas.*
  to claw: *kaku.*

claws: *káka'guas.*

clay: *odda' sabana.*

clean: *gasgas, klaru, lempiesa, na'gasgas.*
  clean (intestines): *fokse.*
  clean (with soap): *habuni.*

cleaning: *yinabbao.*

cleanliness: *lempiesa.*

cleanse: *fa'gasi.*

clear: *desmonte, klaru, manana.*
  all clear: *kaiyio'.*
  clear (liquid): *nao'ao.*
  clear land: *abahu.*
  clear throat: *katkat, kokkok.*

clearing
  a clearing: *manana.*

clearness: *klaridát.*

cleave: *puta', tupa.*

cleaver: *machetten matadót.*

clef: *klabu.*

cleft: *ka'ka'.*

clench: *akihom, akka'.*

clergyman: *inamte.*

clerk: *eskribiente, tenderu.*

clever: *malate', tomtom.*

clicking: *talaktak.*

cliff: *kantít, ladera, paderón.*

climate: *klema, klima.*

climax
  sexual climax (slang): *makaka.*

climb
  climb on top of: *kahulo'gue.*
  climb up: *ékulo', kahulo'.*
  climb up (the tree): *feddos.*

climbed
  climbed up: *mameddos.*

climber: *lakkao, lekkao.*

cling: *apecheng, mañostieni.*
  cling to: *chetton.*

clinic: *ospitát.*

clink: *talaktak, tilingteng, tingteng.*

clip: *chiget, labbon.*
  clip of bullets: *kattuchu.*

clitoris
  clitoris (slang): *kresta.*

cloak: *kapa.*

clobber: *fa'om, saragati.*

clock: *relós.*

clogged
  clogged up: *mañongsong.*

Clorox: *ná'mafnas.*

close: *hihot, huchom.*
  close to: *fi'on.*

closed
  become closed: *machom.*

closest: *yamágigi.*

closet: *aparadót.*
  clothes closet: *tanso'.*

cloth: *indiana, manta.*
  ironing cloth: *saosao magagu.*
  type of cloth: *kambrai, laniya, seda.*

clothe: *minagagu.*

clothes: *bestidu, chinina, labada, linakse, magagu, muda.*
  change clothes: *muda.*
  clothes closet: *aparadót.*
  clothes for women: *bestida.*
  clothes hanger: *kana' magagu.*
  clothes pin: *chiget.*
  clothesline: *fanala'an, talen manala'.*
  work clothes: *bahakke.*

clothing: *bagai, muda.*

cloud: *mapagahes.*

clouds
  rain clouds: *homhom uchan.*

cloudy: *lebbok, lubradu, nubladu, nupbladu.*

clown: *burego'.*

club: *fa'om, galuti, inetnon.*

clubs: *bastos.*

237

cluck: *toktok, totot.*
clumsy: *chapós, kadabet.*
cluster: *montón.*
clutch: *chule'.*
clutched: *chinile'.*
coal: *katbon.*
coalition: *aliansa.*
coarse: *bastos.*
coast: *chepchop tasi, kosta, uriyan tasi.*
coat: *kot, saku.*
cob
  corn cob: *kakalotes.*
cobweb: *tararañas.*
cock: *gayu.*
  cock (firearm): *kasa.*
  cock (young): *poyu.*
  cock-eyed: *kitánlaña', kitan.*
cockfight: *gayera, palitada.*
cockfighter
  cockfighter (m): *gayeru.*
cockpit: *gayera, rueda.*
cockroach: *kukuracha.*
cockscomb: *krestan gayu.*
cocksure: *siguru.*
cocoa: *kakáo.*
coconut: *gafo', kannu'on, ma'son, niyok, niyok kannu'on, pontan, tahu.*
  coconut (without any meat): *aplok.*
  coconut (young): *daddek.*
  coconut candy: *bukayu.*
  coconut dumpling: *ahu.*
  coconut fibre: *gunot.*
  coconut husker: *heggao, hehgao.*
  coconut milk: *lechen niyok.*
  coconut oil: *lañan niyok, tika.*
  coconut palm: *niyok.*
  coconut plant: *haigue.*
  coconut shoot: *penka.*
  grated coconut: *kinamyo.*
  green coconut: *manha, manna.*
  husk of coconut: *punot.*
  leaf of coconut tree: *hagamham.*
  make coconut oil: *tika.*
  meatless coconut: *bóbolong.*
  ripe coconut: *na'gao.*
cocoon: *alitos ababang.*
Cocos Island: *Dano'.*
cod: *bakaláo.*
  cod liver oil: *bakaláo.*
code: *kódigu, lai.*
coffee: *kafé.*
  coffee pot: *kafetera.*
coffin: *ata'út.*
cohere: *chetton.*

coincide: *konfotme.*
coins: *moneda.*
  coins (money): *sensiyu.*
coitus: *baggai, dalle, kichi, paireha, puspus, sirek, umá'uyu.*
colander: *kulanda.*
cold: *fugu, mañom, manengheng.*
  bad cold: *sagu.*
  cold region: *tano' manengheng.*
collaborate: *áfa'maolek.*
collaborator: *á'ayuda, ayudante.*
collapse: *mayamak, poddong.*
collar: *kueyon chinina.*
collect: *hokka, na'etnon, na'montohon, na'monton, rikohi.*
collection: *etnon, koleksión, koleru, montohon.*
  collection box: *kahon limosna.*
collector: *kolektót.*
college: *kolehio, kolehu.*
collide: *ásufa', átotpe.*
  collide with: *totbos, totpe.*
collier: *katboneru.*
colonel: *koronét.*
colonize: *sagayi.*
color: *kulót, penta.*
  shade of color: *changa.*
  solid color: *rasu.*
colorful: *míkulot.*
coloring: *tumu.*
colorless: *kachang.*
colt: *patgon kabayu.*
column: *fila, kolumna, lucha.*
comatose: *afatigáo.*
comb: *paine, paineta.*
  comb (chicken): *kresta.*
combat: *mumu.*
combination: *etnon.*
combine: *na'daña'.*
combined: *daña'.*
combustible: *songgiyon.*
combustion: *guafi.*
come: *maila', mamaila', matto.*
  come into: *kákalom.*
  come to: *fatto.*
comedian: *komidiante.*
comedy: *komeya.*
comfort: *kombenensia, konsoladu, konsolasión.*
comical: *santa'.*
comics: *kameks.*
comma: *koma.*
command: *fina'maolek, kapitani, komanda, manda, nombra, otden, tago'.*

commander: *komanda, tátago'.*
commemorate
to commemorate: *gopte.*
commence: *tuka, tutuhon.*
commend: *rekomenda.*
commerce: *kometsio.*
commission: *ínteres, aturisa, katgo.*
commission (someone): *enkatga.*
commissioner: *atkadi, komísina.*
commit: *kometi.*
committee: *komiti.*
commode: *kómoda.*
common: *otdinariu.*
common coot: *pulattat.*
communion
communion rail: *komotgatorio, kumotgatorio.*
holy communion: *komuñón.*
receive communion: *kómotgan.*
community: *komunidá.*
companion: *ga'chong, kompania.*
company: *kompania.*
comparative
comparative degree: *-ña.*
comparative prefix: *tak-.*
compare: *akompara, kompara.*
comparison: *akomparasión, komparasión.*
compass
compass (mariner's): *kompás.*
compassion: *indothensia.*
compel: *afuetsas.*
compensate: *apasi.*
compete: *achá'igi, champa, kompetensia, kompiti.*
compete with: *kontra.*
competent: *kompetente, kualifikáo.*
competition: *kompetensia, kompitisión.*
competitor: *enimigu, kompetidót, kontrariu, ribát.*
compile: *daña'.*
complain: *kehayi.*
complaint: *keha.*
complete: *funhayan, kabales, kumple, kumplidu, monhayan, munhayan.*
completed: *echo, kompletu.*
completely: *kompletamente.*
complexion
type of complexion: *murena.*
complicated: *gaddon, komplikáo.*
complication: *ginaddon.*
compliment: *komplimenta, komplimentu, tuna.*
complimentary: *atendidu.*

comply: *kumple.*
compositor: *impresót.*
comprehend: *komprende.*
comprehensible: *komprendiyon, tungu'on.*
compress: *chiget, hemmot, peha.*
compromise: *kompremeti, kompromisu.*
comptroller: *kontadót.*
compulsory: *opbligáo.*
compute: *katkula, mangfong.*
comrade: *amiga, ga'chong, próhimu.*
comrades: *afañe'los.*
conceal: *atok, disimula, na'atok, na'na', oropa.*
concealed: *ti annok.*
concede: *atmiti, sedi.*
conceited: *mama'ma'gas.*
conceive: *hasso, mapotge', na'hasso.*
conceive (child): *sumugo'.*
conception: *mapotge'.*
concerned: *ínteres.*
conclude: *ditetmina.*
concluded: *kumplidu.*
concord: *inákomprende.*
concrete: *kónkore', konkrit, paddet.*
concur: *konfotme.*
concussion: *pangpang.*
condemn: *desaprueba, kondena.*
condemnation: *kondenasión.*
condenser: *kondensa.*
condition: *estáo, kondisión.*
condition (referring to soil): *klima.*
conditioned: *arekláo.*
condole: *konsuela.*
condom
condom (slang): *bossat.*
condone: *asi'i, despensa.*
conduct: *dirihi, kondukta, kondukta, manea.*
confederacy: *aliansa.*
conference: *konfirensia.*
confess: *kónfesat.*
confession: *konfesión.*
confessional: *konfesonario.*
confessor: *konfesót.*
confessors: *konfesores.*
confide: *konfia.*
confidence: *konfiansa, siguridát.*
configuration: *botto.*
confine
to confine: *pongle.*
confinement: *minidiyi.*

confirm
confirm (in Catholic church): *konfitma.*
confirmation: *konfitmasión.*
conflagrated: *hanon.*
conflagration: *guafi, kimasón, kumasón.*
conform: *konfotma, konfotme.*
confront: *konfronta.*
confront (one another): *áfana'.*
confused: *aburidu, gaddon.*
confusion: *enkebukáo, kombalachi, yinaoyao.*
congeal: *tulondron.*
conger eel: *hakmang palús.*
congratulate: *filisita, komplimenta.*
congregate: *rikohi.*
congregation: *etnon, montohon.*
congress: *kongresu.*
congressman: *kongresisto.*
connect: *chetton, na'chetton, tokche.*
connected
closely connected: *umáchetton.*
connector: *ná'chetton.*
conquer: *konkista.*
conquest: *biktoria, fangganna.*
conscience: *konsensia.*
consecrate: *konsagra.*
consecrated: *sagradu.*
consecration: *konsagrasión.*
consecutive: *sigidu.*
consent: *konsentimento, konsiente, petmiti.*
consequence: *hiniyong.*
conserve: *utas.*
conserves: *konsetba.*
consider: *konsidera.*
considerate: *konsideradu.*
consideration: *konsiderasión.*
consist
consist of: *konsiste.*
consolation: *konsoladu, konsolasión, konsuelu.*
console: *riberensia.*
constabulary: *polisia.*
construct: *fa'tinas.*
construction: *konstraksion.*
consult: *konsutta.*
consumable: *gastáo.*
consume: *chocho, konsuma, lachai, pañot.*
consume (too much): *dafflokgue.*
consume something: *kanno'.*
consumed: *boka, kinanno'.*

consumption: *soksok.*
consumptive: *tibi.*
contagious: *kontahiosu, takme.*
contagiousness: *malumót.*
contain: *konsiste.*
container: *atupat, dudu, sahguan, tebbot.*
container (large can): *kántaru.*
empty container: *ánbasihu, basihu, basiu.*
tuba container: *bóbolong.*
water container: *suhu.*
contaminate: *na'ye, tatme.*
contaminated: *nina'ye, tinatme.*
contemplate: *konsidera, kontempla.*
contempt
show contempt: *chichi'i.*
contemptible: *despresiáo, despresiapble.*
contemptuous: *despresiáo.*
contend: *achá'igi.*
content: *kontento.*
contentment: *kinentento, kontentamento.*
contents: *sinahguan.*
contest: *huegu.*
continent
continent (land): *kontinensia.*
continuation: *kontinuasión.*
continue: *konsigi, kontinua, petsigi, sigi.*
continuous: *humahnanao.*
contraband: *kontrabando, na'lifet.*
contract: *kontrata, tratos.*
work contract: *pakiáo.*
contracted: *maheddo.*
contractor: *kontratista.*
contradict: *chanda, kontradisi, puni, resiste.*
contradiction: *kontradiksión.*
contrary
to the contrary: *maolekña.*
contrast: *akompara, kompara.*
contrasting: *komparasión.*
contribute: *fa'buresi, faboresi.*
contribute (money): *limosna.*
contribution: *kontribusión.*
contrite: *sotsot.*
control: *desponi, gobietna, guaguat, manea, suheta.*
controversy: *ináguaguat.*
contusion: *dinigridu, magomgom.*
conundrum: *misterio.*
convene: *na'etnon, na'montohon, rikohi.*

convenience: *kombenensia.*
convenient: *kombeniente.*
convent: *kombento.*
convention: *kombension.*
conversation: *kombetsasión.*
converse: *ádingan, kombetsa, kuentos.*
  converse with: *kuentusi.*
conversion: *konbetsión.*
convert: *kombiette.*
convey: *fitma.*
convict tang: *kichu.*
convince: *kombense, sohyo'.*
convoy: *akompañamento.*
convulsed: *kalamle.*
convulsion: *mañague'.*
cook: *chahan, fa'tinas, fattinas,*
  kusineru, na'lagu, na'masa.
  cook (by boiling): *sotne.*
  cook (in water): *chankocha.*
  cook Spanish rice: *balensiana.*
cooked: *masa.*
cooker: *fáfa'tinas.*
cookie: *guyuria.*
cool: *fresko.*
  become cool: *mapao.*
  cool off: *mapao, na'mapao.*
  cool-headed: *su'anu.*
coop: *kasiyas.*
cooperate
  cooperate with: *áfa'maolek.*
cooperation: *ko'operasión.*
cooperative: *ko'operatibu.*
copper: *kopble.*
copra: *sine'so'.*
  make copra: *so'so'.*
copy: *dilitrea, eyak, kopia.*
coral: *acho' ñañak, acho' tasi.*
  coral rock: *cho'cho'.*
  type of coral: *acho' dagon haya.*
cordial: *fiét.*
core: *korasón.*
cork: *kocha, kotcha.*
corn: *eskomme, mai'es, puspus.*
  corn silk: *batbas mai'es.*
  ear of corn: *masotka.*
  green corn: *ilotes.*
  sweet corn: *ilotes.*
corned beef: *katnen notte.*
corner: *banda, birada, birada, renkón,*
  rinkón.
  corner (of building): *eskina.*
cornet: *kotneta.*
cornish
  dark cornish (chicken): *regong.*

corporal: *kóporat, kabu.*
corporeal: *káporat.*
corpse: *kadabet, matai.*
corpulent: *chebot, yommok.*
corral: *chikeru, kollat.*
correct: *dinanche, kurihi, na'ádanche,*
  na'dinanche, na'tunas.
correspond: *koresponde, koresponde.*
correspondence: *katta, korespondensia.*
corridor: *koredót.*
corrupt: *na'atborutáo.*
cost: *gasto, ginasta, kosta.*
  cost of freight: *fleti.*
costly: *guaguan.*
costume: *kastom.*
cot: *kama, kat, katre.*
cottage: *kabaña.*
cotter pin: *kuña.*
cotton: *átgidon, laniya.*
cough: *lo'lo'.*
council: *konsilio.*
councilman: *akonseheru.*
counsel: *akonseha, kuka, pinagat.*
counselor: *á'akonseha, abugáo,*
  abugadu, akonseheru, konseheru.
count: *mamfong, tufong.*
countable: *tufungon.*
counter: *estante, tachi, tapblita.*
  counter-sink: *punsón.*
counteract: *ataha.*
countermand: *diroga.*
counterweight: *kontrapesa.*
country: *bariu.*
countryman: *paisanu.*
couple: *empatma.*
  couple of: *loskuantos, noskuantos,*
  unos kuantos.
couplet: *pat, tetno.*
courage: *animu, subetbia.*
courageous: *animosu, baliente,*
  mama'lahi, subetbiu.
court: *kotte, plasa.*
  court of justice: *fanhusgayan.*
courteous: *atendidu, atento, respetayon,*
  su'abi.
courtesy: *afabilidát, fabót, kotdisia.*
cousin
  cousin (f): *prima.*
  cousin (m): *primu.*
cover: *bándaras, tampe.*
  cover a bet: *kasa, kubre.*
  cover up: *oropa, tampe.*
  to cover: *hulof.*

covered
covered with: *kubietto.*

covering: *funda, onno'.*

coverlet: *hafyen katre.*

covet: *agara, apudera, diseha.*

covetous: *padok.*

cow: *baka, bakiya, guaka.*
milking cow: *lechera.*

coward: *dangnge', kokañao, kubatde.*

cowfish: *danglon.*

cowlick: *rimulinu.*

cowrie
cowrie shell: *karakót.*
small cowrie: *cheggai.*

crab: *ña'ot, apótalang, atópalang, hagáf.*
coconut crab: *ayuyu.*
crab (generic term): *panglao.*
crab (soft-shelled): *hagahaf.*
crab trap: *ókkodon panglao.*
ghost crab: *aguhi, haguihen aguas.*
ghost crab (ocypoda arenaria): *haguihi.*
golden crab: *panglao oros.*
hermit crab: *umang, umang duk, umang maknganiti, umang Yu'us.*
land crab: *panglao tunas.*
mangrove crab: *akmangao.*
robber crab: *ayuyu.*
rock crab: *hagahaf.*
spotted sea crab: *atmangao.*
stuffed crab: *ka'he.*
type of crab-cardisoma (gecarcinidae): *panglao tunas.*
type of crab-carpilius maculatus: *panglao oros.*
type of crab-scylla serrata: *akmangao.*

crack: *ka'ka', ngulo'.*
crack (bones of a joint): *chekchek.*
crack (on the head): *maffak.*
crack (the bones of a joint): *chakchak, chakka'.*
crack in seam: *giga'.*
crack open: *mapta', pokka'.*

cracked: *ma'pe'.*
cracked skin: *ka'ka'mata'.*

cracker: *biskuchu, krakas.*

crackling
crackling (of dry leaves): *kalaskas.*

cradle: *kuna.*
cradle (in one's arms): *turoru.*

crafty: *fayi.*

crag: *paderón.*

cram: *hemmot.*
cram tightly (into a hole): *sohmok.*

cramped: *kalamle.*

crane: *licheng.*

crank: *koranko'.*

cranky: *muñeru.*

cravat: *kotbata.*

crave: *diseha, tanga.*

craving: *disehu, tinanga.*

crawl: *ba', bumá', kúnanaf.*
to crawl: *toru.*

crayon: *korehong.*

crazy: *á'baba', ó'duko', atmariáo, kaduka, kaduku, kuka', loka, loku.*
crazy (slang): *á'langa'.*

cream: *leche, mantikan leche.*

crease: *makalehlo.*

create: *fa'tinas, kriadu, na'faloffan, na'huyong.*

created: *mana'huyong.*

creation: *nina'huyong.*

creator: *fáfa'tinas, kreadót, nána'huyong.*

credentials: *sédulas.*

credit: *kréditu.*

creditor
creditor (m): *akredót.*

creed: *kredu.*

creep: *kúnanaf, kahat, kahatgue, sikat.*

creeper: *akankang.*

crescent: *kresiente.*

crest: *kresta.*
crest-wyandott (chicken): *kresta i rosa.*

crevice: *ka'ka'.*

crew: *marineru.*
crew cut: *dasai adotfo.*

crib: *bilén, kunao.*
baby crib: *kuna.*

cricket: *ga'ga' sirenu, griyos.*
male cricket: *guriyos.*

crime: *isao.*

criminal: *kriminát.*

cripple: *makabebi.*

crippled: *kohu, manko.*

crisis: *predikamento.*

crispy: *dokngos, kaspa, tostos.*

criss-cross: *encros.*

criticize: *kritisisa, tacha.*

crochet: *dibuhu, ganchiyu.*
crochet needle: *gansiyu.*
one who crochets: *fáfamfok.*

crock: *hara, tinaha.*

crocodile: *kaimán.*

crook: *fáfa'baba.*

crooked: *ebang, echong, ekklao, matahlek, natahlek.*

crop: *kosecha.*

cross: *kilu'os.*
  cross legs: *ágaode, gaode.*
  cross over: *krusa.*
  cross-eyed: *kitan.*
  crossbeam: *dotmiente, kabayeti, tiheras.*
  make a cross: *ekkes.*
  sign of cross: *pot i siñat.*

crossroad: *dinga', dinga' chalan.*

crossway: *pasaderu.*

crotch: *afa'fa'.*

crouch: *deha.*

crow
  crow (of rooster): *o'o'.*
  Marianas crow: *aga.*

crowbar: *bareta.*

crowd: *buyada, katdumi, linahyan.*
  crowd in: *si'eng.*

crowded: *bohbo, motmot.*

crown: *korona.*
  crown (of the head): *rimulinu.*

crucifix: *kilu'os, krusifio.*

crucify: *klaba.*
  to crucify: *krusifika.*

cruel: *kruet, malamaña, matditu, sakat, tái'ase', táilayi.*
  be cruel: *na'táilayi.*

cruelty: *kruetdát.*

crumb: *pidasu.*

crumble: *tiges.*

crumbled: *maheffong.*

crumbly: *mangto'.*

crumple: *apédelok, hemmot.*

crumpled: *yá'balak.*

crunch: *na'getmon.*

crunchy
  crunchy sound: *getmon.*

crush: *figes, higef, tiges, tugot.*

crutch: *bákulu.*

cry: *kasao, kati, tanges.*
  cry for: *katiyi, tangse.*
  cry out: *gagak, gigek.*
  cry-baby: *kakte.*
  cry-baby (m): *muñeru.*

crystal: *krestát.*
  crystal (dinner ware): *kristát.*

Cuba: *Kubanu.*

Cuban: *Kubanu.*

cuckold: *kabrón.*

cucumber: *pipinu.*
  sea cucumber: *balate', talen moddong.*

cud: *amme.*

cudgel: *fa'om, galuti.*

cuff: *afulu.*
  cuff link: *mankuetnas.*

cuisine: *kusina.*

culpable: *katgueti.*

cultivate: *kuttiba.*
  cultivate land: *gualo'.*

cultural: *kutturát.*

culture: *kuttura.*

cumbersome: *makkat.*

cumbrous: *makkat.*

cummerbund: *faha.*

cunning: *fáfa'baba.*

cup: *na'yan, potsuelu, pusuelu, tasa.*
  cup of gold: *kopa di oru.*
  glass cup: *basu.*

cupboard: *tapblita.*

curable: *amtiyon.*

curacao milkweed: *asensión.*

curate: *paroku.*

curdle: *kottadu.*

cure: *remediu.*
  cure sickness: *amte.*

cured: *inamte.*

curer: *ná'magong.*

Curia Romana: *Santa Madre i Eklesia.*

curious: *embilikeru, kuriosu.*

curl: *mulatu.*

curlew: *dulili, kalalang.*

curly
  curly hair: *mulata, mulatu.*

currency: *salape'.*

current: *koriente.*

curry: *karí.*

curse: *disecha, matdisi, mattetsio.*
  curse at: *chatfinu'i.*

cursed: *matditu.*

cursing: *chátfino'.*

curtain: *kuttina.*

curtained
  be curtained: *makuttinayi.*

curve: *birada, ebang, echong, kabo', kutba, pusada.*

curved: *ekklao, pakke'.*

cushion: *kúsion, kotchon.*

cuspidor: *fano'la'an.*

custard apple: *anonas.*

custodian: *enkatgáo, subrekatgo.*

custom: *bisio, kustumbre, maña, pengnga', pennga', usu.*

customary: *mana'payon, payon, regulatmente.*

customs: *réditu.*

cut: *cha'lak, chachak, tahu, tasahos, tinaga', utot.*
  cut (in slice): *dibana.*
  cut (with a knife): *se'se'.*
  cut (with one stroke): *gabbe.*
  cut curves: *lapbla.*
  cut down (a woods): *desmonte.*
  cut each other: *átaga'.*
  cut grass: *guassan.*
  cut into slices: *pika.*
  cut lip: *machaba'.*
  cut off: *despunta, ma'tot, manko.*
  cut off (bunch of bananas): *honggo'.*
  cut off (esp. hair): *dasai, laklak.*
  cut off (point): *despongga, upong.*
  cut off ear: *mocha.*
  cut on foot: *ma'akgak.*
  cut open: *ipe'.*
  cut the belly open: *chungat.*
  cut tuba: *risaka.*

cutlery: *ramienta.*

cutter: *chachak, tátaga'.*

cutting: *tahu.*

cuttlefish: *nosnos.*

cyclone
  tropical cyclone: *pakyo.*

cylinder: *silindro.*

cymbal: *símbalu.*

cyst: *cho'le, dohlan.*

d: *de.*

dad: *tata.*

daddy: *tata.*

dagger: *puñát.*

daikon: *daikon.*

daily: *di'ario, kada dia, kada ha'ani.*

dainty: *espót.*

dairy: *lechera.*

damage: *dañu, difekto.*

damaged: *dañáo.*

damnation: *kondenasión.*

damp: *úmidu, fotgonñaihon, maggem, masmas.*

dampen: *na'fotgon.*

dampened: *mumáñaña'.*

damsel fish: *fohmo', fohmo' gadudok.*
  damsel fish (gray): *doddo.*

dance: *baila, dansa.*
  stick dance: *bailan fayao.*

dancer: *bailadót.*
  dancer (f): *bailadora.*

dandruff: *kaspa.*

danger: *piligro.*

dangerous: *piligro, piligrosu.*

dare: *ariesga, atotga, atrebi.*

daring: *atotgante, atrebidu, bátbaru, baliente.*
  daring (f): *subetbia.*
  daring (m): *subetbiu.*

dark: *didok, homhom.*

darkened: *hinemhom.*

darkness: *hinemhom.*

darling: *kiridu.*

darn: *lato', sotse.*

dart: *pechao.*

dash: *malagu, manugong, petsan, pinalala.*
  dash (away): *pechao.*
  dash (liquid on something): *cho'me.*

date
  date (noting time): *fecha.*
  date of birth: *fechan mafañagu.*

daub: *emplasta.*

daughter: *ákkaga, haga, iha.*
  daughter of: *hagan.*
  daughter-in-law: *yetna.*

dauntless: *animosu.*

dawdler: *tatnon.*

dawn: *atba, chakchak, chakchak manana, kinahulo' atdao, machakchak kattan, ogga'an, pa'go manana.*
  break of dawn: *machakchak.*

dawning: *machakchak.*

day: *dia, ha'ani.*
  day after tomorrow: *agupa'ña, inakpa'ña, nakpa'ña.*
  day before yesterday: *nigapña.*
  day break: *pa'go manana.*

daybreak: *chakchak manana, machakchak kattan.*

daylight: *dia, manana.*

days: *dias.*

daytime: *dia, manana.*

dead: *matai.*
  dead person: *difunto.*

deaf: *tangnga.*

deafening: *ná'tanga.*

deafness: *tinangnga.*

deal: *kontrata, tratos.*
  make a deal: *tratos.*

dealer: *bankera, kometsiante.*

dear: *magofli'e', nena.*

death: *finatai, kumekematai, minatai.*
  death quiver: *mañague'.*
  death throes: *fatigáo.*

debar: *fa'hiyong.*

debase: *fohyan.*

debate: *atgumento, debati, diskuti.*

debilitated: *debet, mamaitaguan.*

debris: *ántupa.*

debt: *dada'da', de'uda, dibi.*

debtor: *fihadót.*
debtor (f): *fihadora.*

decay: *betmehu, lamas.*
tooth decay: *dumang.*

decayed: *potlilu.*

deceased: *difunto.*

deceit: *linipa, mandagi.*

deceitful: *embusteru.*

deceive: *fa'baba, tesgue.*

deceiver: *chapuseru, fáfa'baba.*

December: *Disiembre, Umayangan.*

decent: *asientadu, disente.*

deception: *fina'baba, traisión.*

decide: *disidi.*

decimal: *désimu, desimát.*

decimate: *desminuyi.*

decision: *disisión, huisio, sentensia.*

deck: *paneta.*
deck (of ship): *kubietta.*

declaration: *deklarasión.*

declare: *agangñaihon, aklara, deklara, proklama.*

decline: *re'usa, renunsia.*

decorate: *adotna, beste, florisi.*

decoration: *beste, gatbesa.*

decorous: *asentadu.*

decoy: *pugi.*

decrease: *kaguan.*

decrepit: *yá'balak.*

dedicate
to dedicate: *gopte.*

dedicated: *dibotu.*

deed: *aksión, fina'tinas.*

deep: *ancho, apuya' tasi, didok, feman, taddong, tahdong.*

deepen: *na'lámoddong.*

deeper: *háttalom.*

deer: *binadu.*

deface: *desfigura.*

defaced: *desfiguráo.*

defeat: *a'ñao, bense, fa'om, ganna, igi, ikak.*

defeated: *mapedde.*

defecate: *da'os, masinek.*
defecate on: *tatke.*
need to defecate: *ma'atde.*

defect: *difekto.*

defend: *difende, guatdia, na'liheng, protehi.*

defender: *abugáo, abugadu, difensót, gannadót, protektót.*

defer: *dura.*

deference: *onra.*

deficient: *ti kahulo'.*

deficit: *malingu.*

defile: *na'ye.*

defiled: *nina'ye.*

define: *difina.*

definite: *metton, siguru.*

definitely: *etdichu, siempre, téneki, tíeneki.*

definition: *definisión, sustansia.*

deflated: *mahañas.*

deflower: *desbuetga.*

deform: *desfigura.*

deformed: *desfiguráo.*

defraud: *dugeruyi, laime, trampasi.*

defrauded
be defrauded: *mafa'baba.*

dehydrated: *dokngos, tostos.*

deify: *fa'yi'os.*

delay: *bumasta, ditieni, dura, na'parannaihon, po'lonnaihon, taka'.*

delayed
delayed so long: *inapmam.*

delegate: *delegadu.*

delete: *kansela, na'mafnas.*

deliberately: *bulontariamente, hasngon.*

delicate: *chekka', dilikáo.*

delicious: *dilisiosu, mannge'.*

delight: *magof.*

delinquent: *dilenkuente.*

deliver: *diliba, entrega, na'i.*

deliverance: *liberasión.*

delivery: *patto.*

delouse: *fakkot, sesse.*

deluded: *mapulakes.*

deluge: *dilubio, milak.*

deluxe: *supiriót.*

demand: *afuetsas, dimanda, insiste.*

demandant: *akusadót.*

demander: *dimandadót.*

demented: *atmariáo, kaduka, kaduku.*

democracy: *demokrasia.*

demolish: *destrosa, disasi.*

demolition: *minayulang.*

demon: *birak, dimonio, taotaomo'na.*

demonstrate: *chachalani, fa'nu'i.*

demoralize: *na'atborutáo.*

demure: *yómahlao.*

den: *chonchon.*

denial: *mandagi, padakdak.*
  denial (m): *embusteru.*
denominate: *na'fa'na'an.*
denote: *indika.*
denounce: *matdisi.*
dense: *potpot.*
dent: *daloggai.*
dented: *bulengngo', daloggai,*
  maheffong.
dentist: *dentista.*
deny: *ñega, dagi, niega, puni.*
depart: *dingu, hanao.*
  depart for: *malak.*
  depart with: *dipatta.*
department: *dipattemente.*
departure: *ádingu, despidida, inádingu.*
depend: *embatga.*
  depend on: *apela, dipende.*
dependable: *angokkuyon.*
dependence: *dipendensia.*
dependent: *dipendiente.*
depending
  depending on: *konsiste.*
depends
  depends upon: *sigún.*
depimple: *poddak.*
depopulate: *dipotta.*
deport: *dipotta.*
deposit: *dipusita, pigo'.*
depot: *dipósitu, estasión.*
depressed: *inatditi.*
depression: *tinemba.*
depth: *moddong, tinaddong.*
deride: *mofeha.*
descend: *tumunok.*
descendant: *disendente, tátatte.*
descendants: *disendensia.*
descent: *bahada.*
describe: *eksplika.*
description: *deskripsíon.*
desecrate: *na'mancha.*
desert: *dingu, disetto, disietto.*
deserve: *miresi.*
design: *botdadura, obra, penta, pinenta,*
  planu.
designate: *ditetmina, senñala.*
desirable: *ná'malago'.*
desire: *diseha, disehu, guinaiya,*
  malago', muto', tinanga.
  desire (sexual): *ugo'.*
desired
  be desired: *ná'malago'.*
desirous: *disiosu, na'malago'.*

desk: *banko, lamasa.*
despair: *desparadu.*
desperado: *desparadu.*
desperate: *desesperáo, desparadu,*
  despiráo, táininangga.
despise: *chatguaiya, fa'hiyong,*
  faichanak.
despoil: *desbuetga.*
despondency: *triniste.*
despotic: *rekto.*
dessert: *fina'mames.*
destination: *destinasión.*
destiny: *destinu.*
destitute: *kara', na'ma'se', táisaga.*
destitution: *ha'ilas.*
destroy: *desmurona, destrosa, disasi,*
  na'falingu, yamak, yulang.
  destroy by fire: *potne.*
destruction: *destrosu, inale',*
  minayulang.
detach: *chappak, despega, na'hanao.*
detached: *mappa.*
detain: *po'lonñaihon, tane'.*
detect: *gacha'.*
detectable: *konosidu.*
detective: *sikretu.*
detergent: *habon.*
determination: *ditetminasión.*
determine: *ditetmina, gobietna.*
detest: *chatli'e'.*
detrimental: *dañosu.*
deuce
  deuce game: *ti chumá'igi.*
device: *ramienta, trastes.*
devil: *aniti, diablo, dimonio,*
  maknganiti, manganiti, satanás,
  Hudas.
  devil (expletive): *diantre.*
devilfish: *afula', fanihen tasi, hafula'.*
devilish: *tulisán.*
devilment: *diablura.*
devise: *na'huyong.*
devoted: *dibotu.*
devotion: *dibosión, nobena.*
devotionary: *dibosionario.*
devour: *chocho.*
  devour something: *kanno'.*
devoured: *boka.*
devout: *dibotu, yini'usan.*
dew: *chi'ok, chi'op.*
dexterity: *finayi.*
dexterous: *kalamya, makalamya.*
diabetes: *daibites.*

diagonal
diagonal line: *sesgáo.*

dial
dial (of clock or watch): *kannai.*

dialect: *dialekto, lengguahi, tunada.*

diameter: *diametro.*

diamond: *diamante.*

diamonds: *oros.*

diaper: *pañales, sade'.*
put diaper on: *sade'.*

diarrhea: *kinilak, nina'ye masisinik.*
have diarrhea: *da'os, nina'ye
masisinik.*

dice: *dais.*

dictate: *dikta.*

dictionary: *diksinario, diksionario.*

die: *kumematai, matai.*
die down: *chagua.*

diesel: *diso'.*

diet: *dieta.*
impose diet: *pes.*

difference: *diferensia.*

different: *diferentes, otro.*

differentiate: *diferensiát, distengge.*

difficult: *chátsaga, komplikáo, makkat,
mappot.*

difficulty: *difikuttát, ginaddon,
minappot.*

diffused: *machalehgua'.*

dig
dig (with a digging iron): *bareta.*
dig up: *guahi.*
to dig: *guaddok.*

digest: *na'tunok.*

digging iron: *bareta.*

dignified: *dikno.*

dignity: *diknidát, pekka'.*

dilate: *aomenta.*

diligent: *butmuchachu, dilihente.*

dilute: *liti.*

dim: *homhom.*

dime: *riát.*

diminutive: *díkike', po'yet.*

dimple: *hadok, máhadok.*

dine: *na'talo'ani.*

ding: *tingteng.*

dining place: *guma' fañochuyan.*

dinner: *na' talo'ani, sena.*

dip: *totche.*
dip out: *sohgue.*
dip water (with container): *suhu.*

diploma: *diploma.*

diplomat: *diplomátiku.*

dipper
dipper (liquid): *dudu.*

dipsomaniac: *butlacheru.*

direct: *dirihi, ditetmina, gobietna,
kondukta, leklek, manea, na'hanao,
otden.*
direct (by influence or counsel):
desponi.

direction
change direction: *bira.*

directional prefix: *san-.*

director: *direktót.*

directory: *direktorio.*

dirt: *akong, edda', fache', kulakong,
odda'.*

dirtiness: *kuchinada.*

dirty: *ápplacha', akong, hoplat, kalakas,
kossos, kuchinu, kulakong,
lakulakong, máskara, sokkos.*
dirty face: *máskara.*
make dirty: *mayabok.*

disable: *yamak.*

disagree: *aguaguati, resiste.*

disagreeable: *chátpa'go, chura, mahatot.*

disagreement: *yinaoyao.*

disappear
disappear (command): *falingu.*

disappeared: *malingu.*

disappointed: *desganáo.*

disapprove: *desaprueba, yama.*

disapproved: *desaprebáo.*

disarm: *disatma.*

disarrange: *trabuka.*

disarranged: *desarekláo.*

disarrangement: *destempláo.*

disassemble: *desatma, disasi.*

disaster: *desgrasia, destrosu, hinigua,
ira, kebra.*

disbelief: *chathinengge.*

disbursement: *gasto.*

discard: *destieru, yute'.*

discharge: *humuyong.*

dischargee
dischargee (from hospital): *atta.*

disciples
the disciples: *apóstoles, disípulu.*

discipline: *disiplina, guaguat.*

disciplined: *arekláo.*

disciplining: *rekto.*

disclose: *baba, diskubre.*

discomfort: *chinatsaga.*

disconnect: *ádespatta, apatta,
na'adespatta, na'hanao.*

disconsolateness: *minahalang.*
discontented: *ti kontento.*
discount: *deskuenta.*
discourage: *desgusta, deskonsuela.*
discouraged: *desganáo.*
discourteous: *desatento, mata'pang,*
    presemida.
discover: *diskubre, fakcha'i.*
discrimination: *diskriminasión.*
discuss: *diskuti.*
disease
  skin disease: *yafyaf.*
disengage: *libetta, na'adespatta.*
disfiguration: *desfiguradu.*
disfigure: *desfigura.*
disfigured: *desfiguráo, malahechura.*
disfigurement: *desfiguradu.*
disgrace: *desonra, desonro.*
disguise: *fa'otro.*
disgust: *desagunáo, desgusta.*
  show disgust: *asaina.*
disgusted: *desganáo, desgusto.*
dish: *na'yan, platu.*
  type of dish: *maguan.*
dishearten: *desgusta.*
disheartening: *desganáo.*
dishevel: *trabuka.*
dishonest: *desonesto.*
dishonor: *desonra, desonro.*
disjoined
  become disjoined: *mappa.*
dislike: *nokieru.*
dislocate: *appleng, chefchef, desbira.*
dislocated: *ákaleng.*
dismember: *chinachak.*
dismiss: *litira, ritira, suspende.*
dismissal: *despidida, ritirada.*
disobedient: *átaktak.*
disorder: *desareklo.*
disorderly
  disorderly manner: *desarekladu,*
    direchas kuetdas.
  disorderly way: *direchas kuetdas.*
dispatch: *despacha.*
dispel: *chalapon.*
dispensation: *dispensa.*
dispense
  dispense with: *tumaya'.*
disperse: *chalapon.*
dispersed: *mapgao.*
display: *mostra.*
displease: *desgusta.*
disposal: *despuesto.*

dispose
  dispose of all: *lachai.*
disposition: *dispusision, henio.*
  feeling disposition: *muto'.*
dispossess: *amot.*
dispute: *resiste.*
disregard: *deskuidu, disatende, disecha.*
disrespectful: *desatento, tunante.*
dissemble: *disimula.*
dissembler: *hipokritu, kado'*
    mama'maolek.
dissimilarity: *diferensia.*
dissipate: *chalapon.*
dissolute: *malaña', sángganu.*
dissolve: *diliti.*
distance: *áchago', distansia, ináchago'.*
distant: *chago'.*
distasteful: *mala'et.*
distemper: *destempla.*
distill: *estila.*
distillery: *fanestilayan.*
distinguish: *distengge, estampo', tungo'.*
distinguished: *afamáo, distenggidu.*
distort: *desfigura.*
distract: *distrakto, na'tatnon.*
distracting: *tane'.*
distraction: *distraksión.*
distribute: *na'i.*
district: *bariu, distritu.*
distrust: *deskonfiansa, dudosu,*
    suspecha.
disturb: *atborota, estotba, estraña,*
    inturompe.
disturbance: *aburidu, atborotu, yaoyao.*
disturbed: *inatborota.*
disunite: *na'adespatta, na'atarantáo.*
ditch: *guinaddok, kannat.*
divan: *sofá.*
dive: *busu, li'of.*
diver: *buseru, líli'of.*
diversion: *dibetsión.*
divert: *bira.*
divide: *ápatte, dibidi, kompatte, patte.*
divided: *apattáo.*
dividend: *pattida.*
divine: *dichosu.*
diviner: *dibinu.*
diving board: *bátalan.*
divisible: *dibibiyon.*
division: *dibisión.*
divorce: *dibotsia, na'adespatta,*
    umáyute', yinite'.

divulge: *baba.*
divulged: *machalehgua'.*
dizziness: *atarantáo, bulachon ulu,*
    matarabiran tano'.
    cause dizziness: *failek, kalek,*
    pina'lek.
dizzy: *bulachu.*
do: *bida, cho'gue.*
    do (something): *uyu.*
    do (something) again: *agonta'lo.*
    do (something) repeatedly: *kokoti.*
    do again: *numa'lo.*
    do deliberately: *hasnguni.*
    do not: *cha'-mu.*
docile: *fa'na'guiyon, manso.*
dock: *pantalán.*
doctor: *á'amte, dokto, médiku,*
    praktikante.
    herb doctor: *siruanu.*
    herb doctor (f): *suruhana.*
doctrine: *dottrina.*
document: *dukumento.*
dodge: *letke, suhayi.*
doff: *safu.*
dog: *ga'lagu.*
    wild dog: *ga'lagon machalek.*
doll: *muñeka.*
dollar: *pesu.*
dolled up: *mamuda.*
dolphin: *dofen, tuninos.*
domestic: *trastes guma'.*
domesticated: *manso.*
dominate: *ma'gasi.*
domineering: *ti sungunon.*
dominions: *propiedát.*
domino: *dómina.*
don't: *cha'-, cha'-mu, chacha'-, ti*
    guáilayi.
    don't (imperative): *munga.*
donate: *na'i.*
    donate (money): *limosna.*
donation: *chenchule', donesion,*
    ensimasión, ika, koleksión, nina'i,
    regalu.
donkey: *buliku.*
doomsday: *uttimon i tano'.*
door: *ohan potta, potta.*
dormitory: *domitorio, dotmitorio,*
    guma'.
dots: *lonnat.*
dotted: *dondon.*
double: *dinga', dopble, dubli.*
    double cross: *trampasi.*
doubt: *dinida, duda, hekkua'.*

doubtful: *duda.*
doubtfulness: *dinida.*
doubting: *infiét.*
doubtless: *klaru.*
douche: *labatorio, ta'pang.*
dough: *hechura, yinaka'.*
doughnut: *boñelos, boñelos manglo'.*
    banana doughnut: *boñelos aga'.*
    breadfruit doughnut: *boñelos lemmai.*
    shrimp doughnut: *boñelos uhang.*
    sweet potato doughnut: *boñelos*
    kamuti.
    yam doughnut: *boñelos dagu.*
dove: *paluma.*
    dove cote: *palumat.*
    fruit dove: *totot.*
    ground dove: *apaka', paluman kunao,*
    paluman kutbata.
down: *papa'.*
    farther down: *gé'papa'.*
    go down: *tótonok.*
    way down: *yapápapa'.*
downpour: *matmo.*
downward: *gé'papa', papa'.*
doze
    doze off: *malinguñaihon.*
dozen: *dusena.*
draft: *manglo'.*
drag: *arastra, batangga, halla, saggue'.*
    drag (something): *bátsala.*
dragon: *dragón.*
dragonfly: *dulalas.*
drain
    drain pus: *te'te'.*
drama: *programa.*
drapery: *kuttina.*
draw: *penta, tapbla.*
    draw match: *siobo'.*
    draw out: *faidok.*
    draw through: *ensatta.*
    to draw (pictures): *yunga'.*
drawer: *kahon.*
drawing: *yunga'.*
dread: *halang.*
dreadful: *ti atanon.*
dream: *guinifi.*
    bad dream: *pesadiya.*
    dream of: *guifi.*
dreamer
    daydreamer: *desmuronu.*
dreaming
    daydreaming: *desmurón.*
dreary: *mata'pang.*
dredge: *dreya.*

dregs: *bagasu, mohmo, pigo'.*

drench: *sumai.*

drenched: *fotgon, masmai, sohgon.*

dress: *bestida, bestidura, chinina.*
  dress up: *kachet, katsa.*

dressed
  dressed up: *mamuda.*

dressing table: *tukadót.*
  dressing table: *tukadót.*

dressmaker: *mudista.*

dried: *inangglo'.*

drift
  cause to drift: *hasa.*
  drift away: *kílili.*

drifted
  drifted away: *hinasa.*

drill: *baró, barohu, busisi.*
  drill (hand): *broka.*
  drill (soldiers): *etsisio.*

driller: *baró.*

drink: *gimen.*
  drink (soup): *o'o'.*
  give drink: *boyo'.*
  mixed drink: *punche.*

drinker: *gekmen.*

drinking place: *fanggiminan.*

drip: *tu'o', tuho'.*

drive: *draiba, sugon.*
  drive away: *sugon.*
  drive in: *na'dochon.*

driver: *draiba.*

drone
  drone at: *bilengbingi.*

drool: *babas.*

droop: *baha'.*

drooping: *kana'.*

drop: *basnak, poddong.*
  drop (liquid): *to'he, to'i.*
  drop (of liquid): *gota.*
  drop down: *yute'.*

dropping: *poppo.*

droppings: *take'.*

drown: *lumos, matmos.*

drowsy: *dotmiladu, matokngaihon, matuhok.*
  be drowsy: *matuhokñaihon.*

drudge: *macho'cho'.*

drug: *amot.*

drum: *tambot.*
  drum (can): *tanke.*
  drum for: *tanken.*

drunk: *bulachu, teles.*

drunkard: *bulacheru, butlacheru.*

drunken: *teles.*

drunkenness: *binilachu.*

dry: *angglo', tala'.*
  dry season: *fañomnagan.*
  dry up: *appan, tai'ai, tala'.*
  make dry: *tai'ai.*

dubious: *duda, dudosu.*

duck
  duck (fowl): *nganga'.*
  duck under: *nehong.*
  to duck: *ñehom.*

duct: *tubu.*

due: *dibi.*

dull: *ñaño', éhinasso, daffe', lolu, táipunta.*
  dull point: *bulengngo'.*

dumb: *taktamudu, tattamudu, uda, udu.*

dump: *rimotke, sagan basula, yute'.*

dumpling: *pilota.*

dun: *kopbla.*

dunce: *tarugu.*

dunk: *totche.*

dupe: *fa'baba, iridáo, pa'las, trampasi.*

duplicate: *duplika.*

durable: *durapble, fitme, ma'ok, mesngon.*

duration: *durao, mina'ok.*

during
  during (preposition): *duranten.*

dust: *potbos.*
  to dust: *saffe.*

duster: *brochas, saffe.*

Dutch: *Holandes.*

dutiful: *ɔsgon.*

duty: *opbligasión.*
  be on duty: *totno.*

dwarf: *nanu.*

dwell: *saga.*

dwelling: *fansagayan, guma'.*

dye: *tumu.*

dyer: *títumu.*

dying: *kumekematai.*
  dying agent: *títenta.*

dynamite: *dinamita, kaiako'.*

dynamo: *dinamu.*

dysentery: *hinaga', masisinek haga'.*

e: *e.*

each: *kada.*
  each time: *kada.*

eager: *apuráo, empeñáo, empeñosu.*

eagerness: *ansias.*

eagle: *ágila.*
  eagle-eye: *le'an.*

ear: *talanga.*
  ear (cauliflower): *gachu.*
  ear wax: *kulakong talanga.*
  ear-twist: *atilek.*
early: *maga, taftaf.*
earmark: *seññala.*
earn: *ganna.*
earring: *alitos.*
earth: *tano'.*
earthquake: *linao.*
ease: *alibia, osiosu.*
east: *gé'kattan, hátkattan.*
  east (in Saipan): *haya.*
  east (in Guam and Rota): *kattan.*
  go east: *kákattan.*
  move east: *kákattan.*
  way east: *yakáttatan.*
Easter: *Pasgua.*
easterly: *gé'kattan, hátkattan.*
eastward: *gé'kattan, hátkattan.*
  eastward movement: *kákattan.*
easy: *ñálalang, faset, libianu, ti mappot.*
eat: *ñamñam, chocho.*
  eat meat: *fatda'.*
  eat savagely: *tucho'.*
  eat something: *kanno'.*
  to eat raw food: *fala'.*
eaten: *boka.*
  eaten up: *kinanno'.*
eater: *kakno'.*
  eater of raw food: *fakla'.*
eating: *kumida.*
  prohibit eating: *pes.*
eccentric: *táiga'chong.*
ecclesiastic: *eklesiastiku.*
echo: *eku.*
eclipse: *kinilís.*
economical: *puchu.*
economy: *ekonomia.*
Eden: *paradisu.*
edge: *banda, kanto, renkón, rinkón, uriya.*
edging: *sinta.*
edible: *kannu'on, mámakanno'.*
edibles: *na'.*
editor: *editót.*
editorial: *editoriát.*
educate: *eduka, fa'na'gue, kuttiba.*
education: *edukasión, ineyak.*
educator: *fáfa'na'gue.*
eel: *asuli, hakmang kulales.*
  conger eel: *asulen palos.*
  gray eel: *ñotak.*
  type of eel (family muraenidae):

    hakmang pakpada.
  type of eel-anguilla marmorata (family anguillidae): *asuli.*
  type of eel-conger noordziek (family congridae): *asulen palos.*
  type of eel-conger noordzieki (congridae): *hakmang palús.*
  type of eel-echidna nebulosa (muraenidae): *hakmang titugi.*
  type of eel-elaps (genus myrichthys): *hakmang kulales.*
  type of eel-gymnothorax meleagris (family muraenidae): *hakmang.*
  type of eel-gymnothorax pictus (family muraenidae): *títugi.*
  type of eel-lycodontis picta: *ñotak.*
  type of eel-myrichthys maculosus (family ophichthidae): *hakmang lisayu.*
  white eel: *asulen palos.*
effect: *hiniyong, huyong.*
effective: *efektibu.*
effeminate
  effeminate person: *lao'an.*
efficient: *míhinilat.*
effort: *animu, empeñu.*
effortless: *libianu.*
egg: *chada', gueru, kuates, matkrusidu, matkusidu.*
  egg shell: *kaskaran chada', lassas chada'.*
  egg yolk: *agaga' chada', yema.*
  rotten egg: *gueru.*
eggnog: *flamenko.*
eggplant: *birenghenas.*
eggs: *kulales.*
  crab eggs: *ña'ot.*
  fish eggs: *figan, ña'ot, kulales.*
egoism: *egoismo.*
egotistic: *interesáo.*
Egypt: *Éhipto.*
eight: *ocho.*
eighth: *oktabu.*
eighty: *ochenta.*
  eighty-one: *ochenta i unu.*
either: *masea, maseha.*
ejaculate: *mañugo'.*
eject: *tumo'la'.*
elastic: *lastek.*
elasticity: *mueyi.*
elate: *ánima.*
elbow: *tommo, tommon kannai, tommon kodu.*
  to elbow: *sokkok.*
elders
  elders (pl): *mañaina.*

elect: *ilihi, tancho'.*
election: *botasión.*
electricity: *elektrisidá.*
elegant: *gatbo.*
elephant: *elifante.*
elevation: *linekka'.*
eleven: *onse.*
 eleven points: *fuera sin buenas.*
elf: *duendes.*
eligible: *kualifikáo, nombrayon.*
eliminate: *na'mafnas, na'suha.*
elocution: *inádingan.*
elongate: *ekstende, na'anakko'.*
elope: *falagu.*
else: *otro, sinó.*
elude: *eskapa, eskapayi.*
embargo: *embatka.*
embarrass: *na'mamahlao.*
embarrassed: *mamamhlao.*
 become embarrassed: *mumamamhlao.*
embarrassing: *ná'mamahlao.*
embassy: *embahadát.*
embellish: *na'gatbo.*
ember: *pínigan, tesson.*
embitter: *na'layo'.*
emblem: *figura.*
embrace: *alabadu, braseha, toktok.*
 embrace each other: *ágo'te,*
 ámantieni, ásostieni.
embroider: *botda.*
 one who embroiders: *bíbotda.*
embroidery: *botdáo, botdadura,*
 mabotda.
emerge: *huyong.*
emigrant: *emigrante.*
eminent: *tákkilo'.*
emperor
 emperor (m): *emperadót.*
empire: *imperio.*
employ: *emplea, na'sietbe, okupa, usa.*
employed: *moseria.*
employee: *empleáo, empleháo.*
employer: *amu.*
employment: *cho'cho', emplehu,*
 empleo, ofisiu.
empower: *aturisa.*
empty: *basia, chuda', gueku, kasko,*
 panko'.
empty container: *basiu.*
enact: *otdena.*
enamor: *atgimat, inamuradu.*
enamored: *amuráo, enamoráo.*
enchanted: *enkantáo.*

encircle: *dudok, likoku'i, ridondeha,*
 uriyayi.
 encircle with arms: *braseha.*
enclose: *aridondeha.*
encompass: *abrasa, enggatsa, uriyayi.*
encounter: *umásodda'.*
encourage: *ánima, abiba, na'matatnga,*
 su'on.
encyclopedia: *ensaiklopidia.*
end: *fakpo', finakpo', punta.*
 at the end: *infín.*
 the end: *fin.*
endeavor: *na'késiña.*
endless: *táifinakpo', táihinekkok.*
endlessness: *táiuttimo.*
endorse: *endotsa.*
endure: *aguanta, kontinua, sungon.*
enduring: *mesngon.*
enemy: *enimigu, kontrariu.*
energetic: *trabadót, trabahadót.*
energy: *alentos, alimenta, alimento,*
 fuetsa, minetgot.
enervate: *sottayi.*
enfeebled: *mamaitaguan, yafai.*
engage: *enggansa.*
engagement
 engagement period: *plasu.*
engine: *mákina.*
engineer: *enhinieru, enyineria.*
England: *Englatera.*
English: *Engles.*
engrave: *matka, rinaya.*
engraver: *matkadót.*
enhance: *insima, masubi.*
enigma: *misterio.*
enjoy: *gosa, ya-.*
enlarge: *aomenta, ekstende, estiende,*
 lumámeggai, masubi, na'lámoddong.
enlist: *enggancha, rehistra.*
enlistment: *rikohida.*
enliven: *konsuela, na'magof.*
enlivening: *ná'brabu.*
enough: *bastante, nahong, sufisiente.*
 enough (command): *para.*
enraged: *bubu, lalalo'.*
enrich: *kuttiba.*
enroll: *rehistra.*
enrollment: *rikohida.*
ensue: *tatte.*
ensure: *asigura.*
entangle: *gadde'.*
entangled: *gaddon, kokas, matahlek,*
 matalek, matraba.

entanglement: *ginaddon.*
enter: *halom, kákalom.*
entertainment: *dibetsión.*
enthusiastic: *apuráo.*
entice: *eppok, fanoppok, pugi, tenta.*
enticer: *títienta.*
entire: *enteru, entieru, todu.*
entirely: *puru.*
entrails: *tilipas.*
entrance: *entrada, fanhaluman, potta.*
entrapped
  be entrapped: *goddon.*
entreat: *rikuesta, suplika.*
entreaty: *ginagao, pitisión.*
entrust: *dipende, embatga, enkatga.*
envelope: *sobre.*
envious: *hosguan, ti kontento.*
envisage: *hasso, na'hasso.*
envision: *fanhasso.*
envy: *embidia, inigo', ugo'.*
enwrap: *royu.*
epidemic: *epidemia, peste, sagu.*
epidermis: *lassas.*
epilepsy: *repot.*
episode: *estoria, hemplo.*
epoch: *siklo.*
equal: *acháguasguas, achaigua, chilong, parehu.*
equalize: *na'chilong.*
equator: *apuya' tasi.*
equip: *na'huyungi.*
equipment: *aparatos, eramienta, ramienta, trastes.*
equivocate: *dagi.*
era: *ayu na tiempo.*
eradicate: *funas, na'mafnas.*
erase: *funas, na'mafnas.*
eraser: *iresa, musigomo'.*
erect: *tachu, tisu, tohge, tunas.*
erection: *tison chili.*
errand
  send on errand: *tago'.*
error: *inabak, lachi, linachi.*
eruct: *tugap.*
escape: *eskapa, eskapayi, falagu, falaguaihon.*
eschew: *nukeru.*
escort: *akompaña, akompañamento, dalak, esgaihon, ga'chungi, kompañeru.*
escorting: *inesgaihon.*
especially: *espesiatmente, kololo'ña, kuastaria, kululo'ña, lá'yiyi, mayotmente, muchumas.*

essential: *fondamento, impottante, nisisario, prisisu.*
establish: *establesi, po'lo.*
establishment: *fondasión.*
estate: *propiedát.*
  real estate: *propiedát.*
esteem: *estima, kréditu, respeta.*
estimate: *balua, faila'muni, taha.*
estimation: *estimasión.*
etch: *rinaya.*
eternity: *tinaichi.*
eucharist: *óstia.*
eunuch: *kappon.*
Europe: *Europa.*
European: *Europeo.*
evacuate: *abandona.*
evade: *eskapayi, suhayi.*
evaluate: *balua.*
evangelist: *ebanghelista.*
evaporate: *appan, magap.*
eve: *nochebuena.*
even: *tanto.*
  even if: *asipudera, maskeseha.*
  even though: *áchokka', maseha, maskeseha, ombres.*
  even up: *empas, siobo'.*
  not even: *áchokka'.*
evening: *nochebuena, noches, pupuenge, tulanoche.*
event: *estoria, hemplo, kasu, sinisedi.*
eventually: *alosuttimo, gi úttimo, pot uttimo.*
ever
  ever since: *desde ki, deste ki.*
  not ever: *nunka.*
every
  every day: *kada dia, kada ha'ani.*
  every time: *kada.*
everything: *todu, todu esta.*
everywhere: *todu i lugat.*
evidence: *ebidensia, ibidensa, pruebasión.*
evident: *patente.*
evil: *baba, mala.*
  evil spirit: *ná'ma'a'ñao.*
eviscerate: *destilipas, guakse.*
exact: *akto, dimanda, dinanche, eksakto, espisifiku, propiu.*
exactly: *etdichu, perfekto, prifekto.*
exaggerate: *na'dankolo.*
examination: *chinagi.*
examine: *eksamina, sensura.*
examiner: *abiriguadót, imbestigadót.*

example: *ehemplo, modelu.*
for example: *pot i hemplo, tatkomu.*
exceed: *upos.*
exceedingly: *maloffan.*
excellent: *eksalente.*
except: *fuera, sin, solamente.*
excess: *letke, minampos.*
do in excess: *gaddai.*
excess of: *pinat.*
excessive: *fotte.*
excessively: *dalai, maloffan.*
exchange: *átulaika, a'go, troki, tulaika.*
exchangeable: *tulaikayon.*
exchanger
exchanger (m): *bankeru, kombalacheru.*
excitable: *háguinafi.*
excited: *apuráo, ma'agoddai.*
exclamation: *eksklamasión.*
exclude: *fa'hiyong, fa'sahnge, na'suha.*
excluding: *fuera, sin.*
excrement: *inapplacha', take'.*
exculpate: *despensa.*
excursion: *biahi, hinanao.*
excusable: *asi'iyon.*
excuse: *asi'i, despensa, dispensa, eskusa, plasu.*
executioner: *betdugu, betduhu.*
executive: *eksakatibu.*
exercise: *ehetsisio, etsisio.*
exhale
exhale (sharply): *foffo.*
exhaust: *sa'pet.*
exhausted: *kansadu, malachai.*
exhausted (physically): *yafai.*
exhaustion: *sina'pet.*
exhibit: *mostra.*
exhort: *pagat.*
exile: *destieru.*
exist: *eksiste, gágaige, lála'la'.*
existence: *bida, lina'la'.*
expand: *aomenta, ekstende, estira.*
expectation: *esperansa.*
expectorate: *tumo'la'.*
expedite: *alulayi, apura.*
expediter: *ná'chaddek.*
expedition: *espedisión.*
expeditious: *apretáo, apretát.*
expend: *gasta, na'sietbe.*
expenditure: *gasto, ginasta.*
expense: *gasto, kosta.*
expensive: *guaguan.*
experience: *eksperensia, lina'mon, pinayon.*

experienced: *amtao, ansianu, eksperensiáo, praktiku, susedi.*
expert: *ekspert, meyeng.*
explain: *eksplika, esplika, na'manana, sanganiyi.*
explainable: *eksplikáo.*
explanation: *mapula', sustansia.*
expletive
expletive (mild): *puñeta.*
explicable: *eksplikáo.*
explode: *pangpang.*
exploded: *pakpak.*
explore: *diskubre.*
explosion: *pakpak, pangpang.*
export: *ekspotta.*
expose: *na'annok, tala'.*
expose (someone) inadvertently: *gencha'.*
exposed: *annok.*
expound: *eksplika.*
express: *ekspresia, espresa.*
expulsion: *madúlalak.*
exquisite: *dilisiosu, mannge'.*
extend: *aomenta, ekstende, estiende, na'anakko', tokche.*
extending
extending upward: *ébaba'.*
extension: *ekstensión.*
exterior
exterior of: *sanhiyong.*
external
the external: *sanhiyong.*
extinguish: *na'mafnas, puno'.*
extinguish (fire with liquid): *bisi.*
extinguish partially (fire): *chagua.*
extinguisher: *bomban guafi, bomban kimasón.*
fire extinguisher: *puno' guafi, puno' kimasón.*
extol: *fama, tuna.*
extravagance: *gastadót.*
extravagant: *dimasiáo.*
extreme: *mampos, uttimo.*
extremely: *maloffan, sen.*
extremely (intensifier): *gof.*
eye: *átadok, mata.*
floating eye: *bisko.*
eyeball: *átadok, mata.*
eyebrow: *sehas.*
eyeglass
eyeglass wearer: *miganchio'.*
eyeglasses: *antihos, antiohos, antios.*
eyelash: *bábale', bábali.*
eyelid: *bábali, lassas átadok.*

eyes: *matan achiak.*
  blue eyes: *matan katu.*
  cat eyes: *matan katu.*
  close eyes: *achigo'.*
eyesight
  eyesight (poor): *chátmata.*
f: *efi.*
fable: *fábulas.*
fabric: *yatdas.*
fabrication: *fábrika, fakteria.*
face: *fana', fasu, kara, mata.*
  boy's face: *matan lahi.*
  face (each other): *áfana'.*
  face mask: *masko', tampen mata.*
  face shape: *maskaran mata.*
  to face certain direction: *talak-.*
facial feature: *maskaran mata.*
facilitate: *alibia, apura.*
facility: *fasilidát.*
facsimile: *modelu.*
fact: *akto, fakto, minagahet.*
factory: *fábrika, fakteria.*
fad: *ná'moda.*
fade: *pasmo.*
faded: *mafnas.*
  faded (color): *pasmo.*
fail: *guahlo', ti kahulo'.*
  fail to notice: *laisen.*
faint: *lálangu, mamaitaguan.*
fainted: *tisu.*
fair: *feria, husto, tái'interes.*
faith: *hinengge.*
faithful: *dichosu, fiét.*
fall: *basnak, lotgon.*
  about to fall: *so'on.*
  fall down: *matomba, mayamak, poddong.*
  fall down (noisely): *palangpang.*
  fall on: *palo'po'.*
  fall over: *matomba.*
fallen
  be fallen: *matomba.*
false: *fatso.*
falsehood: *digeria, dugeria.*
falsify: *fatsea.*
falsity: *linachi.*
fame: *onra.*
familiar
  be familiar with: *la'mon.*
familiarize: *payuni.*
family: *familia.*
famine: *ha'ilas, mataiñalang.*
famished: *ambre.*
famous: *afamáo, famáo, famosu.*

fan: *bohao, geha, goha, goia, gue'ha, gueha.*
  fan (Japanese style): *abaniku.*
  fan belt: *korehas.*
  fan flower: *nanasu.*
  to fan: *bohao, goia.*
fancy: *fanhasso, na'hallom.*
fang: *kotniyos.*
fantail bird: *chuchurika.*
fantasy: *fantasma.*
far: *chago'.*
  how far: *chi-.*
Farallon de Pajaros: *Farallon de Pajaros.*
fare: *kosta.*
farewell: *adiós, despidida, inádingu.*
  bid farewell: *despidi.*
farm: *gualo', lancheria, lancho.*
farmer: *lancheru, simenterera, simentereru.*
  good farmer: *gúagualo'.*
farming: *gualo'.*
fart: *do'do'.*
  fart (slang): *mamuga'.*
farther: *achago'ña.*
farthest: *uttimo.*
  farthest away: *yaguátutu.*
  farthest back: *yatáttiti.*
  farthest down: *yapápapa'.*
  farthest east: *yakáttatan.*
  farthest front: *yamó'nana.*
  farthest inside: *yahálolom.*
  farthest north: *yalágugu.*
  farthest outside: *yahúyoyong.*
  farthest south: *yaháyaya.*
  farthest up: *yahúlulo'.*
  farthest west: *yalúchachan.*
fascinated
  be fascinated: *kaotiba.*
fascination: *inenkanta.*
fashion: *fa'tinas, moda.*
fast: *ayunat, ayunu, bibu, binibu, chaddek, duru, guse', láguse', sahyao, sigidas.*
  fast day: *ha'anen apsinensia.*
fasten: *aprendes, godde, luluki, manohu, prende.*
  fasten (with a lock): *kandalu.*
fastidious: *espót, fastidiosu.*
fat: *chebot, loddo', manempeya, mantika, sebu, yommok.*
  chicken fat: *empeya.*
  fat (fried): *cháchalon.*
fate: *destinu.*

father: *saina, tata.*
  father-in-law: *sogro.*
  to father: *liles, paireha.*
fathom: *brasa.*
fatigue: *afatigáo, fatigáo, fatiga.*
fatigued: *kansadu, yayas.*
fatten: *na'yommok.*
  fatten up: *seba.*
faucet: *grifu.*
fault: *difekto, inechong.*
faulty: *gáidifekto.*
favor: *bona, fabót, lipa.*
  in favor of: *afabót.*
favorable: *faborapble.*
favorite: *mafa'boreresi, magófatan.*
  favorite (child): *kiridu.*
favoritism: *aras.*
fear: *kinibatde, mina'a'ñao, susto.*
fearless: *fa'a'ñao, matatnga,*
  táima'a'ñao.
feasible: *na'siñayon.*
feast: *gupot.*
feather: *pulu.*
  feather-brained: *tattamudu.*
featherless: *hingao.*
feathers
  grow feathers: *manempluma.*
February: *Febreru, Maimo.*
feces: *pinekso', take'.*
  bloody feces: *masisinek haga'.*
  odor of feces: *paotake'.*
fecundity: *fottalisa.*
fed up: *baya', empachu.*
  fed up with: *sosongte.*
federal: *federát.*
federation: *aliansa.*
Federico palm: *fadang.*
feeble: *dangnge', dolle, pedde.*
  feeble-minded: *á'baba'.*
feed: *na'boka, na'yommok.*
  feed (by hand): *chugo'.*
feel: *siente.*
feelers: *batbas uhang.*
feeling: *sentimiento.*
  feeling disposition: *muto'.*
feet: *addeng.*
feign: *fa'-, kado', pritende.*
feint: *laime.*
  to feint: *hannan.*
felicitate: *filisita.*
fellow: *próhimu.*
  fellow man: *próhimu, tiguang-.*
fellow men: *afañe'los.*

felony: *felunia.*
female: *palao'an.*
females: *famalao'an.*
fence: *chikeru.*
  rail fence: *rehas.*
  to fence: *kollat.*
fern: *amaru, chacha.*
ferocious: *daddao, matditu.*
fertile: *háfañagu, tekcha'.*
  fertile (for reproduction): *meppa'.*
fertility: *fottalisa.*
fertilizer: *abonu.*
  fertilizer (inorganic): *fottalisa.*
fervent: *apuráo.*
fester: *fañugo', mañugo'.*
festivity: *gupot.*
fever: *kalentura.*
  scarlet fever: *eskatlatina.*
few: *dídide', noskuantos, unos kuantos.*
fiance: *nobiu.*
fib: *dagi.*
fiber tree: *pokse'.*
fibre: *pokse'.*
fibrous: *mípilu.*
fickle: *a'guyon, kakaroti.*
fiddle: *labbet.*
fidelity: *amista.*
field: *guinassan, plasa, tirenu,*
  yinabbao.
  field (used for planting): *kaña.*
  small field: *sabaneta.*
fiendish: *inaniti, sinasalaguan.*
fierce: *daddao, malamaña, matditu,*
  tái'ase'.
fiery: *maipe.*
fiesta: *gupot.*
fifteen: *kinse.*
fifth: *kinto.*
fifty: *sinkuenta.*
  fifty-one: *sinkuenta i unu.*
fig
  fig plant: *higos.*
fight: *baggai, kombati, mumu, palitada.*
  fight (to the finish): *balentia.*
  fight off: *fohyan.*
fighter: *gá'mumu, kombateru.*
figuration: *botto.*
figure: *botto, figura, hechura, táhtaotao.*
  figure out: *kedanchiyi, suma, tasa.*
figurine: *figurín.*
filament: *mecha.*
file: *lima.*
filefish: *hagon faha.*

Filipino: *Tagalu.*
   Filipino (slang Guam): *atot.*
   Filipino (slang): *lintek.*
fill: *na'sénbula, siniyi.*
   fill full: *hemmot.*
   fill up: *lotge.*
filled: *bohbo.*
   filled (by pregnancy - slang): *haspok.*
film: *fiom.*
filter: *kúladot, kula.*
filth: *kulakong, potkeria.*
filthy: *akong, hoplat, kossos, kuchinu,*
   máskara.
   filthy face: *máskara.*
final: *uttimo.*
finalize: *finalisa, na'fakpo'.*
finally: *pot fin.*
find: *fakcha'i, sodda'.*
fine: *amen, finu, maolek, mutta.*
finger
   finger (generic term): *kálulot.*
   index finger: *tátancho'.*
   little finger: *kálanke'.*
   middle finger: *kálulot talo'.*
fingernail: *pápakes.*
fingers
   fingers (paralyzed): *haku.*
finish: *fakpo', funhayan, kélachai,*
   monhayan.
   about to finish: *kélachai.*
   finish (already): *munhayan.*
   finish off: *lachai.*
finished: *echo, kompletu, makpo'.*
fire: *guafi, kimasón, kumasón, yokyok.*
   camp fire: *foggera.*
   fire (a gun): *paki.*
   fire extinguisher: *bomban guafi,*
   bomban kimasón.
   fire truck: *trak guafi, trak kimasón.*
   fire-arm (small): *paki.*
   to start fire: *u'os, yugi.*
firebrand: *tesson.*
firecracker: *kuetes.*
firefly: *donggat.*
fireplace: *hali'an.*
firewood: *hayon matutong.*
   collect firewood: *ngayu.*
firm: *kompania, mahetok, sugat.*
firmament: *fitmamento.*
first: *finéne'na, fine'na, primét,*
   prinsipiu.
   apply first aid: *amte.*
   be first: *finéne'na, mo'na.*
   first (m): *primeru.*
   first of all: *finéne'na.*

fiscal
   fiscal year: *añu feskat.*

fish: *guihan, kátokcha'.*
   catch fish: *peska.*
   fish by poisoning: *guasa'.*
   fish eggs: *figan.*
   fish trap: *gigao, nasa.*
   pickled fish: *asnentukon.*
   sliced fish: *sásime'.*
   stone fish: *nufo'.*
   surgeon fish: *patgon tátaga'.*
   to fish: *peska.*
   to fish by line: *étupak.*
   turkey fish: *guihan pabu.*
   type of fish: *alimasat, danglon, fayao,*
   gaddas, iriko', lesso', sassa, talapia.
   type of fish-(family mullidae):
   sakmoneti.
   type of fish-(family serranidae):
   gadao.
   type of fish-(family sphyraenidae):
   alu.
   type of fish-abudefduf sordidus:
   doddo.
   type of fish-acanthocybium solandri
   (family scombridae): *uahu.*
   type of fish-acanthurus glaucpareius
   (acanthuridae): *satan apaka'*
   dadalak-ña.
   type of fish-acanthurus guttatus
   (acanthuridae): *hamoktan.*
   type of fish-acanthurus guttatus (family
   acanthuridae): *hamottan.*
   type of fish-acanthurus
   metoprosophron (family
   acanthuridae): *guasa'.*
   type of fish-amphiprion (family
   pomacentridae): *fohmo' gadudok.*
   type of fish-any member of the
   families platychephalidae: *macheng.*
   type of fish-arothron nigropunctatus:
   buteten malulasa.
   type of fish-aulostomus chinensis
   (family aulostomidae): *ba'yak.*
   type of fish-balistoides viridescens
   (family balistidae): *pulonnon*
   sasadu.
   type of fish-bothus mancus: *tampat.*
   type of fish-caesio caerulaureus:
   bonita.
   type of fish-caranx ignobilis (family
   carangidae): *tarakitu.*
   type of fish-chaetodon auriga:
   ababang amariyu.
   type of fish-chanos chanos: *agua.*
   type of fish-cheilinus chlorurus (family
   labridae): *ga'das.*
   type of fish-cheilinus undulatus (family
   labridae): *tangison.*

type of fish-chelon vaigiensis (family
mugilidae): *laiguan.*
type of fish-cirrihtus pinnulatus:
aluda.
type of fish-clarias batrachus (family
clariidae): *ito'.*
type of fish-coryphaena hippurus:
dofen.
type of fish-cowfish: *toriyu.*
type of fish-ctenochaetus striatus
(acanthuridae): *sata.*
type of fish-ctenochaetus striatus
(family acanthuridae): *odda.*
type of fish-diodon hystrix (family
diodontidae): *buteten tituka'.*
type of fish-epinephalus elongatus
(serranidae): *gadao mama'te.*
type of fish-euthynnus affinis yaito:
mákaro'.
type of fish-family acanthuridae:
hiyok, tataga' halu'u.
type of fish-family apogonidae: *lanse.*
type of fish-family balistidae:
pulonnon, pulonnon attilong.
type of fish-family canthigasteridae:
buteten pento, buteti.
type of fish-family carangidae:
hachuman, i'e', mamulan, tarakitiyu.
type of fish-family carcharhinidae:
halu'on unai, halu'u, katsunesitu.
type of fish-family dasyatidae: *afula',*
fanihen tasi, hafula'.
type of fish-family exocoetidae
(flyingfishes): *gaga.*
type of fish-family hemiramphidae:
hankot.
type of fish-family holocentridae:
cha'lak, sísi'ok, sagámilon, saksak,
saksak sumulo'.
type of fish-family kyphosidae: *guili.*
type of fish-family labridae: *á'aga,*
gatdas, palakse'.
type of fish-family leiognathidae:
guaguas, kahao.
type of fish-family lutjanidae:
kaka'ka', mafute'.
type of fish-family mugilidae: *pi'os.*
type of fish-family mullidae:
bábasbas.
type of fish-family of acanthuridae
(convict tang): *kichu.*
type of fish-family pomacentridae:
fohmo'.
type of fish-family priacanthidae:
mama'gas.
type of fish-family scaridae: *atuhong,*
foge', ha'yan, laggua.
type of fish-family scombridae:
daibang.

type of fish-family scorpaenidae:
ñufo', nufo'.
type of fish-family siganidae: *dagge',*
mañahak.
type of fish-family sphyraenidae: *alon*
laiguan.
type of fish-family thunnus saliens:
bunitu.
type of fish-family zanclidae: *ababang*
gupalao.
type of fish-fistularia petimba
(fistularidae): *ba'yak.*
type of fish-gaterin diagrammus:
lagu.
type of fish-generic term for small fish:
pegge'.
type of fish-gnathodentex aureolineatus
(family lutjanidae): *saligai.*
type of fish-hepatus leucopareius
(family acanthuridae): *guaknas.*
type of fish-hippocampus: *kabayon*
tasi.
type of fish-holocentrus tierra
(holocentridae): *saksak fetda.*
type of fish-holocentrus unipunctatus
(family holocentridae): *lessok.*
type of fish-istiophorus genus: *saoara'.*
type of fish-katsuwonus pelamis:
kacho', tuna.
type of fish-kuhlia rupestris (family
kuhlidae): *umatang.*
type of fish-kuhlia taeniura (family
kuhlidae): *atinget.*
type of fish-kyphosus vaigiensis (family
kyphosidae): *guilen puenge.*
type of fish-lutjanus argentimaculatus
(family lutjanidae): *tagafen saddok.*
type of fish-lutjanus bohar (family
lutjanidae): *tagafi.*
type of fish-lutjanus gibbus (family
lutjanidae): *fáfa'et.*
type of fish-lutjanus kasmira (family
lutjanidae): *funai.*
type of fish-lutjanus kasmira
(lutjanidae): *buninas.*
type of fish-lutjanus vaigiensis (family
lutjanidae): *bu'a.*
type of fish-megalops cyprinoides:
pulan.
type of fish-morotaxis grandoculis
(family lutjanidae): *matan hagon.*
type of fish-mulloidichthys auriflamma
(family mullidae): *sakmoneten*
maninen.
type of fish-naso lituratus (family
acanthuridae): *hangon.*
type of fish-naso sp.: *patgon hugupao.*
type of fish-naso unicornis
(acanthuride): *patgon tátaga'.*

type of fish-naso unicornus (family acanthuridae): *tátaga'.*

type of fish-neomyxus chaptalii: *aguas.*

type of fish-neothunnus albacora macropterus: *maguro'.*

type of fish-oxymonacanthus longirostris (family monacanthidae): *hagon faha.*

type of fish-parupeneus trifasciatus (family mullidae): *sakmoneten acho'.*

type of fish-petroscirtes mitratus (family blenniidae): *atot.*

type of fish-pitroscirtes mitratus (family blennidae): *hatot.*

type of fish-polydactylus sexfilis (family polynemidae): *bukadutse.*

type of fish-pranesus insularum (family atherinidae): *giñu.*

type of fish-pseudobalistes flavomarginatus (family balistidae): *pulonnon sasadu.*

type of fish-pterois antennata (family scorpaenidae): *nufo' pabu.*

type of fish-pterois sp.: *guihan pabu.*

type of fish-rhinecanthus rectangulus: *pulonnon lagu.*

type of fish-salmo salar (family salmonidae): *satmón.*

type of fish-saurida gracilis: *alon le'u.*

type of fish-scolpsis cancellatus (family lutjanidae): *sihek.*

type of fish-scomberoides santi-petri (family carangidae): *hagi.*

type of fish-siganidae: *ha'tan.*

type of fish-siganus punctatus (family siganidae): *hiteng.*

type of fish-siganus spinus (family siganidae): *sesyon.*

type of fish-spratelloides delicatulus (family dussumieridae): *aletses.*

type of fish-strongylura gigantea (belonidae): *pulos.*

type of fish-strongylura gigantea (family belonidae): *palos.*

type of fish-thalassoma trilobata (family labridae): *lalacha' mamati.*

type of fish-thrissina baelama (family engraulidae): *faya.*

type of fish-trachurops crumenophthalmus: *atulai, haiteng.*

type of fish-upeneus vittatus (family mullidae): *sakmoneten le'ao, ti'ao.*

fisherman: *pépeska, pípeska, peskadót, talayeru.*

fishermen: *peskadores.*

fishing: *étokcha', kátokcha', tahu.*
(type of) fishing: *gadi.*
bottom fishing: *étupak.*
fishing line: *gugat, katgat, kotdét.*
fishing pole: *pisao.*
go fishing: *pumeska.*
good fishing: *katna.*
set fishing net in position: *langse.*
type of fishing: *édipok, lulai, lumulai, sulo'.*

fishy
fishy smell: *paomata'.*

fissure: *ka'ka'.*

fist: *trompón.*

fit: *aplikáo, apropósitu, aya, kualifika, omlat, ulat, umaya.*
fit into: *ulat.*

fitted: *kompetente.*

five: *sinko.*

fix: *arekla, fa'maolek, na'maolek.*
fix in position: *planta.*

fixable: *arekláo, areklayon, atmayon.*

fixer: *á'arekla, ná'maolek.*

fizz: *besbes.*

flabby: *ñáfula, ñaohan.*

flag: *bandera.*
flag pole: *hastan bandera.*

flame: *manila'.*
flame tree: *atbot, atbot det fuegu.*

flank: *barigada.*

flannel
flannel (cloth): *laniya.*

flapped: *palappa.*

flapping
flapping noise: *palappa.*

flash: *besbes.*

flashlight: *kandet.*
flashlight: *denke'.*

flask: *buteya, frasko, taru.*

flat: *pasadu.*
flat car: *karu.*

flatfish: *tampat.*

flatten: *pannas.*

flattened
be flattened: *mapannas.*

flatter: *ñuña, dangse, fa'ande', fa'chada', uga.*

flatulence: *hinatme manglo'.*

flaunt: *banidosa, banidosu, bumaranka, dumeskarada.*

flavor: *na'gáisabot, sabót.*
flavor (pleasing): *gusto.*

flaw: *difekto.*

flea: *potgas.*

flee: *falagu.*

fleeting: *fáfa'pos, ti ma'ok.*

flesh: *katne, masisu, sensen.*

fleshy: *chebot, pápada, yommok, yomsan.*

flexible: *ñaba', fléksible, ga'ma.*

flick
flick (with fingertip): *deska.*

flies
full of flies: *latdon.*

flight
take flight: *malagu.*

flighty
flighty person: *gekpo.*

flimsy: *kanifes.*

fling: *aguet, blanko, daggao, yotte.*

flint: *asga', yokyok.*

flip
flip (with fingertip): *deska.*
flip card: *handa.*

flirt
flirt with: *andi'i.*

flirtatious: *dudos.*

flirting: *umá'ande'.*

float: *gama, ma'ya.*

floater
good floater: *gakma.*

flock: *katdumi.*

flood: *dilubio, milak, na'sénbula.*
flood with (something): *baya'.*

flooded: *naga.*

floor: *pisu, satge.*
porch floor: *totta.*

floors
floors (of building): *bibenda.*

flopped: *palappa.*

florist: *floreru.*

flounder
flounder (fish): *tampat.*

flour: *arina.*

flourish: *mamflores.*

flower: *flores, mai'ana.*
flower bud: *kapuyo'.*
type of flower: *asusena, breablanka, chucharita, dama di noche, flores Krismas, kámia, ka'mang, kopa di oru, leston, lirio, natdo, puti tainobiu, rosa.*
type of flower-oleander: *adetfa.*
type of flower-rose: *rosát.*

flowerpot: *maseta.*

flowing: *milak.*

flu: *mañom.*

fluent: *pinalakse'.*

flunk: *poddong.*

flush: *tagga'.*

flushing: *atagga'.*

flute: *flauta.*
flute player: *flautista.*

fly: *barigeta, gupu, lalo'.*
fly killer: *puno' lalo'.*
fly swatter: *panak lalo', puno' lalo'.*
type of fly: *lalo' guaka, lalo' lagu.*

flycatcher: *chuguangguang.*

flyer: *gekpo.*

flying fish: *gaga.*

foam: *bo'an, bu'o', espuma.*

focus: *fokos.*

foe: *enimigu, kontrariu.*

fog: *afao, asgon.*
fog up: *na'asgon.*

fold: *dopbla.*

foliage: *hagon.*

folk: *familia, nasión, rasa, taotao.*

follow: *dalak, dalaki, dalalaki, rastreha, tattiyi.*

follower: *apóstoles, disípulu.*

following: *sigiente.*

folly: *babarias, binaba.*

fond
fond of: *chechet, guaiya.*

fondness: *guinaiya.*

fontanel: *kákagong.*

food: *inakpa'an, ko'lao, latiria, nénkanno'.*
boiled food (starchy): *sinetnan.*
food (carried as supplies): *tengguang.*
food classifier: *na'.*
food sac: *ábuni.*
prepared food: *fina'tinas.*
take food: *ko'lao.*
type of food: *adobu, ahu, alaguan, atmayas, bibenka, champuladu, charakiles, eskabeche, fritada, gollai chotda, ilotes, kélaguen, paksiú, sassa, suman, tinaktak, trosu.*
unprepared food: *na'yan mata'.*

fool: *atmariáo, fa'baba, kaduka, kaduku, salamanka, táisentidu, tolleng, tonto, totko, tulisán.*
fool around: *mama'baba, panggengge'.*

fooled
be fooled: *mafa'baba, mapulakes.*

foolish: *áttamos, ó'duko', bruta, hafkao, nesio, tonto.*

foolishness: *babarias, batbaridat, binaba, diablura.*

foot: *addeng, patas.*
  club foot: *chanko.*
  foot (measurement): *pi'ai, pie.*
footprint: *rastro.*
footprints: *fegge'.*
footrest: *fanggacha'an.*
footstep: *pasu, pokkat.*
footstool: *bankon addeng, fanapu'an,*
  oddas.
footwear
  footwear (generic): *dogga.*
for: *para.*
forage: *sakati.*
forbearance: *indothensia, minesngon.*
forbid: *chomma', empidi, pribi, prohibi,*
  pruibi.
forbiddance: *prohibisión.*
force: *afuetsas, alentos, alimento,*
  fuetsa, minetgot, nina'siña, nombra.
forced: *opbligáo.*
forceps: *tinasa.*
fore: *punta.*
forebear: *guelo'.*
forebearing: *tái'ine'son.*
forecast: *predika.*
forefinger: *tátancho'.*
forehead: *ha'i.*
foreigner: *estrangheru.*
foreman: *átguaset, bosong, fotman,*
  kápurat, kabesiyu, ma'gas, tátago'.
forest: *bundak, halom tano'.*
foretaste: *antisipasión.*
foretell: *adibina.*
forever: *tiot tiempo.*
forge: *fragua, fueyes.*
forget: *maleffa.*
  forget it: *para hafa.*
forgetful: *átaktak, hámaleffa, tákleffa.*
forgivable: *asi'iyon.*
forgive: *asi'i, despensa.*
forgiveness: *inasi'i, ma'ase', mina'ase',*
  petdón.
  have forgiveness: *gái'ase', gáima'ase'.*
forgiving
  forgiving person: *yo'ase'.*
fork: *ténidot.*
  fork (of the tree): *dinga'.*
form: *fa'tinas, fotma, hechura, otganisa,*
  táhtaotao.
  form (of face): *máskara.*
formal: *fotmat, solemne.*
formality: *fotmalidát.*
formation: *fotmasión.*

former: *finéne'na.*
forsake: *dingu.*
forsaken: *abandonáo.*
fort: *kastiyu.*
fortunate: *afottunáo, fottuna.*
fortunately: *grasias adios.*
fortune: *fottuna.*
forty: *kuarenta.*
  forty-one: *kuarenta i unu.*
forward: *sigi.*
forwardness: *táisetbe.*
foul: *kuchinu.*
  foul ball: *supi.*
  foul mouth: *desparateru.*
foundation: *fondasión, simiento.*
four: *kuatro.*
fourteen: *katotse.*
fourth: *kuatta, kuatto.*
fox: *ga'lagon machalek.*
fracture: *ka'ka'.*
fractured: *mafgo', mahlok.*
fragile: *hámafak.*
fragment: *enggranét, ritasos.*
fragrant: *paopao.*
frail: *dangnge', dolle, kadabet, pedde.*
frame: *kuadru.*
  picture frame: *kuadru.*
France: *Fransia.*
franchise: *botu.*
Franciscan
  Franciscan friar: *kapuchinu.*
frank: *franko, magahet, onesto.*
frankfurter: *churisos.*
frankincense: *insensio.*
frankly: *frankamente.*
frankness: *sinseramente.*
fraud: *digeria, linipa, traisión.*
freckle: *dondon, pekas.*
free: *dibatde, franko, saka, suetto.*
  free to act: *obra.*
  free-loader: *ankas.*
  set free: *deskata.*
freed: *kahaya.*
freedom: *konsentimento, libettát,*
  minalulok.
freeze: *mama'ais.*
freezer: *rifa.*
freezing: *fugu.*
freight: *fleti.*
French: *Franses.*
frequent: *fihu, sesso, sessuyi.*
  frequent urge to urinate: *pisagon.*
frequently: *kada ratu.*

fresh: *fresko.*

freshen
freshen up: *rifresko.*

frictionless: *finu, mahlos.*

Friday: *Betnes.*

fried: *inaflitu.*

friend: *ágofli'e', átungo', abok, adai, amigu, dai, ga'chong, kompañeru, kume', lai.*
friend (f): *amiga.*

friendless: *táiga'chong.*

friendliness: *inátungo'.*

friendly: *amapble, chihet.*

friends
be friends: *áfa'maolek.*

friendship: *inágofli'e'.*

frigate: *frigata.*
frigate bird: *fakte, ga'ga' manglo'.*

fright: *kinibatde, linihan, mina'a'ñao.*

frighten: *aminasa, asusta, espanta, fa'ñague, hongang, huppa.*

frightened: *asustáo, espantáo, lu'an, luhan, ma'a'ñao.*

frightful: *ná'ma'a'ñao.*

frigid: *fugu, manengheng.*

frisk: *takka'.*

fritters: *boñelos.*

frivolous: *áttamos.*

frock: *bestidura, sutana.*

frog: *kairo'.*

from: *desde, ginen.*
from (preposition): *gi.*

frond: *hagon.*

front: *mo'na.*
in front of: *me'nan.*
way front: *yamó'nana.*

froth: *bo'an, espuma.*

frown: *matan lalalo'.*

frozen: *mama'ais.*

frugal: *manakihom.*

fruit: *inasahan, to'a.*
fruit (on a plant): *tinekcha'.*
fruit (sweet): *fruta, gulusina.*
spoiled fruit: *lañayon.*

fruitful: *meppa', tekcha'.*

fry: *aflitu.*

frying pan: *kaserola, la'uyan manaflitu.*

fudges: *fatches.*

fulfill: *kumple.*

full: *bokka', bula, mafnot, motmot.*
full (from food): *haspok.*
full moon: *gualafon.*
full of: *lahyan, unmanada.*
full up: *motmot.*

fume: *fiúm.*

fun: *minagof.*

function: *fonksión.*

fund: *fondo.*

fundamental: *fondamento.*

funeral: *entieru.*

fungus
skin fungus: *gupo'.*
type of fungus: *donggat, talangan hayu.*

funnel: *embudu.*

funny: *ná'chalek.*
funny act: *manggua'.*
funny man: *santa'.*

fur: *pulon ga'ga'.*

furious: *fehman, impetosu.*

furnish: *na'huyungi, pribeni.*

furniture: *trastes halom guma'.*

further: *chago'ña, hat-, lage'-, lahát-.*

furthermore: *ombres.*

fuse: *fiús.*

fuss: *atborotu, atborutáo, enkebukáo, kombalachi, plaito, yaoyao, yinaoyao.*

fussy: *chacha', ga'plaito.*

future
future marker: *u.*
future tense marker: *para.*

g: *ge, he.*

gabby: *ñongñong.*

gable: *kabisera.*

gaff: *gancho.*

gag: *bossat, uha'.*

gaiety: *konsuelu, minagof.*

gain: *ganansia, ginanna, taka'.*

gait: *pokkat.*

gall bladder: *lála'et.*

gallinule: *pulattat.*

gallon: *galón.*

gallop: *malagu, pares.*
to gallop: *galoppe.*

gamble: *huega, hugando.*

gambler: *á'aposta, gamboleru, hógado*

gambling: *pa'iket.*

game: *huegu, hugando.*
type of game: *batu, estuleks, pasabara, tángganu, yanken.*

gang: *kompañeru.*

gangrene: *kanggrena.*

gangrenous: *kanggrena.*

gap: *kaguan.*

gape: *angla'a', langnga', nga'nga'.*

garb: *bestidura.*

garbage: *ánkanno'.*
garbled
  garbled speech: *pahya'.*
garden: *hatdín, kaña.*
gardener: *hatdineru.*
gardening: *gualo'.*
gargle: *gátgaras, mokmok.*
garlic: *ahos.*
garment: *bestidura, túniku.*
garnish: *beste, na'beste.*
garrulous: *ga'kumuentos, pichipichi.*
garter: *ligas.*
gas: *gas, gasilina.*
gash: *utot.*
gaslight: *kandet gas.*
gasoline: *gas, gasilina, gatsilina.*
gasp: *guha.*
  gasp (air): *suspiros.*
gate: *tranka.*
gateway: *tranka.*
gather: *hokka, na'etnon, na'montohon, na'monton, rikohi.*
gathering: *etnon, hunta, linahyan, miteng, montohon.*
gaudy: *ande', banidosa, banidosu, míkulot.*
gauze: *gasa.*
gay: *magof.*
gear: *giha.*
gecko: *achiak.*
gelid: *manengheng.*
geneaology: *rasa.*
general: *henerát.*
  in general: *henerát.*
generation: *henerasión.*
generator: *yenereta.*
generous: *goftao.*
gentian violet: *amot lila.*
gentle: *benikno, máñaña'.*
gentleman: *kabayeru, señót, señoritu.*
gentlemanly: *respetayon.*
gentleness: *siniabi.*
genuflect: *kottesia.*
genuine: *magahet.*
geographic: *yeográfiku.*
geography: *yeografia.*
geometry: *yeometria.*
germ: *ulo'.*
German: *Alemán.*
Germany: *Alemania.*
germinate: *dokko', la'chok.*
get: *hentan.*
  get away: *láttanao.*
  get close: *arima.*

get down: *tunok.*
get even: *emmok.*
get here: *mamaila'.*
get out: *huyong, láttanao.*
get up: *fakmata, kahulo'.*
gewgaw: *hugeti.*
ghastly: *boksion, chupon, kalang matai.*
ghost: *bíkulo', birak, duendes, espiritu, ná'ma'a'ñao, plantasma, taotaomo'na.*
giant: *gante, higante.*
gibber: *chátkuentos.*
giddy: *hafkao.*
giddyap: *ali, lácheddek.*
gift: *chenchule', ika, nina'i, regalu.*
  gift (to sweetheart): *prenda.*
  wedding gift: *a'ok.*
gill: *aguas, atgayas.*
  gill (of fish): *guasang.*
  gills: *atkayadas.*
  hook by gill: *atgayas.*
gilt: *puetkasita.*
gin: *hiniebra.*
ginger: *hasngot, kámia, mango'.*
  ginger (edible): *hasmín.*
girl: *ákkaga.*
girlfriend: *nobia.*
give: *na'i, presenta.*
  give (in exchange for): *despacha.*
  give abundantly: *letke, okte, seba.*
  give away excess: *alatga.*
  give in: *fatani.*
  give oneself away: *gencha'.*
  give out: *alatgayi.*
gizzard: *moyeha.*
glad: *magof.*
gladden: *na'magof.*
glance: *atan, inatan.*
  glance off: *supi.*
glare: *lamlam, mañila', mina'lak.*
glass: *krestát.*
  broken glass: *ma'pe' espehos.*
  drinking glass: *basu.*
  piece of glass: *ma'pe' espehos.*
gleam: *inina.*
glee: *alegria.*
gliding: *paya'ya'.*
glittering: *ma'lak.*
global
  global shape: *bolabola, dollan.*
globe: *inadamelong, lámpara.*
  lamp globe: *tubu.*
globular: *adamelong.*
gloomy: *homhom.*
glorification: *silebrasión.*

glorified: *glorifikáo.*
glorify: *glorifika, silebra.*
glorifying: *glorifikáo.*
glorious: *dikno.*
glory: *gloria.*
  morning glory: *abubu.*
glossy: *lamlam.*
glove: *guantes, gurobo'.*
glow: *figan.*
glue: *dangse, enggrudu, kola.*
glutinous: *dangson.*
glutted: *haspok, malulok.*
glutton: *ambiento, kakno'.*
  glutton (for drink): *gekmen.*
gnat: *ga'ga' sirenu, kunitos, ságamai.*
gnaw
  gnaw on something: *kanno'.*
go: *fa'pos, hanao, lahu.*
  go ahead: *sigi mo'na.*
  go and get: *falaggue.*
  go away: *sappe.*
  go beyond: *upos.*
  go by way of: *esgen, sigen, sumigen,*
    umesgen.
  go fishing: *éguihan.*
  go inside for: *halomgue.*
  go on: *sigi.*
  go simultaneously: *gigu.*
  go to: *falak, malak.*
goat: *chiba.*
  goat call: *nani.*
goatfish: *bábasbas, sakmoneten acho',*
    sakmoneten le'ao, sakmoneten
    maninen, sakmoneti.
  goatfish (small): *ti'ao.*
goblet: *kopa.*
goblin: *duendes.*
God: *Asaina, Dios, Yu'us.*
goddaughter: *hada.*
godfather: *kompaire, ninu, patlinu.*
godlike: *yini'usan.*
godmother: *kumaire, matlina, nina.*
godparent: *matlina, patlinu.*
godson: *hadu.*
goggles: *antiohos.*
goiter: *buchi.*
gold: *oru.*
golden shower: *kana' fistula.*
goldish: *inoru na kulot.*
gondola car: *bagón.*
gone
  far gone: *sala'.*
gonorrhea: *enkotdio.*
good: *bibu, buenu, maolek.*
  become good: *mumaolek.*

good (as in approval): *buen.*
good afternoon: *buenas tatdes.*
good at: *meyeng.*
good condition: *na'maolek.*
good day: *buenas dias.*
good evening: *buenas noches.*
good for you: *buen echu.*
good looking: *atanon.*
good morning: *buenas dias.*
good thing: *grasias adios.*
good time: *motgan, mutero', tuhos.*
good-bye: *adjós, inádingu.*
  say good-bye: *despidi.*
  very good: *binibu.*
goodness
  goodness gracious: *nánalao.*
  my goodness: *nánalao.*
goods: *fektos.*
goof around: *mama'baba.*
goose: *ganso.*
  goose pimples: *apigasa.*
gore: *kánghelon.*
gorge: *dafflokgue.*
gorged: *malulok.*
gosh: *karamba.*
gospel: *bangheliu, ebanghelio, pinagat.*
gossip: *agangñaihon, apbladoria,*
    atbladoria, eskándalu, telefon
    alaihai.
gossiper: *apbladót, atbladót, atbladora,*
    gotgot, sakne.
  gossiper (f): *apbladora.*
got up: *mameddos.*
gouge: *asuela.*
gourd: *kalamasa, tagu'a.*
govern: *desponi, gobietna, ma'gasi.*
government: *gobietno.*
governor: *gobietnadót, gobietno, tátago'.*
gown: *bestida, bestidura.*
grab: *chule', habao, hakot.*
  grab (something): *cho'cho'.*
grabbed: *chinile'.*
grace: *fabót, grasia.*
graceful: *grasiosu.*
gracious: *bunita.*
  gracious (m): *bunitu.*
grade: *gradu.*
gradual: *adumídide'.*
graduate: *graduha.*
graduated
  be graduated: *graduha.*
graduation: *graduha.*
graftage
  graftage of vine: *gias.*

grain
grain plant: *trigu.*
grammar: *gramática.*
grand: *gatbo, tagalo'.*
granddaughter: *nieta.*
granddaughter (great, great):
tataranieta.
grandfather: *bihu, guello.*
grandmother: *biha, guella.*
grandparent: *guelo'.*
grandson: *nietu.*
grandson (great, great): *tataranietu.*
granite: *alutong.*
grant: *atmiti, na'i.*
granule: *engggranét.*
grape: *ubas.*
grapefruit: *kahet ma'gas.*
grapevine
by the grapevine: *telefon alaihai.*
grasp: *chule', gini'ot, go'he, go'te, gu'ot,
mantieni, sustieni.*
grasped: *chinile'.*
grass: *cha'guan, chara.*
bermuda grass: *atmagosu.*
type of grass: *ínifok, laso' katu,
maigo' lalo'.*
type of grass-napier grass: *napa.*
grasshopper: *apacha', apacha' matai.*
green grasshopper: *apacha' suette.*
grate: *etses.*
grate (coconut): *kamyo.*
grateful: *pinitiyiyi.*
gratefulness: *gratu.*
grater: *etses.*
coconut grater: *kamyo.*
gratification: *gratifikasión.*
gratify: *finaboresi, gratifika.*
gratifying: *interesante.*
grating: *rehas.*
grating (voice): *lossos.*
gratis: *dibatde, grates.*
gratitude: *agradesimiento, gratifikasión,
gratu, inagradesi.*
gratuitously: *dibatde.*
grave: *graba, naftan.*
grave marker: *lápida.*
gravel: *baras, kaskahu.*
gravid: *mapotge'.*
gravy: *satsa.*
gray
gray (color): *kulot apu.*
gray-tailed tattler: *dulili.*
grayish: *inapu na kulót.*
graze: *pasto.*

grazing land: *pastahi.*
grease: *mantika, sebu.*
grease gun: *asaitera.*
to grease: *palai.*
greasy: *manempeya, mantika.*
great: *dánkolo, krisidu.*
great scott: *karamba.*
great-granddaughter: *bisnieta.*
great-grandfather: *bisabuello.*
great-grandmother: *bisabuella.*
great-grandson: *bisnietu.*
so great: *tatfoi.*
greater: *lámudong.*
greatest: *mampos.*
greatly: *sen.*
greed: *kudisio.*
greedy: *ambiento, chattao, gatgat,
girek, gulosu, hambrento, kudisio,
latga, otguyosu, padok, tragón.*
green
green (color): *betde.*
greenish: *binetde.*
greet: *felisita, saluda.*
greeting: *bien binidu, saludu.*
grenade
hand grenade: *balan granada,
terudang.*
griddle: *kommat.*
gridiron: *alamlen manunu.*
grief: *lutu, pesadumbre, piniti.*
full of grief: *triste.*
grieve
grieve for: *pinitiyi.*
grill: *alamlen manunu.*
grin
grin (showing teeth): *chiche'.*
grind: *gulek, mulinu, tutong.*
grinder: *gulek, mulinu.*
grindstone: *guasa'on, moyong, mulinu.*
grip: *akihom, gini'ot, mañostieni.*
gristle: *gekmon, kustrafas, sankarón.*
grizzled: *chunge'.*
groan: *manugong, uchon, ugong,
umugong.*
groceries: *fektos.*
grocery store: *metkáo.*
groin: *aflagu.*
groom: *nobiu.*
groove: *karít.*
grope: *siente, takka'.*
grouchy: *muñeru.*
ground: *odda', rasón, tano'.*
ground-cherry: *tumates cha'ka.*
soft ground: *fokfok, luño'.*

group: *grupu, gurupu, inetnon,
  katdumi, linahyan, na'etnon,
  na'montohon.*
  group of: *pinipon, pupon.*
grouper: *aluda, gadao.*
grovel: *sufa'.*
grow: *dokko', la'chok.*
  grow root: *manhale'.*
growing
  growing up: *kinahulo'.*
growl: *gonggong.*
growling
  growling (of dog): *so'on.*
grudge: *malisia.*
gruel: *atmayas.*
grumble: *gonggong.*
grunt: *uchon.*
Guam: *Guahan.*
guarantee: *garentia.*
guard: *á'adahi, adahi, difende, guatde,
  guatdia, polisia, protehi, pulan,
  sinague'.*
  keep guard: *pulan.*
guardian: *difensót, protektót.*
guava: *abas.*
guess: *danche, dibina, diha', hallom.*
  cause to guess: *diga.*
  guess size: *takfiha.*
  try to guess: *kédanche.*
guest: *kombidáo, kombiti.*
Guguan: *Guguan.*
guide: *chalani, dirihi, kondukta, leklek,
  manea, pilotu, sugon.*
  guide (by the hand): *pipet.*
  guide (with a rudder): *timón.*
  to guide: *giha.*
guidepost: *tapbleru.*
guileless: *inosente.*
guilt: *isao.*
guiltless: *tái'isao.*
guilty: *isao, lachi, punu'on.*
guitar: *gitala.*
gulch: *kañada.*
gull: *fa'babayon, fa'ga'ga'on.*
gullet: *guliya.*
gullible: *fa'babayon, fa'ga'ga'on.*
gulp: *galamok, kalamot.*
  gulp down (without chewing): *pañot
  ales.*
gum: *danges, fokson.*
gun
  gun barrel: *kañutu.*
  machine gun: *kikanyio'.*
  sound of gun shot: *tiru.*

gurgling: *bulokbok.*
gusty: *guaifon.*
gutter: *maktan.*
  gutter (roof): *fanoktan.*
  rain gutter: *kannat hanom.*
h: *hache.*
habit: *bisio, hábitu, kustumbre, maña,
  usu.*
habitation: *habitasión.*
habitual: *mana'payon, payon,
  pinayongguan.*
habituate: *akostombra, payuni.*
hacienda: *hasienda.*
hack: *taga'.*
haggard: *debet, tufai.*
hair: *gapotulu, pulu.*
  gray hair: *chunge'.*
  hair bun: *akeyo'.*
  hair spray: *amot gapotulu.*
  long hair: *koche'.*
  to give haircut: *dasai.*
  unkempt hair: *kala'u.*
haircut: *laklak.*
  type of haircut: *dasai adotfo, dasai
  dakngas, dasai malachai, dasai
  tapbla, dasai San Visente.*
hairless
  hairless (body): *hingao.*
hairpin: *chiget, kányase'.*
  large hairpin: *atkiya.*
hairy: *batbuda, batbudu, mípilu,
  mepplo, peludu.*
half: *lamitá, media, mediu.*
  half day: *mediu dia.*
  half-and-half: *lamitá.*
  half-breed: *meskláo, mestisa, mestisu.*
halfbeak: *hankot.*
hall: *sala.*
halt: *ataha, cho, na'para.*
halter: *bossat.*
ham: *hammon.*
Hamburg
  Hamburg (chicken): *bulaskes.*
hammer: *masu, mattiyu.*
hammock: *amaka.*
hamstring: *deskareta, kedera.*
hand: *kannai.*
  hand over: *chule' magi, hague'.*
  hand-feed: *chotge.*
  to hand-carry: *kílili.*
hand grenade: *terudang.*
handbag: *balakbak.*
  handbag (made from weaving):
  tisage'.

handcuff: *posa.*
handful: *puñu.*
handkerchief: *pañu.*
handle
  handle (of tool): *tokpong.*
  make handle for: *tokpungi.*
handslap: *pantek.*
handsome: *atanon, bunitu.*
  slightly handsome: *bunituyan.*
handy: *kómodu.*
hang: *á'kalaye', chanka', kahlang, kalang, kana', makana'.*
  hang (to death): *ñaka'.*
  hang on to: *mañostieni.*
  hang up: *kana'.*
hanger
  clothes hanger: *kana' magagu.*
happened
  happened to: *susedi.*
happening: *estoria, hemplo, sinisedi, susiadét.*
happiness: *felisidát, konsuelu, minagof.*
happy: *felís, magof.*
harass: *akachayi, kasse.*
harbor: *báhia, puetto.*
hard: *chátsaga, duru, mahetok, makkat, mappot, sugat.*
  hard-working: *butmuchachu.*
hardened: *mumahetok.*
hardly: *apenas, chat, chat-, chatta'.*
hardship: *difikuttát, ginaddon.*
hardy: *mahayu.*
harelip: *a'pe', pire'.*
harm: *aña, baketasu, dañu, fakkai, fueges, garutasu, lamen, na'famadesi, na'lamen, pethuisiu.*
harmful: *ná'lamen, ná'tailayi.*
harmless: *manso.*
harmonica: *bibek, hamónika.*
  mouth harmonica: *belembao pachot.*
harness
  put on harness: *onse.*
harp: *atpa.*
harpoon: *fisga, hatpón.*
harsh: *bastos, táklalo'.*
  harsh (voice): *lossos.*
harvest: *gutai, hinekka, kosecha.*
  harvest (corn): *ko'ko'.*
  to harvest: *kosecha.*
  to harvest root crop: *hali.*
haste: *chinaddek.*
hasten: *alulayi, apreta, apura, pinalala.*
hasty: *apretáo, apretát, apuráo.*
hat: *tuhong.*

hatched: *mapulakes.*
hatchet: *achita, hachita.*
hatching: *kumuleka.*
hate: *chatli'e'.*
hated: *machatatan.*
hateful: *machatatan, ti guaiyayon.*
hatred: *desgusto, ináchatli'e'.*
haughty: *subetbiu.*
haul: *halla, katga, loffan, saggue'.*
  haul up: *na'kahulo'.*
hauled: *maloffan.*
haunch: *ñanggo, lomu.*
haunt: *chonchon, fa'ñague.*
  to haunt: *pena.*
have: *gái'iyo, guaha.*
  cause to have: *na'gai-.*
  have plenty: *láguaha.*
  have something (prefix): *gai-, ka-.*
  have to: *debidi, ministét.*
haven: *fandeskansayan.*
hawk: *ágila.*
  hawk up: *kakak.*
hay: *sakati.*
hazard: *atotga, atrebi.*
hazardous: *piligrosu.*
haze: *afao, asgon.*
hazy: *mumaya'.*
he: *gue', guiya, ha.*
head: *amu, kabesa, ulu.*
  head of family: *tronko.*
  head shawl: *mantiya.*
  head up: *na'ágihilu'i.*
headache: *malinek ulu.*
headman: *kabesiyu.*
headrest: *baroti.*
headstrong: *manatma.*
heal: *homlo', na'homlo'.*
healed: *magong, maso'.*
healer: *á'amte, ná'homlo', ná'magong.*
healing: *latto'.*
health: *brinabu, salút.*
healthy: *brabu, la'la'.*
heap: *amontona, monton, okso'.*
  heap up: *na'ágitilu'i.*
hear: *hungok.*
heard
  be heard: *hongga.*
hearken: *ékungok.*
heart: *korasón, patnitos.*
  cut heart out of coconut palm: *patnitos.*
  heart attack: *ataken korasón.*
heartbeat: *potso.*

heartfelt: *sinseru.*

hearts: *kopas.*

heat: *na'maipe.*
  be in heat: *mahaga'.*

heathen: *paganu.*

heaven: *langet.*

heavenly: *linangitan.*

heavy: *makkat.*

heck: *lato'.*

heckle: *kahna.*

hectare: *hektaria.*

hedge: *kollat cha'guan.*

hedonist: *luhuriosu.*

heed: *atende, atituyi, hungok.*

heedless: *deskuidáo, táihinadahi.*

heel
  heel (of foot): *dédeggo.*
  heel (of shoes): *takong.*

height: *attura, linekka'.*

heir: *irideru.*

heliotrope
  wild heliotrope: *batbena.*

hell: *enfietno, infietno, sasalaguan, tináifondo.*

hellish: *inaniti, sinasalaguan.*

hello: *buenas dias, hoe'.*
  hello (informal greeting): *hafa dai, hafa dei.*

helmet: *tappe', tuhong tappe'.*

help: *ábiu, akudi, aosiliu, apasigua, asiste, ayuda, fa'che'chu'i, goggue, saguan, sague', sukoru.*
  help (someone) out: *kubre.*
  help out: *áfa'maolek, reskata.*

helped: *kahaya.*

helper: *á'ayuda, asistente, ayudante, hotnaleru.*

hem: *dobladura.*

hemorrhoids: *pudos, tininu.*

hen
  brood hen: *ponedera.*
  hen (chicken): *punidera.*
  hen (young): *poya.*
  setting hen: *kuleka.*

henceforth: *para mo'na.*

her: *-ña.*

herb: *amot.*

herd: *manada.*

herder: *pastót.*

herdsman: *bakeru.*

here: *gaige, guini, magi, uhu.*
  here is: *estague', estaguiya.*
  over here (place in the direction of the speaker): *guini magi.*

over here (place next to the speaker): *este magi.*

hereafter: *pues.*

heritage: *erensia, rénsia.*

hermaphrodite: *mamflorita.*

hermit: *etmitanu.*

heron
  reef heron: *chuchuko'.*

herrings
  round herrings: *aletses.*

hesitate: *na'tatte.*

hex: *kahna, kahnayi.*

hibernate: *maigo'.*

hibiscus: *flores rosa, mapola, rosa.*

hiccup: *fonton.*

hide: *atok, disimula, homme, kueru, na'atok, na'na'.*
  hide by covering: *oropa.*
  hide oneself: *atto'.*
  hide-and-seek (game): *di'ao, di'u.*

hideous: *ti atanon.*

hiding place: *fanatukan.*

high: *bileng, lokka', tákkilo'.*
  high mass: *misan kantada.*

highborn: *nopble.*

higher: *gé'hilo'.*

highway: *chalan.*

hill: *okso'.*

hilly: *bokka', okso', pinatokso'.*
  hilly place: *fina'okso'.*

hinder: *estotba.*

hindrance: *atkagueti, estotbo.*
  hindrance (of marriage): *impedimento.*

hinge: *bisagra.*

hint: *na'tungo'ñaihon.*

hip: *ñanggo, kaderas, lomu.*

hips: *dagan.*

hire: *emplea, enggansa.*

hirsute: *mepplo.*
  hirsute (f): *batbuda.*
  hirsute (m): *batbudu.*

his: *-ña.*

hiss: *chechet.*

history: *historia, istoria.*

hit: *faggas, galuti, panak, planasos, sapblasos.*
  be hit: *toka.*
  cause to hit: *dekkes.*
  hit (a target): *danche.*
  hit (in the face): *trukos.*
  hit down: *tugua'.*
  hit with the fist: *paniti.*
  try to hit: *kédanche.*

hitch-hike: *ensahi.*

hive
    wasp hive: *chonchon sasata.*

hives: *lokklok haga'.*

hoard: *fa'la'mon, manadahi.*

hoarse: *afagao, lossos.*

hoax: *dugeruyi, tolleng.*

hob: *tapblita.*

hocus-pocus: *ta'hafkao.*

hoe: *asada, fusiños, piku.*

hoist: *atbola, pesa, tachu.*
    hoist or raise with a tackle: *hatsa.*

hold: *go'he, go'te, gu'ot, kotma,*
    mantieni, sustieni.
    hold down: *hoño', hokse, klaba,*
    sokka.
    hold fast: *toktok.*
    hold hands: *ágo'te, ámantieni.*
    hold on to: *mañostieni.*
    hold up: *po'lonñaihon.*

hole: *adotgan, hoyu, le'yok, maddok,*
    ngulo'.
    deep hole: *lupok.*
    water hole: *le'yok.*

holiday: *gupot.*

Holland: *Holandes.*

hollow: *ñudu, gueku.*
    hollow sounding: *baobao, mongmong.*

holy: *sagradu, santo.*
    holy person: *santolón, santolona,*
    sinantusan.
    holy portrait: *lámina.*
    holy water: *agua bendita.*
    holy week: *simana santa.*
    Holy Ghost: *Espiritu Santo.*
    Holy Spirit: *Espiritu Santo.*
    Holy Trinity: *Santisima Trinidát.*

homage: *onra.*

home: *guma'.*

homer: *homoráng.*

home run
    a home run: *homoráng.*
    make a home run: *humomran.*

homocidal: *pekno'.*

homosexual: *mamflorita.*

honest: *anes, diberas, franko, magahet,*
    onesto.

honesty: *me'nan Yu'us, tininas.*

honey: *anibat, miét.*
    honey-eater (bird): *égigi.*

honeybee: *abeha.*

honor: *onra, respeta.*

honorable: *dikno, respetayon.*

hoof: *pápakes.*

hook: *gancho, haguet.*
    catch with a hook: *laguet.*

hoop: *sancho, suncho.*

hop: *chulugaigai, ká'dideng,*
    kakaronde', kakaroti, ta'yok, tala'yok.

hope: *diseha, esperansa, pudera.*
    hope for: *tanga.*
    hope to: *puedi.*

hopeless: *desesperáo, táininangga.*

hopscotch: *ká'dideng.*

horizon: *kanton langet.*

horn: *bibek.*
    horn (musical): *kotneta.*
    horn (of animal): *kánghelon.*

horrid: *ti atanon.*

horrified: *susto.*

horror: *kinibatde, mina'a'ñao,*
    ná'ma'a'ñao.

horse: *kabayu.*
    sea horse: *kabayon tasi.*

horsefly: *lalo' guaka.*

horseman: *kabayeru.*

hose: *tilipas.*

hospital: *espitát, ospitát.*

host: *mento', taotao guma'.*

hostess: *mayidoma, mento'.*

hot: *figan, fina'maipe, maipe.*
    hot (spicy): *pika.*

hothead: *embidiosu.*

hound: *ga'lagu.*

hour: *ora.*
    hour hand: *orario.*

house: *guma', hasienda.*
    thatched house: *saguale'.*

housefly: *lalo'.*

how
    how (question word): *hafa taimanu,*
    taimanu.
    how long: *kuantos.*
    how many: *kuanto.*
    how much: *kuanto.*
    that is how: *taiguihi.*
    this is how: *taiguini.*

howl: *éssalao.*

hudges: *fatches.*

hue: *kulót.*

hug: *toktok.*
    hug (by having arms meet together):
    abrasu.

huge: *dánkolo, higante, krisidu,*
    tamong.

huh: *ha.*

hum: *kanta.*

human being: *taotao.*

humane: *umanidát.*
humanity: *umanidát.*
humble: *humitde, tákpapa', umitde.*
humid: *úmidu, maggem.*
humiliate: *na'mamahlao, umiya.*
humiliated
become humiliated: *mumamahlao.*
humility: *umidát.*
humor
bad humor: *malumoradu.*
humorous: *manggua', ná'chalek.*
humorous person: *santa'.*
hump: *buso'.*
humpback: *badu.*
hunchback: *badu.*
hundred: *sien.*
five hundred: *kinientos.*
one hundred: *siento.*
hunger: *ha'ilas.*
hungry: *ñalang, ambre.*
hunk: *pidasu.*
hunt: *peska.*
to hunt for crabs: *épanglao, gualaf.*
hunter: *pépeska, pípeska, peskadót.*
hunters: *peskadores.*
hunting: *pumeska.*
hunting (with light): *sulo'.*
hurl: *blankeha, blanko, daggao, yotte.*
hurrah
hurrah (shout): *biba.*
hurried: *apretát, bibu, chaddek, láguse'.*
hurriedness: *inalula.*
hurry: *énsahi, alula, alulayi, apreta,
apura, guse', láguse', na'chaddek,
pinalala, prikura, sahyao, sigidas.*
hurry there: *gúaguatu.*
hurry up: *ésinahyao, area, insigidas,
lácheddek, lahyao.*
hurt: *aña, baketasu, batakasu,
chetnudan, fakkai, fueges, garutasu,
lamen, latigasu, na'chetnudan,
na'famadesi, na'lamen, puti.*
hurt feelings: *layo'.*
husband: *asagua, esposu.*
husbandry: *gualo'.*
hush: *famatkilu, mamatkilu, pákaka',
silensio.*
husk: *gugan.*
coconut husk: *punot.*
husk (coconut): *kacha'.*
place to husk coconuts: *fangacha'an.*
husking: *kacha'.*
husky: *loddo'.*
hussy: *mahadera, tulisán.*

hustle: *na'chaddek.*
hut: *kabaña, palapala, sade'gani.*
hybrid
hybrid (m): *mestisu.*
hydrophobia: *rabia.*
hymn: *gosu, kantiku.*
hypocrisy: *hipokrisia.*
hypocrite: *hipokritu, kado'
mama'maolek.*
hypodermic
hypodermic needle: *dulok.*
I: *hu, i, yo'.*
I (emphatic): *guahu.*
ice: *ais.*
ice box: *ais baks, kahon ais.*
ice cream: *ais krim, binatten tiratira.*
ice pick: *alesna.*
ice plant: *fabrikan ais.*
icon: *lámina.*
icy: *fugu.*
idea: *idea.*
identical: *eksakto.*
identification: *aidentifikasión.*
identify: *aidentifika.*
idiot: *á'duko', atmariáo, duka', duko',
kaduka, kaduku, táisentidu, totko.*
idiotic: *á'duko', á'tamos, bruta.*
idle: *osiosu.*
idleness: *ginago'.*
idler: *flohu, gago'.*
idol: *ídolu.*
idolatry: *idolatria.*
idolize: *adora.*
if: *akasu, anggen, asta ki, enkasu,
komon, komu, sienkasu, yanggen.*
ignite: *songge, u'os, yugi.*
ignite (a fire): *totnge.*
ignorance: *iknoransia.*
ignorant: *iknorante, inosente.*
ignore: *disecha, iknora.*
iguana: *hilitai.*
ill: *malangu.*
ill-born: *chátmafañagu.*
ill-tempered: *mathenio.*
illegal: *ilegát.*
illegitimate: *ilehítimu.*
illiterate: *iknorante, modoru.*
illness: *minalangu.*
illuminate: *ina.*
illuminated: *manila'.*
image: *hechura, imahen.*
imagine: *hasso, imahina, na'hallom,
na'hasso.*

imbecile: *á'duko', á'tamos, duka', duko'.*
imbecilic: *bruta.*
imbibe: *gimen.*
imitate: *eyak.*
imitation: *dinalalak, imitasión.*
imitator: *á'ada', akda'.*
immature: *chátmasa, hoben.*
  immature (mind): *gada'.*
immeasurable: *taiche'.*
immediately: *imidiatamente, insigidas.*
immense: *taiche'.*
immerse: *ñokñok, supok.*
immigrant: *estrangheru, imigrante.*
immoral: *desonesto.*
immortal: *inmottát, táifinatai.*
immovable: *táikinalamten.*
impair: *yamak.*
impart: *na'i patte.*
impartial: *tái'interes.*
impassable
  become impassable: *machom.*
impatience: *tenhos.*
impatient: *tenhos.*
impede: *chomma'.*
impediment: *atkagueti, impedimento.*
imperfect: *ti kabales.*
imperishable: *táifinatai.*
impertinent: *impetinente.*
impetuous: *empitosu, guse', impetosu.*
implement: *kosas, trastes.*
implore: *táyuyot.*
import: *impotta.*
important: *impottante.*
imposition: *enggañu.*
impossible: *imposipble.*
impotent: *impotente.*
impounded: *mamantieni.*
impoverished: *popble.*
impregnate: *na'chetnudan.*
impress: *bense, figes, imprenta, impresa.*
imprint: *imprenta.*
improbable: *imposipble.*
improve: *adilanta, lumámaolek, na'lámaolek, na'latfe'na.*
improvement: *adilanto, fina'maolek, inadelanta, kinalamten, nina'maolek, progresu, sinibi.*
imprudence: *deskuidu.*
imprudent: *imprudensia.*
impudence: *ekpe.*
impudent: *táirespetu.*

impulsive: *impetosu.*
in: *giya, halom, sanhalom.*
  in case: *enkasu, infín, komon, komu, noseha ki, sienkasu.*
  in fact: *subes.*
  in spite of: *-guan.*
inanimate: *táiha'ani.*
inattention: *deskuidu.*
inattentive: *desganáo, mirón, táigue.*
inauguration: *inaogarasión.*
incapable: *chátsaga.*
incapacitated: *chátsaga.*
incessantly: *sin parát.*
inch: *potgada.*
inches: *potgadas.*
incident: *sinisedi.*
incinerated: *hanon.*
incise: *utot.*
incite: *abiba, kuka, na'layo'.*
inclination: *inklinao.*
inclose: *enggatsa.*
include: *konsiste, kuenta, na'saonao.*
included: *kontodu, saonao.*
including: *kontodu, tanto.*
incognito: *burego'.*
incoherent: *ti komprendiyon.*
income: *nina'halom.*
incomparable: *tái'achaigua, tái'atparehu, táiparehu.*
incomplete: *ti kabales.*
incomprehensible: *ti komprendiyon.*
inconvenience: *atborotu, enkebukáo, inkombinensia.*
inconvenient: *inkombiniente.*
incorrect: *gáidifekto.*
incorrigible: *táiremediu, ti chuma'on.*
increase: *añadi, aomenta, atisa, hatsamiento, lumámeggai, masubi, subida.*
  increase by large quantity: *muttiplika.*
increasing: *mamta'.*
incredible: *ná'manman.*
incriminate: *akusa.*
incurable: *sala', táiremediu.*
indecent: *deskaráo, deskaradu, desonesto.*
indeed: *magahet.*
indefatigable: *mahayu.*
indefinite: *indefinitu.*
indelible: *ti mamafnas.*
independent: *independiente, tái'inangokko.*

index: *lista.*
indicate: *indika.*
indication: *indikasión.*
indifferent: *fatani, para ke, para kehi.*
indigenous: *natibu.*
indigent: *popble, táisaga.*
indirect: *indirekto.*
indoctrinate: *doktrina.*
indolent: *bagu, flohu, gago'.*
indubitable: *asiguráo.*
induce: *su'ok.*
indulge: *logra.*
  indulge (heartily): *dafflokgue.*
indulgence: *indothensia, indulensia.*
industrious: *brabu, bumuchachu,*
  bunmuchachu, butmuchachu,
  karetatibu, trabadót, trabahadót.
industry: *industria.*
inebriated: *teles.*
inexpensive: *baratu.*
inexperienced: *hoben, tái'eksperensia.*
infant: *neni, patgon.*
infantry: *batayón.*
infants: *famagu'on.*
infect: *tatse.*
infected: *mañetnot.*
infer: *hokka.*
inferior: *mámatago'.*
infernal: *inaniti.*
inferno: *enfietno.*
infertile: *cha ttano', kansadu.*
infiniteness: *táiuttimo.*
infinitive marker: *-um-.*
infinity: *táifinakpo', táihinekkok,*
  táiuttimo.
infirmary: *emfetmeria, ospitát.*
inflame: *dagga', mañila'.*
inflammable: *songgiyon.*
inflammation: *tinaohan.*
  inflammation (of gum): *fokson.*
inflate: *na'espongha.*
influence: *sohyo'.*
influenza: *sagu.*
infold: *afuyot, balutan, falulon, fuyot.*
inform: *infotma.*
information: *infotmasión, notisia.*
informed
  be informed: *hungok.*
infrequent: *apenas, hassan.*
infuriate: *na'bubu.*
ingrate: *enggratu.*
inhabit: *sagayi.*

inhale
  inhale vapor: *sahuma.*
inharmonious: *disentunáo, disentunadu.*
inherit: *doti.*
inheritance: *doti, erensia, irensia,*
  rénsia.
initiated: *ansianu.*
injure: *aña, fakkai, fueges, garutasu,*
  lamen, na'chetnudan, na'famadesi,
  na'lamen.
injured: *baketasu, chetnudan, dañáo.*
injurious: *dañosu, mílachi, ná'lamen,*
  ná'tailayi.
injury: *che'tan, chetnudan, dañu.*
injustice: *inechong, inhuestisia.*
ink: *tinta.*
  ink maker: *tinteru.*
  ink well: *tinteru.*
inlet: *ensenada, sagua'.*
inner: *gé'halom.*
innocent: *inosente, tái'isao.*
inoperable: *mayulang.*
inquisitive
  inquisitive (m): *kuriosu.*
insane: *kaduku, kuka'.*
inscription: *títula.*
insect: *ga'ga'.*
  insect spray: *puno' lalo'.*
  small insect: *ga'ga' dikike', kunitos.*
  type of insect: *ababang kahet,*
    alakrán, chíchiget.
  type of insect-acridiidae family:
    apacha' matai.
  type of insect-coleoptera buprestidae:
    San Ignasio.
  type of insect-coleoptera lampyridae:
    donggat.
  type of insect-coleoptera tytiscidae:
    hagan hanom.
  type of insect-hemiptera pentatomidae:
    ga'ga' mutong.
  type of insect-licustidae: *apacha'*
    suette.
  type of insect-odonata: *dulalas.*
  type of insect-orthoptera gryllidae:
    guriyos.
  type of insect-orthoptera mantidae:
    masu.
  type of insect-orthoptera phasmidae:
    apahigai.
  type of insect-orthoptera tettigoniidae:
    apacha' a'me'.
inseparable: *inseparable.*
insert: *introdusi, luño', na'halom.*
inside: *háttalom, halom, sanhalom.*
  get inside: *hatme.*

go inside further: *gé'halom.*
inside out: *átlibes.*
to turn inside out: *baleng, la'mok.*
way inside: *yahálolom.*
went inside: *humalom.*
insignia: *galon.*
insignificant: *despresiapble.*
insinuate: *na'tungo'ñaihon.*
insipid: *desabridu.*
insist: *insiste, petdika.*
insolent: *saguat.*
insomnia: *desbeladu.*
inspect: *inspekta, sensura.*
inspection: *rikonosimento.*
inspector: *inspekta.*
inspire: *ánima, abiba, na'matatnga.*
instant: *momento.*
instantly: *gotpe.*
instead
  instead of: *alugat di, embes di,
  enlugat di, potno.*
instigate: *atborota.*
institute: *instituyi.*
instruct: *chalani, fa'na'gue.*
instructed: *machachalani.*
instruction: *chinachalani.*
instructor
  instructor (m): *ma'estro.*
instrument: *instrumento, ramienta.*
insult: *ale', botlehu, inale', insutta,
  insutto, mofeha, na'layo'.*
insulter: *botlonu.*
insurance: *siguridát.*
insure: *asigura, na'lámaolek.*
insured: *asiguráo.*
insurrection: *inatborota.*
intact: *kabales.*
integrate: *na'daña'.*
integrity: *minaolek.*
intellect: *hinasso.*
intelligent: *intelihente, kabilosu,
  ménhalom, míhinallom, malate',
  tomtom.*
intend: *hasngon, intensiona.*
intense: *apuráo.*
intensify: *insima.*
intensive: *tákkalom.*
intention: *intensión, minito'.*
  one's intention: *entonses na.*
intentionally: *bulontariamente,
  hasngon.*
intercede: *adinganiyi.*
intercept: *inturompe.*

interchange: *átulaika.*
intercourse: *ábale', inábale'.*
  have intercourse: *umá'uyu.*
  have intercourse (slang): *baggai,
  baketa.*
  sexual intercourse: *kichi.*
interest: *ínteres, ínteres.*
  arouse interest: *inadayao.*
interested: *ínteres.*
interesting: *interesante.*
interfere: *atropeya, entalu'i, umentalo'.*
  interfere with: *inturompe, taggam.*
interior: *interiót, intetno, sanhalom.*
intermission: *inentalu'i.*
intern: *interinu.*
internal: *intetno, sanhalom.*
interpret: *sanganiyi.*
  interpret for: *esplikayi.*
interpretation: *mapula'.*
interpreter: *intétpiti.*
interrogate: *abirigua, faisen.*
  interrogate closely: *eksamina.*
interrogator: *abiriguadót.*
interrupt: *bumasta, chaba, chabba,
  chanda, inturompe.*
intersection: *dinga' chalan.*
intertwined: *ádaose.*
intestines: *tilipas.*
into: *halom, sanhalom.*
intoxicated: *bulachu, teles.*
  intoxicated (slightly): *bileng.*
intoxication: *binilachu.*
intrepid: *animosu.*
intricate: *gaddon.*
introduce: *introdusi, presenta.*
introduction: *introdusión.*
intruder: *bilikeru.*
inundation: *milak.'*
invade: *hatme.*
invaluable: *táipresiu.*
invasion: *hinatme.*
invent: *atma, fa'tinas, imbenta,
  na'huyong.*
invention: *imbension.*
inventive: *imbentibu.*
inventor: *imbentót, imbentadót.*
invert: *bira.*
inverted: *mabira.*
invest: *po'lo.*
investigate: *eksamina, imbestiga,
  rikonosi.*
  to investigate (slang): *guaddok.*
investigation: *imbestigasión.*
  under investigation: *enkaosa.*

investigator: *imbestigadót.*
invisible: *ti annok.*
invitation: *imbitasión.*
invite: *agangi, imbita, kombida, sohyo', solisita.*
inviting: *kombidáo.*
invoice: *risibu.*
involve: *afekta, saonao.*
involved
  be involved: *saonao.*
  involved (in a tangle): *gaddon.*
inward: *háttalom.*
iodine: *amot agaga'.*
irk: *atborota, estotba.*
iron: *lulok, prensa.*
  iron (clothes): *prensa.*
  steam iron: *ná'mahlos.*
ironwood tree: *gagu.*
irresponsible: *deskuidáo.*
irreverent: *desatento.*
irritable: *hámaniente.*
irritant: *pápago'.*
irritate: *estotba.*
island: *isla.*
  small island: *isleta.*
isolate: *apatta, dipatta, disetto, fa'sahnge.*
isolated: *apattáo, chinago', mámaisa.*
it: *guiya.*
Italian
  Italian (m): *Italianu.*
Italy: *Italia.*
itch: *makaka.*
itchy
  feel itchy: *makaka.*
item: *áttikulu.*
its: *-ña.*
ivory: *matfet.*
j: *hota.*
jack
  jack (cards): *sota.*
  jack crevally: *hagi.*
  jack-in-the-box tree: *nonnak.*
jackass: *buliku.*
jacket: *kot, saku.*
  life jacket: *satbabida.*
jackfruit: *lanka, nanka.*
jail: *kalabosu, katset, tribunát.*
  to jail: *pongle.*
jam
  jam tightly: *hemmot.*
January: *Eneru, Tumaiguini.*
Japanese: *Chapanes, Hapones.*

jar: *hara, taru.*
jasmine: *hasmín.*
jaw: *achamcham, kihadas, kriadas.*
  pop jaw: *kifan.*
jawbone: *kriadas.*
  jawbone (lower): *achamcham.*
jealous: *hosgon, hosguan, tenhos.*
  be jealous (sexual): *ekgu'i, ugo'.*
  jealous (sexual): *ekgo'.*
jealousy: *inigo'.*
jeep: *sahyan, yip.*
Jello: *yello.*
jerk: *chaflek.*
  jerk loose: *gomgom, kamkam.*
jerking: *so'on.*
jest: *chansa, frihonada.*
jester: *frihón.*
  jester (f): *frihona.*
jesting: *frihonada.*
Jesuit: *Hesuitas, Suitas.*
Jesus
  baby Jesus: *Ñiñu, Niñu.*
Jew: *Hudios.*
jewel: *alahas.*
jewelry: *alahas, halahas.*
jew's-harp: *belembao.*
jilting
  cause jilting: *pokto, potto.*
jingle: *tingteng.*
job: *cho'cho', emplehu, empleo, hotnát, ofisiu, pusisión.*
Job's tears: *bilén.*
  job's tears: *bilén.*
jog: *toyo'.*
join: *atani, fanetnon, saonao.*
joined: *daña'.*
joint: *kuyontura.*
joist: *suleras.*
joke: *éssitan, óssitan, chansa, essitani, frihonada.*
joker: *chanseru, frihón, frihona, frihonera, ga'uméssitan.*
joking: *frihonada.*
jolt: *otto, toyo'.*
jolting: *matulongtong.*
Jose
  nickname for Jose: *Ping, Pinke'.*
jostle: *otto, sokkok, toyo'.*
journal: *gaseta.*
journey: *biahi, hinanao, karera, rumbo.*
jowl: *pápada.*
joy: *minagof.*
Judas: *Hudas.*

judge: *hues.*
  to judge: *husga.*
judgment: *huisio, sentensia.*
  good judgment: *kotdura.*
  Judgment Day: *dia dethuisio.*
judo: *yudo'.*
jug: *hara, taru.*
juggle: *tamyao, tangyao.*
juggling: *tamyao, tangyao.*
juice: *chugo'.*
  squeeze juice on: *fotge.*
juicy: *mesgo'.*
July: *Julio, Semo.*
jump: *ta'yok.*
  jump over: *goppe.*
jumper: *gekpan, geppan.*
junction: *dinga', dinga' chalan.*
June: *Junio, Mananaf.*
jungle: *bundak, halom tano'.*
junk: *embarasos, trompesón.*
jurisdiction: *aturidát.*
jurisprudence: *lai.*
just: *husto.*
  just because: *gúailayi.*
justice: *hustisia.*
jute
  wild jute: *tuban chá'ka.*
k: *ka.*
kapok: *atgodon di Manila.*
karate: *karate'.*
katydid: *apacha' a'me'.*
keel: *kiya.*
keen: *kalaktos.*
  keen edge: *akadidok.*
keep: *chengle.*
  keep on: *konsigi.*
  keep out: *afuera.*
keg: *barilitu, tina.*
kernel: *fenso'.*
kerosene: *petroliu, pritoliu.*
kettle: *katdiritu, takurí.*
  large kettle: *katderón.*
key: *yabi.*
  piano key: *tekla.*
keyhole: *maddok yabi.*
khaki: *kaki.*
kick: *patek, sabate'.*
  kick out: *rimata.*
  kick-the-can (game): *kankarakere'.*
kicker: *paktek.*
kid: *patgon.*
kidding
  act of kidding: *le'le'.*
  no kidding: *basta hiya'.*

kidney: *riñón.*
kids: *famagu'on.*
kill: *buena, puno', talonan.*
  kill (by poison): *tatse.*
killer: *betduhu, pípino'.*
kilogram: *kilu.*
kilometer: *kilumetro.*
kind: *amapble, klasi, mames.*
kindness: *fabót, grasia, inágofli'e'.*
king: *rai.*
kingdom: *raino.*
kingfisher: *sihek.*
kings: *reyes.*
kink: *kinke.*
kinky: *kinke.*
kinsman: *parientes.*
kinswoman: *parientes.*
kiosk: *kiosko.*
kiss: *chiku.*
kitchen: *kusina, sagan mama'tinas.*
kite: *papaloti.*
  box kite: *maru.*
  type of kite: *golondrina, sapisapi,*
    saranggola.
kitten: *katu, patgon katu.*
knead: *yaka'.*
  knead dough: *amasa.*
knee: *tommo.*
  knee cap: *bayogu.*
kneel: *dimu.*
knife: *se'se'.*
  knife (table): *se'se' kubetto.*
  long knife: *padarao'.*
  small knife: *nabaha.*
knock: *addak, dakdak, dakot.*
  knock down: *fa'om, planasos,*
    sapblasos, tomba, yagai.
  knock in: *na'dochon.*
  knock-kneed: *sambo.*
knocker: *á'addak.*
knoll: *okso'.*
knot: *ñudu, godde, gramaderu,*
  tramoha.
  a knot: *nudu.*
  knot (nautical): *miyas.*
  type of knot: *to'chong.*
know: *kétungo', komprende, la'mon,*
  tungo'.
  about to know: *kétungo'.*
  know well: *ápayuni.*
knowledge: *tiningo'.*
knowledgeable: *manungo'.*
known: *konosidu, kunisidu.*
knuckle: *bayogu.*

Korean: *Choseng.*
l: *eli.*
lab: *labatorio.*
labor: *hotnát, macho'cho', patto.*
laboratory: *labatorio.*
laborer: *hotnaleru.*
laborious: *sa'pet.*
lace: *botdáo, enkahi.*
  lace shoes: *hotne.*
  lace trim: *inkahi.*
lack: *eskases.*
lacking: *fatta.*
lackluster: *kachang.*
ladder: *gua'ot.*
ladle: *kicharón, kucharón.*
lady: *señora, señorita.*
  first lady: *asaguan maga'lahi,*
  maga'haga.
lagoon: *hagoe, laguna.*
lake: *hagoe.*
lamb: *kinilu, kotderu.*
lame: *kohu, makabebi.*
lament: *pinitiyi, umugong.*
lamentable: *ná'fañotsot.*
lamentation: *lamentasión.*
lamp: *fallot, kandet, kinké.*
lampshade: *pantaya.*
lance
  lance (used on land): *lansa.*
lancet: *lanseta.*
land: *frinkas, tano'.*
  flat land: *yanu.*
  public land: *estáo.*
landmark: *mohón.*
lane: *pasadura.*
langouste: *mahongang.*
language: *lengguahi, palabra.*
lank: *masoksok.*
lap: *hoflak.*
  hold on lap: *sadde.*
lard: *mantika, sebu.*
large: *dánkolo, krisidu, tamong.*
larger: *lámudong.*
lariat: *lasu.*
larynx: *gekmon.*
lascivious: *garañón.*
lash: *latigasu.*
  lash down: *gramaderu, tramoha.*
lasso: *goddas.*
  lasso for: *fa'lasuyi.*
last: *kulu, sungon, taka', uttimo.*
  always last: *kilu.*
  at last: *pot fin.*

lasting: *durapble, fitme, ma'ok,*
  mesngon.
late: *atrasáo, sala'.*
later: *despues, despues di, tumátatte.*
lather: *bu'o'.*
Latin: *Latinu.*
lattice: *rehas.*
laud: *fama, tuna.*
laudable: *famáo, tunayon.*
lauded
  be lauded: *matuna.*
laugh: *chalek.*
  cause to laugh: *na'chalek.*
  laugh at: *chatge, mofeha.*
laughable: *ná'chalek.*
laughter: *chalek.*
launch: *bapót situ.*
laundress: *labandera.*
laundry: *labadu.*
  laundry (hand): *bateha.*
laundryman: *labanderu.*
lava
  lava rock: *hommon.*
lavatory: *fama'gasiyan, labadót,*
  nagase'.
lavish: *despetdisiáo.*
law: *lai.*
lawful: *ligát, lihítimu.*
lawn: *cha'guan.*
lawsuit: *kaosa.*
lawyer: *abugáo, abugadu.*
lax: *kallo.*
laxative: *ná'masinek.*
lay
  lay (egg): *mañada'.*
  lay down a protecting cover upon
    which something is placed : *hafye.*
  lay hold of: *falaggue.*
laziness: *ginago'.*
lazy: *bagu, flohu, gago', osiosu.*
  lazy person: *balibagu.*
lead: *chalani, dirihi, kapitani,*
  kondukta, kurihi, manea, plomu.
  lead (by the hand): *pipet.*
leaden: *plomisu.*
leader: *fagu, fo'i, kabesiyu.*
  leader (wire for fishing line): *fagot.*
leaf: *hagon, ohas.*
  tear off leaf: *toto.*
league: *aliansa, inetnon, legua.*
leak: *sume', tu'o', tuho'.*
leakage: *sume'.*
lean: *masoksok.*
  lean against: *apo', aso'.*

leaning: *aso'.*
leap
   leap over: *goppe.*
leaps
   move by leaps: *pares.*
learn: *komprende.*
learned: *fayi, mítitanos.*
learner: *estudiante.*
learning: *tiningo'.*
lease: *ariendo, empeña.*
   break lease: *desempeña.*
   lease (house):   *atkila.*
   lease (land):   *arienda.*
leasehold: *inkilinatu.*
least
   at least: *achok, sikera.*
leather: *kueru.*
leave: *hanao.*
   leave at the same time: *gigu.*
   leave behind: *dingu.*
   leave wife: *yinite'.*
leaven: *libadura.*
lecture: *lektura.*
leek: *nira'.*
left: *abandonáo, tetenhan.*
   left (direction):   *akague.*
   left over: *sopbla, tétenan.*
   left-handed: *akague fafayiña.*
leftover: *tehnan, tetenhan.*
   leftover food: *ngatnan.*
   leftover of (something):   *án-.*
leg: *patas.*
   crooked leg: *kohu.*
   leg (human):   *addeng.*
legal: *ligát.*
legalize: *ligalisa.*
legalized: *lihítimu.*
legging: *polainas.*
legislature: *konsilio, leyeslatura.*
legitimate: *lihítimu.*
legs
   cross legs: *na'ágaole.*
   legs of crab: *kálulot.*
leisure: *bakante, dibettáo, dibette, libettáo, osiosu.*
   to give leisure: *libette.*
lemon: *lemon reat.*
lemonade: *lemonada.*
lend: *na'ayao.*
length: *inanakko'.*
lengthen: *ekstende, na'anakko', na'apmam, na'lá'anakko'.*
lenient: *góflamen, máñaña', pasensia.*
lens: *lente.*

Lent: *ayunat, kuaresma.*
lentils: *monggos.*
leper: *atektok, lasarinu, lepra, nasarinu.*
leprosy: *atektok, leprosu, nasarinu.*
less: *menos.*
lessened: *menggua.*
lesson: *estudio, leksión.*
lessor: *arendatariu.*
let: *po'lo ya, sedi.*
   let (someone do something):   *na'-.*
let's
   let's (do something):   *nihi.*
letter: *katta.*
   letter (of alphabet):   *letra.*
   write letter (to someone):   *kattayi.*
level: *nebét.*
   level (carpenter's):   *mubét, nubét.*
lever: *baro'.*
liar: *dakon, embusteru.*
liberate: *deskasa, deskata, dibiette, libetta, libette, na'libre, saka.*
liberation: *liberasión.*
liberty: *konsentimento, libettát.*
lice: *gurupos.*
   full of lice: *lottot.*
   lice (insect):   *hutu.*
license: *lisensia, lisensia.*
lichen: *lumot, yetbas bihu.*
lick: *hoflak, hopba.*
lid: *tampe.*
lie: *dagi, dinagi, fábulas, mandagi, padakdak.*
   lie down: *asson, fano'pok, o'pok.*
   lie down on back: *to'to.*
   lie down on stomach: *oppop.*
   lie down with: *assohne.*
   lie on: *lálacha'.*
   to lie down (on the floor or ground):   *gálilek.*
lieu
   in lieu of: *átulaika.*
life: *bida, lina'la'.*
lifeless: *táiha'ani.*
lifesaver: *satbabida.*
lift: *hatsa, kéhatsa, kahat.*
   able to lift up: *langak.*
   lift head: *lulo'.*
   lift up: *sadda'.*
light: *inina, manana.*
   flash light at: *denke'.*
   light (in weight):   *ñálalang.*
   light bulb: *tubon ilektrik.*
   light up: *na'fañila'.*
lighted: *manila', songge.*

lightning: *lamlam.*
  bolt of lightning: *talangan hulu,*
    troson lamlam.
  lightning bug: *donggat.*
like: *ga'-, gofli'e', kalang, ya-.*
  like better: *ga'ña-, ga'o-.*
  like this: *asi komu.*
  to like dearly: *guaiya.*
likeableness: *minames.*
liked: *magófatan.*
likeness: *achaigua.*
lily: *lirio.*
limb: *patas.*
limbo: *limbo.*
lime: *afok, lemon.*
  lime kiln: *hotnon afok.*
  put lime: *afuki.*
limestone
  limestone (soft): *afok.*
limit: *chi-.*
limitation: *minidiyi.*
limitless: *taiche'.*
limp: *ká'dideng.*
  limp (when walking): *ke'yao.*
limping: *chanko.*
line: *inátattiyi, kotdón, liña, lucha,*
    raya.
  fishing line: *kotdét, tupak.*
linen: *lienso, linu.*
liniment: *amot palai.*
lining: *sábanas.*
linneus: *ayuyu.*
lion: *lión.*
lion fish: *nufo' pabu.*
lip: *labios.*
  lower lip: *ámamang, amang.*
lips: *labios.*
  puckered lips: *muyo'.*
lipstick: *bene', pentan labios.*
  apply lipstick: *bene'.*
liquefy: *lago'.*
liquid: *ná'fache'.*
  full of liquid: *misen.*
liquor: *agi, aguayente, arak, inestila,*
    likót, maneska.
list: *lista.*
listen
  listen to: *ékungok.*
listless: *indiferente.*
litany: *litania, litanias.*
literate: *manungo'.*
litter: *anggariya, lechon.*
little: *díkike'.*
  little bit: *-ñaihon.*
  little while: *ratu.*

live: *lála'la'.*
liver: *hígadu, sassa.*
  chopped liver: *sassa.*
living: *lála'la'.*
  living room: *sala.*
lizard
  lizard (large monitor lizard): *hilitai.*
  small lizard: *guali'ek.*
  small lizard (lives in houses): *achiak.*
load
  load on: *na'makatga.*
loader: *katgadót.*
loading: *katgamento.*
loafer: *bagamondo, flohu, gago',*
    sángganu.
loam: *fache'.*
loathe: *chatli'e'.*
loathesome: *ná'massa'.*
lobe: *alitos.*
lobster: *mahongang.*
  slipper lobster: *pápangpang.*
  type of lobster-(family scylarridae):
    pápangpang.
locate: *espiha.*
location: *lugát, pusisión.*
lock: *andaba, aseradura, kandalu,*
    seladura, seradura.
  lock in or out: *kandalu.*
  wrist lock: *kotma.*
loco: *á'langa'.*
lodging: *apusento.*
lofty: *lokka'.*
log: *trosu.*
logging: *trumosu.*
loin: *lomu, palitiya.*
  loin cloth: *sade'.*
loins: *ñanggo, áttayo'.*
loiter: *lailai.*
loneliness: *minahalang.*
lonely: *mahalang, táiga'chong.*
long: *anakko', laguas.*
  long for: *malago', tanga.*
longing: *ansias, disehu, tinanga.*
look: *li'e'.*
  look at: *atan.*
  look for: *bando, espia, espiha, ilao.*
  look for hole: *éngulo'.*
  look out: *adahi.*
  look secretly: *atan seguet.*
  look up: *ngaha'.*
looking-glass: *espehos, espeos.*
looks: *kakko', trahi.*
loony: *bruta.*
loose: *ñaohan, giga', kallo, mappla'.*
  loose-jointed (when walking): *ke'yao.*

loosen: *afloha, gomgom, kamkam, lusu, na'kallo, sottayi.*
  loosen more: *na'lákallo.*
lop: *gabbe.*
loquacious: *mefno'.*
Lord: *saina, Asaina.*
lose
  lose color: *pasmo.*
  lose sleep: *desbela.*
loss: *dañu, finalingu, pétdidu, pethuisiu.*
lost: *abak, há'abak, malingu, petdidu.*
  get lost (command): *falingu.*
lot
  lot (of land): *sitio.*
  lot of: *buyada.*
lots
  lots of: *bula, meggai, unmanada.*
  to have lots of: *miña.*
lottery: *rifa.*
loud: *a'gang.*
loudness: *ina'gang.*
louse: *hutu.*
  small louse: *eyaf.*
lousy: *míhitu, mehto.*
louver: *pensiana, petsiana, ponsiana.*
lovable: *amante, guaiyayon.*
love: *guaiya, guinaiya.*
  love (platonic): *gofli'e'.*
  love affair: *águaiya.*
lovely: *amante.*
lover: *nobia.*
  lover (m): *anobiu, kiridu.*
lovers: *amantes.*
loving
  loving (m): *kariñosu.*
low: *ébaba', épapa', étigu, baha'.*
  low pitch: *rata.*
lower: *gé'papa', na'tunok.*
  lower (with pulley): *licheng.*
lowly: *humitde.*
loyal: *fiét.*
loyalty: *amista.*
lubricate
  lubricate anus: *lilengga.*
lubricated: *lasge'.*
luck: *suette.*
luckily: *grasias adios.*
lucky: *afottunáo, felís, fottuna, suette.*
luggage: *maleta.*
lull: *na'kemaigo'.*
lumber: *maderas, tapbla.*
  warped lumber: *binadu.*
lumberjack: *hacheru.*

luminous: *ma'lak.*
lump: *buso', cho'le.*
  lump (on the head): *diso', kuku.*
lunacy: *loka, loku.*
lunatic: *atmariáo, kaduka, kaduku, lunátiku.*
lunch: *amotsa, na' talo'ani.*
  box lunch: *tengguang.*
  eat lunch: *na'talo'ani.*
lung: *gofes.*
lure: *katnada, pugi, su'ok.*
  set out lure for: *katnadayi.*
  to lure: *ponne, pugi.*
lurk: *ñehom.*
lust: *ekgu'i.*
luster: *lamlam, mina'gas, mina'lak.*
lusterless: *changa.*
lustful: *fotte, garañón.*
lusty: *fotte, la'la'.*
luxury: *ginéfsaga.*
lying
  lying across: *atrabisáo.*
lymph
  lymph glands (swollen): *chinatguat.*
m: *emi.*
macaroni: *makaroni.*
machete: *machette..*
  long machete: *bolu, machetten anakko', padarao'.*
machine: *mákina.*
  machine gun: *kikanyio'.*
machinery: *atma, makineria.*
machinist: *makinista.*
mackerel
  type of mackerel: *hachuman.*
mad: *bubu, lalalo'.*
madam: *señora, tan.*
magazine: *lepblo.*
maggot: *ulo'.*
magic: *atte.*
  magic power: *pakto.*
magical: *enkantáo.*
magician: *á'atte.*
magistrate: *tátago'.*
magnet: *aseru, maknitu.*
magnetic: *maknitu.*
magnificent: *dikno.*
magnify: *aomenta.*
magnitude: *botto.*
maiden: *bithen, donseya.*
mail: *katta.*
maim: *ma'tot.*
main: *mayót, prinsipát.*

mainly: *mayotmente.*
mainspring: *kuetdas.*
majestic: *dikno.*
major: *mayót.*
  major domo: *mayotdomu.*
majority: *mayoria.*
make: *fa'tinas, fama'-, fattinas, fotma, muna'-, otganisa.*
  make (someone do something): *na'-.*
  make believe: *fa'-.*
make-up
  put make-up on: *kachet, katsa.*
maker: *fáfa'tinas.*
male: *lahi.*
males: *lalahi.*
malevolence: *malisia.*
malice: *hinasnguni, malisia.*
malicious: *malisiosu.*
mallard: *nganga' palao.*
malodorous: *mutong.*
maltreat: *mattrata.*
maltreatment: *abusu, hineño', mattratu, minattrata.*
man: *lahi, lai, taotao.*
  man (single): *señoritu.*
  man of: *lahen.*
  old man: *bihu.*
manage: *desponi, manea, maneha.*
manageable: *faset.*
management: *inenkatga.*
manager: *mániya, ma'gas.*
mandolin: *bandulina, mandolina.*
mane: *pulon tengho.*
maneuver: *mobimiento.*
manger: *bilén.*
mango
  mango (fruit): *mangga.*
mangrove
  mangrove fern: *apehu, lakngayao.*
  mangrove hopper: *hatot, macheng.*
  mangrove tree: *mangle, mangle hembra.*
manhandle: *estropeha.*
maniac: *atmariáo.*
manifest: *fa'nu'i, manifesta, manifesto.*
manifestation: *manifestasión.*
manifesto: *manifesto.*
manioc: *mendioka.*
manly: *mama'lahi.*
manner: *manera, modu.*
mannerly: *respetayon.*
manta ray: *afula', fanihen tasi.*
mantel: *tapblita.*

mantilla: *mantiya.*
mantis: *apacha', apahigai.*
mantle: *mecha.*
manufacture: *fábrika, fakteria.*
manure: *abonu, take', take' ga'ga'.*
many: *bohbo, buyada, kantidá, lahyan, matmo, meggai, unmanada.*
  many times: *meggai na biahi.*
map: *mapa.*
mar: *na'áplacha'.*
marathon: *marasón.*
marble: *matmot, pongga.*
marbles
  game of marbles: *falu.*
  marbles (play): *biyát.*
  marbles (playing): *tama'.*
march: *isisio, matcha.*
March (month): *Matso, Umátalaf.*
marine: *marinu.*
mariner: *ga'ga' tasi.*
mark: *eskama, estampo', matka, siñát, siñala.*
  mark (coin): *matko.*
marker
  boundary marker: *mohón.*
market: *metkáo, tenda.*
marksman: *potso.*
Marpe: *Makpe'.*
marriage: *ákkamo', kasamiento, matrimoniu.*
  marriage agreement: *ginitos finiho'.*
married: *ákkamo', kasamiento.*
  get married: *umákkamo'.*
  married person: *kasáo.*
marrow: *balaso'.*
marry: *ásagua, umákkamo', umásagua.*
marsh: *sesonyan.*
  marsh snipe: *dulili.*
martyr: *mattet.*
martyrdom: *mattet.*
mash: *tiges.*
mask: *bufón, máskara, masko'.*
  face mask: *antihos, antios.*
mason: *átbanet, masón.*
mass: *botto, misa, misan mo'na, misan tátalo'puengi, misan talo', misan tatte.*
  low mass: *misan risada.*
  mass bell: *marimata.*
  midnight mass: *misan gayu.*
massage: *lasa, ye'te', yettek.*
  massage (with the feet): *ugot.*
massaged: *malasa.*
mast: *layak, pahlo, palu.*

master: *amu, ma'gas, saina.*
masterly: *meyeng.*
mastic: *galagala.*
masticate: *ngangas.*
masturbate: *leklok.*
mat: *guafak.*
match: *aya, echan, fósforu, maches,*
   tetno.
  match head: *asga'.*
  match-maker: *ná'daña'.*
matching
  matching area: *maná'echan.*
matchless: *tái'achaigua, tái'atparehu,*
  táichilong.
mate: *asagua, ga'chong.*
material: *matiriát, trastes.*
materialize
  cause to materialize: *materialisa.*
mathematics: *kuentas.*
matrimony: *matrimoniu.*
matrix: *matrís.*
matter: *kasu.*
  matter (from eyes): *mugo'.*
mattock: *achita, asada.*
mattress: *kotchon.*
mature: *gái'idat, guaha idát.*
  mature (fruit): *to'a.*
Maug: *Maug.*
maxim: *atpahon.*
may: *siña.*
May: *Makmamao, Mayu.*
maybe: *buente, fa'na'an, kasi, puedi,*
  será, siña buente, siña ha'.
mayor: *atkadi, mayót.*
me
  me (emphatic): *guahu.*
  me (transitive object pronoun): *yo'.*
meadow: *sabaneta.*
meager: *masoksok.*
meal: *kumida, na' oga'an, sentada.*
  light meal: *mirenda.*
  morning meal: *amotsa.*
mean: *hasngon.*
meaning: *sustansia.*
meantime: *entretanto.*
meanwhile: *entretanto, mientras.*
measure: *braseha, hemi, kuatta, taba'.*
  measure (something): *midi.*
measurement: *midida.*
  unit of measurement: *arias, ganta.*
measuring stick: *sase'.*
measuring tool: *midida.*
meat: *katne, sensen.*
  meat pie: *empañada, empanada.*
  meat scraps: *sankarón.*

mechanic: *makinista.*
medal: *eskapulario, milaya.*
medallion: *eskapulario, milaya.*
meddle: *éntalo', entalu'i.*
meddler: *bilikeru, embilikeru.*
mediator: *negosiante.*
medicine: *amot, amot chetnot maipe,*
  amot dagga', amot makpong, amot
  mapga', amot sinagu, amot tininu.
medium: *medianu.*
meek: *humitde, umitde.*
meekness: *siniabi.*
meet
  meet with: *ásodda'.*
meeting: *hunta, miteng.*
melancholy: *triniste.*
melody: *melodia, sotfa.*
melon: *melon.*
  type of melon: *pipinu.*
melt: *diliti, diriti, fa'hanom, lago',*
  na'lago'.
member: *miembro.*
memorize: *dimimoria.*
men: *lalahi.*
menace: *aminasa, aminasu, espanta,*
  espanto, fa'ñague, huppa.
menacing: *aminasáo.*
mend: *empatma, hetbana, na'maolek,*
  patche, sosse, sotse.
  mend (clothes): *limenda.*
mender: *lálakse.*
mendicant: *gakgao.*
menstruate: *rekla, rumekla.*
menstruating: *mahaga'.*
menstruation: *rekla.*
mention: *hentra, mensiona, mentra,*
  mientra, yama.
mentionable: *sakngan.*
merchandise: *benta, efektos, fektos.*
merchant: *kometsiante.*
merciful: *klemente, ma'ase'.*
  be merciful: *gái'ase', gáima'ase',*
  na'ma'ase'.
  merciful person: *yo'ase'.*
merciless: *malagradesidu, malamaña,*
  sakat.
mercury: *asugi.*
mercy: *klemensia, ma'ase', mina'ase'.*
  for mercy sake: *misirikotdia.*
  have mercy: *gái'ase', gáima'ase'.*
merit: *kréditu, méritu, meti.*
mermaid: *Sirena.*
merriment: *alegria.*

merry: *felís.*
merthiolate: *amot agaga'.*
mess: *trabuka.*
message: *anunsiu, infotmasión, notisia.*
messed up: *machalonchon.*
messenger: *tentago'.*
messy: *kala'u.*
mestizo: *mestisa.*
metal: *lulok, metát.*
  metal sheet: *piesan metát, teppang.*
  sheet metal: *plancha.*
meter: *metro.*
metropolis: *siudá.*
mettle: *animu.*
Mexican
  Mexican (f): *Meksikana.*
  Mexican (m): *Meksikanu.*
Mexico: *Méksiku.*
Micronesian
  Micronesian (bird): *sasngat.*
middle: *éntalo'.*
midget: *che'che', po'yet.*
midnight: *tátalo' puenge.*
midrib: *ba'yak, nuhot.*
midwife: *pattera.*
might: *alentos, alimento, fuetsa,*
  guse'ña, minetgot, nina'siña, noseha
  ki, siña.
mighty: *ná'siña.*
mildew: *pekas.*
mile: *miyas.*
military: *militát.*
militia: *milisia, milisianu.*
milk: *leche.*
  full of milk: *lechera.*
  milk cow: *fokse.*
milkfish: *agua.*
milking cow: *lechera.*
milksop: *pachang.*
mill
  sugar mill: *trapichi.*
millepora: *acho' dagon haya.*
millet: *sibada.*
million: *miyón.*
  one million: *un miyón.*
millionaire
  millionaire (m): *miyonario.*
millstone: *acho' mulinu, manu, metati,*
  mitati, moyong.
mimic: *eyak.*
mimick: *adda'.*
mimicker: *á'ada', akda'.*
mimickry: *adda'.*

mince: *pika, taktak.*
mind: *hinasso, konsensia, osge.*
mine: *mina.*
mine (possessive): *-hu.*
mingle
  cause to mingle: *na'daña'.*
mingled: *daña'.*
miniature: *menót.*
minion: *mafa'boreresi.*
minister: *ministro, pale'.*
ministers: *mamale'.*
minor: *menót, menót di idát.*
minority: *menót.*
minus: *fuera, na'sahnge, na'suha.*
minute: *minutu.*
  for a minute: *naya.*
  minute hand: *minuteru.*
miracle: *milagro.*
miraculous: *milagrosu.*
mire: *fache'.*
mirror: *espehos, espeos.*
mirth: *konsuelu, minagof.*
miscarriage: *chátfañagu.*
mischance: *dimalas.*
mischievous: *águaguat, dañosu,*
  pikatdiha, tarugu.
miser: *meskinu, Chinu.*
miserable: *miserable, ná'ma'ase'.*
miserly: *gake'.*
misery: *misería, pinadesi.*
misfortune: *desgrasia, dimalas,*
  dinimalas, disdicha, inale'.
mishap: *aksidente.*
mislead: *na'lachi.*
miss: *ákkaga, señorita.*
  miss (each other): *álaisen.*
missal: *misát.*
missed: *fatta.*
missing: *malingu.*
missionary: *misioneru.*
mist: *afao, asgon, tasyan.*
mistake: *lachi, linachi.*
mister: *señót, señoritu, ton, tun.*
mistreat: *mattrata.*
mistress: *ama.*
  having a mistress: *achakma'.*
mistrust: *deskonfiansa.*
misty: *tette.*
misunderstanding: *chinatkinemprende,*
  inabak.
mite: *gotgohu, potgas.*
mitigate: *na'kayada.*
mitt: *guantes.*
  mitt (baseball): *mitto'.*

mitten: *guantes.*

mix: *ña'ña', batte, liti, meskla, templa.*
mix up: *yalaka'.*

mixable: *templáo.*

mixer: *batidót, ná'daña'.*

mixing
mixing (of liquid with solid): *sopas.*

mixture: *dinaña', liniti, meskla, templada.*
mixture (of liquid and solid): *sopas.*

moan: *kasao, manugong, ugong.*

moaning: *inigong.*

moat: *guinaddok.*

mock: *antula, botleha, despresia, insutta, mofeha.*

mocker: *á'ada', botlonu.*
mocker (f): *botlona.*
mocker (m): *botlón.*

mockery: *botlehu, despresio.*

mode: *manera, modu.*

model: *figura, modelu.*

moderate: *moderatu, regulát.*

moderation: *moderasión.*

modern: *modetno, nuebu.*

modest: *modesto, yómahlao.*

moist: *úmidu, masmas.*

moisten: *na'fotgon.*

moisture: *úmidu.*

molar: *akankang.*
molar tooth: *ákakam.*

mold: *betmehu, hotma, plantiyas.*
mold (covered with): *linimutan.*
to mold: *hotma.*

moldy: *inapulaihan, linimutan.*

mole: *do'an, lonnat.*

molest: *mattrata, molestia.*

molestation: *mattratu.*

mollusk
type of mollusk: *salang.*

molt: *gosne, manggosña, manggosne.*

moment: *momento, unratu.*
a moment: *un momento.*
for a moment: *naya.*

momentary: *ti apmam.*

monastery: *monasterio.*

Monday: *Lunes.*

money: *kopble, salape'.*

mongo bean: *monggos.*

mongol-eyed: *bá'chigo', bátchigo'.*

monk: *monhe.*

monkey: *macheng, saro'.*

monster: *ná'ma'a'ñao.*

monstrance: *santisimu.*

monstrous: *ná'ma'a'ñao.*

month: *mes.*
coming month: *mamamaila' na mes.*
last month: *ma'pos na mes.*
month after next: *otroña na mes.*
month before last: *ma'posña na mes.*
next month: *otro na mes.*

monument: *monumento.*

mooch
mooch food: *silok.*

moocher: *ankas, bagamondo, limosneru, mangle.*

mood: *henio.*

moon: *pulan.*
new moon: *sinahi.*

moorish idol: *ababang gupalao.*

mop: *lampasu.*
mop handle: *tokpong lampasu.*

moray eel: *hakmang, hakmang titugi, títugi.*

more: *-ña, hat-, kinu, lage'-, lahát-, meggaiña.*
little more: *piku.*
more (slightly): *la-.*
more than: *mas di, mas ki.*

moreover: *adimás, tras.*

morning: *chatanmak, ogga'an, pa'go gi egga'an.*

morning glory: *alaihai tasi, alalak tasi.*
beach morning glory: *alalak.*

moron: *á'duko', duka', duko', morón, tulisán.*

moronic: *bruta.*

morsel: *bokáo.*

mortal: *mottát.*

mortar: *liniti, lusong.*
mortar and pestle: *putot.*

mortgage: *atmoneda, empeña, impeña.*

mosquito: *ñamu.*
mosquito coil: *oddo, senko, senko'.*

moss: *lumot.*

most
most (superlative): *mas.*

moth: *bábale', bábali.*

mother: *nana.*
mother (church): *madre.*
mother superior: *madre superiora.*
mother-in-law: *sogra.*

motherhood: *koreha.*

motion: *kinalamten, mosión.*
motion (irregular): *lailai.*

motive: *motibu, punto.*

motor: *motu.*

motorcycle: *botosaiko', botosaikot, motosaikot, otobái'.*

motorscooter: *otobái'.*

moult: *manempluma.*

mound: *fina'ekso', loma, okso', puha.*

mount: *hotde.*

mountain: *sabana.*

mourn: *piniti.*

mourning: *lutu.*
  mourning dress: *lutu.*

mouse: *cha'ka, cha'kan dikike'.*

moustache: *bigoti.*

mouth: *pachot, sukos, sukos babui.*
  mouth-to-mouth feeding: *mohmo.*
  open mouth (wide): *a'a'.*
  open-mouthed: *nga'nga'.*

mouthful: *bokáo.*

move: *aranka, kalamten, kanya, muebi,
  na'kalamten, rempua, rempuha.*
  don't move: *kietu.*
  move away: *láttanao, suha.*
  move forward: *atbansa.*
  move from: *kaikai.*
  move out: *láttanao.*
  move quickly: *sigidas.*

movement: *mobimiento.*

movie: *káchido', mubi.*

mow: *yabbao.*

Mrs.: *doña.*

much: *bula, meggai.*

mucilage: *enggrudu.*

mucous: *mukos.*

mucus: *mukos.*

mud: *bañaderu, fache'.*
  mud-hole: *bañaderu.*

muddy: *ataska, kossos, lebbok, máskara.*

muffler
  muffler (of engine): *máfura, mafla.*

mule: *mula.*

mullet: *laiguan, pi'os.*
  baby mullet: *aguas.*

multiplication: *muttiplikát.*

multiply: *muttiplika.*

mumble: *gonggong.*

mumbo jumbo: *ta'hafkao.*

mumps: *buchi.*

municipality: *munisipát.*

murder: *puno'.*

murderer: *pípino', pekno'.*

murderous: *pekno'.*

muscle: *gugat.*
  arm muscle: *kodu.*

muscular: *fuetsudu, loddo', mahegat,
  masahegat, masegat, masisu, maso'.*
  muscular appearance: *kuetpo.*

mush: *atuli.*

mushroom
  mushroom (generic): *payon duendes.*

music: *dandan, músika, son.*
  play music: *dandan.*

musician: *dandera, danderu.*

muskmelon
  muskmelon (generic term): *melon.*

muslin
  unbleached muslin: *manta.*

must: *debi, debidi, ministét, téneki.*

mustache: *batbas.*

mustard: *mostasa.*
  mustard plant: *mostasa.*

mutation: *tinilaika.*

mute: *uda, udu.*

mutter: *guenggueng.*

mutton: *katnen kinilu.*

my: *-hu.*

myopic: *chátmata.*

myrrh: *mira.*

mysterious: *enkantáo.*

mystery: *misterio.*

n: *eni.*

nab: *hakot.*

nail: *atani, lulok, luluki.*
  small nail: *tachuelas.*

naive: *inosente.*

naked: *sin magagu.*

name: *na'an.*
  family name: *apiyidu.*
  name (someone): *fa'na'an.*
  name card: *tatheta.*

nap: *maigo'ñaihon, siesta.*

nape: *espinasu, kueyu, tongho.*

napkin: *setbeyeta.*

narrative: *pasu.*

narrow: *anggosto, estrecho, ma'i'ot.*

nasal
  nasal speech: *ongngo'.*

nasty: *kuchinu.*

nation: *nasión.*

national: *nasionát.*

nationality: *nasionát.*

native: *natibu.*

Nativity: *Natibidát.*

natural: *naturát.*

naturally: *naturát.*

naught: *seru, taya'.*

naughty: *águaguat, átaktak.*

nausea: *bulachon ulu, chatguahu,
  chatguiya.*

nauseated: *asayon, atsayon, massa'.*
  become nauseated: *tumáiganas.*

nauseous: *ná'massa'.*
navel: *apuya'.*
navigable: *máma'ya.*
navigator: *nabegadót.*
navy
    navy steward: *marinon mantikiya.*
Nazarene: *Nasarinu.*
Nazareth: *Nasarét.*
near: *fi'on, hihot.*
nearby: *uriya, uriya.*
nearly: *kanna', kasi, katna'.*
nearsighted: *chátmata.*
neat: *aliñao, espót, gasgas, pachuchang.*
    neat (f): *bunita.*
necessary: *impottante, ministét,*
    nisisario, nisisita, prisisu.
necessitous: *nisisitáo.*
necessity: *nisisidát.*
neck: *aga'ga', kueyu, tongho.*
    stiff neck: *lekngai.*
    stuffed neck of chicken: *motsiyas.*
neckerchief: *kotbata.*
necklace: *kadena, lisayu.*
necktie: *kotbata.*
need: *nisisidát, nisisita.*
needful: *nisisario.*
needle: *haguhan kannai, haguhan*
    mákina, haguhan manlakse.
    large needle: *lanseta.*
    needle (generic): *haguha.*
needle's eye: *atadok haguha.*
needlefish: *palos, pulos.*
needy: *miche', nisisitáo, popble, táisaga.*
negative: *des-.*
neglect: *deskuida, maleffa.*
negligence: *deskuidu.*
negligible: *despresiapble.*
negotiation: *negosio.*
negotiator: *negosiante.*
negrito: *nigritos.*
negro: *bakuko', negro, nekglo, nigritos.*
neighbor: *bisinu.*
neighborhood: *bisinu.*
nephew: *subrinu.*
nest: *ala, chonchon.*
    bee's nest: *chomchom abea.*
nest swiftlet: *yayaguak.*
net: *chenchulu, lagua', talaya.*
    closing net: *langse.*
    gill net: *tekken.*
    hand net: *lagua'.*
    mosquito net: *kábiyon.*
    throw net: *talayan mañahak, talayan*
    ti'ao.

neutral: *nutrát.*
never: *ni ngai'an, nunka, tatnai, taya',*
    taya' nai.
    never again: *hamás.*
    never mind: *dialu, para hafa.*
nevertheless: *sinembatgo.*
new: *nuebu.*
    new (article): *simpeng.*
    the New Year: *Añu Nuebu.*
news: *asunto, nobidát.*
newspaper: *gaseta.*
next
    next to: *checho, fi'on, unbanda.*
nibble: *denka.*
nice: *bunita, bunitu, gatbo,*
    pachuchang.
niche: *nichu.*
nick: *chebbang.*
    nick (blade): *tengteng.*
nicked
    nicked (blade): *mafte'.*
nickname: *Olo'.*
    nickname (someone): *fa'na'an.*
    nickname for Adelia: *Delan.*
    nickname for Alfonsina: *Ina.*
    nickname for Ampara: *Paro'.*
    nickname for Amparo: *Ampan,*
    Charo'.
    nickname for Andersina: *Sina.*
    nickname for Andrea: *Dea'.*
    nickname for Antonia: *Onin, Tona'.*
    nickname for Antonio: *Antong, Ton,*
    Tong.
    nickname for Anunciacion: *Uncha'.*
    nickname for Asuncion: *Conchita,*
    Tina.
    nickname for Barbara: *Baran.*
    nickname for Benaventura:
    Benbenidu.
    nickname for Benedicta: *Dikta.*
    nickname for Bernadita: *Benet, Dita,*
    Nadet.
    nickname for Bernardo: *Nado'.*
    nickname for Bonifacio: *Bancho'.*
    nickname for Candelaria: *Anda.*
    nickname for Candido: *Kalen.*
    nickname for Carmen: *Ame', Mame',*
    Milen, Min.
    nickname for Catalina: *Ninan.*
    nickname for Cecilia: *Chilang.*
    nickname for Concepcion: *Cholai',*
    Chonai', Chonke'.
    nickname for Consolacion: *Chong.*
    nickname for Cornelio: *Elo', Nelong.*
    nickname for David: *Bik.*
    nickname for Dolores: *Ling, Lola,*

Lole'.
nickname for Dorotea: *Dolot, Doreng.*
nickname for Emelia: *Émilin,*
   Melang.
nickname for Emelia or Maria: *Lia'.*
nickname for Escolastica: *Atika, Kula.*
nickname for Esperansa: *Ancha',*
   Anchon.
nickname for Estefania: *Chopia,*
   Fansen, Nia'.
nickname for Faustino: *Tinung.*
nickname for Francisca: *Kai', Kika',*
   Siska, Tika.
nickname for Francisco: *Kiko', Ko',*
   Pakitu, Tiku.
nickname for Herman: *Mang.*
nickname for Hermana: *Manan.*
nickname for Ignacio: *Acho', Chacho',*
   Inas.
nickname for Isabel: *Bek.*
nickname for Isidora: *Dorang, Lalan.*
nickname for Jacinto: *Titu.*
nickname for Jesus: *Bai', Chu',*
   Chumbai', Chumen, Umbai'.
nickname for Joaquin: *Kin, Kindo',*
   Kinkeng.
nickname for Jose: *Pepe, Pileng, Pin,*
   Ping, Pinke', Pinkile'.
nickname for Josepha: *Epa', Pai'.*
nickname for Juan: *Bang, Iku, Kuku.*
nickname for Juana: *Iyang.*
nickname for Juliana: *Tanan.*
nickname for Leonardo: *Dado', Ding.*
nickname for Lorenzo: *Encho'.*
nickname for Lucia: *Chian.*
nickname for Luisa: *Chicha', Icha'.*
nickname for Magdalena: *Nenan.*
nickname for Manuel: *Manúng, Ne'.*
nickname for Manuela: *Lela'.*
nickname for Margaret: *Aget.*
nickname for Margarita: *Adet, Tete'.*
nickname for Maria: *Kita'.*
nickname for Maria (diminutive):
   Marikita.
nickname for Maximo: *Mimo', Timo'.*
nickname for Miguel: *Ge', Genge'.*
nickname for Natividad: *Da, Dalen.*
nickname for Nicolas: *Kulas, La'.*
nickname for Oliva: *Biban, Iba.*
nickname for Pedro: *Dudong, Dung.*
nickname for Priscilla: *Pechang.*
nickname for Ramon: *Bo.*
nickname for Rosa: *Chai', Ocha'.*
nickname for Rufina: *Ina'.*
nickname for Soledad: *Daidai.*
nickname for Susana: *Chana'.*
nickname for Teresa: *Checha'.*
nickname for Teresita: *Titan.*
nickname for Thomas: *Tima'.*

nickname for Vicente: *Bénkile',*
   Tente'.
niece: *subrina.*
niggardly: *chattao, gake', meskinu.*
night: *noches, puengi, tulanoche.*
   last night: *painge.*
nightcap: *kepes.*
nightingale: *ga'ga' karisu.*
nightmare: *pesadiya, pesatdiya,*
   pisadiya.
nil: *ni hafa.*
nimble: *kalamya.*
nine: *nuebi.*
ninety: *nobenta.*
   ninety-one: *nobenta i unu.*
ninth: *nebenu.*
nip: *akka', denka, despunta.*
nipple: *akado', cháflaki, chipón.*
nit: *lotsa.*
no: *ahe', diahlo, dialu, munga.*
   no choice: *sininbatgo.*
   no matter: *ni taimanu.*
   no method: *sióganai'.*
   no more: *hokkok.*
   no thanks: *diahlo, dialu.*
   no way: *sióganai'.*
nobility: *diknidát, nobilidát.*
noble: *dikno, matua, nopble.*
nobody: *ni hayi, ni unu.*
nod: *sikat.*
nodding: *sikat.*
noddy
   common noddy: *fahang.*
node: *gahu, gao.*
noise: *a'gang, buruka, ina'gang, ridu.*
   loud noise: *palangpang, ruidu.*
noisy
   noisy (f):   *burukenta.*
   noisy (m):   *burukento.*
   noisy person: *kakte.*
nominate: *tancho'.*
nominee: *kandidatu.*
nonchalant: *fresko.*
none: *hokkok, manai-, ni hafa, tai-,*
   taya'.
nonsense: *appleng, batbaridat,*
   disparati, pirada, tonteria, tonto.
noodle: *utdón.*
noon: *talo'ani.*
normal: *otdinariu, regulát.*
north: *gé'lagu, háttagu, notte.*
   go north: *dádagu, ládagu.*
   move north: *dádagu, ládagu.*
   north (in Saipan):   *kattan.*

north (in Guam and Rota): *lagu.*
way north: *yalágugu.*
northerly: *háttagu.*
northward: *gé'lagu, háttagu.*
  northward movement: *dádagu,*
    ládagu.
nose: *gui'eng.*
  blow nose: *ngofngof.*
  flat nose: *bulengngo', maheffong,*
    ongngo'.
  long nose: *bulenchot.*
  malformed nose: *dado'.*
  nose bleed: *mahagga' gui'eng.*
  nose ring (of animal): *atgoya.*
  pointed nose: *bulenchok.*
  runny nose: *sagu.*
noseless: *ongngo'.*
nosey: *atrebimiento, embilikeru,*
    kamten.
nostril: *maddok gui'eng.*
not: *des-, munga, sin.*
  not (negative marker): *ti.*
  not even: *ni.*
  not ever: *ni ngai'an.*
  not have (plural): *manai-.*
  not have (prefix): *tai-.*
  not in the least: *tampoku.*
  not yet: *trabiha.*
notably: *maloffan.*
notch: *ipe'.*
note: *nota.*
  note (music): *sotfa.*
  note down: *apunta.*
notebook: *lepblo.*
noteworthy: *espesiát.*
nothing: *kasko, ni hafa, seru, taya'.*
  nothing else: *nada mas.*
notice: *asunto, faila', notisia, ripara.*
  take notice: *dia'.*
notification: *notifikasión.*
notify: *abisa, infotma, notifika, ripotte.*
notwithstanding: *sin enao.*
nought: *ni hafa.*
novelty: *nobidát.*
November: *Nobiembre, Sumongsong.*
novena: *nobena.*
now: *pa'go.*
  now and then: *guaha na biahi, pa'go*
    yan ayu.
nowhere: *ni manu.*
nowise: *ni kuanto, ni taimanu.*
nude: *kesnudu.*
nudge: *dekka', ette, sokkok, toyo'.*
nuisance: *estotbo, hásupak, ná'chatsaga,*
    pirada.

null: *nulu.*
nullify: *ñega.*
numb: *ma'etdot, ti manieniente.*
number: *númiru.*
nun: *etmana, madre, mongha.*
nuptial celebration: *fandanggo.*
nurse: *á'amte, emfetmera.*
nursemaid: *emfetmera.*
nurture: *poksai.*
nut: *pipitas, totniyu.*
nutgrass: *cha'guan Umatac.*
nutriment: *nénkanno'.*
nutrition: *alimenta, sustansia.*
nutritious: *alimentosu.*
o: *o.*
o'clock: *ala.*
oaf: *títires.*
oar: *tulos.*
oarlock: *toleti.*
oath: *prinemeti.*
obdurate: *mahetok.*
obediant: *tagu'on.*
obedient: *obidiente, osgon.*
obeisance: *onra.*
obese: *chebot, loddo', yommok.*
object: *ophetu, pine'lo, yama.*
  object to: *chanda.*
objective: *punto.*
obligated: *opbligáo.*
obligation: *afuetsáo, opbligasión.*
obligatory: *fuetsáo.*
oblige: *finaboresi, opbliga.*
oblivion: *minaleffa.*
obscure: *homhom.*
  make obscure: *na'maya'.*
obscured: *maya'.*
  become obscured: *mumaya'.*
observant: *atitu.*
observe
  observe (as spectator): *egga'.*
obstacle: *apstrakto, embarasos,*
    impedimento.
obstetrician: *pattera, patteru.*
obstinate: *águaguat, nesio.*
obstruct: *chomma'.*
obstruction: *apstrakto, atkagueti,*
    impedimento.
obtain: *hentan.*
obtuse: *táipunta.*
occasion: *okasión.*
occasionally: *antohu, guaha na biahi,*
    trasoras.
occupancy: *okupasión.*

287

occupant: *okupante, sumagágayi.*
occupation: *ofisiu, okupasión, pusisión.*
occupied: *okupáo.*
occupy: *okupa.*
occurrence: *estoria, hemplo, sinisedi, susiadét.*
ocean: *tasi.*
octave: *oktaba.*
October: *Fagualo', Oktubre.*
octopus: *gamson.*
odd: *táiga'chong.*
  odd (not even): *nones.*
odds
  give odds: *yeba.*
  give odds (gambling): *logru.*
  odds maker: *lílogru.*
odious: *ná'massa'.*
odor: *paguan, pao.*
  fleshy odor: *paomata'.*
  urine odor: *paosadang.*
of: *pot.*
off limits: *pribidu.*
offend: *isague, ofende.*
offense: *isao, ofensa.*
offensive: *ná'massa'.*
offer: *ofresi, ofresimiento.*
offering: *inefresi, ofresimiento.*
office: *ofisina.*
officer: *ofisiát.*
official: *ofisiát.*
offshoot: *sinisu.*
offspring: *tátatte.*
often: *fihu, sesso, sessuyi, tantos di, tenga.*
  often (prefix): *ha-.*
  often times: *fihu, sesso.*
oh: *ai, o.*
oil: *asaite, luga'.*
  coconut oil: *tika.*
  holy oil: *santos olios.*
  oil (for frying): *sirásime'.*
  oil (generic): *laña.*
  oil can: *asaitera.*
oilcloth: *uli.*
ointment: *engguente, hunto, ingguente, palai.*
okay: *amen, buenu, esta, hu'u.*
okra: *okra.*
old: *amko'.*
  very old: *antiguayon.*
olden times: *antiguamente.*
Oleai: *Oleai.*
oleander: *adetfa.*
olives: *olibas.*

omen: *siñát.*
ominous: *desfaborable.*
omit: *lagua', omiti.*
on: *giya.*
once: *un bi'ahi.*
  at once: *insigidas.*
one: *unu.*
  one (indefinite article): *un.*
  one (telling time): *una.*
  one of group: *atgon.*
oneself: *maisa.*
onion: *nira', rakkio', tamanege'.*
  onion (generic): *siboyas.*
only: *úniku, solamente.*
  only (intensifier): *ha'.*
ooze: *mañugo'.*
opal: *opela.*
open: *atbuetto, baba, bala', baleng.*
  open (wide): *puga'.*
  open eye wide: *atalak.*
  open up: *baleng, la'mok, pulakes.*
opened: *atbietto, binaba.*
opener
  bottle opener: *baban boteya.*
opening: *atbettura.*
operate: *manea, opera.*
operation: *operasión.*
operator: *draiba.*
opinion: *hinasso, upiñón.*
opponent: *enimigu, kontrariu.*
opportunity: *opottunidát.*
oppose: *yama.*
opposite: *átlibes.*
oppressed: *inatditi.*
oppression: *hineño', inhuestisia, minattrata.*
option: *inayek.*
opulent: *fottuna, gófsaga, míguinaha, riku.*
or: *pat, sinó.*
orange: *kahet.*
  orange (color): *kulot kahet.*
orangeish: *kinahet na kulot.*
oration: *orasión.*
orator: *kuikuentos.*
orchestra: *músiku.*
orchid: *siboyas halomtano'.*
ordain: *otdena.*
order: *enkatga, fina'maolek, inarekkla, mana'huyong, otden.*
  an order: *inenkatga.*
orderly: *arekláo.*
ordinal marker: *mina'-.*

ordinary: *otdinariu, regulatmente.*
organ: *atmoniu.*
organize: *fotma, otganisa.*
orgasm: *mañugo'.*
orient: *oriente.*
oriental: *oriente.*
origin: *prinsipiu.*
original: *orihinát.*
ornament: *alahas, beste, botlas, gatbesa.*
oscillation: *ritumbo.*
other: *otro.*
otherwise: *sinó.*
ouch: *ai.*
ought
  ought to: *debidi.*
our: *-mami, -ta.*
ours: *-mami, -ta.*
oust: *dúlalak.*
out: *háttiyong.*
  move out further: *gé'hiyong.*
outcast: *mayute'.*
outcome: *fin, huyong.*
outcry: *éssalao, kati.*
outer: *gé'hiyong.*
  the outer part: *sanhiyong.*
outgoing
  outgoing person: *matala'.*
outline: *obra.*
outmaneuver: *salamanka.*
outside: *háttiyong, huyong, sanhiyong.*
  outside of: *fuera di.*
  way outside: *yahúyoyong.*
outsider: *estrangheru.*
outspoken: *franko.*
outward: *háttiyong.*
outwit: *dugeruyi, salamanka.*
oval: *adamelong.*
oven: *hotno.*
  oven (underground): *chahan.*
over
  be over: *fakpo'.*
overbearing: *ti sungunon.*
overcoat: *saku.*
overcome: *fita', hinilat, hulat, igi.*
overdo: *go'dan, hasnguni, kebranta.*
overextend: *go'dan.*
overflow: *alatga, machuda', milak.*
overindulge: *go'dan.*
overloaded: *katgadu.*
overpower: *aña, a'ñao, fita', fueges, ganna, hulat, igi, talonan, yagai.*
overpowered: *hinilat.*
overrun: *chiget.*

overshadow: *homme.*
oversight: *finalaguaihon.*
oversleep: *ba'an.*
overtask: *sa'pet.*
overturned: *mabira.*
overwhelm: *a'ñao.*
overwork: *kebranta, sa'pet.*
ovum: *chada'.*
owe: *dibi.*
owner: *ama, dueñu.*
ox: *nubiyu.*
  ox (young): *toreti.*
oyster: *tapon.*
p: *pe.*
pace: *pasu, pokkat.*
pacific: *pasífiku.*
  Pacific man-o-war: *fakte, ga'ga' manglo', lu'ao.*
  Pacific golden plover: *dulili.*
pacifier: *chupón.*
pacify: *komplasi.*
pack: *paketi.*
  mule pack: *aparehu.*
  pack (into a hole): *sohmok.*
package: *paketi.*
pad: *kúsion.*
paddle: *poksai.*
padlock: *adaba, andaba, aseradura, kandalu, seradura.*
pagan: *moru, paganu.*
page: *ohas, plegu.*
  page (of paper): *páhina.*
pail: *batde.*
pain: *eyok, pinadesi, piniti, puti, sage', sinilo'.*
  severe pain: *manehyok, maneyok.*
painful: *sage'.*
  painful joints: *mamuti.*
paint: *penta, pentura.*
  paint white: *blankeha.*
paintbrush: *pensét.*
painter: *pípenta, pentot.*
painting: *pinenta, yunga'.*
pair: *pares, pat, tetno.*
pal: *ágofli'e', átungo', abok, amiga, amigu.*
palace: *palasyo.*
palate: *páladat.*
  cleft palate: *dado'.*
pale: *betmehu, boksion, chupon, deskuluráo, pasmo.*
  become pale: *chapon, chipon.*
palette: *paleta.*

palm
  Manila palm: *pugua' China.*
  palm (of coconut): *patma.*
  palm (of the hand): *patma.*
  palm tree: *federiku, gafo'.*
  Palm Sunday: *Damenggon Ramos.*
palo-maria tree: *da'ok.*
pan: *la'uya, satten.*
  large pan: *katderu.*
pancake: *panket.*
  rice pancake: *bibenka.*
pandanus: *aka'on, akgak, akson, kafo', pahong.*
panic: *linihan.*
pant: *guha.*
panties: *katsunes, pantes, saromata'.*
pantry: *dispensiya, haichio'.*
pants: *katsunes.*
  without pants: *sin laso'.*
papa: *tata.*
papaya: *papaya, tronkon papaya.*
paper: *papet.*
  toilet paper: *chirigame', etgue, papet etgue.*
parable: *ehemplo, parábola.*
parachute: *parasiút, rakka'.*
paradise: *paradisu.*
paragraph: *parafu.*
parallel: *alapát, atparehu.*
paralysis: *inutet, paralítiku.*
paralytic: *paralítiku.*
paralyzed: *inutet.*
  fingers (paralyzed): *haku.*
parasite: *didinak.*
parasol: *payu.*
parcel: *paketi.*
pardon: *asi'i, despensa, dispensa, inasi'i, mina'ase', petdón.*
pardonable: *asi'iyon.*
pare: *sufan.*
  pare off: *go'naf.*
parents: *mañaina, saina.*
parochial: *parókia.*
parrot
  parrot (bird): *loru.*
parrot fish: *ha'yan, laggua.*
  large parrot fish: *atuhong.*
  small parrot fish: *foge', palakse'.*
parsimonious: *gake', manakihom, meskinu.*
parsma berry: *mansanita.*
parson: *inamte.*
part: *granu, miembro, patte, pattida, pidasu.*
  part (from a whole): *empe'.*

parted: *siparáo.*
participate: *saonao.*
particle: *las, pidasitu.*
  linking particle: *na.*
particular: *cha'tan, pattikulát, propiu.*
parting: *inádingu.*
partition: *dibisión, luga.*
partner: *ágofli'e', átungo', amigu, ga'chong, kompañeru.*
parturition: *patto.*
party: *fiesta, gupot.*
  party (political): *pattida.*
pass: *upos.*
  pass over: *krusa.*
  pass through: *esek, isek.*
passage: *fanhaluman, pasaderu.*
passageway: *fanfa'pusan, fanlugayan, potta.*
passenger: *pasaheru.*
passion: *pasión.*
passion fruit: *dutse.*
passive marker: *ma-.*
passport: *pasapotte.*
past: *apmam, ma'pos, pasáo.*
  past time: *maloffan.*
  past time (recent): *halacha.*
paste: *enggrudu.*
pasteurize: *pasturisa.*
pastors: *mamale'.*
pastry: *boñelos, postre.*
  pastry (sweet): *fina'mames.*
pasture: *fanpastuyan, pastahi, pasto.*
pat: *padda'.*
  pat repeatedly: *pampan.*
patch: *empatma, hetbana.*
  patch (tire): *limenda.*
  patch up: *patche.*
patent: *patente.*
path: *chalan, kayi, kayon, pasaderu.*
  make a path: *fa'chalani, miche'.*
pathetic: *na'ma'se'.*
patience: *pasiensia.*
patient: *pasensia, tái'ine'son.*
patio: *patiu.*
patriarch: *patriatka.*
patrimony: *rénsia.*
patriotism: *patriotiku.*
patrol: *polisia.*
patrolman: *guatdia.*
patron: *patrón.*
patronage: *fabót.*
pattern: *modelu, padrón.*
pauper: *tákgagao.*

pause: *inentalu'i, pumara.*
pavillion: *palapala.*
  small pavillion: *kiosko.*
paw: *patas ga'ga'.*
  to paw the earth: *guahof.*
pawn: *empeña.*
pay: *abona, apasi.*
  pay attention to: *osge.*
  pay up: *na'empas.*
payday: *pagamento.*
paymaster: *pagadót.*
pea
  beach pea: *akankang manulasa.*
peace: *minaggem, pas.*
  make peace: *aplaka.*
peaceful: *mahgong, pasífiku.*
  more peaceful: *lámahgong.*
peacefulness: *ginéfsaga.*
peak: *punta.*
peanut: *kakaguates.*
pear: *peras.*
pearl: *petlas.*
peas: *chícharos.*
  pigeon peas: *lanta'as.*
peasant: *simenterera.*
  peasant (m): *simentereru.*
pebbles: *baras.*
peck: *denka, denkot.*
pecking
  pecking (sound): *taktak.*
peculiar: *sahnge.*
peddle: *bende gi chalan.*
peek
  peek at: *adu, ngelo'.*
peel: *ette, lassas, ma'i'eng, pulakes,*
    sufan, u'os.
  peel off: *la'la', pappa, tupa.*
peeled
  be peeled (of sore scab): *malatte'.*
peep: *adu.*
  peep at: *éngelo', ngelo'.*
peeping tom: *nge'lo'.*
peer: *acháguasguas, achátaotao,*
    achahet.
peerless: *tái'achaigua, tái'atparehu,*
    táichilong.
peg: *pekke, tarugu.*
pellet: *petdigón, pidigón.*
  shotgun pellet: *balan petdigón.*
pen: *chikeru.*
  fountain pen: *pluma.*
penalize: *kondena.*
penalty: *mutta, pena.*
penance: *pinitensia.*

pencil: *lapes.*
penetrate: *dochon, hatme.*
penis: *chili, chimboko', chingcheng,*
    dódole', iyon lahi, laso'.
  penis (slang): *malaña', malakes.*
  word for penis: *kungkung.*
penny: *memos, meyu, séntimos.*
Pentecost: *Pentekostes.*
penurious: *gake', meskinu.*
people: *taotao.*
pepper: *donne' ti'ao, pimienta,*
    primienta.
  bell pepper: *donne' gollai.*
  chili pepper: *donne' pika.*
  hot pepper: *donne'.*
  pepper (ground): *plimenta.*
  small pepper: *donne' sali.*
  sweet pepper: *pimentos.*
perceive: *li'e'.*
perceptible: *tungu'on.*
perception: *siniente.*
perceptive: *akli'e'.*
perch: *sa'hang.*
perfect: *perfekto, prifekto.*
perform: *cho'gue, huega, hugando.*
performance: *programa.*
perfume: *paopao.*
perfunctory: *mamo'lo.*
perhaps: *buente, fa'na'an, kasi, será,*
    siña buente, siña ha', siakasu.
  perhaps (contrary to fact): *puedi.*
peril: *piligro.*
perilous: *piligro, piligrosu.*
period: *punto, tétmenu.*
  period (of time): *siklo.*
periodic: *periodiku.*
perish: *kumematai.*
perishing: *kumekematai.*
periwinkle: *chuchurika.*
perjure: *chátmanhula.*
permanent: *pendiente, petmamente,*
    prendiente.
  permanent wave: *mulata.*
permeable
  permeable (by water, air, etc.):
    tánkala.
permission: *lisensia, petmisu.*
permissive: *katgueti.*
permit: *aotorisa, aturisa, konsiente,*
    lisensia, petmiti.
perplexed: *manman.*
persecuted: *mapetsigi.*
persecution: *pinetsigi.*
persevere: *potfia.*
  persevere in: *usuni.*

persist: *insiste, kontinua, petdika, petsigi, potfia.*
  persist in: *prikura, usuni.*
persistent: *empeñosu, saguat.*
persistently: *sin parát.*
person: *petsona, taotao.*
personally: *mismo.*
perspicacious: *sábio.*
perspicacity: *sábio.*
perspiration: *masahalom.*
perspire: *masahalom.*
persuade: *bense, eppok, fanoppok, kombense, su'ok, tienta.*
pertinacious: *águaguat.*
pertinent: *pettanesi.*
perverse: *águaguat, nesio, pikatdiha.*
pest: *dañu, ná'chatsaga, peste.*
pester: *achaki, molestia.*
pestle: *fayao, lommok.*
pet: *ga'-.*
petiole: *kálile'.*
petition: *ginagao, pitisión.*
petrol: *gas, gasilina.*
petroleum: *petroliu, pritoliu.*
petticoat: *kamisola, lipes, lupes.*
phantom: *fantasma.*
Pharisee: *Fariseo.*
phenomenon: *sinisedi.*
philosophy: *filosifia.*
phlegm: *flema, lakulakong.*
phone: *telefón.*
  to phone: *dengua'.*
phonograph: *funógrafu.*
phosphorus: *fósforu.*
photograph: *fotografu.*
photographer: *fotograferu, litratista.*
photography: *fotografia, litratista.*
phrase: *frasa.*
physalia: *abubon pápago'.*
physic nut: *tubatuba.*
physician: *á'amte, dokto, médiku, praktikante.*
piano: *pianu.*
pick: *hokka, iteng, tife'.*
  pick (bunch): *ga'om.*
  pick (leaves by hand): *to'to'.*
  pick (tool): *piku, sakapiku.*
  pick (with pole or stick): *dekka', dossok, gaole.*
  pick at: *dekka', denka.*
  pick ears: *dekka'.*
  pick fruit: *famfe', fanggan, mamfe'.*
  pick nose: *dekka'.*
  pick out: *ayek.*
  pick teeth: *gue'gue'.*

pickaback: *ombo'.*
pickax: *achita, asada, hachita.*
pickle: *asne, enkattidu.*
pickled: *inasne.*
picnic: *piknik.*
picture: *fotografu, litratu, pinenta.*
pie: *pai, pastet.*
  meat pie: *empañada, empanada.*
piece: *empe', enggranét, granu, pidasu, ritasos.*
  piece of: *entot.*
pier: *pantalán.*
pierce: *dochon, dossok, getmon, hotne, sihòk, siok, tokcha'.*
  pierce repeatedly: *dongdong.*
  pierce through: *na'adotgan.*
pig: *babuen lansa, babui, lechon.*
  type of pig: *babuen baksia', babuen kuaresma.*
  wild pig: *babuen halom tano', babuen machalek.*
  young pig: *puetkasita.*
pig's call: *bu, nena'.*
pigeon: *paluma.*
pigeon-toed: *patuleku, sambo.*
piggyback
  carry piggyback: *ombo'.*
píglet: *lechon.*
pigpen: *chekeru, chikeru.*
pigsty: *chikeru.*
pile: *amontona, pilapat.*
piled
  piled up: *ádaose, abuttáo.*
piles: *gágalak, tininu.*
pilgrim: *piligrinu.*
pill: *kápsulas, kátsulas, pétduras, pitduras.*
pillage: *despetdisia.*
pillar: *haligi, hotkon.*
pillow: *alunan, atmohada.*
  pillow case: *botsan alunan, fundan alunan.*
  wooden pillow: *alunan hayu.*
pilot: *pilotu.*
pimple: *otdon.*
pimples
  goose pimples: *apigasa.*
pin: *átfilet, atfilet kabesa, atfilet makandalu.*
  pin against: *klaba, sokka.*
  pin down: *kobra.*
  pin up hair: *atkiya.*
  pin-wheel: *ga'ga' manglo'.*
pince-nez: *antihos.*

pincers: *dáma'gas, pincho, tinasa.*
pinch: *de'on.*
  pinch (on the thigh): *chagga'.*
pincher: *chíchiget, déde'on.*
pine
  pine tree: *pinu.*
  screw pine: *kafo'.*
pineapple: *piña.*
pink
  pink (color): *kulot di rosa.*
pinkish: *kinilot di rosa.*
pinto: *pento.*
pious: *dibotu, santolón, santolona.*
pipe
  drain pipe: *tubu.*
  pipe (for tobacco): *chigando'.*
pique: *piké.*
pirate: *pirata.*
pistol: *paki, pistola, rubetbet.*
piston: *piston.*
pit: *hoyu, kannat, maddok.*
pitch: *blanko, daggao, yotte.*
  pitch (underhand): *tira.*
  pitch in: *ambos, ambros.*
pitcher: *hara.*
pitchfork: *tenidot basula.*
pitiful: *ná'ma'ase', na'ma'se'.*
pitiless: *kret.*
pitted: *dondon.*
pity: *ma'ase'.*
  have pity: *gái'ase', gáima'ase'.*
placate: *aplaka, fatani, komplasi.*
place: *dipusita, lugát, mamo'lo, pega, po'lo, puesto, sa'ang, sa'hang, saga, sitio.*
  have place: *gáilugat.*
  place for (something): *sagan.*
  place in: *sahguan, sini, siniyi.*
  place in (something) for: *sahguani.*
  place where: *fan...an.*
placenta: *pares.*
plague: *peste.*
plain: *sabana, sabaneta, yanu.*
plains: *planas.*
plaintiff: *kaosadót.*
plait: *akeyo', filak, mamfok.*
plan: *planeha, planu.*
plane
  plane (carpenter's): *espiyu, supiyu.*
planet: *planeta.*
plank: *bátalan, tablón, tapblón.*
plant: *na'la'la', tanom, tatme, tinanom.*
  plant nursery: *plantet.*
  type of plant: *abahakat, aka'on, akaparas, asensión, bebe'*

Underwood, chaiguan, deres, dutse, fadang, flores asusena, flores rosát, gaogao uchan, kahet dankolo, mansanan paotake', pokse', santán, take' uchan, trigu.
type of plant-abrus precatorius: *kulales halom tano'.*
type of plant-abutilon: *matbas.*
type of plant-acacia farnesiana: *aroma, kandaroma.*
type of plant-acacia kauaiensis: *tronkon boforeng, tronkon sósigi.*
type of plant-achyranthes aspera: *chichiton.*
type of plant-acrosticum aurem: *lakngayao.*
type of plant-acrostium aureum: *apehu.*
type of plant-adenanthera pavonina: *kulales.*
type of plant-adenostemma: *cha'guan mannok.*
type of plant-agave vivipara: *lirio di palu.*
type of plant-ageratum conyzoides: *mumutong.*
type of plant-aglaia mariannensis: *mapuñao.*
type of plant-albizia lebbeck: *tronkon mames.*
type of plant-aleurites moluccana: *lumbang.*
type of plant-allium cepa: *siboyas.*
type of plant-allium sativum: *ahos.*
type of plant-allophylus timorensis: *nget.*
type of plant-alocasia indica: *piga'.*
type of plant-alternanthera: *chucharita.*
type of plant-alyxia torresiana: *nanagu.*
type of plant-amaranthus: *kilites.*
type of plant-amaranthus tricolor: *enmosa biaha.*
type of plant-ammannia coccinea: *astetema.*
type of plant-anacardium occidentale: *kasoe.*
type of plant-ananas comosus: *piña.*
type of plant-annona muricata: *laguaná.*
type of plant-annona reticulata: *anonas.*
type of plant-annona squamosa: *ates.*
type of plant-antidesma bunius: *biknai.*
type of plant-arachis hypogaea: *kakaguates.*
type of plant-areca catechu: *pugua'.*

type of plant-arenga pinnata: *kabon Negro.*

type of plant-artemisia vulgaris: *yetbas Santa Maria.*

type of plant-artocarpus altilis: *lemmai.*

type of plant-artocarpus heterophyllus: *nanka.*

type of plant-artocarpus integra: *lemasa.*

type of plant-artocarpus mariannensis: *dokdok.*

type of plant-asclepias curassavica: *asunsion.*

type of plant-asplenium nidus: *galak, galak fedda'.*

type of plant-averrhoa bilimbi: *pikue.*

type of plant-averrhoa carambola: *bilembines.*

type of plant-bambusa arundinacea: *pi'ao, pi'ao palao'an.*

type of plant-bambusa blumeana: *pi'ao tituka.*

type of plant-barringtonia asiatica: *puteng.*

type of plant-barringtonia racemosa: *lagansát.*

type of plant-bauhinia: *flores mariposa.*

type of plant-benincasa hispida: *kondót.*

type of plant-beta vulgaris: *asetga, remolacha.*

type of plant-bikkia mariannensis: *gaosali.*

type of plant-bixa orellana: *achoti.*

type of plant-blechum brownei: *yetbas babui.*

type of plant-bleekeria mariannensis: *lángiti.*

type of plant-boerhaavia tetrandra: *dafao.*

type of plant-brassica: *nappa'.*

type of plant-brassica juncea: *mostasa.*

type of plant-bruguiera gymnorrhiza: *mangle machu.*

type of plant-caesalpinia major: *pakao.*

type of plant-caesalpinia pulcherrima: *kabayeros.*

type of plant-caesalpinia sappan: *sibukáo.*

type of plant-cajanus cajan: *lanta'as, lenteha Franchesa.*

type of plant-caladium bicolor: *Korason di Santa Maria.*

type of plant-calanthe: *siboyas halomtano'.*

type of plant-callicarpa candicans:

hamlak, kualitai, palapan hilitai.

type of plant-calophyllum inophyllum: *da'ok, palu maria.*

type of plant-camellia sinensis: *cha.*

type of plant-canarium: *breablanka.*

type of plant-canavalia microcarpa: *lodosong tasi.*

type of plant-canavalia rosea: *akankang tasi.*

type of plant-capparis cordifolia: *atkaparas.*

type of plant-capsicum: *donne' pika.*

type of plant-capsicum annuum: *donne'.*

type of plant-capsicum frutescens: *donne' sali.*

type of plant-carica papaya: *tronkon papaya.*

type of plant-carinta herbacea: *tamanes hateng.*

type of plant-cassia alata: *akapuku.*

type of plant-cassia alate: *take' biha.*

type of plant-cassia fistula: *kana' fistula.*

type of plant-cassia occidentalis: *amot tumaga', mumutong sapble.*

type of plant-cassia sophera: *amot tumaga' karabao.*

type of plant-cassia tora: *mumutong palao'an.*

type of plant-cassytha filiformis: *agasi, mai'agas.*

type of plant-casuarina equisetifolia: *gagu.*

type of plant-catharanthus roseus: *chuchurika.*

type of plant-ceiba pentandra: *atgodon di Manila.*

type of plant-celosia argentea: *krestan gayu.*

type of plant-cenchrus echinatus: *laso' katu.*

type of plant-cerbera dilatata: *chuti.*

type of plant-cestrum diurnum: *tentanchinu.*

type of plant-cestrum nocturnum: *dama di noche.*

type of plant-chenopodium album: *kilites.*

type of plant-chenopodium ambrosioides: *apasoti.*

type of plant-chrysanthemum morifolium: *mansaniya.*

type of plant-chrysopogon aciculatus: *ínifok, palai'i.*

type of plant-citrullus vulgaris: *chandia.*

type of plant-citrus aurantifolia: *lemon.*

type of plant-citrus aurantium: *kahet.*
type of plant-citrus grandis: *kahet ma'gas, lalangha, setlas.*
type of plant-citrus limon: *lemon reat.*
type of plant-citrus medica: *sitron.*
type of plant-citrus reticulata: *kahet dikike', lalanghita.*
type of plant-claoxylon marianum: *katot.*
type of plant-cleome viscosa: *monggos paluma.*
type of plant-clerodendruin inerme: *lódigao.*
type of plant-clitorea ternatea: *paokeke.*
type of plant-clitoreaternatea: *kapa de la raina.*
type of plant-cocos nucifera: *niyok.*
type of plant-codiaeum variegatum: *leston puyitos.*
type of plant-coffea arabica: *kafé.*
type of plant-coix lachryma-jobi: *bilén.*
type of plant-colocasia esculenta: *papao, suni.*
type of plant-colubrina asiatica: *gáso'so'.*
type of plant-commelina diffusa: *siemprebiba.*
type of plant-corchorus aestuans: *tuban chá'ka.*
type of plant-cordyline fruticosa: *baston San Jose.*
type of plant-crescentia alata: *hikara, houka.*
type of plant-crinum asiaticum: *piga' palayi.*
type of plant-cucumis melo: *melon.*
type of plant-cucumis sativus: *pipinu.*
type of plant-cucurbita moschata: *kalamasa.*
type of plant-curcuma longa: *mango'.*
type of plant-cyathea lunulata: *chacha.*
type of plant-cycas: *federiku.*
type of plant-cyclosorus spp.: *chacha.*
type of plant-cynodon dactylon: *gramaderu.*
type of plant-cyperus kyllingia: *butonsiyu, cha'guan lemmai.*
type of plant-cyperus rotundus: *cha'guan Umatac.*
type of plant-davallia solida: *pugua' machena.*
type of plant-delonix regia: *atbot, atbot det fuegu.*
type of plant-derris: *bagen.*
type of plant-desmodium gangeticum: *ates aniti, tumates aniti.*

type of plant-desmodium triflorum or oxalis corniculata: *apsom.*
type of plant-desmodium umbellatum: *palaga hilitai.*
type of plant-dicranopteris linearis: *man.*
type of plant-digitaria spp.: *umok.*
type of plant-dioscorea alata: *dagu.*
type of plant-dioscorea bulbifera: *makna huegu.*
type of plant-dioscorea esculenta: *nika, nikan simarón.*
type of plant-dioscorea numularia: *dagon haya.*
type of plant-diplanthera uninervis: *cha'guan tasi.*
type of plant-discocalyx megacarpa: *ottot.*
type of plant-dodonaea viscosa: *lampuayi.*
type of plant-dolichos lablab: *cheribiyan apaka', chuchumeku.*
type of plant-donaxarundiformis: *sanban.*
type of plant-echinochloa colonum: *cha'guan agaga'.*
type of plant-eclipta alba: *títimu.*
type of plant-elaeocarpus joga: *yogga'.*
type of plant-elatostema calcarea: *tupon ayuyu.*
type of plant-elephantopus mollis: *papago' halom tano'.*
type of plant-entada: *lodosong.*
type of plant-entada pursaetha: *bayogon dankolo, gayi.*
type of plant-erythina corallodendron: *tronkon gaogao.*
type of plant-eugenia javanica: *makupa.*
type of plant-eugenia palumbis: *agate'lang.*
type of plant-eugenia reinwardtiana: *á'abang.*
type of plant-euphorbia hirta: *golondrina.*
type of plant-euphorbia neriifolia: *hilenggua i baka.*
type of plant-ficus cairica: *higos, higu.*
type of plant-ficus prolixa: *nunu.*
type of plant-ficus tinctoria: *hoda, tage'te'.*
type of plant-flagellaria indica: *bayogon halom tano'.*
type of plant-freycinetia mariannensis: *fianiti.*
type of plant-frutescens capsicum var grossum: *donne' gollai.*
type of plant-gaillardia: *gayadea.*

type of plant-geniostoma micranthum:
maholok hayu.
type of plant-geniostona micranthum:
nanasu.
type of plant-glochidion: *chosgo.*
type of plant-gomphrena globosa:
butón agaga'.
type of plant-grewia crenata: *angilao.*
type of plant-hedyotis sp.:   *paode'do'.*
type of plant-heliotropium indicum:
batbena, betbena.
type of plant-heliotropium ovalifolium:
hunek tasi.
type of plant-heritiera littoralis: *ufa.*
type of plant-hernandia sonora:
nonnak.
type of plant-hibiscus abelmoschus:
ka'mang.
type of plant-hibiscus esculentus:
okra.
type of plant-hibiscus mutabilis:
mapola.
type of plant-hibiscus rosa-sinensis:
flores rosa, guma' mela.
type of plant-hibiscus sabdariffa:
roseli.
type of plant-hibiscus tiliaceus: *pagu.*
type of plant-hippobroma longiflora:
hiteng.
type of plant-hyptis capitata: *batunes.*
type of plant-indigofera suffruticosa:
aniles.
type of plant-inocarpus fagiferus:
budu.
type of plant-ipomoea aquatica: *flores chichirika, kankong.*
type of plant-ipomoea batatas:
kamuti.
type of plant-ipomoea hederacea:
fofgo.
type of plant-ipomoea littoralis: *lagon tasi.*
type of plant-ipomoea pes-caprae:
alalak tasi.
type of plant-ipomoea tiliaefolia:
alalak.
type of plant-ipomoea tuba: *alaihai tasi.*
type of plant-iresine: *mai'ana.*
type of plant-jasminum: *hasmín.*
type of plant-jasminum sambac:
sampagita.
type of plant-jatropha curcas:
tubatuba.
type of plant-jatropha multifida:
Santa Ana.
type of plant-jussiaea suffruticosa:
títimu.
type of plant-lagenaria siceraria:

tagu'a.
type of plant-lagerstroemia:
melindres.
type of plant-lansium domesticum:
langsan.
type of plant-lawsonia intermis:
sinamomu.
type of plant-lepturus repens: *lasaga.*
type of plant-leucaena leucocephala:
tangantangan.
type of plant-limnophila fragrans:
gege sansoñan.
type of plant-limnophila indica: *gege.*
type of plant-luffa cylindrica:
pachodak.
type of plant-lumnitzera littorea:
bakauaine, nganga'.
type of plant-lycopodium phlegmaria:
Kotdon di San Fransisco.
type of plant-lygodium scandens:
alambriyu.
type of plant-macaranga thompsonii:
pengua.
type of plant-macuna gigantes: *gaye'.*
type of plant-malachra capitata:
pagagu.
type of plant-mammea odorata:
chopak.
type of plant-manihot esculenta:
mendioka.
type of plant-manilkara zapodilla:
chiku.
type of plant-maranta arundinacea:
arurú, sagu.
type of plant-maytenus thompsonii:
luluhot.
type of plant-medinilla rosea: *gafos.*
type of plant-melanolepis
multiglandulosa: *alom.*
type of plant-melastoma mariana:
gafo'.
type of plant-melia azedarach:
para'isu.
type of plant-melochia: *sayafi.*
type of plant-melochia villosissima:
atmahayan.
type of plant-melothria guamensis:
ahgaga.
type of plant-mentha arvensis: *yetbas buena.*
type of plant-merremia peltata:
lagon.
type of plant-messerschmidia argentea:
hunek.
type of plant-microsorum punctatum:
galak dálalai.
type of plant-microsorum scolopendria:
kahlao, sese.
type of plant-mirabilis jalapa:

marabiya.
type of plant-miscanthus floridulus:
nette, tupon nette.
type of plant-momordica charantia:
atmagosu.
type of plant-morinda citrifolia:
ladda.
type of plant-moringa oleifera: *katdes,*
maronggai.
type of plant-morus alba: *seda.*
type of plant-mucuna: *gaogao díkike'.*
type of plant-mucuna gigantea:
bayogon dikike', gaggao dálalai.
type of plant-mucuna gigantes:
gayetan.
type of plant-muntingia calabura:
mansanita.
type of plant-musa textilis: *ábaka.*
type of plant-mushroom: *payon*
duendes.
type of plant-nephelium: *logan.*
type of plant-nephrolepis: *amaru.*
type of plant-nervilia aragoana:
sayáihagon.
type of plant-nicotiana tabacum:
chupa.
type of plant-nipa: *nipa.*
type of plant-nopalea cochinel: *hila'*
guaka.
type of plant-ochrosia oppositifolia:
fago'.
type of plant-ocimum basilicum:
atbahakat.
type of plant-olitorea ternatea:
bukiki.
type of plant-ophioglossum pendulum:
leston.
type of plant-opuntia or nopalea
cochinelifera: *lenggua i baka.*
type of plant-oryza sativa: *fa'i.*
type of plant-pachyrrhizus erosus:
híkamas.
type of plant-pandanus fragrans:
akson.
type of plant-pangium edule: *lasret,*
raoel.
type of plant-peperomia pellucida:
pótpopot.
type of plant-peperomia spp.:   *potpot*
palao'an.
type of plant-persea americana:
alageta.
type of plant-phaseolus angularis:
monggos ayuke'.
type of plant-phaseolus mungo:
monggos.
type of plant-phaseolus sp.:   *akankang*
kalaton, fioles.
type of plant-phaseolus vulgaris:

abuchuelas.
type of plant-phragmites karka:
karisu.
type of plant-phyllanthus acidus:
ibba'.
type of plant-phyllanthus amarus:
maigo' lalo'.
type of plant-phyllanthus marianus:
tronkon gaogao uchan.
type of plant-physalis angulata:
tumates cha'ka.
type of plant-physalis lanceifolia:
tumates kaputi.
type of plant-piper betel: *pupulu.*
type of plant-piper guahamensis:
pupulon aniti.
type of plant-pisonia grandis: *ómumu.*
type of plant-pithecellobium dulce:
kamachili.
type of plant-plumeria obtusifolia:
kalachucha.
type of plant-plumeria rubra: *flores*
Mayu.
type of plant-polyscias fruticosa:
kapua.
type of plant-polyscias scutellaria:
platitos.
type of plant-portulaca oleracea:
botdo lagas.
type of plant-portulaca quadrifida:
huba det poyu.
type of plant-premna obtusifolia:
ahgao.
type of plant-pseudelophantopus
spicatus: *pápago'.*
type of plant-psidium guavaja: *abas.*
type of plant-psophocarpus
tetragonolobus: *sigidiyas.*
type of plant-psychotria mariana:
aplohkateng.
type of plant-pterocarpus indicus:
nana.
type of plant-punica granatum:
granada.
type of plant-ramalina farinacea:
yetbas bihu.
type of plant-raphanus raphanistrum:
radis.
type of plant-rhizophora: *mangle.*
type of plant-rhizophora mucronata:
mangle hembra.
type of plant-rhus taitensis: *lamahu.*
type of plant-ricinus communis:
agaliya.
type of plant-saccharum officinarum:
tupu.
type of plant-sandoricum koetjape:
santót.
type of plant-sansevieria sp.:   *tigre.*

type of plant-scaevola taccada:
nanasu.
type of plant-sechium edule: *chaioti.*
type of plant-serianthes nelsonii:
hayon lagu.
type of plant-sesamum orientale:
ahonholi.
type of plant-sesbania grandiflora:
katurai.
type of plant-sesuvium portulacastrum:
chara.
type of plant-sida spp.:   *eskobiya.*
type of plant-similar in taste to
broccoli: *kádagan.*
type of plant-solanum guamense:
birenghenas halom tano'.
type of plant-solanum lycopersicum:
tumates, tumates ubas.
type of plant-solanum melongena:
birenghenas.
type of plant-sporobolus virginicus:
hatopa.
type of plant-stictocardia tiliaefolia:
abubu.
type of plant-stizolobium: *akankang*
dankolo.
type of plant-suriana maritima:
nietkot.
type of plant-synedrella nodiflora:
cha'guan Saigón.
type of plant-tacca leontopetaloides:
gapgap.
type of plant-taeniophyllum
mariannensis: *kamuten nanoffe.*
type of plant-tamarindus indica:
kalamendo'.
type of plant-tarenna sambucina:
sumak.
type of plant-tarenna sambucina or
timonius nitidus: *sumak ladda.*
type of plant-telosma cordata: *mit*
leguas.
type of plant-teramnus labialis:
cha'guan kakaguetes.
type of plant-terminalia catappa:
talisai.
type of plant-terminalia litoralis:
talisai ganu.
type of plant-thespesia populnea:
banalu, kílulok, kilu.
type of plant-timonius nitidus:
maholok layu.
type of plant-triphasia trifolia: *lemon*
China.
type of plant-tristiropsis obtusangula:
fai'a.
type of plant-triumfetta procumbens:
masiksik hembra.
type of plant-triumfetta semitriloba:
masiksik lahi.

type of plant-typhonium cuspidatum:
paotake'.
type of plant-urena lobata: *dádangse.*
type of plant-veitchia merrillii:
pugua' China.
type of plant-vernonia cinerea:
cha'guan Santa Maria.
type of plant-vigna marina: *akankang*
manulasa.
type of plant-vitex negundo: *lagunde,*
tronkon agalonde.
type of plant-vitis vinifera: *ubas.*
type of plant-wedelia biflora:
masiksik.
type of plant-wikstroemia elliptica:
gapet atayaki.
type of plant-xanthosoma violacea:
sunen Honolulu.
type of plant-xylocarpus granatum:
lalanyok.
type of plant-zea mays: *mai'es.*
type of plant-zingiber zerumbet:
hasngot.
type of plant-Indian chrysanthemum:
yetban Santa Maria.
plaster: *emplasta.*
plastic: *plastek.*
stiff plastic: *karái.*
plasticity: *plastek.*
plate: *na'yan, platitu, platu.*
platform: *eddas, pisu, satge.*
platter: *bandeha, platón.*
play: *dimimoria, huega, hugando.*
play out: *aiutgayi.*
play up to: *ámama.*
playboy: *luhuriosu.*
plaza: *plasa.*
plea: *solisita.*
plead
plead with: *bense.*
pleasantry: *frihonada.*
please: *fan, ombre, pot fabot.*
pleasing: *agradapble, asientadu, bunita,*
interesante.
pleasure: *gusto, minagof.*
pleat: *pleges, prende.*
plebescite: *botasión, botu.*
pledge: *aras, huramento, impeña,*
prinemeti, promesa, prometi.
pledge by oath: *hula.*
plentiful: *abundante, kantidá,*
monchón.
plenty: *abundansia, bula, lahyan,*
manada, meggai, unmanada.
plenty of: *matmo.*

plexiglass: *karái, seluloit, seroroidu.*
pliable: *ñaba'.*
pliers: *alikates, penche', tinasa.*
plot: *planu.*
plover: *pulattat.*
 Pacific golden plover: *dulili.*
plow: *aladu, asada.*
 plow a row: *sutko.*
 to plow: *asada.*
pluck
 pluck (feathers): *potgue.*
plug up: *songsong.*
plugged up: *mañongsong.*
plumeria: *flores Mayu, kalachucha.*
plump: *baobao, chebot, yommok, yomsan.*
plymouth rock: *pilon dulili.*
 plymouth rock (barred): *buremos.*
plywood: *benne.*
pneumonia: *pasmo.*
pocket: *botsa.*
pocketknife: *nabaha.*
pod: *baina.*
poinciana: *atbot, atbot det fuegu.*
point: *punta, punto, tancho', tantos.*
 fine point: *akadidok.*
 point (broken): *ma'pong.*
 point at: *apunta.*
pointed
 make pointed: *lasgue.*
poison: *binenu, binenuyi, hina.*
poisoner: *bíbinenu, híhina, tátatse.*
poisonous: *binenu.*
poke: *dekka', dossok, tatnon, toyo'.*
poker
 poker chips: *tanto.*
pole: *dekka', desguas, dossok, estaka, gaole, hasta, pahlo, palu, tulos, tupak.*
 bean pole: *balas.*
police: *polisia.*
polio: *lítiku.*
polish: *na'mahlos.*
polished: *lamlam.*
polite: *respetáo, respetayon.*
 polite particle: *fan.*
political: *polítiku.*
poll: *botu.*
pollute: *na'ye, tatme.*
polluted: *nina'ye.*
pollution: *inapplacha'.*
pomade: *luga', pumada.*
pomegranate: *granada.*

pomelo: *lalangha, setlas, sitron.*
pompano: *hagi.*
pompous: *fafatta.*
poncho: *kapután, pancho.*
pond: *hagoe.*
ponderous: *makkat.*
pony: *patgon kabayu.*
poor: *chinatsaga, miche', popble, táisalape'.*
 poor (pl): *mamopble.*
 poor people: *poblekanu.*
pop: *pakpak.*
 pop off: *matgan.*
pope: *papa, Santo Papa.*
popular: *magéftungo', suena.*
population: *populasión.*
porcelain: *losa.*
porch: *baranda, kahida.*
porcupine fish: *buteten tituka'.*
pores: *maddok tátaotao.*
pork: *katnen babui.*
porous: *ngulo', tánkala.*
porpoise: *tuninos.*
porridge: *atuli.*
port: *puetto.*
portable: *chuli'on.*
porter: *katgadu.*
portion: *patte, pattida, rasion.*
portly: *chebot, yommok.*
Portuguese Man of War: *abubon pápago'.*
pose: *posa, pumós.*
 pose for: *posturayi.*
position: *attura, cho'cho', pusisión, títula.*
positive: *siguru.*
possess: *gai-.*
possible: *posipble.*
possum
 play possum: *fa'maigu'i.*
post: *estaka, estasión, ofisiu, tapbleru.*
 fence post: *haligi.*
postpone: *mahñao.*
posture: *attura, kuadra, postura.*
pot: *charera, la'uya, satten.*
 huge pot: *kalái, kalahi.*
 small pot: *katdiritu.*
pot pourri: *chamos kadu.*
pot roast: *adubáo, estufáo.*
potato: *batatas.*
 sweet potato: *kamuti.*
pouch: *puchu.*
poultice: *amot nifen, emplasto.*

poultry: *mannok.*

pound: *acha, attan, lommok, tongtong, tulongtong, tutong, tutu.*
pound (something against something): *fongfong.*
pound (weight): *libra.*
pound against: *tulongtong.*

pounder: *á'addak, tutong.*

pour: *batdeha.*
pour (liquid) out: *chuda'.*
pour briskly: *cho'me.*
pour in: *atte.*
pour out: *basia.*

pout: *muyo'.*

poverty: *misería, pinepble.*

powder: *potbos.*
gun powder: *kaiako', pótbula.*

powdery: *mangto'.*

power: *alentos, alimento, finette, fuetsa, minetgot, nina'siña, pudét.*

powerful: *fotte, míhinilat, metgot.*

powerless: *daffe'.*

pox: *betguelas.*

practicable: *na'siñayon.*

practical: *praktikát.*

practice: *praktika.*

practitioner: *praktikante.*

prairie: *sabaneta.*

praise: *aplasu, tinina.*
praise highly: *fama, tuna.*

praiseable: *famáo.*

praised
be praised: *mafama, matuna.*

praiseworthy: *tunayon.*

pratfall: *mata'chong pannas.*

pray: *fanaitai.*
pray for: *tayuyuti.*
pray to: *táyuyot.*
praying pose: *benditu.*

prayer: *tináyuyot, tinaitai.*
prayer director: *techa.*
prayer time: *orasión.*

praying mantis: *masu.*

preach
preach to: *pagat.*

preacher: *pale'.*

preachers: *mamale'.*

preaching: *pinagat.*

precarious: *piligrosu.*

precede: *fo'naigue, na'fo'na.*

precinct: *distritu.*

precious: *presiosu.*

precipice: *ladera.*

precise: *dinanche, espisifiku.*

precisely: *prifekto.*

precocious: *adilantáo.*

predacious: *tekcho'.*

predatory: *tekcho'.*

predestine: *otdena.*

predicament: *predikamento.*

predict: *adibina, predika.*

prefer: *ga'ña-, ga'-, ga'o-, na'fo'na, priferi.*

preferable: *preferable.*

pregnant: *balutan, iridáo, mañini, mambula, mapotge'.*

prejudiced: *pethudika.*

premises: *premisias.*

preoccupied
preoccupied mind: *desmurón.*

preparation: *preparasión.*

prepare: *aparehu, kuadra, pripara, proponi.*

prepared: *preparáo.*

prerequisite: *ministét.*

prerogative: *direcho.*

prescribe: *otden.*

present: *laknos, nina'i, presenta, presente, regalu.*
present (money): *chenchule'.*
present time: *presente.*

preserve
preserve food in sugar: *konsetba.*
preserve in: *prikura.*

president: *presidente.*

press: *chiget, presa.*
press (clothes with an iron): *asienta.*
press against with fingers: *yemme'.*
press down: *foyon, hoño', hokse.*
to press: *puhot.*

pressure: *hoño'.*

presume: *hallom, humallom, pine'lo.*

presumption: *pine'lo.*

pretend: *fa'-, kado', pritende.*
pretend to have: *fa'guaha.*

pretense: *eskusa.*

pretty: *atanon, bunita, bunitu, géfpa'go, gatbo, pachuchang, uges.*

prevaricate: *dagi.*

prevent: *ataha, chomma', empidi.*
prevent doing: *tane'.*

previous: *halacha, maloffan.*
previous to: *antes di.*

previously: *halacha.*

price: *presiu.*

priceless: *táipresiu.*

pride: *binanidosu.*
pride-of-barbados: *kabayeros.*

priest: *pale'*.
parish priest: *kura*.
student priest: *sasetdoti*.
priests: *mamale'*.
primary: *prinsipát*.
primer: *kattiya*.
primitive: *antigu*.
primogeniture: *primerisa*.
prince: *prinsipi*.
princess: *prinsesa*.
principal: *prinsipát*.
principally: *prinsipatmente*.
printer: *impresót*.
prints
flower prints (of cloth): *chita*.
prior
prior to: *antes di*.
prison: *kalabosu, katset, presu, tribunát*.
prisoner: *kastigáo*.
prisoner (m): *presuneru*.
privilege: *direcho, pribilehu*.
prize: *premiu*.
probable: *siña*.
probably: *guse'ña, kasi*.
probe: *imbestiga*.
prober: *imbestigadót*.
problem: *achaki, ginaddon, predikamento, problema*.
procession: *lukao*.
proclaim: *bandoñaihon, deklara, proklama*.
proclamation: *programa*.
procure: *ganye, prokura*.
produce: *na'faloffan, produkto, produsi*.
product: *finañagu, produkto*.
productive: *meppa'*.
profanity: *chátfino'*.
professional: *profesót*.
professor: *profesót*.
proffer: *ofresi*.
proficient: *kompetente, profisiente*.
profit: *ínteres, benefisiu, bentaha, ganansia, ginanna*.
profound: *didok, fehman, feman, taddong, tahdong*.
profusion: *abundansia*.
progenitor
progenitor (m): *guelo'*.
progeny: *simiya, tátatte*.
program: *huegu, programa*.
progress: *adilanta, adilanto, kinalamten, progresu*.

prohibit: *empidi, pribi, probidu, prohibi, pruibi*.
prohibited: *pribidu, pruibidu*.
prohibition: *prohibisión*.
project: *planu*.
proliferation: *sotgan*.
prolific: *meppa', sotgan, tekcha'*.
prolong: *ditieni, ekstende, na'apmam*.
promise: *ho'ye, inefresi, prinemeti, promesa, prometi, promisu*.
promote: *atbansa, sague'*.
promote in rank: *subi*.
promotion: *subida*.
prompt: *guse', listo*.
promptly: *insigidas*.
pronounce: *pronunsia*.
pronunciation: *prononsasión*.
proof: *ebidensia, espiritu, ibidensa, prueba, pruebasión*.
prop: *apoyu*.
propagate: *pupblika*.
propagated: *famta'*.
propagation: *pineksai*.
propel: *chonnek, poksai, su'on*.
propel boat: *tulos*.
propeller: *propela, toropela*.
proper: *asientadu, chumilong, kombieni, propiu*.
property: *propiedát*.
prophecy: *prófesias*.
prophesy: *adibina*.
prophet: *profeta*.
proportion: *chinilong, propotsión*.
proportionate: *chilong*.
proposal: *inefresi, mosión*.
marriage proposal: *ginitos finiho'*.
propose: *ofresi*.
proposition: *inefresi, proposisión*.
proprietor: *dueñu*.
prosecutor: *abugadu*.
prosperous: *fottuna*.
prosthesis: *postisu*.
prostitute: *laputa, puta*.
prostrate: *dilok*.
protect: *adahi, ampara, difende, guatdia, hulof, na'liheng, protehi*.
protection: *proteksión, sinague'*.
protector: *á'adahi, difensót, patrón, protektót*.
protein: *totche*.
protest: *protesta, protesta*.
Protestant: *protestante*.
protestation: *protestasión*.

protract: *ekstende.*
protruded
  protruded lips: *muyo'.*
protruding: *po'dak, potsan.*
proud: *banidosu, presonidu.*
prove: *prueba.*
proverb: *atpahon.*
provide: *na'i, na'nahong, pribeni.*
provided
  provided that: *solamente.*
province: *probensia.*
provisions: *mantensión, probensión.*
  provisions (food): *tengguang.*
proximity: *uriya.*
  in proximity: *uriya.*
prudent: *mítitanos.*
prune: *despongga.*
pruned: *ma'tot, manko.*
pry: *espeki, tupa.*
  pry loose: *gomgom, kamkam, pa'kes, so'so'.*
  pry open: *uha'.*
puberty: *sottera.*
pubic region: *mennong.*
public: *pupbliku.*
publicize: *anunsia, deklara, na'matungo', proklama, pupblika.*
pucker: *makalehlo.*
puckered
  puckered lips: *iba'.*
puckering
  puckering of lips: *iba'.*
pudding: *pudeng.*
  corn pudding: *kalamái.*
  rice pudding: *bibenka.*
puddle: *fache'.*
pudges: *fatches.*
puff: *guaife.*
puffer fish: *buteti.*
  spotted puffer fish: *buteten pento.*
pug-nose: *mafongfong.*
pull: *bátsala, batangga, halla, saggue'.*
  pull (a tooth): *tife'.*
  pull along: *arastra.*
  pull out: *bo'ok, bokbok, faidok.*
  pull seedling: *potto.*
  pull up (in a fold or folds): *heddo, limangga.*
  to pull (by the hair): *gapot.*
puller
  nail puller: *bokbok lulok.*
pulley: *licheng.*
pulpit: *pútpitu.*
pulse: *potso.*

pulverize: *lommok, na'mangto', tutu.*
pulverulent: *mangto'.*
pumice: *ñañak.*
pump: *bomba.*
pumpkin: *kalamasa.*
pumpknot: *diso'.*
punch: *dommo', faggas, paniti, punsón, seku, takos, trompada, trompunasu, tronko.*
  punch (in the face): *trukos.*
puncture: *dulok, tinekcha', tucha.*
punish: *aña, batakasu, fueges, garutasu, kastiga, lamen, yoggua.*
  punish (by burning): *yoggua.*
punishable: *kastigáo.*
punished: *baketasu.*
  be punished: *maloria.*
punishment: *kastigu, mattirio, pena.*
pup: *ga'lagitu.*
puppet: *muñeka.*
puppy: *ga'lagitu.*
purchase: *abona, bona, fahan.*
  purchase on credit: *fiha.*
purchaser: *kompradót.*
pure: *gasgas, sensiyu.*
puree: *atuli.*
purgative: *potga.*
purgatory: *potgatoriu.*
purge: *potga.*
purified: *klaru.*
purify: *na'gasgas, purifika.*
purloin
  purloin openly: *embatga.*
purple
  purple (color): *kulot lila.*
purplish: *linila.*
purpose: *hangai, minito'.*
purposely: *hasngon, propósitu.*
purse: *pottamuneda.*
  put in purse: *botsiyu.*
pursue: *dúlalak, petsigi, tattiyi.*
pursuit: *pinetsigi.*
pus: *chugo'.*
push: *chonnek, su'on.*
  push gently: *choffe.*
put: *dipusita, mamo'lo, pega, po'lo, sa'ang, sa'hang.*
  put down: *na'ha'yan.*
  put forth: *laknos.*
  put in: *dochon, sahguan, siniyi.*
  put in (something) for: *sahguani.*
  put into: *sini.*
  put on something: *hatme.*
putrefy: *lamas.*

putty: *galagala.*
puzzled: *inabak.*
pyorrhea: *fokson.*
quadrant: *kuadrante.*
quail
  painted quail: *bengbeng.*
quake: *mayengyong.*
qualification: *kualifikasión.*
qualified: *kompetente, kualifikáo.*
qualify: *kualifika.*
quality: *kualidát.*
quarantine: *kuarentena.*
quarrel: *aguaguati, buya, desgusto,
  mumu, munon pachot, plaito, resiste.*
quarry: *fanachu'an, mina.*
quarters: *kuattét.*
quay: *pantalán.*
queasy: *eskerosu.*
queen: *laraina, raina, raraina.*
queer: *estrañu.*
question: *abirigua, faisen, finaisen,
  kuestión.*
  question marker (general): *kao.*
  question word: *hafkao.*
  to question: *kuestiona.*
questionable: *duda, suspecháo.*
quick: *bibu, guse', insigidas, kalamya,
  láguse', listo, sahyao, sigidas.*
quicklime: *afok.*
quicksilver: *asugi.*
quiet: *fátkilu, kayada, ketu, pas,
  silensio.*
  be quiet: *famatkilu, kietu, pákaka'.*
  being quiet: *mamatkilu.*
  quiet down: *mapao.*
quilt: *hafyen katre, subrekama.*
quit: *basta, para.*
quitting time: *litirada.*
quiver: *chaflek, laolao, naonao.*
quota: *kuota.*
quotative marker: *hun.*
r: *eri.*
rabbit: *koneo.*
rabbit fish: *dagge', ha'tan, hiteng,
  mañahak, sesyon.*
rabies: *rabia.*
race: *achá'ikak, karera.*
  race (breed): *rasa.*
racket: *buruka.*
radiance: *mina'gas.*
radiant: *lamlam, ma'lak.*
radio: *rediu.*
radish: *radis.*

raffle: *diga, rifa.*
raft: *batsa.*
rafter: *barakilan.*
rag: *talapos.*
rail
  Guam rail (bird): *ko'ko'.*
  guard rail: *langle.*
railing: *langle, rehas.*
raiment: *chinina.*
rain: *ame', uchan.*
  blowing rain: *satpon.*
  heavy rain: *matmo.*
  rain water: *hanom sinaga.*
rainbow: *isa.*
raincoat: *kaputón, pancho.*
rainy: *cháta'an.*
  rainy season: *fanuchanan, tiempon
  uchan.*
raise: *hatsamiento, poksai.*
  about to raise: *kéhatsa.*
  pay raise: *subre.*
  raise (with pulley): *licheng.*
  raise in salary: *subi.*
  raise up: *hatsa, kahat, na'kahulo',
  tachu.*
raisins: *pasas.*
rake: *balle, eskoba, painen basula.*
ramble: *la'on.*
rampart: *muraya.*
ramrod: *baketa.*
ranch: *lancheria, lancho.*
rancher: *lancheru.*
rancid: *mahange', ransio.*
rank: *gradu, títula.*
rap: *addak, dakdak, dakot.*
rapacious: *hambrento.*
rapid: *bibu.*
rapier: *espada, sapble.*
rare: *hassan.*
rarely: *apenas, eskasu, halak, hassan.*
rascal: *kakaroti, kariteru, mahaderu,
  píkaru, pendehu, petbetso, saragatte,
  satbahi, tulisán.*
rash: *satna.*
  skin rash: *bosbos, satpuyidos.*
rat: *cha'ka, cha'kan akaleha', cha'kan
  yomson.*
rate: *kosta.*
rather
  rather than: *adimás, debet.*
ration: *pattida, rasion.*
rational: *rasonapble.*
rattle: *alapika, chalaochao, chaochao,
  dilingdeng, kalaskas, matraka,
  talaktak.*

ravage: *despetdisia.*

ravenous: *girek, gulosu.*

raw: *mata', ti masa.*

rawhide: *kueru.*

ray

  ray (from the sun): *somnak.*

  sting ray: *afula', fanihen tasi, hafula'.*

raze: *arasa, emplasta.*

razor: *nabaha.*

re

  re-: *ta'lo.*

  re- (a prefix denoting again): *agon-.*

  re-examine: *ribisa.*

reach: *fatto, hago', taka'.*

  reach for: *hagu'i.*

  reach into: *cho'cho'.*

read: *fanaitai, taitai.*

reader: *fáfanaitai, tátaitai.*

reading: *tinaitai.*

ready: *esta, listo.*

  make ready: *na'masa.*

real estate: *frinkas.*

reality: *akto, fakto.*

realize: *fanhasso, hasso, na'hasso, rialisa.*

really: *agon, guaña, ha', huguan, lá'yiyi, mismo.*

reap: *kosecha.*

rear: *tatte.*

reason: *asunto, eskusa, motibu, rasón.*

  the reason: *mina', muna'.*

reasonable: *gáihinasso, rasonapble.*

rebellion: *inatborota.*

recall: *na'mahñao.*

recede

  recede (water): *appan.*

receipt: *rinisibi, risibu.*

receivable: *agradesidu, atgradesidu, atgradesiyon.*

receive: *aksepta, miresi, risibi.*

received: *inaksepta.*

recently: *halacha, maloffan.*

reciprocal marker: *a-, afan-, umá.*

reckless: *arebatáo, bronka, bronko, deskuidáo, táihinadahi.*

recklessness: *tái'inadahi.*

reckon: *mangfong.*

recline: *asson.*

  recline on back: *to'to.*

recognizable: *konosidu.*

recognize: *tungo'.*

recommend: *rekomenda.*

recommendation: *rekomendasión.*

recompense: *inagradesi, rekompensa.*

reconcile: *komplasi, na'afa'maolek.*

record: *nota.*

  record (phonograph): *plaka.*

  record player: *funógrafu.*

recoup: *deskita.*

recover

  recover (from sickness): *homlo'.*

recovered: *magong.*

recovery: *hinemlo'.*

recreation: *dibetsión, huegu, hugando.*

rectify: *kurihi, na'dinanche, rektifika.*

rectum: *gálabok.*

red

  red (color): *agaga'.*

  red pyle game (chicken): *siamo'.*

reddish: *inagaga'.*

  reddish (color): *atagga'.*

redeem: *goggue, ridima.*

redeemed: *kahaya.*

redeemer: *satbadót.*

reduce: *ribaha.*

reduction: *rinibaha.*

reed

  reed pipe: *tubon pi'ao.*

reef: *ribentasón, rubentasón.*

reefer: *rifa.*

reek: *lammok.*

reel: *plaka.*

reenlist: *re'enggancha.*

refer: *riferi.*

  refer to: *mensiona.*

referee: *ampaia', hues, sentensiadót.*

referendum: *botu.*

referential focus marker: *-i.*

reflector: *donggat, riflekta.*

reform: *na'fañotsot, rifotma.*

reformatory: *rifotmatoriu.*

reformed: *mañotsot.*

refrain

  refrain (from an action): *mahñao.*

refresh: *na'mapao, rifresko.*

refreshment: *rinefresko.*

refrigerator: *ais baks, kahon ais.*

refuge: *liheng.*

refusal: *pinini.*

refuse: *inapplacha', re'usa, renunsia, trompesón.*

regality: *regalu.*

regardless: *maseha, sin enao.*

region: *lugát.*

register: *rehistra.*

  register book: *kanóniku.*

registration: *rehistrasión, rikohida.*
registry: *rehistrasión.*
regret: *na'fañotsot, sentimiento.*
regrettable: *ná'fañotsot.*
regular: *regulát.*
regulate: *gobietna, manea.*
regulation: *areklamento, areklo.*
regurgitate: *muta'.*
regurgitation
to cause regurgitation: *gua'gua'.*
rehearsal: *ensayu.*
reimburse: *apasi.*
reiterate: *taplong.*
reject: *re'usa, renunsia.*
rejection: *pinini.*
relate: *eksplika.*
relative: *parientes.*
relax: *deskansa, libette, na'tunas.*
relaxed: *ñaba'.*
release: *diskuti, entrega, lusu, sotta.*
released
be released: *masotta.*
relevant: *aplikáo.*
reliance: *konfiansa.*
relief: *alibiu.*
relieve: *alibia, lumámagof, remedia.*
religion: *rilihón, rilihión.*
religious: *dibotu.*
religious (m): *rilihiosu.*
relinquish: *abandona, destieru.*
rely
rely on: *angokko, dipende.*
remainder: *sopbla, sopplo, tétenan, tetenhan.*
remains: *sopbla, tétenan.*
remarkable: *atituyiyon.*
remedy: *remediu.*
to remedy: *remedia.*
remember: *hasso.*
remembrance: *memorias, rikuetdo.*
remind: *na'hasso.*
remission: *mina'ase'.*
remit: *rimiti.*
remnant: *ritasos.*
remonstrate: *protesta.*
remonstration: *protesta.*
remote: *chinago'.*
remove: *apatta, despega, na'suha, remoebi, rimotke, safu.*
remove for each other: *apula'i.*
remunerate: *apasi.*
rend: *tupa.*
render: *cho'gue.*

renew: *renueba, ribisa.*
renounce: *protesta, renunsia.*
renovate: *rifresko.*
rent: *ariendo, atkilón, atkila.*
rental: *ariendót, ariendo, atkilón.*
renter: *ariendót, atkilón.*
renunciation: *protesta.*
repair: *arekla, na'maolek.*
repairable: *atmayon.*
repairman: *á'arekla, ná'maolek.*
repeal: *diroga.*
repeat: *agonta'lo, ripiti, ta'lo, taplong.*
repeatedly: *tantos di.*
do repeatedly: *ataka.*
repent: *fañotsot, masga.*
cause to repent: *na'fañotsot.*
repentance: *sinetsot.*
repentant: *sotsot.*
repented: *mañotsot.*
replace
replace someone: *kuentayi.*
replacement
replacement for: *kuentan.*
replenish: *na'bula, rifresko.*
replica: *replika.*
reply: *kontesta, kontestasión, oppe, replika.*
report: *inánokcha', keha, ripotte.*
report on: *fa'aila', kehayi.*
repose: *deskansa, deskanso.*
represent: *representa.*
representative: *delegadu.*
reprimand: *lalatde, reprende.*
reproach: *achaka, inhuria, kritisisa.*
reprove: *lalatde.*
reptile: *tákpapa'.*
repugnant: *ti guaiyayon.*
reputation: *reputasión.*
request: *gagao, ginagao, rikuesta, solisita.*
request for permission: *faisini.*
requiem: *misan ánimas.*
require: *afuetsas, dimanda, nisisita.*
required: *afuetsáo, fuetsáo.*
rescue: *na'liheng, reskata.*
rescue from danger: *goggue.*
rescue or deliver from danger: *satba.*
rescued: *libre, liheng.*
rescuer: *satbadót.*
research
make research: *estudiayi.*
resemble: *gapi, manosge, osge, umáchuli.*

reserve: *risetba.*

reservoir
  reservoir (water): *dipositon hanom.*

residence: *risidensia.*

residential area: *lugát.*

resign: *risáin, risikna.*

resinous: *dangson.*

resist: *aguanta, resiste.*

resolution: *resolusión.*

resolve: *disidi, proponi.*

resound: *oppan.*

respect: *respeta, respetu, saludu.*

respectful: *respetáo, respetayon.*

respond: *oppe, responde, ripresta.*

response: *respondo.*

responsibility: *opbligasión, responsabilidát.*

responsible: *responsapble.*
  be responsible for: *la'mon.*
  hold responsible: *malakuenta.*

rest: *deskansa, deskanso, saga.*

restaurant: *guma' fañochuyan.*

restless: *apuráo, kamten.*

restore
  restore order: *atmayi.*

restrain: *gobietna.*
  restrain oneself: *aguanta.*

restrict: *pribi.*

restricted: *opbligáo, pribidu, pruibidu.*

restroom: *kommon.*

result: *finañagu, resutta.*
  as a result: *humuyongña.*

resurrection: *resureksión.*

retain
  retain by force: *go'te, gu'ot.*

retaliate: *deskita.*

retaliator: *benggadót.*

retard: *ditieni.*

retarded: *ba'ba', modoru, retatdo.*

retch: *uha'.*

reticulum: *mundonggo.*

retire: *ritira.*

retired: *ritiráo.*

retirement: *ritiru.*

retreat: *ritira.*
  a retreat: *fanhalluman.*

retriever: *fáfa'nu'i.*

return: *na'lo, numa'lo, ritirada, tuma'lo.*
  one who returns: *biradót.*
  return (something): *ritira.*
  return (something) borrowed: *na'na'lo.*

reveal: *baba, diskubre, na'annok, na'tungo'.*

revenge: *bengga, emmok.*
  get revenge: *deskita.*

revengeful: *benggansa.*

revenger: *benggadót.*

revenue: *aduana, apas kontribusión, réditu.*

revere: *riberensia.*

reverence: *onra, respetu, riberensia.*

reverse: *ato'.*

reversed: *mabira.*

review: *ribisa, sensura.*

revile: *inhuria.*

revise: *renueba, ribisa.*

revive: *homlo', numa'lo, remedia.*

revoke: *diroga, na'mahñao, richasa, rimati.*

revolution: *mumon linahyan, rebolusión.*

revolve: *kílulok, líkoko', líliko'.*

revolver: *pistola, rubetbet.*

revolving: *rebolusión.*

revulsion: *kalakas.*

reward: *agradesimiento, gratifikasión, inagradesi, premiu.*

rheumatism: *reuma, riuma, ruma.*

Rhode Island red: *rodo'.*

rhythm: *kompás.*

rib: *kustiyas.*

ribbon: *leston.*

ribs: *bariya.*

rice: *fa'i.*
  cooked rice: *hineksa'.*
  jungle rice: *cha'guan agaga'.*
  red rice: *hineksa' agaga'.*
  rice cake: *potu.*
  rice field: *fama'ayan, famahayan, fanfa'iyan.*
  rice pudding: *bibenka, potu.*
  rice soup: *alaguan.*
  shelled rice: *tinitu.*
  Spanish rice: *balensiana.*
  uncooked rice: *pugas.*

rich: *gófsaga, míguinaha, mespe', riku.*
  be rich of (something): *dafflok, malulok.*

riches: *guinaha, rikesa.*

rickrack: *trensiyas.*

ricochet: *rebotbida, ritachi.*

riddle: *adibina.*

ride: *ma'udai.*
  ride together: *ankas.*

rider: *máma'udai.*

ridge: *ga'tot, loma.*
  ridge (of a roof): *pipong, pupong.*

ridicule: *antula, botleha, botlehu,*
    despresia, insutta, mofa, mofeha.
    one who ridicules: *botlón, botlona.*
    ridicule (by imitating): *adda'.*

rifle: *paki.*

right: *dinanche, direcho, meti.*
    just right: *anai maolilek.*
    right (direction): *agapa'.*
    right side up: *atderecho, direcho.*
    right-handed: *agapa' fafayiña.*

righteous: *husto.*

rigid: *tisu.*

rigor: *difikuttát.*

rigorous: *atdet, rekto.*

rim: *aniyu.*
    iron rim: *yantas.*

rind: *lassas.*

ring: *aniyu, aras.*
    ring bell: *dandan, dilingdeng.*
    ring for the finger: *aniyon kannai.*

ringlet: *mulatu.*

ringworm: *gupo'.*

rinse: *ta'pang.*
    rinse (in clean water): *hinagua.*
    rinse (urine): *ta'pang.*

riot: *atborotu.*

rip: *sisi, sokkai, titek, tupa.*
    rip off: *chappak.*
    to rip off: *pappa.*

ripe: *masa.*

ripen
    make ripen: *nunok.*

rise
    sudden rise: *kinahulo'guan.*

risk: *ariesga, atotga, atrebi.*

risky: *piligro, piligrosu, riesgo.*

rites
    last rites: *biatiku.*

rival: *ribát.*

rive: *tupa.*

river: *saddok.*

rivet: *ribet, rimacha, rimachi.*

road: *chalan, katsada.*
    gravel road: *chalan kąskáo.*
    paved road: *chalan simento.*

roadblock
    set up roadblock: *futot.*

roam: *la'on, mamokkat.*

roaming: *pasiando.*

roar: *ruidu.*

roast: *adubáo.*
    pot roast: *trosu.*

rob: *sakke.*

robber: *chekle', ladrón, sakke.*

robe: *sutana, sutana.*

robust: *fotte, krisidu, la'la'.*

rock: *acho', chungat, hommon.*
    cause to rock: *chukan.*
    rock (in one's arms): *turoru.*
    type of rock: *lakte'.*
    type of rock-pumice: *ñañak.*

rockfish: *ñufo'.*

rocking: *lailai.*

rocky: *baranka, mí'acho'.*

rod: *tekkeng.*
    steel rod: *bariya.*

rogue: *fáfa'baba, kariteru, mahaderu,*
    píkaru, petbetso, saragatte, tulisán.

roll: *royu.*
    cause to roll: *na'gálilek.*
    roll (between two things): *yílulok.*
    roll on: *lálacha'.*
    roll up: *royu.*
    roll up (shorten): *heddo, limangga.*
    to roll (on the floor or ground):
        gálilek.

roller: *rora'.*
    steam roller: *pesson.*

Rome: *Roma.*

roof: *atof, atof sin, sin, techo.*
    roof frame: *atboladura.*
    roof of coconut palm: *higai.*
    roof of vehicle: *totda.*
    to roof: *afte.*

room: *apusento, kampo, kuatto.*
    make room: *na'kapát.*
    room divider: *biombo.*

roomy: *ancho, fedda', magguak.*

roost: *fanmaigu'an.*

rooster: *gayu, tandan.*

root
    root (of a plant): *hale'.*
    root crop: *dagge'.*
    root crops: *misen.*
    root out: *faidok.*
    sprout root: *manhale'.*
    take root: *fanhale'.*

rooting
    rooting (pig): *mañufa'.*

rope: *ábaka, kotdón, tali.*
    coil of rope: *madea, madeha, royon*
        tali.
    long rope: *talen moddong.*
    manila rope: *káñamu.*
    rope maker: *trabadót.*
    type of rope: *ga'pet.*

rosary: *lisayu.*

rose: *flores rosát, flores rosa, rosát.*

rot: *lamas.*

Rota: *Luta.*
  Rota island: *Rota.*
Rotanese: *Gilita.*
rotten: *lamas, potlilu.*
rough: *bastos, le'yok, makalaton.*
  rough (surface): *kalaton.*
round: *adamelong, aridondo, bes, biahi, ridondo.*
  not round: *dekabuko'.*
  round trip: *birada, buetta, dibuetta.*
  round up (animals): *éssugon.*
roundabout
  go a roundabout way: *ridondeha.*
rounds: *sigidu.*
rouse
  rouse (someone): *pangon.*
rove: *mamokkat.*
roving: *pasiando.*
row: *fila, inátattiyi, ingglera, lucha, poksai.*
  to row: *tuleti.*
royalty: *nobilidát.*
rub: *bruñi, hopyat, lampasu, palai, yílulok.*
  rub (gently): *hulos.*
  rub against: *lagas.*
  rub out: *funas.*
rubber: *goma, musigomo'.*
rubbish: *ántupa, basula, yekte'.*
  rubbish man: *basuleru.*
ruckus: *aburidu.*
rudder: *timón.*
rudder fish: *guilen puenge, guili.*
rude: *mata'pang, táilayi.*
rudeness: *táisetbe.*
rug: *atfombra.*
rugged: *bastos.*
ruin: *destrosa, disasi.*
rule: *areklamento, areklo, gobietna, ma'gasi, manda, nombra, raya.*
ruler: *maga'lahi, regla, rula.*
  ruler (for measurement): *sase'.*
rumble: *gonggong.*
rumen: *mundonggo, pansa.*
rumor: *rumót.*
rump: *dagan.*
run: *achá'ikak, malagu.*
  run (imperative): *falagu.*
  run over: *chiget.*
runner: *fáfalagu.*
rupture
  inguinal rupture: *chinada'.*
ruse: *laime, trampas.*

rush: *manugong, pinalala, tugong.*
  rush at: *sufa'.*
  rush violently: *petsan.*
Russia: *Rusia.*
rust: *take' lulok.*
rustle: *kalaskas, kaskas.*
rustling
  rustling sound: *palappa.*
rut: *karít.*
  rut (of a wheel): *rastro.*
ruthless: *kret.*
s: *esi.*
saber: *espada, sapble.*
sack: *ala, kostat, puchu, surón.*
  burlap sack: *kabán, ganggoche.*
  gunny sack: *piku.*
  small sack: *botsiyu.*
sacrament: *óstia, sakramento.*
sacred: *sagradu.*
sacrifice: *sakrifisia, sakrifisiu.*
sacrilege: *sakrilehu.*
sacristan: *sakrestan.*
sacristy: *sakristia.*
sad: *piniti, táiminagof, triste.*
sadden: *na'piniti.*
saddle: *siyan kabayu.*
sadistic: *sakat.*
sadness: *triniste.*
safe: *kaha, safo'.*
safeguarded: *libre, liheng.*
safety: *siguridát.*
sag: *iningak.*
  cause to sag: *hagom, hugom.*
sage: *méhnalom.*
sagging: *kana'.*
said: *ilék-, masangan.*
  the said: *dichu.*
sail: *la'yak, lumayak.*
sailfish: *saoara'.*
sailor: *bayineru, marinu.*
sails: *layak.*
saint: *santolón, santolona, sinantusan.*
  saint (f): *santa.*
  saint (m): *san, santo.*
saints: *santos.*
Saipan: *Saipan.*
salable: *bendiyon.*
salad: *ensalada.*
salary: *apas, suetdo.*
sale: *baratura.*
  put on sale: *na'lábaratu.*
saleable: *kori.*
salesman: *bíbende, benteru.*

saliva: *to'la'.*
salmon: *satmón.*
salon: *salón.*
saloon: *salón.*
salt: *asiga, inasigayan.*
salted: *ma'asne.*
  salted fish: *satmuera.*
  salted meat: *satmuera.*
  something salted: *inasne.*
saltern: *salinas.*
salty: *fa'et, ma'asen.*
salute: *saluda, saludu.*
salvation: *satbasión.*
salve: *hunto, ingguente.*
Samaritan: *Samaritanu.*
same: *parehu.*
  at same time: *achágigu.*
sampan: *champan.*
sample: *mostra, muestra.*
San Roque: *San Roque.*
sanctified: *sagradu.*
sanctify: *santifika.*
sanction: *sedi.*
sand: *unai.*
sandal: *chankletas, sandalias.*
sandbank: *nane'.*
sandburr: *españa.*
sandcrab: *haguhi.*
  sandcrab (generic): *haguihi.*
sanderling: *dulili.*
sandpaper: *papet aseru.*
sandpiper
  commom sandpiper: *dulili.*
  sharp-tailed sandpiper: *dulili.*
sandwich
  sandwich in: *afuyot, fuyot.*
sandy: *mí'unai.*
sap: *chugo'.*
  coconut sap: *tuba.*
sarcasm: *botlas, botleha, botlehu, despresio, kinasse.*
sarcastic: *kinasse.*
sardine: *satdinas.*
Sariguan: *Sariguan.*
sarong: *bagai.*
sashimi: *sásime'.*
sass: *responde, respondo.*
sassy: *ekpe, fresko.*
satan: *aniti, diablo, maknganiti, manganiti, satanás, Hudas.*
sated: *haspok.*
satiate: *na'haspok, singao.*
satiated: *baya', binaya', digula, empachu, haspok, malulok.*

satin: *rasu, satén.*
satisfied: *nahong, satisfecho.*
satisfy: *na'magof, na'satisfecho.*
saturate: *sumai.*
saturation: *hinatme.*
Saturday: *Sábalu.*
satyr: *garañón.*
sauce: *kaddo, satsa.*
  make sauce (hot): *fa'denne'.*
  sauce (hot): *fina'denne'.*
  sauce pan: *kaserola, la'uyan káddo.*
saucer: *platitu, tasa.*
saucy
  be saucy: *responde.*
sauntered: *laoya.*
sausage: *churisos.*
sautee: *gisa.*
savage: *malamaña, matditu, tái'ase'.*
savanna: *sabaneta.*
save: *goggue, na'libre, satba.*
saved: *kahaya, libre, liheng.*
  be saved: *masotta.*
savior: *nána'libre, sásatba, satbadót.*
savory: *gáisabot.*
saw: *chachak, chachak trumosu, sisi.*
  electric saw: *makinan chachak.*
  rip saw: *chachak mañisi.*
sawdust: *aserín.*
sawhorse: *kabayon katpenteru, kabayu.*
sawmill: *makinan chachak.*
say: *alok, ilék-, késangan, sangan, sangani.*
saying: *refran.*
scab: *latte'.*
scabbard: *baina.*
scabbed
  be scabbed: *malatte'.*
scabrous: *kalaton.*
scad
  big eye scad (mature): *haiteng.*
  big eye scad (small): *atulai.*
scaffold: *andami.*
scale: *go'naf, pesadót.*
  fish scale: *go'naf.*
  to scale: *go'naf.*
scaliness: *gusan.*
scallion: *nira'.*
scallop: *lapbla.*
scalp: *lassas ulu.*
scaly: *gofgufan.*
scamper: *hotde.*
scandal: *eskándalu, isao.*
scandalize: *eskandalisa.*

scar: *ánmaso'on, amasohan, paladan.*
scarce: *hassan.*
scarcity: *eskases, hassan.*
scare: *aminasa, espanta, fa'ñague, hongang, huppa.*
one who scares: *fáfa'ñagui.*
scarecrow: *espantahu, espanto.*
scared: *espantáo, luhan, ma'a'ñao.*
be scared: *mahongang.*
scarf: *atmadót, kotbata, pañelu, pañu, pañuelu.*
scary: *bubulao.*
scat: *sappe.*
scatter: *biba, chalapon.*
cause to scatter: *pugao.*
scatter (drops or particles): *rega.*
scattered: *direcha iskietda, machalapon.*
scattered (flock, group, etc.): *mapgao.*
scattered (in large numbers): *piesa.*
scent: *paguan, pao.*
sceptre: *setro.*
scheme: *obra, planu.*
scholar: *eskuelante, estudiante.*
scholastic: *akadémiku.*
school: *eskuela, umeskuela.*
public school: *eskuelan rai.*
school (of fish): *katdumi, salungai.*
schoolhouse: *eskuela.*
schooner: *goleta.*
scimitar: *espada, sapble.*
scion: *sinisu.*
scissors: *tieras, tiheras.*
scold: *lalatde, reprende.*
scoop
rice scoop: *paletan hineksa'.*
scorch: *tosta.*
scorched: *akong, dokngos, hinanon, kimadu, kimasón, kulakong, kumadu, kumasón.*
score: *kinahulo', tantos.*
scorpion fish: *ñufo', nufo', nufo' pabu.*
scoundrel: *brutu, mahaderu, píkaru, petbetso, tulisán.*
scour: *egues, guakse.*
scourge: *latigasu, peste, yoggua.*
scow: *champan.*
scowl: *atalaki.*
scram: *suha.*
scrap: *ántupa, trompesón.*
scrape: *egues, guasguas, guesgues, ka'guas, kaleku, pa'kes, so'so'.*
scrape (with thrusting motion): *so'so'.*
scraper: *eskrepa', guesgues, pesson.*

scratch: *guakse, ka'guas, kassas.*
scratch surface: *kaleku.*
to scratch the ground: *guahof.*
scratcher: *káka'guas.*
scrawny: *masoksok.*
scream: *gagak, kati.*
screen
to screen: *ame', choffe, lehnge.*
wire screen: *ame'.*
screened: *magéfatan.*
screw: *totniyu, totniyu.*
screw driver: *destotniyadót.*
screw pine: *aka'on, akgak, kafo', pahong.*
scribe: *eskribiente.*
scribner: *eskribiente.*
scroll: *royu.*
scrotum: *dódole', dammot.*
swollen scrotum: *pinatu.*
scrub: *bruñi, gua'guas, guakse, guesgues, hotyat.*
scrub brush: *taoase'.*
scrutinize: *eksamina, kula.*
scuffle: *mama'che'cho'.*
scum: *ñatas, espuma, pongpong, poppo.*
scythe: *tugua'.*
sea: *tasi.*
sea dog: *ga'ga' tasi.*
sea gull: *fahang.*
sea horse: *kabayon tasi.*
sea slug: *salang.*
sea urchin: *la'on.*
seabass: *gadao.*
seacoast: *uriyan tasi.*
seafood
salted seafood: *bagón.*
seal: *seyu.*
seam: *kostura, linakse.*
seamstress: *kosturera, lálakse, sastre.*
sear: *chamosga.*
search: *espia, espiha, ilao.*
search for: *aligao, buska.*
search for (something): *e-, o-.*
search in bushes: *gaddo'.*
search in woods: *gaddo'.*
seashore: *chepchop tasi, chepchop unai, kanton tasi, kosta, uriyan tasi.*
seasick: *bulachon tasi.*
seaside: *kosta, uriyan tasi.*
season: *sakkan.*
dry season: *tiempon somnak.*
hot season: *fañomnagan.*
season for: *sagu.*
wet season: *fanuchanan, tiempon uchan.*

seat: *banko, siya, ta'chong.*

seaweed
type of seaweed: *ado', chaiguan, lamot, lo'u, lumot.*

sebright
sebright (chicken): *sinisa.*

seclusion: *ánineng.*

second: *sigunda, sigundayi, sigundo.*
for a second: *naya.*
second from: *sigundon.*
second hand: *segondariu.*
second-hand: *usáo.*

secrecy: *sinikretu.*

secret: *sikretu.*

secrete: *disimula, na'atok, na'na'.*

secretive
be secretive: *fatkiluyi.*

sections: *gahu.*

secure: *gramaderu, tramoha.*

security: *inasigura, siguridát, sigurida.*

sedan: *sahyan, sidán, tumobet.*

sediment: *mohmo, pigo'.*

seduce: *tenta.*

see: *diha', kéli'e', le', li'e'.*
about to see: *kéli'e'.*
see there: *dia'.*
see-saw: *siso'.*

seed: *ba'ba', hutu, pipitas, simiya.*
seed (of pandanus): *fenso'.*

seedling: *dinekko', haigue, sapo', simiya.*

seek: *aligao, buska, espia, espiha.*

seer: *profeta.*

seesaw: *balansa.*

seine: *chenchulu.*

seize: *aresta, chule', mantieni.*

seized: *chinile'.*

seldom: *apenas, eskasu, hassan.*

select: *adapta, adopta, ayek, tancho'.*

selection: *ga'o-, inayek, sileksion.*

selective: *cha'tan.*

self
self (reflexive): *maisa.*
self-control: *hinilat maisa.*
self-opinionated: *atguyosu, otguyosu.*
self-reliance: *siguridát.*

selfish: *chattao, gake', interesáo, meskinu, otguyosu, táilayi.*

selfishness: *ínteres.*

selfless: *goftao.*

sell: *bende.*

seller: *bíbende.*

semen: *chugo'.*

seminarian: *siminariu.*

seminary: *akademia.*

senate: *senadu.*

senator: *senadót.*

send
send away: *despacha.*
send for: *agangi.*

senna: *amot tumaga'.*

sense: *sensia, siente.*
common sense: *gáisensia.*

sensible: *gáihinasso.*

sensitive: *sentidu.*

sentence: *sentensia, yoggua.*

sentiment: *sentimento, sentimiento.*

sentinel: *sentinát.*

separable: *siparáo.*

separate: *ádespatta, apatta, desapatta, desparati, na'adespatta, sipara, umádespatta.*
cause to separate: *kompatte.*
separate from: *dipatta.*

separated: *apattáo, mappa, siparáo.*

separation: *ádingu, siparasión.*
separation of liquids: *huganom.*

September: *Lumamlam, Septembre.*

sepulcher: *naftan.*

serenade: *serenata.*

serenity: *ginéfsaga.*

sergeant: *sarento.*

serious: *atdet, fehman, feman, fotmat, graba, sinseru, solemne, tahdong.*
serious look: *malaktos.*

seriousness: *fotmalidát, sinseramente.*

sermon: *pinagat, setmon.*

serpent: *setpiente.*

servant: *kriadu, mosu, muchachu, setbente, sietbo, sitbiente, tentago'.*

serve: *cho'guiyi, setbe, sietbe.*
serve (food): *na'yan.*

service: *setbisiu.*

serving: *putahi.*

sesame: *ahonholi.*

session: *sesion.*

set: *na'fata'chong, planta, po'lo.*
set aside: *fa'sahnge.*
set in between: *na'éntalo'.*
set the table: *planta i lamasa.*
set up: *planta.*

settle: *disidi, sagayi.*

seven: *siete.*

seventh: *séptimu.*

seventy: *sitenta.*
seventy-one: *sitenta i unu.*

sever: *dibidi, utot.*

several: *loskuantos, noskuantos, unos kuantos.*

severe: *addet, atdet, malaktos.*

sew: *lakse, sotse.*

sewing machine: *makinan manlakse.*

sex organ: *mennong.*
  sex organ (f): *chonchon.*

sexual intercourse: *dalle, sirek.*

shack: *palapala, sade'gani.*

shacking up: *achakma'.*

shade: *homme, lehngon, sombra.*

shaded: *nuhong.*
  shaded area: *ñehngon.*

shadow: *ánineng.*

shadowy: *nuhong.*

shady: *lehngon, nuhong.*

shaft: *latgeru.*

shaggy: *batbuda.*

shake: *chalaochao, chaochao, laolao,*
    mayengyong, yengyong, yokyok.
  shake hands: *ágo'te, ámantieni.*
  shake out: *kalankangi.*

shaking: *belembao.*

shallow: *nátata.*

sham: *kado', pritende.*

shame: *na'mamahlao.*
  shame (f): *desonra.*
  shame (m): *desonro.*

shamefaced: *mamahlao, mamalao,*
    yómahlao.

shameless: *deskaráo, saguat.*

shampoo: *luga'.*

shank: *espiniya.*

shanty: *palapala.*

shape: *fa'tinas, fotma, hechura,*
    otganisa, táhtaotao.

share: *ápatte, ankas, dibidi, kabo',*
    kompatte, patte, pattida, rasion.
  share (something): *ambos, ambros.*
  share bet: *yeba.*

sharer: *ga'chong.*

shark: *halu'u.*
  baby shark: *katsunesitu.*
  sand shark: *halu'on unai.*
  type of shark-sphyrnalewinii
    (sphyrnidae): *ulon matiyu na*
    halu'u.

sharp: *kadidok, kalaktos.*
  sharp point: *akadidok.*
  sharp-eyed: *le'an.*
  sharp-sighted: *akli'e', géfmata.*

sharpen: *lasgue, tasme.*
  to sharpen: *guasa'.*

sharpener
  sharpener (for metal tools): *guasa'on.*

sharpshooter: *potso.*

shatter: *maffak, pokka'.*

shave: *batbas.*
  shave (sideburn): *traskila.*
  shave the head: *boyo', madakngas.*

shawl: *pañelu, pañolón.*

she: *gue', guiya, ha.*

sheaf: *manohu.*

shear: *dasai, laklak.*

shearwater: *paya'ya', paya'ya'.*

sheath: *baina.*

sheep: *kinilu, obehas.*

sheer: *kanifes.*

sheet: *fundan katre, plegu.*
  bed sheet: *subrekama.*

shelf: *tapblita.*

shell: *káskara, tagong.*
  bullet shell: *kara', káskara.*
  sea shell: *koncha.*
  shell (of a coconut): *ha'iguas.*
  shotgun shell: *balan petdigón.*
  small shell: *do'gas.*
  trumpet shell: *kulo'.*
  type of shell: *karakót.*
  type of shell-cypraeidae: *cheggai.*

shelling: *kampo'.*

shelter: *ñagong, fanlihengan, guma',*
    liheng, nagong.
  to shelter: *hulof.*
  typhoon shelter: *sade'guani.*

sheltered: *liheng.*

shelve: *sa'hang.*

shepherd: *pastót.*

shield: *difende, guatdia, protehi.*
  shield from: *choffe.*
  to shield: *lehnge.*

shift: *a'go.*

shin: *kaniya, satnot.*
  hit on shinbone: *satnot.*
  shinbone: *to'lang satnot.*

shine
  shine on: *ina.*

shingle: *teha.*

shinny: *feddos.*

shiny: *lamlam.*
  very shiny: *lámlalam.*

ship: *bapót, batko, moddong.*
  small ship: *guleta.*
  to ship: *na'makatga.*

shipwrecked
  shipwrecked person: *naofragu.*

shirt: *chaleku, chinina, magagu.*

shoal: *nátata.*

shoals: *nane'.*

shoat: *balakiyu, puetkasita.*

shock: *susto.*
  electric shock: *gini'ot.*
shocked: *manghang.*
shoemaker: *sapateru.*
shoes: *sapatos.*
  small shoes: *sapatiya.*
shoestring: *godden sapatos.*
shoot: *paki.*
  shoot (of a plant): *sinisu.*
  shoot at: *flecha.*
  shoot forth: *dokko', la'chok.*
shooter: *oia'.*
  good shooter: *potso.*
  shooter (marbles): *bákulu.*
shopkeeper: *bíbende.*
shore: *kosta.*
short: *ébaba', étigu, kádada'.*
  make short: *ngisot.*
  short in length: *ngisot.*
  short time: *ratu.*
  short while: *ti apmam.*
shortage: *chatda'.*
shorten: *na'kádada', ngisot.*
shorts: *kansunsiyu.*
shotgun: *eskopeta.*
should: *debi, debidi.*
  should not: *cha'-.*
shoulder: *apaga.*
  shoulder blade: *palitiya.*
shout: *éssalao, kati.*
  shout at: *essalaogue.*
shove: *chanda, chonnek, su'on.*
shovel: *pala.*
  to shovel: *pala.*
show: *fa'nu'i, indika, manifesta.*
  show off: *ande', banidosa, banidosu, fatta.*
  show off to: *andi'i.*
  show up: *fatto, mamaila'.*
shower: *baño.*
  shower room: *fano'makan.*
  take a shower: *o'mak.*
showy: *ande', banidosa, banidosu, dudos.*
shred: *ritasos, talapos.*
shreds: *hilachas.*
shrew
  shrew (family soricidae): *cha'ka.*
shriek: *gagak.*
shrimp: *uhang.*
  type of shrimp-enoplometopus antillensis: *uhang tasi.*
shrine: *kapiya, kotpos, monumento.*
shrivel: *heddo.*

shrivers: *konfesores.*
shrubbery: *montesiyu.*
shrunk: *maheddo.*
shuffle: *balaha, chulugaigai.*
  shuffle (cards): *amara.*
shun: *laisen.*
shut: *huchom.*
  shut off: *puno'.*
  shut up: *famatkilu, ketu, silensio.*
shutter: *ohan bentana.*
shy: *mamahlao, mamalao, manachang, yómahlao.*
sibling: *che'lu.*
siblings: *mañe'lo.*
  be siblings: *fañe'lo.*
sic: *tirayi.*
sick: *malangu.*
  sick bay: *ospitát.*
sickened: *massa'.*
  sickened (from repetition): *empachu.*
sickening: *ná'malangu.*
sickle
  cut with sickle: *kamma'.*
  sickle: *kamma'.*
sickly
  sickly person: *hámlangu.*
sickness: *minalangu, sinilo'.*
  type of sickness: *dinalak, makpong, tinacho'.*
side: *banda, unbanda.*
  be at side of: *echóngñaña.*
  on the side: *unbanda.*
  side (portion of body): *kálaguak.*
  side by side: *alapát, atparehu.*
  side with: *abona, aguguiyi, alaba, lipa.*
  this side of: *magen.*
sides
  take sides: *aguguiyi.*
sieve: *kóladot.*
sieze: *aprehende, sustieni.*
sift: *kula.*
sigh: *suspiros.*
sight: *fanatan.*
sightseer: *pasiadót, pasiadora.*
sign: *fitma, señát, siñát.*
  traffic sign: *tapbleru.*
signal: *alof, señát, sikno.*
  give signal: *señas.*
signature: *fitma.*
signboard: *tapbleru.*
significant: *siknifikante.*
signification: *siknifikasión.*
signify: *siknifika.*

313

silence: *finatkilu, mamatkilu, silensio.*
silent: *fátkilu, kayada, maggem, mamatkilu, pákaka', pas.*
be silent: *famatkilu, silensio.*
silent (person): *fáfatkilu.*
silhouette: *botto, butto.*
silk: *seda.*
silk tree: *seda.*
silly: *bábaba, hafkao.*
act silly: *mama'baba.*
silly (m): *tonto.*
silver: *plata.*
silver (as a form of money): *salape'.*
silver plate: *platea.*
silverside: *giñu.*
silversmith: *plateru.*
silverware: *kubietto.*
silvery: *kulot salape', plinata na kulot.*
similar: *achaigua, kulang, parehu.*
be similar: *koresponde.*
similarly: *ombres.*
similative affix: *achá-.*
simple: *ti mappot.*
simpleton: *táitiningo'.*
simultaneous: *sumísiha.*
simultaneously: *achágigu.*
sin: *isao.*
mortal sin: *isao dankolo, isao ma'gas.*
original sin: *isao orihinat.*
venial sin: *isao ñalalang, isao dikike'.*
since: *desde, ginen.*
sincere: *feman, fiét, magahet, onesto, sinseru.*
sincerity: *sinseramente.*
sing: *kanta, lalai.*
Singapore: *Singgapót.*
singed: *kimasón, kumasón.*
singer: *kantót, kantora.*
single: *mámaisa, sensiyu.*
sink: *fama'gasiyan, fondo, labadót, mafondo, nagase', supok*
cause to sink in: *luño'.*
sink in: *makño'.*
sinker: *katgaderu, plomu.*
put sinker on: *plomuyi.*
sinner: *í'isao, gá'isao, pekadót, pikadót.*
sip: *gimen, taña', tamtam.*
sir: *señót, ton, tun.*
sire: *paireha.*
siren: *busina.*
sissy: *pachang.*
sister: *che'lu.*
sister-in-law: *kuñada.*
sisterhood: *konfradia.*

sisters: *mañe'lo.*
sit: *mata'chong.*
sit down (command): *fata'chong.*
sit down on: *fata'chohnge.*
sitar: *sítara.*
site: *sitio.*
sitting
sitting cross-legged on the floor: *ta'chong pannas.*
sitting room: *sala.*
situation: *estáo, situasión.*
six: *sais.*
sixteen: *dies i sais.*
sixty: *sisenta.*
sixty-one: *sisenta i unu.*
size: *botto, mineddong, moddong.*
sizzle: *besbes.*
skate: *afula', fanihen tasi, hafula'.*
skeleton: *kalabera, to'lang.*
sketch: *obra.*
skid: *lálacha', lagas.*
skill: *lina'mon, pinayon.*
skilled: *praktiku.*
skillet: *la'uyan manaflitu.*
skillful: *ansianu, ekspert, meyeng.*
skin: *lassas.*
irritate skin: *pago'.*
leather skin: *kueru.*
scaly skin: *gufan, gufgufan, gusan.*
skin back foreskin: *baleng, la'la', la'mok.*
to skin: *pappa.*
wrinkled skin: *makalehlo.*
skinned
be skinned: *malassas.*
skinny: *dálalai, laguas, masoksok, soksok.*
skip: *ta'yok.*
skip (with one leg): *ká'dideng.*
skipjack: *tarakitiyu, tarakitu.*
baby skipjack: *i'e'.*
large skipjack: *mamulan.*
skirt: *lupes, sukato'.*
skoal: *kampai'.*
skull: *ha'iguas, kabesa, kalabera.*
sky: *langet.*
slack: *flohu.*
slacken: *afloha, kallo, lusu, na'flohu, na'kallo.*
slacken for: *sottayi.*
slacken speed: *e'kat.*
slackening: *kayada, kayada.*
slam: *panak.*
slander: *enredos, eskándalu, fa'hiyong, kalumnia.*

slanderer: *apbladót, enredadót.*
slanderer (m): *atbladót.*
slang: *appleng.*
slant: *eggeng.*
slanted
   slanted eyes: *matan achiak.*
slap: *lapbla, padda', patmada, trompada.*
   slap at: *salibao.*
slash: *chinachak, gabbe.*
slaughterer: *matadót, mataderu.*
slaughterhouse: *guma' matansa, matansa.*
slave: *esklabu.*
slay: *puno'.*
sleep: *deskansa, deskanso, maigo'.*
   sleep walking: *pisadiya.*
sleeper
   light sleeper: *fáfakmata, fákmata.*
sleeping
   sleeping pill: *amot muna'maigo'.*
   sleeping soundly: *maffong.*
sleepless: *desbeláo.*
sleeplessness: *desbeladu.*
sleepy: *matuhok.*
sleepyhead: *dotmilón, gá'maigo'.*
sleeve: *manggas.*
slender: *dálalai.*
slice: *chinachak, dibana, ribana, saha, tasahos.*
sliced meat: *tasahos.*
slicer: *chachak, tátaga'.*
slick: *lakse', lasge'.*
slicker: *kaputón, pancho.*
slide: *lálacha', lagas, slait, soberidai', sulon.*
sliding
   sliding smoothly: *lakse'.*
slightly: *chat.*
   slightly (prefix): *chat-.*
slim: *dálalai.*
slime: *fache'.*
sling: *a'fe, atupat, faine, yotte.*
slingshot: *flecha, katupat, paken goma.*
slip: *kamisola, lagas, palaga', sulon.*
   half slip: *lupes a'paka'.*
   slip (underwear): *lipes.*
   slip away: *falaguaihon, masge', maske'.*
   slip of vine: *gias.*
slipper: *chankletas, kocha, kotcha, sandalias.*
   Japanese slipper: *yore'.*
slippers: *sapatiya.*

slippery: *fanlatu'an, lakse', lasge'.*
   slippery (surface): *palakse'.*
   slippery place: *fansuluyan.*
slit: *ngulo'.*
slob: *boddek.*
slope: *bahada, eggeng.*
sloppy: *diháo, dihada.*
slothful: *flohu, gago', paosa.*
slovenly: *diháo, dihada.*
slow: *ñateng, é'kahat, despasio, e'kat.*
   slow-witted: *átaktak, tattamudu.*
slowpoke: *bahu, paosa.*
slug: *planasos, salang, salang, sapblasos.*
   land slug: *salang, tágula.*
   sea slug: *balate'.*
sluggish: *manman.*
slumber: *deskansa, deskanso, maigo'.*
sly: *fayi, saragatte.*
smack: *planasos, sapblasos.*
small: *balaskes, bulaskes, chibe', díchicheng, díkike', hagui, pachakati.*
   small portion: *pidasitu.*
   small pox: *betguelas.*
small bell: *kampaniya.*
smaller: *menos.*
smart: *fayi, kabilosu, ménhalom, malate', tomtom.*
smash: *faggas, tiges.*
   smash flat: *pannas.*
smear: *emplasta, na'fache', palai.*
smegma: *padong.*
smell: *paguan, pao.*
   cause to smell: *ñaño'.*
   smell (something): *nginge'.*
smile
   smile (toothy): *chiche'.*
smiley: *chatgon.*
smiling: *ñangñang.*
smoke: *asu.*
   smoke cigarette: *chupa.*
   smoke out: *asgue, oddo, pohne.*
   smoke out (something): *fohne.*
   smoke stack: *chuminea.*
smoker
   heavy smoker: *chekpa.*
smoking
   act of smoking out: *pohne.*
   act of smoking out (something): *fohne.*
   smoking area: *fañupayan.*
smooth: *finu, mahlos, malulasa, na'mahlos.*
   smooth out: *hulos.*

smudge: *asu, emplasta, oddo.*

smuggle: *kontrabando, na'lifet.*

smutty: *kossos, máskara.*

snack: *merienda, mirenda, se'pe, sentada.*
  snack bar: *guma' fañochuyan.*

snag: *inkahi.*
  snag (cloth): *sokkai.*

snail: *akaleha'.*
  snail (large, land): *dengdeng.*

snake: *kolepbla, tákpapa'.*
  snake eel: *hakmang lisayu.*

snap: *kotchetes, maktos.*
  snap off: *gutos.*

snapped
  snapped off easily: *kaspa.*

snapper: *bonita, bu'a, buninas, fáfa'et, funai, kaka'ka', mafute', matan hagon, saksak sumulo', saligai, sihek, tagafen saddok, tagafi.*

snare: *ókkodu, desguas, goddas, salamanka.*

snared
  be snared: *toka.*

snatch: *ato', chule', habao, hakot.*

snatched: *chinile'.*

sneak: *kahat, kahatgue, sikat.*

sneer: *muyu'i.*

sneeze: *achom, hachem, hatcheng, humatcheng.*

sniff: *nginge'.*
  cause to sniff: *ñaño'.*
  sniff out: *énginge'.*

snob: *mata'pang.*

snooper: *bilikeru.*
  snooper (m): *embilikeru.*

snore: *lannan.*

snoring: *lossos.*

snort: *foffo.*

snot: *mukos.*

snout: *sukos.*

snow: *niebi.*

snuff box: *bayogon dankolo.*

so: *entonses, ke, o, ya.*
  so long as: *kuentat ki.*
  so many: *kuando.*
  so many times: *tantos di.*
  so much: *kuando.*
  so much of: *tantos di, tatfiét, tatfoi.*
  so much time: *tantos di.*
  so that: *kosa ki.*

soak: *sumai.*

soaked: *fotgon, masmai, sohgon.*

soap: *habon.*
  bath soap: *habon umo'mak.*
  laundry soap: *habon mama'gasi.*

soapy
  soapy (fish): *guaguas, kahao.*

soaring: *paya'ya'.*

sob: *kasao, kati, tanges.*

sociable: *atendidu, dádaña'.*

social: *sosiát.*

sock: *dommo', paniti, seku, takos, trompada, trompunasu, tronko.*
  sock (in the face): *trukos.*

socks: *meyas.*
  put socks on: *mineyas.*

sodality: *sodáliti.*

sofa: *sofá.*

soft: *ga'ma, máñaña'.*
  soft (voice): *despasio, ñangon.*
  soft-hearted: *maggem.*

softball: *bola.*

soften: *lago', na'máñaña'.*

softened: *mumáñaña'.*

soil: *edda', mayabok, odda', tano'.*
  sticky soil: *hago'.*
  watery soil: *ñohmon.*

sold: *mabende.*

soldier: *sindalu.*

sole: *úniku, mámaisa.*
  shoe sole: *suelas.*

solemn: *solemne, yini'usan.*

solicit: *rikuesta, solisita.*

solid: *enteru, metgot, sugat, táigueku.*

solidified: *mumahetok.*

solitariness: *minahalang.*

solitary: *mámaisa, táiga'chong.*

soluble: *diritiyon.*

somber: *solemne.*

sombrero: *tuhong.*

some: *palu, pumalu.*
  some time ago: *halacha.*

someone: *fulanu.*

somersault: *dilok cha'ka, sakadatche', salamanka.*

somerset: *dilok cha'ka, sakadatche'.*

sometimes: *guaha na biahi, pa'go yan ayu.*

somnambulism: *pisadiya.*

son: *ihu.*
  son of: *lahen.*
  son-in-law: *yetno.*

song: *kanta, son.*
  folk song: *kantan Chamorrita.*

soon: *ti apmam.*

sooner: *guse'ña.*

soot: *tesna.*

soothe: *riberensia, uga.*

sophisticated: *su'abi.*

soporific: *amot muna'maigo'.*

sorcerer: *á'atte, kahna.*

sorceress: *bruha.*

sore: *chetnot, hirida, irida, mama'chigo'.*
chronic sore: *ganggosu.*

sorrow: *lutu, pesadumbre, piniti, sentimiento.*

sorrowful: *ná'fañotsot.*

sort: *klasi, sattea.*

soul: *ánimas, anti.*

sounds
soft sounds: *kaskas.*

soup: *kaddo, sopas.*

sour: *apson, kákalek, ma'aksom, ná'failek.*
make sour: *na'ma'aksom.*
sour stomach: *failek.*

source: *hale'.*

sourface: *malakara.*

soursop: *laguaná.*

south: *gé'haya, háttaya, sut.*
go south: *kákaya.*
move south: *kákaya.*
south (in Saipan): *luchan.*
south (in Guam and Rota): *haya.*
way south: *yaháyaya.*

southerly: *háttaya.*

southward: *gé'haya, háttaya.*
southward movement: *kákaya.*

souvenir: *rikuetdo.*

sow: *panandera, parandela, rega, riega, satpe.*
sow (with litter): *puetka.*

sowing: *siembra.*

sown field: *siembra.*

soy sauce: *kechap.*

space: *kampo.*

spacious: *ancho, fedda'.*

spade: *espada, pala.*
to spade: *pala.*

spades: *espadas.*

Spain: *España.*

Spaniard: *Españót.*

Spanish: *Españót.*

spank: *balas, sakudi, sakutassu, saolak, sapblasos, yagai.*
spank (with a belt): *korehas.*
to spank: *ba'ba'.*

panked
be spanked: *maloria.*

spanking: *látigu, latigasu, pega ni duru, sinaolak.*

spare: *masoksok, na'libre.*
spare time: *lugát.*

spark: *chispas, estreyas.*

sparkle: *estreyas.*

sparkling: *ma'lak.*

speak: *ádingan, fino', kombetsa, kuentos, sangan, sangani.*
speak of: *mientra.*
speak to: *adingani, kuentusi.*

spear: *fisga, lansa, tokcha'.*
spear gun: *paken fisga.*
spear gun (commercial type): *paken tokcha'.*
spear gun (local made): *pachinko'.*

spearfishing: *étokcha'.*

special: *espesiát.*

specific: *espisifiku, propiu.*

speck: *chasko.*

speckled: *dondon.*

spectator: *espektadót.*

specter: *birak, plantasma, taotaomo'na.*

speculate: *atotgayi.*

speech: *lengguahi, sinangan.*
unclear speech: *ngokngok.*

speechless: *uda, udu.*

speed: *chinaddek, finalagu, sahyao.*
speed up: *apreta.*

speedy: *apretáo, apretát, sahyao.*

spell: *deletrea.*
spell out: *dilitrea.*

spend: *gasta, na'sietbe, usa.*

spender: *gastadót.*

spendthrift: *gastadót, gastadora, latga.*

sperm: *leche.*

sphere: *inadamelong.*

spherical: *adamelong.*

spice
type of spice: *kanela.*

spider: *sanye'ye'.*
large spider: *apayu'ak.*
large spider (generic): *apayuhak.*
spider shell: *toru.*

spiderweb: *tararanas.*

spill: *chuda'.*
spill (liquid): *cho'me.*

spin: *kílulok, líkoko', líliko', na'kílulok.*

spine: *espinasu.*

spinning
spinning smoothly: *paha.*

spirit: *ánimas, animu, anti, espiritu.*
evil spirit (baby talk): *bíkulo'.*

spiritual: *espirituát.*

spit: *to'la'.*
  spit at: *to'la'i.*
  spit out: *tumo'la'.*
  spit out (mouthful): *boyo', boyok, luga'.*
spittle: *to'la'.*
spittoon: *fano'la'an.*
splash: *palaspas.*
splatter: *chispas.*
spleen: *pahariya.*
splendid: *gatbo, tagahlo', tagalo'.*
splendor: *mina'lak.*
splice: *empatma, tokche.*
splint: *estiyas.*
  put on splint: *ha'fe.*
splinter: *estiyas.*
split: *ipe', ma'pe', mapga', mapta', matitek, na'adespatta, puta', sisi, tupa.*
  split (a bet): *ambos, ambros.*
  split (with an ax): *gachai, pakngas.*
  split evenly: *ápatte, dibidi.*
  split widely open: *mamuga'.*
spoiled: *baba, desabridu, deskalentáo.*
spoke: *espiga.*
  spoke (bicycle): *bariya.*
sponge: *espongha.*
sponger: *mangle.*
spook: *birak, duendes, fáfa'ñagui.*
spool: *karetiya.*
  spool of thread: *karitét.*
spoon: *kichala, kicharón, kuchala.*
  small spoon: *kucharita.*
sport: *huegu.*
spot: *chatko, mancha.*
  spot (with a light): *denke', ina.*
  weakest spot: *buena.*
spotted: *dondon, pekas, pellon, pento.*
spouse: *asagua, esposu, kasáo.*
spout
  down spout: *maktan.*
sprained: *appleng.*
spray: *satpon.*
  spray out: *bohbo.*
spread: *machalapon.*
  spread apart: *puga', sasa'.*
  spread out: *huto'.*
spring: *bo'bo', matan hanom, mueyi.*
springy: *getpan.*
sprinkle: *rega, riega, satpe, tette.*
  sprinkle (of water): *te'i.*
sprout: *dokko', la'chok, manokcha'.*
sprouting: *dinekko', lina'chok, po'dak.*
spur
  spur (of chicken): *éspolon.*

spurs
  riding spurs: *espuelas.*
spurt: *chispas.*
  spurt of liquid: *bosbos.*
sputum: *to'la'.*
spy: *espai.*
spyglass: *lagabista.*
squalid: *kuchinu.*
squander: *despetdisia, satpa.*
squandering: *despetdisiáo.*
square: *kuadráo.*
  square (carpenter's): *kuadrante.*
squash: *kalamasa.*
  large squash: *kondót.*
  long squash: *kalabasa.*
squat: *deha.*
squeaky: *chekchek.*
squeamish: *chacha', eskerosu.*
squeegee: *guesgues.*
squeeze: *fokse, fuñot, fugo', gunom, higef, hugom.*
  squeeze between fingers: *yemme'.*
  squeeze pimple: *poddak.*
  squeeze together: *si'eng.*
squeezed: *mafgo'.*
squid: *nosnos.*
squirrel fish: *cha'lak, lessok, sísi'ok, sagámilon, saksak, saksak sumulo'.*
squirt: *besbes, petsan.*
stab: *bulokbok, dulok, si'ok, sihok, sine'se', siok, tokcha'.*
stable: *estable, kabayerisa.*
stack
  stack deck: *amara.*
  stack up: *adonse, na'ápalo'po'.*
stacking
  stacking deck: *amarasión.*
staff: *baston.*
stag: *toron binadu.*
stage: *eddas.*
stagger: *kabesada, matulaihon.*
staggering: *so'on.*
stain: *chatko, mancha, na'mancha.*
stainer: *títenta, títumu.*
stairs: *gua'ot.*
stairway: *gua'ot.*
stake: *estaka.*
  stake (gambling): *parada.*
stale: *mahange'.*
  stale-smelling: *ransio.*
stalk: *kahat, kahatgue, sikat.*
  stalk of fruit: *rasimu.*
stall: *gani.*
stalwart: *metgot.*

stamina: *minetgot, nina'siña.*

stamp: *estampa, estampo', figes, seyu, tiges.*

stand
 stand (on toes): *deggo, le'yok.*
 stand in: *kuentan.*
 stand up: *tachu, tohge.*

staple
 large staple: *kasungái.*
 staple food: *agon.*

star: *estreyas, luseru, puti'on, puti'on chatanmak, puti'on chatanmak.*
 star apple: *bilembines.*

starch: *asiento, ugas.*
 bad starch: *kalapang.*
 making of starch: *ugas.*
 starch (for ironing): *átbidon.*
 type of starch: *inigas.*

starchy
 starchy food: *saibok.*

stare: *atalak.*
 stare blankly: *manman.*

starling bird: *sali.*

start: *tuka, tutuhon.*
 start motion: *kalamten.*
 start to: *keke, kumeke, mangeke-.*

startled: *mahngang, manghang.*

starvation: *ha'ilas.*

starved: *ambre.*

state: *estadu, raino, yama.*

statement: *deklarasión, sinangan.*

station: *estasión.*

stations: *estasiones.*

stative verb: *gaige.*

statue: *botto, butto, estatua, imahen, lápina.*

statuette: *estatua.*

status: *estáo, gradu.*

stay: *saga.*
 stay so long: *inapmam.*

steal: *sakke.*
 steal away: *falaguaihon.*
 steal openly: *embatga.*

stealer: *chekle', sakke.*

steam: *asu.*
 let off steam: *lipa.*

steam roller: *pesson.*

steel: *aseru, lulok.*

steep: *bokka', didok.*

steer: *nubiyu, sugon, toreti, toriyu.*
 steer (with a rudder): *timón.*
 to steer: *giha.*
 young steer: *nubiyitu.*

steerer: *timoneru.*

steering wheel: *manggo.*

stem: *kákale', kákayu, nuhot, tronko.*
 stem of fruit: *rasimu.*

step: *pasu, pokkat.*
 a long step: *inagua'.*
 step aside: *suha.*
 step on: *gatcha'.*
 step over: *adanggua', agua', lagua'.*

stepfather: *pairastro.*

stepmother: *mairastra.*

stepping stone: *fanggacha'an.*

steps: *gua'ot.*

stepson: *entinadu.*

sterile: *ba'ba', esterit, pasadu, táiminaolek.*
 sterile (f): *machora.*
 sterile male: *gueru.*

stern: *malaktos, táklalo'.*

stevedore: *katgadót.*

steward: *kamareru.*

stewardess: *kamarera, mayidoma.*

stick: *balas, hayu, pítuma, tánganu, tonnas.*
 fire stick (partly burned): *tesson.*
 match stick: *palitu.*
 stick (for stick dance): *palitu.*
 stick (used for picking): *dekka', dossok, gaole.*
 stick in: *dochon.*
 stick on: *pega.*
 stick through: *na'adotgan.*
 stick to: *chetton.*

sticker: *dádangse.*

stickerburr: *ínifok.*

sticky: *dádangse, dangson.*

stiff: *tisu.*

stifle: *chiget.*

still: *ha', sinembatgo, trabiha.*
 keep still: *kietu.*
 still water: *malinao.*
 still-hunt: *kahat, kahatgue, sikat.*

sting: *inakka'.*

stinger
 bee stinger: *títokcha'.*

stingy: *gake', mai'imot, meskinu.*

stink: *lammok, mutong, poksión.*
 stink bug: *ga'ga' mutong.*

stipend: *apas.*

stir: *batte, lehgua', yalaka'.*
 stir (liquid): *liti.*
 stir up: *na'kalamten.*
 to stir: *chalehgua'.*

stirrup: *estribu.*

stitch: *botda, lakse, puntada, sotse.*

stockings: *meyas.*
stockpile: *estiba.*
stocky: *chebot, yommok, yomsan.*
stoker: *foggoneru.*
stole: *estola.*
stomach: *estómagu, pansa, tuyan.*
stone: *acho', hali'an.*
  sling stone: *acho' atupat.*
stonefish: *ñufo'.*
stoop: *nehong.*
stooped
  stooped person: *ohlo'.*
stop: *basta, bumasta, chuga, na'para, para.*
  about to stop: *so'on.*
  stop by: *saga, sugo'.*
  stop-off: *estasión.*
stopped up: *machom.*
stopper: *songsong.*
store: *dipusita, tenda.*
storekeeper
  storekeeper (m): *tenderu.*
storm: *chubasko, hinigua, pakyo.*
stormy: *papakyo.*
story: *estoria, hemplo, pasu, sinangan.*
  story (of building): *bibenda.*
stout: *chebot, figo', loddo', metgot, yommok, yomsan.*
stove: *foggon.*
  electric stove: *foggon denke', foggon elektrisida.*
straddle: *sa'dang.*
straggle: *mama'tatte.*
straight: *tisu, tunas.*
straighten: *na'tunas.*
strain: *estira, kula.*
strainer: *kóladot, kúladot.*
strand: *hinila.*
strange: *estrañu, nuebu, sahnge.*
  look strange: *na'sangi.*
stranger: *estrangheru.*
strangle: *ñukot.*
strap: *korehas, tirante.*
  strap on: *bándera.*
stratagem: *atte, trampas.*
straw: *ngasan.*
stray
  stray (animal): *atsadu.*
strayed: *petdidu.*
streaked: *rayaó.*
stream: *saddok.*
street: *chalan, kayi, kayon.*
strength: *alentos, alimento, finette, fuetsa, minetgot, nina'siña.*
  have strength: *gáiminetgot.*

strengthen: *ánima, na'fitme.*
strengthening: *ná'brabu.*
strenuous: *atdet.*
stretch: *estira.*
stretcher: *agaliya, andas, anggariya.*
strict: *addet, atdet, estrikto, rekto.*
stride: *inagua'.*
strife: *ináguaguat.*
strike
  cause to strike: *dekkes.*
  strike down: *tugua'.*
  to strike (match): *u'os, yugi.*
string: *ensatta, godde, halon, hilu.*
  string beans: *fioles.*
stringer: *kattuchu.*
stringy: *mípilu.*
strip: *sintas.*
  strip off: *pappa.*
striped: *rayaó.*
strive: *famai'che'cho'.*
stroll: *mamokkat, pasehu, pinekkat.*
  stroll idly: *la'yao.*
strolled: *laoya.*
strong: *figo', fotte, ma'ok, mahayu, mahegat, matatnga, metgot.*
  strong (spirit): *atdet.*
  strong enough: *langak, sungon.*
strongest part: *fáfayi.*
structure: *estroktura.*
struggle: *famai'che'cho', mama'che'cho'.*
strut: *banidosu, tohne.*
  strut (f): *banidosa.*
stubborn: *águaguat, átaktak, chátilu, manatma, subetbia, tarugu.*
stuck: *chengle, chenglong.*
  stuck in throat: *ga'otgan.*
  stuck on: *oggan.*
  stuck together: *umáchetton.*
  stuck-up: *mama'ma'gas, otguyosu.*
stud: *suleras.*
  wall stud: *piderecho.*
student: *eskuelante, estudiante.*
studious: *estudiosu.*
study: *analisa, estudia, estudio.*
stuff: *hemmot.*
stuffed: *digula, paola.*
stumble: *alenken, basnak.*
  cause to stumble: *gua'deng, tolleng.*
  stumble and fall: *poddong.*
stumbled: *matompo', salamanka.*
stumbling: *so'on.*
stung
  stung by bees: *dongdong.*
stunted: *ba'ba'.*

stupefied: *mahngang.*

stupid: *á'baba', éhinasso, bábaba, bruta, loka, loku, modoru, taktamudu, tarugu, tattamudu.*

stupidity: *babarias, binaba, tonteria.*

sturdy: *figo', metgot.*

stutterer: *tattamudu.*

sty: *otdon.*

suave: *su'abi.*

subdivision: *dibisión.*

subdue: *hulat, suheta.*

subdued: *hinilat.*

subject: *suhetu.*

sublime: *gatbo, linangitan, ná'manman, tagalo'.*

submarine: *bapót lumi'of, batkon lumi'of, supmarinu.*

submerge: *ñokñok, fondo, li'of, supok.*

submerged: *mañokñok.*
  become submerged: *mafondo.*

submissive: *osgon.*

submit: *entrega.*

subordinate: *dipendiente, mámatago'.*

subsequently: *tumátatte.*

subside: *kayáo, mafondo.*

substitute: *a'go, tahgue.*
  substitute (for someone): *kuentayi.*
  substitute for: *kuenta.*

substitution
  substitution for: *kuentan.*

subtract
  subtract (mathematics): *resta.*

subtraction: *restát.*

succeeding: *sigiente.*

succession
  in succession: *sigilu.*

successive: *sigidu, sigiente.*

successively: *sigidu.*

succor: *asiste, sague', sukori, sukoru.*

such
  such as: *kalang, komu, tatkomu.*

suck: *chopchop, soppla, susu.*
  suck in (as in smoking): *soppla.*
  suck thumb: *chigando'.*

suckle: *susu.*

sudden
  sudden movement: *gotpeha.*

suddenly: *derepente, gotpe.*

sue: *keha, kehayi.*

suffer: *padesi.*
  cause to suffer: *sa'pet.*

sufferance: *indothensia.*

suffering: *chinatsaga, pinadesi.*

suffice: *basta.*

sufficient: *bastante, nahong, sufisiente.*

suffocate: *lumos, sufoka.*

suffrage: *botu.*

sugar: *asukat.*
  sugar apple: *ates.*
  sugar cane: *tupu.*
  sugar palm: *kabon Negro.*

sugary: *minames.*

suicide: *pinino' maisa'.*

suit: *aya, bestidu, saku, trahi.*

suitable: *aplikáo, apropósitu, asientadu, umaya.*

suitcase: *balakbak, balisa, katpeta, maleta.*

suitor: *nobiu, pretendiente.*

sultry
  sultry condition: *tiempon somnak.*

sum: *tanto, tutát.*
  sum up: *tutát.*

Sumatra
  black Sumatra (chicken): *kuba.*

summary: *sumaria.*

summer: *fañomnagan, tiempon somnak.*

summon: *agang, sita.*
  summon chickens: *kórorot.*

sun: *atdao.*

sunburned: *daggua.*

Sunday: *Damenggo.*

sundown: *pineddong atdao, pineddong somnak.*

sunk: *mañokñok.*
  be sunk in: *makño'.*

sunlight: *ininan atdao, somnak.*

sunny
  sunny day: *gófha'an.*

sunrise: *kinahulo' atdao.*

sunset: *lemlem taotao, minachom atdao.*

sunshine: *somnak.*

superb: *estrabiyu, gatbo, tagahlo', tagalo'.*

supercargo: *subrekatgo.*

superficial: *máma'ya.*

superfluous: *dimasiáo.*

superimpose: *gé'hilu'i.*

superior: *ma'gas, supiriót.*

superlative: *itmás.*
  superlative prefix: *ya-.*

superlatively: *maloffan.*

superstition: *chathinengge.*

supervise: *manea.*

supper: *sena.*

supplant: *suplenta.*

supplicate: *rikuesta, suplika.*

supplier: *ná'guaha.*

supplies: *mantensión, probensión.*

supply: *ábiu, na'huyungi, na'nahong, suplika.*

support: *ábiu, apoyu, asuguat, go'he, go'te, gu'ot, na'apo', na'fata'chong, oddas, sague', supotta.*

suppose: *humallom, kalumnia, suponi.*

supposed: *dipotsí.*

suppository: *hilengga, lengga, lilengga.*

suppress: *fatkiluyi, hoño'.*

suppurate: *fañugo', mañugo'.*

supreme
the Supreme Being: *Yu'us.*

sure: *asiguráo, diberas, fitme, fotte, hu'u, siguru.*

surely: *siempre, téneki, tíeneki.*

surf: *napu.*

surfeit: *manada, singao.*

surgeon: *dokto, médiku.*
surgeon fish: *guasa', hamottan, hangon, hiyok, hugupao, odda, tataga' halu'u.*

surmise: *hallom.*

surname: *apiyidu, apuyidu.*

surpass: *igi, upos.*

surpassingly: *maloffan.*

surprise: *higef.*
surprise (from changes): *lemlem.*

surprised: *manman.*

surrender
cause to surrender: *halang.*

surround: *aridedót, uriyayi.*

surrounding: *uriya.*

surveyor: *agramensót.*
surveyor (f): *agramensora.*

susceptible: *sentidu.*

suspect: *humallom, sokne, suspecha, suspechosu.*

suspend: *na'parannaihon, suspende.*
suspend (with a strap): *chanka'.*

suspender: *tirante.*

suspicion: *suspecho.*

suspicious: *suspecháo.*
be suspicious: *suspechosu.*
be suspicious of infidelity: *ekgu'i, ugo'.*

sustain: *na'apmam, sungon.*

sustenance: *nénkanno'.*

Susupe: *Susupe.*

swaddle: *balutan.*

swallow: *pañot.*
swallow (without chewing): *pañot ales.*
swallow up: *chinepchop.*
swallow whole: *galamok, kalamot.*

swallowed up: *mafondo.*

swamp: *sesonyan.*

swapper: *kombalacheru.*

swarm: *bosbos.*
swarm at: *bosbusi.*

swat
swat at: *salibao, yabbao, yalibao.*

swathe: *balutan.*

sway
cause to sway: *chukan.*

swayback: *panda.*

swaying: *belembao, lailai.*

swear: *diberas, hula.*
swear at: *chatfinu'i.*

sweat: *masahalom.*

sweater: *franela.*

sweep: *balle, lempiesa.*

sweeper: *báballe.*

sweet: *mames, minames.*

sweetheart: *kiridu, nobia, nobiu.*

sweetlips fish: *lagu.*

sweets: *dutse.*

sweetsop: *ates.*

swell: *banna, na'espongha.*
swell up: *espongha, umespongha.*

swelling: *pokpok.*
swelling (from bee sting): *bocha.*

swift: *alula.*

swiftlet: *payesyes.*

swiftness: *chinaddek, inalula.*

swim: *ñangu, nangu, o'mak.*

swindle: *digeruyi, dugeruyi, pa'las, trampasi.*

swindler: *digeru, dugeru, fáfa'baba, tramposu.*

swine: *babui.*

swing: *amaka, chukan, turoru.*
swing (hips): *chaole.*

swivel: *sárukang.*

swollen: *banna, bohbo, mambula.*

sword: *espada, sapble.*
sword fight: *chambara'.*
sword grass: *nette.*

swordfish: *saoara'.*

syllabify: *delekora.*

syllable: *sílaba.*

symbol: *símbulu.*

symbolize: *representa.*

symmetrical: *simetrikát.*
sympathizer: *konsoladót.*
sympathizing: *pinitiyiyi.*
sympathy: *inágofli'e', konsoladu, konsolasión, ma'ase'.*
symptom: *señát, siñát.*
synagogue: *sinagoga.*
synonym: *sinónimu.*
syringe: *lilengga.*
syrup: *anibat, atnibat.*
thick syrup: *tiratira.*
system: *sistema.*
systematize: *sistema.*
t: *te.*
T-shirt: *fanela, franela.*
tabernacle: *tabinákulu.*
table: *lamasa.*
set table: *sahyan.*
tablecloth: *hafyen lamasa, manteles, tampen lamasa.*
tablet
tablet (medicine): *kátsulas.*
taciturn: *fátkilu.*
tack: *atachuelas, tachuelas.*
thumb tack: *atachuelas.*
tacking: *botdo.*
tackle
tackle (for pulling): *licheng.*
tactless: *tafo'.*
taffy: *panocha.*
tag
tag (someone): *tachi.*
tag-along: *pudos.*
Taga: *Taga'.*
tail
tail of an animal: *dádalak.*
tailor: *kostureru, lálakse, sastre.*
taint: *na'ye.*
tainted: *nina'ye.*
take: *aksepta, ato', chule', embatga.*
take (someone): *konne'.*
take (something) away: *amot.*
take down: *baha'.*
take oath: *hula.*
take off (hat): *safu.*
take off for each other: *apula'i.*
take out: *laknos.*
try to take: *kéchule'.*
taken: *chinile'.*
talapia: *talapia.*
tale: *estoria, hemplo.*
tale bearer: *gotgot.*
talent: *talento.*
talk: *ádingan, kombetsa, kuentos.*
talk back: *responde.*

talk silly: *bumábaba.*
talk to: *adingani, kuentusi.*
talk too much: *fábila di chispas.*
talkative: *ñangnang, ñongñong, ga'kumuentos, mefno', pichipichi.*
tall: *lokka'.*
tall and slender: *naile.*
taller: *lámudong.*
tallow: *sebu.*
tamales
bunch of tamales: *atahu.*
tamarind: *kalamendo'.*
tambourine: *pandereta.*
tame: *manso, na'manso.*
tamp: *fongfong.*
tangerine: *kahet dikike', lalanghita.*
tangled
tangled (by twisting): *kokas.*
tangled up: *matraba.*
tank: *tanke, tanko.*
tank for: *tanken.*
tap: *grifu.*
tap (blood): *sanggra.*
tap (tree sap): *fakte.*
tap water: *hanom grifu.*
tapioca: *mendioka.*
tapping: *talaktak.*
taps
heel taps: *chapeta, tachuelas.*
tar: *atkitrán.*
tardy: *atrasáo.*
tarnished: *tinake'.*
taro: *piga', sunen Honolulu.*
taro (generic): *suni.*
type of taro: *baba', piga' palayi, sunen agaga', sunen sisonyan, sunen Hapón.*
wild taro: *papao.*
tarpon: *pulan.*
tart: *kákalek, ma'aksom.*
task: *cho'cho'.*
tassel: *espiga.*
tasseling
tasseling (corn): *manespiga.*
taste: *gusto, taña'.*
taste of: *sabót.*
tasteless: *desabridu, táisabot.*
tatter: *talapos.*
tattered: *yá'balak.*
tattle: *fa'aila', kehayi.*
tattle-tale: *fakla', sakne.*
tattoo: *tatu.*
taunt: *mofeha.*
taunter: *botlonu.*

taut
  make taut: *estirante.*
tavern: *kantina.*
taw: *oia'.*
tax: *kontribusión.*
taxable: *aduanayon.*
taxes: *aduana, apas kontribusión, réditu.*
TB: *tibi.*
tea: *cha.*
  tea leaf: *baston San Jose.*
  tea plant: *cha.*
teach: *eduka, fa'na'gue.*
teachable: *fa'na'guiyon.*
teacher: *fáfa'na'gue, ma'estro.*
teakettle: *charera.*
tear: *lago'.*
  tear (to pieces): *yaya.*
  tear off: *ette, sisi, sokkai, titek, tupa.*
tease: *akachayi, kasse, mofeha, palacha'.*
teaser: *akacha.*
teaspoon: *kucharita.*
teat: *akado'.*
teen
  teen-ager: *hobensitu.*
  teen-ager (m): *sotteritu.*
teeter-totter: *balansa, siso'.*
teeth: *nifen.*
  decayed teeth: *dumang.*
telegram: *kapble, telegrama.*
telephone: *dengua', telefón.*
telescope: *teleskopiu.*
  small telescope: *lagabista.*
television: *telebikbik.*
tell
  one who tells tales: *fakla'.*
  tell (something): *sangan, sangani.*
  tell for: *sanganiyi.*
  tell off: *na'ha'yan.*
  tell on: *faila'.*
temper
  lose temper: *sinilo'.*
  short tempered (m): *impetosu.*
  temper tantrum: *kurahi.*
temperament: *émpito, henio.*
temperamental: *empitosu.*
temperate: *regulát.*
temperature
  check temperature: *graduha.*
  take temperature: *graduha.*
temple: *sentidu, templo.*
tempo: *kompás.*
temporarily: *hiya'.*

tempt: *tenta, tienta.*
temptation: *tentasión.*
tempted: *tinienta.*
tempter: *títienta.*
ten: *dies.*
tenacious: *figo', metgot, saguat.*
tender: *dilikáo, máñaña'.*
  became tender: *mumáñaña'.*
tendon: *gugat, kustrafas.*
tennis racket: *panak tenes.*
tense: *tisu.*
tent: *ten, tento'.*
tenth: *désimu.*
tepid: *kalentadu, tíbiu.*
terminal: *plasan batkon aire.*
terminate: *tetmina.*
terminated: *makpo'.*
tern
  white tern: *chunge'.*
terrain: *tirenu.*
terrible: *teripble.*
terrified: *susto.*
territorial: *teritoriát.*
territory: *puesto, teritoriu.*
terror: *kinibatde, mina'a'ñao.*
test: *aprueba, chagi, chinagi, tamtam.*
testament: *testamento.*
testicle: *bolabola, dódole', dammot, dollan, laso'.*
  testicle (slang): *ábuni.*
testicles
  swollen testicles: *pinatu.*
testifier: *testigu.*
testify: *klaruyi, testiguyi.*
testimony: *testimoniu.*
testy: *mathenio.*
than: *kinu.*
thank
  thank God: *grasias adios.*
  thank you: *si Yu'us ma'ase'.*
thankful: *óhala.*
thankless: *ingratu, malagradesidu.*
thanks: *agradesimiento, gratifikasión.*
that: *ayu, yuhi.*
  that (demonstrative): *enao.*
that's
  that's all: *ayu ha', enao ha'.*
  that's it: *ayu ha', enao ha'.*
  that's right: *etdichu kichu.*
thatched
  thatched roof: *higai.*
the
  the (definite article): *i.*

their: -ñiha.
theirs: -ñiha.
theme: suhetu.
then: despues, entonses, pos, pues,
    tieneki.
there: gi guatu, guatu, guenao, guihi.
    over there: ayu guatu, enao guatu,
        guenao guatu, guihi guatu.
    there exists: guaha.
    there is: ayugue', eyugue', guaha, ka-.
    there is (toward addressee): énague'.
    to there: guatu guenao, guatu guihi.
thermometer: tétmomentro.
    thermometer (medical): graduha.
thermos: tetmosa.
    thermos bottle: temos.
they: ma, siha.
thick: loddo', potpot.
    thick (liquid): te'ok.
thief: chekle', ladrón, pakcha, sakke.
    thief (polite): kamten.
thigh: cháchaga', petna, pietna.
thighs
    place on thighs: sadde.
thimble: doddak.
thin: kanifes, masoksok.
thing: hinafa, pine'lo.
    thing (inanimate): kosas.
things: pumalu.
think: fanhasso, hasso.
    cause to think: na'hasso.
    think over: konsidera.
third: tetsét, tetseru.
thirst: mina'ho.
thirsty: ma'ho, ma'o.
thirteen: tresse.
thirty: trenta, trienta.
    thirty-one: trienta i unu.
this
    this (demonstrative pronoun): ini.
    this (demonstrative): este.
    this is all: este ha'.
    this is it: este ha'.
thorn: laktos, títuka'.
thorny: mítituka'.
thoroughfare: fanlugayan.
though: maskeseha.
thought: hinasso.
thoughts: hallom.
thousand
    one thousand: mit.
thread: halon, taraha.
    basting thread: hilon chotda.
    spool of thread: karetiyan hilu.
    thread (needle): hotne.

threadfin: bukadutse.
threat: aminasu, espanto.
threaten: aminasa, espanta, fa'ñague,
    hanhan, huppa, ta'an.
threatening: aminasáo.
three: tres.
thresh: tafye.
thrift: iniho'.
thrifty: manakihom, puchu, yódahi.
thrive: na'latfe'na.
throat: guetgueru.
throne: tronu.
throw: aguet, blankeha, blanko,
    daggao, yotte.
    low throw: rata.
    throw (underhand): tira.
    throw against (something): foyang.
    throw away: kéyute', yute'.
    throw down: foyong, tugua'.
    throw for: tirayi.
    throw to: tirayi.
    throw up: muta'.
thrust: chonnek, sine'se', sokkok, su'on.
    thrust in: dochon.
thumb: dáma'gas.
    thumb-sucker: chigando'.
thump: otto.
thunder: hulu, ruidu.
    roll of thunder: talangan hulu.
thunderbolt: troson lamlam.
Thursday: Huebes.
tick
    tick (insect): garapatas.
ticket: biyeti, tiket.
tickle: kadidak.
tickling: kadidak.
ticklish: kadidakon.
ticks
    full of ticks: lottot.
tide
    ebb tide: kinekuyong tasi.
    high tide: hafnot.
    incoming tide: hafno', hafnot.
    low tide: ma'te, mama'te.
tidy: aliñao.
tie
    tie down: atgoya, gramaderu, kotma.
    tie game: siobo', ti chumá'igi.
    tie on: manohu.
    tie up: godde.
    to tie: traba.
tiger: tígiri.
tight: mafñot, mafnot.
    make tight: na'lámafnot, ngisot.

tighten: *na'lámafnot.*
tighten up: *fuñot, funot.*
tile: *teha.*
till
  till soil: *gualo'.*
tilt: *dilok, ma'ngak.*
  cause to tilt: *ungak.*
tilted: *aso'.*
time: *bes, biahi, ora, ora, tétmenu,*
  tiempo.
  have time: *gáilugat.*
  long time: *kaiha.*
  the time being: *presente.*
  time required: *taka'.*
  what time: *ki ora.*
timid: *kubatde, manso, muñeru,*
  yómahlao.
timorous: *yómahlao.*
tin: *estaño, plancha, sin.*
  tin roof: *atof sin.*
tinder: *mecha.*
Tinian: *Tinian.*
tinkle: *tingteng.*
tiny: *chibe', chikitu, díchicheng, díkike'.*
  tiny part: *pidasitu.*
tip: *grates.*
tippler: *bulacheru.*
tipsy: *teles.*
tiptoe: *le'yok.*
  to tiptoe: *deggo.*
tire: *goma, rueda, taia'.*
  flat tire: *panko'.*
  rubber tire: *taia'.*
tired: *kansadu, sosongte, yayas.*
  tired (physically): *mahgef.*
titillate: *kadidak.*
title: *títula.*
titter: *chakka', chekchek.*
TNT: *dinamita.*
to: *asta, para.*
toad: *irana, kairo', tot.*
toadfish: *ñufo'.*
toast: *na'tosta, tosta.*
  toast (in drinking): *brinda, kampai'.*
toaster
  toaster (for tortillas): *kommat.*
tobacco: *chupa.*
  chewing tobacco: *amme, amaska,*
  labana.
  tobacco field: *fañupayan.*
  tobacco twist: *paliyu.*
today: *pa'go.*
toddy: *tuba.*
toe: *dáma'gas.*

toenail: *pápakes.*
together
  be together: *daña'.*
toil: *facho'cho', macho'cho'.*
toilet: *kommon.*
toilsome: *sina'pet.*
token: *prenda, rikuetdo, siñát.*
tolerance: *indothensia.*
tolerate: *sungon.*
tomato: *tumates, tumates aniti.*
  cherry tomato: *tumates kaputi,*
  tumates ubas.
tomb: *naftan.*
tombstone: *lápida.*
tome: *tomu.*
tomorrow: *agupa'.*
ton: *tinilada.*
  ton (2000 lbs.): *tonelada.*
tone: *son, tonu, tunada.*
tongs: *tinasa.*
tongue: *hula', lenggua.*
  slip of tongue: *pinalakse'guan.*
  stick tongue out at someone:
  hula'gue.
tonight: *lámo'na.*
tonsils: *tumates aga'ga'.*
too: *lokkue'.*
  have too much fun: *motgan, mutero',*
  tuhos.
  too bad: *sióganai'.*
  too much: *dalai, pinat.*
tool: *eramienta, kosas, ramienta, trastes.*
  digging tool: *kubu.*
  type of tool: *si'i.*
tools
  hand tools: *ramenta.*
tooth: *akankang, nifen.*
  broken tooth: *mafte'.*
  canine tooth: *kotniyos.*
  chipped tooth: *doffe'.*
  missing tooth: *doffe'.*
toothbrush: *guesgues nifen.*
toothpaste: *amot guesgues nifen.*
toothpick: *dekka' nifen, gue'gue'.*
top: *pongga.*
  get on top of: *ékulo'.*
  put on top of: *gé'hilu'i.*
  spinning top: *tulompo.*
topic: *asunto.*
torch: *a'ef, achón.*
  torch (usually used when fishing):
  hachón.
  torch-fishing: *sulo'.*
torment: *totmento.*

torn: *matitek.*
tornado: *rimulinu.*
torpedo: *toropidu, totpidu.*
torpid: *ti manieniente.*
tortillas: *titiyas.*
tortoise: *haggan.*
torture: *sina'pet, yoggua.*
   torture (by burning): *yoggua.*
toss: *daggao, tira, yotte.*
   toss up: *tira.*
total: *tanto, tutát.*
tote: *uma.*
toted: *maloffan.*
totter: *kabesada, laolao.*
tottering: *belu.*
touch: *pacha, siniente.*
   touch (slightly): *ette.*
   touch lightly: *ette.*
toucher: *pakcha.*
touchy: *mathenio, sentidu.*
tough: *figo', metgot, sugat.*
tour: *pasehu.*
tourist: *pasiadót, pasiadora.*
toward: *asta.*
towards
   towards (directional): *para.*
towel: *tu'aya.*
tower: *tori.*
town: *siudát, songsong.*
toy: *hugeti.*
   toy with: *hugando.*
trace: *chasko, dilitrea.*
trachoma: *bayila', puten matan Saipan.*
track: *rastreha, rastro.*
   track down: *rastreha.*
tract: *tirenu.*
   tract (of land): *distritu.*
trade: *kometsio, tulaika.*
trader: *kometsiante.*
tradition: *kustumbre, maña.*
traditional: *tradisionát.*
trail: *kayi, kayon, tattiyi.*
trailer: *trela.*
train: *kola.*
trained
   well trained: *mahayo'.*
traitor: *traidót.*
tranquil: *trankilu.*
tranquility: *ginéfsaga.*
transcend: *upos.*
transfer: *katga, loffan, transferi.*
transferred: *maloffan.*
transform: *konsagra.*

transgression: *kontradiksión.*
transitory: *fáfa'pos, ti ma'ok.*
translate: *pula', sanganiyi, translada.*
translation: *mapula'.*
translator: *intétpiti.*
transmit: *na'faloffan.*
transom: *trabisañu.*
transparent
   transparent (liquid): *nao'ao.*
transplant: *transplanta.*
transport: *katga, loffan, transpotta.*
transportation: *transpottasión.*
   means of transportation: *udai.*
transported: *maloffan.*
transubstantiation: *konsagrasión.*
trap: *ókkodu, lasu.*
   crab trap: *nasan panglao.*
   set trap: *atma.*
   trap for: *fa'lasuyi.*
trapped
   be trapped: *toka.*
   be trapped (with a snare): *goddon.*
trash: *basula, yekte'.*
   trash can: *fanyuti'an, sagan basula.*
   trash man: *basuleru.*
travel: *buetta, karera, rumbo.*
   travel over: *kubre.*
traveler: *biaheru, pasiadót, pasiadora.*
traveling: *pasiando.*
traverse: *atrabisáo.*
tray: *bandeha.*
treacherous: *traidót.*
treason: *finaila'iyi, traisión.*
treasure: *tesoru.*
treasurer: *kaheru, tresureru.*
treasury: *tresurát.*
treat: *trata.*
   treat badly: *mattrata.*
treatment: *kriansa.*
tree: *tinaitai, tronkon hayu.*
   shade tree: *mayao.*
   type of tree: *aka'on, akgak, chopak,*
     fago', gaogao díkike', hoda, hunek,
     ibba', ifek, ifet, kafo', katurai, ladda,
     mapuñao, maronggai, nunu, paipai,
     panao, pinu, tronkon mames,
     tronkon pugua'.
   type of tree-canagium odoratum:
     alangilang.
   type of tree-pandanus: *pahong.*
   type of tree-pemphis acidula: *nigas.*
trellis: *balas.*
tremble: *laolao.*
trench: *guinaddok, kannat, trenchera.*

trepang: *balate'.*
trespass: *hatme.*
tress: *akeyo', filak.*
trestle: *kabayu.*
trial: *kotte.*
triangle: *batingting, traianggo'.*
triangular: *traiangula.*
tribe: *familia.*
tribute: *tribu.*
trick: *atte, dugeruyi, enggañu, fa'baba, fina'baba, laime, salamanka, tolleng, traiduti, trampas, trampasi.*
  dirty trick: *kuchinada.*
tricked
  be tricked: *mafa'baba.*
trickery: *fáfa'baba.*
trickster: *á'atte, salamanka.*
trigger fish: *pulonnon, pulonnon lagu, pulonnon sasadu.*
  black trigger fish: *pulonnon attilong.*
trim: *batbas, dasai, labbon.*
Trinity: *Trinidát.*
trinket: *hugeti.*
trinkets: *tilentines.*
trip: *biahi, hinanao, karera, rumbo.*
  cause to trip: *gua'deng.*
  to trip: *tolleng, tompo'.*
tripe: *mundonggo.*
tripling: *tripulasión.*
tripped: *matompo', salamanka.*
  be tripped: *matohleng.*
triumph: *biktoria, fangganna.*
troop: *tropa.*
tropic bird: *chunge'.*
  tropic bird: *chunge'.*
tropics: *tano' maipe.*
trot: *pares.*
trouble: *achaki, atborotu, enkebukáo, estraña, molestia, plaito, yanto, yinaoyao.*
troublemaker: *áchibao, akacha, buskaplaiteru, buskaplaito, kombateru, palacha'.*
troublesome: *akacha, atborutáo, enkebukáo, palacha', yinaoyao.*
troublesomeness: *atborotu.*
trough: *kanoa, tappe'.*
trousers: *katsunes.*
trowel: *paleta.*
truant: *fattista.*
truck: *trak.*
true: *fiét, klaru, magahet.*
truly: *anes, guaña.*

trumpet: *kotneta.*
trumpet fish: *ba'yak.*
truncate: *destronka.*
trunk: *ba'út, tronko.*
trunkfish: *danglon.*
trust: *angokko, apela, dipende, embatga, hongge, konfiansa.*
trustful: *angokkuyon.*
trustworthy: *angokkuyon.*
truth: *minagahet.*
truthful: *angokkuyon, franko, magahet, onesto, táidinakon.*
try: *chagi, na'késiña.*
  to try: *kotte.*
  try (for first time): *estrena.*
  try out: *tamtam.*
  try to: *keke, kumeke, mangeke-.*
  try to do (something): *ke-.*
tub: *katderu, tap, tarái'.*
tubercular: *tibi.*
tuberculosis: *soksok, tibi.*
tuberose: *asusena, flores asusena.*
tuck: *heddo, limangga.*
  tuck in: *chiget, pekke.*
Tuesday: *Mattes.*
tug: *halla, saggue'.*
tumbler: *basu.*
tumult: *ira.*
tuna: *mákaro', maguro', tuna.*
  large tuna: *daibang.*
  tuna (blue): *kacho'.*
  tuna (white): *kacho', bunitu.*
tune: *sotfa, tonu, tunada.*
  tune (engine): *templa.*
tuning: *templada.*
tunnel: *adotgan, bókugo'.*
turbulent: *guaifon.*
turkey: *pabu.*
turkey fish: *nufo' pabu.*
turmeric: *mango'.*
turn: *bira, tarabira, totno, tutno.*
  one who turns: *biradót.*
  turn (as a screw): *totniyu.*
  turn around: *mabira.*
  turn down: *ribaha.*
  turn inside out: *guakse.*
  turn into (prefix): *mama'-.*
  turn off: *puno'.*
  turn on: *na'la'la'.*
  turn over: *puha.*
  turn over again: *tarabira.*
turnabout: *bira.*
turnip: *daigo', daikon, rabanos, takuán.*
turnover: *pastet.*
  turnover (pastry): *buchibuchi.*

turnstone: *dulili.*
turtle: *haggan.*
turtle dove: *paluman sinisa.*
tusk: *kotniyos.*
tweak: *de'on.*
   tweak (by the ear): *atilek.*
tweezer: *chiget.*
tweezers: *pincho, tinasa.*
twelve: *dosse.*
twenty: *bente.*
   twenty-one: *bente i unu.*
twig: *balas, ramas.*
twilight: *lemlem taotao.*
twin: *dinga'.*
twine: *hilu.*
   ball of twine: *madea.*
twinkle: *chalamlam, señas.*
   twinkle of light: *donggat.*
twinkling: *donggat.*
twirl: *rimulinu.*
twirling: *belemba.*
twist: *chaflalak, tahlek.*
   twist (rope): *traba.*
   twist (something): *chaflilek.*
twisted: *ákaleng, matahlek.*
twitch: *chaflek.*
two: *dos.*
twofold: *dopble.*
type: *klasi.*
typewriter: *makinan mangge'.*
typhoon: *pakyo.*
   typhoon condition: *papakyo.*
typical: *regulát.*
u: *u.*
ugly: *chátpa'go, chura.*
ultimate: *uttimo.*
ultimately: *alosuttimo, gi úttimo, pot uttimo.*
umbrella: *payu.*
umpire: *ampaia', hues.*
unadulterated: *sinseru.*
unafraid: *mesge'.*
unbelievable: *ná'manman.*
unbend: *na'tunas.*
unbound: *suetto.*
unchanging: *táikinalamten.*
uncivil: *mata'pang.*
uncle: *tihu.*
unclean: *ápplacha', deskaráo.*
unconcerned: *fatani.*
unconscious: *lálangu, mamaitaguan, tisu.*
uncooked: *mata', ti masa.*

unction: *ólios.*
   extreme unction: *santos olios.*
undecided: *atarantáo.*
under: *bahu.*
underline: *raya.*
undermine: *sekpapa'i.*
underneath
   put underneath: *gé'papa'i.*
undershirt: *chaleku, franela.*
   baby's undershirt: *kamisita.*
undershorts: *kansunsiyu.*
   undershorts (for males): *katsunsiyu.*
underskirt: *kamisola, lipes.*
understand: *komprende.*
understandable: *komprendiyon.*
underwear
   underwear (f): *katsunes.*
undisturbed: *trankilu.*
undulation: *dansa.*
unearth
   to unearth: *guahi.*
uneasy: *massa'.*
unfairness: *dugeria.*
unfaithful: *traidót.*
unfathomable: *desfonda.*
unfeigned: *sinseru.*
unfertile: *pasadu.*
unfinished: *tétenan.*
unfit: *inutet, táiguailayi.*
unfold: *huto'.*
unfriendly: *presemida, táilayi.*
ungrateful: *ingratu, malagradesidu.*
unhampered: *dafflok, malulok.*
unhappiness: *triniste.*
unharness: *na'tunas.*
unheedful: *átaktak.*
unicorn fish: *tátaga'.*
uniform: *chilong, unifotme.*
uninhabited: *disetto.*
uninjured: *táichetnot.*
unintelligent: *lolu.*
uninteresting: *mata'pang.*
unique: *úniku, espesiát, táiparehu.*
unite: *fanetnon.*
united: *daña'.*
university: *unibetsiha.*
unlearned: *iknorante.*
unless: *solamente, solu.*
unlettered: *iknorante.*
unload: *deskasa, deskatga, diskatga.*
   unload (weapon): *deskata.*
unmindful: *átaktak.*
unnatural: *subrenaturát.*

unobtrusive: *yómahlao.*
unoccupied: *anokupáo, bakante.*
unpleasant: *chátpa'go, chura.*
unprepared: *despribináo, despribinidu.*
unproductive: *cha ttano'.*
unquestionably: *etdichu.*
unreal: *fatso.*
unripe: *chátmasa.*
unroll: *baba.*
unroof
  unroof (a house): *desafte.*
unruly: *ti gobietnayon.*
unsaddle: *desaparehu.*
unsavory: *desabridu.*
unselfish: *geftao, goftao.*
unserviceable: *inutet.*
unsoiled: *gasgas.*
unstained: *táimancha.*
unsymmetrical: *dekabuko'.*
untamed: *machalek, matditu.*
untidy: *desarekladu, kala'u.*
untie: *lusu, pula'.*
until: *asta, asta ki.*
  until when: *asta ngai'an.*
untrammeled: *dafflok, malulok.*
untruthfulness: *dinagi.*
untutored: *iknorante.*
unusual: *estrañu, sahnge.*
unwrap: *pula', pulakes.*
up: *hulo'.*
  further up: *gé'hilo'.*
  go up: *kókkolo'.*
  up to: *asta.*
  up to (someone): *la'mon.*
  way up: *yahúlulo'.*
upgrade
  upgrade in rank: *subi.*
uplift: *atbola.*
upright: *husto, tumachu, tunas.*
uprising: *inatborota, mumon linahyan.*
uproar: *atborotu.*
uproot: *bo'ok, bokbok, halle'.*
  uproot (weeds): *ha'lak.*
  uproot seedling: *potto.*
upset: *atborota.*
upside-down: *átlibes.*
upward: *gé'hilo'.*
urge: *bense, eppok, insiste, petdika.*
  urge on: *guse'.*
urgent: *prisisu.*
urinal: *bátadot, fanme'miyan, na'yan me'me'.*
urinate: *me'me'.*
  need to urinate: *ma'empon.*

  place to urinate: *fanme'miyan.*
  urinate on: *me'i.*
urine: *me'me'.*
  smell of urine: *paosadang.*
urn: *pasu.*
us: *-mami, ham, hit.*
  us (emphatic, inclusive): *hita.*
  us (possessive, inclusive): *-ta.*
usable: *usáo.*
use: *aprobecha, na'setbe, na'sietbe, usa, yuma.*
  use (for first time): *estrena.*
  use sparingly: *uho'.*
  use up: *gasta.*
used: *usáo.*
  get used to: *ápayuni.*
  used to: *payon.*
  used to be: *estaba.*
useful: *kómodu.*
useless: *táibali, táiguailayi.*
usual: *otdinariu, payon, regulatmente.*
usually: *kada ratu, tatde ti, tenga.*
utilization: *aplikasión.*
utilize: *na'sietbe, usa.*
utter: *ádingan, ekspresia, kuentos, sangan, sangani.*
utterance
  soft utterance: *ñangon.*
uvula: *gatganta.*
vacant: *bakante.*
vacation: *bakasión.*
vaccinate: *bakuna.*
vaccination: *bakuna.*
vagabond: *bagamondo, bagu.*
vagina: *bebe', dódole', iyon palao'an.*
  vagina (slang): *chada', cheggai pápaguan.*
vale: *bayi.*
valiant: *animosu.*
valise: *balisa.*
valley: *kañada.*
valor: *minatatnga.*
valorous: *animosu.*
valuable: *presiosu.*
value: *agradesi, bali, presiu.*
valve: *bukiya.*
vanished: *malingu.*
vanity: *banidát.*
vanquish: *a'ñao, igi.*
variable: *a'guyon, bariapble.*
variation: *diferensia, tinilaika.*
variety: *klasi.*
various: *diferentes.*

varnish: *banes, batnís.*
vase: *floreru.*
vast: *taiche'.*
vat: *kalahi.*
vegetable: *gollai.*
vehicle: *kareta, sidán, trak, tumobet.*
  small vehicle: *sahyan.*
veil: *belu, panelón.*
vein: *gugat.*
vend: *bende.*
vendable: *bendiyon.*
veneration: *respetu.*
venereal disease: *enkotdio, suki.*
vengeful: *benggansa, benggatibu,*
  embidia.
venomous: *binenu.*
ventilate: *aire, goia, gueha.*
  ventilate manually: *bohao.*
ventilated: *guinaife.*
venture: *atotga, atrebi, bentura.*
venturesome: *bátbaru.*
venturous: *atotgante.*
veranda: *baranda, kahida.*
verbalizer: *-um-.*
verbose: *ga'kumuentos.*
verdict: *huisio.*
verify: *aprueba.*
vermin: *ga'ga'.*
verruca: *du'an, du'an nanaso'.*
verse: *betso.*
versed: *profisiente.*
vertical: *tumachu.*
very: *era, gof, ha', mampos, mismo, sen.*
  the very: *dichu.*
vesper: *béspira.*
vest: *chaleku.*
vestibule: *antikamara.*
vestment: *silisiu, sutana.*
vestry: *sakristia.*
veteran: *beteranu.*
vex: *akachayi, atborota, estotba, guahi,*
  kasse, na'bubu.
  to vex: *gapi, guafi.*
vexation: *cháthinallom, estotbo,*
  linalalo'.
vial: *fraskitu.*
vibrate: *laolao, yengyong.*
vibration
  vibration (caused by loud noise):
  ritumbo.
vice: *bisio, isao.*
vicinity: *bisinu, uriya.*
vicious: *bisiosu, daddao.*

vicissitude: *ginaddon.*
victim: *biktima, iridáo.*
victorious: *biktoriosu.*
victory: *biktoria, fangganna, ginanna.*
view: *na'annok.*
vigil: *béspira, bela.*
  keep vigil: *mamulan.*
vigorous: *la'la'.*
vigorously: *duru.*
village: *songsong.*
villain: *pikatdiha.*
villainy: *pikatdiha.*
vine: *cha'guan, cheribiyan apaka',*
  chuchumeku, kákale'.
  crawling vine: *flores kunanaf.*
  type of vine: *akankang, botdo lagas,*
  chaioti, kulales, lodosong, lodosong
  tasi, luluhot, mai'agas, nietkot, nupi.
vinegar: *binakle.*
viola: *biola.*
violation: *isao, kontradiksión.*
violetish: *bineleta.*
violin: *labbet.*
virgin: *bithen, donseya.*
virtue: *bittot.*
virtuous: *bitu'osu, táibisio.*
visible: *li'e'on.*
visit: *bisita, fattoigue.*
  visit briefly: *sugo'.*
  visit excessively: *silok.*
visitor: *bisita.*
vital: *impottante.*
  vital organs: *munidensia.*
vitamins: *baitamina.*
vivacious: *aktibu, la'la'.*
vocalist
  vocalist (f):   *kantora.*
  vocalist (m):   *kantót.*
voice: *bos.*
  changing voice: *ñedok.*
  husky voice: *afagao.*
void: *nulu.*
volcanic: *botkán, botkanu.*
volcano: *botkán, botkanu.*
voluble: *pinalakse'.*
volume: *ñangon, tomu.*
voluntarily: *bulontariamente.*
voluntary: *bulontát, bulontariu.*
volunteer: *bulontariu.*
vomit: *muta'.*
  cause to vomit: *gue'gue'.*
vote: *bota, botu.*
  vote for: *bota.*

voting ticket: *balotu.*

vow: *hula, huramento, prinemeti, promesa, prometi.*

voyage: *biahi, hinanao, karera, rumbo.*

voyager: *biaheru.*

voyeur: *nge'lo'.*

wad: *hemmot, yilulok.*

wag
  wag (tail): *chaole.*

wage: *apas, suetdo.*

wager: *aposta, parada, tatos.*

wagon: *karetón.*

wahoo: *uahu.*

waist: *sintura.*

waistband: *faha, pretina.*

waistcoat: *chaleku.*

waistline: *sintura.*

wait: *nangga, nenggue.*
  cause to wait: *fa' i ninok, faininok.*
  wait-a-bit: *pakao.*

waiter: *kamareru.*

waitress: *kamarera.*

wake: *bela, pahngon.*
  to wake (someone) up: *pangon.*
  wake (of a ship): *rastro.*
  wake up: *fakmata, makmata, pahngon, ya'ho.*
  wake up (late): *ba'an.*

wakefulness: *desbeladu.*

waken: *makmata.*

waking up: *kinahulo'.*

walk: *channo, lahu, mamokkat, pinekkat.*
  walk (command): *famokkat.*
  walk fast: *énsahi.*

walking
  walking briskly: *essinahyao, insinahyao.*
  walking stick: *apahigai.*

wall: *liga, luga.*

wallet: *katpeta, pottamuneda.*

wallop: *planasos, sapblasos, yagai.*

wallow: *chukan, fanfachi'an.*

waltz: *batso.*

wan: *boksion.*

wander: *la'on, lailai.*
  wander around: *pasehu.*

wanderer: *piligrinu.*
  wanderer (f) : *pasiadora.*
  wanderer (m) : *pasiadót.*

want: *diseha, malago', nisisita.*

war: *bataya, batiya, gera.*

wardrobe
  clothes wardrobe: *aparadót.*

warehouse: *dipósitu.*

wares: *fektos.*

warm: *kalentadu, tíbiu.*
  make warm: *ha'me.*
  warm liquid: *tébiu.*
  warm up: *na'maipe.*

warn: *akonseha.*

warning: *abisa, amonestasión.*

warrior: *gereru, sindalu.*

warship: *batkon gera.*

wart: *du'an, du'an nanaso'.*

was: *estaba.*

wash: *fa'gasi.*
  wash (by rubbing): *hopyat.*
  wash (with soap): *habuni.*
  wash basin: *fama'gasiyan, mama'gasiyan.*
  wash out: *hinagua.*
  wash surface: *batdeha.*

washboard: *batehan mama'gasi.*

washer: *chapeta, fa'gas.*
  washer (metal): *arandela.*

washpan: *palanggana.*

washtub: *bateha.*

wasp: *gonggong.*

waste: *despetdisia, despetdisio, gasta, ginasta, lástima, na'lástima, táibali, trompesón.*

wasteful: *despetdisiáo.*

watch: *egga', li'e', relós.*
  watch out: *adahi, kuidáo.*
  watch over: *esgaihon, mamulan, pulan.*

watcher: *guatdia.*

water: *agua, chepchop tasi, hanom.*
  calm water: *malinao.*
  deep water: *mattinan, rubentasón, sahagu.*
  rough water: *chaochao, langat.*
  shallow water: *salasa.*
  to dip water in bucket: *lupok.*
  water supply: *aguada.*

waterhole: *banaderu.*

watering hole: *fanggiminan.*

watermelon: *chandia.*

watery: *fotgon, hinanom, kinilak, masmai.*
  become watery: *aguahnon, aguanon, guahnom.*

wave: *napu.*
  big wave: *langat.*
  receding wave: *risaki.*
  wave action: *salida.*
  wave away: *salibao, yabbao.*
  wave goodby: *ayu'os.*

waver
  cause to waver: *chukan.*
wavering: *dansa.*
wax: *danges.*
waxing: *sahi.*
way: *manera, modu.*
  long way: *kaiha.*
we: *ham, hami, hit, hita, in.*
  we (inclusive): *ta.*
weak: *ñama', chekka', daffe', daife',
  dangnge', dolle, pachakati, pedde.*
  weak-hearted: *kokañao.*
weakened: *mamaitaguan, mumáñaña',
  yafai.*
  weakened (person): *mayaye', patot.*
weakling: *dangnge', dolle, pachang,
  pedde.*
weal: *diso', pili'ao.*
wealth: *guinaha, rikesa.*
wealthy: *fottuna, géfsaga, gófsaga,
  míguinaha, riku.*
wean: *gunos.*
weapon: *atmas.*
wear
  wear out: *gasta.*
weariness: *afatigáo, fatigáo.*
weary: *ñañas, mahgef, yayas.*
weather: *tiempo.*
  good weather: *gófha'an.*
weave: *filak, mamfok, tufok.*
weaver: *fáfamfok, mámamfok, títufok.*
web
  spider web: *tararañas.*
webbing: *tinifok.*
wed: *ásagua, umákkamo', umásagua.*
wedding: *kasamiento.*
  wedding celebration: *fandanggo.*
  wedding party: *komplimentu.*
  wedding ring: *aras.*
wedlock: *matrimoniu.*
Wednesday: *Metkoles.*
weed: *cha'guan.*
  to weed: *ha'lak.*
  weed out (grass): *ripasa.*
weeding: *ripasa.*
week: *pa'go na simana, simana.*
  coming week: *mamamaila' na
  simana.*
  last week: *ma'pos na simana.*
  next week: *otro na simana.*
  week after next: *otroña na simana.*
  week before last: *ma'posña na
  simana.*
weep: *kasao, kati, tanges.*
  weep for: *katiyi, tangse.*

weigh: *pesa.*
  weigh (by lifting): *tanteha.*
  weigh (using the hand): *tahlang.*
weight: *minakkat, pesada.*
  estimate weight: *tahlang.*
weighty: *makkat.*
welcome: *bien binidu, buen binidu,
  saluda.*
weld: *sotda.*
welding
  welding machine: *makinan mañotda.*
well: *ke, maolek, tupo'.*
  as well: *ombres.*
  be well-known: *mafama.*
  be well-liked: *mafama.*
  become well: *mumaolek.*
  well then: *entonses, pues po'lo.*
  well-disposed: *faborapble.*
welt: *diso', pili'ao.*
went: *ma'pos.*
west: *gé'lichan, háttichan.*
  go west: *dódichan, lódichan.*
  move west: *lódichan.*
  way west: *yalúchachan.*
  west (in Saipan): *lagu.*
  west (in Guam and Rota): *luchan.*
westerly: *gé'lichan, háttichan.*
westward: *gé'lichan, háttichan.*
  westward movement: *lódichan.*
wet: *fotgon, masmai, masmas.*
whack
  whack at: *salibao, yabbao, yalibao.*
whale: *bayena.*
whaler: *bayineru.*
whales: *salungai.*
wharf: *pantalán.*
what: *ha, hafa.*
  for what: *pot hafa.*
  what for: *para hafa, pot hafa.*
  what kind: *hafa na klasi.*
whatever: *kuatkuera.*
whatnot: *renkonera.*
wheal: *ga'tot, paladan, pili'ao.*
wheat: *trigu.*
wheedle: *fa'ande', uga.*
wheel: *rueda.*
wheelbarrow: *karetiya.*
wheeze: *guha, lossos.*
when: *annai, komu, yanggen.*
  that is when: *ayu nai, enao nai.*
  this is when: *este nai.*
  when (question word): *ngai'an.*
  when (relative): *nai.*
  when (subordinator): *anai, gigon.*

where: *amanu.*
  that is where: *ayu nai, enao nai.*
  this is where: *este nai.*
  where (question word): *mangge, manu nai.*
  where (relative): *nai.*

whether: *maseha.*

whetstone: *guasa'on.*

whey: *huganom, huguahnom.*

which: *amanu, manu.*
  which (relative): *ni.*

whichever: *kuatkuera, manu.*

while: *mientras.*
  a while: *ti apmam.*
  for a while: *-ñaihon, naya.*

whim: *antohu.*

whimper: *kasao.*

whip: *balas, kuatta, sakudi, sakutassu, saolak, sapblasos, yagai.*
  to whip: *ba'ba', kuattasu.*

whipping: *latigasu, sinaolak.*

whirl: *rimulinu.*

whirlwind: *rimulinu.*

whisker: *batbas guihan, bigoti.*

whiskers: *batbas.*

whisper: *ñangon.*

whistle: *bibek.*
  whistle (with lips): *cheffla.*
  whistle at: *chefflague.*

white: *á'paka.*
  egg white: *á'paka' chada'.*
  turn white: *chapon.*
  white (color): *blanka.*

whiten: *enkola.*

whiteness: *ina'paka'an.*

whitish: *ina'paka', ina'paka'an.*

whittle: *lasgue, saha.*

who: *hai.*
  who (question word): *hayi.*
  who (relative): *ni.*

whoa: *cho, la.*

whoever: *hayi ha'.*

whole: *entieru.*

wholehearted: *sinseru.*

whore: *laputa, puta.*

why: *pot hafa, pot ke motibu, sa' hafa.*
  that is why: *enao na.*
  that is why (something is done): *ayu na.*
  this is why: *este na.*

wick: *mecha.*

wide: *ancho, fedda'.*

widen: *na'ancho.*

wider: *lá'ancho.*

widow: *bi'uda, gaddai chili.*

widower: *bi'udu.*

width: *finedda', inancho.*

wife: *asagua.*

wig: *postisu.*

wild
  wild (animals): *machalek.*

wile: *laime, trampas.*

will: *irida.*
  will (future marker): *bai.*

willingly: *bulontariamente.*

wilted: *maggem, malayu.*

win: *ganna.*
  to win: *dalle.*
  win by conquest: *logra.*

wind: *manglo'.*
  break wind: *do'do'.*
  to wind: *kuetdasi.*
  western wind: *béndabat.*

winding: *natahlek.*

window: *bentana.*
  window sash: *kuadron bentana.*

windy: *guaifon.*

wine: *binu.*

wing: *pappa.*

wink: *achetge, chalamlam, señas.*

winner: *biktoriosu, gakna, gaknadót, gatnadót.*

wipe: *lampasu, saosao.*
  wipe anus: *etgue.*
  wipe out: *funas, na'mafnas.*

wiped out: *mafnas.*

wire: *alamle, uaia'.*
  barbed wire: *alamlen tituka'.*

wisdom: *finayi, kotdura, tinemtom.*

wise: *fayi, méhnalom, mítitanos.*
  three wise men: *reyes.*
  wise man: *profeta.*

wiser: *láfedda'.*

wish: *diseha, pudera.*
  wish feeling: *mohon.*
  wish for: *malago', tanga, ya-.*
  wish to: *puedi.*

witch: *bruha.*
  witch doctor: *kákahna, kákana.*

with
  with (prep.): *kon.*

withdraw: *risikna.*

within: *dentro.*

without: *fuera, sin.*

withstand: *langak, sungon.*

witness: *testigu.*

wizard: *á'atte, bruha.*

wolf: *lobu.*

woman: *palao'an.*
old woman: *biha.*
woman (single): *señorita.*
womanizer: *gaddai bebe'.*
womb: *matrís.*
women: *famalao'an.*
wood: *hayu.*
wood shaving: *ánlasgue, ánsupiyu.*
woods: *bundak, halom tano'.*
wool: *lana.*
wooly: *peludu.*
word: *fino', palabra.*
words: *finiho', fino'lagu.*
native words: *fino'haya.*
work: *bida, cho'cho', cho'gue, emplehu, empleo, facho'cho', hotnát, macho'cho', nina'huyong, obra, ofisiu.*
work fast: *pakiáo.*
worker: *fáfacho'cho'.*
working
working age: *polista.*
world: *tano'.*
worm: *gigek, ulo'.*
wormseed: *apasoti.*
worn: *gastadu.*
worn out: *amko', gastáo, gastadu, ginasta, tufai, yá'balak.*
worry: *atborotu, cháthinasso, enkebukáo, plaito.*
worse
made worse: *sinilo'.*
worsen: *kifan.*
worsen (the wound): *taohan.*
worship: *adora, adorasión.*
worth: *bali.*
worthiness: *diknidát.*
worthless: *despresiapble, táibali.*
wound: *chetnot, hirida, irida, lamen, na'chetnudan.*
to wound: *fañetnot.*
treat wound: *amte.*
wounded: *chetnudan, hiridáo, iridáo.*
wrap: *falulon.*
wrap around: *bándaras, cha'flilek.*
wrap in: *afuluyi.*
wrap up: *afuyot, balutan, fuyot.*
wrasse: *á'aga, ga'das, palakse'.*
large wrasse: *tangison.*
wrathful: *hosguan.*
wreath: *korona.*
wreck: *destrosa, destrosu, disasi, yulang.*
wrestle: *áffulo', fulo'.*
arm wrestle: *kodu.*

hand wrestle: *makodu.*
wrestle (with someone): *umáfulo'.*
wrestling: *áffulo'.*
wretched: *ná'ma'ase'.*
wring: *chaflalak, fugo'.*
wrinkle: *ginetton, makalehlo.*
wrinkled
wrinkled (clothes): *kala'u.*
wrinkled skin: *machaflakos, makachichi.*
wristwatch: *relós.*
write: *fitma, mangge', tuge'.*
write to (someone): *tugi'i.*
writer: *eskribiente, títuge'.*
writing: *eskritura.*
wrong: *lachi.*
wrongful: *mílachi.*
y: *yu.*
yam: *dagon haya, dagu, makna huegu.*
type of yam: *dagon a'paka', dagon anakko', dagon halom tano', dagon lila, dagon lulok, dagon Lukas, nika, nikan asumsion.*
wild yam: *gaddo'.*
yam (hairy root): *nikan asumsion.*
yam (rabbit): *dagon kunehu.*
yam (red): *dagon agaga'.*
yam (shoulder): *dagon apaga.*
yard
yard (measurement): *bara, yatdas.*
yard (of a house): *kabisera.*
yardage: *magagu.*
yarn
ball of yarn: *madea.*
coil of yarn: *madeha.*
yawn: *magap.*
yaws: *duya'.*
yeah: *hu'u.*
year: *añu, sakkan.*
coming year: *mamamaila' na sakkan.*
last year: *ma'pos na sakkan.*
next year: *otro na sakkan.*
year after next: *otroña na sakkan.*
year before last: *ma'posña na sakkan.*
yearn: *mahalang.*
yearning: *na'malago'.*
years: *años.*
yeast: *libadura, ná'espongha.*
yellow: *amariyu.*
yellow butterfly fish: *ababang amariyu.*
yellowish: *inamariyu.*
yes: *hu'u, hunggan, no.*
yesterday: *nigap.*

yet: *lao, naya, sinembatgo, trabiha.*
yield: *entrega, iningak, produkto.*
yielding: *máñaña'.*
yoke: *yugu.*
  to yoke: *onse.*
yolk
  double yolk: *kuates.*
  egg yolk: *agaga' chada', yema.*
you: *en, hamyo, hao.*
  you (emphatic sing.): *hagu.*
  you (sing.): *un.*
young: *hoben.*
  young (fruit): *gada'.*
youngsters: *hóbenes, manhoben.*
your: *-miyu, -mu.*

yours
  yours (possessive pl.): *-miyu.*
  yours (possessive sing.): *-mu.*
youth: *hobensitu.*
zeal: *esmeru.*
zero: *seru.*
zigzag: *botdo.*
  zigzag cut: *lapbla.*
zinc: *sin.*
zip
  to zip up: *yippa.*
zipper: *yippa.*
zoom: *besbes, pechao.*
  zoom by: *chispas.*